P9-DEY-586

lonely planet

Denmark

Northern
Jutland
p240

Central Jutland
p205

Southern
Jutland
p185

Funen
p157

Zealand
p93

Copenhagen
p42

Bornholm
p141

Møn,
Falster &
Lolland
p126

THIS EDITION WRITTEN AND RESEARCHED BY

Carolyn Bain, Cristian Bonetto

New Carlisle Public Library
New Carlisle, IN 46552

Contents

PLAN YOUR TRIP

Welcome to Denmark ... 4
Denmark Map 6
Denmark's Top 15 8
Need to Know 16
What's New 18
If You Like... 19
Month by Month 21
Itineraries 25
Outdoor Activities 30
Travel with Children.... 35
Regions at a Glance.... 38

ON THE ROAD

COPENHAGEN 42
Around Copenhagen ... 91
Ishøj 92
Charlottenlund 92
Klampenborg 92
Lyngby 92

ZEALAND.......... 93
Øresund Coast 96
Rungsted 96
Helsingør 97
Inland Towns 101
Hillerød............... 101
Fredensborg 103
North Coast.......... 104
Hornbæk.............. 104
Gilleleje 106
Tisvildeleje........... 107
Fjord Towns 108
Roskilde 108
Lejre 113
Southern Zealand..... 114
Køge 114
Vallø 119
Sorø 119
Trelleborg............. 122
Vordingborg........... 124

MØN, FALSTER & LOLLAND......... 126
Møn................. 128
Stege 129
Ulvshale & Nyord 131
Keldby 131
Elmelunde 132
Møns Klint & Around.... 132
Klintholm Havn........ 134
Western Møn.......... 134
Bogø.................. 135
Falster 135
Nykøbing F 136
Marielyst 137
Lolland.............. 138
Maribo 139
Around Lolland........ 140

BORNHOLM 141
Rønne................. 143
Åkirkeby.............. 145
Interior Woodlands 146
Dueodde 146
Snogebæk............. 147
Nexø 147
Svaneke 148
Gudhjem & Melsted..... 150

AARHUS P208

VIKING SHIP MUSEUM P109

Contents

Around Gudhjem
& Melsted 152

Sandvig & Allinge........ 153

Hammershus Slot 154

Hammeren............. 155

Christiansø 155

FUNEN 157

Odense.............. 159

Around Funen 168

Kerteminde 168

Ladby 169

Egeskov Slot 170

Faaborg 170

Svendborg............. 173

Tåsinge................ 175

Langeland 177

Rudkøbing 178

Northern Langeland 178

Southern Langeland 179

Ærø................. 180

Ærøskøbing............ 181

Marstal................ 183

Søby 184

**SOUTHERN
JUTLAND......... 185**

Kolding................ 186

Esbjerg................ 188

Fanø 191

Ribe................... 193

Wadden Sea
National Park 198

Rømø 198

Tønder 200

Møgeltønder 202

Sønderborg............. 203

Als.................... 204

**CENTRAL
JUTLAND......... 205**

Aarhus 208

Djursland 221

Ebeltoft 221

Grenaa 223

Around Djursland 223

The Lake District 224

Silkeborg 224

Ry 228

Himmelbjerget 229

The Interior 230

Jelling................. 230

Givskud 231

Billund & Legoland...... 231

Randers 234

Rebild Bakker &
Rold Skov.............. 235

Viborg................. 237

Central West Coast ... 238

Hvide Sande 238

**NORTHERN
JUTLAND......... 240**

Aalborg................ 241

Frederikshavn.......... 248

Sæby 249

Skagen................ 251

Råbjerg Mile 255

Hirtshals 255

Hjørring 257

Løkken 257

Hanstholm............. 259

Klitmøller.............. 260

UNDERSTAND

Denmark
Today 262

History 264

The Danish Lifestyle .. 273

Danish Design........ 276

Food & Drink 279

Literature, Film & TV .. 285

SURVIVAL GUIDE

Directory A–Z 290

Transport............ 297

Language............ 304

SPECIAL FEATURES

Itineraries 25

Outdoor Activities 30

The Danish
Lifestyle............273

Danish Design.......276

Welcome to Denmark

Denmark seems to have cemented its position at or near the top of every global quality-of-life survey. Take a look around, and it's not hard to see why.

Happiness & Hygge

It's heart-warming to know there's still a country where the term 'fairy tale' can be used freely – from its most enduring literary legacy to its fine textbook castles. In a nutshell, Denmark gets it right: old-fashioned charm embraces the most avowedly forward-looking design and social developments, and wins it a regular chart-topping place on lists of both the most liveable *and* the happiest nations on earth. You won't have to search hard to find some much-prized *hygge,* an untranslatable and uniquely Danish trait that has a profound influence on the locals' inestimable happiness. *Hygge* is social nirvana in Denmark: a sense of cosiness, camaraderie and contentment.

History & Impact

The world first took notice of Denmark more than a millennium ago, when Danish Vikings took to the seas and ravaged vast tracts of Europe. How things have changed. These days Denmark captures the global imagination as the epitome of a civilised society, and it punches above its weight on many fronts: progressive politics, urban planning, sustainability, design, architecture. Recent global crushes freshly exported from Copenhagen include city cycling culture, the New Nordic culinary movement, and brilliantly addictive TV drama series.

Equality of Life

While many countries are noticeable for the ever-increasing gap between the 'haves' and 'have-nots', Denmark seems to be populated by the 'have enoughs', and the obviously rich and obviously poor are few and far between. This egalitarian spirit allows the best of the arts, architecture, eating out and entertainment to be within easy reach of all. Indeed, the best catchword for Denmark might well be 'inclusive' – everyone is welcome and everyone is catered to, be they young, old, gay, straight, male, female, and whether they travel with kids, pets or bikes in tow, or with a mobility issue or handicap. Cities are compact and user-friendly, infrastructure is clean and modern, and travel is a breeze.

The Danish Aesthetic

Denmark's landscapes are understated – pure and simple, often infused with an ethereal Nordic light. Such landscapes are reflected in the Danish design philosophy towards fashion, food, architecture, furniture and art. Simplicity of form and function come first, but not at the expense of beauty. And so you'll find moments of quintessential Danish loveliness on a sandy beach, beside a lake, admiring a Renaissance castle, or in a candlelit cafe that has perfected the art of *hygge.*

Why I Love Denmark

By Carolyn Bain, Author

My first experience of Denmark came as a teenager, living there for a year as an exchange student. My first youthful Danish loves were the pastries, the furniture design and the long summer nights. These days I return with the same passions, enriched with an adult appreciation for Denmark's egalitarianism, its belief that cities belong to people not cars and its endless quest for *hygge*. It helps that everything is easy on the eye – the unfairly attractive locals, yes, but also the architecture, the landscapes and the interior design. I think that secretly, most cities want to grow up to be Copenhagen – and if they don't, they should.

For more about our authors, see page 320.

Above: Country home near Egeskov Slot (p170), Funen

Denmark

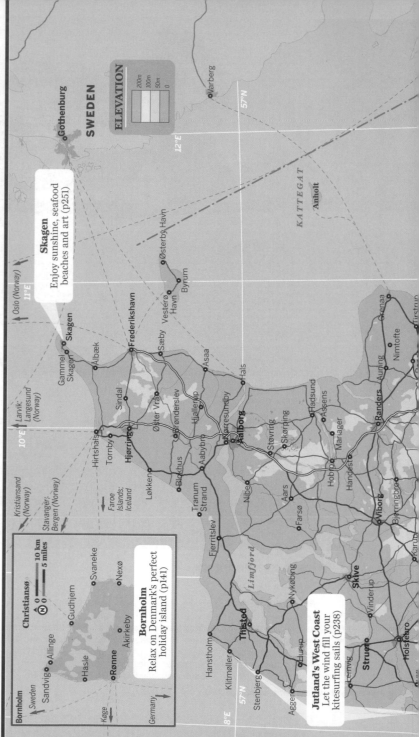

0 .... 100 km
0 ...... 50 miles

Bornholm
Relax on Denmark's perfect holiday island (p141)

Bornholm
Sweden
Sandvig o Allinge
Hasle o
o Svaneke
Gudhjem o
Christiansø
o Nexø
Akirkeby o
Rønne o
Germany
Køge

0 ...... 10 km
0 ...... 5 miles

Skagen
Enjoy sunshine, seafood beaches and art (p251)

SWEDEN

Gothenburg

ELEVATION
200m
100m
50m
0

Varberg

KATTEGAT
Anholt

Oslo (Norway)
Larvik; Larggesund (Norway)
Kristiansand (Norway)
Stavanger; Bergen (Norway)
Faroe Islands; Iceland

Skagen
Gammel Skagen
Albæk
Frederikshavn
Sæby
Vesterø Havn
Byrum
Østerby Havn

Sindal
Øster Vrå
Brønderslev
Hjallerup
Asaa
Hals
Aalborg
Gæsumdby

Hirtshals
Tornby
Hjørring
Løkken
Blokhus
Tranum Strand
Fjerritslev
Aabybro
Nibe
Aars
Farsø
Støvring
Skørping
Hobro
Mariager
Hadsund
Assens
Randers
Aurning
Nimtofte
Grenaa
Hurstrup
Hadsund
Handest

Limfjord
Løgstør
Nykøbing
Skive
Vinderup
Viborg
Bjerringbro
Karup

Hanstholm
Klitmøller
Thisted
Stenbjerg
Agger
Vestervig
Struer
Lemvig
Holstebro

Jutland's West Coast
Let the wind fill your kitesurfing sails (p238)

57°N
8°E
10°E
11°E
12°E
57°N

Helsingør
Visit Hamlet's majestic castle (p97)

Copenhagen
Envy the locals' sky-high quality of life (p42)

Aarhus
Explore Denmark's surprising second city (p208)

Ærø
Hear seafaring tales and cycle rural bike lanes (p180)

Silkeborg
Ponder the great outdoors and bog-body mysteries (p224)

Legoland
Embrace your inner child (p231)

Ribe
Soak up centuries of history (p193)

GERMANY

Denmark's
Top 15

Copenhagen

1 You may find it hard to suppress your envy for residents of Scandinavia's coolest capital (p42). While this 850-year-old harbour town retains much of its historic good looks (think copper spires, cobbled squares and pastel-coloured gabled abodes), the focus here is on the innovative. Denmark's high-achieving capital is home to a thriving design scene, a futuristic metro system, and clean, green developments. Its streets are awash with effortlessly hip shops, cafes and bars; world-class museums and art collections; brave new architecture; and no fewer than 15 Michelin-starred restaurants. Below left: Cafes, Nyhavn

Danish Dining

2 Sure, some trendspotters predicted the end of New Nordic cuisine's time in the global spotlight – but then Noma (p75) popped up to reclaim the title of world's number one restaurant in 2014 (after temporarily losing the crown). New Nordic (p279) isn't going anywhere, and its effects are being warmly felt. Emboldened by the attention and praise lavished on Danish produce and innovative chefs, food producers are re-embracing old-school culinary delights. Expect new spins on beloved rye breads and pastries, smørrebrød (open sandwiches), smoked fish, and even humble pork-and-potato dishes. Below right: Herring dish at Aamanns Takeaway (p77)

CHRISTER FREDRIKSSON / GETTY IMAGES ©

Nyhavn

IMAGE BY MICHAEL TALALAEV / GETTY IMAGES ©

2

CHRISTIAN ASLUND / GETTY IMAGES ©

Cycling

3 Is Denmark the best nation for bicycle touring in the world? Probably, thanks to its national network of cycle routes, terrain that is either flat or merely undulating, and a culture committed to two-wheeled transport. But you needn't embark on tours of the country to enjoy cycle touring. The cities are a breeze to pedal around, and many have public bike-sharing schemes with free (or cheap) bike usage. More than 50% of Copenhagen commuters travel by cycle. It's easy to follow their lead, especially with new initiatives like Cykelslangen (p57), an elevated bike lane over the harbour.

Bornholm

4 Bornholm (p141) is a Baltic beauty lying some 200km east of the Danish mainland, located closer to Germany and Sweden than to the rest of Denmark. This island holds a special place in the hearts of most Danes, and is beloved for its plentiful sunshine, glorious beaches, endless cycle paths, iconic *rund-kirker* (round churches), artistic communities, fish smokehouses and idyllic thatched villages. If that's not enough to lure you, the island is developing a reputation for outstanding restaurants and local edibles. Above right: Hammerhus Slot (p154), Bornholm

Ærø

5 Denmark has been likened to a china plate that's been dropped and smashed into pieces. Each fragment represents an island – and there are 406 of them. The midsized islands, each with their own distinctive character, are the most fun to explore, and south of Funen there's a whole archipelago of them, making it a prime sailing destination. Steeped-in-time Ærø (p180) is an utterly idyllic slice of Danish island life: visit for seafaring heritage, rural bike lanes, cobblestoned villages, sandy beaches and postcard-perfect bathing huts. Opposite top: Sailing boats in Ærø harbour

Summer Music Festivals

6 There's a fat calendar of summer festivals (p21) countrywide, from folk music in Tønder to riverboat jazz around Silkeborg. The capital lets loose at its largest event, Copenhagen Jazz Festival, but also celebrates electronic beats at Strøm. Meanwhile in Aarhus, NorthSide helps build the city's music-fest street cred. But it's the festivals outside the cities that draw the biggest crowds: Roskilde rocks with Scandinavia's largest music festival, and Skanderborg hosts Denmark's 'most beautiful' Smukfest. Right: Music fans at Roskilde Festival (p112)

DIVERSE IMAGES/UIG / GETTY IMAGES ©

Legoland

7 A theme park (p231) that celebrates the 'toy of the century' (as judged by *Fortune* magazine in 2000) in the country in which it was invented ('the world's happiest nation' according to a Gallup World Poll). You've got to believe Legoland will be something special – and it is. Theme parks, waterparks and an inspired new cultural centre (designed to resembling gigantic Lego bricks) make this region Happy Families HQ in a country that's overflowing with child-friendly attractions.

Shakespeare at Kronborg Slot

8 Something rotten in the state of Denmark? Not at this 16th-century castle (p97) in Helsingør, made famous as the Elsinore Castle of Shakespeare's *Hamlet*. Kronborg's primary function was as a grandiose toll house, wresting taxes from ships passing through the narrow Øresund between Denmark and Sweden. The fact that Hamlet was a fictional character hasn't deterred legions of sightseers from visiting the site. It's the venue for glorious summer performances of Shakespeare's plays during the HamletScenen festival.

JOHN ELK / GETTY IMAGES ©

TERJE RAKKE / GETTY IMAGES ©

Skagen

9 Skagen (p251) is an enchanting place, both bracing and beautiful. It lies at Denmark's northern tip and acts as a magnet for much of the population each summer, when the town is full to capacity yet still manages to charm. In the late 19th century artists flocked here, infatuated with the radiant light's impact on the rugged landscape. Now tourists flock to enjoy the output of the 'Skagen school' artists, soak up that luminous light, devour the plentiful seafood and laze on the fine sandy beaches. Above: Grenen, Skagen

Bog Bodies

10 Two stars of the early Iron Age are the intact bodies of men who lived around 300 BC and were exhumed from Denmark's peat bogs after their two-millennia-long slumber; their discovery bring us tantalisingly close to ancient societies. The bodies also provide compelling historical who- and why-dunnits: were they human sacrifices, executed prisoners, or victims of murder perhaps? Tollund Man rests in a museum in bucolic Silkeborg (p224); Grauballe Man lies in the magnificent new construction housing Aarhus' Moesgård Museum (p209). Above top right: Tollund Man

Ribe

11 Compact postcard-perfect Ribe (p193) is Denmark's oldest town, and it encapsulates the country's golden past in exquisite style, complete with imposing 12th-century cathedral, cobblestone streets, skewed half-timbered houses and lush water meadows. Stay overnight in atmospheric lodgings that exude history (low-beamed rooms in a wonky 1600s inn, or in converted jail cells), and take a free walking tour narrated by the town's nightwatch-man – the perfect way to soak up the streetscapes as well as tall tales of local characters.

DDR DIE BILDAGENTUR DER FOTOGRAFEN GMBH / ALAMY ©

Danish Design

12 Denmark is a world leader in applied design (p276), characterised by cool clean lines, graceful shapes and streamlined functionality. These concepts have been applied to everything from concert halls to coffee pots to Lego blocks. The result has not just been great artistic acclaim but also big business; iconic brands include Bang & Olufsen (sleek stereos), Bodum (kitchenware), Georg Jensen (silverware and jewellery) and Royal Copenhagen Porcelain. Then there are the furniture designers and fashion houses. Credit cards ready? Above left: Georg Jensen– designed bowl

Beaches

13 Denmark comes alive in summer, and the country's 7314km of coastline and its smorgasbord of islands (all 406 of them) draw locals for wholesome pursuits and a dose of vitamin D. True, water temperatures may be a little unkind, but long sandy strands such as Bornholm's Dueodde (p146) or northern Jutland's Skagen (p251) easily fulfil seaside-holiday fantasies. Other stretches, especially at towns like Hvide Sande (p238) and Klitmøller (p260) along Jutland's wild west coast, crank up activities harnessing the wind's power. Above right: Dueodde, Bornholm

Viking History

14 The Vikings (p265) ensured that the Danes were known and feared throughout northern Europe from the 8th to 11th centuries, but battle and bloodlust is far from the whole story. The Vikings were not just plunderers but successful traders, extraordinary mariners and insatiable explorers. Getting a feel for the Viking era is easy, whether visiting the ship-burial ground of Ladby (p169), the Viking forts of Zealand, the longship workshops at Roskilde or the many museums that seek to re-create the era with live re-enactments. Opposite top: Viking Ship Museum (p109), Roskilde

Aarhus

15 Always the brides-maid, never the bride – Aarhus (p208), the second-largest city in Denmark, labours in the shadows of Copenhagen in terms of tourist appeal, but this is a terrific city in which to spend a couple of days. It has a superb dining scene, thriving nightlife (much of it catering to the large student population), a waterfront undergoing transformation, picturesque woodland trails and beaches along the city outskirts, along with one of the country's finest art museums, turning heads thanks to its crowning glory, *Your Rainbow Panorama*.

PHOTOPOP / VISIT AARHUS ©

Need to Know

For more information, see Survival Guide (p289)

Currency
Danish krone (Dkr)

Language
Danish (English widely spoken)

Visas
Generally not required for stays of up to 90 days. Not required for members of EU or Schengen countries.

Money
ATMs widely available. Credit cards accepted in most hotels, restaurants and shops.

Mobile Phones
Bring a GSM compatible phone; local SIM cards are widely available. Mobile coverage is widespread.

Time
Central European Time (GMT/UTC plus one hour)

When to Go

Warm to hot summers, cool winters
Mild to hot summers, cold winters

Aalborg
GO May–Sep

Aarhus
GO May–Sep

Copenhagen
GO year-round

Odense
GO May–Sep

Bornholm
GO Jun–mid-Sep

High Season
(mid-Jun–mid-Aug)

➡ Long daylight hours, with A-list concerts, festivals and theme parks in full swing

➡ Busy campgrounds, beaches, sights and transport

➡ Accommodation prices peak

Shoulder
(May–mid-Jun, mid-Aug–Sep)

➡ A good time to travel, with generally mild weather and fewer crowds

➡ Spring offers local produce, flowers and a few festivals

➡ Autumn has golden landscapes and cosy nights

Low Season
(Oct–Apr)

➡ Cool and wet with short daylight hours, but *hygge* (cosiness) is in full swing

➡ Big cities have Christmas lights, ice-skating rinks and *gløgg* (mulled wine)

➡ Reduced hours for sights; outdoor attractions closed

Useful Websites

Visit Denmark
(www.visitdenmark.com) Info ranges from the practical to the inspirational.

Visit Copenhagen (www. visitcopenhagen.com) All the capital's highlights.

Rejseplanen (www.rejseplanen. dk) Great journey planner.

Denmark.dk (www.denmark.dk) Informative on diverse subjects.

Lonely Planet (www.lonely planet.com/denmark) Info, hotel bookings, forums etc.

Important Numbers

There are no area codes in Denmark.

Denmark country code	☏45
International access code	☏00
Emergency (police, fire, ambulance)	☏112
Directory assistance (local)	☏118
Directory assistance (international)	☏113

Exchange Rates

Australia	A$1	Dkr5.36
Canada	C$1	Dkr5.26
Euro zone	€1	Dkr7.44
Sweden	Skr1	Dkr0.81
Japan	¥100	Dkr5.44
New Zealand	NZ$1	Dkr4.78
UK	UK£1	Dkr9.31
USA	US$1	Dkr5.78

For current exchange rates see www.xe.com.

Daily Costs

Budget
less than Dkr800

➡ Dorm bed: Dkr150–300

➡ Double room in budget hotel: Dkr500–650

➡ Cheap meals: under Dkr125

➡ Bike hire: free in some places or Dkr100 per day

➡ 24-hr City Pass for Copenhagen transport: Dkr80

Midrange
Dkr800–1500

➡ Double room in midrange hotel: Dkr700–1500

➡ Three-course menu in restaurant: Dkr300

➡ Train ticket Aarhus–Copenhagen: Dkr382

➡ Museum admission: Dkr50–110

Top End
more than Dkr1500

➡ Double room in top-end hotel: Dkr1500 and up

➡ Main course in top-end restaurant: Dkr250 and up

Opening Hours

Opening hours vary throughout the year. We've provided high-season opening hours; hours will generally decrease in the shoulder and low seasons.

Banks 10am-4pm Monday to Friday

Bars 4pm-midnight, to 2am or later Friday & Saturday

Cafes 8am-5pm or midnight

Restaurants noon-10pm

Shops 10am-6pm Mon-Friday, to 4pm Saturday, some Sundays

Supermarkets 8am-9pm

Arriving in Denmark

Copenhagen International Airport, Kastrup

Train Every 10 minutes (Dkr36, 12 minutes) connecting the airport to Copenhagen Central Station (København Hoved-banegården).

Taxi It's a 20-minute journey between the airport and city centre; cost is Dkr250-300.

Metro Line M2 runs 24 hours from the airport (station: Lufthavnen) to many neighbourhoods (eg Christianhavn, Kongens Nytorv, Nørreport, Frederiksberg) but doesn't run through Copenhagen Central Station.

Getting Around

Transport in Denmark is reasonably priced, quick and efficient. Your best friend is the journey-planning website www.rejseplanen.dk (download the Rejseplanen app to your phone).

Train Reasonably priced, with extensive coverage of the country and frequent departures.

Car Denmark is perfect for touring by car. Can be hired in larger towns. Drive on the right.

Bike Extensive bike paths link towns throughout the country. Bikes can be hired in every town.

Bus All large cities and towns have a local and regional bus system. Long-distance buses run a distant second to train.

Ferries Boats link virtually all of Denmark's populated islands.

For much more on
getting around,
see p297

What's New

Capital Food Scene

The next wave of Modern Danish hotspots in Copenhagen include Clou (p74) and Rebel (p74). Classic Danish cuisine gets competent new twists at Øl & Brød (p76), which also boasts Denmark's best collection of akvavit and snaps. The Copenhagen branch of Kadeau (p75) received its first Michelin star in 2013. Copenhagen Street Food (p74) has opened up inside a warehouse on Paper Island; it's a food market made up of food trucks and stalls, right opposite the Danish Playhouse.

Aarhus' Arsenal

Denmark's second city is growing in stature, with its harbourfront continuing its transformation, and an incredible new home for Moesgård Museum opened in 2014. Plus: it's the European Capital of Culture in 2017. (p209)

Everything is Awesome in Billund

The rise (and rise) of Lego continues, with the Lego House 'experience centre' under construction in Billund (Lego HQ) set to open in 2016. Its design: in a word, awesome! (p232)

World Heritage Additions

In 2014, Unesco admitted two new Danish sites to its World Heritage List: the natural wonderland of Wadden Sea National Park, and the history-rich white cliffs of Stevns Klint. (p118)

A New Story in Odense

This town is transforming itself into a city, with some big ideas and grand projects. It started in mid-2014 with the closure of a main arterial road, allowing the historic heart to reconnect.

Animal Encounters, Copenhagen

Animal lovers will want to check out the new aquarium Den Blå Planet (p63), in a stunning futuristic-looking building, and the Arctic Ring at Copenhagen Zoo (p61), where a tunnel takes you through the polar bears' swimming pool.

Zealand Newbies

The new M/S Museet for Søfart (p99), dockside in Helsingør, is the architecturally stunning new national maritime museum. Danmarks Borgcenter (p124) in Vordingborg is home to a striking, high-tech 'castle centre' on Scandinavia's largest castle site.

Roskilde Rocks

The new Rock and Roll Museum in Roskilde will open in 2015, with plans to include interactive exhibits that will give visitors the chance to record and mix tunes, and play to a virtual Roskilde Festival crowd. (p111)

Bathing Beauties

Sea bathing gets scenic, with a beautiful new public pavilion built on the Faaborg waterfront, and a designer concrete pool opened in the North Sea shallows at remote Nørre Vorupør. (p259)

For more recommendations and reviews, see lonelyplanet.com/denmark

If You Like...

Islands

Bornholm Lose yourself in nature on this Baltic summer playground (p141)

Møn Tackle the brilliant-white cliffs of Møns Klint (p132)

Slotsholmen Politics, ruins and drama define Copenhagen's most imposing inner-city island (p50)

Læsø See salty traditions and unwind in a salt bath (p250)

Lolland Explore Maribo's charm, as well as blockbuster family attractions (p139)

Ærø Cycle between towns rich in seafaring tradition (p180)

Fanø Observe the metaphorical distance between industrial Esbjerg and beguiling Fanø (p191)

Rømø Choose from gentle (horse riding) or windwhipped (blokarts and kitebuggies) (p199)

Viking History

Roskilde Five Viking ships discovered at the bottom of Roskilde Fjord are displayed at the Viking Ship Museum (p109)

Lejre Explore the fascinating experimental archaeology centre 'Land of Legends' (p113)

Ladby Discover an unearthed ship grave, where a chieftain was laid to rest in a warship (p169)

Trelleborg See a circular fortress constructed in the 10th century, and built to a precise mathematical plan (p122)

Ribe An informative museum as well as a fun village re-creation – with warrior training! (p195)

Jelling The royal seat of King Gorm during the Vikings' most dominant era (p230)

Aalborg The Viking burial ground at Lindholm Høje (p243)

Copenhagen Rune stones and unearthed Viking loot on show at Nationalmuseet (p45)

Fabulous Food

Copenhagen For any Scandi treat you may desire (p70)

Lammefjorden Denmark's famous 'vegetable garden' has made Dragsholm Slot a destination dining favourite (p113)

Bornholm Stays true to its roots with hot fish smokehouses, but adds to its arsenal with a league of food artisans (p146)

Skagen Fun fish auctions, prawns fresh off the boats, or fancy-pants dining (p254)

Aarhus Denmark's second-largest city has a growing dining scene plus budget meals (p216)

Møn Smoked fish, locally brewed suds and artisan ice cream served right on the farm (p132)

Funen Pastures and orchards (and roadside produce stalls) in the 'garden of Denmark' (p172)

Family Attractions

Copenhagen Start with headliners like Tivoli amusement park (p45) and Den Blå Planet (p63) aquarium

Billund Plastic-fantastic Legoland (p231), with a Lalandia (p232) mega-waterpark as its neighbour

Odense The city that gave birth to children's lit by way of Hans Christian Andersen (p159)

Vordingborg Let kids loose at a museum where they can hunt for ghosts amid castle ruins (p124)

Randers Home to a magnificent man-made rainforest full of critters (p234)

Djursland A family mecca with amusement parks, theme parks, safari parks and beaches (p224)

Lolland More waterparks and safari parks to explore, and more beaches (p140)

Outdoor Activities

Copenhagen Jogging, cycling and kayaking tours, and an architect-designed swimming spot on the main canal (p61)

Lake District Hills, beech forest, lakes and rivers – and canoe-hire places that can build you your own paddling itinerary (p225)

Bornholm An island full of cycling trails and worthy destinations to cycle between (p141)

Hvide Sande Coach those wild winds into windsurf sails and kites, or waterski a fun course (p239)

Rebild Bakker Walking trails and bike tracks in rural forests (p235)

Klitmøller Waves to conquer and winds to tame thanks to surfing and windsurfing schools (p260)

Rømø Horse ride along the shoreline, or kitebuggy and blokart across the sand (p199)

Svendborg Sail the South Funen Archipelago on an old wooden sailing ship (p173)

Architecture & Design

Copenhagen The architecture and design mother lode. Modern architectural marvels include the Black Diamond library extension, Operaen (p83), and contemporary art museums such as Arken (p92), Louisiana (p91) and Ordrupgaard (p92)

Aalborg A striking waterfront centre (p241) designed by and dedicated to Jørn Utzon, plus an art museum (p243) designed by Finnish great Alvar Aalto

Kolding The Trapholt museum of modern art, applied art and furniture design is a gem, and incorporates Arne Jacobsen's prototype summerhouse (p187)

Tønder A converted water tower showcases the fabulous chairs of design hero Hans Wegner (p201)

Aarhus A modernist, Jacobsen-designed town hall, an art museum topped by a rainbow walkway, and the Moesgård Museum (p209)

Billund Watch the new Lego House take shape – a genius design that resembles a stack of gigantic Lego bricks (p232)

Helsingør New design from Bjarke Ingels – this one is a maritime museum cleverly built in and around a dry dock (p99)

Top The 'Black Diamond' extension of Det Kongelige Bibliotek (p54), Copenhagen
Bottom Moesgård Museum (p209)

Month by Month

TOP EVENTS

Riverboat Jazz Festival, June

Roskilde Festival, July

Copenhagen Jazz Festival, July

Aarhus Festival, August

Christmas, December

February

Midwinter in Denmark may be scenic under snow and in sunshine, but it's more likely grey and gloomy, with a few events to brighten the mood. A midterm school holiday sees many locals head north to ski.

✲ Vinterjazz

Danes love their summer jazz festivals; in mid-February, those suffering from jazz withdrawal can get a fix from this smaller-scale event (www.jazz.dk) held at cosy venues countrywide.

✲ Copenhagen Fashion Week

Models and style connoisseurs make Copenhagen shine during the twice-yearly Fashion Week (early February and early August).

The associated Fashion Festival (www.copen hagenfashionfestival.com) brings the finery to a more accessible level – lots of shopping, sales, shows and parties.

April

Spring has sprung! Warmer, drier days bring out the blossoms, and attractions that were closed for the winter reopen: Legoland at the start of April, Tivoli midmonth.

✲ CPH:PIX

Held over two weeks from mid-April, this is Copenhagen's feature-film festival (www.cphpix.dk). Expect flicks from Denmark and abroad, as well as a busy program of film-related events.

✲ Sort Sol

The marshlands of the west-coast Wadden Sea provide food and rest for millions of migratory birds, and in late March and April (and again in September/October) huge formations of starlings put on a brilliant natural show known as the 'Sort Sol' (Black Sun).

May

The sun comes out on a semipermanent basis, more warm-weather attractions open, and the events calendar starts filling as Danes throw off winter's gloom. Tourists have yet to arrive in great numbers.

✲ Aalborg Karneval

In late May, Aalborg kicks up its heels hosting the biggest Carnival celebrations in northern Europe (www.aalborgkarneval.dk), when up to 100,000 participants and spectators shake their maracas and paint the town red.

✲ Ølfestival

Specialist beer and micro brewing are booming in Denmark. This is the country's largest beer festival (http://beerfestival.dk), held around mid-May in the capital and drawing over 13,000 thirsty attendees.

June

Hello summer! Denmark's festival pace quickens alongside a rising temperature gauge and longer daylight hours. The main tourist season begins in earnest in late June, when schools break for a seven-week vacation.

Copenhagen Distortion

Known to get a little crazy, Distortion (www.cphdistortion.dk) is a celebration of the capital's nightlife, with the emphasis on clubs and DJs. It's a five-day mobile street party, rolling through a different Copenhagen neighbourhood each day.

Sculpture by the Sea

Aarhus' southern beachfront is transformed into an outdoor gallery courtesy of this month-long event (www.sculpturebythesea.dk), with dozens of sculptures from Danish and foreign artists displayed beside (and in) the water. It's held biennially (odd-numbered years).

Riverboat Jazz Festival

Jutland's bucolic Lake District, centred on Silkeborg, comes alive with five days of jazz (www.riverboat.dk). It's not quite New Orleans but you can buy a ticket and take a cruise down the river, or stroll the streets and enjoy the free performances.

Midsummer Eve

The Danes let rip on the longest night of the year (23 June), known as Sankt Hans Aften (St Hans Evening), with bonfires in parks, gardens and, most popular of all, on the beaches. They burn an effigy of a witch on the pyre, sing songs and get merry.

Top One of Copenhagen's many Christmas fairs (p24)
Bottom Festival fans at Aalborg Karneval (p21)

✕ Sol over Gudhjem

Bornholm is home to Denmark's biggest one-day cook-off (the name translates as 'Sun over Gudhjem'). It sees some of the country's best chefs battle it out using local produce. It's a hit with visitors and is broadcast on TV. (p152)

🎵 NorthSide Festival

A three-day mid-month music event (www.north side.dk) in Aarhus that's building a big reputation – line-ups rival the legendary Roskilde Festival.

July

Many Danes take their main work holiday during the first three weeks of July, so expect busy seaside resorts, chock-a-block camping grounds and near-full coastal hotels – book ahead to join in on the beachy summer-holiday vibe.

🎵 Skagen Festival

Skagen acts as a magnet in summer, drawing well-heeled holidaymakers to Jutland's far-northern tip. Held over four days in late June/early July, this festival (www.skagenfestival. dk) entertains with quality folk and world music.

🎵 Roskilde Festival

Roskilde is rocked by Scandinavia's largest music festival (www.roskilde-festival. dk) for four days in early July, with major international acts and some 75,000 music fans (most camping on-site). It's renowned for its relaxed, friendly atmosphere. (p112)

🎵 Copenhagen Jazz Festival

This swingin' party (www. jazzfestival.dk) is the biggest annual entertainment event in the capital. For your sensory pleasure there are 10 days of Danish and international jazz, blues and fusion music, with 500 indoor and outdoor concerts. (p65)

🎵 Viking Moot

You can unleash your inner pillager at a Viking-style market (www.moesmus. dk) outside Aarhus in late July. There are crafts, food and equestrian events, plus Vikings of all nationalities competing in mock battles.

🎵 Rebild Festival

One for the Americans, the Rebild Festival (www.re-bildfesten.dk) is an annual July 4th celebration (held since 1912) that is among the biggest outside the USA. It's held in the forested hills of Rebild Bakker and features musicians, politicians and entertainers, as well as high-profile guest speakers (Danish and American).

August

Summer continues unabated, with beaches and theme parks packed to the gills, and the populace determined to wring every last ray of sunshine out of the season. Schools resume around mid-month.

☆ Hamlet Summer Plays

Helsingør's grand Kronborg Slot was made famous as the Elsinore Castle of

Shakespeare's *Hamlet*. Every summer it hosts outdoor productions – the Shakespeare Festival does more than just perform *Hamlet,* putting on different plays by the Bard each year (www.hamletscenen.dk).

🎵 Copenhagen Pride

Out and proud since 1996, this five-day festival (www. copenhagenpride.dk) brings Carnival-like colour to the capital, culminating in a gay-pride march. Needless to say, there's lots of dancing and flirting.

🎵 Tønder Festival

Regarded as one of Europe's best folk-music festivals, this south-Jutland shindig (www.tf.dk) draws some 20,000 attendees to its celebration of folk and roots music, and is renowned for its friendly, fun atmosphere.

🎵 Smukfest

This midmonth music marvel in Skanderborg bills itself as Denmark's most beautiful festival (www. smukfest.dk), and is second only to Roskilde in terms of scale. It takes place in lush parkland in the scenic Lake District and attracts up to 40,000 music fans.

🎵 Aarhus Festival

Denmark's second city dons its shiniest party gear at the end of August, when this festival (www. aarhusfestival.com) transforms the town for 10 days, celebrating music, food, short film, theatre, visual arts and outdoor events for all ages (many of which are free).

✗ Copenhagen Cooking

The world's foodie lens seems trained on Copenhagen of late, and this food festival (Scandinavia's largest) focuses on the gourmet end of the food spectrum and is held in venues and restaurants throughout the city. Aside from the summer edition, a month-long winter version takes place each February. See www. copenhagencooking.dk.

✯ HC Andersen Festivals

Of course Odense honours its homegrown literary hero. This week-long program (www.hcafestivals.com) in mid-August features plenty of Hans Christian Andersen (HCA) performances and lectures, plus concerts, comedy and family-friendly events. It's bookended by the local flower festival and a short-film shindig, too.

✯ Strøm

Copenhagen's week-long electronic music festival (www.stromcph.dk) is considered the best of its kind in Scandinavia. Events include workshops and masterclasses, concerts, raves and parties.

September

The summer madness drops off as abruptly as it began, and crowds have largely disappeared. Good weather is still a chance, but by month's end many big outdoor attractions have wrapped things up for another year.

◉ Art Copenhagen

This major art fair sees the participation of around 60 art galleries from across Nordic Europe and beyond, showcasing a good number of contemporary artists from Denmark, Sweden, Norway, Finland, Iceland and the Faroe Islands.

✯ Copenhagen Blues Festival

If the shorter days have you feeling blue, this five-day international event (www. copenhagenbluesfestival. dk) should suit, with more than 50 toe-tapping concerts staged at venues around the capital.

October

Summer is a distant memory, with the weather crisp and cool and the countryside taking on a golden tinge. Business travellers outnumber those travelling for pleasure.

◉ Kulturnatten (Culture Night)

Usually held on the second Friday in October, this wonderful, atmospheric event (www.kulturnatten.dk) sees Copenhagen's museums, theatres, galleries, libraries and even Rosenborg Slot throw open their doors through the night with a wide range of special events.

✯ Halloween

Historically Halloween hasn't been a big Danish

tradition, but it coincides with the midterm break, so the country's big theme parks fire up for the week and highlight the fright factor (in a family-friendly way, of course). Tivoli and Djurs Sommerland both come to the party.

December

Sure, the weather is cold and damp, but Denmark cranks up the *hygge* (cosiness) and celebrates Christmas in style: twinkling lights, ice-skating rinks, and gallons of warming *gløgg* (mulled wine).

🔒 Christmas Fairs

Fairs are held countrywide throughout December, with booths selling sometimes-kitschy arts and crafts and traditional Yuletide foodie treats. For an idyllic, olden-days atmosphere, visit somewhere with a strong connection to the past: Den Gamle By in Aarhus, or historic Ribe in southern Jutland.

◉ Tivoli

Copenhagen's Tivoli reopens for Christmas with a large market and buckets of schmaltz. Attractions include special Christmas tableaux, costumed staff and theatre shows. Fewer rides are operational but the traditional *gløgg* and *æbleskiver* (spherical pancakes) ought to be ample compensation.

Itineraries

 Denmark's Classic Hits

The beauty of Denmark's compact size is that it never takes too long to get from A to B. To cover the classic sites, start in **Copenhagen** and soak up the riches (cultural, culinary, retail) of the capital. From there, it's a short hop west to **Roskilde** to investigate Denmark's royal and Viking heritage. Further west, **Odense** offers up fairy-tale charm in abundance and plenty of ways to connect with the city's famous native son, Hans Christian Andersen. Stop in **Kolding** for a polished mix of the old and cutting-edge, en route to history-soaked **Ribe**, Denmark's oldest town, oozing chocolate-box appeal. From here, you can pause on the history lessons for a hefty dose of childhood nostalgia at **Legoland**, then some lakeside R&R in **Silkeborg** (go canoeing or do a cruise through the picturesque lakes of the area). Squeeze in a quick hop north to luminous **Skagen** for art, beaches and fresh seafood. Finally, stop by cosmopolitan **Aarhus**, the country's second city. It holds a few surprises – not least its rainbow-topped art museum – and from here, you can take a ferry to northern Zealand for an easy and scenic return to Copenhagen.

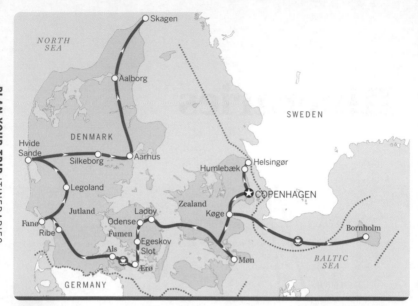

 Denmark in Detail

Designate **Copenhagen** some quality time in your itinerary, and make a couple of day trips outside the capital to check out the superb modern art at the Louisiana Museum in **Humlebæk** and magnificent castles such as Kronborg Slot at **Helsingør**. Head south to potter about pretty, historic **Køge**, then catch a ferry out to the Baltic bombshell of **Bornholm** – spend a few days exploring the island's bike trails, sandy beaches and gastronomic treats. Once you're back on Zealand, head further south to **Møn**, an enchanting island with some of the country's most dramatic scenery – the white-chalk cliffs of Møn rise sharply over a jade-green sea and are as pretty as a picture.

Head back across southern Zealand to reach the island of Funen. **Odense** is a must-see for its various tributes to hometown-hero Hans Christian Andersen, but take time to visit the Viking ship grave at **Ladby**, and the marvellous Renaissance treats at **Egeskov Slot**. A day or two on the friendly old seafaring island of **Ærø** will recharge your batteries.

Onward west – a ferry can take you from Ærø to **Als**, and on to southern Jutland, where you can reach **Ribe** for history lessons with a decidedly friendly face (mock Viking settlements, a nightwatchman's tour of the cobbled streets), plus some outstanding bird-watching nearby. Jump on a boat out of Esbjerg for the 12-minute trip to idyllic **Fanø**, and take a pause in Sønderho.

A detour to **Legoland** is essential – this place will blow your mind with its astounding creations made from the humble plastic brick. Then it's back to the west coast for more mind-blowing activity – this time courtesy of North Sea winds, perfect for kitesurfing in **Hvide Sande**.

From here, wend your way east to leafy, lakeside **Silkeborg**, then on to **Aarhus** for top-notch museum-mooching and noshing. The rejuvenated northern city of **Aalborg** warrants a stop for its Utzon architecture and a Viking burial ground, but the best comes last at cinematic **Skagen**, hugging Denmark's northernmost tip. Make time to admire the artwork, indulge in fine seafood, soak in the incredible northern light and dip a toe in the angry seas.

Above: Kronborg Slot
(p97)
Right: Silkeborg (p224)

THOMAS E. GUNNARSSON / GETTY IMAGES ©

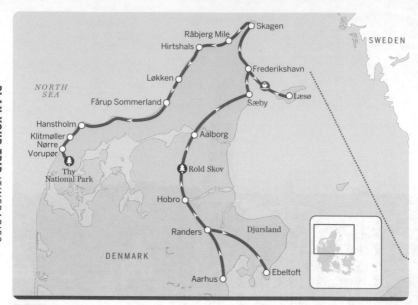

Northern Exposure

2 WEEKS

Why should Copenhagen get all the attention? For some off-the-beaten-track seaside R&R, the underrated further reaches of northern Jutland beckon, with plenty of quirky treats alongside the expected sun, sea, sand and seafood.

Start from **Aarhus,** with its fine dining, ace festivals and snazzy museums (particularly rainbow-topped ARoS and head-turning new Moesgård), and head north, stopping in **Randers** for a man-made rainforested dome and a left-field dose of Elvis kitsch courtesy of a replica Graceland. With kids in tow, a detour to the safari parks and sandy beaches of Djursland is a must – but there's lots for grown-ups here, too, particularly in the gourmet hotspots at Femmøller outside **Ebeltoft**.

Sleepy **Hobro** offers history in the shape of a 10th-century Viking ring fortress, while **Rold Skov** lets you cut loose on forested mountain-bike trails. and **Aalborg** puts on her best face to impress you with a rejuvenated waterfront and the final design from revered architect Jørn Utzon. At sweet **Sæby** you can connect with Danish literature and go back for seconds at bountiful seafood buffets.

From **Frederikshavn**, catch a ferry to the island of **Læsø** to take a step back in time (salt baths optional). Next is **Skagen**, a delightful slice of seaside life with a winning art museum, boutique hotels and alfresco dockside dining. Southwest of Skagen, the walkabout sand dunes of **Råbjerg Mile** let you know mother nature is still in charge, while in **Hirtshals** you can admire more of her handiwork at a huge aquarium. Relax in **Løkken** – but not too much. Nearby **Fårup Sommerland** can get your heart pumping with amusement rides and a waterpark.

Heading south, stop to inspect WWII-era bunkers and devour a fab fishy dockside lunch in **Hanstholm** before a visit to quirky 'Cold Hawaii': the small surfing village of **Klitmøller**, where you can get wet and windblown in various ways. Be sure to stop by the new sea baths at nearby **Nørre Vorupør** and take to some walking or cycling trails through the dune heaths of **Thy National Park**. You'll return to Aarhus with the cobwebs well and truly blown away.

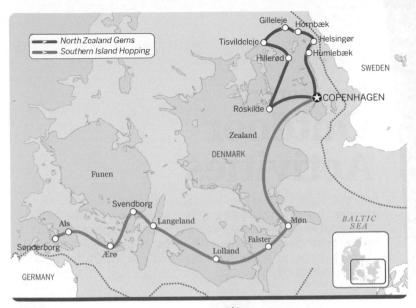

North Zealand Gems
Southern Island Hopping

 ## North Zealand Gems

1 WEEK

An easy and accessible circuit of north Zealand offers glam beaches, royal remains, fairytale castles, Viking ships and cutting-edge architecture.

Start in fjord-side **Roskilde**, where you can see Viking longships and pay your respects to Denmark's past kings and queens at the country's finest cathedral. North from here is magnificent Frederiksborg Slot, which dominates the town of **Hillerød**. It's hard to decide which is more impressive, the baroque interiors or the regal grounds.

For northern light and sunbathing, head to the beaches: the chic bathing hotels of **Tisvildeleje** are worth a stop, as are the sculptures between **Gilleleje** and Hornbæk. **Hornbæk** is where the young and gorgeous go to catch some sun.

Further along the coast is historic Kronborg Slot in **Helsingør**, more than just the home of Hamlet. Helsingør's newest drawcard is the stunningly designed national maritime museum. Take the coastal road south to **Humlebæk** and the Louisiana Museum – its architecture rivals its contemporary art collection. A short drive along the 'Danish Riviera' leads to **Copenhagen**.

 ## Southern Island Hopping

1 WEEK

Most travellers between **Copenhagen** and Jutland take the quickest, direct route across Funen, but this meandering option is for those after rural retreats and quiet villages, with small ferries providing island-hopping potential.

From the capital make a beeline south to **Møn**, then across to **Falster** and on to **Lolland**. This trio is known as Denmark's 'South Sea Islands'. While they may lack the coconut palms associated with that label, they offer a fine glimpse of Scandinavian island life: fields, sandy beaches and rustic manor houses. Allocate time to Møn's chalky cliffs, Marielyst's glorious beach (on Falster), and Lolland's theme parks.

Western Lolland connects to **Langeland** by ferry – and now you're in the South Funen Archipelago. This stretch of green connects by road to Funen, and from **Svendborg**'s harbour you can catch a ferry to **Ærø**, an island well worth a visit for its maritime history, bike lanes, farmhouses and picture-perfect bathing huts. Ferry on to **Als**, connected by road to Jutland proper at the larger town of **Sønderborg**. And now you're in the southeast corner of Jutland, with a whole peninsula to explore…

Plan Your Trip

Outdoor Activities

Although small (and very flat), Denmark has great diversity for activities, from island-hopping cycling adventures to Lake District canoeing. The sea, never far away, offers fishing, sailing, windsurfing and beachgoing, while the national parks and hiking trails offer walkers a chance to stretch their legs. And everywhere, the cycling opportunities are outstanding.

Best of the Outdoors

Best Time to Go

June to August. Having been cooped up for most of the winter, Denmark comes alive in summer, shaking off winter's grey blanket to catch a Scandi tan. May and September can also be good, weatherwise.

Best Cycling

For long-distance pedalling, any of the 11 national cycling routes is a fine choice. Leisurely island cycling is outstanding on Bornholm or Ærø. Looking to catch some air? Forested Rold Skov has good mountain-biking tracks.

Best Walking

Scenic short walks take in the white cliffs of Møns Klint, or the bucolic Lake District. For a longer ramble, the Hærvej Route covers Jutland's spine, while Øhavssti incorporates the South Funen Archipelago.

Best on the Water

Sailors flock to Svendborg – from here there's an archipelago to explore. Canoeists will love the lakes and rivers of the Lake District (regional hub: Silkeborg). Wind-powered watersports are big on the west coast – try Hvide Sande or Klitmøller.

Cycling

Denmark is a superb country for cyclists, with more than 12,000km of signposted cycle routes and relatively quiet country roads that wend through attractive, gently undulating landscapes.

As well as the Danes' widespread use of cycling as a means of commuting, you'll also see locals (and tourists) enjoying cycling holidays. The big draw for touring cyclists are the 11 national routes, which are in excellent condition, but there are also oodles of regional and local routes to get you pedalling. The routes are well suited to recreational cyclists, including families with children.

Danish cyclists enjoy rights that, in most other countries, are reserved for motorists. There are bicycle lanes along major city roads and through central areas, road signs are posted for bicycle traffic, and bicycle racks can be found at grocery shops, train stations and many other public places. Drivers have an incredibly accommodating attitude towards cyclists.

When bicycle touring, accommodation is easy to find, be it at a small country inn or campground. One advantage of Denmark's small scale is that you're never far from a bed and a hot shower.

For quality rental bikes, Copenhagen and Aarhus are your best starting points, but you can generally rent bikes in every town enquire locally. Note: you are not legally required to wear a helmet. Bikes are allowed on most trains, some buses and all ferries.

Cycling Routes

Signs along cycling routes are blue, with a white bike symbol. Note that many routes crisscross each other, so it's possible to combine routes.

➡ **National routes** White route number in a red square. North–south routes have uneven numbers; east–west routes are even. There are two circular routes (10 and 12).

➡ **Regional routes** White route number on a blue background, with numbers 16 to 99.

➡ **Local routes** White route number on a blue background, with numbers 100 to 999.

Planning & Resources

The best way to tour Denmark by bike is by grabbing a map and planning it yourself. Tours, not surprisingly, are also available and are well run, although they tend to be rather pricey.

For planning, a fantastic resource is the Cyclistic website (http://cyclistic.dk/en/). The best overview map is the *Cycling Map of Denmark* (Dkr95), a 1:500,000-scale map that shows all the national routes. (Note that it's great for general planning, but not detailed enough to use on the trail.)

Each county produces its own detailed 1:100,000 cycle touring maps; many of them come with booklets detailing accommodation, sights and other local information. These maps are in Danish, German and English, cost around Dkr129, and are available at tourist offices or online via the Danish cycling federation,

Dansk Cyklist Forbund (its shop is at http://shop.dcf.dk).

Websites

Visit Denmark (www.visitdenmark.com) A good starting point, with loads of useful information on its cycling-dedicated pages (including cycling with kids). It also outlines 25 great 'panorama cycling routes' of 15km to 40km length, broken into East Coast and West Coast Denmark.

Cyclistic (http://cyclistic.dk/en/) Fabulous resource, combining route-finding for cyclists with attractions and practical information along the way (sights, accommodation, food etc).

Dansk Cyklist Forbund (www.cyklistforbun det.dk) Website of the Danish Cycling Federation. There is well-hidden info in English – under 'Alt om cykling', click on 'På tur i Danmark og verden', then 'På tur i Danmark'. A link at the bottom of the page takes you to 'Biking in Denmark' and some useful info.

Cycle Guide DK (http://cycleguide.dk) Copenhagen-focused, but with good advice on safety issues, and cycling culture and etiquette.

Cycling Embassy of Denmark (www. cycling-embassy.dk) Has a great range of information and some cool stats, too – for example, nine out of 10 Danes own a bicycle; 45% of all Danish children cycle to school.

Swimming

Although the water temperature would worry even brass monkeys most of the year, enjoyable seaside swimming can be had in the warmer months (July and August). The quality of the beaches is outstanding as the majority have clean water, silky sand and plenty of room.

CYCLING BORNHOLM

Out in the Baltic, magical Bornholm is ideal for exploring by bike. More than 230km of bike trails cover main roads, extensive forests, former train routes and fine sandy beaches. There's a multitude of picturesque coastal hamlets and medieval round churches, and the excellent local food and drink are a great reward for pedalling.

Consider burning some calories from Gudhjem to Østermarie and on to Svaneke, cycling via factories producing chocolates, toffees and sweets; smokehouses; farm shops; a dairy; and a microbrewery. The island's tourist offices stock a free cycling booklet, outlining 21 routes of varying difficulty across the island.

DENMARK'S NATIONAL CYCLING ROUTES

ROUTE NO	ROUTE NAME	DISTANCE	DESCRIPTION
1	Vestkystruten (West Coast Route)	560km (70% sealed)	Begins in Rudbøl (by the German border) and runs to Skagen along the windswept west coast of Jutland, taking in sandy beaches, tidal flats and dunes.
2	Hanstholm–Copenhagen	420km (80% sealed)	Begins in the north Jutland fishing port of Hanstholm and runs southeast across central Jutland to Ebeltoft. The Ebeltoft–Odden ferry allows you to pick up the route again through northern Zealand to Copenhagen.
3	Hærvejsruten (Hærvej Route)	450km (78% sealed)	Heads from Skagen along the backbone of Jutland to Padborg on the German border. From Viborg it follows the Hærvej, or Old Military Road. See also www.haervej.dk.
4	Søndervig–Copenhagen	310km (90% sealed)	Runs from Søndervig on the west Jutland coast, east to Hou, then by ferry (via Samsø) across to Kalundborg, and east across Zealand to finish in Copenhagen.
5	Østkystruten (East Coast Route)	650km (90% sealed)	The longest route begins in Skagen and runs the length of Jutland, hugging the east coast to finish at Sønderborg.
6	Esbjerg–Copenhagen	330km (92% sealed)	Begins in Esbjerg and runs east through Funen and Zealand to finish in Copenhagen. Note: cyclists are not permitted on the 18km Storebælt bridge linking Funen and Zealand; you will need to take a train.
7	Sjællands Odde–Rødbyhavn	240km (90% sealed)	A family-friendly route that begins at Odden in northwest Zealand and travels south through north Falster and Lolland to end at Rødbyhavn.
8	Sydhavsruten (South Sea Route)	360km (95% sealed)	This trail sweeps across southern Denmark and requires a couple of island-hops. It begins in Rudbøl, traverses Jutland to Als, crosses to southern Funen, Langeland, Lolland, Falster and ends at Møns Klint.
9	Helsingør–Gedser	290km (92% sealed)	This route has links with Sweden and Germany thanks to ferry connections at its start (Helsingør) and end (Gedser) points. It follows the east coast of Zealand before tracking south through Møn and Falster.
10	Bornholm Rundt (Around Bornholm)	105km (90% sealed)	Bornholm is an idyllic island encircled by a popular cycling route.
12*	Limfjordsruten (Limfjord Route)	610km (90% sealed)	The route hugs both sides of the Limfjord in northern Jutland, from the Kattegat to the North Sea. Ferry and bridge 'shortcuts' across the fjord are possible.

*Note: there is no route 11.

Generally speaking the Baltic waters (east coast) will be a degree or two warmer than those of the North Sea (west coast). If you're swimming on the west coast of Jutland, caution needs to be taken with currents and undertows, otherwise the waters are generally calm and child-friendly.

Aside from the miles of beaches (no place in Denmark is more than 52km from the beach), most towns have a family-focused aqua centre with heated pool (look for the *svømmehal*, or swimming hall). These are getting more grandiose, offering plenty of other ways to wrinkle your skin (waterslides, jacuzzis, saunas, kids' play area, day spas).

There are also huge summertime waterparks – incredibly popular are the aqua playlands of Lalandia (p140) (Billund and Lolland) and Sommerland (p224), attached to amusement parks at Fårup near Løkken, and Djursland.

Watersports

The wild winds of Jutland's west coast have gained plenty of attention from windsurfers and kitesurfers, and the consistently good conditions attract many European enthusiasts to Klitmøller (aka 'Cold Hawaii', a nickname we love) and Hvide Sande.

Not only do these towns hold numerous contests each year, but they boast great terrain for all skill levels. Experts can carve up the wild North Sea breakers, while beginners can master the basics on the inland fjords.

At both Klitmøller and Hvide Sande, outfits offer gear rental and lessons in windsurfing and kitesurfing. There are other watersports on offer, too – surfing, and paddle boarding. At Hvide Sande there's also a cool water-skiing course, which skiers navigate using cable rope-tows.

Sailing

Denmark's long (7314km) and varied coastline and 406 islands are made for sailing, something the Danes embrace enthusiastically.

The island-speckled, sheltered cruising area between Jutland's east coast and Sweden is very popular. The mixture of sea, calmer inshore waters and still fjords, combined with scores of pretty, cobbled and often historic harbours (more than 350 marinas) makes sailing a perfect way to explore the country. Yachts and motorboats equipped with all the necessary safety, living and navigational equipment can be hired – prices vary considerably by season and size of craft.

Charter a yacht through **Scancharter** (www.scancharter.com) or **JIM Søferie** (www.jim-soeferie.dk). The latter website also has a few tour suggestions. If hiring your own craft sounds too much like hard work, major towns along Funen's southern coast offer sailing cruises around the islands of the South Funen Archipelago. Svendborg is an excellent yachting hub.

Canoeing & Kayaking

Canoeists and kayakers can paddle the extensive coastline and fjords or the rivers and lakes. White water is about the only thing that's missing in mountain-free Denmark.

The country's best canoeing and kayaking can be experienced along the rivers Gudenå (in Jutland) and Suså (in Zealand). The idyllic forests and gentle waterways of

TOP BEACHES

Our authors have travelled the length and breadth of Denmark to give you their favourite spots to take a dip.

Copenhagen (Islands Brygge) Not technically a beach, but slap-bang in Copenhagen's main canal, this designer outdoor pool comes with downtown views and delectable eye candy.

Zealand (Tisvildeleje) Sandbars, shallows and chic hotels on Zealand's north coast 'riviera'.

Møn, Falster & Lolland (Marielyst, Falster) Endless sandy beaches and a family-friendly holiday vibe.

Bornholm (Dueodde) Soft endless sand, epic skies and a Nordic forest backdrop.

Funen (Vesterstrand, Ærø) Swim and/or sunset-watch among the brightly painted bathing huts outside Ærøskøbing.

Southern Jutland (Rømø) Miles of west-coast emptiness, plus hair-raising speed-machine activities down south.

Central Jutland (Hvide Sande) Colourful wind- and kitesurfers harnessing the North Sea wind.

Northern Jutland (Skagen) Wild winds and shifting sands to the west, calm family-friendly waters to the east, and everywhere are the blue hues that inspired artists.

'TIS THE SEASON

If you're thinking about visiting Denmark to partake of the outdoors, it's worth bearing in mind a few things. There's an old joke that Denmark has two winters – a green one and a white one – but that is rather unkind. While it's true the weather can be fickle, the summer season most reliably runs from mid-June to mid-August. That's when there are enough travellers around to ensure regular departures of boat cruises or frequent schedules of windsurfing classes etc, and hence there's a wider range of activity options during this two-month window. Depending on weather and demand, however, many operators may open in May and remain open until mid/late September.

And in winter...? Denmark is *not* a destination for winter-sports enthusiasts. The country's highest post is a trifling 171m. That's not to say that Danes don't love (or excel at) snowbound activity – it's just that many of them head north to Norway to engage in it.

central Jutland's prized Lake District are perfect for cycling, rambling and, especially, canoeing – multiday canoeing-and-camping adventures are possible here. You can hire canoes and equipment in Silkeborg. The lakes are generally undemanding as far as water conditions go, although some previous experience is an advantage.

Canoeing the small coves, bays and peninsulas of several Danish fjords is also an option, including Limfjorden in northern Jutland, and the fjords of Zealand: Roskilde Fjord, Holbæk Fjord and Isefjord.

Walking

There's not much wilderness in wee Denmark (especially in comparison to its larger, more mountain-endowed neighbours), and walking and hiking is not as widespread a phenomenon as cycling. But rambling is popular nonetheless, and all local tourist offices will be able to point you in the direction of a local area with walking trails.

In Jutland, there are some picturesque trails through the forested Rold Skov area, the Mols Bjerge and Thy national parks, and the bucolic Lake District. The Hærvej (www.haervej.dk), the Old Military Road, is a 250km historic route from the German border north to Viborg. It's been converted into a popular, well-maintained cycling, hiking and horse-riding trail; the website has information about facilities along the route.

The 220km Øhavssti (Archipelago Trail) is a long-distance walking trail spanning Funen and the islands to its south. It snakes its way from west to east Funen along the southern coast, then travels northern Langeland. It concludes with a delightful 36km stretch across Ærø's countryside.

Shorter walks at or around scenic landmarks include the base of the chalk cliffs at Møns Klint; along the coast at Stevns Klint; to Grenen sand spit, Denmark's northernmost point; and around 147m Himmelbjerget, one of Denmark's highest peaks.

Plan Your Trip
Travel with Children

Denmark is prime family-holiday territory, especially in high season when family-filled camper vans hit the road to celebrate the summer break. Theme parks, amusement parks, zoos and child-friendly beaches are just part of the story – businesses go out of their way to woo families, and children are rarely made to feel unwelcome.

Denmark for Kids
What to See & Do

Entry to most museums is free for kids, and you won't have to minimise your time in cultural attractions lest your offspring start climbing the walls – almost everywhere has displays and activities designed especially to keep kids entertained.

Travellers with children should enquire at local tourist offices – all regions have places where kids are king, from huge indoor swim centres to play centres and petting farms.

The larger theme parks and animal parks aren't particularly cheap, but most attractions have family passes and packages. Free entertainment can come in the form of long sandy beaches, parks and playgrounds.

Where to Stay

In high season (mid-June to mid-August) camping grounds are hives of activity, and many put on entertainment and activity programs for junior guests.

Hostels are exceedingly well set up for, and welcoming to, families. Rooms often sleep up to six (in bunks); there will invariably be a guest kitchen and lounge facilities. Farm stays may offer a rural idyll and/or the chance to get your hands dirty.

Best Regions for Kids
Copenhagen
Capital attractions include funpark-meets-fairy-tale Tivoli (p45), polar bears at the zoo (p61), and the colourful fish of Den Blå Planet (p63).

Møn, Falster & Lolland
Chalk cliffs and a mind-bending geology centre (p133) on Møn, beaches and a medieval village (p136) on Falster, and a safari park (p140) and waterpark (p140) on Lolland.

Funen
Odense pays homage to the tales of Hans Christian Andersen (p159). Plus there's a moat-encircled castle (p170) with mazes and marvels, and bunkers and battleships at a 1950s fort (p179).

Central Jutland
Plastic fantastic Legoland (p231) – need we say more? Close by are a huge waterpark and a safari park, plus family canoeing opportunities, beaches and loads more amusement parks.

Northern Jutland
Sandy strands and shifting sand dunes that will put your sandcastles to shame, plus a mega-aquarium (p255) that reveals just what lies beneath.

In resorts, summer houses are available at a reasonable price (usually by the week). In cities that are emptier due to the summer exodus, business hotels may drop their rates and add bunks to rooms to woo family business.

Where to Eat

On the whole, Danish restaurants welcome children with open arms. Virtually all offer high chairs, many have a *børnemenu* (children's menu) or will at least provide children's portions, and some have play areas. Two family-focused chains to look for are the steak chain **Jensen's Bøfhus** (www.jensens.com), and the US-influenced **Bone's** (www.bones.dk), with a menu of spare ribs, burgers and barbecued chicken. Both chains offer extensive kids menus and all-you-can-eat ice-cream bars – bonus!

Self-catering will be a breeze if you are staying somewhere with kitchen facilities – larger supermarkets will stock all you'll need (including baby items), but may have shorter hours than you might expect. There are oodles of prime picnic spots.

Transport

Naturally, having your own set of wheels will make life easier, but public transport shouldn't be dismissed – on trains, children under 12 years travel free if they are with an adult travelling on a standard ticket (each adult can take two children free).

A cycling holiday may be doable with slightly older kids, as the terrain is flat and distances between towns are not vast. Larger bicycle-rental outfits have kids trailers and kids bikes for rent.

Children's Highlights

Culture Vultures

Copenhagen Nationalmuseet (p45) has a brilliant hands-on children's section, while kids are spoiled at Louisiana (p91) with a wing of their own, where they can create artistic masterpieces.

Zealand The superb Viking Ship Museum (p109) in Roskilde displays five Viking ships; there's also Viking shipbuilding and the chance to go on a longboat cruise. M/S Museet for Søfart (p99)

(National Maritime Museum) in Helsingør has vivid, interactive exhibitions.

Funen At Fyrtøjet (p159) (The Tinderbox) in Odense, kids get to explore the world of Hans Christian Andersen through storytelling and music. Egeskov Slot (p170) is a must – the summer program includes evening concerts, ghost hunts and fireworks.

Central Jutland Aarhus' art museum (p208) will wow kids with its giant *Boy* sculpture and awesome rooftop rainbow walkway. Kvindemuseet (p212) has hands-on kids' exhibits in its 'History of Childhood' section.

Funparks & Theme Parks

Copenhagen Tivoli (p45) is a charming combination of amusement rides, flower gardens, food pavilions, carnival games and open-air stage shows. Bakken (p92) is its poor relation but still provides loads of old-fashioned fun.

Møn, Falster & Lolland Lalandia (p140) on Lolland really undersells itself with the label 'waterpark'.

Central Jutland Legoland (p231) is the big daddy of Danish theme parks, joined by a new Lalandia (p232) as its neighbour. Aarhus has Tivoli Friheden (p213) for rides and games, and Djurs Sommerland (p224) has the blockbuster combo of waterpark and amusement park in one superpopular attraction.

Northern Jutland Djurs Sommerland's northern sister is Fårup Sommerland (p257), equally popular and home to a waterpark and amusement rides.

Animal Encounters

Copenhagen The zoo (p61) houses a multitude of critters, and some lovely new architect-designed homes for them – including a new polar bear enclosure with glass tunnel. Den Blå Planet (p63) takes its fishy business seriously.

Møn, Falster & Lolland Knuthenborg Safari Park (p140) on Lolland has a drive-through savannah area for a taste of Africa (but without the good weather).

Bornholm Sommerfugle og Tropeland (Butterfly Park , Tropical Land; www.sommer fugleparken.dk; Gammel Rønnevej 14; adult/child Dkr90/60; ☺10am-5pm daily mid-May-late Oct) showcases jungle climates and has 1000 butterflies.

Funen Odense Zoo (p159) has a new African area. Kerteminde's aquarium (p168) is home to seals, porpoises and fine-finned fish.

Central Jutland Randers Regnskov (p234) is a sultry, dome-enclosed tropical zoo taking you to Africa, Asia and South America. At Skandinavisk Dyrepark (p224) you can assess a full collection of Scandi species, including polar bears and brown bears. Ree Park (p221) has animals from all corner of the globe. Silkeborg's Aqua (p225) has an abundance of fish and cute otters.

Northern Jutland Aalborg has a quality zoo (p243), while Hirtshals is home to one of the largest aquariums (p255) in northern Europe.

Time Travel

The Danes have a seemingly limitless enthusiasm for dressing up and re-creating history, and they do it well in countless open-air museums and re-created Viking camps and medieval villages, all with activities for youngsters.

Zealand The experimental archaeology centre of Sagnlandet Lejre (p113), 'Land of Legends', is fascinating. Danmarks Borgcenter (p124) in Vordingborg lets kids explore medieval castle life and the world of kings using iPad technology.

Møn, Falster & Lolland Falster's Middelalder-centret (p136) re-creates an early-15th-century medieval village.

Bornholm Oh look, it's another ye-olde village: Bornholms Middelaldercenter (p152) re-creates a medieval fort and village.

Funen Den Fynske Landsby (p162) is a re-created olden-days country village with the requisite costumes and farmyard animals.

Southern Jutland Ribe VikingeCenter (p195) re-creates the Viking era in Denmark's oldest town; finish the day with a walk alongside the town's nightwatchman.

Central Jutland Den Gamle By (p208) (The Old Town) in Aarhus is a photogenic open-air museum. Hobro has a Viking-era farmstead (p236) to complement its Viking fortress.

Best Fresh-Air Fun

Copenhagen Amager Strandpark (p61) is a sand-sational artificial lagoon, with acres of sandy beach. Playground facilities and shallow water make it ideal for children. Plus, you can't visit Copenhagen and *not* take a canal boat trip (p62).

Zealand Roskilde's Viking Ship Museum (p109) runs sailing trips on the fjord. The beautiful beaches of northern Zealand are great for outdoor summertime fun.

Møn, Falster & Lolland The Falster beach resort of Marielyst (p137) is marketed as a family-oriented 'activity town'; take a boat trip to see the white cliffs of Møns Klint (p132).

Bornholm The calm and shallow waters of the sweeping beach at Dueodde (p146) suit families to a T.

Funen The grounds of Egeskov Slot (p170) are full of mazes, museums and diversions, while Svendborg's Maritimt Center Danmark offers sailing trips on ancient wooden ships.

Southern Jutland For older kids, Rømø's southern beach (p199) is full of wind-blown speed treats: land-yachts or blokarts – buggies with attached parachutelike kites.

Central Jutland Canoeing and camping in the picturesque Lake District (p224) is an undeniably wholesome family pursuit.

Northern Jutland Loads of beaches, mega-sand dunes at Rubjerg Knude (p258) and Råbjerg Mile (p255), and a tractor-pulled bus ride (p252) to Denmark's northernmost tip.

Planning
When to Go

The best time for families to visit Denmark is the best time for any traveller – between May and September. Local school holidays run from late June to mid-August. On the plus side, at this time, good weather is likely (though never assured), all attractions and activities are in full swing and your kids are likely to meet other kids. On the downside, beaches and attractions are busy, and campgrounds and hostels are heavily in demand (and also charge peak prices).

Useful Websites

The official websites visitdenmark.com and visitcopenhagen.com have pages dedicated to family holidays – lists of kid-approved attractions, child-friendly restaurants, ace playgrounds in the capital and much more.

Regions at a Glance

Copenhagen

Food
Design
Museum & Galleries

New Nordic or Old Danish

Copenhagen is one of the world's hottest culinary destinations, home to visionary chefs concocting uniquely Nordic dishes. At the other end of the spectrum, old-school cafes and historic restaurants allow you to discover traditional favourites like smørrebrød (open sandwiches).

Top Marks for Design

Check out architectural show-stealers like the Black Diamond library extension and Operaen; admire the town planning that makes this city so damn user-friendly; and browse museums dedicated to local output that changed the way the world designs and decorates.

Calling Culture Vultures

For a whistle-stop tour through the country's history, nothing beats the Nationalmuseet; fine art excels at Statens Museum for Kunst and Ny Carlsberg Glyptotek. Out of town you can ogle modern art in modern architectural marvels, then check out the art scene in fab city galleries.

p42

Zealand

Castles
Viking History
Beaches

Crowning Glories

Most visitors gravitate to Helsingør's magnificent Kronborg Slot, otherwise known as Elsinore, home of Shakespeare's indecisive antihero, Hamlet. But don't ignore Frederiksborg Slot, a glorious Dutch Renaissance–style confection. Divine Dragsholm Slot combines food and finery with aplomb.

Investigate the Viking Era

Got a thing for rugged, hirsute marauders? Be wowed by Viking ships at Roskilde, ponder the enigmatic ring fortress at Trelleborg, and get swept into the Iron Age lifestyle at the archaeology centre outside Lejre.

Coastal Capers

Gorgeous white-sand beaches line the northern coast, and summer beachgoers create a sunshine-and-ice-cream vibe in favourite spots such as Hornbæk and Tisvildeleje. Coastal trails give access to the stunning landscapes of Stevns Klint.

p93

Møn, Falster & Lolland

Landscapes
Family Attractions
Arts & Crafts

Elevated Heights

You may notice that Denmark is rather flat. So Møn's striking white chalk cliffs, rising 128m above a jade-green sea, are beloved of scenery-seekers. The cliffs are one of Denmark's most famous landmarks – take a boat trip to check them out.

Fun for the Whole Family

This island trio attracts summer-sun-seeking families, and there are oodles of attractions aiming to enrich the holiday experience: interactive museums, a mega-waterpark, zoo, safari park and re-created medieval village.

Møn Artistry

Møn is a magnet for artists and potters, keen to tap into the inspiration offered by cliffs, coastline and clay soils. Their works are on display in various studios and galleries, but you can admire wondrous art from an altogether different era in ancient, fresco-adorned churches.

p126

Bornholm

Beaches
Food
Cycling

Bathing Beauties

This Baltic outpost is encircled by beaches, but Dueodde justifiably hogs the limelight: a vast stretch backed by pine trees and expansive dunes. Its soft sand is so fine-grained it was once used in hourglasses and ink blotters.

Culinary Offerings

This productive island is home to historic fish smokehouses, first-class organic produce, a brace of fine-dining restaurants (Kadeau is a New Nordic star), and an ever-expanding league of food artisans, creating treats from ice creams and caramels, to hams and microbrews.

Cycling Bliss

More than 230km of bike trails cover main roads, forests, former train routes and beaches. There are a multitude of picturesque coastal hamlets and medieval round churches, and the excellent local food and drink are your reward for pedalling some gently undulating landscape.

p141

Funen

Castles
Fairy Tales
Islands

To the Manor Born

Dozens of castles and manor houses dot Funen. The big daddy of them all is splendid Egeskov Slot, complete with moat and drawbridge, a doll's house beyond compare, and summertime evening fireworks.

Once upon a Time...

A baby was born to a cobbler and a washerwoman, in 1805 in Odense. That baby went on to write fairy tales known and loved the world over. Odense honours home-grown Hans Christian Andersen in all manner of ways, including museums dedicated to the man and sculptures from his most famous stories.

Island-Hopping

This region includes a bevy of islands (90 of 'em!), some home to people, some just to birds, rabbits and deer. Island-hopping by ferry or yacht is a salt-sprayed pleasure, as is exploring nautical-but-nice Ærø.

p157

Southern Jutland

Historic Villages
Nature
Design

Picturebook Destinations

You want thatch-roofed houses, blooming gardens and cobblestone streets lined with boutiques, galleries and cafes? You need Ribe (Denmark's oldest town), Møgeltønder and the island of Fanø on your itinerary. Careful, you might overdose on quaintness.

Bird-Watching Bliss

Stretching along Jutland's west coast is the marshy Wadden Sea National Park, ripe for exploration. Its tidal rhythms provide opportunities for seal-spotting, winter oyster-collecting and bountiful bird-watching.

Unlikely Designer Destinations

Admire Utzon architecture in modern Esbjerg, a brilliant design museum in suburban Kolding and, in a converted water tower in Tønder, a Wegner chair collection that will have design buffs drooling.

p185

Central Jutland

Activities
Family Attractions
Art

The Great Outdoors

Truly something for everyone: the Lake District has canoeing and rambling; the wild west coast offers first-class wind- and kitesurfing; and Rold Skov has excellent mountain biking. Aarhus is perfect for city cycling, while Djursland has long, pristine beaches.

Legoland & Loads More

Did someone say Lego? Yes, this is the spiritual home of the wondrous plastic brick. There's also some cool kid-oriented stuff in Aarhus, Randers has a brilliant man-made rainforest, and Djursland is prime holiday turf, brimming with amusement and safari parks.

Modern Art Marvels

Modern art struts its stuff in this region – prime viewing is *Your Rainbow Panorama* atop Aarhus' outstanding ARoS. You can admire (don't touch!) gobsmacking glassworks in Ebeltoft, appreciate Asger Jorn's repertoire in Silkeborg and ponder conceptual art in Herning.

p205

Northern Jutland

Landscapes
Beaches
Food

Mother Nature's Finest

Visitors can witness the region's natural beauty without needing to rough it: the shifting sands, the luminous light, the raging winds, the clashing waters. You'll understand why artists and writers have felt inspired here.

Beachy Keen

Both the east and west coasts draw holidaymakers to long sandy stretches – sometimes windy and woolly on the west, more sheltered on the east. Northernmost Skagen combines the best of both worlds, but Løkken, Tornby Strand and Frederikshavn have shore appeal.

Fresh Catch

At the *røgeri* (smokehouse) in Hanstholm, harbour-side buffets of Sæby, chic restaurants of Skagen and the smart menus around Aalborg, you're left in little doubt – seafood is king here. And it's a worthy monarch, fresh as can be.

p240

On the Road

Northern Jutland p240

Central Jutland p205

Southern Jutland p185

Funen p157

Zealand p93

⊗ **Copenhagen** p42

Bornholm p141

Møn, Falster & Lolland p126

Copenhagen

Includes ➡

Copenhagen 42
Around Copenhagen . . 91
Ishøj 92
Charlottenlund 92
Klampenborg 92
Lyngby 92

Best Places to Eat

➡ Noma (p75)

➡ Kadeau (p75)

➡ Kanalen (p75)

➡ Höst (p71)

Best Places to Drink

➡ Ved Stranden 10 (p78)

➡ 1105 (p78)

➡ Ruby (p78)

➡ Mikkeller (p80)

➡ Lidkoeb (p80)

Best Places to Stay

➡ Hotel Nimb (p67)

➡ Hotel D'Angleterre (p68)

➡ Hotel Guldsmeden (p69)

➡ CPH Living (p69)

Why Go?

Copenhagen is the coolest kid on the Nordic block. Edgier than Stockholm and worldlier than Oslo, the Danish capital gives Scandinavia the X factor. Just ask style bibles *Monocle* and *Wallpaper* magazines, which fawn over its industrial-chic bar, design and fashion scenes, and culinary revolution. This is where you'll find New Nordic pioneer Noma, (once again) voted the world's best restaurant in 2014, and one of 15 Michelin-starred restaurants in town – not bad for a city of 1.2 million.

Yet Copenhagen is more than just seasonal cocktails and geometric threads. A royal capital with almost nine centuries under its svelte belt, it's equally well versed when it comes to world-class museums and storybook streetscapes. Its cobbled, bike-friendly streets are a *hyggelig* (cosy) concoction of sherbet-hued town houses, craft studios and candlelit cafes. Add to this its compact size, and you have what is possibly Europe's most seamless urban experience.

When to Go

Arguably, the best time to drop by is from May to August, when the days are long and the mood upbeat. Events such as Distortion in June, Copenhagen Jazz Festival in July, and both Strøm and Copenhagen Pride in August give the city a fabulous, festive vibe. On a more negative note, many of Copenhagen's top restaurants close for several weeks in July and August.

Golden foliage and cultural events (including Art Copenhagen and Kulturnatten) make autumn appealing, while late November and December counter the chill with Yuletide markets, twinkling lights and *gløgg* (mulled wine).

History

Copenhagen was founded in 1167 by tough-as-nails Bishop Absalon, who erected a fortress on Slotsholmen Island, fortifying a small and previously unprotected harbourside village.

After the fortification was built, the harbourside village grew in importance and took on the name Kømandshavn (Merchant's Port), which was later condensed to København. Absalon's fortress stood until 1369, when it was destroyed in an attack on the town by the powerful Hanseatic states.

In 1376 construction began on a new Slotsholmen fortification, Copenhagen Castle, and in 1416 King Erik of Pomerania took up residence at the site, marking the beginning of the city's role as the capital of Denmark.

Still, it wasn't until the reign of Christian IV, in the first half of the 17th century, that the city was endowed with much of its splendour. A lofty Renaissance designer, Christian IV began an ambitious construction scheme, building two new castles and many other grand edifices, including the Rundetårn observatory and the glorious Børsen, Europe's first stock exchange.

In 1711 the bubonic plague reduced Copenhagen's population of 60,000 by one-third. Tragic fires, one in 1728 and the other in 1795, wiped out large tracts of the city, including most of its timber buildings. However, the worst scourge in the city's history is generally regarded as the unprovoked British bombardment of Copenhagen in 1807, during the Napoleonic Wars. The attack targeted the heart of the city, inflicting numerous civilian casualties and setting hundreds of homes, churches and public buildings on fire.

Copenhagen flourished once again in the 19th and 20th centuries, expanding beyond its old city walls and establishing a reputation as a centre for culture, liberal politics and the arts. Dark times were experienced during WWII with the Nazi occupation, although the city managed to emerge relatively unscathed.

During the war and in the economic depression that had preceded it, many Copenhagen neighbourhoods had deteriorated into slums. In 1948 an ambitious urban renewal policy called the 'Finger Plan' was adopted; this redeveloped much of the city, creating new housing projects interspaced with green areas of parks and recreational facilities that spread out like fingers from the city centre.

A rebellion by young people disillusioned with growing materialism, the nuclear arms race and the authoritarian educational system took hold in Copenhagen in the 1960s. Student protests broke out on the university campus and squatters occupied vacant buildings around the city. It came to a head in 1971 when protesters tore down the fence of an abandoned military camp at the east side of Christianshavn and began an occupation

COPENHAGEN

COPENHAGEN IN...

Two Days

Start with a canal and harbour tour, then soak up the salty atmosphere of Nyhavn on your way to Designmuseum Danmark (p56). Lunch on celebrated smørrebrød at Schønnemann (p74) before heading up the historic Rundetårn (p49) for a bird's-eye view of the city. That done, stock up on Danish design at Illums Bolighus (p85), Hay House (p86) or Stilleben (p86), then pick a restaurant in Vesterbro's buzzing Kødbyen (literally 'Meat City') precinct. Once fed, cap the night with shameless fun and Danish *hygge* (cosiness) at Tivoli (p45). On day two, brush up on your Danish history at Nationalmuseet (p45), lunch at produce market Torvehallerne KBH (p79), break free from the rat race at Christiania (p57) before New Nordic feasting at Kanalen (p75) or Kadeau (p75). If the night is still young, kick on with cocktails at Ruby (p78) or 1105 (p78), or late-night sax at La Fontaine (p84).

Four Days

If you have a third day, escape the city with a trip to art museum Louisiana (p91). Lunch there before heading back into the city to snoop around Rosenborg Slot (p59), then head straight to Ved Stranden 10 (p78) for a well-earned glass of vino. Fine-dine at Höst (p71) or keep it simple and juicy at Cock's & Cows (p71). Kick-start day four with masterpieces at Statens Museum for Kunst (p58) or Ny Carlsberg Glyptotek (p48), then spend the rest of the day treading the grit-hip streets of Nørrebro, home to street art, eclectic bars, and the city's most beautiful cemetery, Assistens Kirkegård (p60). If you get hungry, slip into Manfreds og Vin (p77) for local produce cooked simply and skillfully.

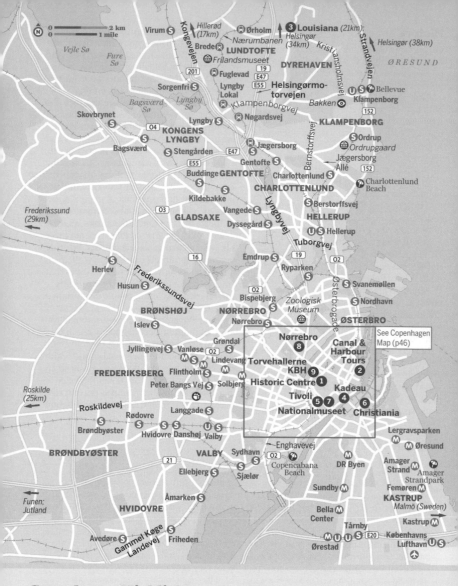

Copenhagen Highlights

1 Hunt down Danish design and fashion at **Hay House** (p86), **Henrik Vibskov** (p86) and **Wood Wood** (p86) in the **historic centre**

2 See city architecture on a **canal and harbour tour** (p63)

3 Be inspired at modern art museum **Louisiana** (p91)

4 Treat your taste buds to New Nordic cuisine at restaurants like **Kadeau** (p75)

5 Indulge in thrills and spills at vintage amusement park **Tivoli** (p45)

6 Let your hair down in the free-spirited neighbourhood of **Christiania** (p57)

7 Learn about the Vikings at **Nationalmuseet** (p45)

8 Seek out bars, boutiques and the resting place of Hans Christian Andersen in **Nørrebro** (p58)

9 Sip and sup your way through Copenhagen's temple to artisan food and drink, **Torvehallerne KBH** (p79)

of the 41-hectare site, naming this settlement Christiania.

In recent decades, major infrastructure projects, enlightened city planning, and a wave of grassroots creativity have helped transform Copenhagen from a provincial Scandinavian capital into an enlightened, international trendsetter. In 2014, the city was once more declared the world's most liveable by influential magazine *Monocle,* as well as the world's healthiest by American broadcaster CNN. Such enviable honours are in no small part propelled by the city's highly developed cycling culture, one that now sees over half of the city's denizens do their daily commuting on a bike saddle. And it doesn't stop there, with Copenhagen now planning to become the world's first CO_2-neutral capital by 2025.

◉ Sights

One of the great things about Copenhagen is its size. Virtually all of Copenhagen's major sightseeing attractions – Tivoli, Nationalmuseet, Statens Museum for Kunst, Marmorkirken, Nyhavn, Rosenborg, Christiansborg, Christiania and Amalienborg – are in or close to the medieval city centre. Only the perennially disappointing Little Mermaid lies outside of the city proper, on the harbourfront.

◉ Rådhuspladsen & Tivoli

The sweeping central square of Rådhuspladsen, flanked on one side by the city hall (or rådhus) and on another by metro construction works, marks the heart of Copenhagen. The bustling pedestrian shopping street Strøget begins at the northeast side of Rådhuspladsen, while the historic pleasure garden, Tivoli, twinkles to the southwest.

★**Tivoli Gardens**　　　　AMUSEMENT PARK
(Map p52; www.tivoli.dk; adult/child under 8yr Dkr99/free; ⊗11am-10pm Sun-Thu, 11am-12.30am Fri, 11am-midnight Sat early Apr-late Sep, reduced hrs rest of yr; 🚻; 🚌2A, 5A, 9A, 12, 26, 250S, 350S, 🚇S-train København H) Dating from 1843, tasteful Tivoli wins fans with its dreamy whirl of amusement rides, twinkling pavilions, carnival games and open-air stage shows. Visitors can ride the renovated, century-old **roller-coaster**, take in the famous Saturday evening **fireworks display** or just soak up the storybook atmosphere. A good tip is to go on Fridays during the summer season, when the open-air Plænen stage hosts free rock concerts from Danish bands

(and the occasional international superstar) from 10pm – go early if it's a big-name act.

Indeed, Tivoli is at its most romantic after dusk, when the fairy lights are switched on, cultural activities unfold, and the clock tower of the neighbouring Rådhus soars in the moonlight like the set of a classic Disney film.

Each of Tivoli's numerous entertainment venues has a different character. Perhaps best known is the open-air pantomime theatre, built in 1874 by Vilhelm Dahlerup, the Copenhagen architect who also designed the royal theatre. Tivoli's large concert hall features performances by international symphony orchestras and ballet troupes, as well as popular musicians. While the many open-air performances are free of charge, there's usually an admission fee for the indoor performances – check the website for venue details, line-ups and prices.

Amusement ride tickets cost Dkr25 (some rides require up to three tickets), making the multiride ticket (Dkr199) better value in most cases.

Outside the main summer season, Tivoli also opens for around three weeks around Halloween and from mid-November to early January for Christmas. For up-to-date opening times, see the Tivoli website.

★**Nationalmuseet**　　　　MUSEUM
(National Museum; Map p52; www.natmus.dk; Ny Vestergade 10; ⊗10am-5pm Tue-Sun; 🚻; 🚌1A, 2A, 11A, 33, 40, 66, 🚇S-train København H) **FREE** For a crash course in Danish history and culture, spend an afternoon at Denmark's National Museum. It has first claims on virtually every antiquity uncovered on Danish soil, including Stone Age tools, Viking weaponry, rune stones, and medieval jewellery. Among the many highlights is a finely crafted 3500-year-old Sun Chariot, as well as bronze *lurs* (horns), some of which date back 3000 years and are still capable of blowing a tune.

You'll find sections related to the Norsemen and Inuit of Greenland, and an evocative exhibition called 'Stories of Denmark', covering Danish history from 1660 to 2000. Among the highlights here are recreated living quarters (including them an 18th-century Copenhagen apartment) and a whimsical collection of toys, including a veritable village of doll houses. The museum also has an excellent **Children's Museum**, as well as a classical antiquities section complete with Egyptian mummies. For a little cerebral relief, find refuge in the decent museum cafe and well-stocked gift shop.

Copenhagen

A map of Copenhagen showing neighborhoods including NØRREBRO, NØRREBRO, VESTERBRO, FREDERIKSBERG, KØDBYEN, and VESTERBRO.

Labeled locations and streets:

NØRREBRO

Fuglebakken
Hillerødgade
Norrebroparken
Nørrebros Runddel
Mimersgade
Tibirkegade
Jagtvej
Sjællandsgade
Fredrik Bajers Plads
Nørre Allé
Jagtvejsgade
Horsloholmsgade
48
61
55
Charlottes Gade
Prinsesse
4
Assistens Kierkegård
Møllegade
73
47
72
68
66
Borups Allé
Ågade
Struenseegade
Rantzausgade
NØRREBRO
58
Kapelvej
Griffenfeldsgade
Baggesensgade
Blågårds Plads
Korsgade
Dronning Louises Bro
Kongs Georgs Vej
Holder Danskes Vej
62
Nordre Fasanvej
Guldborgvej
Lollandsvej
Bentzonsvej
Langelandsvej
A Møllers Have
Sindshvilevej
Roarsvej
Helgesvej
Rolfsvej
Folkvarsvej
Nyelandsvej
Åblvd
Peblinge Sø
Steenwinkelsvej
Rosenørns Allé
Nørre Søgade
Hostrupsvej
Thorvaldsenvej
Frederiksberg
Forum
29
28
VESTERBRO
Howitzvej
60
Sylows Allé
Danasvej
Niels Ebbesens Vej
Kampmannsgade
Grundtvigsvej
Gammel Kongevej
Falkoner Allé
FREDERIKSBERG
Sankt Jørgens Sø
Vesterport
21
Frederiksberg Runddel
49
Frederiksberg Allé
Amicisvej
Nyvej
Madvigs Allé
Mynstersvej
Alhambravej
Skt Knuds Vej
Vodroffsvej
Værnedamsvej
11
Ved Vesterport
33
Frederiksberg Have
Zoo (250m)
Pile Allé
Jacobys Allé
Kochsvej
Henrik Ibsens Vej
Platanvej
Kingosgade
42
65 69
30
Helgolandsgade
54
39
24
71
23
Vesterbrogade
26
FREDERIKSBERG
Matthæusgade
Gasværksvej
35
KØDBYEN
18
57
80
79
Enghavevej
Istedgade
59
74
Absalonsgade
Eskildsgade
56
53
51
Flæsketorvet
70
45
15
67
VESTERBRO
17
Søndermarken
Rahbeks Allé
Ny Carlsberg Vej
75
Enghave Plads
Vesterfælledvej
Flensborggade
Sønder Blvd
Dybbølsgade
Dybbølsbro
Gamle Carlsberg Vej
6
Alsgade
41
Ingerslevgade
Dybbølsbro
Vigerslev Allé
Enghave

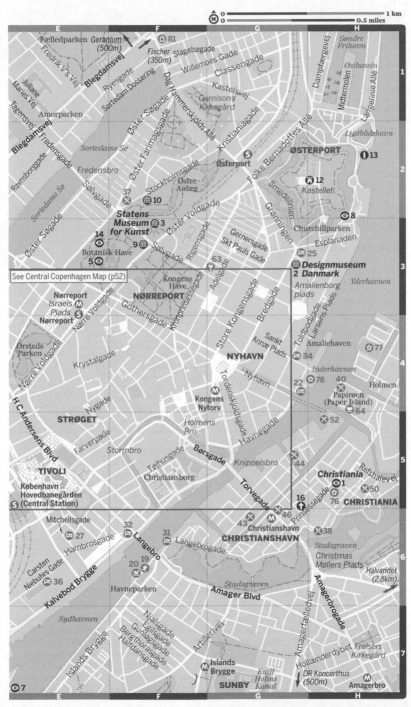

Copenhagen

◎ **Top Sights**
1 Christiania.................................H5
2 Designmuseum Danmark G3
3 Statens Museum for Kunst F3

◎ **Sights**
4 Assistens Kirkegård C2
5 Botanisk Have E3
6 Carlsberg Visitors Centre A6
7 Cykelslangen E7
8 Gefion Fountain H2
9 Geologisk Museum F3
10 Hirschsprung....................................F2
11 Imax Tycho Brahe Planetarium D5
12 Kastellet H2
13 Little Mermaid H2
14 Palmehus E3
15 V1 Gallery D6
16 Vor Frelsers Kirke G5

◎ **Activities, Courses & Tours**
17 Baisikeli D7
18 DGI-byen D6
19 GoBoat F6
20 Islands Brygge Havnebadet F6
21 Nordic Noir Tours D5

◎ **Sleeping**
22 71 Nyhavn Hotel G4
23 Andersen Hotel D6
24 Axel Guldsmeden D5
25 Babette Guldsmeden G3
26 Bertrams Guldsmeden C6
27 Cabinn City E6
28 Cabinn Express C4
29 Cabinn Scandinavia...........................D4
30 Carlton Guldsmeden C5
31 CPH Living F6
32 Danhostel Copenhagen City F6
33 Radisson BLU Royal Hotel D5
34 Scandic Front G4
35 Tiffany D6
36 Wakeup Copenhagen E6

◎ **Eating**
37 Aamanns Takeaway F2
   Alberto K ....(see 33)
38 Bastionen + Løven.............................H6
39 Cofoco D5
40 Copenhagen Street Food H4

41 Dyrehaven C7
42 Granola C5
43 Kadeau G6
44 Kanalen G5
45 Kødbyens Fiskebar..............................D6
46 Lagkagehuset G6
47 Laundromat Cafe D2
48 Manfreds og Vin................................C2
49 Mielcke & Hurtigkarl A5
50 Morgenstedet...................................H5
51 Mother D6
52 Noma...H5
53 Nose2Tail..D6
54 Øl & Brød D5
55 Oysters & Grill C2
56 Paté Paté D6
57 Pony B6
58 Pop – et Spiseri D3
59 Siciliansk Is.....................................C6
60 Sokkelund..A4

◎ **Drinking & Nightlife**
   Bakken ....(see 53)
61 Coffee Collective C2
62 Coffee Collective Frederiksberg B3
63 Culture Box G3
64 Den Plettede Gris H4
65 Falernum C5
66 Kassen D3
67 KBIII D6
68 Kind of Blue D2
69 Lidkoeb C5
   Malbeck ....(see 47)
70 Mesteren & Lærlingen D6
71 Mikkeller D6
72 Nørrebro Bryghus D2
73 Rust...D2
74 Sort Kaffe & Vinyl C6

◎ **Entertainment**
75 Dansehallerne..................................A6
76 Loppen H5
77 Operaen H4
78 Skuespilhuset H4
79 Vega Live B6

◎ **Shopping**
80 Designer Zoo....................................B6
81 Normann Copenhagen F1

★ **Ny Carlsberg Glyptotek** MUSEUM
(Map p52; www.glyptoteket.dk; Dantes Plads 7, HC Andersens Blvd; adult/child Dkr75/free, Sun free; ⏱11am-5pm Tue-Sun; 🚌1A, 2A, 11A, 33, 40, 66, Ⓡ S-train København H) Fin de siècle architecture dallies with an eclectic mix of art at Ny Carlsberg Glyptotek. The collection is divided into two parts: Northern Europe's largest booty of antiquities, and a collec-tion of 19th-century Danish and French art. The latter includes the largest collection of Rodin sculptures outside of France, and no less than 47 Gauguin paintings. These are displayed along with works by Cézanne, Van Gogh, Pissarro, Monet and Renoir.

At the museum's heart is a glass-domed conservatory, replete with palm trees and a cafe that's especially welcoming in the winter.

An added treat for visitors is the August/ September Summer Concert Series (admission around Dkr75), which sees classical music performed in the museum's concert hall, which is evocatively lined by life-size statues of Roman patricians. Concerts usually commence at noon on Sunday.

Rådhus   HISTORIC BUILDING
(City Hall; Map p52; ⊘ 7.45am-5pm Mon-Fri, 10am-1pm Sat; ☑ 12, 26, 33, 1A, 2A, 11A, 40, 66, ☒ S-train København H) **FREE** Completed in 1905, Copenhagen's national romantic-style town hall is the work of architect Martin Nyrop. The building's most famous resident is the curious **Jens Olsen's World Clock** (Map p52; ⊘ 9am-5pm Mon-Fri, 10am-1pm Sat) **FREE**, designed by astromechanic Jens Olsen (1872–1945) and built at a cost of one million kroner. Not only does it display local time, but also solar time, sidereal time, sunrises and sunsets, firmament and celestial pole migration, planet revolutions, the Gregorian calendar and even changing holidays! You can also climb the 105m city hall **tower** (admission Dkr20; ⊘ tour 11am & 2pm Mon-Fri, noon Sat, min 4 people) for a view of the city.

The building's architecture is influenced by both medieval Danish and northern Italian architecture, the latter most notable in the central, fountain-studded **courtyard** (⊘ 9am-4pm daily). Adorning the facade above the main entrance is a golden statue of Bishop Absalon, who founded the city in 1167.

⊙ Strøget & the Latin Quarter

Stretching from Rådhuspladsen to Kongens Nytorv, pedestrian shopping street Strøget – roughly pronounced 'stroll' – weaves its way through Copenhagen's historical core. Technically consisting of five continuous streets, this is the city's 'Main Street' – a restless ribbon of shoppers, camera-toting tourists and street performers of varying talent. At its western end, it's a tacky medley of souvenir stores, mediocre fashion brands and kebab shops. The scene improves further east towards Kongens Nytorv, where you'll find flagship design and department stores, as well as luxury fashion boutiques. This said, many of these retail stores peddle ubiquitous global brands, broken up by average, over-priced cafes and restaurants. Our suggestion? Walk down it once, then slip into the side streets for an altogether more inspiring and intimate vibe.

Rundetårn   HISTORIC BUILDING
(Map p52; www.rundetaarn.dk; Købmagergade 52; adult/child Dkr25/5; ⊘ 10am-8pm late May-late Sep, reduced hrs rest of year; observatory usually 7-9pm Tue & Wed Oct & Mar, 6-9pm Tue & Wed Nov-Feb; ☑ 5A, 14, 11A, Ⓜ Nørreport) Haul yourself to the top of the 34.8m-high, red-brick 'Round Tower' and you will be following in the footsteps of such luminaries as King Christian IV, who built the tower in 1642 as an observatory for famous astronomer Tycho Brahe. You'll also be following in the hoofsteps of Tsar Peter the Great's horse and, according to legend, the track marks of a car that made its way up the tower's spiral ramp in 1902.

While we can't verify the latter claim, we can attest to the inspiring panorama of rooftops and spires from the top.

The tower still functions as an excellent stargazing platform, making it the oldest functioning observatory in Europe. Visitors wanting to view the night sky from the 3m-long telescope mounted within the rooftop dome should call ahead to confirm opening times and days, as they can vary.

Latin Quarter   NEIGHBOURHOOD
(Map p52; ☑ 11A, 5A, 6A, 14, Ⓜ Nørreport) Stretching east from Vor Frue Plads along Store Kannikestræde and Skindergade to Købmagergade, and north up Fiolstræde to Nørre Voldgade, the Latin Quarter gets its nickname from the presence of the old campus of Københavns Universitet (Copenhagen University) and the secondhand bookshops and cafes that grew up around it. It's a wonderful place for ambling, with postcard-pretty nooks including **Gråbrødretorv** (Grey Friars' Square), dating from the mid-17th century.

Founded in 1479, the university has largely outgrown its original quarters, with faculties now spread across the city.

Vor Frue Kirke   CHURCH
(Map p52; www.koebenhavnsdomkirke.dk; Nørregade 8; ⊘ 8am-5pm, closed during services & concerts; ☑ 11A) Founded in 1191 and rebuilt three times after devastating fires, Copenhagen's current cathedral dates from 1829, its neoclassical looks the work of CF Hansen. Sporting high-vaulted ceilings and columns, it's home to sculptor Bertel Thorvaldsen's statues of Christ and the apostles, completed in 1839 and considered his most acclaimed works. The sculptor's depiction of Christ, with comforting open arms, remains the most popular worldwide model for statues of Jesus. In May 2004, the cathedral hosted

the wedding of Crown Prince Frederik to Australian Mary Donaldson.

Sankt Petri Kirke
CHURCH

(Map p52; ☎33 13 38 33; Sankt Pedersstræde 2; ◎11am-3pm Wed-Sat) Another handsome place of worship in the Latin Quarter is Sankt Petri Kirke, a German church that dates from the 15th century, making it the oldest church building in the city.

Nikolaj Kunsthal
GALLERY

(Map p52; ☎33 18 17 80; www.nikolajkunsthal.dk; Nikolaj Plads 10; adult/child Dkr20/free, Wed free; ◎noon-5pm Tue, Wed & Fri-Sun, to 9pm Thu; ☐1A, 2A, 15, 19, 26, 350S, Ⓜ Kongens Nytorv) Built in the 13th century, the church of Skt. Nikolaj is now home to the Copenhagen Contemporary Art Centre, which hosts around half a dozen exhibitions annually. Exhibitions tend to focus on modern-day cultural, political and social issues, explored in mediums as diverse as photography and performance art. The centre also houses a snug, well-regarded Danish restaurant called Maven.

Kunstforeningen GL Strand
GALLERY

(Map p52; ☎33 36 02 60; www.glstrand.dk; Gammel Strand 48; adult/child Dkr65/free; ◎11am-5pm Tue & Thu-Sun, to 8pm Wed; ☐1A, 2A, 11A, 26, 40, 66) The HQ of Denmark's artists' union continues to foster emerging and forward-thinking talent with five to six major exhibitions of modern and contemporary art each year. The work of both Danish and international artists is explored, with an underlying emphasis on current and emerging trends in the art world.

Strædet
STREET

(Map p52; Strædet; ☐11A) Running parallel to crowded Strøget, Strædet is one of Copenhagen's eye-candy shopping streets. It's technically made up of two streets, Kompagnistræde and Læderstræde, dotted with independent jewellers and antique silver shops, and some snug cafes to boot.

Domhuset
BUILDING

(Map p52; Nytorv; ◎8.30am-3pm Mon-Fri; ☐11A) Built in 1815, Copenhagen's neoclassical courthouse was designed by CF Hansen, also responsible for Vor Frue Kirke. It's linked by its own 'bridge of sighs' to cells across the road on Slutterigade. The words inscribed above the courthouse steps, 'Med Lov Skal Man Land Bygge' (With Law Shall One Build the Land), are taken from the Jutland Code that codified laws in Denmark in 1241.

You can take a peek inside, although casual visitors are not encouraged.

◉ Slotsholmen

A small island separated from the city centre by a moat-like canal, Slotsholmen is the seat of national government and a veritable repository of historical sites. Its centrepiece is imposing palace **Christiansborg Slot**, home to Folketinget (the Danish parliament) and various government offices.

Several short bridges link Slotsholmen to the rest of Copenhagen. If you walk into Slotsholmen from Ny Vestergade, you'll cross the western part of the canal and enter Christiansborg's large main courtyard, which flanks the royal stables. The courtyard's equestrian feel is further enhanced by a **statue of Christian IX** (1863–1906) on horseback.

The stables and buildings surrounding the main courtyard date back to the 1730s when the original Christiansborg palace was built by Christian VI to replace the more modest Copenhagen Castle that previously stood there.

The west wing of Christian VI's palace went up in flames in 1794, was rebuilt in the early 19th century and was once again destroyed by fire in 1884. In 1907 the cornerstone for the third (and current) Christiansborg palace was laid by Frederik VIII. Upon completion, the national parliament and the Supreme Court moved into new chambers there.

★ Thorvaldsens Museum
MUSEUM

(Map p52; www.thorvaldsensmuseum.dk; Bertel Thorvaldsens Plads; adult/child Dkr40/free, Wed free; ◎10am-5pm Tue-Sun; ☐1A, 2A, 11A, 26, 40, 66) What looks like a colourful Greco-Roman mausoleum is in fact a museum dedicated to the works of illustrious Danish sculptor Bertel Thorvaldsen (1770–1844). Heavily influenced by mythology after four decades in Rome, Thorvaldsen returned to Copenhagen and donated his private collection to the Danish public. In return the royal family provided this site for the construction of what is a remarkable complex housing Thorvaldsen's drawings, plaster moulds and statues. The museum also contains Thorvaldsens' own collection of Mediterranean antiquities.

De Kongelige Repræsentationslokaler
HISTORIC BUILDING

(Royal Reception Rooms; Map p52; www.ses.dk; adult/child Dkr80/40; ◎10am-5pm daily May-

Sep, closed Mon rest of yr, guided tours in Danish 11am, in English 3pm; ☐1A, 2A, 9A, 11A, 26, 40, 66) The grandest part of Christiansborg is De Kongelige Repræsentationslokaler, an ornate Renaissance hall where the queen holds royal banquets and entertains heads of state. Of particular note are the riotously colourful wall tapestries depicting Danish history from Viking times to today. Created by tapestry designer Bjørn Nørgaard over a decade, the works were completed in 2000. Keep an eye out for the Adam and Eve–style representation of the queen and her husband (albeit clothed) in a Danish Garden of Eden.

Christiansborg Slotskirke   CHURCH

(Map p52; ⊙10am-5pm Sun, daily Jul; ☐1A, 2A, 9A, 11A, 26, 40, 66) Tragedy struck CF Hansen's austere, 19th-century neoclassical church on the day of the 1992 Copenhagen Carnival. A stray firework hit the scaffolding that had surrounded the church during a lengthy restoration and set the roof ablaze, destroying the dome. Miraculously, a remarkable frieze by Bertel Thorvaldsen that rings the ceiling just below the dome survived. The restorers went back to work and the church reopened in 1997.

Teatermuseet   MUSEUM

(Theatre Museum; Map p52; ☑33 11 51 76; www. teatermuseet.dk; Christiansborg Ridebane 18; adult/child Dkr40/free; ⊙11am-3pm Tue-Thu, 1-4pm Sat & Sun; ☐1A, 2A, 9A, 11A, 26, 40, 66) Dating from 1767, the wonderfully atmospheric Hofteater (Old Court Theatre) has hosted everything from Italian opera to local ballet troupes, one of which included fledgling ballet student Hans Christian Andersen. Taking its current appearance in 1842, the venue is now the Theatre Museum, and visitors are free to explore the stage, boxes and dressing rooms, along with displays of set models, drawings, costumes and period posters tracing the history of Danish theatre.

Royal-watchers will enjoy peeking into the royal boxes – Christian VIII's entertainment area comes equipped with its own commode.

Ruinerne under Christiansborg   RUINS

(Ruins under Christiansborg; Map p52; www.ses.dk; adult/child Dkr40/20; ⊙10am-5pm daily, closed Mon Oct-Apr, guided tours in English noon Sat, in Danish noon Sun; ☐1A, 2A, 9A, 11A, 26, 40, 66) A walk through the crypt-like bowels of Slotsholmen, known as Ruinerne under Christiansborg, offers a unique perspective on Copenhagen's long history. In the basement of the current palace, beneath the tower, are

the remains of two earlier castles. The most notable are the ruins of Absalon's fortress, Slotsholmen's original castle, built by Bishop Absalon in 1167.

De Kongelige Stalde   MUSEUM

(Royal Stables; Map p52; ☑33 40 10 10; www. kongehuset.dk; adult/child Dkr40/20; ⊙10am-5pm daily Jul, 1.30-4pm daily May, Jun & Sep, closed Mon Oct-Apr, guided tours in English 2pm Sat, in Danish 2pm Sun; ☐1A, 2A, 9A, 11A, 26, 40, 66) Gallop your way through a collection of antique coaches, uniforms and riding paraphernalia, some of which are still used for royal receptions. You can also eye-up the royal family's carriage and saddle horses.

Folketinget   PARLIAMENT

(Map p52; ☑33 37 32 21; www.thedanishparliament.dk; Rigsdagsgården; ⊙guided tours in English 1pm Sun-Fri Jul–mid-Aug, reduced hrs rest of yr; ☐1A, 2A, 9A, 11A, 26, 40, 66) FREE Folketinget is where the 179 members of the Danish parliament debate national legislation. Guided tours also take in Wanderer's Hall, which contains the original copy of the Constitution of the Kingdom of Denmark, enacted in 1849. Outside the summer high season, tours generally take place at 1pm on Sundays and public holidays – dates are listed on the website, where you can also book tour tickets.

Kongernes Lapidarium   MUSEUM

(Lapidarium of the Kings; Map p52; www.kongerneslapidarium.dk; Frederiksholms Kanal 29; adult/child 4-17yr Dkr50/25; ⊙10am-5pm daily May-Sep, closed Mon rest of yr; ☐1A, 2A, 9A, 11A, 26, 40, 66, ⚑Det Kongelige Bibliotek) Housed in Christian IV's old brewery, an extraordinary building dating from 1608, the Lapidarium of the Kings features original royal sculptures from Denmark's castles and gardens. Among these are the original, 18th-century sandstone figures from Normandsdalen at Fredensborg Slot, unique in their depiction of common Norwegians and Faroese. Even more extraordinary is French sculptor JFJ Saly's 18th-century equestrian statue of Frederik V, more than 20 years in the making and more expensive than the entire Amalienborg Palace when completed.

Considered one of the most beautiful equestrian statues in the world, the work had to be cut and reassembled to simply fit inside the museum. It's a tight squeeze, with a mere four centimetres between Frederik V's laurel wreath and the ceiling. Close by stands AC Lamoureux's dramatic 17th-century sculpture of Christian V on horseback,

Copenhagen Central

Gothersgade

Botanisk
Have

4
Rosenborg
Slot

50

Frederiksborggade

54

82

89

Vendersgade

Nansensgade

Rømersgade

73

88

126

Norre Farimagsgade

Israels
Plads

63

Linnesgade

NØRREPORT

M Nørreport

Nørreport
S

Øster Voldgade

Norre Voldgade

Frederiksborggade

Rosenborggade

65

Abenrå

Gothersgade

80
Hauser
Plads

Hausergade

Pusterviq

Landemærket

Rosengården

Kultorvet

111

Ørsteds
Parken

Norre Voldgade

Teglgårdstræde

Larslejsstræde

Nørregade

Fiolstræde

25

119

31

Købmagergade

52

Krystalgade

LATIN
QUARTER

Niels Hemmingsensgade

66

Københavns
Universitet

32

Kannikestræde

Vor
Frue Plads

Gråbrødretorv

105

94

53

36

Sankt Pedersstræde

92

Studiestræde

35

Klosterstræde

129

Larsbjørnsstræde

STRØGET

Skindergade

74

Vimmelskaftet

33

Gammeltorv

Nygade

Badstuestræde

Nabolosstræde

23

45

48

Vester Voldgade

Vestergade

Frederiksberggade (Strøget)

Nytorv

17

Sluttergade

Knabrostræde

108

97

Vindebrogade

5
Thorvaldsens
Museum

103

Kompagnistræde

104

Magstræde

Jernbanegade

56

Rådhuspladsen

55

95

Lavendelstræde

Længangstræde

109

46

Nybrogade

Stormbro

Christiansborg
Slot

Copenhagen
Visitors
Centre

40

Vesterbrogade

H C Andersens Blvd

39

20

29

Regnbuepladsen

Rådhus
(City
Hall)

Bag Rådhuset

Stormgade

Frederiksholms Kanal

Industriens
Hus

6
Tivoli Main Entrance

Tivoli
Gardens

72

Nationalmuseet

2

Ny Vestergade

Vester Voldgade

Ny Kongensgade

Bernstorffsgade

93

51

59

TIVOLI

Dantes
Plads

Ny Carlsberg
Glyptotek

3

København
Hovedbanegården
S (Central Station)

85

110

Tietgensgade

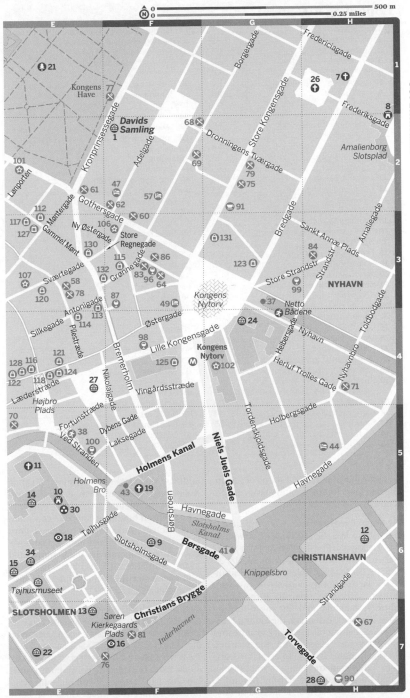

Copenhagen Central

⊙ Top Sights
1	Davids Samling	F2
2	Nationalmuseet	D6
3	Ny Carlsberg Glyptotek	C7
4	Rosenborg Slot	D1
5	Thorvaldsens Museum	D5
6	Tivoli Gardens	A6

⊙ Sights
7	Aleksander Nevskij Kirke	H1
8	Amalienborg Slot	H2
9	Børsen	F6
10	Christiansborg Slot	E5
11	Christiansborg Slotskirke	E5
12	Dansk Arkitektur Centre	H6
13	Dansk Jødisk Museum	E7
14	De Kongelige Repræsentationslokaler	E5
15	De Kongelige Stalde	E6
16	Det Kongelige Bibliotek	F7
17	Domhuset	C5
18	Folketinget	E6
19	Holmens Kirke	F5
20	Jens Olsen's World Clock	B6
21	Kongens Have	E1
22	Kongernes Lapidarium	E7
23	Kunstforeningen GL Strand	D5
24	Kunsthal Charlottenborg	G4
25	Latin Quarter	C3
26	Marmorkirken	H1
27	Nikolaj Kunsthal	E4
28	Overgaden	H7
29	Rådhus	B6
30	Ruinerne under Christiansborg	E6
31	Rundetårn	D3
32	Sankt Petri Kirke	B4
33	Strædet	D5
34	Teatermuseet	E6
35	Vor Frue Kirke	C4

⊙ Activities, Courses & Tours
36	Bike Copenhagen With Mike	A4
37	Canal Tours Copenhagen	G3
	Christianshavns Bådudlejning og Café	(see 90)
38	Copenhagen City Sightseeing	E5
39	Copenhagen Free Walking Tours	B6
40	CPH:cool	A6
41	Kayak Republic	G6
42	Københavns Cyklerbørs	B1
43	Netto-Bådene	F5

⊙ Sleeping
44	Copenhagen Strand	H5
45	First Hotel Kong Frederik	B5
46	First Hotel Twentyseven	C6
47	Generator Hostel	F2
48	Hotel Alexandra	A5
49	Hotel d'Angleterre	F3
50	Hotel Kong Arthur	A1
51	Hotel Nimb	A7
52	Hotel Skt Petri	C3
53	Hotel SP34	A4
54	Ibsens Hotel	A1
55	Palace Hotel	B5
56	Square	A5
57	Wakeup Copenhagen	F2

⊙ Eating
58	42° Raw	E3
59	Andersen Bakery	A7
60	Atelier September	F3
61	Big Apple	E2
62	Bistro Pastis	F2
63	Bottega della Pasta	B2
64	Brasserie Granberg	F3
65	Brdr.Price	C2
66	Café Hovedtelegrafen	D3
67	Cafe Wilder	H7
68	Ché Fè	F2

the first equestrian-themed statue of a Scandinavian king. Its 20th-century bronze replica now graces Kongens Nytorv.

Det Kongelige Bibliotek — LIBRARY

(Royal Library; Map p52; ☑ 33 47 47 47; www.kb.dk; Søren Kierkegaards Plads; ⊙8am-7pm Mon-Sat Jul & Aug, to 10pm rest of year; ⊟1A, 2A, 9A, 11A, 26, 40, 66, ⓢDet Kongelige Bibliotek) FREE Scandinavia's largest library consists of two very distinct parts: the original, 19th-century red-brick building and the head-turning 'Black Diamond' extension, the latter a leaning parallelogram of sleek black granite and smoke-coloured glass. From the soaring, harbour-fronting atrium, an escalator leads up to a 210-sq-metre ceiling mural by celebrated Danish artist Per Kirkeby. Beyond it, at the end of the corridor, is the 'old library'

and its Hogwarts-like northern Reading Room, resplendent with vintage desk lamps and classical columns.

Aside from housing a complete collection of all Danish printed works produced since 1482, Denmark's national library also hosts fascinating, temporary art, photography and history exhibitions. It's also home to decent cafe Øieblikket (p72) and modern Danish restaurant Søren K (p72).

Dansk Jødisk Museum — MUSEUM

(Map p52; ☑ 33 11 22 18; www.jewmus.dk; Kongelige Bibliotekshave (Royal Library Garden); adult/child Dkr50/free; ⊙10am-5pm Tue-Sun Jun-Aug, 1-4pm Tue-Fri, noon-5pm Sat & Sun rest of yr; ⊟1A, 2A, 11, 40, 66, 350S) Designed by Polish-born Daniel Libeskind, the Danish Jewish Museum occupies the former Royal Boat House, an early

69 Clou...F2
70 Cock's & Cows........................E5
71 Damindra H4
   Grød...................................(see 63)
72 Grøften...................................A6
   Hallernes Smørrebrød ....(see 63)
73 Höst..A2
74 La Glace..................................C4
75 Meyers Bageri G2
76 Øieblikket................................E7
   Omegn................................(see 63)
77 Orangeriet................................F1
78 Palæo......................................E3
79 Rebel.......................................G2
80 Schønnemann.........................D2
81 Søren K....................................F7
82 Sticks 'N' Sushi.........................A1
83 The Yogurt Shop.......................F3
   Torvehallerne KBH ....(see 63)
84 Union Kitchen...........................H3
85 Wagamama...............................B7
86 Wokshop Cantina.....................F3

⊙ **Drinking & Nightlife**
87 1105...F3
88 Bankeråt...................................A2
89 Bibendum A1
90 Christianshavns Bådudlejning og
   Café.......................................H7
   Coffee Collective ....(see 63)
91 Forloren Espresso....................G2
92 Jailhouse CPH B4
93 Library Bar................................A7
94 Never Mind...............................A4
   Nimb Bar..............................(see 51)
95 Oscar Bar & Cafe C6
96 Palæ Bar..................................F3
97 Ruby..D5
98 Sunday.....................................F4
99 Union Bar.................................G3

100 Ved Stranden 10 ....E5

⊙ **Entertainment**
101 Cinemateket E2
102 Det Kongelige Teater G4
103 Grand Teatret............................B5
104 Huset KBH................................C5
105 Jazzhouse.................................D4
106 Jazzhus Montmartre..................F3
107 Københavns Musikteater E3
108 La Fontaine...............................D5
109 Mojo...C6
110 Tivoli Koncertsal.......................B7

⊙ **Shopping**
111 Botanisk Haves Butik...............C1
112 Bruuns Bazaar..........................E3
113 By Malene Birger.......................E3
114 Day Birger Mikkelsen................E4
115 Filippa K...................................F3
116 Georg Jensen...........................E4
117 Han Kjøbenhavn.......................E3
118 Hay House................................E4
119 Henrik Vibskov..........................C3
120 Hoff..E3
121 Illum...E4
122 Illums Bolighus.........................E4
123 Klassik Moderne Møbelkunst ...G3
124 Le Klint.....................................E4
125 Magasin....................................F4
126 Piet Breinholm – The Last Bag...........A2
127 Pop Cph....................................E3
128 Royal Copenhagen Porcelain.....E4
129 Stilleben....................................D4
130 Storm..E3
131 Susanne Juul.............................G3
   Unika by Arla........................(see 63)
132 Wood Wood E3

17th-century building once part of Christian IV's harbour complex. The transformed interior is an intriguing geometrical space, home to a permanent exhibition documenting Danish Jewry. You'll find the entrance on the Royal Library Garden, behind the Kongelige Bibliotek (Royal Library).

Holmens Kirke   CHURCH
(Church of the Royal Danish Navy; Map p52; www.holmenskirke.dk; Holmens Kanal 9; ⊙10am-4pm Mon, Wed, Fri & Sat, to 3.30pm Tue & Thu, noon-4pm Sun; ☐1A, 2A, 11, 29, 350S) Queen Margrethe II took her marriage vows here in 1967, and while much of the present Dutch Renaissance-style structure dates from 1641, the church's nave was originally built in 1562 to be used as an anchor forge. Converted into a church for the Royal Navy in 1619, the building's burial chapel contains the remains of Admiral Niels Juel, who beat back the Swedes in the crucial 1677 Battle of Køge Bay. Other highlights include an intricately carved 17th-century oak altarpiece and pulpit.

Børsen   HISTORIC BUILDING
(Map p52; Børsgade; ☐1A, 2A, 9A, 40, 350S) Not many stock exchanges are topped by a 56m-tall spire formed from the entwined tails of four dragons. Børsen is one. Constructed at the eastern corner of Slotholmen in the early 17th century, its elegant Dutch Renaissance design features richly embellished gables and an eye-catching copper roof. Opened during the bustling reign of Christian IV, this still-functioning chamber of commerce is the oldest in Europe, though generally not open to the public.

⊙ Nyhavn to the Little Mermaid

Built to connect Kongens Nytorv to the harbour, the canal of Nyhavn (pronounced new-hown) was long a haunt for sailors and writers, including Hans Christian Andersen, who lived there for most of his life at, variously, numbers 20, 18 and 67. These days Nyhavn is defined by smitten tourists, brightly coloured gabled town houses, herring buffets and foaming ale. Behind the bustle is the blue-blooded quarter of Frederiksstaden, home to Denmark's much-loved royal family, the Vatican-esque pomp of Marmorkirken, the commendable Designmuseum Danmark, as well as the top-tier art galleries and antique shops flanking Bredgade and Store Kongensgade. At its northern end sits the ancient fortress of Kastellet, kept company by one of Copenhagen's most anticlimactic sights, the Little Mermaid.

★ Designmuseum Danmark MUSEUM
(Map p46; www.designmuseum.dk; Bredgade 68; adult/child Dkr75/free; ⊙11am-5pm Tue & Thu-Sun, to 9pm Wed; 🚇1A) The 18th-century Frederiks Hospital is now the outstanding Denmark Design Museum. A must for fans of the applied arts and industrial design, its fairly extensive collection includes Danish silver and porcelain, textiles, as well as the iconic design pieces of modern innovators like Kaare Klint, Poul Henningsen and Arne Jacobsen. Also on display are ancient Chinese and Japanese ceramics, and 18th and 19th-century European decorative arts.

Designmuseum Danmark lies 250m north of Marmorkirken.

Amalienborg Slot PALACE
(Map p52; ☎33 12 21 86; dkks.dk/amalienborgmuseet/amalienborg; Amalienborg Plads; adult/child Dkr90/free; ⊙10am-4pm daily May-Oct, reduced hrs rest of yr; 🚇1A, 26) Home of the current queen, Margrethe II, Amalienborg Slot consists of four austere, 18th-century palaces around a large cobbled square. The changing of the guard takes place here daily at noon, the new guard having marched through the city centre from the barracks on Gothersgade at 11.30am. One of the palaces features exhibits of the royal apartments used by three generations of the monarchy from 1863 to 1947, its reconstructed rooms decorated with gilt-leather tapestries, trompe-l'oeil paintings, family photographs and antiques.

They include the study and drawing room of Christian IX (1863–1906) and Queen Louise, whose six children wedded into nearly as many royal families – one ascending the throne in Greece and another marrying Russian Tsar Alexander III. The neoclassical Gala Hall features statues of Euterpe and Terpsichore created by a young Bertel Thorvaldsen.

Marmorkirken CHURCH
(Marble Church; Map p52; ☎33 15 01 44; www.marmorkirken.dk; Frederiksgade 4; dome adult/child Dkr35/20, church admission free; ⊙church 10am-5pm Mon, Tue, Thu & Sat, 10am-6.30pm Wed, noon-5pm Fri & Sun, dome 1pm & 3pm daily mid-Jun–Aug, 1pm & 3pm Sat & Sun rest of yr; 🚇1A) Consecrated in 1894, the neobaroque Marble Church (offi-

---

COPENHAGEN FOR FREE
. . . .

Copenhagen has a reputation for being heavy on the budget, but many of its top sights are free for at least one day of the week. So zip up that wallet and head to these spots, all of which are free all week unless a particular day is specified.

➡ Assistens Kirkegård (p60)

➡ Christiania (p57)

➡ Churches, including Marmorkirken (p56)

➡ Davids Samling (p59)

➡ Den Hirschsprungske Samling (p60) (free on Wednesday only)

➡ Folketinget (p51)

➡ Nationalmuseet (p45)

➡ Ny Carlsberg Glyptotek (p48) (free on Sunday only)

➡ Statens Museum for Kunst (p58)

➡ Thorvaldsens Museum (p50) (free on Wednesday only)

➡ V1 Gallery (p61)

cially Frederikskirken) is one of Copenhagen's most imposing architectural assets. Its grandiose dome – measuring more than 30m in diameter and inspired by St Peter's in Rome – can be climbed on weekends. The church was ordered by Frederik V and drawn up by Nicolai Eigtved. Construction began in 1749 but spiralling costs saw the project mothballed. Salvation came in the form of Denmark's wealthiest 19th-century financier CF Tietgen, who bankrolled the project's revival.

The church's exterior is ringed by statues of Danish theologians and saints.

Kunsthal Charlottenborg MUSEUM

(Map p52; ☑ 33 74 46 39; www.kunsthalcharlotten borg.dk; Nyhavn 2; adult/child Dkr60/free, after 5pm Wed free; ☺ 11am-5pm Tue & Thu-Sun, to 8pm Wed; ☐ 1A, 15, 19, 26, 350S, Ⓜ Kongens Nytorv) Fronting Kongens Nytorv, Charlottenborg was built in 1683 as a palace for the royal family. Home to Det Kongelige Kunstakademi (Royal Academy of Fine Arts) since 1754, it keeps culture vultures flocking with its rotating exhibitions of contemporary art from both Danish and international artists.

Kastellet FORTRESS

(Map p46; ☐ 1A, ⚲ Nordre Toldbod) The star-shaped fortress of Kastellet was originally commissioned by Frederik III in 1662. Today it is one of the most historically evocative sites in the city, its grassy ramparts and moat surrounding some beautiful 18th-century barracks, as well as a chapel occasionally used for concerts. On the ramparts is a historic windmill and some excellent views to the Little Mermaid, the harbour and, in the other direction, Marmorkirken.

Just beyond the fortress' southeastern edge is Anders Bundgaard's monumental Gefion Fountain (Gefionspringvandet; Map p46), depicting the Norse goddess Gefion steering some rather stoic oxen.

Aleksander Nevskij Kirke CHURCH

(Map p52; ☑ 33 13 60 46; Bredgade 53; ☺ only for services; ☐ 1A) Completed in 1883, golden-domed Alexander Newsky Kirke flaunts a Russian Byzantine style, complete with marble staircase, mosaic floors and Byzantine-style frescoes. The bronze chandelier was a gift from Tsar Alexander III, who commissioned the church.

☉ Christianshavn

The setting for parts of the novel and movie *Miss Smilla's Feeling for Snow*, Christians-

DON'T MISS

CYKELSLANGEN: THE CYCLING SNAKE

Two of the Danes greatest pasions – design and cycling – meet in spectacular fashion with **Cykelslangen** (Map p46), or Cycle Snake. Designed by local architects Dissing + Weitling, the 235-metre-long cycling path evokes a slender orange ribbon, its gently curving form contrasting dramatically against the area's block-like architecture. The elevated path winds its way from Bryggebro (Brygge Bridge) west to Fisketorvet Shopping Centre, weaving its way over the harbour and delivering a cycling experience that's nothing short of whimsical. To reach the path on public transport, catch bus 30 to Fisketorvet Shopping Centre. The best way to reach it, however, is on a bike, as Cykelslangen is only accessible to cyclists.

havn channels Amsterdam with its glittering canals, outdoor cafes and easy-going attitude. Located on the city's eastern flank, the quarter was established by Christian IV in the early 17th century as a commercial centre and also a military buffer for the expanding city. That it recalls Amsterdam is no coincidence: its network of boat-lined waterways is modelled after those in Holland. Equally reminiscent of free-minded Amsterdam is the area's most famous attraction, the alternative, pot-scented neighbourhood of Christiania.

★ Christiania NEIGHBOURHOOD

(Map p46; www.christiania.org; Prinsessegade; ☐ 9A, 2A, 40, 350S, Ⓜ Christianshavn) Escape the capitalist crunch at Freetown Christiania, a dreadlocks-heavy commune straddling the eastern side of Christianshavn. Since its establishment by squatters in 1971, the area has drawn nonconformists from across the globe, attracted by the concept of collective business, workshops, and communal living. Explore beyond the settlement's infamous 'Pusher St' – lined with shady hash and marijuana dealers – and you'll stumble upon a semi-bucolic wonderland of whimsical DIY homes, cosy gardens, and a handful of craft shops, eateries, beer gardens and music venues.

Before its development as an alternative enclave, the site was an abandoned 41-hectare military camp. When squatters took over, police tried to clear the area. They failed. The hippie revolution was at its peak and waves of alternative folk continued to pour in.

Bowing to public pressure, the government allowed the community to continue as a social experiment. Self-governing, ecology-oriented and generally tolerant, Christiania residents did, in time, find it necessary to modify their 'anything goes' approach. A new policy was established that outlawed hard drugs, and the heroin and cocaine pushers were expelled.

The main entrance into Christiania is on Prinsessegade, 200m northeast of its intersection with Bådsmandsstræde. From late June to the end of August, 60- to 90-minute guided tours (Dkr40) of Christiania run daily at 3pm (weekends only September to late June). Tours commence just inside Christiania's main entrance on Prinsessegade.

Vor Frelsers Kirke   CHURCH
(Map p46; www.vorfrelserskirke.dk; Sankt Annæ Gade 29; church free, tower adult/child Dkr40/10; ⊙ 11am-3.30pm, closed during services, tower 10am-7.15pm Mon-Sat, 10.30am-7.15pm Sun Jun-Sep, reduced hrs rest of yr; ⬜ 9A, 2A, 40, 350S, Ⓜ Christianshavn) It's hard to miss this 17th-century church and its 95m-high spiral tower. For a soul-stirring panoramic city view, make the head-spinning 400-step ascent to the top – the last 150 steps run along the outside rim of the tower, narrowing to the point where they literally disappear at the top. Inspired by Borromini's tower of St Ivo in Rome, the colourful spire was added in 1752 by Lauritz de Thurah. Inside, the church wows with its elaborately carved pipe organ from 1698 and an ornate baroque altar.

Dansk Arkitektur Centre   GALLERY
(Danish Architecture Centre; Map p52; ☑ 32 57 19 30; www.dac.dk; Strandgade 27B; exhibition adult/child Dkr40/free, 5-9pm Wed free; ⊙ exhibition & bookshop 10am-5pm Mon, Tue, & Thu-Sun, to 9pm Wed, cafe from 11am Mon-Fri, 10am-4pm Sat & Sun; ⬜ 2A, 19, 47, 66, 350S, Ⓜ Christianshavn) You'll find the Danish Architecture Centre inside Gammel Dok, a 19th-century harbourside warehouse. Aside from an excellent bookshop and panoramic cafe, the centre runs changing exhibitions on Danish and international architecture. On Sundays from May to September, the centre also runs two-hour walking tours of the city (Dkr125). See the website for tour themes and details.

Overgaden   GALLERY
(Map p52; ☑ 32 57 72 73; www.overgaden.org; Overgaden Neden Vandet 17; ⊙ Tue, Wed & Fri-Sun

1-5pm, to 8pm Thu; ⬜ 2A, 9A, 40, 350S, Ⓜ Christianshavn) **FREE** Rarely visited by tourists, this non-profit art gallery runs about 10 exhibitions annually, putting the spotlight on contemporary installation art and photography, usually by younger artists. The gallery also runs a busy calender of artist talks, lectures and film screenings. See the website for upcoming events.

◉ Nørreport to Nørrebro

Straddling the city's shallow lakes, with Nørreport to the south and Nørrebro to the northwest, are two of Copenhagen's most intriguing areas. Nørreport's star strip is Nansensgade, a low-key street studded with a handful of atmospheric cafes, bars and independent boutiques. Across the water, livelier Nørrebro subverts the pristine Nordic stereotype with its dense, sexy funk of art-clad 19th-century tenements, multicultural crowds, thronging cafes, bars and clubs, and independent fashion boutiques.

While streets such as Elmegade, Blågårdsgade, Ravnsborggade and Sankt Hans Torv have long offered a fix of Nørrebro cool, a more recent Nørrebro magnet is Jægersborggade, to the west of the strangely enchanting cemetery Assistens Kirkegård. Once a notorious drug strip, it's now best known for top-notch dining, coffee, local design and fashion.

★ Statens Museum for Kunst   MUSEUM
(Map p46; www.smk.dk; Sølvgade 48-50; special exhibitions adult/child Dkr110/free; ⊙ 10am-5pm Tue & Thu-Sun, to 8pm Wed; ⬜ 6A, 26, 42, 173E, 184, 185) **FREE** Denmark's National Gallery straddles two contrasting, inter-connected buildings: a late-19th-century 'palazzo' and a sharply minimalist extension. The museum houses medieval and Renaissance works, and impressive collections of Dutch and Flemish artists including Rubens, Breughel and Rembrandt. It claims the world's finest collection of 19th-century Danish 'Golden Age' artists, among them Eckersberg, Krøyer and Hammershøi, foreign greats like Matisse and Picasso, and modern Danish heavyweights including Per Kirkeby, Richard Mortensen and Asger Jørn. Among the contemporary stars are Danish/Norwegian duo Elmgreen and Dragset, and Vietnamese-born Danish artist Danh Vo.

The museum also has an extensive collection of drawings, engravings and lithographs representing the works of such prominent artists as Degas and Toulouse-Lautrec, as well as a strikingly colourful geometric cafe created by designer Peter Lassen and artist Bjørn Nørgaard. Check the website for upcoming temporary exhibitions.

★**Rosenborg Slot** CASTLE
(Map p52; dkks.dk; Øster Voldgade 4A; adult/child Dkr90/free, incl Amalienborg Palace Dkr125/free; ⊙10am-5pm daily Jun-Aug, 10am-4pm daily May, Sep & Oct, reduced hrs rest of yr; ▣6A, 11A, 42, 150S, 173E, 184, 185, 350S, Ⓜ Nørreport) A 'once-upon-a-time' combo of turrets, gables and moat, the early-17th-century Rosenborg Slot was built between 1606 and 1633 by King Christian IV in Dutch Renaissance style to serve as his summer home. Today, the castle's 24 upper rooms are chronologically arranged, housing the furnishings and portraits of each monarch from Christian IV to Frederik VII. The pièce de résistance, however, is the basement Treasury, home to the dazzling crown jewels, among them Christian IV's glorious crown and the jewel-studded sword of Christian III.

Feeling cramped at Rosenborg, King Frederik IV built a roomier palace in the 18th century, in the town of Fredensborg, north of the city. In the years that followed, Rosenborg was used mainly for official functions and as a place in which to safeguard the monarchy's heirlooms. In the 1830s the royal family decided to open the castle to visitors as a museum, while still using it as a treasury for royal regalia and jewels.

Although information panels are scarce, smartphone users with a scanner app can download information about collection highlights via the exhibition barcodes. If you don't have a smartphone – or if you simply want more extensive coverage of the collection – catalogues are available at the ticket office, either for hire (Dkr10) or purchase (Dkr25).

Kongens Have PARK
(King's Gardens; Map p52; ▣6A, 11A, 42, 150S, 173E, 184 185, 350S, Ⓜ Nørreport) **FREE** The oldest park in Copenhagen was laid out in the early 17th century by Christian IV, who used it as his vegetable patch. These days it has a little more to offer, including immaculate flower beds, romantic garden paths, and a marionette theatre with free performances during the summer season (2pm and 3pm Tuesday to Sunday). Located on the northeastern side of the park, the theatre occupies one of the neoclassical pavilions designed by Danish architect Peter Meyn.

★**Davids Samling** MUSEUM
(Map p52; ☑33 73 49 49; www.davidmus.dk; Kronprinsessegade 30; ⊙10am-5pm Tue & Thu-Sun, to 9pm Wed; ▣1A, 11, 15, 26, 350S) **FREE** Davids Samling is a wonderful curiosity of a gallery

---

THAT LITTLE MERMAID

Little Mermaid (Den Lille Havfrue; Map p46; ▣1A, ⬛Nordre Toldbod) New York has its Lady Liberty, Sydney its (Danish-designed) Opera House. When the world thinks of Copenhagen, chances are they're thinking of the Little Mermaid. Love her or loathe her (watch Copenhageners cringe at the very mention of her), this small, underwhelming statue is arguably the most photographed sight in the country, as well as the cause of countless 'is that it?' shrugs from tourists who have trudged the kilometre or so along an often windswept harbourfront to see her.

In 1909 the Danish beer baron Carl Jacobsen was so moved after attending a ballet performance based on the Hans Christian Andersen fairy tale 'The Little Mermaid' that he commissioned sculptor Edvard Eriksen to create a statue of the eponymous lady-fish to grace Copenhagen's harbourfront. The face of the famous statue was modelled after the ballerina Ellen Price, while Eline Eriksen, the sculptor's wife, modelled for the body.

The Little Mermaid survived the Great Depression and the WWII occupation unscathed, but modern times haven't been so kind to Denmark's leading lady, with several decapitations and lost limbs at the hands of vandals and protesters trying to make various political points.

Partly in response to this, Carlsberg commissioned Danish artist Bjørn Nørgaard to create a new Little Mermaid in 2006. The result is a 'genetically altered' mermaid, sitting only a few hundred metres from the original. While there's no doubt that Eriksen's creation may be the prettier sibling, Nørgaard's misshapen creation is arguably truer in spirit to Andersen's rather bleak, twisted fairy tale, in which the fish-tailed protagonist is physically and emotionally tormented...and never gets her man.

housing Scandinavia's largest collections of Islamic art, including jewellery, ceramics and silk, and exquisite works such as an Egyptian rock crystal jug from AD 1000 and a 500-year-old Indian dagger inlaid with rubies. And it doesn't end there, with an elegant selection of Danish, Dutch, English and French art, porcelain, silverware and furniture from the 17th to 19th centuries.

The collection was bequeathed to the museum by the barrister Christian Ludvig David, who died in 1960, and it is maintained by the foundation he founded. Fittingly, the museum is housed in David's former home, a neoclassical mansion dating from 1806.

Hirschsprung   MUSEUM

(Map p46; ☑ 35 42 03 36; www.hirschsprung.dk; Stockholmsgade 20; adult/child Dkr75/free, Wed free; ☺ 11am-4pm Tue-Sun; ☐ 6A, 14, 40, 42, 43, 150S) Dedicated to Danish art of the 19th and early 20th centuries, Den Hirschsprungske Samling is a little jewel-box of a gallery, full of wonderful surprises for art lovers unfamiliar with the classic era of Danish oil painting. Originally the private holdings of tobacco magnate Heinrich Hirschsprung, the museum contains works by 'Golden Age' painters such as Christen Købke and CW Eckersberg, a notable selection by Skagen painters PS Krøyer and Anna and Michael Ancher, and also works by the Danish symbolists and the Funen painters.

Assistens Kirkegård   CEMETERY

(Map p46; ☑ 35 37 19 17; http://assistens.dk; Kapelvej 4; ☺ 7am-10pm Apr-Sep, to 7pm Oct-Mar; ☐ 5A, 350S) You'll find some of Denmark's most celebrated citizens at this famous cemetery, including philosopher Søren Kierkegaard, physicist Niels Bohr, author Hans Christian Andersen, and artists Jens Juel, Christen Købke and CW Eckersberg. It's a wonderfully atmospheric place to wander around – as much a park and garden as it is a graveyard. A good place to start is at the main entrance on Kapelvej, which has an office (10am to 4pm weekdays) where you can pick up a brochure mapping famous grave sites.

Botanisk Have   GARDENS

(Botanical Gardens; Map p46; http://botanik.snm. ku.dk; main entrance Gothersgade 140; ☺ 8.30am-6pm daily May-Sep, 8.30am-4pm Tue-Sun Oct-Apr; ♿; ☐ 6A, 11A, 14, 40, 42, 150S, 173E, 184, 185, Ⓜ Nørreport, Ⓡ S-train Nørreport) Restorative and romantic, Copenhagen's Botanic Garden lays claim to the largest collection of living plants in Denmark. You can amble along tranquil trails punctuated with quotes from Danish poets and writers (in Danish), escape to warmer climes in the 19th-century Palmehus (Map p46; ☺ 10am-3pm May-Sep, closed Mon Oct-Apr) glasshouse, and even pick up honey made by the garden's own bees at the gorgeous little gift shop (Map p52; ☺ 10am-5pm Apr-Sep, to 3.30pm Tue-Sun rest of yr). At the garden's northwest corner lies the old-fashioned Geologisk Museum (Geology Museum; Map p46; Øster Voldgade 5-7; adult/child Dkr40/free; ☺ 10am-1pm Tue-Fri, 1-4pm Sat & Sun), worth a trip for its exhibition of botanical drawings, dazzling mineral displays and riotously colourful staircase mural by revered Danish artist Per Kirkeby.

◉ Vesterbro to Frederiksberg

It is hard to imagine two more disparate neighbours than leafy, middle-class Frederiksberg and gritty, urban Vesterbro, but both promise an intriguing handful of sights, not to mention some must-try restaurants, bars and cafes.

Vesterbro begins at the western side of København H (Central Station) with the city's most infamous thoroughfare, Istedgade. At its 'station end', the strip is Copenhagen's seedy red light district, littered with sex shops, massage parlours, junkies, stiletto-strapped prostitutes and lower range hotels. Further west, Istedgade transforms into one of the city's most interesting streets, lined with independent boutiques and Middle Eastern grocery shops, as well as cafes and bars filled with Vesterbro creative types.

South of Istedgade awaits Kødbyen (literally 'Meat City'). Dubbed Copenhagen's 'Meatpacking District', this one-time industrial site has developed into one of the city's trendiest districts, with an ever-increasing booty of industrial-cool restaurants and bars.

North of Istedgade lies Vesterbrogade, a mainstream shopping street with supermarkets and midrange fashion stores. Turn right where Vesterbrogade meets Frederiksberg Allé and you'll hit atmospheric Værndamsvej. Known locally as Copenhagen's 'Little Paris', it's a super-cute strip with a handful of buzzing cafes, wine bars, restaurants and fashion boutiques.

Further west, respectable Frederiksberg is where you'll find two of the city's most popular tourist attractions – the zoo and the Carlsberg Visitors Center. It's also home to contemporary-art hot spot Ny Carlsberg Vej 68, not to mention Copenhagen's most romantic park, Frederiksberg Have – home to culinary gem Mielcke & Hurtigkarl.

Carlsberg Visitors Centre BREWERY

(Map p46; ☑33 27 12 82; www.visitcarlsberg. dk; Gamle Carlsberg Vej 11, Vesterbro; adult/child Dkr80/60; ☺10am-5pm Tue-Sun; ☑18, 26) Adjacent to the architecturally whimsical Carlsberg brewery, the Carlsberg Visitors Center explores the history of Danish beer from 1370 BC (yes, they carbon-dated a bog girl who was found in a peat bog caressing a jug of well-aged brew). Dioramas give the lowdown on the brewing process and en route to your final destination you'll pass antique copper vats and the stables with a dozen Jutland dray horses. The self-guided tour ends at the bar, where you can knock back two free beers.

Zoo ZOO

(☑72 20 02 00; www.zoo.dk; Roskildevej 32, Frederiksberg; adult/child Dkr160/95; ☺10am-6pm Jun & Aug, to 8pm Jul, reduced hrs rest of yr; ☑4A, 6A, 72) Located up on Frederiksberg (Frederik's Hill), Copenhagen Zoo rustles and rumbles with over 2500 of nature's lovelies, including lions, zebras, hippos and gorillas. The zoo's state-of-the-art elephant enclosure was designed by English architect Sir Norman Foster, while the newer Arctic Ring enclosure allows visitors to walk right through the polar-bear pool for some spectacular close encounters with those cuddly looking beasts.

V1 Gallery ART GALLERY

(Map p46; ☑33 31 03 21; www.v1gallery.com; Flæsketorvet 69-71, Vesterbro; ☺noon-6pm Wed-Fri, to 4pm Sat during exhibitions; ☑10, 14) **FREE** Part of the Kødbyen (Vesterbro's 'Meatpacking District'), V1 is one of Copenhagen's most progressive art galleries. Cast your eye on fresh work from both emerging and established local and foreign artists. Some of the world's hottest names in street and graffiti art have exhibited here, from Britain's Banksy to the USA's Todd James and Lydia Fong (aka Barry McGee).

Imax Tycho Brahe Planetarium PLANETARIUM

(Map p46; ☑33 12 12 24; www.tycho.dk; Gammel Kongevej 10, Vesterbro; adult/child Dkr144/94; ☺noon-7.40pm Mon, 10.45am-7.40pm Tue-Thu & Sun, 10.45am-8.50pm Fri & Sat; ☑9A, ☒S-train Vesterport) Explore the heavens at Copenhagen's planetarium, with its state-of-the-art equipment capable of projecting more than 7500 stars, planets and galaxies in its domed Space Theatre. The centre also screens IMAX and 3D/4D films on subjects ranging from sea monsters to Irish rockers U2. While the films are narrated in Danish, English-language headphones are available at the ticket counter (Dkr20).

The planetarium was named after the famed Danish astronomer Tycho Brahe (1546–1601), whose creation of precision astronomical instruments allowed him to make exact observations of planets and stars, and paved the way for the discoveries made by later astronomers.

🏃 Activities

You'll be forgiven for wanting to damn the Danes. Despite their high-level intake of tobacco, alcohol and fat, svelte bodies are the norm on Copenhagen streets. So what's their secret? A passion for physical activity. Top of the list is cycling, which combines ecofriendly transport with a decent workout. Beyond the pedal are a number of fine swimming options...allowing the locals to flaunt those frustratingly fine figures.

Beaches

If brisk water doesn't deter you, the greater Copenhagen area has several bathing spots. The water is tested regularly and if sewage spills or other serious pollution occurs, the beaches affected are closed and signposted.

Amager Strandpark BEACH

(www.amager-strand.dk; ☒; ☒Øresund, Amager Strand) This is a sand-sational artificial lagoon to the southeast of the city centre, with acres of beach and, during summer, a festive vibe most days with cafes and bars. Playground facilities and shallow water make it ideal for kids. The beach is also home to Helgoland (www.amager-strand.dk; ☺non-members 10am-6pm daily late Jun-Aug) **FREE**, a vintage-inspired sea bathing complex with multiple pools open to non-members from late June to the end of August.

Swimming Pools

Whether you're after indoor laps or a harbour splash, Copenhagen has you covered; the following are Copenhagen's most central swimming options.

DGI-byen POOL, GYM

(Map p46; www.dgi-byen.dk; Tietgensgade 65, Vesterbro; day pass adult/child Dkr65/45, day pass before 9am Mon-Fri Dkr45/30; ☺6.30am-10pm Mon-Thu, 6.30am-7.30pm Fri, 9am-7pm Sat, 9am-6pm Sun; ☒; ☑1A, 820, ☒København H) An extravagant indoor swim centre with several pools, including a grand ellipse-shaped

LOCAL KNOWLEDGE

TUE HESSELBERG FOGED, ARCHITECT

My favourite neighbourhood...

...is Islands Brygge. It used to be a working-class area, with industry along the harbour. Now it's like the Copacabana of Copenhagen. During summer, it's packed with near-naked people jumping into the harbour. The water is clean and you can swim in the centre of the city. It's a symbol of Copenhagen and what it can do. It's free and accessible to all. Just hanging out here in July and August is a must-do.

A perfect day in Copenhagen...

...would start in my favourite park, Kongens Have. There are always loads of people hanging out there on beautiful days. Across the street, I'd stop at Cinemateket, run by the Danish Film Institute. They only show good-quality classics and art-house films. Further out, I'd head to the Ny Carlsberg Vej 68 art precinct. It's home to Galleri Nicolai Wallner, one of the coolest galleries in Copenhagen.

The coolest thing about Copenhagen

...are festivals such as Distortion, which turns the city into one big block party. It's getting bigger and bigger each year and it's worth coming to Copenhagen just to experience it. It's what I love most about the city – the best parts are the temporary parties.

As told to Cristian Bonetto

affair with 100m lanes, a deep 'mountain pool' with a climbing wall, a hot-water pool and a children's pool. If you've forgotten your togs or towels, they can be hired for Dkr25 each (bring photo ID as a deposit). There's also a small gym on the premises.

Islands Brygge Havnebadet　　　POOL
(Map p46; Islands Brygge; ⊙7am-7pm Mon-Fri, 11am-7pm Sat & Sun Jun-Aug; 🚼; ☐5A, 12, Ⓜ Islands Brygge) **FREE** Copenhagen's coolest outdoor pool complex sits right in the central city's main canal. Water quality is rigorously monitored, and the lawns, BBQ facilities and eateries make it a top spot to see and be seen on a warm summer day, whether you get wet or not. In 2014, plans were underway for winter-friendly saunas and thermal baths, as well as a sixth pool.

Boating

GoBoat　　　BOATING
(Map p46; ☑40 26 10 25; www.goboat.dk; Islands Brygge 10; boat hire 1/3hr Dkr395/999; ⊙10am-sunset; 🚼) *What could be more 'Copenhagen' than sailing around the harbour and canals in your own solar-powered boat? You don't need prior sailing experience and each comes with a built-in picnic table (you can buy supplies at GoBoat or bring your own). Boats seat up to eight and rates are per boat, so the more in your group, the cheaper per person.

The rental kiosk sits right beside Islands Brygge Havnebadet.

Christianshavns Bådudlejning og Café　　　BOATING
(Map p52; ☑32 96 53 53; www.baadudlejningen. dk; Overgaden neden Vandet 29; boats per hr Dkr100; ⊙10am-sunset May–mid-Sep) *If you want to explore Christianshavn's historic canals, Christianshavns Bådudlejning og Café rents out rowing boats on the canal just beside Christianshavns Torv. An added bonus is the waterside cafe/bar (p80) on the premises.

Cycling

Hiring a bike is easy in Copenhagen. In addition to the rental rates, expect to pay a refundable deposit of around Dkr500 for a regular bike, Dkr1000 for a mountain bike or tandem. Tours are also available.

Baisikeli　　　CYCLING
(Map p46; ☑26 70 02 29; http://baisikeli.dk; Ingerslevsgade 80, Vesterbro; bicycles per 6hr/week from Dkr50/270; ⊙10am-6pm) Baisikeli is Swahili for bicycle, and the profits from this rental outlet are used to ship 1200 much-needed bikes to African communities annually. It's located beside Dybøllsbro S-train station and just south of the Kødbyen restaurant and bar precinct in Vesterbro.

Københavns Cyklerbørs　　　CYCLING
(Map p52; www.cykelboersen.dk; Gothersgade 157; bicycles per day/week Dkr75/350; ⊙8.30am-5.30pm Mon-Fri, 10am-2pm Sat, plus 6-9pm Sat & Sun May-Aug) Close to the Botanisk Have (Bo-

tanical Gardens) on the northwest edge of the city centre.

☞ Tours

You can't visit Copenhagen and *not* take a canal boat trip. Not only is it a fantastic way to see the city, but you see a side of it land-lubbers never see. There are two outfits that operate guided canal tours during summer – Canal Tours Copenhagen and Netto-Bådene. Be aware that, in most boats, you are totally exposed to the elements (which can be quite elemental in Copenhagen harbour, even during summer). Both operators offer tours in covered, heated boats from October to March.

Copenhagen City Sightseeing   TOUR
(Map p52; ☎32 66 00 00; www.citysightseeing.dk; ticket booth Ved Stranden, opposite Christiansborg Slotskirke; tickets adult/child from Dkr175/85; ☉ departures every 30 to 60min, 9.30am-6pm daily, mid-May–mid-Sep, shorter hrs and routes rest of yr) A hop-on/hop-off double-decker bus with three themed tours: Mermaid, Carlsberg and Christiania. Multilingual tape recordings make sure everyone gets the picture. The two-day 'Bus & Boat combo' (adult/child Dkr225/110) also covers Canal Tours Copenhagen.

Canal Tours Copenhagen   BOAT TOUR
(Map p52; ☎32 66 00 00; www.stromma.dk; adult/child/family Dkr75/35/190; ☉9.30am-9pm late Jun–late Aug, reduced hrs rest of yr; ⊕) Canal Tours Copenhagen runs one-hour cruises of the city's canals and harbour, taking in numerous major sights, including Christiansborg Slot, Christianshavn, the Royal Library, the Opera House, Amalienborg Palace and the Little Mermaid. Embark at Nyhavn or Ved Stranden. Boats depart up to six times per hour from late June to late August, with reduced frequency the rest of the year.

Netto-Bådene   BOAT TOUR
(Map p52; ☎32 54 41 02; www.havnerundfart.dk; adult/child Dkr40/15; ☉tours 2-5 per hr, 10am-7pm Jul & Aug, to 5pm Apr-Jun & Sep–mid-Oct; ⊕) Netto-Bådene operates good-value one-hour cruises of Copenhagen's canals and harbour. Embarkation points are at Holmens Kirke and Nyhavn. From mid-July to August, boats also depart from the Little Mermaid. Check the website for timetable updates.

Kayak Republic   KAYAK TOUR
(Map p52; ☎30 49 86 20; www.kayakrepublic.dk; Børskaj 12; per person 150-575 kr; ☉10am-8pm) ⌀ Kayak Republic runs two-hour and full-day kayak tours along the city's canals.

WORTH A TRIP

DEN BLÅ PLANET

Den Blå Planet (www.denblaaplanet.dk; Jacob Fortlingsvej 1, Kastrup; adult/child 3-11yr Dkr160/95; ☉10am-9pm Mon, to 6pm Tue-Sun; ☐5A, Ⓜ Kastrup) Designed to look like a whirlpool from above, Copenhagen's new, aluminum-clad aquarium is the largest in northern Europe. The space is divided into climatic and geographic sections, the most spectacular of which is 'Ocean/Coral Reef'. Home to swarms of Technicolor tropical fish, the exhibition is also home to the centre's largest tank, a massive 4,000,000-litre showcase brimming with sharks, stingrays and other majestic creatures. If possible, visit the aquarium on a Monday evening, when it's at its quietest and most evocative.

The Blue Planet is also home to a notable cafe by prolific food figure Claus Meyer, with good pastries, updated versions of Danish classics, and decent coffee to boot.

Den Blå Planet lies 7km southeast of central Copenhagen and is easily reached by bus or metro.

They also rents out kayaks for self-guided outings (single kayak per one/two hours Dkr150/250).

Nordic Noir Tours   WALKING TOUR
(Map p46; http://nordicnoirtours.com; per person Dkr150, if booked online Dkr100; ☉Borgen tour 2pm Sat, The Killing/The Bridge tour 4pm Sat) Fans of Danish TV dramas *Borgen, The Bridge* and *The Killing* can visit the shooting locations on these themed 90-minute walks. Tours commence at Vesterport S-train station. Bookings are not required, though tickets purchased online at least 48 hours in advance are Dkr50 cheaper.

Copenhagen Free Walking Tours   WALKING TOUR
(Map p52; www.copenhagenfreewalkingtours.dk) FREE Departing daily at 11am and 2pm from outside Rådhus (City Hall), these free, three-hour walking tours take in famous landmarks and interesting anecdotes. Tours are in English and require a minimum of five people. Free 90-minute tours of Christianshavn depart at 4pm Friday to Monday from the base of the Bishop Absalon statue on Højbro Plads.

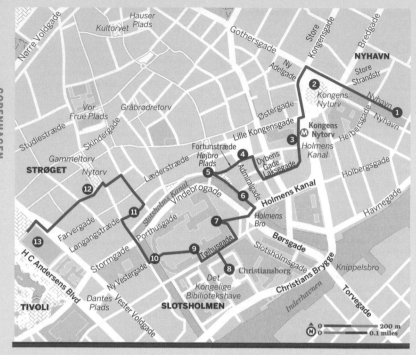

City Walk
Copenhagen: Cobbles & Cosiness

START NYHAVN
FINISH RÅDHUSPLADSEN
DISTANCE 2.7 KILOMETRES
DURATION 2 HOURS

Start your stroll at iconic ❶ **Nyhavn**, eyeing up its coloured townhouses and imagining a past filled with sailors and women of 'ill repute'. Commissioned by Christian V, the canal was constructed by Swedish war prisoners in the 17th century to connect the harbour to ❷ **Kongens Nytorv**, Copenhagen's largest square. At the southern end of the square stands the ❸ **Magasin department store** (p87), an example of French Renaissance Revival architecture. Built in 1894, it replaced the Hotel du Nord, which was home to Hans Christian Andersen between 1838 and 1847.

Continue south into Laksegade, turning right into Nikolajgade. The street leads to ❹ **Nicolaj Kunsthal** (p50), a contemporary art space set inside Copenhagen's third oldest church. Head west down Fortunstræde to ❺ **Højbro Plads**, home to a statue of Copenhagen's founder, Bishop Absalon. Close by is superlative wine bar ❻ **Ved Stranden 10** (p78). Stop for a swill, then cross the canal at Holmens Bro. In front of you is ❼ **Christiansborg Slot** (p50), home to the Danish parliament. Head through the archway to the left of the palace, then through the second archway on your left. Awaiting is the ❽ **Royal Library Garden**, built on top of Christian IV's old naval port, Tøjhushavnen. Head back through the archway, continuing south to the late-baroque ❾ **Riding Ground Complex**, the only remnant from the original Christiansborg Palace. The riding ground leads out to the 18th-century ❿ **Marble Bridge**. Cross it, turning right into Frederikshoms Kanal until you reach ⓫ **Magstræde**, Copenhagen's oldest street. Wander down it, turning left into Knabrostræde and then left again at Brolæggerstræde. The street spills into Nytorv, home to Copenhagen's pink-stucco court house ⓬ **Domhuset** (p50). Head down Slutterigade to the left of the building, at the very end of which soars the architectural flourish that is ⓭ **Rådhus** (p49).

CPH:cool WALKING TOUR

(Map p52; ☑ 29 80 10 40; www.cphcool.dk; Vesterbrogade 4A) Generally running for two hours, these walking tours cover themes like gastronomy, shopping, architecture and design. Prices vary according to the number of participants and tours start outside the Copenhagen Visitors Centre at Vesterbrogade 4A, opposite Tivoli amusement park.

Bike Copenhagen With Mike CYCLING TOUR

(Map p52; ☑ 26 39 56 88; www.bikecopenhagen withmike.dk; Skt Peders Stræde 47; per person Dkr299) If you don't fancy walking, Bike Mike runs three-hour cycling tours of the city, departing from Skt Peders Stræde 47 in the city centre, just east of Ørstedsparken (which is southwest of Nørreport station). The tour cost includes bike and helmet rental. Seasonal options are also offered, including a Saturday evening 'Ride & Dine' tour from June to September. Cash only.

✦✦ Festivals & Events

Vinter Jazz MUSIC

(www.jazz.dk/en/vinter-jazz) Toe-tap your blues away at this smaller scale version of Copenhagen's summertime jazz festival. Usually kicking off on the first Friday of February, it runs for 17 days, with events held across the city.

CPH:PIX FILM

(www.cphpix.dk) Held over two weeks in April, this is Copenhagen's feature film festival. Sit down to a comprehensive programme of flicks from Denmark and abroad, as well as a busy schedule of film-related events, including director and actor Q&As.

Dronning Margrethe II's Birthday ROYAL

On 16 April, Danes celebrate the birthday of their much-loved queen. If she is celebrating in town, you will find her greeting the crowds from the balcony of Amalienborg Slot at noon as soldiers in full ceremonial dress salute her.

Distortion MUSIC

(www.cphdistortion.dk) Taking place over five heady days in early June, Copenhagen Distortion celebrates the city's street life and club culture. Expect raucous block parties and top-name DJs spinning dance tracks in bars and clubs across town.

Skt Hans Aften CULTURAL

(St Hans Evening) The Danes let rip on the evening of 23 June – the shortest night of the year – with bonfires in parks, gardens and, most popular of all, on the beaches. Join them in burning an effigy of a witch on a pyre, singing songs and getting merry.

Copenhagen Jazz Festival MUSIC

(jazz.dk) Copenhagen's single largest event, and the largest jazz festival in northern Europe, hits the city over 10 days in early July. The programme covers jazz in all its forms, with an impressive line-up of local and international talent.

Kulturhavn CULTURAL

(www.kulturhavn.dk) For three days in early August, Copenhagen takes culture to the harbour and waterways with a wide programme of theatre, dance, music, sports and parades on the 'beach' at Islands Brygge, as well as at Sydhavnen, Papirøen, Refshaleøen and other waterside locations. Most events are free.

Copenhagen Pride GAY & LESBIAN

(www.copenhagenpride.dk) Rainbow flags fly high during the city's five-day queer fest in August. Expect live music and merry revellers in the city centre, fabulous club parties, cultural events and the obligatory Pride parade, the latter taking place on the Saturday afternoon.

Strøm MUSIC

(www.stromcph.dk) Copenhagen's electronic music festival runs for a week in August. Considered the top festival of its kind in Scandinavia, its 60-plus events include workshops and masterclasses, concerts, raves and parties across the city.

Copenhagen Cooking FOOD

(www.copenhagencooking.dk) Scandinavia's largest food festival serves up a gut-rumbling programme spanning cooking demonstrations from A-list chefs, to tastings and foodie tours of the city. Events are held in venues and restaurants across town, usually in August. A month-long winter edition takes place in February.

Art Copenhagen ART

(www.artcopenhagen.dk) This major, three-day art fair in September involves around 60 art galleries from Scandinavia and beyond. Showcasing a good number of contemporary artists from Denmark, Sweden, Norway, Finland, Iceland and the Faroe Islands, the event usually takes place at Forum Copenhagen.

Copenhagen Blues Festival MUSIC

(www.copenhagenbluesfestival.dk) For five days in late September or early October, Copenhagen

COPENHAGEN FESTIVALS & EVENTS

❶ CYCLING: 101

Copenhagen is one of the world's great biking centres, and hitting the peddle is a convenient way of exploring the city. To ensure your ride is safe and stress-free (and to avoid aggravating local cyclists), familiarise yourself with the following basic rules:

➡ Keep right unless overtaking another cyclist

➡ Do not cycle on footpaths or pedestrianised streets

➡ Walk your bicycle across crosswalks

➡ Signal right (right arm stretched out low) before turning right, signal left (left arm stretched out low) before turning left, and use the stop signal (hand raised by your side) when making an atypical stop on the cycle path, or if stopping to turn left at a main intersection

➡ Do not turn right on a red light

➡ Stop and give way to pedestrians needing to cross the bike path to get on and off buses

➡ Give way to bus passengers crossing cycle lanes to reach the pavement

➡ Texting while cycling is illegal, as is riding while inebriated

➡ Lock your bike – bike theft occurs

celebrates the moody sounds of the blues with this international music festival. The line-up includes both Danish and international acts.

Kulturnatten CULTURAL
(Culture Night; www.kulturnatten.dk) Usually held on the second Friday in October, Culture Night sees the city's museums, galleries, theatres and libraries throw open their doors from 6pm to around midnight to those with a Kulturpas (Culture Pass; Dkr90), with no shortage of special events. Public transport is also free with the Kulturpas.

CPH:DOX FILM
(www.cphdox.dk) CPH:Dox is an acclaimed international documentary film festival, and the largest of its kind in Scandinavia. Its diverse programme takes to cinemas across the city. The festival takes place over 11 days from early to mid-November.

Tivoli CULTURAL
(www.tivoli.dk) From mid-November to early January, Tivoli gets into the Christmas spirit with a large Yuletide market, costumed staff and theatre shows. Fewer rides are operational but the mulled wine and *æbleskiver* (small doughnuts) are ample compensation.

🛏 Sleeping

Copenhagen's accommodation options span everything from the floating chic of CPH Living, to the classic Danish design aesthetics of the Radisson Blu Royal Hotel. The city's design legacy is not limited to higher-end establishments, with both WakeUp Copenhagen and Generator Hostel injecting style and sass into the city's more budget-conscious offerings.

With both WakeUp Copenhagen and Generator Hostel being exceptions, most of the city's main budget hotels are centred on the western side of the Central Station, around Vesterbrogade and the fruitier parts of Istedgade. Ironically, what was once a relatively downtrodden part of town is now home to one of its trendiest districts, Kødbyen, now filling up with some of Copenhagen's hottest eateries and bars.

The hotel rates quoted in listings here include service charge and value-added tax (VAT). It's a good idea to book in advance – rooms in many of the most popular mid-range hotels fill quickly, particularly during the convention season (typically from August to October) when prices increase significantly too. At other times, prices for rooms fluctuate greatly, depending on the time of year or even the time of week, with most hotels tempting guests with special offers throughout the year. Copenhagen's hostels often fill early in summer so it's best to make reservations in advance. You will need a hostelling card to get the advertised rates at hostels belonging to the **Danhostel** (www.danhostel.dk) organisation.

The Copenhagen Visitors Centre can book rooms in private homes (Dkr350/500 for singles/doubles); there is a Dkr100 booking fee if you book via the tourist office when you arrive, otherwise it is free online. This office also books unfilled hotel rooms at discounted rates of up to 50% (sometimes even more). These discounts, however, are based on supply and demand, and are not always available during busy periods.

🛏 Rådhuspladsen, Tivoli & Around

Danhostel Copenhagen City   HOSTEL €
(Map p46; ☑ 33 11 85 85; www.danhostel.dk/copenhagencity; HC Andersens Blvd 50; dm/d Dkr225/610; @ 🛜; 🚇 1A, 2A, 11A, 12, 33, 40, 66) With interiors by design company Gubi and a cafe-bar in the lobby, this friendly, ever-popular hostel is set in a tower block overlooking the harbour, just south of Tivoli Gardens (did we mention the views?). Both the dorms and private rooms are bright, light and modern, each with their own bathroom. Book ahead.

Cabinn   HOTEL €
(www.cabinn.com; s/d/tr Dkr545/675/805; @ 🛜) Well managed, functional and cheap, the Cabinn chain has four hotels in Copenhagen, the most central being **Cabinn City** (Map p46; ☑ 33 46 16 16; Mitchellsgade 14; @ 🛜; 🚇 5A, 9A, 11A, 30, 🚆 S-train København H), just south of Tivoli. Although small and anonymous, rooms are comfortable, with cable TV, phone, free wi-fi and private bathroom. Both **Cabinn Scandinavia** (Map p46; ☑ 35 36 11 11; Vodroffsvej 57, Frederiksberg; 🚇 2A, 68, 250S, Ⓜ Forum) and **Cabinn Express** (Map p46; ☑ 33 21 04 00; Danasvej 32, Frederiksberg; @ 🛜; 🚇 3A, 30, Ⓜ Forum) are less than 2km west of Tivoli, while the newer **Cabinn Metro** (☑ 32 46 57 00; Arne Jakobsens Allé 2; Ⓜ Ørestad) is a short walk from Ørestad metro station, and close to the airport.

★ Hotel Alexandra   HOTEL €€
(Map p52; ☑ 33 74 44 44; www.hotelalexandra.dk; HC Andersens Blvd 8; s/d from Dkr750/950; @ 🛜; 🚇 2A, 10, 11A, 12, 26, 250S, 🚆 S-train Vesterport) The furniture of Danish design deities such as Arne Jacobsen, Ole Wanscher and Kaare Klint grace the interiors of the refined yet homely Alexandra. Recently renovated, rooms are effortlessly cool, each decked out in mid-century Danish style. Contemporary concessions include flatscreen TVs. Staff are attentive, and the hotel's refined retro air makes a refreshing change from all that white-on-white Nordic minimalism.

First Hotel Twentyseven   HOTEL €€
(Map p52; ☑ 70 27 56 27; www.firsthotels.com; Løngangstræde 27; s/d from Dkr930/1100; @ 🛜; 🚇 11A, 12, 33) The rooms might be a little small, but the minimalist styling and cool furniture fit the hipster bill at this super-cool Scandi number. Perks include sleek, black-slate bathrooms, friendly staff, and decent cocktails in the popular ground-floor bar (request a room away from the bar if you're a light sleeper).

First Hotel Kong Frederik   HOTEL €€
(Map p52; ☑ 33 12 59 02; www.firsthotels.com; Vester Voldgade 25; s/d from Dkr880/960; @ 🛜; 🚇 5A, 6A, 10, 11A, 14, 🚆 S-train Vesterport) There's something rather baronial about black-and-gold Kong Frederik, its interiors a mix of dark woods, antique furnishings and paintings of Danish royalty and hunting scenes. The well-appointed rooms come in three themes: Classic, Romantic and Library (the latter featuring silvery 'bookshelf' wallpaper). The staff are genuinely friendly and there's a Nespresso machine in the communal reading room.

Square   HOTEL €€
(Map p52; ☑ 33 38 12 00; www.thesquarecopenhagen.com; Rådhuspladsen 14; s/d from Dkr925/1030; ✷@ 🛜; 🚇 2A, 12, 26, 250S, 🚆 S-train Vesterport) Pimped with Jacobsen chairs and red leather, The Square is an excellent three-star hotel with designer flair and amenities generally associated with greater expense and more stiffness. Standard rooms are a little small but well equipped, and some have sterling views of the main square – plus all the city's main sights are within walking distance.

★ Hotel Nimb   BOUTIQUE HOTEL €€€
(Map p52; ☑ 88 70 00 00; www.nimb.dk; Berns torffsgade 5; r from Dkr2600; @ 🛜; 🚇 2A, 5A, 9A, 12, 26, 250S, 350S, 🚆 S-train København H.) Located at Tivoli, this boutique belle offers 17 individually styled rooms and suites fusing clean lines, beautiful art and antiques, luxury

TOP EXPERIENCES FOR KIDS

➡ Tivoli (p45)

➡ DGI-byen (p61)

➡ Nationalmuseet (p45)

➡ Canal Boat Tour (p63)

➡ Den Blå Planet (p63)

fabrics and high-tech perks such as Bang & Olufsen TVs and sound systems. All rooms except three also feature a fireplace, while all bar one come with views over the amusement park. In-house perks include a savvy cocktail lounge with crackling fire.

Radisson BLU Royal Hotel HOTEL €€€
(Map p46; ☑33 42 60 00; www.radissonblu. com; Hammerichsgade 1; s/d from Dkr1745/1845; P ❈ @ ⚆; ☐2A, 5A, 9A, 12, 26, 250S, 350S, ☐S-train København H) Centrally located and famous among the design cognoscenti (Arne Jacobsen designed it and room 606 – a tidy Dkr5500 per night – has been left intact), this multistory hotel of 260 rooms is popular with well-to-do business travellers and visiting dignitaries. Service is peerless, there's a full-service gym, and the excellent Alberto K restaurant on the 20th floor is a culinary high.

Palace Hotel HOTEL €€€
(Map p52; ☑33 14 40 50; www.scandichotels.com; Rådhuspladsen 57; rm incl breakfast from Dkr1300; ❈ @ ⚆; ☐12, 26, 33, 11A, ☐S-train København H.) Bang on Rådhuspladsen and housed in a landmark 1920s, Anton Rosen–designed building, the Palace skilfully balances historic architecture with contemporary detailing. Rooms are elegantly pared back, with sleek bathrooms and shades of pastel or grey breaking up the Scandinavian white.

🛏 Strøget & Around

★ Generator Hostel HOSTEL €
(Map p52; www.generatorhostel.com; Adelgade 5-7; dm Dkr230-325, rm Dkr800-1070; @ ⚆; ☐11A, 350S, Ⓜ Kongens Nytorv) A solid choice for 'cheap chic', upbeat, design-literate Generator sits on the very edge of the city's medieval core. It's kitted out with designer furniture, slick communal areas (including a bar and outdoor terrace) and friendly, young staff. While the rooms can be a little small, all are bright and modern, with bathrooms in both private rooms and dorms.

Hotel SP34 BOUTIQUE HOTEL €€
(Map p52; ☑33 13 30 00; www.brochner-hotels.dk; Skt Peders Stræde 34; rm from Dkr1255; ⚆; ☐5A, 6A, 14, 10, 11A, ☐S-train Vesterport) Urbane SP34 is one of Copenhagen's newest boutique options. Tans and subtle pastels underline the communal areas, among them a plush, light-drenched lounge, Modernist-inspired reading room, and svelte lobby bar. The 118 rooms keep things smart and simple, with

slate-coloured walls, muted accents and REN bathroom amenities. Nibble on organic produce at breakfast, and sip complimentary vino between 5pm and 6pm.

Hotel d'Angleterre HOTEL €€€
(Map p52; ☑33 12 00 95; www.dangleterre.com; Kongens Nytorv 34; rm from Dkr2750; ❈ @ ⚆ ≋; Ⓜ Kongens Nytorv) Hitting the scene in 1755, the neoclassical d'Angleterre is Copenhagen's most glamorous slumber palace. Fresh from an ambitious facelift, it's once again fit for royalty and mere mortal sybarites. Regal portraits, fireplaces and Art Nouveau flourishes keep things suitably posh in the public areas, while the hotel's rooms and suites deliver contemporary twists on classic luxury, with powdery accents, luxurious fabrics, and marble bathrooms.

The hotel's rebirth also includes an extraordinary, 2,000-square-foot tile-and-marble pool, part of the hotel's luxury spa. Other hotel perks include the city's first dedicated champagne bar, and Michelin-starred nosh spot Marchal.

Hotel Skt Petri HOTEL €€€
(Map p52; ☑33 45 91 00; www.hotelsktpetri. com; Krystalgade 22; rm from Dkr1160; @ ⚆; ☐11A, Ⓜ Nørreport) Admittedly, the design-conscious Skt Petri is showing a little wear and tear in parts. That said, rooms remain comfortable, their neutral tones sexed up with boldly coloured bedhead art panels. Request a room on level four or higher for the best outlook. Sweat it out in the fitness centre or throw diet to the wind at the hotel's trendy bread-and-beer concept bar.

🛏 Nyhavn

Copenhagen Strand HOTEL €€
(Map p52; ☑33 48 99 00; www.copenhagenstrand.dk; Havnegade 37; rm incl breakfast from Dkr1060; @ ⚆; ☐11A, 66, Ⓜ Kongens Nytorv) 🍃 In a converted 19th-century warehouse, the appealing Strand overlooks Copenhagen Harbour. Rooms are classically styled in wood, brass and shades of royal blue. Standard rooms are smallish but cosy; the executive rooms and suites come with harbour views.

Scandic Front HOTEL €€
(Map p46; ☑33 13 34 00; www.scandichotels.dk; Sankt Annæ Plads 21; rm from Dkr1200; ❈ @ ⚆; ☐11A, 66 Ⓜ Kongens Nytorv) Conveniently plonked to the rear of Nyhavn and overlooking the harbour, Front is light, bright and sexed-up with a bold colour scheme (although

the orange carpets that grace some rooms are probably best avoided). Admittedly, the rooms are looking a little worn these days, though we do love the pebble-floored bathrooms, amiable staff and handy little on-site gym.

71 Nyhavn Hotel
HOTEL €€€
(Map p46; ☑ 33 43 62 00; www.71nyhavnhotel.com; Nyhavn 71; rm from Dkr1050; @ 🛜) Housed in a striking 200-year-old canalside warehouse, atmospheric 71 Nyhavn offers great views of both the harbour and Nyhavn canal. Rooms facing Nyhavn are quite small, while those without the magical view compensate with more space. The hotel is popular with business travellers, and therefore can be a bargain on weekends.

🛏 Christianshavn

CPH Living
FLOATING HOTEL €€
(Map p46; ☑ 61 60 85 46; www.cphliving.com; Langebrogade 1C; r incl breakfast from Dkr1000; 🛜; 🚍 5A, 12) Located on a converted freight boat, Copenhagen's only floating hotel consists of 12 stylish, contemporary rooms, each with harbour and city views. Perks include modern bathrooms with rainforest shower, and a communal sundeck for summertime lounging. Breakfast is a simple continental affair, while the central location makes it an easy walk to the city centre, Christianshavn and the harbour beach at Islands Brygge.

🛏 Nørreport

Ibsens Hotel
BOUTIQUE HOTEL €€
(Map p52; ☑ 33 13 19 13; www.ibsenshotel.dk; Vendersgade 23; s/d from Dkr740/870; @ 🛜; 🚍 5A, 40, 350S Ⓜ Nørreport) ✈ A true boutique hotel, Ibsens is a sound choice for discerning urbanites. Local creativity defines everything from the striking textiles to the artwork. Rooms are minimalist yet plush, with muted tones, designer fixtures and blissful beds. Book early for the best rates.

Hotel Kong Arthur
HOTEL €€
(Map p52; ☑ 33 11 12 12; www.kongarthur.dk; Nørre Søgade 11; rm from Dkr1220; @ 🛜; 🚍 5A, 40, 350S Ⓜ Nørreport) ✈ The 155-room Kong Arthur merges understated elegance with quirky period details such as suits of armour. Rooms are a soothing white, splashed with contemporary art and including attractive bathrooms. Some overlook the waters of Peblinge Sø. The new in-house spa – home to a hot tub, sauna, and aroma steam bath – is free for guests who book rooms directly on the hotel website.

🛏 Vesterbro

★ Hotel Guldsmeden
BOUTIQUE HOTEL €€
(www.hotelguldsmeden.dk) ✈ The simply gorgeous Guldsmeden hotels include **Bertrams** (Map p46; ☑ 70 20 81 07; Vesterbrogade 107; s/d from Dkr895/995; 🚍 6A, 3A), **Carlton** (Map p46; ☑ 33 22 15 00; Vesterbrogade 66; s/d from Dkr695/795; 🚍 6A), **Axel** (Map p46; ☑ 33 31 32 66; Helgolandsgade 7-11; s/d Dkr765/895; 🚍 6A, 26, 🚉 S-train København H.) and newcomer **Babette** (Map p46; ☑ 33 14 15 00; Bredgade 78; s/d from Dkr795/945; 🛜; 🚍 1A). Only the latter is not in Vesterbro, instead located between Amalienborg and Kastellet on the northern side of the city centre. All four deliver subtle, Balinese-inspired chic, with raw stone, bare wood, four-poster beds and crisp white linen.

Needless to say, the Guldsmeden chain has become a classic choice for discerning, style-conscious travellers.

Andersen Hotel
HOTEL €€
(Map p46; ☑ 33 31 43 44; www.andersen-hotel.dk; Helgolandsgade 12; s/d from Dkr1255/1435; 🛜; 🚍 6A, 26, 🚉 S-train København H.) White-on-white gives way to bold, playful design at new-school Andersen. Rooms are simple yet skilfully pimped with smile-inducing details, from geometric blankets and cushions, to Mad Men-style rugs and chairs, and text wall murals (you might even find a rubber duck in the bathroom). If you're a light sleeper, request a room facing the internal courtyard.

Service is genuine and friendly, and the hotel is a quick walk from Central Station and Vesterbro's popular bars, restaurants and boutiques. Booking well in advance can see prices drop as low as Dkr850 for a single and Dkr1030 for a double.

Wakeup Copenhagen
HOTEL €€
(Map p46; ☑ 44 80 00 10; www.wakeupcopenhagen.com; Carsten Niebuhrs Gade 11; rm Dkr450-1500; @ 🛜; 🚍 11A, 🚉 S-train København H.) An easy walk from Central Station and Tivoli, this is one of two Wakeup Copenhagen branches in town, well known for offering style on a budget (assuming you've booked online and in advance). The foyer is an impressive combo of concrete, glass and Arne Jacobsen chairs, while the 500-plus rooms are sharp and compact, with flat-screen TV and capsule-like showers.

Wakeup's second **branch** (Map p52; ☑ 44 80 00 00; Borgergade 9; 🛜) enjoys an even more central location close to Nyhavn.

Tiffany
HOTEL €€

(Map p46; ☑33 21 80 50; www.hoteltiffany.dk; Colbjørnsensgade 28; s/d from Dkr745/895; @ 🔊; ⓡS-train København H.) The Tiffany, which proudly bills itself as a 'Sweet Hotel', is a pleasant little place filled with character. The 30 rooms each have a TV, phone, trouser press, bathroom, and kitchenette with a refrigerator, microwave oven and toaster. Service is kind and considerate, and it's an easy walk from Central Station and the hip cafes, bars and restaurants of the Vesterbro neighbourhood.

🛏 Greater Copenhagen

Charlottenlund Fort
CAMPGROUND €

(☑39 62 36 88; www.campingcopenhagen.dk; Strandvejen 144B; camping per adult/3-12yr/0-2yr Dkr100/45/20; ⊘early Mar–mid-Oct; ⓡS-train Svanemøllen, then bus 14) Eight kilometres north of central Copenhagen, this friendly camping ground, on Charlottenlund beach, is set in the tree-lined grounds of an old, moat-encircled coastal fortification. Space is limited so book ahead. Facilities include showers and a coin laundry on-site; a bakery and a supermarket are just a few hundred metres away.

To get here, take S-train line A, B or C to Svanemøllen station and switch to bus 14 (ask the driver to let you off at the camping ground).

Danhostel Copenhagen Amager
HOSTEL €

(☑32 52 29 08; www.copenhagenyouthhostel. dk; Vejlands Allé 200, Amager; dm Dkr160, s/d Dkr490/530; ℙ@🔊; ⓜBella Center) In an isolated part of Amager just off the E20, about 5km southeast of the city centre, this is one of Europe's largest hostels, with 528 beds in a series of low-rise wings containing rooms of two-bed and five-bed rooms. There's a laundry and guest kitchen. To get here, take the metro to Bella Center.

✖ Eating

Copenhagen remains one of the hottest culinary destinations in Europe, with more Michelin stars than any other Scandinavian city.

Beyond New Nordic cult restaurants like Noma, Geranium and Kadeau, contemporary Danish innovation is also driving a growing number of casual, midrange eateries, from Höst and Manfreds og Vin, to Kødbyens Fiskebar and Kadeau's baby brother, Pony.

Yet it's not all sea buckthorn, *skyr* (strained yoghurt) curd and pickled quail eggs, with old-school Danish fare still a major player on the city's tables. Indeed, tucking into classics such as *frikadeller* (meatballs), *sild* (pickled herring) and the iconic Danish open sandwich (smørrebrød) at institutions such as Schønnemann is an integral part of the Copenhagen experience.

Keep in mind that the Danes are not Mediterranean, meaning that if you like to eat late, you'll have trouble finding a place to accommodate you after about 10pm. That said, Copenhageners love to eat out, so make sure to reserve a table at popular nosh spots, especially later in the week. Many restaurants now offer easy online reservations on their websites.

✖ Rådhuspladsen & Tivoli

Andersen Bakery
BAKERY €

(Map p52; ☑33 75 07 35; www.andersenbakery. com; Bernstorffsgade 5; pastries from Dkr10, gourmet hot dog Dkr50; ⊘6.30am-7pm Mon-Fri, 7.30am-7pm Sat & Sun; 🔊; ▣2A, 5A, 9A, 250S, ⓡS-train København H) Pastry peddler Andersen puts the sticky in sublime. The vaguely healthy wholewheat *kanelsnegle* (cinnamon snail) is an instant perk-me-up, while fans of blue cheese cannot afford to miss the Danablu Horn, a sweet-and-salty revelation involving Danish blue cheese, honey and walnuts in a horn-shaped bread concoction. If it's lunch, stuff your face with the Grand Danois, Andresen's celebrated gourmet hot dog.

You'll find the bakery right opposite the central train station.

Grøften
DANISH €€

(Map p52; ☑33 75 06 75; www.groeften.dk; smørrebrød Dkr69-135, mains Dkr145-385; ⊘noon-10pm daily early Apr-late Sep, reduced hrs rest of yr; 🔊; ▣2A, 5A, 9A, 97N, 250S, ⓡS-train København H) If you're getting your thrills at Tivoli, jolly Grøften is a handy place to refuel. Sure it's a bit touristy, but it's been here since 1874, making it a bit of a local institution. Reminisce about the good old days over smørrebrød classics like hand-peeled shrimps with lemon and mayonnaise, or tackle the mains, which includes gutsy, no-nonsense meat and fish dishes.

Wagamama
JAPANESE €€

(Map p52; www.wagamama.dk; Tietgensgade 20; mains Dkr95-135; ⊘noon-9pm daily; 🔊; ▣1A, 2A, 5A, 9A, 11A, ⓡS-train København H) Yes, it's a ubiquitous UK chain, but we still love Waga-mama for several reasons: the food is fresh and flavoursome, the place is open all week, and it's a short walk from the central station. Pique the appetite with tasty gyoza or vibrant seaweed salad, then slurp your way through steamy bowls of ramen noodles.

Although part of the Tivoli complex, Wagamama is accessible to all from Tietgensgade.

★ **Alberto K**   MODERN DANISH €€€
(Map p46; ☑ 33 42 61 61; www.alberto-k.dk; Hammerichsgade 1; 5/7 courses Dkr750/950; ⊘ 6-9.45pm Mon-Sat; ☐ 5A, 6A, 26, ☒ S-train Vesterport, København H) Perched on the 20th floor of the Radisson Blu Royal Hotel, Alberto K is a culinary high, both literally and metaphorically. Award-winning head chef Jeppe Foldager marries modern French techniques with local produce from small producers, producing arresting dishes that are vibrant and seductive. Arne Jacobsen cutlery and furniture pay tribute to the hotel's celebrated designer, while the restaurant's wine cellar is an oenophile's delight.

✗ Strøget & Around

Cock's & Cows   BURGERS €
(Map p52; ☑ 69 69 60 00; http://cocksandcows.dk; Gammel Strand 34; burgers Dkr89-129; ⊘ noon-9.30pm Sun-Thu, to 10.30pm Fri & Sat; ☐ 1A, 2A, 26, 40, 66) When burger-lust hits, satiate your urges at Cock's. In a setting best described as American diner meets Danish Modernist (picture red leather booths against Poul Henningsen lamps), energetic staff deliver fresh, made-from-scratch burgers that are generous and insanely good. The meat is Danish and charcoal grilled, and there's a veggie burger for herbivores. Make sure to order a side of the onion rings.

Palæo   INTERNATIONAL €
(Map p52; www.palaeo.dk; Pilestræde 32; dishes Dkr59-89; ⊘ 8am-8pm Mon-Fri, 10am-7pm Sat, 11am-5pm Sun; ☎; ☐ 11A, ☒ Kongens Nytorv) Fast-food, Flintstones-style is what you get at Palæo, a trendy eat-in/take-away joint peddling so-called 'primal gastronomy'. Dishes are inspired by the palaeolithic diet, which means carb-light creations like hot dogs with egg-based wrappers (not buns) and risottos that give rice the flick for celeriac kernels. But if you're thinking mung bean mediocrity, thing again: behind the menu is Michelin-starred chef Thomas Rode Andersen.

La Glace   BAKERY €
(Map p52; www.laglace.dk; Skoubougade 3; cake slices Dkr57, pastries from Dkr36; ⊘ 8.30am-6pm Mon-Fri, 9am-6pm Sat, 10am-6pm Sun, closed Sun Easter-Sep; ☐ 11A) Copenhagen's oldest *konditori* (pastry shop) has been compromising waistlines since 1870. Succumb to a slice of the classic *valnøddekage* (walnut cake), a sinful concoction of crush and caramelised walnuts, whipped cream and Mocca glacé. Alternatively, betray your personal trainer with the *sportskage* (crushed nougat, cream and caramelised profiteroles).

★ **Höst**   MODERN DANISH €€
(Map p52; ☑ 89 93 84 09; http://cofoco.dk/da/restauranter/hoest; Nørre Farimagsgade 41; mains Dkr195-215, 3-course set menu Dkr295; ⊘ 5.30-9.30pm daily; ☐ 40, ☒ Nørrebro) Höst's phenomenal popularity is a no-brainer: warm,

---

SØLLERØD KRO

Søllerød Kro (☑ 45 80 25 05; www.soelleroed-kro.dk; Søllerødvej 35, Holte; 2-/3-course lunch Dkr375/475, 4-/6-course dinner Dkr775/995; ⊘ noon-2.30pm & 6-9.30pm Wed-Sun) Not all of Copenhagen's Michelin stars are inner-city dwellers. One of them lives in Holte, an unassuming outer suburb 19km north of the city centre. We're talking about Søllerød Kro, a one-star Michelin restaurant set in a beautiful 17th-century thatched-roof inn. The kitchen's creations are nothing short of extraordinary, pushing modern Danish creativity to new, enlightened heights.

Here, dehydrated artichokes might be paired with hazelnut milk & smoke, while roasted foie gras could come with beets and an elderberry jus. The balancing of flavours and textures is quite often breathtaking, as are the wine pairings for each course.

Yet, despite the fame, adulation and classically chic interiors, Søllerød Kro keeps its feet firmly on the ground, ditching pomp and attitude for a genuine hospitality that's as much a highlight as its degustation menus.

To get here from Copenhagen, catch S-train (Line E) north to Holte station, from where bus 195 will drop you off 150m from the restaurant (tell the driver you're going to Søllerød Kro). Journey time is around 35 minutes.

award-winning interiors, mere-mortal prices, and New Nordic food that's equally fabulous and filling. The set menu is great value, with three smaller 'surprise dishes' thrown in, and evocative creations like salted Faroe island scallops with corn, raw plums, pickled black trumpet mushrooms and wild garlic. The 'deluxe' wine menu is significantly better than the standard option.

Book ahead, especially later in the week.

Brdr.Price
INTERNATIONAL €€

(Map p52; ☑38 41 10 20; http://rosenborggade. brdr-price.dk; Rosenborggade 15-17; cafe mains Dkr145-195, restaurant mains Dkr175-265; ☺cafe noon-midnight Sun-Thu, to 1am Fri & Sat, restaurant 5.30-10pm Sun-Wed, to 10.30pm Thu-Sat; ☎; ☒6A, 11A, 150S, M Nørrebro) Siblings Adam and James Price host a cult-status TV cooking show (Adam also created TV series *Borgen*), and their noshery turns prime produce into mood-enhancing comfort grub. Join foodies, *Borgen* fans and the odd poet in the bistro-style cafe for standouts like pillow-soft pulled pork served burger-style. Downstairs in the restaurant, chintzy chandeliers make a suitable match for old-school fare like lobster thermidor.

Bistro Pastis
FRENCH €€

(Map p52; ☑33 93 44 11; http://bistro-pastis.dk; Gothersgade 52; salads & sandwiches Dkr115-145, mains Dkr165-285; ☺11.30am-3pm & 5.30-10.30pm Mon-Sat; ☒11A, 350S) Paging both Paris and NYC with its lipstick-red banquettes and white subway tiles, upbeat Pastis is just the ticket for a post-shopping Gallic bite or a more substantial dinner date. Feel fancy over a light *salade chèvre chaud* (grilled goat's cheese salad with pickled walnuts and raisins) or delve into warming classics like bouillabaisse (fish soup with Gruyère cheese).

Café Hovedtelegrafen
DANISH €€

(Map p52; ☑33 41 09 86; www.cafehovedtele grafen.dk; Købmagergade 37; dishes Dkr99-159; ☺10am-4pm daily; ☒11A, M Nørreport, Kongens Nytorv) Nosh while scanning city rooftops at this light-drenched cafe, perched atop the Post & Tele Museum. It's a hit with suit-and-ties and lunching ladies, all debriefing over fresh, well-made classics like smørrebrød (open sandwiches) and marinated herring, vibrant salads, and one seriously mouthwatering burger. If the weather's on your side, head in early for a table on the terrace.

42° Raw
VEGETARIAN €€

(Map p52; ☑32 12 32 10; www.42raw.com; Pilestræde 32; meals Dkr88-128; ☺7am-8pm Mon-Fri, 10am-6pm Sat, 11am-5pm Sun; ☑; ☒11A) ✔ Treat your body at this hip, healthy eat-in or takeaway. The deal is raw food, served in vibrant, textured dishes like 'raw' lasagne, Thai noodles, and sexed-up salads where strawberries mix it with watermelon and chilli. The handful of breakfast options include yoghurt and porridge, best washed down with organic coffee or a freshly squeezed juice or smoothies. Your mama will thank us.

Sticks 'N' Sushi
JAPANESE €€

(Map p52; ☑33 11 14 07; www.sushi.dk; Nansensgade 47; nigiri per piece from Dkr21, sushi/sashimi sets from Dkr105; ☺11am-10pm Sun-Thu, to 10.30pm Fri & Sat; ☒40, 5A, 350S, M Nørreport) The original and still the sexiest contemporary sushi place in Copenhagen, with especially good tuna tartare and hamachi carpaccio options. Other branches crop up in various areas of the city – check online for a comprehensive listing of locations.

🍴 Slotsholmen

Øieblikket
CAFE €

(Map p52; Søren Kierkegaards Plads 1; soup & salads Dkr40-45, sandwiches Dkr50-55; ☺8am-7pm Mon-Fri, 9am-6pm Sat; ☎☑; ☒9A, ☖ Det Kongelige Bibliotek) The Royal Library's ground-floor cafe delivers a short menu of cheap, fresh bites, with one soup, a couple of salads and sandwiches, and no shortage of naughty cakes and pastries for a mid-afternoon high. The coffee is good and the harbourside deckchairs are a top spot to soak up some rays on those sunny summer afternoons.

Søren K
MODERN DANISH €€

(Map p52; ☑33 47 49 49; Søren Kierkegaards Plads 1; lunch dishes Dkr85-175, dinner mains Dkr190; ☺noon-4pm & 6-10pm Mon-Sat; ☎; ☒9A, ☖ Det Kongelige Bibliotek) Bathed in light on even the dourest of days, the Royal Library's sleek, waterside fine-diner revels in showing off top-notch regional ingredients. Seasonal menus deliver delicate, contemporary takes on Nordic flavours, from smoked herring with gel of cress, egg yolk and radish, to Norwegian lobster with cucumber, apple and sesame, to buckwheat ice-cream with buttermilk and woodruff. Whatever the season, expect flavours that are clean and pure.

✕ Nyhavn to the Little Mermaid

Meyers Bageri
BAKERY €

(Map p52; www.clausmeyer.dk; Store Kongensgade 46; pastries from Dkr20; ⊘7am-6pm Mon-Fri, to 4pm Sat, to 1pm Sun; 🚇1A, 26, Ⓜ Kongens Nytorv) Sugar and spice and all things nice is what you get at this pocket-sized organic bakery, owned by the founding father of the New Nordic food movement, Claus Meyer. Only flour produced in-house is good enough for these sticky morsels, among them golden apple croissants, *blåbærsnurrer* (blueberry twists), and a luscious *kanelsnægel* (cinnamon snail) laced with *remonce* (creamed butter and sugar filling).

You'll find another outlet in the basement of department store Magasin (p87).

Atelier September
CAFE €

(Map p52; http://atelier-september.dk; Gothersgade 30; dishes Dkr30-125; ⊘8am-6pm Mon-Sat; 🕿; 🚇11A, Ⓜ Kongens Nytorv) It might look like a *Vogue* photo shoot with its white-on-white interior, black-clad staff, and impossibly beautiful clientele, but Atelier September is very much a cafe. Kitted out with art, erudite magazines, and colourful crockery, it peddles gorgeous espresso and a short list of simple, inspired edibles. Standouts include sliced avocado on rye bread, topped with lemon zest, chives, paprika and peppery olive oil.

The Yogurt Shop
YOGHURT €

(Map p52; www.theyogurtshop.dk; Ny Adelgade 7; yoghurt Dkr45-53; ⊘7.30am-6pm Mon-Fri, 10am-4pm Sat; 🕿; 🚇11A, Ⓜ Kongens Nytorv) Hay-designed chairs, flickering tea lights, and piles of fashion mags – in Denmark, even yoghurt vendors make style editors weep. Join fashionistas and the virtuous as you decide just how to customise your yoghurt treat. Skyr, Greek and lactose-free yoghurt? Raspberry-ginger puree or strawberry-chilli puree? Granola topping, or fresh fruit and nuts? First World problems never tasted so good.

Big Apple
SANDWICHES €

(Map p52; Kronprinsessegade 2; sandwiches Dkr50, salads Dkr55; ⊘8am-6pm Mon-Fri, 9am-6pm Sat & Sun; 🕿; 🚇11A, Ⓜ Kongens Nytorv) Concrete floors, rustic communal tables, and splashes of vibrant green keep things Nordic and natural at this popular sandwich peddler. The bread is vegan, toasted and stuffed with combos like goat's cheese, avocado, cucumber and homemade pesto. Liquids include freshly squeezed juices and fantastic coffee from top local roastery The Coffee Collective. *And* they have soy milk!

Orangeriet
MODERN DANISH €€

(Map p52; 🖉33 11 13 07; www.restaurant-orangeriet.dk; Kronprinsessegade 13; smørrebrod Dkr75, 3-/5-course dinner Dkr375/495; ⊘11.30am-3pm & 6-10pm Mon-Sat, noon-4pm Sun; 🚇11A, 26, 350S) Take a vintage conservatory, add elegant, seasonal menus, and you have Orangeriet. Skirting the eastern edge of Kongens Have, its main man is award-winning chef Jasper Kure, whose contemporary creations focus on simplicity and premium produce. Savour the brilliance in clean, intriguing dishes like rimmed cod with celeriac, cabbage, cress and clam sauce with smoked cod roe. Lunch is a simple affair of smørrebrød. Book ahead.

Brasserie Granberg
FRENCH €€

(Map p52; 🖉33 12 45 32; http://brasseriegranberg.dk; Ny Adelgade 3; mains Dkr125-240; ⊘5-10pm Tue-Fri & Sun, noon-10pm Sat; 🕿; 🚇11A, Ⓜ Kongens Nytorv) A whirl of chandeliers, vintage posters, and crisp white linen, Gallic Granberg is the kind of place you expect to bump into a warbling Edith Piaf. Sink into an armchair, order a perfect G&T, and browse a short, sharp menu of old faithfuls like lobster bisque with cognac, delicate moules frites and obscenely fresh oysters. If it's winter, request a table in the super-snug backroom.

Ché Fè
ITALIAN €€

(Map p52; 🖉33 11 17 21; www.biotrattoria.dk; Borgergade 17A; mains Dkr150-195; ⊘6-10pm Mon-Sat; 🕿; 🚇11A, 26, Ⓜ Kongens Nytorv) 🍃 With its rustic farmhouse chairs, swathes of hessian and colourful ceramics, Ché Fè feels freshly plucked out of a Tuscan hillside. Whatever the weather, expect warm, soulful Italian dishes like housemade pasta with venison, or earthy Tuscan pork sausage with tomato sauce and black chickpeas. The set menu (Dkr250) is good value, especially given that most of the ingredients are organic. Viva Ché Fè!

Union Kitchen
CAFE €€

(Map p52; Store Strandstræde 21; ⊘7.30am-5pm Mon & Tue, to 11pm Wed & Thu, to midnight Fri, 8am-midnight Sat, 8am-5pm Sun; 🕿; 🚇11A, 66, Ⓜ Kongens Nytorv) Just around the corner from Nyhavn is new-school Union Kitchen, where inked staffers look like punk-pop rockers, the colour scheme is grey-on-grey, and the clipboard menu is packed with contemporary cafe grub like homemade

DON'T MISS

SMØRREBRØD AT SCHØNNEMANN

Schønnemann (Map p52; ☑ 33 12 07 85; www.restaurantschonnemann.dk; Hauser Plads 16; smørrebrød Dkr72-178; ⊙ 11.30am-5pm Mon-Sat; ☐ 6A, 11A, Ⓜ Nørreport) A verified institution, Schønnemann has been lining bellies with smørrebrød (open sandwiches) and schnapps since 1877. Originally a hit with farmers in town peddling their produce, the restaurant's current fan base includes revered chefs like Noma's René Redzepi. Two smørrebrød per person should suffice, with standouts including the King's Garden (potatoes with smoked mayonnaise, fried onions, chives and tomato). Make sure to order both a beer and a glass of schnapps to wash down the goodness, and always book ahead (or head in early) to avoid long lunchtime waits.

granola and toasted sourdough with cottage cheese, tomato, thyme and olive oil. Best of all is the 'Balls of the Day', a daily-changing combo of succulent homemade meatballs served with interesting sides.

Wokshop Cantina   THAI €€
(Map p52; www.wokshop.dk; Ny Adelgade 6; noodle dishes Dkr65-129, dinner mains Dkr129-169; ⊙ noon-10pm Mon-Sat; ☐ 11A, Ⓜ Kongens Nytorv) Communal tables and fresh Southeast Asian flavours are what you get at this popular basement cantina, a quick walk from Kongens Nytorv and the Hotel d'Angleterre. Tuck into staples like Thai fish cakes, *tom yam goong* soup, and no shortage of red, green and yellow curries.

Clou   MODERN DANISH €€€
(Map p52; ☑ 36 16 30 00; restaurant-clou.dk; Borgergade 16; 3/5/7-course menu incl wine Dkr850/1300/1600; ⊙ 6-9pm Tue-Sat; ☐ 1A, 11A, 26, Ⓜ Kongens Nytorv) Bucking the casual-dining trend, Michelin-starred Clou luxuriates in its large, linen-clad tables, upholstered armchairs, and bowtied waiters in armbands. That said, the menu is an adventurous, modern affair, with both Nordic and global influences driving knockouts like duck breast served with luscious berries and chestnuts braised in aniseed and maple syrup. As for the wines: they're so impressive that the food is created around them.

Rebel   MODERN DANISH €€€
(Map p52; ☑ 33 32 32 09; www.restaurantrebel.dk; Store Kongensgade 52; dishes Dkr119; ⊙ 5.30-10.30pm Tue-Sat) Award-winning Rebel prides itself on dishing out arresting, modern Danish grub without the fanfare. The black-and-white dining space is relatively small, simple and unadorned, giving all the attention to inspired creations like cured scallops with cucumber and dill, or tender sirloin with rose hip, pickled onions and kohlrabi. Trust the sommelier's wine choices, which include some extraordinary Old and New World drops. There's a minimum order of two dishes per person.

Damindra   JAPANESE €€€
(Map p52; ☑ 33 12 33 75; www.damindra.dk; Holbergsgade 26; lunch dishes Dkr175-398, 7-course dinner tasting menu Dkr750 (min 2 persons); ⊙ 11am-3pm & 5-10pm Tue-Sat; ☐ 11A, 66, Ⓜ Kongens Nytorv) We wouldn't be surprised if Japanese Damindra lands a Michelin star in the next few years. From the buttery sashimi to an unforgettable prawn tempura, dishes are obscenely fresh and mesmerising. The evening 'Chef's Choice' set sushi menu (Dkr398) provides the perfect culinary tour, while desserts such as green-tea ice cream with plum compote and fresh wasabi cream make for a wicked epilogue.

✖ Christianshavn

Copenhagen Street Food   INTERNATIONAL €
(Map p46; http://copenhagenstreetfood.dk; Warehouse 7 & 8, Trangravsvej 14, Papirøen; dishes from Dkr40; ⊙ food stalls generally noon-10pm; ☑; ☐ 11A, 66, ⚲ Papirøen) ✔ Take a disused warehouse, pack it with food trucks and stalls, hipster baristas and a chilled-out bar or two, and you have yourself this hot little newcomer. The emphasis is on fresh, affordable grub, from handmade pasta, tacos and ratatouille, to organic *koldskål* (cold buttermilk dessert). Portions aren't huge but the quality is high.

If the weather's on your side, grab a sunchair and catch some rays by the harbour.

Morgenstedet   VEGETARIAN €
(Map p46; www.morgenstedet.dk; Langgaden; mains Dkr80-100; ⊙ noon-9pm Tue-Sun; ☑; ☐ 2A, 9A, 40, 350S, Ⓜ Christianshavn) ✔ A homely, hippy bolthole in the heart of Christiania, Morgenstedet offers but two dishes of the day, one of which is usually a soup. Choices are always vegetarian and organic, and best devoured in the bucolic bliss of the cafe garden.

Lagkagehuset
BAKERY €

(Map p46; ☑32 57 36 07; www.lagkagehuset.dk; Torvegade 45; pastries from Dkr18, sandwiches Dkr50; ⊙6am-7pm Sat-Thu, to 7.30pm Fri; 🛜; 🖵2A, 9A, 40, 350S, Ⓜ Christianshavn) Right opposite Christianshavn metro station, this is the original (and some would say the best) of the Lagkagehuset bakeries. Handy for a quick bite on the go, its counters heave with luscious pastries, salubrious sandwiches, mini pizzas, and heavyweight loaves of rye bread. You'll find a handful of counter seats as well as free wi-fi (if you insist on Instagramming your *kanelsnegle*).

Cafe Wilder
INTERNATIONAL €€

(Map p52; www.cafewilder.dk; Wildersgade 56; lunch Dkr90-149, dinner mains Dkr179-209; ⊙9am-9.30pm Mon-Wed, 9am-10pm Thu & Fri, 11am-10pm Sat, 11am-9.30pm Sun; 🛜; 🖵2A, 9A, 40, 350S, Ⓜ Christianshavn) This corner classic serves beautiful, generous lunch options like hot smoked salmon salad with organic egg, baked tomatoes and rye croutons. Come evening, tuck into reassuring dishes like butter-roasted poussin with creamy Portobello mushroom risotto. One of Copenhagen's oldest cafes, the place makes several appearances in the cult TV drama series *Borgen*.

Bastionen + Løven
DANISH €€

(Map p46; Christianshavn Voldgade 50; weekend brunch Dkr175, dinner mains Dkr185-215; ⊙11am-9.30pm Tue-Fri, 10am-9.30pm Sat, 10am-2pm Sun; 🛜; 🖵2A, 9A, 40, 350S, Ⓜ Christianshavn) While the elegant wood interior and storybook garden of this old miller's cottage is enough to induce bucolic Nordic fantasies, the reason to head here is the weekend buffet brunch: book one week ahead (it's that popular). The restuarant also serves lunch and dinner, though both are a hit-and-miss affair, with significantly better options in the same price range. Cash only.

★ Noma
MODERN DANISH €€€

(Map p46; ☑32 96 32 97; www.noma.dk; Strandgade 93; degustation menu Dkr1600; ⊙noon-4pm & 7pm-12.30am Tue-Sat; 🖵2A, 9A, 11A, 40, 66, 350S, Ⓜ Christianshavn) Noma is a Holy Grail for gastronomes across the globe. Using only Scandinavian-sourced produce such as musk ox and *skyr* curd, head chef René Redzepi and his team create extraordinary symphonies of flavour and texture. Tables are booked months ahead, so expect to join the waiting list. Tip: parties of four or more have a better chance of landing a table with shorter notice.

★ Kanalen
MODERN DANISH €€€

(Map p46; ☑32 95 13 30; http://restaurant-kanalen.dk; Wilders Plads 2; 6/7 course menu Dkr700/800; ⊙11.30am-3pm & 5.30-10pm Mon-Sat; 🖵2A, 9A, 11A, 40, 66, 350S, Ⓜ Christianshavn) Reborn Kanalen offers an irresistible combination: extraordinary modern Danish food and a canalside location. While the lunch menu delivers competent renditions of Danish classics, it's the dinner menu that takes the breath away. Expect seamless, sophisticated dishes where pillow-soft cod is wrapped in beetroot gel, or where baked plum schmoozes with liquorice and white chocolate sorbet.

While dishes are available a la carte, treat yourself to the degustation menu for a culinary thrill you won't forget.

★ Kadeau
MODERN SCANDINAVIAN €€€

(Map p46; ☑33 25 22 23; www.kadeau.dk; Wildersgade 10a; 4-/8-course menu Dkr550/850; ⊙noon-3.30pm Wed-Fri & 6pm-late Tue-Sun) This is the Michelin-starred sibling of Bornholm's critically acclaimed Kadeau, its outstanding New Nordic cuisine now firmly on the radar of both local and visiting gastronomes. Whether it's salted and burnt scallops drizzled in clam bouillon, or an unexpected combination of toffee, creme fraiche, potatoes, radish and elderflower, dishes are evocative, revelatory and soul-lifting. An equally exciting wine list and sharp, warm service make this place a must. Book ahead.

✖ Vesterbro to Frederiksberg

Dyrehaven
DANISH €

(Map p46; www.dyrehavenkbh.dk; Sønder Blvd 72, Vesterbro; breakfast Dkr28-120, lunch Dkr58-85, dinner mains Dkr125-162; ⊙9am-midnight Mon-Wed, to 2am Thu & Fri, 10am-2am Sat, 10am-midnight Sun, kitchen closes 9pm Sun-Thu, 10pm Fri & Sat; 🛜; 🖵1A, 10, 14) Once a spit-and-sawdust working-class bar (the vinyl booths and easy-wipe floors tell the story), Dyrehaven is now a second home for Vesterbro's cool, young bohemians. Squeeze into your skinny jeans and join them for cheap drinks, simple tasty grub (the 'Kartoffelmad' egg open sandwich is a classic, made with homemade mayo and fried shallots) and some late-night camaraderie.

Siciliansk Is
ICE CREAM €

(Map p46; ☑30 22 30 89; http://sicilianskis.dk; Skydebanegade 3; ice cream from Dkr25; ⊙noon-9pm mid-May–Aug, 1-6pm Apr–mid-May & Sep;

🔲10, 14) Honing their skills in Sicily, gelato meisters Michael and David churn out Copenhagen's (dare we say Denmark's) best gelato. Lick yourself out on smooth, seasonal flavours such as *havtorn* (sea buckthorn) and *koldskål* (a frozen take on the classic Danish buttermilk and lemon dessert). For an unforgettable combo, try *lakrids* (liquorice) with Sicilian mandarin.

Øl & Brød
DANISH €€

(Map p46; ☎ 33 31 44 22; http://mikkeller.dk/ol-brod; Viktoriagade 6; 5-/7-course menu Dkr500/1100; ⊙ 11.30am-10pm Tue-Thu & Sun, to 11pm Fri & Sat; 🔲 6A, 10, 14, 26, 🔲 S-train København H) Modernist Danish furniture, Arne Jacobsen cutlery and a muted palette of greys and greens offer the perfect backdrop to high-end, contemporary smørrebrod. Decide between the five- or seven-course menu (the latter includes matching craft beers) and raise your glass to sophisticated reinventions like dried and smoked goose breast with soft-boiled egg, stewed corn and chervil. The restaurant claims Denmark's largest collection of akvavit and schnapps.

Pony
MODERN DANISH €€

(Map p46; ☎ 33 22 10 00; www.ponykbh.dk; Vesterbrogade 135; dishes Dkr110-185, 4-course menu Dkr450; ⊙ 5.30-10pm Tue-Sun; 🔲 6A) If your accountant forbids dinner at Kadeau, opt for its bistro spin-off, Pony. While the New Nordic grub here is simpler, it's no less stunning, with palate-punching marvels like tartar with black trumpet mushrooms, blackberries and mushroom broth, or lemon sole with cauliflower, pickled apples, kale, almonds and capers. The vibe is convivial and intimate. Book ahead, especially on Friday and Saturday.

Paté Paté
INTERNATIONAL €€

(Map p46; ☎ 39 69 55 57; www.patepate.dk; Slagterboderne 1; dishes Dkr80-130; ⊙ 9am-10pm Mon-Thu, 9am-11pm Fri, 11am-11pm Sat; 🔁; 🔲 10, 14) Another Kødbyen favourite, this pâté factory-turned-restaurant/wine bar gives Euro classics modern twists. While the menu changes daily, signature dishes include refreshing burrata with roasted peach, pesto, chilli and browned butter, and earthy grilled piglet with mojo rojo, *sobrasada* (raw cured sausage), borlotti beans and grilled carrots. Hip and bustling, yet utterly convivial, bonus extras include clued-in staff, a well-versed wine list, and solo-diner-friendly bar seating.

Nose2Tail
DANISH €€

(Map p46; ☎ 33 93 50 45; Flæsketorvet 13; mains Dkr150-190; ⊙ 6-10pm Mon-Thu, to 11pm Fri & Sat;

🔲10, 14) 🍴 Finding its muse in the Danish bars of yesteryear, this basement factory-turned-noshery uses every part of the animal to cook up honest, rustic fare served on wooden chopping blocks. The menu is short and seasonal, the produce mainly local and organic, and the vibe equally cool and cosy – think candlelight flickering on white industrial tiles, old Danish crockery, and crooked old photos.

In the warmer months, long collective tables are set outside, with industrial Kødbyen your gritty, evocative backdrop.

Sokkelund
INTERNATIONAL €€

(Map p46; ☎ 38 10 64 00; http://cafe-sokkelund.dk; Smallegade 36E, Frederiksberg; salads Dkr135-165, mains Dkr165-259; ⊙ 8am-10pm Mon-Fri, 9.30am-10pm Sat, 9.30am-9pm Sun; 🔁; 🔲 9A, 72, 73, 🔲 Frederiksberg) Sokkelund is the quintessential neighbourhood brasserie, kitted out with lovingly worn leather banquettes, newspapers on hooks, and handsome waiters in crisp white shirts. Breakfast, lunch, or dinner, join the steady stream of regulars for flexible bistro bites, including aromatic *moules frites* and some of the juiciest burgers in town. The handcut fries are simply sublime.

Mother
PIZZERIA €€

(Map p46; http://mother.dk; Høkerboderne 9-15; pizzas Dkr75-145; ⊙ 8am-11pm Mon-Fri, 11am-11pm Sat, 11am-10pm Sun; 🔁; 🔲 10, 14) Pizzeria Mother ditches gingham tablecloths for sexy concrete floors, industrial tiles and an X-factor Kødbyen (Meat City) address. The bubbling, thin-crust pie is made with organic sourdough and topped with real-deal ingredients like buffalo mozzarella and prosciutto di Norcia. If there's a wait for a table (likely), pull up a log at Mother's adjoining bar and down an Aperol Spritz.

Granola
CAFE €€

(Map p46; ☎ 40 82 41 20; Værndemsvej 5, Vesterbro; lunch Dkr75-145, dinner mains Dkr135-195; ⊙ 7am-10pm Mon-Fri, 9am-10pm Sat, 9am-4pm Sun; 🔲 6A, 9A, 26) A top spot for breakfast or brunch (head in early on weekends), Granola packs a cool Vesterbro crowd with its retro mix of industrial lamps, terrazzo flooring and 'General Store' cabinets. Start the day with uncomplicated standards like fruit-laced oatmeal, croque monsieur, or pancakes, or head in later for well-rounded classics like moules marinière, braised pork cheek, and Niçoise salad.

Sweet-tooths should leave room for the velvety, Jutland-made ice cream.

Cofoco FRANCO-DANISH €€
(Map p46; ☑ 33 13 60 60; http://cofoco.dk; Abel Cathrines Gade 7; 4-course menu Dkr275; ⊙ 5.30-9.30pm Mon-Sat; ☑ 6A, 10, 14, 26, ☑ S-train København H) One of several good-quality, fixed-menu places owned by the same team, Cofoco offers a glamorous setting and posh nosh like veal tartar with wasabi, pickled gherkins and artichoke, or lobster bisque with salted scallops, pickled pumpkin, pumpkin seeds and tarragon oil. Perfect for a budget-conscious date night.

★Kødbyens Fiskebar SEAFOOD €€€
(Map p46; ☑ 32 15 56 56; fiskebaren.dk; Flæsketorvet 100; mains Dkr215-255; ⊙ 5.30-11pm daily; ☑ 10, 14) Concrete floors, industrial tiling and a 1000-litre aquarium meets impeccable seafood at this Michelin-listed must, slap bang in Vesterbro's trendy Kødbyen ('Meat City' district). Ditch the mains for three or four starters; the oysters are phenomenal, while the silky razor clams, served on a crisp, rice-paper 'shell', are sublime. While you can book a table, dining at the Manhattan-style bar is much more fun.

Mielcke & Hurtigkarl MODERN DANISH €€€
(Map p46; ☑ 38 34 84 36; www.mielcke-hurtigkarl. dk; Frederiksberg Runddel 1, Frederiksberg; small/large degustation menu Dkr800/950; ⊙ 6-9pm Tue-Sat; ☑ 18, 26) Set in a former royal summer house adorned with contemporary murals and a forest soundscape, Mielcke & Hurtigkarl is as dreamy as its menu is heavenly. Head chef Jakob Mielcke's inspired approach to local and global ingredients shines through in creations like smoked oysters with pork and lingonberries, and many dishes use ingredients plucked straight from the kitchen garden.

🍴 Nørrebro & Østerbro

★Manfreds og Vin MODERN DANISH €€
(Map p46; ☑ 36 96 65 93; http://manfreds.dk; Jægersborggade 40, Nørrebro; small plates Dkr75-95, 7-course tasting menu Dkr250; ⊙ noon-3.30pm & 5.30-10pm; ☎☑; ☑ 5A, 18, 350S) On hip strip Jægersborggade, convivial Manfreds is the fantasy local bistro, with passionate staffers, boutique wines, and a menu that favours local, organic produce cooked simply and sensationally. Swoon over nuanced, gorgeously textured dishes like sauteed spinach with lard-roasted croutons and warm poached egg,

or slightly charred broccoli served with cheese cream, pickled onion and toasted bulgur.

Opt for the good-value seven-dish menu, and consider sitting at bar or in the open kitchen, where your meal comes with a free side of staff theatrics and spontaneous banter.

Oysters & Grill SEAFOOD €€
(Map p46; ☑ 70 20 61 71; http://cofoco.dk/en/ restaurants/oysters-and-grill; Sjællandsgade 1B, Nørrebro; mains Dkr155-195; ⊙ 5.30-9.30pm Mon-Thu, to 10pm Fri & Sat, to 9.15pm Sun; ☎; ☑ 5A) Finger-licking surf and turf is what you get at this rocking, unpretentious classic, complete with kitsch vinyl tablecloths and a fun, casual vibe. If you're a seafood fan, make sure your order includes both the ridiculously fresh oysters and the common cockles drizzled with parsley oil. Meat lovers won't to be disappointed either, with cuts that are lust-inducingly tender and succulent. Book ahead.

Aamanns Takeaway DANISH €€
(Map p46; ☑ 35 55 33 44; www.aamanns.dk; Øster Farimagsgade 10; smørrebrød Dkr55-95, dinner mains Dkr90-98; ⊙ smørrebrød 11am-4pm Mon-Sat, noon-4pm Sun, dinner 5-8pm Mon-Fri; ☑ 6A, 14, 40, 42, 150S, 184, 185) Clued-up foodies get their contemporary smørrebrød fix at Aamanns, where open sandwiches are seasonal, artful, and served on Aamanns' own organic sourdough bread (head in before 1pm to avoid waiting). The star option is the beef loin tartar, served with mushroom emulsion, gherkin, pickled beech mushrooms, shallots and mini-potato chips. On weekdays, two simple dinner dishes are also served, one option always being meatballs.

Fischer ITALIAN €€
(☑ 35 42 39 64; hosfischer.dk; Victor Borges Plads 12, Østerbro; pasta Dkr139, dinner mains Dkr189-235; ⊙ 11am-10pm Mon-Fri, 10.30am-10pm Sat & Sun; ☑ 3A) A reformed workingman's bar, neighbourly Fischer serves Italian-inspired soul food like freshly made linguini with bottarga, lemon and mint, or fresh mullet with black cabbage, celery purée and mussels. That it's all seriously good isn't surprising considering that owner and head chef David Fischer worked the kitchen at Rome's Michelin-starred La Pergola. On weekends, brunch is served from 10.30am to 3.30pm.

Laundromat Cafe INTERNATIONAL €€
(Map p46; www.thelaundromatcafe.com; Elmegade 15, Nørrebro; dishes Dkr45-155; ⊙ 8am-midnight Mon-Fri, 10am-midnight Sat & Sun; ☎; ☑ 3A 5A, 350S) Cafe, bookstore, and laundrette in one,

this retrolicious Nørrebro institution is never short of a crowd. It's an especially popular brunch spot, with both 'clean' (vegetarian) and 'dirty' (carnivorous) brunch platters, strong coffee and fresh juices. Breakfast options include porridge and croque madame, while all-day comforters span hamburgers (veggie option included), chilli con carne, and a pear and goat's cheese salad.

Geranium
MODERN DANISH €€€

(☑69 96 00 20; http://geranium.dk; Per Henrik Lings Allé 4, Østerbro; lunch/dinner tasting menu Dkr1250/1550, lighter lunch tasting menu Dkr950; ☺lunch noon-1pm Thu-Sat, dinner 6.30-9pm Wed-Sat; ☑) ✔ Perched on the 8th floor of Parken football stadium, Geranium is one of ony two restaurants in town sporting two Michelin stars (the other is Noma). At the helm is Bocuse d'Or prize-winning chef Rasmus Kofoed, who transforms local ingredients into edible Nordic artworks like venison with smoked lard and beetroot, or king crab with lemon balm and cloudberries. Kronor-conscious foodies can opt for the slightly cheaper lunch menus, while those not wanting to sample the (swoon-inducing) wines can opt for enlightened juice pairings. Book ahead.

★ Pop – et Spiseri
ITALIAN €€€

(Map p46; ☑42 36 02 22; www.pop-etspiseri.dk; Griffenfeldsgade 28, Nørrebro; set menu Dkr600; ☺6-10pm Wed-Fri; ☎; ☑3A, 5A, 12, 66, 350S) Petite Pop is run by four Danish women passionate about Italian nosh. There's no conventional menu; just the one four-course menu with matching wines and coffee for Dkr600. Whether it's *pappa al pomodoro* (Tuscan bread soup) or succulent pork with pan-fried Swiss chard, chanterelle mushrooms and rosemary, expect prized produce and dishes that sing with flavour. Service is knowledgeable and empty wine glasses generously refilled. Book ahead.

🍸 Drinking & Nightlife

Copenhagen is packed with a diverse range of drinking options – slinky cocktail hideouts; rowdy, nicotine-stained *bodegas* (pubs); and everything in-between. The line between cafe, restaurant and bar is often blurred, with many places changing role as the day progresses. Vibrant drinking areas include Kødbyen (the 'Meatpacking District') and Istedgade in Vesterbro, Ravnsborggade, Elmegade and Sankt Hans Torv in Nørrebro, Nansensgade close to Nørreport and the maze of streets to the north of Strøget,

including Pilestræde, around Gråbrødretorv and especially gay-friendly Studiestræde. And, of course, on a sunny day there is always Nyhavn, although there can be a serious risk of encountering a Dixieland jazz band.

★ Ved Stranden 10
WINE BAR

(Map p52; www.vedstranden10.dk; Ved Stranden 10; ☺noon-10pm Mon-Sat; ☎; ☑1A, 2A, 26, 40, 66) Politicians and well-versed oenophiles make a beeline for this canalside wine bar, its enviable cellar stocked with classic European vintages, biodynamic wines and more obscure drops. Adorned with modernist Danish design and friendly, clued-in staff, its string of rooms lend the place an intimate, civilised air that's perfect for grown-up conversation. Chat terroir and tannins over vino-friendly nibbles like olives, cheeses and smoked meats.

★ Forloren Espresso
CAFE

(Map p52; www.forlorenespresso.dk; Store Kongensgade 32; ☺8am-4pm Tue-Fri, from 9am Sat; ☎; ☑1A, 26, 11A, Ⓜ Kongens Nytorv) Coffee snobs weep joyfully into their nuanced espressos and Third-Wave brews at this cute, light-filled cafe, decorated with photography tomes. Bespectacled owner Niels tends to his brewing paraphernalia like an obsessed scientist, turning UK- and Swedish-roasted beans into smooth, lingering cups of Joe. Whatever your poison, pair it with a Danablu Horn, a ridiculously delicious horn-shaped bread stuffed with blue cheese, honey and walnuts.

★ 1105
COCKTAIL BAR

(Map p52; www.1105.dk; Kristen Bernikows Gade 4; ☺8pm-2am Wed, Thu & Sat, 4pm-2am Fri; ☑11A, Ⓜ Kongens Nytorv) Head in before 11pm for a bar seat at this dark, luxe cocktail lounge. It's the domain of world-renowned barman Hardeep Rehal, who made the top 10 at the 2014 Diageo World Class, the unofficial Olympics of mixology. While Rehal's martini is the stuff of legend, 1105's seductive libations include both classics and classics with a twist. Whiskey connoisseurs will be equally enthralled.

Ruby
COCKTAIL BAR

(Map p52; www.rby.dk; Nybrogade 10; ☺4pm-2am Mon-Sat, 7pm-1am Sun; ☑1A, 2A, 11A, 26, 40, 66) Cocktail connoisseurs raise their glasses to high-achieving Ruby. Here, hipster-geek mixologists whip-up near-flawless libations such as the Green & White (vodka, dill, white chocolate and liquorice root) and a lively crowd spill into a labyrinth of cosy, decadent rooms. For a gentlemen's club

TO MARKET, TO MARKET

Since debuting in 2011, food market **Torvehallerne KBH** (Map p52; www.torvehallernekbh. dk; Israels Plads; ⊙10am-7pm Mon-Thu, to 8pm Fri, to 6pm Sat, 11am-5pm Sun) has become an essential stop on the Copengahen foodie trail. A gut-rumbling ode to the fresh, the tasty and the artisanal, its beautiful stalls peddle everything from seasonal herbs and berries, to smoked meats, seafood and cheeses, smørrebrød, fresh pasta, and hand-brewed coffee. You could easily spend an hour or more exploring its twin halls, chatting to the vendors and taste-testing their products. Best of all, you can enjoy some of the city's best sit-down meals here... with change to spare. To help you on your waist-expanding way, we've identified some undisputed highlights.

Grød (Map p52; Torvehallerne KBH, hall 2, stall A8; porridge Dkr40-75; ⊙8am-7pm Mon-Thu, to 8pm Fri, 10am-6pm Sat, 10am-5pm Sun) Perfect for breakfast, Grød turns stodge sexy with its modern takes on porridge. Made-from-scratch options might include porridge with gooseberry compote, liquorice sugar, *skyr* (Icelandic yoghurt) and hazelnuts, or healthier-than-thou grain porridge cooked in carrot juice and served with apple, roasted flaxseeds, raisins and a zingy ginger syrup. If it's later in the day, try the chicken congee with spring onions, coriander and peanuts.

Coffee Collective (Map p52; http://coffeecollective.dk; Torvehallerne KBH, hall 2, stall C1; ⊙7am-8pm Mon-Fri, 8am-6pm Sat & Sun) Save your caffeine fix for Copenhagen's most respected microroastery. The beans here are sourced ethically and directly from farmers. These guys usually offer two espresso blends, one more full-bodied and traditional, the other more acidic and Third-Wave in flavour. If espresso is just too passé, order a hand-brewed cup from the Kalita Wave dripper. There are two other outlets, in Nørrebro (p80) and Frederiksberg (Map p46; Godthåbsvej 34b; ⊙7.30am-9pm Mon-Fri, from 9am Sat, from 10am Sun).

Omegn (Map p52; Torvehallerne KBH, hall 1, stall E2; cheese & charcuterie platter Dkr70-95; ⊙9am-7pm Mon-Thu, to 8pm Fri, to 6pm Sat, 10am-5pm Sun) This Nordic deli stocks the top products from various small-scale Danish farms and food artisans. The cheese selection includes Thybo, a beautiful, sharp cow's milk cheese from northern Jutland. Another good buy is the handcrafted Borghgedal beers from Vejle. Peckish punters can grab a table and nibble on a cheese and charcuterie platter, or go old-school with a warming serve of *skipperlabskov* (beef stew).

Unika by Arla (Map p52; Torvehallerne KBH, hall 1, stall F5; ⊙10am-7pm Mon-Thu, to 8pm Fri, to 6pm Sat, 11am-5pm Sun) Unika by Arla works with small dairies, artisan cheesemakers and top chefs to produce idiosyncratic, Nordic cheeses. Look out for the unpasteurised Kry cheese; according to many connoisseurs, unpasteurised cheeses deliver superior flavour. Equally unique are the apple-based 'dessert wines' from Jutland's Cold Hand Winery, their taste reminiscent of a summery port.

Hallernes Smørrebrød (Map p52; Torvehallerne KBH, hall 1, stall F2; smørrebrød Dkr38-52; ⊙10am-7pm Mon-Thu, to 8pm Fri, to 6pm Sat, 11am-5pm Sun) Not only is the smørrebrød here scrumptious, it – like the beers and schnapps on offer – is well-priced. Grab a spot at the wooden bar, order a Mikkeller beer, and tuck into beautifully presented classics like *fiskefilet* (fish fillet) with remoulade. If it's on the menu, don't go past the roast pork with pickled red cabbage. Order one smørrebrød if you're peckish, two if you're hungry.

Bottega della Pasta (Map p52; Torvehallerne KBH, hall 1, stall E4; pasta Dkr80-110; ⊙10am-7pm Mon-Thu, to 8pm Fri, to 6pm Sat, 11am-5pm Sun) While we prefer to focus on all the Nordic delciousness, we make a concession for this rocking slice of Italy. The pasta is made from scratch, then turned into insanely fine dishes like rich, earthy pasta with parmigiano cream and freshly shaved truffle. The house wine is pleasingly quaffable, and if you're very lucky, you might even score a complimentary, post-prandial limoncello.

COPENHAGEN DRINKING & NIGHTLIFE

vibe, head downstairs into a world of Chesterfields, oil paintings, and wooden cabinets lined with spirits.

★ Coffee Collective
CAFE

(Map p46; http://coffeecollective.dk; Jægersborggade 10, Nørrebro; ☺7am-7pm Mon-Fri, 8am-7pm Sat & Sun; ☐12, 18, 66) In a city where lacklustre coffee is as common as perfect cheekbones, this micro-roastery peddles the good stuff – we're talking rich, complex cups of caffeinated magic. The baristas are passionate about their beans and the cafe itself sits on creative Jægersborggade in Nørrebro. There are two other outlets, at food market Torvehallerne KBH (p79) and in Frederiksberg.

Lidkoeb
COCKTAIL BAR

(Map p46; ☑33 11 20 10; www.lidkoeb.dk; Vesterbrogade 72B, Vesterbro; ☺4pm-2am Mon-Sat, 8pm-1am Sun; ☎; ☐6A, 26) Lidkoeb loves a game of hide and seek: follow the 'Lidkoeb' signs into the second, light-strung courtyard. Once found, this top-tier cocktail lounge rewards with passionate barkeeps and clever, seasonal libations. Slip into a Børge Mogensen chair and toast to Danish ingenuity with Nordic bar bites and drinks like the Koldskål; a vodka-based twist on Denmark's iconic buttermilk dessert. Extras include a dedicated upstairs whiskey bar with over 100 drops.

Mikkeller
BAR

(Map p46; http://mikkeller.dk; Viktoriagade 8B-C, Vesterbro; ☺1pm-1am Sun-Wed, to 2am Thu & Fri, noon-2am Sat; ☎; ☐6A, 10, 14, 26, ☐S-train København H) Low-slung lights, moss-green floors and 20 brews on tap: cult-status Mikkeller flies the flag for craft beer, its rotating cast of suds including Mikkeller's own acclaimed creations and guest drops from microbreweries from around the globe. The bottled offerings are equally inspired, with cheese and snacks to soak up the foamy goodness.

Christianshavns Bådudlejning og Café
CAFE, BAR

(Map p52; ☑32 96 53 53; www.baadudlejningen.dk; Overgaden Neden Vandet 29; ☺9am-midnight daily Jun–mid-Aug, reduced hrs rest of yr, closed Oct-Mar; ☎; ☐2A, 9A, 40, 350S, Ⓜ Christianshavn) Right on Christianshavn's main canal, this festive, wood-decked cafe-bar is a wonderful spot for drinks by the water. It's a cosy, affable hangout, with jovial crowds, strung lights and little rowboats (available for hire) docked like bathtime toys. There's grub for the peckish, and gas heaters and tarpaulins to ward off any northern chill.

Nørrebro Bryghus
BREWERY

(Map p46; ☑38 60 38 60; www.noerrebrobryghus.dk; Ryesgade 3, Nørrebro; ☺11am-midnight Mon-Thu, to 2am Fri & Sat; ☐3A, 5A, 350S) This now-classic brewery kickstarted the microbrewing craze a few years back. Thankfully, the concept remains as alluring as ever, and the place remains a great place to wash down local suds. Rumbling bellies are also accounted for, with the brewery's in-house restaurant serving up tasty, reasonably priced grub like pan-roasted scallops, fish and chips, and risotto.

Kassen
BAR

(Map p46; Nørrebrogade 18B, Nørrebro; ☺8pm-2am Wed, 8pm-3am Thu, 2pm-4am Fri, 8pm-4am Sat; ☐5A) Loud, sticky Kassen sends livers packing with its dirt-cheap drinks and happy-hour specials (Dkr80 cocktails, anyone?). Dkr250 gets you unlimited drinks on Wednesdays, with two-for-one deals running the rest of the week; all night Thursdays, 2pm to 10pm Fridays, and 8pm to 10pm Saturday. Cocktail choices are stock-standard and a little sweet, but all is forgiven with all that change in your pocket. Pours are generous and the crowd mixed and fun.

Kind of Blue
BAR

(Map p46; ☑26 35 10 56; http://kindofblue.dk; Ravnsborggade 17, Nørrebro; ☺4pm-midnight Mon-Wed, to 2am Thu-Sat; ☎; ☐5A) Chandeliers, perfume, and walls painted a hypnotic 1950s blue: the spirit of the Deep South runs deep at intimate Kind of Blue. Named after the Miles Davis album, it's never short of a late-night, hipster crowd, kicking back porters and drinking in owner Claus' personal collection of soul-stirring jazz, blues and folk. You'll find it on Nørrebro's bar-packed Ravnsborggade.

Mesteren & Lærlingen
BAR

(Map p46; Flæsketorvet 86, Vesterbro; ☺8pm-3am Wed-Sat) In a previous life, Mesteren & Lærlingen was a slaughterhouse bodega. These days it's one of Copenhagen's in-the-know drinking holes, its tiled walls packing in a friendly, hipster crowd of trucker caps and skinny jeans. Squeeze in and knock back a rum and ginger (the house speciality) to DJ-spun retro, soul, reggae and country.

Bibendum
WINE BAR

(Map p52; Nansensgade 45; ☺4pm-midnight Mon-Sat; ☎; ☐ 5A, 40, 350S, Ⓜ Nørreport) Cosily set in a rustic cellar on trendy Nansensgade, Bibendum is an oenophile's best friend. Dive in and drool over a savvy list that offers over 30 wines – including drops from Australia, New Zealand, Spain, France and Italy – by the glass. The vibe is intimate but relaxed, and the menu of small plates (Dkr89 to Dkr95) simply gorgeous.

Malbeck
WINE BAR

(Map p46; Birkegade 2, Nørrebro; ⊙ 4pm-midnight Sun-Thu, to 1am Fri & Sat; ◻ 3A, 5A, 350S) Giant industrial lamps, découpage table tops and a convivial buzz set the scene at this respected Nørrebro wine bar. Look out for lesser-known Argentinean drops, and toast twice to the half-price deals on glasses of vino between 4pm and 6pm Sunday to Thursday. If hunger washes over, graze on the likes of cheese, charcuterie and croquettes, or tuck into a juicy slab of steak.

Union Bar
BAR

(Map p52; www.theunionbar.dk; Store Strandstræde 16; ⊙ 8pm-2am Tue-Thu, 4pm-3am Fri, 8pm-3am Sat) Inspired by the speakeasy bars of old New York (even the cocktails are named after 1920s slang), the sneaky Union lies behind an unmarked black door. Ring the buzzer and head down the steps to a suitably dim, decadent scene of handsome bartenders, in-the-know revellers and silky tunes.

Falernum
WINE BAR

(Map p46; ☑ 33 22 30 89; www.falernum.dk; Værnedamsvej 16; ⊙ noon-midnight Sun-Thu, to 2am Fri & Sat; ☎; ◻ 6A, 9A, 26) Worn floorboards and chairs, bottled-lined shelves and soothing tunes give this winning cafe and wine bar a deliciously snug, moody air. You'll find around 40 wines by the glass alone, as well as boutique beers, coffee, and a simple, seasonal menu of sharing plates like osso buco with roasted artichokes and onions, as well as cheeses and chàrcuterie.

Halvandet
BEACH BAR

(☑ 70 27 02 96; www.halvandet.dk; Refshalevej 325, Refshaleøen; ⊙ 10am-midnight Jun-Aug, reduced hrs Apr, May & Sep; ⛴ Refshaleøen) Copenhagen meets Ibiza at this seasonal, harbourfront bar-lounge. Book a mini-cabana, grab a mojito and tan away to sexy lounge tunes. Edibles include sandwiches, grilled meats, seafood and salads, but the real reason to head in is the vibe and music. It's located north of Operaen, at the northern end of Amager.

Bakken
BAR

(Map p46; Flæsketorvet 19-21, Vesterbro; ⊙ 6pm-4am Fri & Sat; ◻ 10, 14) Affordable drinks, DJ-spun disco and rock, and a Meatpacking District address make intimate, gritty Bakken a magnet for attitude-free hipsters.

Bankeråt
BAR

(Map p52; ☑ 33 93 69 88; www.bankeraat.dk; Ahlefeldtsgade 27; ⊙ 9.30am-midnight Mon-Fri, 10.30am-midnight Sat, 10.30am-11pm Sun; ☎; ◻ 40, 12, 66, 68, Ⓜ Nørrebro) ⚐ A snug spot to get stuffed (literally), kooky, attitude-free Bankeråt is pimped with taxidermic animals in outlandish get-ups – yes, there's even a ram in period costume. The man behind it all is local artist Phillip Jensen. But is it art? Debate this, and the mouth-shaped urinals, over a Carlsberg or three.

Library Bar
BAR

(Map p52; ☑ 33 14 92 62; www.librarybar.dk; Bernstorffsgade 4; ⊙ 4pm-midnight Mon-Thu, to 1.30am Fri & Sat; ◻ 2A, 5A, 9A, 97N, 250S, ◻ S-train København H) The Copenhagen Plaza's intimate hotel bar mimics a classic London gentlemen's club, with leather chairs, an open fire and shelves lined with books. A pianist tickles the ivories on Thursdays, with live jazz a regular fixture on Saturday nights from 8pm.

Nimb Bar
COCKTAIL BAR

(Map p52; ☑ 88 70 00 00; www.tivoli.dk/nimb; Bernstorffsgade 5; ⊙ 5pm-midnight Sun-Thu, to 1am Fri & Sat; ◻ 2A, 5A, 9A, 250S, ◻ S train København H) If you fancy chandeliers, quirky murals, and an open fire with your well-mixed drink, make sure this ballroom bar is on your list. Located inside super chic Hotel Nimb, it was kick-started by legendary bartender Angus Winchester. The beer is expensive, but you're here for seasonal, classically styled cocktails. Period.

Oscar Bar & Cafe
GAY

(Map p52; www.oscarbarcafe.dk; Regnbuepladsen 77; ⊙ 11am-11pm Sun-Thu, to 2am Fri & Sat; ☎; ◻ 11A, 12, 26, 33, ◻ S-train København H) In the shadow of Rådhus, this corner cafe-bar remains the most popular gay in the village. There's food for the peckish and a healthy quota of eye-candy between the locals and out-of-towners. In the warmer months, its alfresco tables are packed with revellers, one eye on friends, the other on Grindr.

Jailhouse CPH
GAY

(Map p52; http://jailhousecph.dk; Studiestræde 12; ⊙ 3pm-2am Sun-Thu, to 5am Fri & Sat; ☎; ◻ 5A, 6A, 11A) Trendy, attitude-free and particularly popular with an older male crowd, this themed bar promises plenty of penal action, with uniformed 'guards' and willing guests.

Den Plettede Gris
CAFE

(Map p46; Trangravsvej 5; ☉ 9.30am-6pm Mon-Fri, 10am-6pm Sat & Sun; ☎; 🚇 9A, 🚢 Papirøen) The pocket-sized Spotted Pig on Papirøen (Paper Island) is the latest venture for Danish designer, artist, musician and all-round avant-gardiste Henrik Vibskov. Inside, the space is pure Vibskov, with elastic-band wall sculptures, splashes of pink and red, and an effortlessly cool, chilled-out vibe. Stop by for Swedish-roasted coffee, organic teas and juices, or guzzle boutique beers with ingredients like elderflower.

Warning: weekend opening times can get a little 'freestyle'.

Sort Kaffe & Vinyl
CAFE

(Map p46; ☑ 61 70 33 49; Syydebanegade 4, Vesterbro; ☉ 8am-7pm Mon-Wed, 8am-10pm Thu & Fri, 9am-10pm Sat, 9am-7pm Sun; 🚇 10) This skinny little cafe/record store combo is a second home for Vesterbro's coffee cognoscenti. Join them for velvety espresso, hunt down that limited edition Blaxploitation LP, or score a prized pavement seat and eye-up the eye-candy regulars.

Palæ Bar
PUB

(Map p52; www.palaebar.dk; Ny Adelgade 5; ☉ 11am-1am Mon-Wed, to 2am Thu-Sat, 4pm-1am Sun; 🚇 11A, Ⓜ Kongens Nytorv) The air is thick with tobacco and intriguing conversation at this unapolegtically old-school drinking den. A traditional hit with journalists, writers and politicians, it's not one for asthmatics or vehement non-smokers.

Never Mind
GAY

(Map p52; http://nevermindbar.dk; Nørre Voldgade 2; ☉ 10pm-6am; 🚇 5A, 6A, 11A) Tiny, smoky and often packed to the rafters, Never Mind is a seriously fun spot for shameless pop and late-night flirtation.

Rust
CLUB, LIVE MUSIC

(Map p46; ☑ 35 24 52 00; www.rust.dk; Guldbergsgade 8, Nørrebro; ☉ hrs vary, club usually 11pm-5am Fri & Sat; 🚇 3A, 5A, 350S) A smashing place attracting one of the largest, coolest crowds in Copenhagen. Live acts focus on alternative or upcoming indie rock, hip hop or electronica, while the club churns out hip hop, dancehall and electro on Wednesdays, and house, electro and rock on Fridays and Saturdays. From 11pm, entrance is only to over

18s (Wednesday and Thursday) and over 20s (Friday and Saturday).

Culture Box
CLUB

(Map p46; www.culture-box.com; Kronprinsessegade 54A; ☉ White Box 9pm-late Fri & Sat, Red Box 10pm-late Fri & Sat, Black Box midnight-late Fri & Sat; 🚇 26) Electronica connoisseurs swarm to Culture Box, known for its impressive local and international DJ line ups and sharp sessions of electro, techno, house and drum'n'bass. The club is divided into three spaces: pre-clubbing bar White Box, intimate club space Red Box, and heavyweight Black Box, where big-name DJs play the massive sound system.

Sunday
CLUB

(Map p52; ☑ 53 66 82 28; www.sundayclub.dk; Lille Kongensgade 16; ☉ 11.30pm-5am Fri & Sat; Ⓜ Kongens Nytorv) Club meisters Simon Frank and Simon Lennet are known for whipping up exclusive, cult-status clubs with kinky or subversive twists. Sunday is no exception, with Bangkok lady-boy servers and hedonistic party people with an anything-goes attitude. Lose your inhibitions over electro, rock, hip hop and RnB.

KBIII
CLUB

(Map p46; ☑ 33 23 45 97; www.kb3.dk; Kødboderne 3, Vesterbro; ☉ champagne bar 8pm-late Thu-Sat, club 11pm-4am Fri & Sat; 🚇 1A, 🚆 S-train to Dybbølsbro) KBIII is the biggest club in the kicking Kødbyen (Meat City) district, aptly occupying a giant former meat freezer. Although events span film screenings, live acts, burlesque and release parties, the emphasis is on thumping club tunes from resident and global DJs, with past deck guests including Just Blaze and Secondcity. Come summer, the club's backyard is a buzzing party spot.

☆ Entertainment

Copenhagen is home to thriving live-music and club scenes that span intimate jazz and blues clubs, to mega rock venues and secret clubs dropping experimental beats. Blockbuster cultural venues such as Operaen (Copenhagen Opera House) and Skuespilhuset (Royal Danish Playhouse) deliver top-tier opera and theatre, while cinemas screen both mainstream and art-house flicks. Note: many nightspots don't get the party started until 11pm or midnight.

Most events can be booked through **Billetnet** (☑ 70 15 65 65; www.billetnet.dk), which has an outlet at Tivoli. You can also try **Billetlugen** (☑70 26 32 67; www.billetlugen.dk) . For listings, scan www.aok.dk (mostly in Danish).

Cinemas

First-release movies are shown on about 20 screens in the group of cinemas along Vesterbrogade between Rådhuspladsen and Central Station. Tickets for movies range from around Dkr70 for weekday matinees to around Dkr90 for weekend evenings. As in the rest of Denmark, movies are generally shown in their original language with Danish subtitles.

Cinemateket   CINEMA
(Map p52; www.dfi.dk; Gothersgade 55; ☺9.30am-10pm Tue-Fri, noon-10pm Sat, noon-7.30pm Sun; ☐11A, 350S) Cinephiles flock to the Danish Film Institute's cinema centre, which screens over 60 films per month, including semi-monthly classic Danish hits (with English subtitles) on Sundays. The centre also houses an extensive library of film and TV literature, a 'videotheque' with more than 1500 titles, as well as a shop and restaurant-cafe.

Grand Teatret   CINEMA
(Map p52; ☑33 15 16 11; www.grandteatret.dk; Mikkel Bryggersgade 8; admission Dkr65-85; ☺11am-9.30pm daily; ☎; ☐11A, 12, 26, 33, ◪S-train København H) Just off Strøget, this historic theatre from 1913 screens mainly European art-house films. The onsite cafe serves simple bites like quiche and cake, as well as organic, fair-trade coffee and top-notch teas.

Dance, Opera, Theatre & Classical Music

Located at the main Tivoli entrance,**Tivoli Billetcenter** (☑33 15 10 12; Vesterbrogade 3; ☺10am-8pm Mon-Fri, 11am-5pm Sat & Sun) is good for tickets of any kind. Not only does it sell Tivoli performance tickets, but it's also an agent for **BilletNet**, which sells tickets for concerts and music festivals nationwide.

Operaen   OPERA
(Copenhagen Opera House; Map p46; ☑box office 33 69 69 69; www.kglteater.dk; Ekvipagemestervej 10; ☐9A, ⛴Opera) Designed by the late Henning Larsen, Copenhagen's state-of-the-art opera house has two stages: the Main Stage and the smaller, more experimental Takkeløftet. The repertoire runs the gamut from classic to contemporary opera. Productions usually sell out in advance, so book ahead or you might miss the fat lady singing.

Det Kongelige Teater   BALLET, OPERA
(The Royal Theatre; Map p52; ☑33 69 69 69; http://kglteater.dk; Kongens Nytorv; ☐1A, 11A, 20E, 26, 350S, Ⓜ Kongens Nytorv) These days, the main focus of the opulent Gamle Scene ('old stage') is world-class opera and ballet, including productions from the Royal Danish Ballet. The current building, the fourth theatre to occupy the site, was completed in 1872 and designed by Vilhelm Dahlerup and Ove Petersen. Book tickets in advance.

Skuespilhuset   THEATRE
(Royal Danish Playhouse; Map p46; ☑33 69 69 69; http://kglteater.dk; Sankt Anne Plads 36; ☐11A, Ⓜ Kongens Nytorv) Copenhagen's handsome, contemporary playhouse is home to the Royal Danish Theatre and a world-class repertoire of both homegrown and foreign plays. Productions range from the classics to provocative contemporary works. Tickets often sell out well in advance, so book ahead if you're set on a particular production.

Dansehallerne   DANCE
(Map p46; ☑box office 33 88 80 08; www.danse hallerne.dk; Pasteursvej 20, Vesterbro; ☐1A, ◪S-train Enghave) Dansehallerne is Copenhagen's leading contemporary dance venue. Located in a disused Carlsberg mineral water factory, its two stages showcase over 20 works each year, from both Danish artists and international ensembles. Tickets can be purchased by calling the box office between 1pm and 3pm on weekdays, or online at www.teater-billetter.dk or www.billetten.dk (in Danish).

Københavns Musikteater   MUSIC THEATRE
(Map p52; ☑33 32 55 56; http://kobenhavnsmusik teater.dk; Kronprinsensgade 7; ☐11A, Ⓜ Kongens Nytorv) Push your boundaries at Copenhagen's avant-garde music theatre venue, delivering a wide range of artistic crossover performances. All works include newly composed or reinterpreted compositions, with genres including classical and chamber music, electronica, poetic pop, and rock. Check the website for upcoming performances.

Tivoli Koncertsal   CONCERT HALL
(Concert Hall; Map p52; www.tivoli.dk; Tietgensgade 30; ☐2A, 12, 26, ◪S-train København H) The Tivoli concert hall hosts both Danish and international symphony orchestras, string quartets and other classical-music performances, not to mention contemporary music artists and dance companies. Purchase tickets online or at the Tivoli Billetcenter.

Live Music

★ Jazzhouse
JAZZ

(Map p52; ☑ 33 15 47 00; www.jazzhouse.dk; Niels Hemmingsensgade 10; ⬚ 11A) Copenhagen's leading jazz joint serves up top Danish and visiting talent, with music styles running the gamut from bebop to fusion jazz. Doors usually open at 7pm, with concerts starting at 8pm. On Friday and Saturday, late-night concerts (from 11pm) are also offered. Check the website for details and consider booking big-name acts in advance.

La Fontaine
JAZZ

(Map p52; www.lafontaine.dk; Kompagnistræde 11; ⊙ 8pm-5am daily, live music from 10pm Fri & Sat, from 9pm Sun; ⬚ 1A, 2A, 11A, 26, 40, 66) Cosy and intimate, Copenhagen's jazz-club veteran is a great spot to catch emerging homegrown musicians and the occasional big name. If you're an aspiring jazz star, hang around until late, when the stage is thrown open to songbirds in the audience.

Vega Live
LIVE MUSIC

(Map p46; ☑ 33 25 70 11; www.vega.dk; Enghavevej 40, Vesterbro; ☎; ⬚ 3A, 10, 14) The daddy of Copenhagen's live-music and club venues, Vega hosts everyone from big-name rock, pop, blues and jazz acts to underground indie, hip hop and electro up-and-comers. Gigs take place on either the main stage (Store Vega), small stage (Lille Vega) or the revamped ground floor Ideal Bar. The venue itself is a 1950s former trade union HQ by

---

ALL THAT JAZZ

Copenhagen's Jazz Festival (p65) is *the* biggest entertainment event in the city's calendar, with 10 days of saxy tunes beginning on the first Friday in July. The festival energises the Danish capital like nothing else, bringing not just live music to its streets, canalsides and an eclectic mix of venues, but creating a tangible buzz of excitement in the air.

There are usually over 1200 different concerts held in every available space, from cafes and street corners to the Operaen (Opera House) and Tivoli's Koncertsal – in fact, the city itself becomes one big sound stage. Amble through the city centre on a summer night during the festival and the party mood is nothing short of infectious. Even if you have an instinctive aversion to men in black turtlenecks, expect to be won over by the incredible line-up each year. You'll even find special children's jazz events in Kongens Have, ready to hook the next generation of sax and bass fiends early.

Copenhagen has been the jazz capital of Scandinavia since the 1920s, when the Montmartre Club was one of the most famous in Europe. Revived in 2010 after a long hiatus, the new Jazzhus Montmartre is in good company, with top venues such as La Fontaine, the city's most 'hard-core' jazz club, and Jazzhouse, the largest and most popular, ensuring that legacy remains alive and kicking. The fact that the city is also home to a disproportionately large population of both home-grown and international jazz musicians doesn't hurt either.

Copenhagen's first jazz festival took place in 1978. Since then it has mushroomed into one of Europe's leading jazz events. Over the years, performers have included such renowned names as Dizzy Gillespie, Miles Davis, Sonny Rollins, Oscar Peterson, Ray Charles and Wynton Marsalis. Tony Bennett, Herbie Hancock and Keith Jarrett are regulars, as are Denmark's own Cecilie Norby and David Sanborn.

It's a fun, slightly haphazard scene that brings everyone in the city out to party. Most of the open-air events are free, but you have to buy tickets to the big names in big venues. The music at the Copenhagen Jazz Festival is as varied as the venues. Traditional sounds range from old-fashioned Dixieland jazz and Satchmo-style solo improvisation to the WWII-era swing music that reigned in Duke Ellington and Benny Goodman's day – the Danish free jazz scene also gets a look-in. There's plenty of modern jazz along the lines of that inspired by legendary trumpeter Miles Davis, and you can also find lots of contemporary hybrid sounds: free-jazz, acid jazz, soul jazz, nu-jazz, jazz vocals and rhythm and blues. The festival programme is usually published in May.

If you can't make it to Copenhagen in summer for the main jazz festival, you can take heart that a smaller festival takes place in winter. It's called, not surprisingly, Vinter Jazz (it shares a website with the July festival). Also, not surprisingly, the winter version has a mellower, less-harried vibe.

leading Danish architect Vilhelm Lauritzen. Performance times vary; check the website.

Jazzhus Montmartre
JAZZ

(Map p52; ☑ 70 26 32 67; www.jazzhusmontmartre. dk; Store Regnegade 19A; ☺ 5.30-11.30pm Thu-Sat; ▣ 11A, 350S, Ⓜ Kongens Nytorv) One of Scandinavia's great jazz venues, Jazzhus Montmartre showcases local and international talent. On concert nights, you can also tuck into Italian-inspired, pre-show nosh (3-course set menu Dkr325, charcuterie plate Dkr165) at the cafe-restaurant, run by the team from Michelin-starred restaurant Era Ora.

Huset KBH
LIVE MUSIC

(Map p52; ☑ 21 51 21 51; www.huset-kbh.dk; Rådhusstræde 13; ☺ hrs vary, restaurant 6-9pm Tue-Sat; ☏; ▣ 1A, 2A, 11A, 26, 40, 66) ∅ Huset KBH is an institution, churning out almost 1500 annual events spanning live music, theatre and arthouse film, to poetry slams, cabaret and stand-up comedy. The complex also houses a waste-free restaurant using surplus produce donated from the food industry, with all profits going towards humanitarian projects in Sierra Leone.

Loppen
MUSIC

(Map p46; ☑ 32 57 84 22; www.loppen.dk; Bådsmandsstræde 43; ☺ 8.30pm-late Sun-Thu, 9pm-late Fri & Sat; ▣ 2A, 9A, 40, 350S, Ⓜ Christianshavn) Rocking out in an wooden-beamed warehouse in live-and-let-live Christiania, Loppen delivers both established and emerging acts from Denmark and beyond. Music styles are as eclectic as the crowds, with anything from rock and funk to post-punk and jazz. While gigs generally take place Wednesday to Sunday, always check the website before heading in. Cash only.

DR Koncerthus
CONCERT HALL

(☑ 35 20 62 62; www.dr.dk/Koncerthuset; Emil Holms Kanal 20, Amager; Ⓜ DR Byen) Home of the National Symphony Orchestra and National Chamber Orchestra, Jean Nouvel's bold blue box hosts world-class concerts spanning from classical, chamber and choral music, to rock, pop and experimental sounds. Check the website for a list of upcoming events.

Mojo
BLUES

(Map p52; ☑ 33 11 64 53; www.mojo.dk; Løngangstræde 21C; ☺ 8pm-5am daily; ▣ 1A, 2A, 11A, 26, 40, 66, ▣ S-train København H) East of Tivoli, this is a great spot for blues, with live entertainment nightly and draught beer aplenty.

🛍 Shopping

Most of the big retail names and home-grown heavyweights – among them Illums Bolighus, Georg Jensen and Royal Copenhagen – are centered on the main pedestrian shopping strip, Strøget.

Running parallel to the south of Strøget, pedestrianised Strædet (made up of two streets, Kompagnistræde and Læderstræde) is dotted with interesting jewellery and antique stores. To the north of Strøget, the area of Pisserenden (centred on Studiestræde, Larsbjørnstræde and Vestergade) is good for street style, while the so-called Latin Quarter (from Vor Frue Kirke to Købmagergade) is worth a wander for books and clothing.

Serious fashionistas flock to the area roughly bordered by Strøget, Købmagergade, Kronprinsensgade and Gothersgade, crammed with high-end Nordic labels, trendsetting concept stores and cutting-edge jewellery shops.

North of Nyhavn, exclusive Bredgade and Store Kongensgade are lined with private art galleries and high-end antique stores selling classic, collectable Danish furniture.

For more affordable bric-a-brac, vintage jewellery and kitschy furniture, scour the shops on Ravnsborggade in Nørrebro. Arty Nørrebro is also home to Elmegade and Jægersborggade, two streets pimped with interesting, independent shops.

Further south, the equally fashionable Vesterbro neighbourhood is another good bet for independent fashion designers and homewares, with most of the offerings on and around Istedgade and Værndamsvej.

Illums Bolighus
DESIGN

(Map p52; www.illumsbolighus.dk; Amagertorv 8-10, Strøget; ☺ 10am-7pm Mon-Fri, to 6pm Sat, 11am-6pm Sun; ▣ 11A) Revamp everything from your wardrobe to your living room at this multilevel department store, dedicated to big names in Danish and international design. Coveted goods include fashion, jewellery, silverware and glassware, and no shortage of Danish furniture, textiles and fetching office accessories.

Day Birger Mikkelsen
FASHION, ACCESSORIES

(Map p52; ☑ 33 45 88 80; www.day.dk; Pilestræde 16; ☺ 10am-6pm Mon-Fri, to 5pm Sat; ▣ 11A, Ⓜ Kongens Nytorv) Understated elegance with subtle hippy-chic twists define this Danish fashion heavyweight. The flagship store is a top spot to bag the label's sophisticated women's threads, as well as accessories including jewellery and bags.

Just around the corner you'll find designer Malene Birger's own **shop** (Map p52; 35 43 22 33; www.bymalenebirger.dk; Antonigade 10; 10am-6pm Mon-Fri, to 5pm Sat; 11A, Kongens Nytorv) – she is no longer part of the Day group.

Han Kjøbenhavn   FASHION, ACCESSORIES
(Map p52; www.hankjobenhavn.com; Vognmagergade 7; 11am-6pm Mon-Thu, to 7pm Fri, 10am-5pm Sat; 11A, Kongens Nytorv) While we love the Modernist fitout, it's what's on the racks that will hook you: original, beautifully crafted men's threads that merge Scandinavian sophistication with hints of old-school Danish working-class culture. Accessories include painfully cool eyewear, as well as sublime leathergoods from America's Kenton Sorensen.

Storm   FASHION, ACCESSORIES
(Map p52; htttp://stormfashion.dk; Store Regnegade 1; 11am-5.30pm Mon-Thu, to 7pm Fri, 10am-4pm Sat; 11A, Kongens Nytorv) Storm is one of Copenhagen's most inspired fashion pit stops, with trendsetting men's and women's labels such as Chauncey, Géométrick and Merz b. Schwanen. The vibe is youthful and street smart, with extras including statement sneakers, boutique fragrances, art and design tomes, fashion magazines and jewellery. Obligatory for cashed-up hipsters.

Wood Wood   FASHION, ACCESSORIES
(Map p52; htttp://woodwood.dk; Grønnegade 1; 10.30am-6pm Mon-Thu, to 7pm Fri, to 5pm Sat; 11A, Kongens Nytorv) Unisex Wood Wood's flagship store is a veritable who's who of cognoscenti street-chic labels. Top of the heap are Wood Wood's own hipster-chic creations, made with superlative fabrics and attention to detail. The supporting cast includes solid knits from classic Danish brand SNS Herning, wallets from Comme des Garçons, and sunglasses from Kaibosh.

Henrik Vibskov   FASHION
(Map p52; www.henrikvibskov.com; Krystalgade 6; 11am-6pm Mon-Thu, to 7pm Fri, to 5pm Sat; 11A, Nørreport, S-train Nørreport) Not just a drummer and prolific artist, Danish enfant terrible Henrik Vibskov pushes the fashion envelope, too. Break free with his bold, bright, creatively silhouetted threads for progressive guys and girls, as well as other fashion-forward labels such as Issey Miyake, Walter Van Beirendonck and Denmark's own Stine Goya.

**Piet Breinholm –
The Last Bag**   LEATHER GOODS
(Map p52; www.pietbreinholm.dk; Nansensgade 48; 11am-7pm Fri, by appointment rest of week; 40, Nørreport) Musician-turned-designer Piet Breinholm is famous for his classic leather satchels, available in small or large, and in colours ranging from sensible black to outrageous canary yellow. A handful of other styles are also available, all using high-quality leather sourced from an ecofriendly Brazilian tannery. Samples and faulty goods are sometimes slashed to half-price.

Stilleben   DESIGN
(Map p52; 33 91 11 31; www.stilleben.dk; Niels Hemmingsensgade 3; 10am-6pm Mon-Fri, to 5pm Sat; 11A) Owned by Danish Design School graduates Ditte Reckweg and Jelena Schou Nordentoft, Stilleben stocks a bewitching range of contemporary ceramic, glassware, jewellery and textiles from mostly emerging Danish and foreign designers. A must for design fans and savvy shoppers seeking 'Where did you get that?' gifts.

Hay House   DESIGN
(Map p52; www.hay.dk; Østergade 61, Strøget; 10am-6pm Mon-Fri, to 5pm Sat; 11A) Rolf Hay's fabulous interior design store sells its own coveted line of furniture, textiles and design objects, as well as those of other fresh, innovative Danish designers. Easy-to-pack gifts include anything from notebooks and ceramic cups, to building blocks for style-savvy kids. There's a second branch at Pilestræde 29-31.

Bruuns Bazaar   FASHION
(Map p52; www.bruunsbazaar.com; Vognmagergade 2; 10am-6pm Mon-Thu, to 7pm Fri, to 5pm Sat; 11A, 350S) You'll find both men's and women's threads at the flagship store for Bruuns Bazaar, one of Denmark's most coveted and internationally respected brands. The style is contemporary, archetypal Scandinavian, with a focus on modern daywear that's crisp, well-cut, and classically chic with a twist.

Royal Copenhagen Porcelain   PORCELAIN
(Map p52; 33 13 71 81; www.royalcopenhagen.com; Amagertorv 6; 10am-7pm Mon-Fri, to 6pm Sat, 11am-4pm Sun; 11A, Kongens Nytorv) This is the main showroom for the historic Royal Danish Porcelain, one of the city's best-loved souvenir choices. Its 'blue fluted' pattern is famous around the world, as is the painfully expensive Flora Danica dinner

service, its botanical illustrations the work of 18th-century painter, Johann Christoph Bayer.

Georg Jensen   DESIGN
(Map p52; ☑33 11 40 80; www.georgjensen. com; Amagertorv 4; ☉10am-7pm Mon-Fri, to 6pm Sat, 11am-4pm Sun; ⬚11A) This is the world-famous silversmith's flagship store, selling everything from rings, brooches and watches, to attention-commanding vases and tableware. Popular gifts for less than Dkr300 include moneyclips and business-card holders, as well as Georg Jensen's iconic elephant bottle opener.

Designer Zoo   DESIGN
(Map p46; ☑33 24 94 93; www.dzoo.dk; Vesterbrogade 137, Vesterbro; ☉10am-5.30pm Mon-Thu, to 7pm Fri, to 3pm Sat; ⬚6A) If you find yourself in Vesterbro – and you should – make sure to drop into this supercool design complex. Here, fashion, jewellery and furniture designers, as well as ceramic artists and glass blowers, work and sell their limited edition, must-have creations.

Hoff   JEWELLERY
(Map p52; ☑33 15 30 02; www.gallerihoff.dk; Kronprinsensgade 12; ☉noon-6pm Tue-Thu, to 7pm Fri, to 3pm Sat; ⬚11A, Ⓜ Kongens Nytorv) Ingrid Hoff showcases some of Denmark's most innovative and talented jewellery designers. Each piece is a veritable conversation piece, and though the designers mix gold and silver with acrylic and nylon, this is by no means 'of-the-moment' fashion jewellery but one-off and limited run pieces to covet for a lifetime.

Le Klint   HOMEWARES
(Map p52; ☑33 11 66 63; www.leklint.com; Store Kirkestræde 1; ☉10am-6pm Tue-Fri, to 4pm Sat; ⬚1A, 2A, 11A, 26, 40, 66, Ⓜ Kongens Nytorv) Beautiful lighting is a Scandinavian obsession and Le Klint's handmade, concertina-style lampshades are works of art in themselves. Designed by some of Denmark's most respected designers and architects, the range includes ceiling, table and wall lamps, mostly in classic white.

Filippa K   FASHION
(Map p52; ☑33 93 80 00; www.filippa-k.com; Ny Østergade 13; ☉10am-6.30pm Mon-Fri, to 5pm Sat; ⬚11A, Ⓜ Kongens Nytorv) This is Swedish designer Filippa Knutsson's flagship Danish store, selling her simple, modern, oft-monochromatic men's and women's ranges.

The look is undisputedly Nordic – crisp, clean and uncluttered. Bag everything from jeans and basics, to shirts, sweaters, party frocks and sultry evening gowns.

Klassik Moderne Møbelkunst   FURNITURE
(Map p52; ☑33 33 90 60; www.klassik.dk; Bredgade 3; ☉11am-6pm Mon-Fri, 10am-3pm Sat; ⬚1A, 11A, 20E, 26, 350S, Ⓜ Kongens Nytorv) Close to Kongens Nytorv, Klassik Moderne Møbelkunst is Valhalla for lovers of Danish design, with a trove of classics from greats like Poul Henningsen, Hans J Wegner, Arne Jacobsen, Finn Juhl and Nanna Ditzel – in other words, a veritable museum of Scandinavian furniture from the mid-20th century.

Normann Copenhagen   HOMEWARES, FASHION
(Map p46; ☑35 27 05 40; www.normann-copenhagen.com; Østerbrogade 70; ☉10am-6pm Mon-Fri, to 4pm Sat; ⬚1A, 3A, 14) In a converted cinema in 'white bread' Østerbro, sprawling Normann seduces eyes and wallets with its eye-candy designer goods, from statement bowls, glassware and tea strainers, to furniture, lighting, cushions and more. If it's time to give your life a Scandi makeover, this is the place to do it. Best of all, the shop ships worldwide.

Illum   DEPARTMENT STORE
(Map p52; ☑33 14 40 02; www.illum.dk; Østergade 52; ☉10am-8pm Mon-Sat, 11am-6pm Sun; ⬚11A, 350S, Ⓜ Kongens Nytorv) Fresh from a major makeover, Illum is CPH's answer to Selfridges or Bloomingdales. That said, the range of fashion is rather stock standard, with mainly mainstream local and international brands. Nordic labels worth looking out for include Stine Goya, Dagmar, Filippa K, Acne, Whyred and Won Hundred. The store's renovated atrium is the work of renowned Italian architect Claudio Silvestrin.

Magasin   DEPARTMENT STORE
(Map p52; ☑33 11 44 33; www.magasin.dk; Kongens Nytorv 13; ☉10am-8pm; ⬚1A, 11A, 26, Ⓜ Kongens Nytorv) The city's largest (and oldest) department store covers an entire block on the southwestern side of Kongens Nytorv. Beyond the global fashion brands are a handful of savvy local labels, including Mads Nørgaard, Henrik Vibskov, and Baum und Pferdgarten. Head to the basement for the city's best range of international magazines.

Susanne Juul   HATS
(Map p52; ☑33 32 25 22; www.susannejuul.dk; Store Kongensgade 14; ☉11am-5.30pm Tue-Thu,

COPENHAGEN SHOPPING

to 6pm Fri, 10am-2pm Sat; 1A, 11A, 26, Kongens Nytorv) Crown Princess Mary is known to ride her bike here occasionally, which is hardly surprising given that Susanne Juul is considered one of Copenhagen's finest milliners. The look is classic and refined, from the felt hats and fascinators, to the dapper caps and hats for men. Prices start at around Dkr375 and soar from there.

Pop Cph

FASHION

(Map p52; www.popcph.dk; Møntergade 5; 11am-6pm Mon-Thu, to 7pm Fri, to 5pm Sat; 11A, 350S, Kongens Nytorv) In 2005 Mikkel Kristensen and Kasper Henriksen began hosting parties for Copenhagen's creative community. The parties continue to inspire the duo's burgeoning fashion label: four collections per year combine dinner-party glamour with subversive detailing and hipster staples such as printed graphic tees.

ℹ Information

EMERGENCY

Dial 112 to contact police, ambulance or fire services; the call can be made free from public phones.

Politigården (33 14 88 88; Polititorvet 14) Police headquarters; south of Tivoli.

INTERNET ACCESS

Hovedbiblioteket (Krystalgade 15; 8am-7pm Mon-Fri, 9am-4pm Sat;) The main public library provides computer terminals with internet access, as well as free wi-fi.

INTERNET RESOURCES

Four websites that will link you to a wealth of information:

www.visitcopenhagen.com Copenhagen's official tourism website has a plethora of information on accommodation, sightseeing, events, dining and more.

www.aok.dk An online listings guide to Copenhagen with some English content.

http://cphpost.dk The online edition of the *Copenhagen Post*, with plenty of news and cultural insight. In English.

www.kopenhagen.dk The top website for Copenhagen's art scene, with exhibition listings, news and artist interviews. In English and Danish.

LEFT LUGGAGE

Central Station (5.30am-1am Mon-Sat, 6am-1am Sun) Has a left-luggage office (24 68 31 77; per 24hr luggage per piece Dkr55-65, max 10 days; 5.30am-1am Mon-Sat, 6am-1am Sun) and luggage lockers (per 24hr small/large Dkr50/60, max 72hr). Both are located

at the back of the station, near the exit into Reventlowsgade.

Copenhagen Airport Offers luggage lockers (per 24hr small/large Dkr50/75, max 72hr) In car park 4 (P4), opposite Terminal 2.

MEDICAL SERVICES

Private doctor and dentist visits vary but usually cost from around Dkr1,400. To contact a doctor, call 60 75 40 70.

There are numerous pharmacies around the city; look for the sign *apotek*.

Call 1813 before going to a hospital emergency department to save waiting time. The following hospitals have 24-hour emergency wards:

Amager Hospital (32 34 35 00; Italiensvej 1, Amager) Southeast of the city centre.

Bispebjerg Hospital (35 31 23 73; Bispebjerg Bakke 23) Northwest of the city centre.

Tandlægevagten (1813; Oslo Plads 14) Emergency dental service near Østerport station.

Steno Apotek (Vesterbrogade 6C) A 24-hour pharmacy opposite Central Station.

MONEY

Banks are plentiful, especially in central Copenhagen. Most are open from 10am to 4pm weekdays (to 5.30pm on Thursday). Most banks in Copenhagen have ATMs that are accessible 24 hours.

POST

Post Office (Map p52; Købmagergade 33; 10am-6pm Mon-Fri, to 2pm Sat) A handy post office near Strøget and the Latin Quarter.

København H Post Office (Map p46; Central Station; 9am-7pm Mon-Fri, noon-4pm Sat) Post office in Central Station.

TOURIST INFORMATION

Copenhagen Visitors Centre (Map p52; 70 22 24 42; www.visitcopenhagen.com; Vesterbrogade 4A; 9am-6pm Mon-Sat, to 2pm Sun May, Jun & Sep, 9am-7pm Jul & Aug, 9am-4pm Mon-Fri, to 2pm Sat rest of yr;) Copenhagen's excellent information centre has multilingual staff, as well as a bakery and lounge with free wi-fi and power sockets. It's the best source of information in town – free maps, masses of brochures and guides to take

---

ℹ ON FOOT

We can't stress enough that by far the best way to see Copenhagen is on foot. This has to be the most eminently walkable capital in Europe, with much of the city centre pedestrianised and few main sights or shopping quarters more than a 20-minute walk from the city centre.

away, and booking services and hotel reservations available for a fee. It also sells the Copenhagen Card.

① Getting There & Away

AIR

Copenhagen's user-friendly international airport is Scandinavia's busiest hub, with direct flights to cities in Europe, North America and Asia, as well as a handful of Danish cities.

Located in Kastrup, 9km southeast of Copenhagen's city centre, the airport has good eating, retail and information facilities.

If you're waiting for a flight, note that this is a 'silent' airport and there are no boarding calls, although there are numerous monitor screens throughout the terminal.

BOAT

Copenhagen offers regular direct ferry services to/from Norway. There is also a combined bus-ferry service to Poland and a train-ferry service to Germany.

DB (www.bahn.de) Runs direct ICE trains from Copenhagen Central Station to Hamburg (one way from Dkr635, 4½ hours, several daily), with a ferry crossing between Puttgarden and Rødby.

DFDS Seaways (☑ 33 42 30 10; www.dfdssea ways.com; Dampfærgevej 30) One daily service to/from Oslo (one-way from Dkr750, 17¼ hours) leaves from Søndre Frihavn, just north of Kastellet.

Polferries (☑ 44 45 12 80; www.polferries. com/ferry) Offers one daily bus-ferry combo to/from Poland (one way from Dkr400). Bus 866 connects Copenhagen to Ystad in Sweden (1¼ hours), from where ferries travel to/from Świnoujście, Poland. Ferry crossings take between six and 8½ hours.

BUS

Eurolines (Map p46; ☑ 33 88 70 00; www. eurolines.dk; Halmtorvet 5) Operates buses to several European cities. The ticket office is behind Central Station. Long-distance buses leave from opposite the DGI-byen sports complex on Ingerslevsgade, just southwest of København H (Central Station). Destinations include:

Berlin Dkr329, 7½ hrs, 2 to 3 daily

Paris Dkr699, 19 to 22¼ hrs, 1 to 2 daily

CAR & MOTORCYCLE

The main highways into Copenhagen are the E20 from Jutland and Funen (and continuing towards Malmö in Sweden) and the E47 from Helsingør and Sweden. If you're coming from the north on the E47, exit onto Lyngbyvej (Rte 19) and continue south to reach the heart of the city.

COPENHAGEN CARD

The **Copenhagen Card** (www. copenhagencard.com; 24hr adult/child 10-15 Dkr339/179, 48hr Dkr469/239, 72hr Dkr559/289), available at the Copenhagen Visitors Centre or online, gives you free access to 72 museums and attractions in the city and surrounding area, as well as free travel for all S-train, metro and bus journeys within the seven travel zones.

TRAIN

All long-distance trains arrive at and depart from Københavns Hovedbanegård (Central Station), commonly known as København H, an imposing, 19th-century wooden-beamed hall with numerous facilities, including currency exchange, a post office, lockers and left-luggage facilities, and food outlets. Destinations include:

Odense Dkr276, 1½ hours, at least twice hourly

Aarhus Dkr382, three to 3½ hours, twice hourly

Aalborg Dkr431, 4½ to five hours, at least hourly

① Getting Around

TO/FROM THE AIRPORT
Metro

The 24-hour **metro** (www.m.dk) runs every four to 20 minutes between the airport arrival terminal (the station is called Lufthavnen) and the eastern side of the city centre. It does not stop at København H (Central Station) but is handy for Christianshavn and Nyhavn (get off at Kongens Nytorv for Nyhavn). Journey time to Kongens Nytorv is 14 minutes (Dkr36).

Taxi

By taxi, it's about 20 minutes between the airport and the city centre, depending on traffic. Expect to pay between Dkr250 and Dkr300.

Train

Trains (www.dsb.dk) connect the airport arrival terminal to Copenhagen Central Station (København H) around every 12 minutes. Journey time is 14 minutes (Dkr36). Check schedules at www.rejseplanen.dk.

BICYCLE

Copenhagen vies with Amsterdam as the world's most bike-friendly city. Most streets have cycle lanes and, more importantly, motorists tend to respect them.

Bikes can be carried free on S-trains, but are forbidden at Nørreport station during weekday peak hours. Enter carriages through the middle door and keep your bike behind the red line in

SMART CITY BIKES

In 2014, Copenhagen introduced its next-generation of **Bycyklen** (City Bikes; http://bycyklen.dk). These high-tech 'Smart Bikes' feature touchscreen tablets with GPS, multi-speed electric motors, puncture-resistant tyres and locks. The bikes can be rented from a handful of docking stations dotted across the city, including at Central Station, Vesterport, Østerport and Dybbølsbro S-train stations, and on Rådhuspladsen (City Hall Square). Available 24/7, 365 days a year, rental costs Dkr25 per hour and must be paid by credit card via the bike's touchscreen. For further information and a full list of docking stations, visit the Bycyklen website.

the designated bicycle area. Stay with the bike at all times. Bikes can be carried on the metro (except from 7am to 9am, and from 3.30pm to 5.30pm, on weekdays from September to May). Bike tickets cost Dkr13.

CAR & MOTORCYCLE

Except for the weekday-morning rush hour, when traffic can bottleneck coming into the city (and vice versa around 5pm), traffic in Copenhagen is generally manageable. Getting around by car is not problematic, except for the usual challenge of finding an empty parking space in the most popular places.

That said, Copenhagen's compact size, reliable public transport, and bike-friendly roads make driving unnecessary.

Parking

➨ For street parking, buy a ticket from a kerbside *billetautomat* (automated ticket machine) and place it inside the windscreen. Ticket machines accept credit cards.

➨ Copenhagen parking is zoned (red, green and blue). Those in the central commercial area (red zone) are the most costly (Dkr30 per hour). Blue zone parking, located on the fringe of the city centre, is the cheapest, costing Dkr11 per hour. Closer to the centre, green zone parking costs Dkr18 per hour. These rates are valid between 8am and 6pm, with reduced rates at other times. Parking is free from 5pm Saturday to 8am Monday and on public holidays.

➨ If you can't find street parking, you'll find car parks at the main department stores and at Israels Plads beside the Torvehallerne KBH food market (enter from Linnesgade).

➨ *Parkering forbudt* means 'no parking' and is generally accompanied by a round sign with a red diagonal slash. You can stop for up to three minutes to unload bags and passengers. A round sign with a red 'X', or a sign saying *Stopforbud*, means that no stopping at all is allowed.

Rental

The following car hire companies have booths at the airport in the international terminal. Each also has an office in central Copenhagen.

Avis (☑ 70 24 77 07; www.avis.com; Kampmannsgade 1)

Budget (☑ 33 55 05 00; www.budget.dk; Kampmannsgade 1)

Europcar (☑ 33 55 99 00; www.europcar.com; Gammel Kongevej 13A)

Hertz (☑ 33 17 90 20; www.hertzdk.dk; Ved Vesterport 3)

PUBLIC TRANSPORT

Copenhagen has an extensive public transit system consisting of a metro, rail, bus and ferry network. All tickets are valid for travel on the metro, buses and S-tog (S-train or local train) even though they look slightly different, depending on where you buy them. The free Copenhagen city maps that are distributed by the tourist office show bus routes (with numbers) and are very useful for finding your way around the city. Online, click onto the very handy www.rejseplanen.dk for all routes and schedules

➨ **Metro** (www.m.dk) Currently consists of two lines (M1 and M2). A city circle (Cityringen) line is due for completion in late 2018 or early 2019. Metro trains run around the clock, with a frequency of two to four minutes in peak times, three to six minutes during the day and on weekends, and seven to 20 minutes at night. Both lines connects Nørreport with Kongens Nytorv and Christianshavn. Line M2 (yellow line) runs to the airport.

➨ **S-train** (www.dsb.dk) Known locally as S-tog, Copenhagen's suburban train network runs seven lines through Central Station (København H). Popular tourist towns covered by the network include Helsingør and Køge. Services run every four to 20 minutes from approximately 5am to 12.30am. All-night services run hourly on Friday and Saturday (half-hourly on line F).

➨ **Movia** (www.moviatrafik.dk) The main terminus for Copenhagen's extensive bus system is Rådhuspladsen, a couple of blocks northeast of Central Station. There are seven primary routes, each with the letter 'A' in the route number. These routes run every three to seven minutes in peak hour, and about every 10 minutes at other times. Night buses (denoted by an 'N' in the route number) run on a few major routes between 1am and 5am nightly. Movia also operates the city's commuter ferries, known as

Harbour Buses. There are three routes, servicing 10 stops along the harbourfront, including the Royal Library, Nyhavn and the Opera House.

Tickets

Copenhagen's bus, train, and harbour bus network has an integrated ticket system based on seven geographical zones. Most of your travel within the city will be within two zones. Travel between the city and airport covers three zones.

The cheapest ticket (*billet*) covers two zones, offers unlimited transfers, and is valid for one hour (adult/12 to 15 years Dkr24/12). Children under 12 travel free if accompanied by an adult.

If you plan on exploring sights outside the city, including Helsingør, the north coast of Zealand and Roskilde, you're better off buying a 24-hour ticket (all zones adult/12 to 15 years Dkr130/65) or a seven-day FlexCard (all zones Dkr590).

Alternatively, you can purchase a **Rejsekort** – a touch-on, touch-off smart card that covers all zones and all public transport across the country. Available from the Rejsekort machines at metro stations, Central Station or the airport, the card costs Dkr180 (Dkr80 for the card and Dkr100 in credit). To use, tap the Rejsekort against the dedicated sensors at train and metro stations or when boarding buses and commuter ferries, then tap off when exiting. Only tap off at the very end of your journey – if your journey involves a metro ride followed immediately by a bus ride, tap on at the metro station and again on the bus, but only tap off once you exit the bus.

TAXI

Taxis can be flagged on the street and there are ranks at various points around the city centre. If the yellow *taxa* (taxi) sign is lit, the taxi is available for hire. The fare will start at Dkr37 (Dkr50 from 11pm to 7am Friday and Saturday) and costs Dkr14.20 per kilometre from 7am to 4pm Monday to Friday, and Dkr18.75 from 11pm to 7am Friday and Saturday. The rate at all other times is Dkr15. Most taxis accept major credit cards. Three of the main companies are **DanTaxi** (☑ 70 25 25 25; www.dantaxi.dk), **Taxa** (☑ 35 35 35 35; www.taxa.dk) and **Amager-Øbro Taxi** (☑ 27 27 27 27; www.amagerobrotaxi.dk).

AROUND COPENHAGEN

Many places in the greater Copenhagen area make for quick and easy excursions from the city. If you're hankering for woodlands, lakes, beaches, historic areas or impressive art museums, the mix of destinations that follows should satisfy.

WORTH A TRIP

LOUISIANA MUSEUM OF MODERN ART

Louisiana (www.louisiana.dk; Gammel Strandvej 13, Humlebæk; adult/child Dkr110/free; ⊙ 11am-10pm Tue-Fri, to 6pm Sat & Sun) Even if you don't have a consuming passion for modern art, Denmark's outstanding Louisiana should be high on your 'To Do' list. It's a striking modernist gallery, made up of four huge wings, which stretch across a sculpture-filled park, burrowing down into the hillside and nosing out again to wink at the sea (and Sweden). The collection itself is stellar, covering everything from constructivism, CoBrA movement artists and minimalist art, to abstract expressionism, pop art and photography.

Pablo Picasso, Francis Bacon and Alberto Giacometti are some of the international luminaries you'll come across inside, while Henry Moore's monumental bronzes and Max Ernst's owl-eyed animals lurk between the hillocks of the garden. Prominent Danish artists include Asger Jorn, Carl-Henning Pedersen, Robert Jacobsen and Richard Mortensen. Six to eight temporary exhibitions take place each year, and the museum's evening programme often includes art lectures and live music.

Kids are spoiled with an entire wing of their own, where they can create masterpieces inspired by the gallery's exhibitions, using everything from crayons to interactive computers. With its large sunny terrace and sea views, Louisiana's cultured cafe is a fabulous spot for a reviving coffee, while the museum shop stocks art books, prints and coveted Scandinavian design.

Louisiana is in the leafy town of **Humlebæk**, 30km north of Copenhagen. From Humlebæk train station, the museum is a 1.5km signposted walk along Gammel Strandvej. Trains to Humlebæk run at least twice hourly from Copenhagen (Dkr108, 35 minutes) and Helsingør (Dkr36, 10 minutes). If day-tripping it from Copenhagen, the 24-hour ticket (adult/child Dkr130/65) is much better value.

Alternatively, for those who want to tick off two countries in one visit, Sweden's third largest city, Malmö, is just 35 minutes away by train from Copenhagen Central Station via the majestic Øresund Fixed Link bridge and tunnel.

Ishøj

Arken Museum of Modern Art   MUSEUM
(Ark; www.arken.dk; Skovvej 100, Ishøj; adult/child Dkr95/free; ⊙10am-5pm Tue & Thu-Sun, to 9pm Wed) Modern art fans won't regret making the trip out to the outstanding Arken Museum of Modern Art. The art museum's fine collection of post-1945 art includes several Warhols, works by Jeff Koons and Damien Hirst, as well as creations by celebrated contemporary Danish artists such as Per Kirkeby, Asger Jorn, Jesper Just and Olafur Eliasson. There's plenty to keep children intrigued, too, including the wonderful sandy beach outside.

To get here from Copenhagen, take the S-train southwest to Ishøj station, then bus 128 from there.

Charlottenlund

Charlottenlund is a salubrious coastal suburb just beyond the northern outskirts of Copenhagen. Despite being so close to the city, it has a decent **sandy beach**. Its other attraction is a fine art gallery.

◉ Sights

Ordrupgaard   MUSEUM
(☎39 64 11 83; www.ordrupgaard.dk; Vilvordevej 110, Charlottenlund; adult/child Dkr110/free; ⊙1-5pm Tue-Fri, 11am-5pm Sat & Sun; 圓S-train Klampenborg, then bus 388) Architect Zaha Hadid's slinky glass-and-stone extension put Ordrupgaard on the international map, but this petite art museum, housed in an early-20th-century manor house north of Copenhagen, has always had an enviable collection of 19th- and 20th-century art. The museum also incorporates the former home of pioneering 20th-century Danish designer Finn Juhl, as well as a smart cafe. Ordrupgaard's collection includes works by Gauguin, who lived in Copenhagen for many years.

Other artists in the permanent collection include Renoir, Matisse, as well as homegrown artists of the 'Danish Golden Age', among them JT Lundbye and Vilhelm Hammershøj. The Finn Juhl house is only open weekends September to June.

Klampenborg

Being only 20 minutes from Central Station on S-train line C, Klampenborg is one of the favourite spots for Copenhageners on family outings.

A few hundred metres east of Klampenborg station is **Bellevue beach**, a sandy stretch that gets packed with sunbathers in summer.

◉ Sights

Bakken   AMUSEMENT PARK
(www.bakken.dk; Dyrehavevej 62; multiride wristband adult/child Dkr249/179) An 800m walk west from Klampenborg station is Bakken, established in the 16th century and now the world's oldest amusement park. A blue-collar version of Tivoli, it's a honky-tonk carnival of bumper cars, roller coasters, slot machines and beer halls. See the website for opening times.

Dyrehaven   WALKING, CYCLING
Formally called Jægersborg Dyrehave, Dyrehaven is a 1000-hectare sweep of beech trees and meadows crisscrossed by an alluring network of walking and cycling trails. Now the capital's most popular picnicking area, the grounds were established as a royal hunting ground in 1669. There are still about 2000 deer in the park, mostly fallow but also some red and Japanese sika deer. Among the red deer are a few rare white specimens, descendants of deer imported in 1737 from Germany, where they are now extinct.

Lyngby

The main sight of interest in the Lyngby area is **Frilandsmuseet** (☎41 20 64 55; www.natmus.dk; Kongevejen 100; admission free; ⊙10am-5pm Tue-Sun Jul-Aug, shorter hrs rest of yr) FREE, a sprawling open-air museum of old countryside dwellings that have been gathered from sites around Denmark. Its 50-plus historic buildings are arranged in groupings that provide a sense of Danish rural life as it was in various regions and across different social strata. It's not open all year; check the website for opening times.

Frilandsmuseet is a 10-minute signposted walk from Sorgenfri station, 25 minutes from Central Station on S-train line B. You can also take bus 184 or 191, both of which stop at the entrance.

Zealand

Includes ➜

Øresund Coast 96
Rungsted 96
Helsingør 97
Hillerød 101
Fredensborg 103
Hornbæk 104
Roskilde 108
Køge 114
Sorø 118
Trelleborg 122
Vordingborg 124

Best Places to Eat

➜ Dragsholm Slot (p113)

➜ Babette (p125)

➜ Skipperhuset (p104)

➜ Restaurant Mumm (p113)

➜ Rustica (p108)

Best Places to Stay

➜ Helenekilde Badehotel (p108)

➜ Gilleleje Badehotel (p106)

➜ Vallø Slotskro (p119)

➜ Dragsholm Slot (p113)

➜ Ewaldgården Pension (p113)

Why Go?

Denmark's largest island offers much more than the dazzle of Copenhagen. North of the city lie some of the country's finest beaches, quaintest fishing villages and vainest castles. Here you'll find Helsingør's hulking Kronborg Slot and the striking new Maritime Museum of Denmark, not to mention Hillerød's sublimely romantic Frederiksborg Slot.

West of Copenhagen awaits history-steeped Roskilde, home to a World Heritage–listed cathedral, Scandinavia's top rock music festival and the superb Viking Ship Museum. History also comes to life at nearby Sagnlandet Lejre, an engrossing, hands-on archaeology site.

Further west stands the millennia-old Trelleborg ring fortress, while Zealand's southern assets include medieval Køge, the World Heritage–listed coastline of Stevns Klint, and Vordingborg's cutting-edge museum, Danmarks Borgcenter.

Much of Zealand is easy to get around, and (bonus!) the Copenhagen Card allows free public transport and admission to many attractions.

When to Go

The best time to visit Zealand is between June and August. The weather is at its warmest, the countryside is a luxuriant green, and the region's gorgeous north coast is at its most enticing. Tourist offices and attractions are in full swing, and world-class cultural events such as the Roskilde Festival bring some of the world's top performers. The downside is that you won't be the only one soaking up the sun, sea and culture. Most Danes take their holiday in July, making coastal towns particularly crowded and accommodation scarce. Book ahead.

Outside of summer, May and September are your next best bets, with mild weather, fewer crowds, and most attractions open at full capacity. In winter the days are cold and short and the region's beach towns are mostly shut for the season. Many museums and tourist attractions run to reduced opening hours.

Zealand Highlights

1 Are you in Denmark or the south of France? Ponder the question on the wide golden beach at **Hornbæk** (p105)

2 Snoop around the immense bastion **Kronborg Slot** (p97), setting for Shakespeare's *Hamlet*

3 Explore nautical themes and spectacular architecture at Helsingør's showstopping **Maritime Museum of Denmark** (p99)

4 Continue the castle odyssey at lakeside **Frederiksborg Slot** (p101), one of Denmark's finest historic buildings

5 Let your child run free with an axe at the Iron Age settlement at **Lejre** (p113)

6 Party hard at northern Europe's largest rock music festival in **Roskilde** (p112)

7 Puzzle over the enigmatic remains of the Viking ring fortress at **Trelleborg** (p122)

8 Lose yourself in the narrow, medieval streets of **Køge** (p114), home to Denmark's oldest house

9 Delve into medieval conflict and strategy on one of Denmark's most important historical sites at **Danmarks Borgcenter** (p124) in Vordingborg

ℹ Getting There & Away

Most of northern Zealand can be reached from Copenhagen in less than an hour – quicker if you have your own transport. The Copenhagen Card can be used for many bus or train trips in the area.

Frequent trains head northwards from Copenhagen, but take bus 388 from Klampenborg (the last stop on the C line of the S-train system) north to Helsingør for beautiful coastal views. Helsingør train station handles both Danske Statsbaner (DSB) trains and the privately operated Lokalbanen, which runs a regional service in north Zealand.

The transportation system in the southern part of Zealand is also well linked to Copenhagen and just about all of it can be reached in an hour from the capital. This said, having your own transport is more important down south, since the destinations are more scattered than in the north and a good amount of the region's appeal lies in its pastoral scenery.

If you're travelling across the region between Køge and Korsør using your own transport, the rural Rte 150 makes an excellent alternative to zipping along on the E20 motorway.

ℹ Getting Around

A joint zone fare system (Dkr24 per zone travelled) applies to all Copenhagen buses, DSB/State Railway and S-trains in metropolitan Copenhagen, northern Zealand and as far south as Køge, as well as some privately operated railway routes in the area (within an approximately 40km radius of Copenhagen). It's possible to change between train and bus routes on the same ticket.

Depending on the number of zones crossed, it's often cheaper and more convenient to purchase a 24-hour ticket (all zones adult/child Dkr130/65) or the touch-on, touch-off Rejsekort smart card, which can be topped up as required.

To reach most of the north coast you must switch trains in either Hillerød or Helsingør.

The main east–west train line between Copenhagen and Odense cuts across the central part of Zealand, servicing towns such as Sorø and Korsør. The main north–south route runs from Copenhagen to and from Nykøbing F on Falster, servicing the major southern towns of Køge and Vordingborg.

Many of the train routes in southern Zealand are privately run, and buses usually connect stations to towns and villages not serviced by train. For all public transport routes, timetables and prices, click onto the very useful www.rejseplan.dk.

ØRESUND COAST

This area is sometimes grandly referred to as the Danish Riviera, thanks to its expensive seaside mansions. It's a slightly misleading name, however – if you're dreaming of golden beaches, head for the north coast. The main attractions on north Zealand's eastern shore are a handful of excellent museums and Helsingør's beast of a castle, Kronborg Slot.

The Øresund itself is the sound that separates Denmark from Sweden, just across the water.

Rungsted

If you're a fan of the fantastical, erotic, mordant writings of Karen Blixen (1885–1962), the coastal town of Rungsted holds a treat. Here you can visit Rungstedlund, Blixen's Danish estate, now a museum dedicated to her life and work.

◉ Sights

Karen Blixen Museet   MUSEUM
(www.karen-blixen.dk; Rungsted Strandvej 111; adult/child Dkr60/free; ⊙10am-5pm Tue-Sun May-Sep, 1-4pm Wed-Fri, 11am-4pm Sat & Sun Oct-Apr) Karen Blixen's former home in Rungsted is now the Karen Blixen Museum. Fans of her writing will appreciate how it remains much the way she left it, with photographs, Masai spears, paintings, shields and other mementoes of her time in Africa, such as the gramophone given to Blixen by her lover Denys Finch-Hatton. On her desk is the old Corona typewriter she used to write her novels.

One wing of the museum houses a library of Blixen's books, a cafe, bookshop and an audiovisual presentation on her life. The wooded grounds, set aside as a bird sanctuary, contain Blixen's **grave**, a simple stone slab inscribed with her name.

The museum is opposite the busy yacht harbour, 1.5km from the train station. Walk north up Østre Stationsvej, turn right at the lights onto Rungstedvej and then, at its intersection with Rungsted Strandvej, walk south about 300m.

ℹ Getting There & Away

Trains to Rungsted run every 20 minutes from Copenhagen (Dkr84, 30 minutes) and Helsingør (Dkr60, 25 minutes).

OUT OF RUNGSTED

Karen Blixen (1885–1962) was born in Rungsted, a well-to-do community north of Copenhagen, as Karen Christenze Dinesen. Throughout her life, this unusual woman created an aura of eccentricity around herself, trying on different names, fictionalising her own life, and causing controversy with her 'decadent' writings.

In 1914, aged 28 and eager to escape the confines of her bourgeois family, she married her second cousin Baron Bror von Blixen-Finecke, after having a failed love affair with his twin brother Hans. It was a marriage of convenience – she wanted his title and he needed her money.

The couple moved to Kenya and started a coffee plantation, which Karen was left to manage. It was here that she was diagnosed with syphilis, contracted from the womanising baron (although it's possible that her ill health was caused by arsenic poisoning, taken as medicine for the syphilis she feared she had). The diagnosis was especially damaging psychologically since her father had committed suicide after contracting syphilis when Karen was 10 years old. Blixen came home to Denmark for medical treatment, then returned to Africa and divorced the baron in 1925.

She then lived with the great love of her life, Englishman Denys Finch-Hatton, for six years, until he died in a tragic plane crash in 1932. The couple were played by Meryl Streep and Robert Redford in the Oscar-winning film adaptation of *Out of Africa*, Blixen's autobiography. Soon after his death Blixen left Africa, returning to the family estate in Rungsted where she began to write. Denmark was slow to appreciate her, in part because she used an old-fashioned idiomatic style, wrote approvingly about the aristocracy and insisted on being addressed as 'Baroness' in a country bent on minimising class disparity.

Blixen's first book of short stories, *Seven Gothic Tales*, was published in New York in 1934 under the pseudonym Isak Dinesen. It was only after the book became immensely successful in the USA that Danish publishers took a serious interest.

After the commercial success of *Out of Africa* in both Danish and English, other books followed: *Winter's Tales* (1942), *The Angelic Avengers* (1946), *Last Tales* (1957), *Anecdotes of Destiny* (1958) and *Shadows on the Grass* (1960). Another Oscar-winning film, *Babette's Feast*, was based on her story about culinary artistry in small-town Denmark.

Helsingør

POP 46,400

The main sight at the busy port town of Helsingør (Elsinore) is imposing Kronborg Slot, a brute of a castle that dominates the narrowest point of the Øresund. It was made famous as Elsinore Castle in Shakespeare's *Hamlet*, although the intimate psychological nature of the play is a far cry from the military colossus squatting on the shore.

Beyond Hamlet's pad, Helsingør has no shortage of atmospheric historic streets, laced with half-timbered houses, Gothic churches and a medieval cloister.

Frequent ferries shuttle to and from Sweden, filled with Swedes on a mission to buy cheap (it's all relative) Danish alcohol.

◉ Sights

★ **Kronborg Slot**   CASTLE
(www.kronborg.dk; Kronborgvej; interior incl guided tour adult/child Dkr80/35; ◉10am-5.30pm Jun-Aug, 11am-4pm Apr-May & Sep-Oct, shorter hrs rest of yr; guided tours 11.30am & 1.30pm daily) The Unesco World Heritage–listed Kronborg Slot began life as Krogen, a formidable tollhouse built by Danish king Erik of Pomerania in the 1420s. Expanded by Frederik II in 1585, the castle was ravaged by fire in 1629, leaving nothing but the outer walls. The tireless builder-king Christian IV rebuilt Kronborg, preserving the castle's earlier Renaissance style and adding his own baroque touches. The galleried chapel was the only part of Kronborg that escaped the flames in 1629 and gives a good impression of the castle's original appearance.

Kronborg fell upon more bad luck during the Danish-Swedish wars, with the Swedes occupying the castle from 1658 to 1660 and looting everything of value, including its famous fountain. Following the Swedish attack, Christian V bulked up Kronborg's defences, but the Danish royals gave up trying to make the castle a home. The building became a barracks from 1785 until 1924, when it became a museum (the Swedish government sportingly

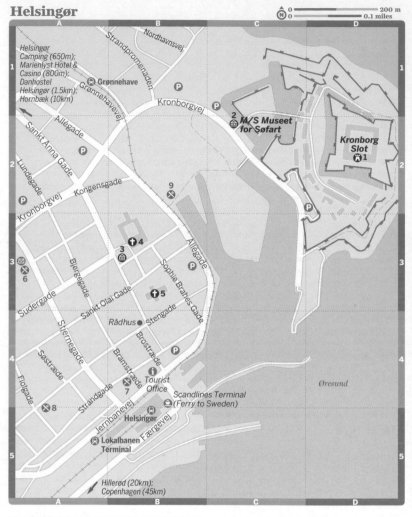

0
N 0
200 m
0.1 miles

Øresund

Helsingør

◎ Top Sights
1 Kronborg Slot D2
2 M/S Museet for Søfart C2

◎ Sights
3 Helsingør Bymuseum B3
4 Sankt Mariæ Kirke &
    Karmeliterklostret B3
5 Sankt Olai Domkirke B3

⊗ Eating
6 Kvickly A3
7 Rådmand Davids Hus B4
8 Rustica A5
9 Spisehuset Kulturværftet B2

returning some looted items). Although it costs to enter the interior, you can cross several swan-filled moats and walk into the dramatic courtyard free of charge, or circumnavigate the castle's mighty sea barriers (open daily until sunset) – a good picnic spot.

➡ Royal Apartments

The Royal Apartments are rather empty today: the king's and queen's chambers, for example, have little in them but marble fireplaces, a few sticks of furniture, and some lavish ceiling paintings, although occasional modern-art exhibitions add an interesting dimension. The most impressive room is the ballroom, the longest in Scandinavia when it was built in 1585. Banquets held here consisted of 65 courses, and each guest was given their own vomiting bucket. Seven of the tapestries that originally adorned the walls – in excellent condition, and with interesting explanations alongside – can be seen in the adjoining Little Hall.

➡ **Casements**

The chilly, low-ceilinged dungeon, which also served as storerooms and soldiers' quarters, stretches underneath a surprisingly large area of the castle. It's suitably dark and creepy, although you'll make better sense of it if you read up on barracks life before heading downwards. Delights include nesting bats, and a statue of the Viking chief Holger Danske (Ogier the Dane), who, legend says, will wake and come to Denmark's aid in its hour of need.

★ **M/S Museet for Søfart**   MUSEUM
(Maritime Museum of Denmark; www.mfs.dk; Ny Kronborgvej 1; adult/child Dkr110/free; ⊙10am-5pm daily Jul & Aug, 11am-5pm Tue-Sun rest of yr) Ingeniously built in and around a dry dock beside Kronborg Slot, Denmark's subterranean Maritime Museum merits a visit as much for its design as for its enlightened, multimedia galleries. The latter explore Denmark's maritime history and culture in dynamic, contemporary ways. Alongside the usual booty of nautical instruments, sea charts and wartime objects, exhibitions explore themes as varied as the representation of sailors in popular culture, trade and exploitation in Denmark's overseas colonies, and the globe-crossing journeys of modern shipping containers.

Interactive displays will have you inking a sailor's tattoo, testing your navigational skills, and even running your own trade company. The museum also houses a contemporary cafe and a fantastic gift shop where maritime-themed gifts mix it with Danish design and fashion pieces.

Sankt Mariæ Kirke & Karmeliterklostret   CHURCH, CLOISTER
(www.sctmariae.dk; Sankt Anna Gade 38; ⊙10am-3pm Tue-Sun) Slip into this medieval church for some rather eclectic 15th-century frescoes, in which frogs, foxes, bulls and rams spring from bizarre-looking faces, and where pipers and lute players burst from giant flowers. Other highlights include an ornate rococo gallery and a 17th-century organ, the latter played by Dieterich Buxtehude (1637–1707), a baroque composer who greatly influenced Bach; the frequent organ concerts are attended by aficionados. Sankt Mariæ Kirke is attached to one of Scandinavia's best-preserved medieval monasteries, Karmeliterklostret.

It's believed that Christian II's mistress, Dyveke (c 1490–1517), is buried here.

Sankt Olai Domkirke   CATHEDRAL
(⊙10am-4pm May-Aug, 10am-2pm Sep-Apr) Surrounded by lime trees, handsome, red-brick Sankt Olai Domkirke is a Gothic cathedral built in 1559. Eclectic features include an over-the-top white-and-gold altarpiece (one of Denmark's largest at 12m high), an ominous black stone slab where the names of wrong-doers were written, and, wedged in an archway, an English cannonball fired en route to the Battle of Copenhagen (1801).

Helsingør Bymuseum   MUSEUM
(www.vaerftsmuseet.dk; Sankt Anna Gade 36; adult/child Dkr30/free; ⊙noon-4pm Tue-Fri & Sun, 10am-2pm Sat) One block north of the cathedral

TO BE OR NOT TO BE

Shakespeare's *Hamlet* (1602) is set in Kronborg Slot in Helsingør ('Elsinore'). Despite the vividness of the play, the Bard had never set foot in Denmark. It's possible that he gleaned details of the imposing new castle from a group of English players who performed in Helsingør in 1585, the year that Kronborg was completed. Shakespeare also included two actual Danish noblemen, Frederik Rosenkrantz and Knud Gyldenstierne (Guildenstern), who visited the English court in the 1590s.

Although the remaining characters are based on a story that was 800 years old in Shakespeare's time, audiences were utterly convinced of the play's authenticity. English merchants trading in Helsingør would visit the castle out of respect for Hamlet: so many visitors wanted to know where the indecisive Dane was buried that 'Hamlet's grave' was built in the grounds of Marienlyst Slot.

Each August the castle plays host to the Shakespeare Festival, which sees some of the world's leading theatre ensembles perform a selection of Shakespeare's works in Kronborg's courtyard. Check www.hamletscenen.dk to see what's coming up.

is Helsingør Bymuseum, built by the monks of the adjacent monastery in 1516 to serve as a sailors' hospital. There's a detailed model of 19th-century Helsingør, with an interesting 15-minute recording about the town's history in Danish, Swedish, German and English. Beyond it is a hotchpotch of exhibits, from old chemists' bottles and medieval pottery, to a few hundred dolls.

Danmarks Tekniske Museum MUSEUM
(www.tekniskmuseum.dk; Fabriksvej 25; adult/child Dkr65/35; ☺10am-5pm Tue-Sun) Southwest of the town centre on an industrial estate, Danmarks Tekniske Museum displays innovative technological inventions from the late 19th and early 20th centuries: early gramophones, radios, motor vehicles and aeroplanes. The latter includes a 1906 Danish-built aeroplane that, it's claimed, was the first plane flown in Europe (it stayed airborne for 11 seconds!). The museum is a 25-minute ride away on bus 802, in the direction of Espergærde.

Hammermøllen HISTORIC BUILDING
(www.hammermollen.dk; Bøssemagergade 21; adult/child Dkr10/free; ☺10am-5pm Tue-Sun) If you don't have a pressing itinerary, consider cycling to Hammermøllen, about 5km west in Hellebæk. This picturesque old smithy was founded by Christian IV in 1765 to hammer out cannons for his battleships, and has also served as a copper mill and textile mill. Admire the thatched roof and waterwheels, and kick back with coffee and cake.

🛏 Sleeping

Danhostel Helsingør HOSTEL €
(☑49 28 49 49; danhostelhelsingor.dk; Nordre Strandvej 24; dm/s/d/tr Dkr225/495/550/595; P ?) This 180-bed hostel is based in a coastal manor house 2km northwest of town, on a little beach looking directly across to Sweden. The run-of-the-mill dorms are in one of the smaller attached buildings. Facilities include a self-catering kitchen, small playground and outdoor ping-pong tables to keep kids amused. From Helsingør, bus 842 (Dkr24) will get you there.

Helsingør Camping CAMPGROUND €
(☑49 28 49 50; www.helsingorcamping.dk; Strandalleen 2; campsites per adult/child Dkr70/35, cabin with bathroom Dkr850; ☺year-round) 🏕 A well-spaced, low-key beachside camping ground east of Danhostel Helsingør and approximately 1.5km northwest of the town centre. Facilities include a shop and laundry, and it's close to one of the area's best beaches. To get here, take bus 842 from Helsingør train station.

Marienlyst Hotel & Casino HOTEL €€
(☑49 21 40 00; www.marienlyst.dk; Nordre Strandvej 2; s Dkr800-1425, d Dkr1000-1625; P @ ? ☼) Stretching along the seafront, Helsingør's four-star hotel features a swimming pool, casino, and views across the sea to Sweden. Rooms are neutrally hued and classically styled, and while they won't win any design awards, all are comfortable and satisfactory.

🍴 Eating

There's a cluster of restaurants and beer gardens around the main square, Axeltorv. For coffee and cake, head for pedestrianised Stengade.

You'll find a **Kvickly** (Stjernegade 25; ☺8am-8pm Mon-Fri, to 6pm Sat & Sun) supermarket and bakery west of Axeltorv.

Rådmand Davids Hus DANISH €
(☑49 26 10 43; Strandgade 70; dishes Dkr38-98; ☺10am-5pm Mon-Sat) What better place to gobble down Danish classics than a snug, lop-sided 17th-century house, complete with cobbled courtyard? Refuel with honest, solid staples like smørrebrød (open sandwiches), herring, and the special 'shopping lunch', typically a generous plate of salad, salmon pâté, and slices of pork, cheese and homemade rye bread. Leave room for the Grand Marnier pancakes.

Spisehuset Kulturværftet INTERNATIONAL €
(www.kulturvaerftet.dk; Allégade 2; meals Dkr45-95; ☺10am-7pm Mon-Fri, to 5pm Sat & Sun; ?) Part of the Culture Yard, a striking waterfront cultural centre housing theatres, exhibition spaces, and the Helsingør library, this casual, light-filled eatery peddles fresh, modern cafe grub. Gaze out over Hamlet's pad while chowing down on open sandwiches, creative soups and salads, or the more substantial daily special. If the view inspires the scribe within, there's free wi-fi, good coffee and nibble-friendly pastries and cookies.

Rustica ITALIAN €€
(☑20 68 56 44; www.rustica.dk; Stengade 26E; mains Dkr179-229; ☺11am-late Tue-Sat) At the far end of a courtyard, up a flight of stairs, Rustica serves beautiful, seasonal dishes in a contemporary rustic setting of whitewashed wooden beams, filament bulbs and long communal tables made by the chef himself. The Italian-inspired menu is reassuringly short, with only a handful of antipasti, mains, pizzas

and desserts, driven by quality produce and an emphasis on clean, natural flavours.

The result is dishes like succulent Danish entrecôte served with herb-laden roast potatoes, vine-ripened tomatoes, peppery rucola, Parmesan, and grilled peppers. The place is just as perfect for a glass of vino, and there's live music twice a month.

ℹ Information

Library (Allégade 2, Kulturværftet; ◷10am-9pm Mon-Fri, to 4pm Sat) Free internet access.

Post Office (Stjernegade 25; ◷10am-5pm Mon-Fri, 10am-noon Sat) Inside the Kvickly supermarket building.

Tourist Office (☑49 21 13 33; www.visitnordsjaelland.com; Havnepladsen 3; ◷10am-5pm Mon-Fri, to 2pm Sat & Sun Jul-early Aug, reduced hrs rest of yr) Opposite the train station.

ℹ Getting There & Away

BOAT

Scandlines (☑33 15 15 15; www.scandlines. dk) sails between Helsingør and Helsingborg in Sweden (person/car plus nine passengers Dkr59/745 return, 20 minutes). Car tickets are cheaper booked online.

CAR

Helsingør is 64km north of Copenhagen and 24km northeast of Hillerød. There's free parking throughout the city, including west of Kvickly supermarket. Parking outside Kronborg Slot costs Dkr10 per hour between 8am and 8pm.

TRAIN

Helsingør train station has two adjacent terminals: the DSB terminal for national trains and the smaller Lokalbanen terminal for the private railway that runs along the north coast.

Trains to Copenhagen (Dkr108, 45 minutes) run about three times hourly from early morning to around midnight. Trains to Hillerød (via Fredensborg Dkr72, 30 minutes) run at least once hourly until around midnight.

The Lokalbanen train from Helsingør to Gilleleje (Dkr72, 45 minutes) runs once to twice hourly until around midnight.

INLAND TOWNS

In the heart of Zealand lie Hillerød and Fredensborg, two small towns built around magnificent – and very different – royal residences. You're free to roam the ornate rooms and soaring towers of the castle at Hillerød, whereas the interior of the more modest palace at Fredensborg is only open in July – the rest of the year, it's the beautiful lakeside gardens that are the main draw.

Hillerød

POP 31,180

Christian IV sure knew how to build a castle. Hillerød, 30km north of Copenhagen, is a modern market town, whose glorious palace elevates it to 'must visit' status. Frederiksborg Slot, sitting on a nest of islands in the middle of an attractive lake, is a vision of copper turrets and baroque gardens, and one of the most impressive attractions in the region.

Hillerød is also a transport hub for north Zealand, with train connections for the beaches on the north coast. The train station is about 500m from the town centre.

◉ Sights

★**Frederiksborg Slot**   CASTLE
(www.frederiksborgmuseet.dk; adult/child Dkr75/20; ◷10am-5pm Apr-Oct, 11am-3pm rest of yr) The impressive Dutch Renaissance–styled Frederiksborg Slot spreads across three islets on the castle lake, Slotsø. The oldest part of the castle dates from the reign of Frederik II, after whom it is named. His son Christian IV was born here and most of the present structure was built by Christian in the early 17th century. With its gilded ceilings, tapestries and fine paintings, the castle's interior is magnificent. Especially dazzling is the Slotskirken (Coronation Chapel), which retains the original interior commissioned by Christian IV.

Spared serious damage in the fire that ravaged the castle in 1859, the chapel is a deliciously ornate confection of curling gold and pink-cheeked cherubs, kept in fine company by a silver pulpit and altarpiece. A setting fit for royalty, Danish monarchs were crowned in the chapel from 1671 to 1840. You can hear the sound of the 17th century each Thursday between 1.30pm and 2pm, when the priceless **Compenius organ** (1610) is played, or at free concerts every Sunday at 5pm in July and August.

Also fairly intact is the **Audience Chamber**, an eye-boggling room containing trompe l'oeil details, a self-indulgent portrait of big-nosed Christian V posing as a Roman emperor, and best of all, a 17th-century elevator chair, which enabled the king to rise graciously through the floor!

Other rooms in the castle were restored to their original appearances in the 19th century. The richly embellished **Riddersha-len** (Knights Hall), once the dining room, is particularly striking – check out the stucco friezes of deer, embedded with real antlers. Also impressive is the Great Hall, a vast ballroom complete with minstrels' gallery, fine tapestries and vivid ceiling carvings.

The rest of the 1st and 2nd floors contain the Museum of National History, a chronologically arranged portrait gallery of kings, noblemen and olden-day celebrities, interspersed with unusual pieces of furniture. It's a lot to digest in one go – you might be better off concentrating on the time periods that interest you. On the 3rd floor is the Moderne Samling **(Modern Collection)**, a collection of 20th- and 21st-century paintings and photography.

Both Frederik II and Christian IV used Frederiksborg as their royal seat, but after Hillerød suffered plague, fire and rampaging Swedes during the 17th century, the throne moved to quieter Fredensborg in the 18th century.

➔ Slotshaven

The castle gardens lie to the north. The formal baroque garden (open from 10am till sunset), visible from the castle windows and made up of perfect terraces and immaculately manicured yew and box, demonstrates that even nature must bend to a king's will. There's also a Romantic garden, Indelukket, where 18th-century rigidity melts into a wilder 19th-century notion of gardening. North again is the oak wood of Lille Dyrehave, which was planted to provide material for boat-building after the Danish fleet was confiscated by England in 1807. You could easily spend a pleasant hour's outing strolling through the three sections.

➔ The Slotsø Ferry

From mid-May to mid-September, the little **Frederiksborg ferry** (adult/child Dkr30/10)

makes a 30-minute round-trip of the castle lake between 11am and 5pm Monday to Saturday, and between 1pm and 5pm on Sunday. It stops at three small piers: one on the edge of Torvet, one near the castle entrance and one by the baroque gardens.

🛏 Sleeping

Accommodation is scarce in Hillerød and fills up quickly even out of high season – book ahead. For a list of accommodation options, head to www.visitnordsjaelland.com.

Danhostel Hillerød   HOSTEL €
(☑ 48 26 19 86; www.hillerodhostel.dk; Lejrskolevej 4; dm/s/d Dkr200/585/620; P @ 🛜) Located 2.5km east of town, this wonderful lakeside hostel comes with comfortable beds and a bucolic setting. The hostel is geared towards school groups and its diversions include ping-pong, air hockey, badminton, pétanque, canoes, and bicycle hire (per day Dkr75). Rooms in the newer building (s/d Dkr700/735) are the largest and brightest, with contemporary toilets, designer furniture and no carpet.

Buses 301, 302 and 305 run from near the hostel to town.

Hillerød Camping   CAMPGROUND €
(☑ 48 26 48 54; www.hillerodcamping.dk; Blytæk-kervej 18; campsite per adult/child Dkr100/50; ⊙ mid-Apr–Sep; P) This wonderful two-star camping ground is about a 20-minute walk directly south of the castle along Slangerup-gade. You can really feel the love – bags of toys for children, a spotless kitchen, a cosy lounge with books and magazines, and even fresh flowers in the toilets.

Hotel Hillerød   HOTEL €€
(☑ 48 24 08 00; www.hotelhillerod.dk; Milnersvej 41; s Dkr620-1135, d Dkr800-1340; P @ 🛜)

DENMARK'S MOST HAUNTED...

Esrum Kloster (www.esrum.dk; Klostergade 11-12, Esrum; adult/child Dkr50/free; ⊙ 11am-5pm Tue-Sun Apr–mid-Oct, 11am-4pm Thu-Sun rest of yr), a monastery 15km north of Hillerød, has a juicy ghost story attached about the demonic Brother Rus, who was employed as the monastery's cook in the 16th century. Wicked old Rus served up decadent dishes and lashings of sinful wine to his fellow monks, in between chasing the serving wenches round the kitchen and having late-night chats with Satan.

Word of this evil-doing got back to the abbot, who had Brother Rus tortured to death on his own cooking grill (on view in the monastery today). A splatter of his blood has defied all attempts to wash it off, and the damned monk has been spotted wandering the monastery in the dead of night.

Bus 390R from Helsingør to Helsinge runs past the monastery.

Rooms at this modern, bungalow-style hotel are pleasant and entirely unmemorable in that Ikea-type of way. Superior rooms keep things cool with air-conditioning, and several rooms feature handy kitchenettes. Hotel Hillerød is about 2km south of the castle.

🍴 Eating

Il Gallo Nero   ITALIAN €€
(☑️48 24 35 33; Torvet 1; brunch Dkr139, pizza Dkr119-139, dinner mains Dkr229-269; ⊘5-10pm daily, plus 11am-3pm Fri-Sun) Run by verified Italians, the Black Rooster serves proper Italian nosh made with prime ingredients. Dishes burst with flavour, from pizzas to mouthwatering à la carte options like delicate spinach, ricotta and tomato crepes, decadent Gorgonzola lasagna, and meaty mains like grilled lamb served *cacciatora* style. The restaurant also serves brunch Friday to Sunday.

Café Vivaldi   INTERNATIONAL €€
(Torvet 11; lunch Dkr95-109, dinner mains Dkr169-199; ⊘10am-10pm Sun-Thu, to 11pm Fri & Sat) Right in the centre of the sloping town square, this is the place to head on a sunny afternoon for people-watching. There's a good choice of light meals – nachos, sandwiches and salads, as well as more substantial offerings such as steaks. The weekend brunch buffet (10am to 1pm), however, is of a rather average quality.

ℹ️ Information

Tourist Office (☑️48 24 26 26; www.visit-nordsjaelland.com; Frederiksværksgade 2A; ⊘9.30am-4pm Mon-Fri May-Sep, also 9.30am-1.30pm Sat late-Jun–early Aug) A short walk from the castle entrance.

ℹ️ Getting There & Away

Direct S-train services run every 10 to 20 minutes between Copenhagen and Hillerød (Dkr108, 40 minutes) on weekdays. On weekends you may need to alight at Gentofte station, from where a connecting bus service continues to Hillerød; total journey time is 55 minutes.

Trains from Hillerød run eastward to Fredensborg (Dkr24, 10 minutes) and Helsingør (Dkr72, 30 minutes), north to Gilleleje (Dkr60, 30 minutes) and west to Tisvildeleje (Dkr60, 30 minutes); all services operate at least hourly.

Buses also link Hillerød with north Zealand towns but they are much slower than the train and cost just as much.

ℹ️ Getting Around

Buses 301 and 302 depart frequently from the train station and can drop you near the castle gate (Dkr24).

Fredensborg

POP 8380

Small, quiet Fredensborg *is* its royal palace, plus the fairytale palace gardens that stretch alongside Denmark's second-largest lake, Esrum Sø. The palace is only open to the public in July, but it's worth a day out here anyway for peaceful greenery, swimming, boating and fishing opportunities.

👁️ Sights

Fredensborg Slot   PALACE
(www.ses.dk; Slotsgade 1; tours adult/child Dkr75/30; ⊘tours (in English) 1.45-3.30pm daily Jul-early Aug) The royal family's summer residence, Fredensborg Slot was built in 1720 by Frederik IV. The main Italian baroque mansion, with its marble floors and a large central cupola, can only be visited in July, when the royal family holidays elsewhere. Whenever the royal family is in residence, the building is flanked by smart Little-Tin-Soldier guards, with white-striped uniforms and bearskin hats. The **changing of the guard** is at noon daily.

Fredensborg Slot's interior is not as impressive as some other Danish royal palaces, and the true highlight is the palace gardens, a blending of baroque formality and a more luxuriant Romantic vision. Interestingly, the name – 'Peace Palace' – commemorates the truce that Denmark had just achieved with its Scandinavian neighbours. Indeed, the country-manor appearance reflects the more tranquil mood of that era, an abrupt contrast with the moat-encircled fortresses of Kronborg and Frederiksborg that preceded it.

The palace is about 1km from the train station, and well signposted.

Fredensborg Slotshave   GARDENS
(⊘Palace Park year-round, Private Garden 9am-5pm Jul) While Fredensborg Slot's **Palace Park**, a 120-hectare spread of soothing woodland, is open to the public year-round, the Private Garden is only accessible in July. During this time, visitors can snoop around the royal family's **Orangery and Herb Garden** (joint ticket to palace, orangery & herb garden adult/child Dkr75/30; ⊘tours (in English) 2.30pm

daily Jul only) on guided tours. The Palace Park itself is crossed by long riding avenues that radiate outwards from the palace. Its most unusual feature is **Normandsdalen**, a circular amphitheatre containing 70 life-sized statues of Norwegian and Faroese folk characters.

The original small wooden dolls of these fishermen, farmers, soldiers and servants were carved by an 18th-century Norwegian postman, Jørgen Christensen Garnaas, who sent them to King Frederik V. Frederik liked them so much he had them made from sandstone.

Esrum Sø   LAKE

About 1km west of the palace gate along Skipperallé, you'll come to heart-fluttering Esrum Sø, Denmark's second-largest lake at 17 sq km. A trail skirts around its shores, or you can explore the water by boat. You'll find a lakeside restaurant, Skipperhuset, as well as **canoes and kayaks** (www.kanokongen. dk; Sørupvej 1; canoe hire 1hr/1-4hrs Dkr150/250; ⊙10am-7pm Jul & Aug) for hire. There's also a summer **ferry** (☑48 48 01 07; www.bådfarte-nesrumsø.dk; return ticket adult/child Dkr100/60; ⊙May-Sep) service to **Gribskov**, a forested area with trails and picnic grounds on the western side of the lake. From Fredensborg train station, bus 371 runs hourly to the lake, on weekdays only.

🛏 Sleeping

Danhostel Fredensborg   HOSTEL €

(☑48 48 03 15; www.fredensborghostel.dk; Østrupvej 3; s Dkr320, d from Dkr490; ⊙Jan–mid-Dec; 🅿🐾) Fredensborg's hostel occupies a prime location just 300m south of the Fredensborg Slot. There are no dorms here – most of its 88 beds are in double rooms (all with washbasin or toilet). Best of all is the large, secluded garden.

🍴 Eating

★**Skipperhuset**   DANISH €€

(☑48 48 10 12; www.skipperhuset.dk; Skipperallé 6; lunch Dkr89-145, dinner mains Dkr195-285; ⊙noon-5pm Tue-Sun mid-Apr–Sep, plus 6-9pm Fri & Sat May-Aug) It's hard to imagine a more idyllic setting for alfresco dining than this restaurant on Esrum Sø. Many of the ingredients are organic, with herbs and vegetables picked fresh from the nearby palace garden. Whether it's new asparagus with poached eggs, herbs and crisp rye bread, or lobster and fish served with brown butter

and seasonal vegetables, expect fresh, nuanced flavours and thoughtful presentation.

Consider booking ahead if heading in for dinner.

Restaurant Under Kronen   DANISH €€

(underkronen.dk; Jernbanegade 1; lunch Dkr59-168, dinner mains Dkr168-188; ⊙9am-10pm) A stone's throw from the palace gates, smart, cafe-style Restaurant Under Kronen serves good-quality, seasonal grub. Danish lunch classics include herring, smoked salmon, smørrebrød (open sandwiches) and tartar, while the smaller dinner menu might include fresh mussels in white wine or cockeral with ratatouille. Brunch is served from 9am to noon on weekends and the attached kiosk peddles cooling ice cream.

ℹ Information

Tourist Office (www.visitnordsjaelland.com; Slotsgade 2; ⊙10am-5pm Mon-Fri, to 2pm Sat & Sun Jul, 10am-4pm Mon-Fri Jun & Aug, shorter hrs rest of yr) Seasonal tourist bureau inside Hotel Fredensborg Store Kro, on the same street as Fredensborg Slot.

ℹ Getting There & Away

Fredensborg is midway between Hillerød (Dkr24, 10 minutes) and Helsingør (Dkr60, 25 minutes). Trains run about twice hourly.

NORTH COAST

Gorgeous white-sand beaches with shallow water and gentle waves line the northern Kattegat coast. Although the scattered small towns and villages only have a few thousand residents in winter, in summer the holiday homes fill and throngs of beachgoers, creating a salubrious sunshine-and-ice-cream atmosphere.

Hornbæk

POP 3500

'Denmark's St Tropez!', shout the tourist brochures. There are two similarities: Hornbæk's Blue-Flag beach, a vast expanse of soft white sand, is just as beautiful as any you'll find in southern France, and the patch certainly attracts more than its fair share of foxy young socialites.

Danish artists first discovered the attractions of this little-known fishing village in the 19th century, with early tourists following hot on their heels. Thanks to some geographical peculiarities, Hornbæk enjoys more sunshine than anywhere in Denmark.

Sights & Activities

Hornbæk Beach BEACH

Hornbæk's gorgeous Blue-Flag beach is the best on the north coast and the town's main attraction. The sand is white and the air scented with salt and wild roses. The beach stretches out to either side of the harbour, and even though it borders the town, it's pleasantly undeveloped, with all the commercial facilities on the other side of the dunes. The eastern side is where the kitesurfers and windsurfers hang out: you'll need your own gear to join them.

From the train station it's a five-minute walk – about 200m – directly north along Havnevej to the harbour. Climb the dunes to the left and you're on the beach.

Hornbæk Plantage WALKING

For an enjoyable nature stroll, Hornbæk Plantage, a public woodland that extends 3.5km along the coast east from Hornbæk, has numerous interconnecting trails branching out on either side of Rte 237. One trail hugs the coast from Lochersvej in Hornbæk to the eastern end of the plantage. There are several areas along Nordre Strandvej (Rte 237) where you can park your car and start your wanderings. A free map *Vandreture i Statsskovene, Hornbæk Plantage* shows all the trails and is available from the tourist office.

Sleeping

Hornbæk Camping DCU CAMPGROUND €

(☑49 70 02 23; www.camping-hornbaek.dk; Planetvej 4; campsite per adult/child Dkr80/50; ☺year-round) Nestling up to the woods of Hornbæk Plantage, this three-star camping ground is about 1.5km southeast of the town centre, off Sauntevej. It has good facilities – smart toilets, huts for hire, and a playground and 'bouncy pillow' for kids.

Hotel Hornbækhus HOTEL €€

(☑49 70 01 69; www.hornbaekhus.com; Skovvej 7; s/d incl breakfast Dkr895/995, without bathroom Dkr725/825; Ⓟ@🛜) Down another green lane full of flowers and birds, this is the grandest hotel in Hornbæk, with the feel of a stately home. Rooms are elegant and classically furnished, and some have their own balconies. There are also cheaper rooms with shared bathrooms available.

Ewaldsgården Guest House GUESTHOUSE €€

(☑49 70 00 82; www.ewaldsgaarden.dk; Johannes Ewalds Vej 5; s/d incl breakfast Dkr565/875; ☺mid-Jun–mid-Aug; Ⓟ@🛜) This 17th-century farmhouse pension is a delight, with a picture-perfect garden and a cosy mix of antiques and cottage-style furnishings. All 12 rooms have washbasins; showers and toilets are off the hall. There's also a simple guest kitchen. Ewaldsgården is a five-minute walk southeast of the train station.

Hotel Villa Strand HOTEL €€

(☑49 70 00 88; www.villastrand.dk; Kystvej 12; s/d incl breakfast Dkr895/995, without bathroom Dkr725/825; ☺Jun–Aug; Ⓟ🛜) If this hotel was any closer to the sea, it would be floating towards Sweden. Rooms in the main building are large, with cool white decor, floorboards and a lofty air. Rooms with shared bathroom facilities are cheaper.

Eating

Fiskehuset Hornbæk SEAFOOD €

(Havenevej 32; dishes Dkr45-75; ☺11am-8pm summer, shorter hrs rest of yr) Hornbæk's harbourside gem is the Fiskehuset, a humble fishmonger-cum-kiosk where punters happily devour the likes of smoked cod's roe, cured herring, smoked mackerel, fresh prawns, *fiskefrikadeller* (fish cakes), mussel soup and all manner of wonderful, fresh, local seafood. Best of all, you'll have change to spare.

Restaurant Søstrene Olsen DANISH, INTERNATIONAL €€

(Øresundsvej 10; lunch Dkr70-175, dinner mains Dkr175-325; ☺noon-4pm & 6-9pm Thu-Mon) Hornbæk is hardly a gourmet mecca, but you will find refined nosh at husband-and-wife team Thorleif and Minne Aagaard's charming thatched cottage right by the beach. With inspiration sourced from numerous cuisines, including Danish, French and Italian, you can expect anything from lunchtime Kalix caviar with blinis, pickled onions and herb cream, to evening homemade tortellini in a decadent Gorgonzola sauce.

Hansens Café DANISH €€

(☑49 70 04 79; Havnevej 19; lunch Dkr72-149, dinner mains Dkr178-238; ☺4pm-midnight Mon-Fri, 1pm-midnight Sat & Sun) Hansens is in the town's oldest house, an earthen-roofed half-timbered building with a pleasant publike atmosphere. The menu changes daily but you can expect to find solid grub such as *fiskefrikadeller* (fishballs) with homemade remoulade or moules marinière.

❶ Information

Tourist Office (☑ 49 70 47 47; www.hornbaek. dk; Vestre Stejlebakke 2A; ☺ 1-5pm Mon & Thu, 10am-3pm Tue, Wed & Fri, 10am-2pm Sat) Inside the library, just behind the northern side of Nordre Strandvej. Offers free internet access.

❶ Getting There & Around

Trains connect Hornbæk with Helsingør (Dkr36, 25 minutes) and Gilleleje (Dkr48, 20 minutes) about once or twice hourly.

Hornbæk Cykeludlejning (☑ 20 78 03 43; Nordre Strandvej 315D; bicycles per day/week Dkr100/600; ☺ 9am-noon & 3-4pm Mon-Wed, to 5pm Thu, 10am-noon Sat & Sun) Rents bicycles.

Gilleleje

POP 6510

A fishing village since the 14th century, Zealand's northernmost town retains a certain timeless character. During WWII, Gilleleje's fishing boats were used to smuggle thousands of Jews to neutral Sweden, but don't expect any such excitement today. Low-key charms include a string of beaches, an early morning harbourside auction, bustling fish restaurants, and a coastal walk to a small monument dedicated to Kierkegaard. Between Hornbæk and Gilleleje is Tegners Museum and Statuepark, devoted to one of Denmark's leading sculptors.

◉ Sights & Activities

Rudolph Tegners Museum & Statuepark   MUSEUM
(www.rudolphtegner.dk; Museumsvej 19, Villingerød; adult/child Dkr50/free; ☺ 11am-6pm Tue-Sun Jun-Aug, noon-5pm Tue-Sun mid-Apr–May & Sep–mid-Oct) One of the first Danish sculptors to discover concrete, Rudolph Tegner (1873–1950) used the wild heathland midway between Gilleleje and Hornbæk as a backdrop for his monumental sculptures, made of plaster, clay, bronze and marble. This museum now displays more than 250 of Tegner's pieces, while the surrounding grounds showcase 14 of his monumental bronze sculptures. The museum also functions as a mausoleum – Tegner is buried in a chamber in the heart of the building. From Gilleleje, bus 362 reaches Museumsvej.

Fyrhistorik Museum på Nakkehoved   MUSEUM
(Fyrvejen 20; adult/child Dkr40/free; ☺ 11am-4pm Tue-Sun mid-Jun–Aug, shorter hrs rest of yr) The eastern lighthouse is now the Fyrhistorik Museum på Nakkehoved, which traces the history of Danish lighthouses from the 16th century. You can get to the lighthouse on the coastal footpath or by turning north off Rte 237 onto Fyrvejen.

Gilleleje Museum   MUSEUM
(Vesterbrogade 56; adult/child Dkr35/free; ☺ 1-4pm Wed-Mon Jun-Aug, 1-4pm Wed-Fri, 10am-2pm Sat Sep-May) This museum on the western side of town runs through Gilleleje's history from the Middle Ages to the advent of summer tourism. It includes a 19th-century fisherman's house.

Beaches   BEACH
Although they aren't as long and golden as those at Hornbæk or Tisvildeleje, beaches surround the town. The one on the western side, a stretch of sand and stone, meets Blue-Flag standards and comes with lifeguards in summer.

Walking Trails   WALKING
Of the two **coastal trails**, the one to the west, which starts near the intersection of Nordre Strandvej and Vesterbrogade, leads 1.75km to a stone **memorial** dedicated to the Danish philosopher Søren Kierkegaard, who used to make visits to this coast.

The trail to the east begins just off Hovedgade and leads 2.5km to the site where two lighthouses with coal-burning beacons were erected in 1772.

⊨ Sleeping

There are no hostels or camping grounds in Gilleleje, but tourist office staff can book rooms in private homes for around Dkr450/800 for singles/doubles, plus a Dkr35 booking fee.

Gilleleje Badehotel   HOTEL €€
(☑ 48 30 13 47; www.gillelejebadehotel.dk; Hulsøvej 15; r incl breakfast from Dkr1090; ℗ 🛜) Kierkegaard was a frequent guest at this luxurious beach hotel. The atmosphere is so richly nostalgic you half expect the hotel to be sepia-tinted, but instead a soothing egg-white colour scheme prevails. All the rooms are bright and sunlit and most have balconies with views of Sweden. The hotel also offers a sauna, steam room and massage treatments. You'll find it 1km west of town.

Eating

Adamsen's Fisk
SEAFOOD €

(Gilleleje Havn; meals Dkr50-79; ⊗11am-9pm, sushi bar 11am-8pm) This popular harbourside takeaway dishes up fish, seafood, sides of chips and more salubrious salads. The fish and seafood are heavily battered, so delicate stomachs and waist-watchers may prefer the grilled options. After selecting your combo, you're given a token which flashes when your order is ready. For those who prefer their fish raw, Adamsen's has a sushi bar next door (10-piece sushi set Dkr130).

Rogeriet Bornholm
SMOKEHOUSE €

(Gilleleje Havn; fish Dkr40-60; ⊗8am-6.30pm Mon-Fri, to 5.30pm Sat & Sun) Close to Adamsen's Fisk, this simple smokehouse sells inexpensive smoked fish by the piece.

Isen
ICE CREAM €

(Vesterbrogade 3; 2 scoops Dkr30; ⊗noon-9pm Mon-Fri, 11am-9pm Sat & Sun Jul & Aug, reduced hrs rest of yr) A stickler for tradition, ice-cream peddler Isen crafts its waffle cones in wrought-iron molds. Filling them is north Zealand's revered Hansen ice cream, made with proper, old-fashioned cream. Needless to say, the result is sublime. Don't let the queues put you off – good things come to the patient!

Restaurant Brasseriet
SEAFOOD €€

(Nordre Havnevej 3; lunch Dkr58-148, dinner mains Dkr188-255; ⊗noon-4pm & 5.30-9pm) By the harbour and featuring a shady courtyard, Brasseriet keeps the lunch crowds purring with its tasty Danish classics, among them succulent *fiskefrikadeller* (fish cakes) with red onion creme tartar. The more limited dinner menu usually includes a daily fish special, as well as a steak and pasta dish. Vegetarians will struggle.

Gilleleje Havn
DANISH €€

(www.gillelejehavn.dk; Havnevej 14; lunch Dkr78-138, dinner mains Dkr170-250; ⊗11.30am-10pm daily) Gilleleje Havn is an excellent modern option, with an open kitchen and Danish-inspired grub. Fish and seafood predominate, with solid choices including lobster-pimped fish soup and Gilleleje Toast, a whisker-licking concoction of fresh seafood salad, shrimp, roe and crab claws on toasted bread. Turf options include a pulled pork sandwich and spare ribs with coleslaw and BBQ sauce.

ⓘ Information

Tourist Office (www.visitnordsjaelland.dk; Gilleleje Stationsvej 10; ⊗10am-5pm Mon-Fri, to

2pm Sat Jul-early Aug, 10am-4pm Mon-Fri May-Jun & mid-Aug–late Sep) At the train station.

ⓘ Getting There & Around

Trains run between Hillerød and Gilleleje (Dkr60, 30 minutes), and between Helsingør and Gilleleje (Dkr72, 45 minutes), once to twice hourly.

Tisvildeleje

Tisvildeleje is essentially a glorious sweep of golden-sand beach with a small seaside village attached. The beach is backed by hills and forests, threaded through with nature trails. You could easily spend several relaxing days here, sunbathing, swimming, strolling through the woods, poking around the town's boutiques, and generally taking things very, very easy.

⊙ Sights & Activities

Beach
BEACH

The Blue-Flag beach, a kilometre-long stretch of pure sand at the foot of the village, is the reason people flock to Tisvildeleje. A shallow-sloping shore and lifeguards at the height of summer make it a favourite with families. There are toilets and an ice-cream kiosk at the edge of the large parking area. Other beaches are accessible a short walk away from town.

Forest Trails
WALKING

From the car park, you can walk along the beach or on a dirt path through the woods, about 3km south to **Troldeskoven** (Witch Wood), an area of ancient trees that have been sculpted into haunting shapes by the wind.

Inland from the beach is **Tisvilde Hegn**, a forest of twisted trees and heather-covered hills that extends southwest for more than 8km. Tisvilde Hegn has numerous trails, including one to **Asserbo Slotsruin**, the moat-encircled ruins of a 12th-century manor house and monastery, near the southern boundary of the forest.

Interestingly, much of this enchanting forest was planted in the 18th century to stabilise sand drifts engulfing the area. Trail maps are available free from the tourist office.

🛏 Sleeping & Eating

Tisvildeleje has a good **bakery** (Hovedgaden 60; ⊗7am-6pm), and there's a grocery shop further up the street. A couple of kiosks, one in town and one at the beach car park, sell burgers, hot dogs, pizzas and ice cream.

Danhostel Tisvildeleje HOSTEL € (☎48 70 98 50; www.helene.dk; Bygmarken 30; dm/s/d Dkr200/680/700; ⊙year-round; P@☎) One kilometre east of town, this modern hostel shares the excellent facilities of the Sankt Helene holiday complex. The grounds cover 12 hectares, with walking trails, sports fields, playgrounds, kids' activities and a decent restaurant, as well as easy access to a sandy beach. By train, get off at Godhavn station, one stop before Tisvildeleje: the hostel is a short walk north.

Bed & Breakfast Hårlandsgård GUESTHOUSE € (☎48 70 83 96; www.haarlandsgaard.dk; Harlands Allé 12; s Dkr420, d Dkr560-600; P) This 18th-century farmhouse, about 1km from town near Godhavn station, has a sunny garden, comfy rooms, and an art gallery in the former stables. Breakfast is an extra Dkr60. It's the house on the right-hand side of the first sharp turn of Harlands Allé.

Tisvildeleje Strand Hotel HOTEL €€ (☎48 70 71 19; www.strand-hotel.dk; Hovedgaden 75; s/d Dkr1050/1350; ⊙late Jun–mid-Aug; P☎) Neutral tones, art books and weathered antiques give the place a chic 'Hamptons' vibe. Rooms are a soothing combo of coconut rug carpets, woollen throws and contemporary charcoal-hued toilets. The three rooms with shared toilet are cheaper (Dkr850). The hotel also has a popular restaurant, though its future management and direction was under review on our last visit.

★**Helenekilde Badehotel** BOUTIQUE HOTEL €€€ (☎48 70 70 01; www.helenekilde.com; Strandvejen 25; r with sea view incl breakfast from Dkr1695, r without sea view incl breakfast from Dkr1395; P☎) Like Tisvildeleje Strand, the interior of this enchanting beachfront hotel was designed by the ballet dancer Alexander Kolpin. The cosy communal areas feature beautiful furnishings, art and the odd vintage suitcase-turned-coffee table, while the rooms themselves are simple yet elegant, with 16 of them looking out over the waves.

Dreamy sea views are also on tap at its casually elegant **restaurant** (lunch Dkr245, 3-course dinner Dkr425; ⊙noon-2pm & 6-8.30pm daily, closed Sun Sep-May), which serves up a daily-changing menu of honest, rustic Danish fare. It's always advisable to book a table in advance, especially from September to May. The hotel is a five-minute walk along a leafy lane (signposted from the station).

Tisvildeleje Cafeen INTERNATIONAL €€ (Hovedgaden 55; mains Dkr129-162; ⊙11am-11pm daily summer, shorter hrs rest of yr) A popular spot, complete with alfresco summertime seating, Tisvildeleje Cafeen delivers a worldly menu spanning salads and burgers, to curry and fish soup. Happy hour runs from 5pm to 7pm Friday to Sunday, with cheaper beer and cocktails. The cafe features live music and DJs on Friday and Saturday nights in summer.

ℹ Getting There & Around

Getting round the coast from Gilleleje to Tisvildeleje by public transport isn't as simple as it might be. From Gilleleje, catch bus 360R to Helsinge, then the train to Tisvildeleje (Dkr36, 50 minutes Monday to Saturday, 80 minutes Sunday). Services run half-hourly to hourly on weekdays, and hourly on weekends. Trains also run between Tisvildeleje and Hillerød (Dkr60, 30 minutes) every 30 to 60 minutes.

FJORD TOWNS

Roskilde Fjord slices its way over 30km inland. Several towns lie scattered around its shores, the best of which is undoubtedly Roskilde itself, an unmissable tourist spot with its fascinating Unesco-blessed cathedral, Viking artefacts and epic annual rock festival.

Roskilde

POP 48,720

In July fans pour into town for the four-day Roskilde Festival, which vies with Glastonbury for the title of Europe's biggest rock festival. Anyone who's anyone on the international scene has played here – past crowds have grunged out to Nirvana, head-banged before Metallica and busted some moves to the Arctic Monkeys.

If you're not a festival fan, pity the poor fools for their warm beer and toilet queues, and relish the town instead. Roskilde is justly famous for its superb Viking Ship Museum and iconic cathedral, the burial site of Danish royalty.

The town itself came to prominence in the Viking Age, when it was the capital of Denmark. Harald Bluetooth built Zealand's first wooden-stave Christian church here in

AD 980. It was replaced by a stone building in 1026 on the instructions of a woman named Estrid, whose husband was assassinated in the stave church after a heated chess match (only in Scandinavia!). The foundations of the 11th-century stone church are beneath the floor of the present-day cathedral.

Medieval Roskilde was a thriving trade centre and the powerhouse of Danish Catholicism, big enough to support the country's grandest cathedral. The town began its decline when the capital moved to Copenhagen in the early 15th century, and its population shrank radically after the Reformation in 1536.

These days, Roskilde is a popular day trip from Copenhagen, a mere 30km away.

◉ Sights

★ **Viking Ship Museum**   MUSEUM
(☑46 30 02 00; www.vikingeskibsmuseet.dk; Vindeboder 12; adult/child May–mid-Oct Dkr115/free, mid-Oct–Apr Dkr80/free, boat trip excl museum Dkr90; ☺10am-5pm late Jun–mid-Aug, to 4pm rest of yr, boat trips daily mid-May–Sep) Viking fans will be wowed by the superb Viking Ship Museum, which displays five Viking ships discovered at the bottom of Roskilde Fjord. The museum is made up of two main sections – the Viking Ship Hall, where the boats themselves are kept; and Museumsø, where archaeological work takes place. There are free 45-minute guided tours in English daily at noon and 3pm from late June to the end of August, and at noon on weekends from May to late June and in September.

➡ **Viking Ship Hall**

Roskilde's Viking-era inhabitants were expecting trouble in the mid-11th century. Five clinker-built ships, all made between 1030 and 1042, were deliberately scuttled in a narrow channel 20km north of Roskilde, presumably to block an attacking army. Once they had been holed and sunk, a mass of stones was piled on top to create an underwater barrier.

In 1962 a coffer dam was built around the barrier and sea water was pumped out. Within four months, archaeologists were able to remove the mound of stones and excavate the ships, whose wooden hulks were in thousands of pieces. These ship fragments were painstakingly reassembled onto skeleton frames in the purpose-built Viking Ship Hall. This brutal-looking minimalist construction becomes something magical inside, where the ghostly boats seem to float once more on the waters of the fjord.

The ships, known as Skuldelev 1, 2, 3, 5 and 6, show off the range of the Viking shipwrights: there's an ocean-going trading vessel, a 30m warship for international raiding, a coastal trader, a 17m warship probably used around the Baltic, and a fishing boat. Carbon dating and dendrochronology have discovered further secrets, including their builders' geographical scope – *Skuldelev 1*, for example, was made in Norway, whereas *Skuldelev 2* came from Dublin.

Interesting displays about the Viking Age put the boats into a historical context, and the basement cinema runs a 14-minute film (in Danish, English, French, German, Italian and Spanish) about the 1962 excavation. There's also a fascinating exhibition and film documenting the nail-biting 2007 voyage of the Havhingsten fra Glendalough from Roskilde to Dublin and back. Based on the 60-oared warship Skuldelev 2, it's the largest Viking ship reconstruction to date (an incredible 340 trees went into its creation).

➡ **Museumsø**

On Museum Island, adjacent to the Viking Ship Hall, craftspeople use Viking-era techniques and tools to build replicas of Viking ships. *Ottar, Havhingsten fra Glendalough, Roar Ege, Helge Ask* and *Kraka Fyr* (reconstructions of Skuldelev 1, 2, 3, 5 and 6 respectively) are moored in the harbour, where you can appreciate their light, flexible designs.

In summer a shipwright, blacksmith, tar-burner, weaver, rope-maker and fletcher demonstrate their crafts. Children can join in the fun by striking coins and painting their own shields.

➡ **Boat Trips**

If you've always had an urge to leap aboard a longboat for a spot of light pillaging, join one of the museum's hour-long boat trips. Traditional Nordic boats are propelled across the water by you and the rest of your shipmates.

From mid-May to the end of September, 50-minute trips run one to three times daily, with an additional two to three trips daily from late June to mid-August, weather dependent. Call ahead to confirm sailing times. Tickets (Dkr90) are additional to the main museum entry ticket.

★ **Roskilde Domkirke**   CATHEDRAL
(www.roskildedomkirke.dk;   Domkirkepladsen; adult/child Dkr60/free; ☺9am-5pm Mon-Sat,

ZEALAND ROSKILDE

Roskilde

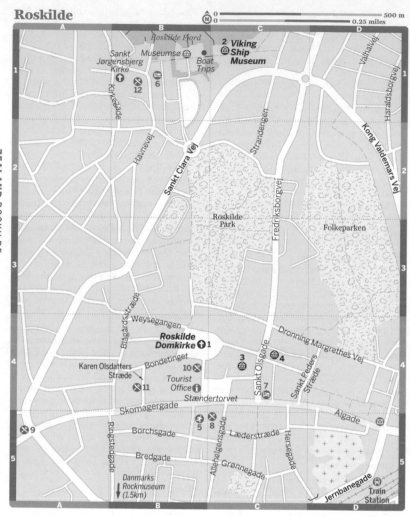

12.30-5pm Sun Apr-Sep, shorter hrs rest of yr) Not merely the crème de la crème of Danish cathedrals, this twin-towered giant is a designated Unesco World Heritage site. Started by Bishop Absalon in 1170, the building has been rebuilt and tweaked so many times that it's now a superb showcase of 800 years' worth of Danish architecture. As the royal mausoleum, it contains the crypts of 37 Danish kings and queens – contemplating the remains of so many powerful historical figures is a moving memento mori.

No fewer than 11 chapels and crypts sprout from the main body of the cathedral. The **chapel of King Christian IV**, off the northern side of the building, contains the builder-king himself. His coffin, surrounded by processing angels, is quite low-key for such an extravagant monarch. Most of the decoration in the chapel – vast, overly dramatic paintings of Christian's life surrounded by trompe l'oeil details – is actually from the 19th century, as the original sepulchre burned down a year before Christian's death. The only contemporary features are the chapel gates, so ornate they were said to have been created by the devil himself (although really the work of Christian's favourite metalsmith Caspar Fincke).

Roskilde

◎ **Top Sights**
1 Roskilde Domkirke................................B4
2 Viking Ship Museum..............................C1

◎ **Sights**
3 Museum for Samtidskunst...................C4
4 Roskilde Museum C4

◎ **Activities, Courses & Tours**
5 Jupiter Cykler..B5

◎ **Sleeping**
6 Danhostel Roskilde B1
7 Hotel Prindsen C4

◎ **Eating**
8 Café Vivaldi...C5
9 Gimle A5
10 Raadhuskælderen B4
11 Restaurant Mumm B4
12 Store Børs B1

There are some fantastic 15th-century frescoes (the largest in Denmark) in the **chapel of the Magi**. It also contains the Renaissance sepulchres of Christian III and Frederik II, the most ornate in the cathedral. They look like antique temples, guarded by halberd-bearing soldiers. Another interesting feature of the chapel is the Royal Column, which shows the heights of visiting princes – from Christian I at a lofty 219.5cm down to titchy Christian VII at 164.1cm.

The neoclassical **chapel of Frederik V** whispers 'death' like no other part of the cathedral. Twelve members of the royal family are interred here, in sepulchres, surrounded by skulls, angels and weeping women.

The **nave** contains Christian IV's private box, and an intricate 17th-century pulpit (1610) made of marble, alabaster and sandstone by Copenhagen sculptor Hans Brokman. A killjoy dean disconnected the mechanism of the wonderful **clock** in the 18th century, annoyed that his parishioners paid more attention to it than to him, but today's church-people have relented. St George slays the dragon on the hour; the poor beast lets out a pitiful wheeze; and two ballad characters ting the bells.

Margrethe I's elegant sarcophagus and the golden altarpiece in the **choir** attract crowds of admirers. We prefer the wonderfully lively 15th-century choir-stall carvings: highlights from the New Testament line the northern side, and fearsome Old Testament tales adorn the south – Joseph being stuffed down a hole, Judith chopping off Holofernes' head, and Noah's family crammed into the ark...

Free concerts on the 16th-century baroque pipe organ are usually held at 8pm on Thursday in June, July and August. It's not unusual for the cathedral to be closed on Saturday for weddings, particularly in spring.

Danmarks Rockmuseum
MUSEUM
(www.danmarksrockmuseum.dk; Rabalderstræde 1) Scheduled to open in mid-2015, the Denmark Museum of Rock Music will deliver a multi-sensory journey through the wild, often transgressive history of rock and roll. Interactive exhibitions will have visitors laying out remixing hits, practising various dance steps, and rocking to a virtual Roskilde Festival crowd. Check the website for opening times and pricing. From Roskilde train station, buses 202A and 212 stop 350m from the museum.

Museum for Samtidskunst
MUSEUM
(samtidskunst.dk; Stændertorvet 3D; adult/child Dkr40/free; ◎ noon-4pm Tue-Sun, to 8pm first Wed of month) Housed in the 18th-century Roskilde Palace (built to be used by Christian VI whenever he was in town) is this cutting-edge contemporary art space. Exhibitions lean towards new media, with often perplexing sound, video or performance installations by both Danish and international artists.

Roskilde Museum
MUSEUM
(www.roskildemuseum.dk; Sankt Olsgade 18; adult/child Dkr25/free; ◎ 11am-4pm) Delve into Roskilde's rich history, from the Stone Age through Harald Bluetooth's legacy and the first railway in Denmark.

🏃 Activities

Jupiter Cykler
CYCLING
(☑ 46 35 04 20; www.jupitercykler.dk; Gullandsstræde 3; per day Dkr100; ◎ 9am-5.30pm Mon-Thu, to 6pm Fri, to 2pm Sat) This centrally located shop rents bikes.

🛏 Sleeping

Roskilde has limited accommodation for its size; being so close to Copenhagen, it's a popular day-trip destination.

Danhostel Roskilde
HOSTEL €
(☑ 46 35 21 84; www.danhostel.dk/roskilde; Vindeboder 7; dm/s/d Dkr250/575/700; 🅿 🛜) Roskilde's modern hostel sits right next door to the Viking Ship Museum, on the waterfront.

ROSKILDE ROCKS

Denmark's answer to Glastonbury and northern Europe's music festival heavyweight, **Roskilde Festival** (www.roskilde-festival.dk) is a four-day binge of bands and booze that rocks Roskilde every summer in late June or early July.

Since 1971 it has attracted the biggest and best international performers – over 160 rock, techno and world-music bands play on seven stages. The line-up in 2014 included The Rolling Stones, Arctic Monkeys, Jack White, Stevie Wonder, and Trentemøller. The promoters are astute at trend-spotting, so expect to also catch hot new bands who haven't yet come into the spotlight.

While the music is the main protagonist, there are plenty of other diversions, including a swimming lake, food workshops, art events, and a naked run! Many people camp from the Sunday before the festival starts, spending four days 'warming up' for the festival proper. Stalls sell everything from tattoos to produce-driven food but you may want to bring some food supplies as prices are high.

Full festival tickets start from Dkr1965 and can be purchased on the official festival website, which has a link to **Billetnet** (www.billetnet.dk). If lugging your own tent along seems bothersome, you can rent one from Dkr825 (excluding festival pass).

Advance sales usually start around October. All 75,000-plus tickets are usually sold by June, so it pays to bag yours early.

Pimped with funky black and white murals, each of the 40 large rooms has its own shower and toilet. Staff are friendly, although the mattress we slept on was frustratingly lop-sided. Cheekily, wi-fi is an extra Dkr20 per hour (Dkr100 per 24 hours).

Roskilde Camping   CAMPGROUND €
(☑ 46 75 79 96; www.roskildecamping.dk; Baunehøjvej 7, Veddelev; campsite per adult/child Dkr85/45; ☺ Apr-Sep) Beautifully situated on the edge of Roskilde Fjord, 4km north of the Viking Ship Museum, this three-star camping ground is family-friendly with good facilities. There's a sandy Blue-Flag beach on the doorstep. From Roskilde train station, catch bus 203 (Dkr24). Journey time is around 25 minutes.

Hotel Prindsen   HOTEL €€€
(☑ 46 30 91 00; www.prindsen.dk; Algade 13; s/d incl breakfast Dkr1395/1495; P @ 🛜) First opened in 1695, the centrally located Prindsen is Denmark's oldest hotel, with former guests including King Frederik VII and Hans Christian Andersen. Rooms are comfortable and classically styled. The carpet-free Nordisk rooms (s/d Dkr1505/1605) are larger than the standard rooms, but not really worth the extra cost. Rates often drop on weekends and public holidays.

🍴 Eating

Gimle   INTERNATIONAL €
(www.gimle.dk; Helligkorsvej 2; meals Dkr49-99; ☺ noon-midnight Tue & Wed, to 2am Thu, to 5am Fri & Sat, 10am-5pm Sun; 🛜 🍽) Gimle covers all bases, from laidback cafe and cultural hub, to live-music venue and weekend nightclub. Pull up a retro chair and munch on simple, tasty grub such as sandwiches, dahl, nachos and burgers (including a vegetarian version). Sunday brunch is served from 10am to 1pm, and wi-fi is free.

Store Børs   DANISH, INTERNATIONAL €€
(☑ 46 32 50 45; www.store-bors.dk; Havnevej 43; lunch Dkr89-198, dinner mains Dkr198-278, 7-course tasting menu Dkr495; ☺ 5-9.30pm Tue-Sat, also noon-3.30pm Sat & Sun) Located down by the harbour, this melon-coloured cottage cooks up some of the town's finest food. The chefs smoke their own fish, use herbs from the restaurant garden, and create soulful evening gems such as fried mackerel with smoked potatoes, tarragon cream and sprouts.

Raadhuskælderen   DANISH, INTERNATIONAL €€
(www.raadhuskaelderen.dk; Stændertorvet; smørrebrød Dkr68-118, dinner mains Dkr188-348; ☺ 11am-9pm Mon-Sat; 🛜) Another reliable nosh spot is this atmospheric restaurant in the cellar of the old town hall (c 1430). Herring platters, shrimps, salads, a burger and open sandwiches feature on the lunch menu. Come dinner, you might see racks of lamb paired with tzatziki and rosemary sauce, or smoked salmon carpaccio prepared with breadcrumbs. Vegetarians may struggle.

Café Vivaldi   INTERNATIONAL €€
(Stændertorvet 8; sandwiches & salads Dkr99-109, mains Dkr169-199; ☺ 10am-10pm Sun-Thu, to 11pm

Fri & Sat) Slap bang on the main square (cathedral views included), this faux-bistro is a good place to sit back and people-watch over abundant servings of tasty cafe grub. Edibles include soup, sandwiches, wraps, burgers and salads, as well as more substantial pasta and meat dishes. It's particularly handy on Sundays, when most of the town shuts down.

Restaurant Mumm   DANISH, INTERNATIONAL €€€
(☑ 46 37 22 01; www.mummroskilde.com; Karen Olsdatters Stræde 9; dishes Dkr120; ☺ 5.30-11pm Mon-Sat) One of Roskilde's more exclusive dining destinations, intimate Mumm melds Danish and global influences to create contemporary tasting dishes like glazed veal sweetbread with pickled onions and malt soil. Four to six dishes should fill most bellies. Book ahead.

❶ Information

Library (www.roskildebib.dk; Dronning Margrethes Vej 14; ☺ 10am-7pm Mon-Fri, 10am-2pm Sat year-round, plus noon-4pm Sun mid-Sep–mid-Apr) Free internet access.

Post Office (Algade 51; ☺ 10am-5.30pm Mon-Fri, to 1pm Sat) Inside the Kvickly supermarket building.

Tourist Office (☑ 46 31 65 65; www.visitroskilde.com; Stændertorvet 1; ☺ 10am-5pm Mon-Fri, to 1pm Sat) The tourist office provides information, as well as accommodation options.

❶ Getting There & Around

CAR
If you're coming from Copenhagen by car, Rte 21 leads to Roskilde. Upon approaching the city, exit onto Rte 156, which leads into the centre. There is a large car park down by the Viking Ship Museum.

TRAIN
Trains between Copenhagen and Roskilde are frequent (Dkr96, 25 minutes).

Lejre

The superb experimental archaeology centre outside Lejre (a tiny village about 8km southwest of Roskilde) is like nothing we've ever seen.

◉ Sights

Sagnlandet Lejre   MUSEUM
(www.sagnlandet.dk; Slangealleen 2; adult/child Dkr130/85; ☺ 10am-5pm daily late Jun–mid-Aug, reduced hrs rest of yr) Easily reached from Lejre train station on bus 233, this experimental

ZEALAND LEJRE

WORTH A TRIP

DRAGSHOLM SLOT
· ·

Fancy a night in a culinary castle? Then pack your bag and your appetite and check in at **Dragsholm Slot** (☑ 59 65 33 00; www.dragsholm-slot.dk; Dragsholm Allé, Hørve; s/d from Dkr1895/1995; ℗). Located at the edge of Zealand's fertile Lammefjorden (Denmark's most famous 'vegetable garden'), its medieval walls are home to **Slotskøkkenet** (Castle Kitchen; 5/7 courses Dkr700/900; ☺ 6-10pm Wed-Sat Jun, 6-10pm Tue-Sat Jul-early Sep, reduced hrs rest of yr), a New Nordic hot spot headed by ex-Noma chef Claus Henriksen. 'Locally sourced' is the catch-cry, from the area's prized carrots to herbs from the castle's own garden. The end result is deceptively simple, with sublime creations such as watercress and crayfish with radish and smoked lard, or candied herbs with skyr and celeriac. Upstairs, the more casual **Lammefjordens Spisehus** (2-course lunch Dkr245, 3-course dinner Dkr345; ☺ noon-3pm & 6-10pm daily) offers cheaper, pared-back Nordic dishes using the same top-notch ingredients (think herb-marinated herring or hay-smoked salmon). Bookings are a must for Slotskøkkenet and recommended for Spisehuset.

Nosh aside, whitewashed Dragsholm is famed for its 800-year history, which includes the imprisonment of Roskilde's last Catholic bishop and the secret burial of a love-struck girl in the castle walls (eerily visible behind a plexiglass panel). While some rooms – spread across the castle and the nearby porter's lodge – feature contemporary styling, most ooze a distinguished baronial air, with anything from canopy beds to fleur-de-lis wallpaper and (in some cases) Jacuzzis. Add to this a string of Late Romantic salons and ballrooms and rambling fairy-tale gardens, and you'll soon be feeling like a well-fed noble. Check the website for dinner and accommodation packages (often cheaper than the official room rates), and request a room with field or garden views.

Dragsholm Slot is 91km west of Copenhagen via motorway 21. Getting here by public transport is very difficult.

archaeology centre is truly fascinating. Enthusiastic re-enactors use ancient technology to test out various theories: how many people does it take to build a dolmen? What plants might have been used to dye clothing? And how do you stop the goats eating your reed roof? Kids can let loose in the hands-on Fire Valley, paddling dug-out canoes, attempting to work a fire drill, and chopping up logs using primitive axes.

The landscape at Lejre is simply beautiful, with rolling hills and lake-filled hollows. A 3km-long path takes you past a Viking Age marketplace, prehistoric burial mounds, a dancing labyrinth and the Iron Age village 'Lethra', through fields of ancient crops, and down to a sacrificial pool and over precarious staked-wood bridges.

❶ Getting There & Away

From Roskilde it's just a short train ride to Lejre station, where bus 233 continues to both Ledreborg Slot and Sagnlandet Lejre (Dkr24).

By car, from Roskilde take Ringstedvej (Rte 14), turn right on Rte 156 and then almost immediately turn left onto Ledreborg Allé. Follow the signs to Ledreborg, 6km away, where a long drive lined by old elm trees leads to the entrance. Sagnlandet Lejre is 2km further west along the same road.

SOUTHERN ZEALAND

While northern Zealand lays claim to most of the island's must-see sites, the island's south is not without its drawcards. You'll find Denmark's best preserved ring fortress at Trelleborg and its oldest half-timbered house in Køge. The region is also home to one of Denmark's most shamelessly charming enchanting hamlets, Vallø, as well as the Unesco World Heritage–listed natural wonder that is Stevns Klint.

Køge

POP 35,770

Køge is a pretty town that, if not worth a special visit, offers a pleasant diversion if you're passing through on your way to Bornholm (by ferry), Stevns Klint, or the south islands.

The one-time medieval trading centre retains a photogenic core of cobbled streets flanked by Denmark's best-preserved 17th- and 18th-century buildings. At its heart is Torvet, the nation's largest square.

You'll find narrow beaches along the bay to the north and south of town, although you'll need to ignore the somewhat industrial backdrop of the modern commercial harbour.

In 1677 a vital naval engagement was fought in the waters off Køge. Known as the Battle of Køge Bay, it made a legend of Danish admiral Niels Juel, who resoundingly defeated the attacking Swedish navy.

◉ Sights

Køge Museum MUSEUM
(📞 56 63 42 42; www.koegemuseum.dk; Nørregade 4) Occupying a half-timbered 17th-century abode, the revamped Køge Museum uses state-of-the-art technology to bring to life its local-history artefacts. One exhibition examines the ill-fated 17th-century battleship *Dannebroge,* while another explores the Strøby Egede grave from 4000 BC. Containing the skeletons of eight children and adults, it's the only mass grave from that era to be found in Europe. The museum is also home to Denmark's biggest coin-hoard, a pile of 17th-century silver unearthed in the courtyard at Brogade 17 by two electricians. The 32kg pile is thought to have been stashed away during the Danish-Swedish wars.

In Hans Christian Andersen's day, a local inn was supposed to have had the words 'God, Oh God in Kjøge' scratched onto a windowpane. Failing to find the inscription, Andersen vandalised a window himself – writing smugly in his diary 'I wrote it, and now it is very legible'. The museum has the glass on show.

KØS MUSEUM
(www.koes.dk; Vestergade 1; adult/18-24yr/child Dkr50/20/free; ⊙10am-5pm Tue-Sun) Køge's Museum of Art in Public Spaces, Køge Skitsesamling is a unique entity, displaying not the artists' finished work, but the notes and scribblings, sketches, models and mock-ups that built up into the final piece. It's fascinating, particularly for non-artists, to see the creative process deconstructed.

Sankt Nicolai Kirke CHURCH
(Kirkestræde 31; admission free, tower adult/child Dkr10/free; ⊙10am-4pm Mon-Fri, noon-4pm Sun, tower noon-4pm daily Jul-Aug) Sankt Nicolai Kirke was named after the patron saint of mariners, and the brick projection (called Lygten) on the upper eastern end of the church tower was used to hang a burning lantern to guide sailors returning to the harbour. In fact, it was

Køge

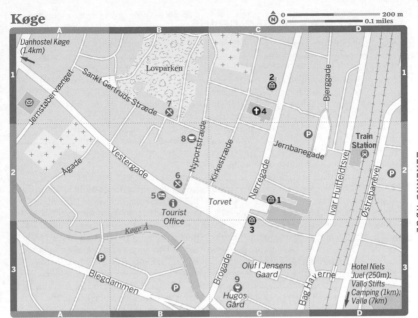

from the top of the tower that Christian IV kept watch on his naval fleet as it successfully defended the town from Swedish invaders during the Battle of Køge Bay.

Dating back to the 14th century, the tower is the oldest part of the church, and from July to early August visitors are able to climb it. Inside the church itself, features worth noting include the ornate 17th-century altar and pulpit, and the carved wooden gallery that raised Køge's nobility above the rabble. The church lies two blocks north of Torvet.

Harbour & Beaches   BEACH

Early risers can watch the fishermen unload herring and eels at the working harbour. The yacht harbour lies 2km to the north, and there are two beaches, lying north and south of the industrial harbour.

The inlet Køge Bay is well-known for the beaches at Solrød and Greve, 8km and 17km north of Køge, respectively. They're a popular escape for the city-dwellers of Copenhagen, just a short ride away on the city's S-train.

🛏 Sleeping

The tourist office can book rooms in private homes for around Dkr500 per double; there's a Dkr25 booking fee.

Køge

◉ Sights

1 Køge Museum	C2
2 KØS	C1
3 Rådhus	C3
4 Sankt Nicolai Kirke	C1

🛏 Sleeping

| 5 Centralhotellet | B2 |

🍴 Eating

| 6 Café Vivaldi | B2 |
| 7 StigAnn | B1 |

🍷 Drinking & Nightlife

| 8 Café T | B2 |
| 9 Hugos Vinkjælder | C3 |

Danhostel Køge   HOSTEL €
(☑ 56 67 66 50; www.danhostel-koege.dk; Vamdrupvej 1; dm Dkr200, r from Dkr380; ⓟ 🛜) In a quiet area 2km northwest of town, this friendly 116-bed hostel offers pleasant, cosy rooms; those upstairs have velux windows with relaxing sky views. The more expensive rooms come with toilets. There's a coin laundry, small playground and breakfast buffet (Dkr60). To get here from Køge, catch bus 101A and get off at Norsvej, from where the hostel is an 850m walk.

KØGE: THE OLD & THE BEAUTIFUL

Storybook buildings pepper the streets of Køge, turning the clock back a few hundred years and firing up the imagination. The Køge Museum (p114) is housed in a building dating back to the early 17th century, wine bar Hugos Vinkjælder contains a medieval brick-built cellar dating to 1300, and the neoclassical **Køge Rådhus** – on the eastern side of Torvet – is said to be the oldest functioning town hall in Denmark. At the back of the town hall is a building erected in 1600 to serve as an inn for King Christian IV, when he travelled from his Copenhagen palace to visit his mother at Nykøbing Slot.

Less heartwarming is a marble **plaque** marked Kiøge Huskors (Kiøge and Kjøge are old spellings of Køge) on the corner building at Torvet 2. It honours the victims of a witch-hunt in the 17th century, when 16 people were burned at the stake, including two residents of an earlier house on this site.

By the southeastern corner of Torvet, Brogade has no shortage of veteran buildings. **Brogade 1** has housed a pharmacy on this site since 1660, while **Brogade 16** is famed as Køge's longest timber-framed house, erected in 1636 by the town's mayor. In 1987 workers in the courtyard at **Brogade 17** unearthed an old wooden trunk filled with over 2000 17th-century silver coins, the largest coin-hoard ever found in Denmark. Some of these are now on display at the Køge Museum. Another 17th-century survivor is **Brogade 23** – built around 1638, its carved cherubs are the work of famed 17th-century artist Abel Schrøder.

Beating them all in the age stakes is the building at **Kirkestræde 20**, which hit the scene in 1527. Denmark's oldest half-timbered house, its 4m-by-5m dimensions once housed a late-19th-century tanner, his wife and 10 children. If you do drop by, also check out **Kirkestræde 3**. Built by Oluf Sandersen and his wife Margareta Jørgensdatter in 1638, the building's date is recorded in the lettering above the gate. Close by, **Kirkestræde 13** dates back to the 16th century, its twisting chimney pot was an advert to passers-by seeking a blacksmith.

Vallø Stifts Camping CAMPGROUND €
(☏ 56 65 28 51; www.valloecamping.dk; Strandvejen 102; campsite per adult/child Dkr78/45; ☺ Apr-early Oct; @ ☎) Only 1km from the centre of Køge, this leafy camping ground is inside a seaside nature reserve. It's ideal for families with young children – there are goats, mini-golf, table tennis, pétanque and playgrounds on-site, and a child-friendly beach just across the road. You can also rent out basic four- to six-person wooden huts (per night Dkr350 to Dkr590), as well as blankets, pillows and bed sheets.

Hotel Niels Juel HOTEL €€
(☏ 56 63 18 00; www.hotelnielsjuel.dk; Toldbodvej 20; s/d incl breakfast Dkr1225/1395; P ☎) Overlooking the harbour a couple of blocks south of the train station, this pleasant hotel/restaurant combo offers 51 well-furnished rooms in two colour schemes: maritime blue or warm-and-earthy. All include phone, minibar and satellite TV. Check the hotel website for discounts and special offers.

Centralhotellet HOTEL €€
(☏ 56 65 06 96; centralhotellet.dk; Vestergade 3; s/d incl breakfast without bathroom Dkr450/795, s/d with bathroom Dkr745/995; P ☎) The apt-ly named Centralhotellet is adjacent to the tourist office, complete with a slick cafe in the lobby. The rooms upstairs are straightforward and admittedly dowdy, while the renovated rooms in a separate wing at the back are lighter and slightly more modern. Four of the doubles have toilets.

✗ Eating

There's a produce, cheese and flower market on Torvet (the main square) on Wednesday and Saturday mornings. Just east of the train station on Havnepladsen is a string of restaurants in restored buildings by the port.

★ Restaurant Arkens SEAFOOD €€
(☏ 56 66 05 05; www.restaurant-arken.dk; Bådehavnen 21; lunch Dkr68-168, dinner mains Dkr158-288; ☺ 11.30am-9pm Mon-Thu & Sun, to 9.30pm Fri & Sat; ☎) This Skagen import has quite a reputation for sterling seafood, and its Køge outpost is no less drool-inducing. It's a case of top ingredients cooked well; superlative choices include the garlic gratin Norwegian lobster tails. There's a savvy choice of wines by the glass, as well as housemade schnapps and beer from Skagen. You'll find Arkens right on Køge marina, 2.5km north of Torvet.

StigAnn EUROPEAN €€

(✐56 63 03 30; www.stigann.dk; Sankt Gertruds Stræd 2; lunch Dkr70-110, dinner mains Dkr195-285; ☺4-10pm Tue, noon-4pm & 5-9.30pm Wed-Sat) One of Køge's best restaurants cooks up ambitious Danish dishes with global twists – think glazed lamb on spicy polenta and port wine sauce with grapes, or fried hake on pea risotto with crispy air-dried ham. Lunch is a simpler Danish affair, with staples like fish cakes with remoulade. Mains are mostly carnivorous.

Café Vivaldi INTERNATIONAL €€

(✐56 63 53 66; www.cafevivaldi.dk; Torvet 30; lunch Dkr95-149, dinner mains Dkr169-199; ☺10am-10pm Sun-Thu, to 11pm Fri, to midnight Sat) This chain 'bistro' is a safe bet for tasty, straightforward cafe nosh like salads, sandwiches, burgers, burritos as well as more substantial meat and fish dishes. Order at the counter. There's seating right on the square.

 Drinking

Hugos Vinkjælder WINE BAR

(Brogade 19; ☺noon-11pm Mon-Thu, noon-2am Fri, 10-2am Sat, 1-6pm Sun) Hugos is a fantastic place, a dark and cosy little wine bar curled up in a 14th-century cellar. The wine list is good, but it's the choice of over 200 beers from around the world that really thrills, including beers from several Danish microbreweries. In summer live jazz bands play in the courtyard around noon on Saturday.

Café T CAFE

(Nyportstræde 17; ☺8am-5.30pm Mon-Fri, to 4pm Sat, 10am-2.30pm Sun) Just off the main square, this oversized doll's house serves coffee, loose-leaf teas, and sweet treats like classic *kanelsnegle* (cinnamon roll) and scones with lemon curd. If you just can't live without the old sofas, retro lamps, or dainty tea sets, buy them; the cafe doubles as a bric-a-brac shop.

ⓘ Information

Library (✐56 65 23 00; www.koegebib.dk; Kirkestræde 18; ☺10am-6pm Mon-Fri, to 2pm Sat) Free internet.

Post Office (Jernstøbervænget 2; ☺8am-6pm Mon-Fri, to 1pm Sat)

Tourist Office (✐56 67 60 01; www.visitkoege. com; Vestergade 1; ☺9.30am-6pm Mon-Fri,

---

RINGSTED'S ROYAL CHURCH

Sankt Bendts Kirke (Sankt Bendtsgade 1; ☺10am-5pm May–mid-Sep, 11am-1pm Mon-Fri & 1-3pm Sat & Sun rest of year) Ringsted is mostly a modern town, with a bustling shopping centre but little in the way of tourist attractions. If you're passing through, however, it's worth stopping at the imposing Sankt Bendts Kirke, Scandinavia's oldest brick church. It was built in 1170 by Valdemar I, partly as a burial sanctuary for his father, Knud Lavard, and partly as a political act, to intertwine the influences of the Valdemar family and the Catholic Church.

Sankt Bendts' most interesting features are its magnificent 14th-century frescoes. These include a series depicting Erik IV (1216–50), whose short and turbulent reign saw him warring against his own family and the local peasantry, before he was assassinated on the orders of his brother Abel. The frescoes of Erik (known as 'Ploughpenny' for the despised tax he levied on ploughs) were painted in a doomed campaign to get the dead king canonised. They show Queen Agnes seated on a throne; on her left Ploughpenny's murderers stab the king with a spear, while on the right the king's corpse is retrieved from the sea by fishermen.

The church was a royal burial place for 150 years: flat stones in the aisle floor beneath the nave mark the graves of Denmark's early royals. An interesting find came from one of these tombs. Queen Dagmar (1186–1213), the first wife of Valdemar II, was a Bohemian princess revered by the Danes. In 1683 her tomb was opened and a small gold cross with finely detailed enamel work was discovered. Now known as the **Dagmar Cross**, it is thought to date from AD 1000. One side shows Christ with arms outstretched on the cross and the other side depicts him with the Virgin Mary, John the Baptist, St John and St Basil. The Byzantine-styled cross is now in the national museum in Copenhagen, with a replica on display in Sankt Bendts Kirke. Copies are traditionally worn by brides who marry in the church.

Note that the church is closed to visitors whenever there are weddings, a particularly common occurrence on Saturdays in April and May.

Ringsted lies 65km southwest of Copenhagen. If driving, take the E20 highway to exit 14. Trains to Ringsted run several times an hour from Copenhagen (Dkr88, 37 to 48 minutes), as well as from Roskilde (Dkr44, 16 to 22 minutes).

STEVNS KLINT: WORLD HERITAGE WONDER

Denmark's number of World Heritage sites increased in June 2014 when both the Wadden Sea and Stevns Klint were added to Unesco's illustrious list. The latter, a fossil-rich chalk and limestone cliff located south of Køge Bugt (Køge Bay), made the list for its superlative geological record of the Chicxulub meteorite. Crashing off the coast of Mexico's Yucatán peninsula around 65.5 million years ago, the meteor is believed to have ended the Cretaceous Period and the age of the dinosaurs. Evidence of the ash cloud that formed on impact, and of the flora pertaining to both the pre- and post-impact periods, is embedded in the thin, grey, horizontal strip of fish clay running along the middle of the cliff face, between the white chalk below and the limestone overhang above.

While visitors are currently unable to get close to the fish clay, the best place to see the stratification, not to mention to soak up the area's extraordinary natural beauty, is in Stevns Klint Højerup, 5km southeast of the town of Store Heddinge. It's here, at the southwest corner of the car park, that you'll find **Stevns Museum** (Højerup Bygade 38; adult/child Dkr25/free; ⊘10am-5pm daily Jul & Aug, 11am-5pm Tue-Sun May, Jun & Sep), which explores the coastline's unique geology. Directly east of the car park, on the edge of the cliff, stands the 13th-century church **Højerup Gamle Kirke** (⊘9am-5pm daily Jun-Sep, shorter hrs rest of yr). In March 1928 the chancel and part of the church's cemetery tumbled into the sea when part of the cliff gave way. As a result, the nave now leads to a small balcony offering a superb view of Stevns Klint and the sea.

To reach the base of Stevns Klint, you'll need to descend 110 steep steps just south of the church grounds. At the bottom, climb the second set of steps (beside the first) to avoid the rockiest part of the beach. The trail leads to the very foot of the cliff, from where it's possible to see the thin layer of fish clay half way up the cliff face.

Back at the top of the cliff, follow the walking trail just north of the church grounds for commanding views of Stevns Klint. The trail itself is beautiful, traversing woods, skirting fields of wheat, and overlooking the deep blue of the Øresund. An easy 1.3km north along the trail is **Stevns Fyr** (Fyrvej, Tommestrup; ⊘lighthouse 11am-3pm Mon-Fri, noon-3pm Sat & Sun; gallery 11am-4pm Mon-Fri, noon-4pm Sat & Sun), a lighthouse dating back to 1878. Beside it, Stevns Fyrcentre hosts temporary art exhibitions. In the spring and autumn, the area is a good spot to observe migratory birds, including cranes.

From Højerup Gamle Kirke, a 3km walk south along the trail leads to the **Koldkrigsmuseum Stevnsfort** (Cold War Museum; Korsnæbsvej 60, Rødvig; underground fortress guided tour adult/child Dkr110/60; ⊘10am-5pm daily Apr-Oct), where daily guided tours (90 minutes) allow access to a top-secret subterranean fortress used in the defence of Denmark and NATO during the Cold War. The tour is in Danish, though a limited number of audio guides are available in English and German.

You don't need to join a guided tour to explore the above-ground fortress area, which includes cannons and a Cold War exhibition in the visitors' centre. If you have a smartphone, consider downloading the free and informative Stevns Klint app (called Kalklandet), which makes for a handy guide to the area.

In Stevns Klint Højerup, **Ishuset Højeruplund** (2 scoops Dkr30; ⊘10am-8pm daily Apr-Aug) sells ice cream and refreshments, while the adjoining restaurant **Traktørstedet Højeruplund** (lunch Dkr85-152, dinner mains Dkr169-225; ⊘noon-8pm Jul & Aug, closed Mon Apr-Jun & Sep, shorter hrs rest of yr) serves classic, competent Danish grub (though very few non-meat options).

Stevns Klint lies 29km southeast of Køge. If driving, take route 261 to Store Heddinge and turn left into Frøslevvej (which becomes Højerupvej). If using public transport, catch bus 253 (Dkr60, 55 minutes) from Køge train station to Højerup, from where Stevns Klint is a 550m walk east along Højerup Bygade. In July and August a free shuttle bus runs several times daily from a few local train stations (including Store Heddinge and Rødvig) to points of interest along the coast, including Stevns Klint, Stevns Fyr and Koldkrigsmuseum Stevnsfort. See stevnsbussen.dk for times and details.

10am-3pm Sat Jul & Aug, 9.30am-5pm Mon-Fri, 10am-1pm Sat rest of yr; ☎) Just off the town's main square, the tourist office offers information and free wi-fi, and can also book accommodation.

❶ Getting There & Away

BOAT

Bornholmer Færgen (☎70 23 15 15; www.faergen.dk; adult/child 12-15/under 11 Dkr290/145/free, car incl 5 passengers Dkr1625) Runs daily, year-round ferries between Køge and Rønne, on the island of Bornholm. From Køge, the ferry departs at 12.30am, arriving in Rønne at 6am. From Rønne, the ferry leaves at 5pm, arriving in Køge at 10.30pm.

CAR

Køge is 42km southwest of Copenhagen and 23km southeast of Roskilde. If you're coming by road take the E47/E55 from Copenhagen or Rte 6 from Roskilde and then pick up Rte 151 south into the centre of Køge.

TRAIN

Køge is the southernmost station on greater Copenhagen's S-train network, at the end of the A line. Trains from Copenhagen (Dkr108, 45 minutes) run three to six times an hour.

❶ Getting Around

Car drivers can park in Torvet, but only for an hour; turn down Brogade, then follow Fændedi-get round for less-restricted free parking off Bag Haverne and north of the harbour.

Vallø

Tiny Vallø is a deeply romantic hamlet with cobblestone streets, a dozen storybook houses and an attractive moat-encircled Renaissance castle, Vallø Slot. Situated in the countryside about 7km south of Køge, Vallø makes a wonderful little excursion for those looking to get off the beaten track.

◉ Sights

Vallø Slot CASTLE, GARDENS
(www.valloe-stift.dk; ⊙8am-sunset (gardens only)) Red-brick Vallø Slot ticks all the 'proper castle' boxes, with pointy turrets and a moat filled with lily pads and croaking frogs. The building has retained its original 16th-century style, although much of it was rebuilt following a fire in 1893. While the castle itself is not open to the public, visitors are free to amble through the beautiful woods and gardens that extend from the castle building all the way to the sea.

On her birthday in 1737 Queen Sophie Magdalene, who owned the estate, established a foundation that turned the castle into a home for 'spinsters of noble birth'. Unmarried daughters of Danish royalty unable to live in their own castles were allowed to live at Vallø, supported by the foundation and government social programs. In the 1970s, bowing to changing public sentiments, the foundation amended its charter and declined to accept new residents. For now, the castle remains home solely to a handful of ageing blue-blooded women who took up residence before 1976.

🍴 Sleeping & Eating

★ Vallø Slotskro INN €€
(☎inn 56 26 70 20, restaurant 56 26 62 66; www.valloeslotskro.dk; Slotsgade 1; menus from Dkr400; ⊙6-9pm Wed-Sat; 🅿) Just outside the castle gate, this 200-year-old inn harbours an elegant restaurant of crisp white linen and decadent Franco-Danish dishes such as quail with foie gras and summer truffles. Alas, the inn's seven double rooms were closed for a revamp during our visit. Check the website for updates and dinner/accommodation packages, as an overnight stay in Vallø makes for an enchanting retreat.

❶ Getting There & Away

Take the train to Vallø station, two stops south of Køge, and from there it's an easy 1.25km stroll east down a tree-lined country road to the castle.

If you're travelling by road take Rte 209 south from Køge, turn right onto Kirkehøjen and then right again onto Vallørækken.

There's a signposted cycle route from Køge that leads into Valløvej.

Sorø

POP 7845

Thick with old timber-framed houses and framed by peaceful lakes and woodlands, Sorø is a soulful, off-the-radar spot. It owes its existence to Sorø Akademi, an elite school for noblemen's sons established by Christian IV. The academy remains a prestigious school to this day; its grounds and lakeside park are open to the public, and make for an idyllic late-afternoon stroll.

During Denmark's 'Golden Age' (1800–50) of national romanticism, Sorø became a haunt for some of the country's most prominent

ZEALAND SORØ

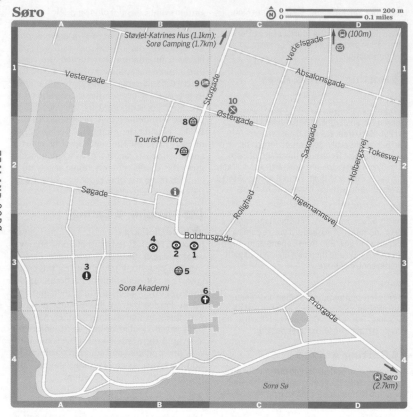

Søro

⊙ Sights

1 Boldhuset...B3
2 Klosterporten..B3
3 Ludvig Holberg Statue...........................A3
4 Ridehuset...B3
5 Sorø Akademi...B3
6 Sorø Kirke...B3
7 Sorø Kunstmuseum...............................B2
8 Sorø Museum..B2

🛏 Sleeping

9 Hotel Postgaarden.................................B1

⊗ Eating

10 Café Tre Konger....................................C1

cultural figures, including Bertel Thorvaldsen, NFS Grundtvig and Adam Oehlenschläger.

⊙ Sights & Activities

For a dose of vintage charm, slip into **Søgade**, a street that's lined with leaning

half-timbered, mustard-yellow houses with red tiled roofs. You'll find it on the west side of the town's main square, Torvet.

Sorø Kirke CHURCH
(⊙9am-4pm) Denmark's largest monastery church, and one of the country's oldest brick buildings, is the 12th-century Sorø Kirke, set snugly on the grounds of the Sorø Academy. The Romanesque interior is simple and harmonious, brightened by **medieval frescoes** of blue, red, orange, green and white geometric patterns, shields and leaves, and lightened by a high 13th-century Gothic ceiling.

Interred in a prime position directly behind the main altar is Bishop Absalon, a member of the influential Hvide family and one of Denmark's most significant medieval statesmen.

Absalon established a Cistercian monastery in Sorø in 1161 and had this church built in the grounds to serve as a family mausoleum. In a display cabinet to the right of the altar are the ivory crosier, gold-and-sapphire ring and silver chalice with which he was buried (extracted from his tomb in the 19th century).

Keeping Absalon company are kings Valdemar IV, Christopher II and Oluf III. Queen Margrethe I, the architect of the 1397 Kalmar Union, was buried here as well, but her remains were later transferred to Roskilde Domkirke (p109). At the end of the left aisle is the marble sarcophagus of the great comic poet and playwright Ludvig Holberg.

The church's grand interior includes a 6m-high 16th-century crucifix by Odense sculptor Claus Berg, carved from a single piece of wood, and a beautifully detailed baroque altar and pulpit. The 16th-century organ is the centrepiece of the Sorø International Music Festival.

Sorø Akademi
HISTORIC BUILDING

After the Reformation, Frederik II decreed that Sorø's monastery should be turned into a school. In 1623, his successor, Christian IV, developed it into the Sorø Academy of Knights, an elite establishment dedicated to the education of the sons of the nobility. Lessons included the art of hunting, behaviour and manners – skills fitting to a noble diplomat.

Although its intake is a little less exclusive these days, Sorø Akademi remains a prominent Danish school and visitors are welcome to stroll through the extensive grounds.

The southern end of Sorø's main street, Storgade, leads directly to the academy via Klosterporten, a medieval gate that once cloistered the monks from the outside world.

Other medieval monastery buildings were replaced with Renaissance structures – thought to be more conducive to learning – in the 17th century. Ridehuset, immediately west of Klosterporten, was built by Christian IV to stable the horses and dogs used for hunting. Boldhuset, just east of Klosterporten, also dates from the reign of Christian IV and now houses the library.

A statue of the Danish playwright Ludvig Holberg (1684–1754), who rescued the school after a financial crisis forced it to close, can be found in the garden area in the western part of the grounds. Picturesque walking trails lead west from the statue down to Sorø Sø.

Sorø Kunstmuseum
MUSEUM

(www.sorokunstmuseum.dk; Storgade 9; adult/child Dkr70/free; ⊙11am-5pm Tue, Wed & Fri-Sun, to 6pm Thu) Flaunting an award-winning extension by Copenhagen-based architects Lundgaard & Tranberg, Sorø Kunstmuseum spans 300 years of Danish art, with works running the gamut from medieval woodcarvings to modern sculpture and photography. While the collection is best known for its 19th-century 'Golden Age' paintings, it also includes the largest collection of Russian icons in Denmark, spanning 1500 to 1900. In recent years, the museum has strengthened its contemporary collection, and its four annual temporary exhibitions showcase both Danish and international artists.

When cultural exhaustion kicks in, recharge at the on-site cafe (cake Dkr25).

Sorø Museum
MUSEUM

(www.vestmuseum.dk; Storgade 17; ⊙10am-4pm Tue-Sun Jul & Aug, shorter hrs rest of yr) FREE Housed in a handsome half-timbered building dating from 1625, Sorø Museum showcases an eclectic booty of regional artefacts, including ancient pottery and the partial reconstruction of a 5,500-year-old Bornholm longhouse. A string of rooms are adorned with period furnishings, including the fetching living room of an aristocrat. There's also a grocery shop from 1880, and the personal belongings of the 19th-century poet BS Ingemann, who taught at Sorø Akademi. Most of the information is in Danish only.

★ Festivals & Events

Sorø International Music Festival
MUSIC

(www.soroemusik.dk) This international music festival is held at Sorø Kirke, with classical concerts held mostly on Wednesday evening throughout July and August; tickets (from Dkr100) are available from the tourist office or at the venue 75 minutes before show time.

Sorø Jazz
MUSIC

(soroejazz.dk) Sorø's ever-growing jazz festival takes place over a week in July, with around 25 concerts performed in various venues across the municipality, including museums, churches and cafes. See the festival website or contact the tourist office for details.

🛏 Sleeping

Sorø Camping
CAMPGROUND €

(☑57 83 02 02; www.soroecamping.dk; Udbyhøjvej 10; campsite per adult/child Dkr79/40; P ⛱) Three-star Sorø camping ground has a gorgeous setting, on the edge of Pedersborg Sø, about 150m north of Slagelsevej. There's a coin laundry, lollipop-making sessions, and a 'bouncy pillow' to keep kids amused. Four- to six-person cabins and apartments (per night Dkr450 to Dkr800) are also available.

ZEALAND SORØ

A 1km-long lakeside trail winds its way into town, or take bus 422.

Hotel Postgaarden
HOTEL €€

(☑57 83 22 22; www.hotelpostgaarden.dk; Storgade 25; s/d incl breakfast Dkr750/925; ℗⊛) A good choice in the centre of town, this refurbished inn-style hotel boasts a 300-year history. Its 18 rooms may not be cutting-edge, but they're pleasant and comfortable. Some face the main pedestrianised street, while others look onto a quiet courtyard. There's a restaurant on-site.

✗ Eating

There are several places to get cheap meals including a bakery and a takeaway pizzeria on Storgade.

Café Tre Konger
INTERNATIONAL €€

(Østergade 3; lunch Dkr89-125, dinner mains Dkr98-238; ⊛11am-10pm Mon-Sat, to 9pm Sun) Set in a converted movie theatre adorned with chintzy chandeliers and velvet drapes, the Three Kings serves fresh and filling comfort grub. Many of the ingredients are made on-site, from the buns used in the fantastic burgers, to the addictive potato wedges. Dinner options include hearty pasta and steak dishes.

On sunny days the leafy courtyard is a perfect spot to wash down a glass or two of local Sorø Bryghus beer.

Støvlet-Katrines Hus
DANISH €€€

(☑57 83 50 80; www.stovletkatrineshus.dk; Slagelsevej 63; lunch Dkr95-165, 5-/8-course dinner Dkr395/635; ⊛noon-4pm & 5.30-9.30pm Mon-Sat, also 11am-1pm first Sun of month) On the western edge of town, fine-dining Støvlet-Katrines Hus occupies the former home of Christian VII's mistress. These days, lust comes in the form of delicious, seasonal dishes such as ashen monkfish with spinach cream and pickled squash, or pickled cherries with vanilla pannacotta, buttermilk and elderflower. Wines competently match each course.

To get here from the centre of town, walk north along Storgade, turning left into Hauchsvej (which becomes Kongebrovej). The restaurant is at the end of the street (on the corner with Slagelsevej).

❶ Information

Library (Storgade 7; ⊛10am-7pm Mon, 10am-6pm Tue, Thu & Fri, 1-6pm Wed, 10am-1pm Sat) Free internet access.

Post Office (Rådhusvej 6; ⊛noon-5pm Mon-Fri, 10am-noon Sat)

Tourist Office (☑57 82 10 12; www.soroe-turistbureau.dk; Torvet 2; ⊛1-5pm Mon, 10am-5pm Tue-Fri, 10am-12.30pm Sat mid-Jun–Aug, shorter hrs rest of yr) Sorø's tourist office is located on the town's main square.

❶ Getting There & Away

CAR
Sorø is 15km east of Slagelse and 16km west of Ringsted via Rte 150 or the E20.

TRAIN
Sorø train station is in Frederiksberg, 3km south of the town centre – buses 421, 422 and 425 run from central Sorø to the train station at least hourly.

Sorø is on the line between Copenhagen (Dkr99, 50 minutes) and Odense (Dkr181, 45 minutes), with trains running approximately every 30 to 60 minutes.

Nearby towns on the same line include Slagelse (Dkr36, 10 minutes), Korsør (Dkr48, 20 minutes), Ringsted (Dkr36, 10 minutes) and Roskilde (Dkr53, 25 minutes).

Trelleborg

The best preserved of the four Viking ring fortresses in Denmark, Trelleborg is 7km west of Slagelse and 22km west of Sorø. Admittedly, Slagelse is rather uninspiring, so consider making Sorø your base if staying overnight. If you choose to stay in Slagelse, contact the Slagelse **tourist office** (☑70 25 22 06; www.visitvestsjaelland.dk; Løvegade 7; ⊛10am-5pm Mon-Fri, to 3pm Sat mid-Jun–Aug, shorter hrs rest of yr) for accommodation options.

⊙ Sights

Trelleborg
ARCHAEOLOGICAL SITE

(www.vikingeborgen-trelleborg.dk; Trelleborg Allé 4; ⊛10am-5pm Tue-Sun Jun-Aug, 10am-4pm Tue-Sat Apr, May, Sep & Oct) **FREE** History buffs will revel in visiting one of the most important Viking Age sites, a ring fortress dating back to AD 980. Before heading across the meadows to the fortress and reconstructed Viking-era buildings, visit the small but informative **museum**, which explains how the fort was built, occupied and abandoned. Displays contain weapons belonging to soldiers at the fort (spearheads, axes, arrowheads and shield bosses), as well as everyday items (pottery, bronze jewellery, locks and keys, combs and loom weights). There are also two skeletons from the graveyard.

➤ The Fortress

Trelleborg was constructed as a circular fortress, built to a precise mathematical plan and home to a garrison of around 500 soldiers, plus craftsmen and some women and children. Huge earthen banks, 17m wide and 6m high, formed a protective wall around the fort. Inside, two streets divided the circle into quarters, each containing four longhouses set around a courtyard. Two nearby streams gave the inhabitants boat access inland and out to the sea.

Trelleborg's impressive scale and strategic position, and the similarly designed forts at Fyrkat, Nonnebakken and Aggersborg, indicate a powerful 10th-century force at work, with immense manpower to command. Dendrochronology has shown that the trees for the palisade (which added an extra defensive layer to the earthen banks) were cut down in AD 980, during the reign of Harald Bluetooth. One theory is that the forts were built by Harald after an uprising led by his son, Sweyn Forkbeard.

Hints of big trouble are littered across Trelleborg. The fort was occupied for a very short space of time, before being abandoned around 990. There are signs of a large fire, and a Viking graveyard lying within the fort's outer defences contains two mass graves, both containing the bodies of men in their 20s and 30s.

Despite the passing of a millennium since its construction, the circular earthen mound is perfectly intact. Naturally, the wooden structures that once stood inside it have long since decayed, but the post holes and gable ends of the buildings have been filled with cement to show the outlines of the house foundations. You can walk up onto the grassy circular rampart and readily grasp the strikingly precise geometric design of the fortress. Grazing sheep imbue the scene with a timeless aura.

➤ Reconstructions

Several Viking-era buildings have been reconstructed at the site, using authentic materials and methods. The most impressive is the replica longhouse, built in 1941 in Viking stave style. Sit quietly on one of the sleeping benches that line the walls, watching the swallows dart through the doorways and the smoke hole, and you half expect one of the fortress's former inhabitants to wander in.

Since it was built, archaeologists have changed their opinion on the external appearance of the longhouse. They now think that there was no outer gallery and that the roof was much lower – still, 10 out of 10 for effort.

A few reconstructed houses are clustered together to form 'Trelletorp', a tiny Viking village, with besmocked interpreters doing chores of the period such as sharpening axes, chopping wood and baking bread. From June to August there are often activities for children, such as archery demonstrations and pottery workshops.

LIFESTYLES OF THE RICH & VIKING

The discovery of Viking artefacts may not be unique to Zealand, but none in Denmark match the richness of those uncovered at the site of a 6th-century Viking manor house on lake Tissø's western shore, between Slagelse and Kalundborg.

The manor-house complex, four times the size of any other so far discovered, is thought to have been a royal estate, holiday home, hunting lodge, banquet house or cult centre (20 Thors' hammers have been found there), or possibly some combination of the above. The absence of any graves at the site leads archaeologists to believe that it wasn't a permanent dwelling-place.

Some experts think the site may have been the ancient seat of Viking kings. Artefacts from England, Ireland, Germany and Norway indicate that the manor house's visitors were heavily involved in military adventures and plundering – and therefore the elite of Viking society.

Over 12,000 items have been found since digs began in earnest in 1995, with the extent and high calibre of the finds causing real excitement. An abundance of Arabian and Nordic coins, beautifully cast silver brooches, animal-entwined bronze pendants, a golden hinge, a tuning-peg for a harp, and top-quality sword handles and stirrups, all dating from 500 to 1050 AD, are just some of the aristocratic treasures found. One of the best places to eye-up some of the booty is at Copenhagen's national museum (p45), home to the most famous find (so far), a massive solid-gold necklace weighing 1.8kg.

ZEALAND TRELLEBORG

THE GREAT BELT

The **Storebælts-forbindelsen** (Great Belt Fixed Link; www.storebaelt.dk; one-way toll motorcycle Dkr125, small/medium/large car Dkr125/235/360) is the stuff that engineers lust over. Spanning a whopping 18km, its combination of two bridges, island and tunnel allow the E20 motorway to connect Denmark's largest and third-largest islands, Zealand and Funen. It's an amazing piece of design and worth an admiring gasp. After all, the highest points in Denmark are the tops of the two 254m pylons on the East Bridge, which joins Zealand to Sprogø Island before carrying cars onwards over the West Bridge to Funen. The bridges look particularly stunning at night, glittering and twinkling against a black backdrop.

Three kilometres to the south on the Zealand side is **Korsør**, a one-time booming ferry town thanks to its position at the narrowest point between Zealand and Funen. The opening of the Storebælts-forbindelsen changed all that, turning the transport hub into another victim of progress. While the town itself has no major drawcards, it is home to the **Korsør By og Overfartsmuseum** (Korsør Town & Ferry Service Museum; www. byogoverfartsmuseet.dk; Søbatteriet 3; ⊙ 11am-4pm Tue-Sun May–mid-Sep) FREE, a museum dedicated to the ferries and icebreakers that traversed the Store Bælt over the past two centuries. (After all, everyone deserves a little love, right?)

Korsør's new train station is 3km north of town, by the Storebælt link. It's on the main line between Zealand and Funen, with trains running roughly every half hour to Copenhagen (Dkr138, one hour) and Odense (Dkr146, 30 minutes). Local buses 460, 901 and 908 connect the train station to Korsør's town centre (Dkr26, 10 to 15 minutes).

❶ Getting There & Away

BUS & TRAIN

Bus 439 runs from Slagelse to Trelleborg (Dkr26, 12 minutes) from Monday to Friday. There are around seven buses per day, with the first leaving Slagelse train station at 7am and the last (to arrive within the museum's opening hours) at 2.56pm (June to August) and 1.56pm (April, May, September and October).

Trains run frequently between Slagelse and Copenhagen (Dkr121, one hour).

CAR

Driving from Slagelse, take Strandvejen to its end at the village of Hejninge and then follow the signs to Trelleborg, 1km further on.

TAXI

From Slagelse, a taxi to the site costs about Dkr190 on weekdays, Dkr220 on weekends. To book one, call **DanTaxi** (☑ 70 25 25 25).

Vordingborg

POP 11,750

Vordingborg's quaintness is deceptive. Now best known as Zealand's gateway to the south islands, the town played a starring role in early Danish history. It was the royal residence and Baltic power base of Valdemar I (Valdemar the Great), famed for reuniting the Danish kingdom in 1157 after a period of civil war.

And it was here that Valdemar II (Valdemar the Victorious) signed the Law of Jutland in 1241, a civil code which declared that legitimate laws must be based on objective and sovereign justice. The code would become the forerunner to Danish national law.

This history is vividly documented at Vordingborg's brand new multimedia museum, Danmarks Borgcenter, located at the very site of Vordingborg's famous medieval fortress. It's here that you'll also find the town's iconic medieval Goose Tower, now part of the museum.

A short drive from town is the Knudshoved Odde peninsula with its grassy lawns and narrow rocky beaches; ideal for a dip if the temperature's right.

◉ Sights

Danmarks Borgcenter MUSEUM
(Danish Castle Centre; www.danmarksborgcenter. dk; Slotsruinen 1; adult/child Dkr115/free; ⊙ 10am-5pm daily) The ruins of King Valdemar the Great's Vordingborg Slot have been given new life with the opening of the Danish Castle Centre, a high-tech museum exploring the castle's history, as well as that of medieval Danish power, politics and castle life. Using interactive iPads, visitors can explore themes such as the tactics used by kings to gain and retain power, as well as learn about the museum's historical artefacts. Among these is an

extraordinary piece of 15th-century chain-mail armor, weighing almost 11 kilograms.

Outside, the iPad guide brings the ruins back to vivid life with digital reconstructions, while dedicated kids' features allow little ones to 'hunt ghosts' among the ruins. Scan your museum ticket to enter and ascend the Gåsetårnet (Goose Tower), the only surviving remnant of a once mighty fortress.

Vor Frue Kirke CHURCH
(Kirketorvet; ⊘10am-3pm Mon-Fri Jun-Aug, to 2pm rest of year) Along the way, on the western side of Algade, is the brick-built Vor Frue Kirke, whose oldest section is a mid-15th-century nave. Inside are elegant frescoes, and a baroque altarpiece created in 1642 by master-carver Abel Schrøder.

🏃 Activities

Knudshoved Odde WALKING
If you have your own transport, Knudshoved Odde, the 18km-long peninsula west of Vordingborg, offers some hiking opportunities in an area known for its 'Bronze Age landscape'. The area features moors and meadows, its flora includes blackthorn, honeysuckle and wild roses. A small herd of American buffalo roam the land, brought in by the Rosenfeldt family who own Knudshoved Odde. There's a car park (Dkr15) halfway down the peninsula on Knudskovvej, where the trail begins.

🛏 Sleeping

Danhostel Vordingborg HOSTEL €
(☑55 36 08 00; www.danhostel.dk/vordingborg; Præstegårdsvej 18; dm Dkr150, s/d Dkr450/600; 🅿) This 66-bed hostel, about 2km north of town, is in a peaceful rural area, surrounded by paths and lakes. Rooms are pleasant and facilities include a coin laundry.

Hotel Kong Valdemar HOTEL €€
(☑55 34 30 95; www.hotelkongvaldemar.dk; Algade 101; s/d incl breakfast Dkr595/795; 🅿🛜) Opposite Gåsetårnet (Goose Tower) and the Danmarks Borgcenter, the Kong Valdemar has a convenient, central location. While the hotel's 60 bland, dowdy rooms could do with a makeover, all come with private toilet.

🍴 Eating

Restaurant Borgen DANISH, INTERNATIONAL €€
(Slotsruinen 1; lunch Dkr80-165, 2-/3-course dinner Dkr295/335; ⊘10am-5pm daily, plus 6-9pm Thu-Sat) Whitewashed, half-timbered walls and black, low-slung lamps set a slick scene at Danmarks Borgcenter's on-site cafe-restaurant.

Local, seasonal produce drive flavourful lunch options like smørrebrød (open sandwiches) and a moreish burger served with onion marmalade and vegetable chips. Dinner is usually only one entree, main and dessert, dictated each day by that morning's top ingredients.

The result might be anything from baked cod with beetroot and garden herbs, to tender veal served with seasonal vegetables and a blackcurrant sauce. The kitchen is always happy to accommodate vegetarians.

Cafe Oscar DANISH, INTERNATIONAL €€
(www.babette.dk; Nordhavnsvej 8; dishes Dkr85-195; ⊘noon-4pm & 5-9pm Tue-Sun Jun-Aug, shorter hrs rest of yr) Seasonal, affordable and snugly set in an old salting hut by the harbour, it's hard not to love Oscar. Run by the team from Babette (you're in capable hands!), its menu is reassuringly short, simple and fresh. Made-from-scratch salads, sandwiches and a gourmet burger spell lunch, while dinner usually offers a soup, pasta dish, meat and fish main. More of a grazer? Opt for the plate of Danish cheese with olives and bread.

★Babette DANISH, INTERNATIONAL €€€
(☑55 34 30 30; www.babette.dk; Kildemarksvej 5; 5-course menu Dkr645; ⊘noon-3pm & 6-9pm Wed-Fri, 6-9pm Sat) If you're in the region it's definitely worth visiting Babette, 1km north of the town centre, for a full gastronomic and aesthetic treat. The restaurant (named after the film Babette's Feast) is known for its original pan-European cuisine, making use of local seasonal ingredients in sometimes unusual combinations – braised Duroc pork belly with fruit syrup, buckthorn and carrots, anyone?

Babette is also blessed with a panoramic surf-and-turf vista. Book ahead.

❶ Information

Post Office (Prins Jørgens Alle 10-12; ⊘10am-5.30pm Mon-Fri, 9am-1pm Sat) In the Kvickly supermarket building, north of Algade.

Tourist Office (☑55 34 11 11; www.visitmoen.dk; Algade 97; ⊘10am-3pm Mon-Fri) Opposite Danmarks Borgcenter and Gåsetårnet. When closed, you can find tourist information at Danmarks Borgcenter.

❶ Getting There & Away

Vordingborg is 28km south of Næstved via Rte 22, and 13km from Møn via Rte 59.

By train, Vordingborg is around 65 to 75 minutes from Copenhagen (Dkr138). If you're en route to Møn, you'll need to switch from the train to the bus at Vordingborg train station.

Møn, Falster & Lolland

Includes ➡

Møn. 128
Stege 129
Ulvshale & Nyord 131
Keldby 131
Elmelunde 132
Møns Klint & Around .132
Klintholm Havn. 134
Western Møn. 134
Bogø. 135
Falster 135
Nykøbing F 136
Marielyst 137
Lolland 138
Maribo 139

Best Places to Eat

➡ La Comida (p137)
➡ Oreby Kro (p136)
➡ Lollesgård (p131)
➡ David's (p130)
➡ Portofino (p134)

Best Places to Stay

➡ Oreby Mølle (p136)
➡ Tohøjgaard Gæstgivern (p134)
➡ Liselund Ny Slot (p133)

Why Go?

Denmark's 'South Sea Islands' may lack the coconut palms and hula skirts usually associated with that phrase, but they *do* offer a fine glimpse of rural Scandinavian island life: rolling fields, sandy beaches and Neolithic tombs.

Møn deserves the most attention: it's perfectly sized, artistically spirited and home to something very unusual for Denmark – cliffs! Four churches exhibit wondrous medieval frescoes, from recognised masterpieces to primitive daubs. Add evocative beaches, enchanted forests and cosy guesthouses, and you've got the perfect island escape.

While less inspiring than Møn, Falster is famous for its beaches, which lure Danish sun worshippers each (short) summer. Further west, Lolland's sprawl of farms and woods is punctuated with Maribo's small-town charm, as well as blockbuster attractions Lalandia waterpark and Knuthenborg Safari Park.

All three islands are easily accessed by road bridges from southern Zealand.

When to Go

To catch a glimpse of Møn's rare orchids, head to the island between May and August. This is a good period in general, as many attractions and restaurants close or reduce their hours outside high season. Falster's famous beaches make July and August crowded, but if lazy beach days and lively bar nights are your thing, these are the months to go. Across the islands, September is ideal, with relatively good weather and fewer crowds, especially at Lolland's family-focused drawcards.

Winter is by far the quietest season, with many coastal businesses shut for the season. The landscape takes on a brooding and melancholy air, which may appeal to more poetic souls.

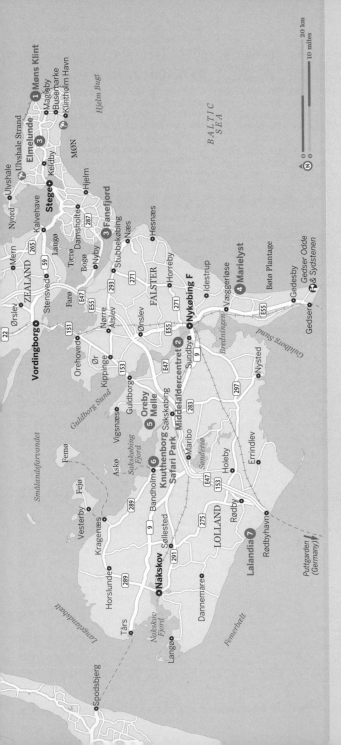

Møn, Falster & Lolland Highlights

1 Track down prehistoric fossils in the gleaming chalk cliffs at **Møns Klint** (p132)

2 Channel your inner knight or maiden at the medieval-themed **Middelaldercentret** (p136), just outside Nykøbing F

3 Absorb the medieval frescoes inside Møn's **Elmelunde Kirke** (p132) and **Fanefjord Kirke** (p134)

4 Tan, splash and just kick back on the sand at **Marielyst** (p137), Falster's premier summer beach resort

5 Indulge in a little elegant slumming at lovingly restored **Oreby Mølle** (p136)

6 Monkey around at the drive-through **Knuthenborg Safari Park** (p140) at Bandholm

7 Make the kids squeal with glee at splash-happy amusement park **Lalandia** (p140)

MØN

POP 9580

Expect to fall head over heels for Møn. By far the most magical of the south islands, its most famous drawcard is its spectacular white cliffs, Møns Klint. Soft, sweeping and crowned by deep-green forest, they're the stuff landscape paintings are made of, which possibly explains the island's healthy headcount of artists.

Yet the inspiration doesn't end there, with beautiful beaches spanning sandy expanses to small secret coves, haunting Neolithic graves and medieval churches adorned with some of Denmark's most whimsical medieval frescoes.

Møn's rich clay soil draws potters to the area (look out for 'keramik' signs along country roads), while its fields and coast inspire the island's handful of culinary must-tries.

So hit the pedal or get behind the wheel (Møn has no trains and the bus service is sketchy), and explore what is bound to become one of your favourite corners of Denmark.

❶ Getting There & Away

Visitors need to take the train to Vordingborg in southern Zealand then switch to a bus. Trains from Copenhagen to Vordingborg (Dkr138, 1½ hours) leave at least hourly until around midnight.

Bus 660R (and occasionally bus 664) from Vordingborg, in south Zealand, to Stege (Dkr48, 45 minutes), on Møn, connects with train arrivals, leaving Vordingborg half-hourly on weekdays and hourly on weekends.

If driving, the E47 highway reaches both Falster and Lolland. For Møn, exit the E47 at exit 41, from where Rte 59 continues east to Møn. Bridges also connect Møn directly to Falster via the small island of Bogø.

❶ Getting Around

Route 287, which cuts across the centre of the island from east to west, is Møn's main road.

Møn

Numerous rural roads branch off it – they can be slow going but fun to explore.

BICYCLE

In Stege bicycles can be rented at **Point S** (Storegade 91; per day Dkr65; ⊙7.30am-5pm Mon-Fri, 9am-1pm Sat). The Min Købmand supermarket in Klintholm Havn also hires out bikes. Maps of cycling routes on Møn can be found at the tourist office in Stege.

BUS

Stege is the departure point for all buses on Møn. Fares depend on the number of zones travelled, with the highest fare between any two places on Møn being Dkr24. Frequency of service varies with the day of the week and the season.

The most frequent service is bus 667, which goes from Stege to Klintholm Havn (Dkr24, 30 minutes) via Keldby, Elmelunde and Magleby.

Bus 678 runs hourly between Stege and Møns Klint (Dkr24, 35 minutes). The last bus to Møns Klint departs Stege at 5.40pm. The last bus back from Møns Klint is at 6.06pm (6.36pm on weekends).

Stege

POP 3830

Møn's main town and gateway, Stege is the island at its busiest. Its single narrow main street contains the island's tourist office, a handful of good cafes, small independent shops, a cinema and (most importantly) a microbrewery. The island is so small that wherever you are, it's only a short drive back here to stock up on supplies.

During the Middle Ages, Stege was one of Denmark's wealthiest provincial towns, thanks to its lucrative herring industry. The entire town was fortified until 1534, when the castle walls were torn down – by citizens who supported a mutinous attacking army. Pieces of the rampart remain here and there, including near the camping ground.

◉ Sights & Activities

There's a signposted cycle path running between Stege and Møns Klint, and in the other direction from Stege to Bogø. The tourist office has maps of walking and cycling routes on the island.

Thorsvang   MUSEUM
(thorsvangdanmarkssamlermuseum.dk; Thorsvangs Allé 7; adult/child Dkr50/25; ⊙10am-5pm mid-Apr–mid-Oct, shorter hrs rest of yr) Fastidiously detailed and highly atmospheric, this collectors' museum recreates 30 old shops and workshops, from a barber, butcher and bakery, to a cinema lobby adorned with vintage film magazines, candy and a 1967 Italian projector. The museum is also home to a small yet fascinating collection of historic motor vehicles, including Ford's final T-Model car (1927) and its first A-Model vehicle (1928).

You'll find Thorsvang 800m southwest of the tourist office in Stege, just off Rte 59.

Stege Kirke   CHURCH
(Provstesstræde; ⊙9am-5pm) It looks as though a demented nine-year-old has been let loose inside Stege Kirke, built in the 13th century by a member of the powerful Hvide family. The interior is covered in endearingly naive 14th- and 15th-century frescoes in red and black paint: monkey-like faces sprout from branches, a hunter chases unidentifiable animals, and a sorrowful man is covered in big blobs...measles? The church has a splendidly carved pulpit dating from 1630.

Empiregården   MUSEUM
(Storegade 75; adult/child Dkr40/free; ⊙10am-4pm Tue-Sun) Part of Møn Museum, Empiregården covers local cultural history. Archaeological finds from the Stone Age to the Middle Ages include ancient skeletons, jewellery and the world's oldest chewing gum, dating back 11,000 years to a settlement

MØN, FALSTER & LOLLAND STEGE

Møn

◉ **Top Sights**
1 Fanefjord Kirke A4
2 Keldby Kirke C3

◉ **Sights**
3 Elmelunde Kirke C2
4 Geocenter Møns Klint D3
5 Grønsalen A4
6 Liselund D2
7 Thorsvang B3

🛏 **Sleeping**
8 Bakkegaard Gæstgiveri D3
9 Camping Møns Klint D3
10 Danhostel Møns Klint D3
11 Liselund Ny Slot D2
12 Nyord B&B A2
13 Pension Elmehøj C3
14 Tohøjgaard Gæstgivern B3

🍴 **Eating**
15 Damme Kro A4
   Liselund Ny Slot Cafe .... (see 11)
   Lollesgård .... (see 12)
16 Møn Is B3

Stege

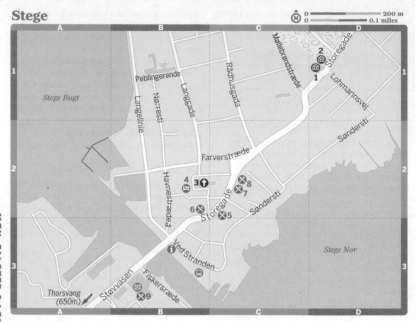

Stege

⊙ Sights
1 Empiregården...D1
2 Mølleporten D1
3 Stege Kirke B2

🛏 Sleeping
4 Motel Stege B2

⊗ Eating
5 Bryghuset Møn......................................C2
6 David's...B2
7 Din Bager C2
8 Kiwi Mini Pris C2
9 SuperBrugsen.......................................B3

north of Vordingborg. Also on display are 19th-century house interiors, toys, coins and pottery.

Mølleporten   HISTORIC BUILDING
(Storegade) Of the three medieval gates that once allowed entry into the town, Mølleporten (Mill Gate) on Storegade is the only one still standing. It's one of the best-preserved town gates in Denmark.

🛏 Sleeping

The tourist office has a brochure with a list of B&Bs on the island. You're welcome to

use the tourist office phone free of charge to book accommodation. Singles/doubles in a private home average Dkr300/400.

Motel Stege   MOTEL €€
(☑55 81 35 35; www.motel-stege.dk; Provst-estræde 4; s Dkr550-650, d Dkr575-750; P🅿🛜) Your best bet in central Stege, Motel Stege offers 12 rooms that are simple yet smart. Those in the main building have a mezzanine level (accessible by ladder), and sleep up to four. Rooms in the annexe have their own kitchenette, while all guests have access to a homely communal kitchen and dining area. Added comforts include a washer and dryer.

🍴 Eating

There's a good bakery, **Din Bager** (Storegade 36; pastries from Dkr11; ⊙5am-5pm Mon-Fri, 6am-2pm Sat, 6am-1pm Sun), and several large supermarkets, including **SuperBrugsen** (Vasen 3; ⊙9am-7pm Mon-Fri, 8am-6pm Sat, 10am-6pm Sun). The most central supermarket is **Kiwi Mini Pris** (Storegade 44; ⊙8am-10pm).

David's   INTERNATIONAL €€
(www.davids.nu; Storegade 11A, Stege; dishes Dkr89-150; ⊙10am-5pm Mon-Fri, to 4pm Sat & Sun) David's open kitchen prepares fabulous, con-

temporary cafe fare. Tuck into the celebrated 'tapas' platter or opt for gems like the roll of smoked salmon and apples with trout mousse and green salad. Housemade cakes keep gluttons happy. Sunny days mean alfresco noshing in the leafy courtyard. No credit cards.

Bryghuset Møn   DANISH, INTERNATIONAL €€
(Storegade 18; lunch Dkr65-115, dinner mains Dkr119-180; ⊙11am-9pm daily Apr–mid-Oct, shorter hrs rest of yr) Tucked away inside Luffes Gård courtyard, Møn's well-known microbrewery serves good-quality lunch grub, including smørrebrød (open sandwiches), butter-fried fish fillet with homemade pickles, and hearty meatballs with red cabbage and cucumber salad. The dinner menu is a more limited affair, usually with one meat and one fish option. Wash it all down with one of the microbrewery's silky beers.

ℹ Information

Library (Møllebrøndstræde 12; ⊙noon-4pm Mon-Fri, 10am-1pm Sat) Free internet access.
Post Office (Støvvasen 3; ⊙11am-5pm Mon-Fri, 10am-noon Sat) Inside the SuperBrugsen supermarket building.
Tourist Office (☑55 86 04 00; www.visit-moen.dk; Storegade 2; ⊙9.30am-4pm Mon-Fri, 9.30am-12.30pm & 2.30-4pm Sat Jun & Aug, 9.30am-5pm Mon-Fri, 9.30am-12.30pm & 2.30-5pm Sat Jul, shorter hrs rest of yr) Has information about the entire island. Internet access costs Dkr10 per 15 minutes.

Ulvshale & Nyord

Møn's best beach, **Ulvshale Strand**, sprawls along Ulvshale peninsula, 6km north of Stege. This pristine stretch of gently sloping white sand is created by pieces of cliff washing around the coast from Møns Klint. The beach is popular with windsurfers and holds a Blue Flag award (an international eco-label for the sustainable development of beaches and marinas). Ulvshalevej runs alongside – and it's edged by one of the few virgin woods left in Denmark (look out for adders). The forest extends to the end of the peninsula, where there's a narrow bridge to the island of Nyord.

Nyord has only been connected to the Møn mainland since 1968. Its former isolation safeguarded it from development, and today the sole village (also named Nyord) is a perfect cluster of 19th-century thatched cottages, surrounded by idyllic gardens. Cars are banned (there's a car park outside), so the loudest sound is the chattering of swallows. Much of the 5-sq-km island, particularly the east, is given over to marshland and salt meadows. There's a **bird-watching tower** about 1km west of the bridge – you can't miss it in this flat landscape. Birds include ospreys, kestrels, rough-legged hawks, snow buntings, ruffs, avocets, swans, black-tailed godwits, Arctic terns, curlews and various ducks.

🛏 Sleeping & Eating

Nyord B&B   GUESTHOUSE €
(☑55 86 32 57; www.nyord-bb.dk; Aksvej 8, Nyord; s/d with bathroom Dkr450/575-775, without bathroom Dkr375/450; ⊙Apr-Oct; 🔊) If it's peace you're after, Nyord B&B has your name all over its farmhouse walls. Owned by affable ex-sailor Niels Andreasen and his family, it's set in Møn's only car-free village, opposite the cosy Lollesgård restaurant. The eight white rooms are simple, clean and comfortable, two with private toilets and none with TVs. Breakfast is an extra Dkr75. Cash only.

Lollesgård   DANISH €€
(☑31 39 99 82; www.lolles.dk; Hyldevej 1, Nyord; lunch Dkr45-125, dinner mains Dkr125-345; ⊙noon-9pm daily summer, shorter hrs rest of yr) Anja Hansen's criminally cosy restaurant showcases top-notch regional produce, from seafood and beef, to charcuterie, cheeses and vegetables. Seasonality and natural flavours define the menu, which might include Lollesgård's famous fried eels with new potatoes and parsley sauce (Dkr340). Lighter lunch dishes include smørrebrød.

Keldby

The Keldby area, about 5km east of Stege, is notable mainly for the superb frescoes in its roadside church. There's also a small farm museum a few kilometres south of Rte 287.

◎ Sights

★**Keldby Kirke**   CHURCH
(Rte 287; ⊙8am-4.45pm) Some of Denmark's most splendid frescoes are splashed across the walls and ceiling of Keldby's 13th-century brick church. The oldest (1275) decorate the chancel walls. An impressive Judgment Day scene, where the saved join the saints and the damned descend into a devil-filled hell, dates from around 100 years later. It's a theme also visited by the 15th-century 'Elmelunde master', whose cool-faced figures are found all over the soaring arches.

Eating

Møn Is ICE CREAM €
(www.moen-is.dk; Hovgårdsvej 4, Stege; 2 scoops
Dkr25; ⊘11am-5pm daily summer, shorter hrs rest
of yr) Ice-cream makers often wax lyrically
about 'fresh ingredients', but it doesn't get
fresher than Møn Is, where you can lick in
full view of the cows that made it all possible. Flavours include seasonal fruit sor-
bets and creamy stunners like liquorice.
Although the farm's address is in Stege, it's
actually 8km southeast of Stege (or 2km
southeast of Kelbyville).

Elmelunde

Ancient fresco-filled churches are a recur-
ring theme in this part of the world. Never-
theless, the church in this rural hamlet,
halfway between Stege and Møns Klint,
is the one after which the most renowned
fresco painter was named. Bus 667 and 678
from Stege stops in front.

Sights

Elmelunde Kirke CHURCH
(Kirkebakken 41; ⊘8am-4.45pm Apr-Sep, to
3.45pm rest of yr) One of Denmark's oldest
stone churches, Elmelunde Kirke dates back
to 1080. The vaults were painted by the
'Elmelunde master', whose awesome frescoes span everything from the Creation to
Christ in judgment. There's a splendid ser-
pent in the Garden of Eden, with a snake-
like body and human head; Herod's soldiers
dressed in medieval armour; a devil leading
the damned into the monstrous mouth of
hell; and several hunting scenes, reminders
of the shortness of human life.

🛏 Sleeping

Pension Elmehøj GUESTHOUSE €
(☑55 81 35 35; www.elmehoj.dk; Kirkebakken
39, Stege; s/d Dkr310/390; ⊘closed Jan-Mar;
🅿@🛜) Situated next door to Elmelunde
Kirke, this pension has 24 off-white bedrooms with shared toilets and showers. You
can bring your own bed linen and towel, or
rent it for Dkr50. The somewhat institution-
al interiors are redeemed by the guest kitch-
en, cosy TV lounge, trampolines, and lovely
host. Children under 12 years of age stay for
half-price; breakfast is an extra Dkr60.

Møns Klint & Around

Sometimes it's a wonder that the whole island doesn't tilt eastwards with the sheer
weight of visitors coming to admire the
gleaming white cliffs of Møns Klint. In
Denmark's rather dull flat landscape, these
striking chalk cliffs, rising sharply above a
jade-green sea, are geographic breathtakers.

The main visitor area, Store Klint, has a
car park (Dkr35), a GeoCenter and a decent
cafe.

◎ Sights & Activities

Møns Klint LANDMARK
The 128m-high chalk cliffs of Møns Klint are
one of Denmark's most spectacular land-

THE ELMELUNDE FRESCOES

Several of Møn's churches are covered in beautiful frescoes, so rich and abundant that
the churches can be likened to medieval art galleries. These frescoes were a means of
describing the Bible to illiterate peasants, and their cartoon-like clarity still gets the stories across today. Scenes run the gamut from light-hearted frolics in the Garden of Eden
to depictions of grotesque demons and the yawning mouth of hell.

After visiting a couple of these churches, you may get a sense of déjà vu. This is because most of the loveliest 15th-century frescoes were painted by the same artist, whose
exact identity is a mystery but who is known as Elmelundemesteren (the 'Elmelunde
master') after the church of the same name. His people have calm emotionless faces,
and the master's palette is one of distinctive warm earth tones: russet, mustard, sienna,
brick red, chestnut brown and pale aqua.

Møn's church frescoes, created by painting with watercolours on newly plastered, still-
wet walls or ceilings, are some of the best-preserved in Denmark, although their survival
is a lucky fluke. Lutheran ministers thought the frescoes too Catholic and whitewashed
over them in the 17th century. Ironically, this preserved the medieval artwork from soiling
and fading, thanks to a protective layer of dust that separated the frescoes from the
whitewash. The whitewash wasn't removed until the 20th century.

marks. Right behind the Geocenter Møns Klint, a boardwalk leading right offers lofty views of the cliffs and sea below. Alternatively, a near-vertical flight of wooden stairs lead straight down to the beach (unsuitable for swimming because of strong tides and rocks). At the bottom, keep your eyes peeled for Cretaceous-period fossils, which you can take to the GeoCenter to be identified by an expert.

You can walk south along the shoreline and then loop back up through a thick, cooling forest of wind-gnarled beech trees for a longer walk lasting about 1½ hours. Needless to say, the views from the clifftop on the way back are extraordinary.

The cliffs themselves were created during the last Ice Age, when the calcareous deposits from aeons of compressed seashells were lifted from the ocean floor. Strangely, the closer you get to the cliffs, the less white they become – up close, there are shades of orange, grey and purple, and layers of grey-black flint. Keep an eye out for peregrine falcons on the cliffs, the only place in Denmark where they nest.

GeoCenter Møns Klint
MUSEUM
(www.moensklint.dk; Stengårdsvej 8, Borre; adult/child Dkr120/80; ⊗10am-6pm late Jun–early Aug, shorter hrs rest of yr) Located at Store Klint, the high-tech GeoCenter Møns Klint manages to make geology utterly engrossing. Imaginative displays (in Danish, German and English) explain how the cliffs were formed, show off an orderly fossil collection and bring other-worldly Cretaceous sea creatures to life. Kids absolutely love the inventive hands-on nature centre, and there are roaming experts to answer any questions. Ponder nature's craftiness at the smart upstairs cafe, which serves coffee, cakes and open sandwiches.

Liselund
GARDENS
(⊗manor house tours 10.30am, 11am, 1.30pm & 2pm Wed-Sun) The ultimate romantic gift, the enchanting garden of Liselund was built by Antoine de la Calmette in the late 1700s as a present for his wife (the name means 'Lise's Grove'). Paths wind their way under chestnut trees, by waterfalls, streams and ponds, up to a viewpoint on the sea cliffs, and past buildings designed to invoke exotic destinations – a Chinese pavilion, Greek 'ruins', an Egyptian pyramid. It's a blissful vision, disrupted occasionally by the raucous shriek of wandering peacocks.

🛏 Sleeping & Eating

Camping Møns Klint
CAMPGROUND €
(⊘55 81 20 25; www.campingmoensklint.dk; Klintevej 544, Børre Møn; campsites per adult/child/tent Dkr90/66/30; ⊗mid-Apr–Oct; @🛜🏊) This massive, family-friendly, three-star site is about 3km northwest of Møns Klint. The camping ground has impressive facilities: a 25m outdoor swimming pool, guest kitchen, coin laundry, tennis court, mini-golf, bike hire (Dkr100 per day), boat hire (Dkr50 per hour), internet cafe and a shop. In high summer there are guided kayak tours (Dkr350) and nature workshops in English, German and Danish.

Danhostel Møns Klint
HOSTEL €
(⊘55 81 24 34; www.danhostel.dk/hostel/danhostel-moens-klint; Klintholm Havnevej 17A, Borre; dm/s/d/tr from Dkr180/340/380/470; 🅿🛜) With lots of shady trees and scurrying hares, this hostel has a pleasant lakeside location 3km northwest of Møns Klint. There are 29 rooms, cosy seating areas and plenty of kids' toys. The hostel also offers bike rental (per day Dkr70). From Stege, take bus 667.

★Liselund Ny Slot
HOTEL €€
(⊘55 81 20 81; www.liselundslot.dk; Langebjergvej 6; s/d incl breakfast Dkr800/1200, 2nd night d Dkr900; 🅿) If the idea of slumbering in a romantic, 19th-century manor house appeals, Liselund Ny Slot has your name all over its art-clad walls. The 17 rooms are simply yet elegantly furnished, with old wooden floorboards and views of the calming gardens. Each room is named after a Hans Christian Andersen fairy tale, and the in-house cafe (cake Dkr25, lunch Dkr85-135; ⊗10am-6pm daily late Jun-early Aug, shorter hrs rest of yr) comes with enchanting lawn seating.

The hotel also offers dinner, though its gourmet ambitions don't quite hit the mark.

Bakkegaard Gæstgiveri
GUESTHOUSE €€
(⊘55 81 93 01; www.bakkegaarden64.dk; Busenevej 64, Busene; s with/without view Dkr390/440, d with/without view Dkr650/550; 🅿@) Artists and the artistically inclined will adore this guesthouse, run by local painters Vivi Schlechter and Uffe Hofmann Andersen. Within walking distance of Møns Klint and set on peaceful grounds with sea views, its 12 cosy rooms are decorated by 13 local artists. The cultural theme continues with a small gallery and occasional art classes, while the in-house cafe/restaurant serves mostly organic, local produce.

Klintholm Havn

This sleepy one-road village wakes up in summer, when the large harbourside holiday resort throws open its doors, German tourist yachts mingle with the Klintholm fishing boats and sun-seekers flock to the long sandy beach. The eastern section is particularly pristine, with light grey sand backed by low dunes and the best surf. The safest swimming is on the stretch west of Klintholm.

A novel way to experience the white cliffs of Møns Klint is on a two-hour boat trip (☑21 40 41 81; www.sejlkutteren-discovery.dk; adult/child Dkr175/90) from Klintholm Havn, at 10am, noon, 2pm, 4pm and 7pm daily from late June to the end of August (noon, 2pm and occasionally 4pm from mid-April to late June).

You can hire bicycles from the Min Købmand supermarket (Thyravej 6; ⊙7am-8pm) for Dkr70 per day.

✗ Eating

Klintholm Røgeri   SEAFOOD €€
(Thyravej 25; lunch/dinner buffet Dkr125/165; ⊙noon-4pm & 6-9pm; 🐾) Head to Klintholm's harbourside smokehouse to tackle a lip-smacking buffet of grilled, smoked and marinated ocean treats. Kids under 12 are charged half-price.

Portofino   ITALIAN €€
(Thyravej 4A; pizzas Dkr59-99, pasta Dkr59-118, mains Dkr128-188; ⊙1-9pm Wed-Mon, 5-9pm Tue Jul–mid-Aug, 5-9pm Thu-Sun rest of yr) Humble Portofino serves satisfying Italian dishes, including authentic pizzas and a just-like-Mamma's pasta *al ragù*. If you're lucky, Tuscan owner Adriano might even serenade you on his electric keyboard.

Western Møn

You'll see more pheasants than people on the narrow country lanes at the western end of Møn: such tourist-free ruralism is very restful. There are a few worthwhile historic sights, but you'll need your own transport as public buses primarily serve Rte 287.

◉ Sights

★Fanefjord Kirke   CHURCH
(Fanefjordvej; ⊙8am-6pm) This 13th-century church is adorned with superb frescoes. The oldest, from 1350, depicts St Christopher carrying Christ across a fjord, but most of the vaults are covered with a cartoon-like 'paupers' Bible by the 'Elmelunde master'. Unique images include a gruesome one of Judas, with two devils pulling out his soul; Mary on doomsday, tipping the judgment scales in humanity's favour; and a gleeful horny-kneed demon listening to two women gossiping!

Passage Graves   HISTORIC SITE
FREE There are 119 megalithic tombs on Møn, dating from 4000 to 1800 BC. Two of the best-known passage graves (*jættestuer*, or 'giants rooms') are Kong Asgers Høj and Klekkende Høj, each about 2km from the village of Røddinge. Northwest of Røddinge, **Kong Asgers Høj** (Kong Asgersvej) is Denmark's largest passage grave, with a burial chamber 10m long and more than 2m wide. Southeast of Røddinge, **Klekkende Høj** is the only double passage grave on Møn: the side-by-side entrances each lead to a 7m-long burial chamber.

The grave is 400m away from a tiny car park through a farmer's field.

Grønsalen   ARCHAEOLOGICAL SITE
A short walk down the road from Fanefjord Kirke (turn left out of the church driveway) is one of Denmark's longest megalithic barrows, Grønsalen. You can't go inside, but you can admire its scale – it's 102m long and surrounded by 145 huge blocks of sparkling, pinkish-hued rock.

🛏 Sleeping & Eating

★Tohøjgaard Gæstgivern   GUESTHOUSE €€
(☑55 81 60 67; www.tohoejgaard.com; Rytsebækvej 17, Hjelm; r Dkr480-700; ⊙mid-Mar–mid-Oct; 🅿🐾) Book ahead to slumber at one of Denmark's most coveted guesthouses: an 1875 farmhouse surrounded by fields, a 4000-year-old burial mound and calming sea views. Six eclectic, individually themed guestrooms are a cosy combo of flea-market finds, books and fluffy bathrobes, while the welcome tray of organic local chocolates, seasonal fruit and juice is a sweet extra touch. Breakfast is an extra Dkr70.

On Fridays and Saturdays, host Christine serves fabulous Scandinavian dinners (two courses Dkr195) at a communal table in the converted milking room. On all other nights, she offers a simpler 'biker's supper' (from Dkr130). The guesthouse lies 9.5km southwest of Stege; if catching public transport, you'll need to walk about 4km to get here.

Damme Kro
DANISH €€

(Fanefjordgade 162, Askeby; lunch Dkr32-112, dinner mains Dkr99-229; ⊙ 4-9pm Tue-Fri, noon-9pm Sat & Sun) Trainers and cardiologists don't exist in the world of Damme Kro, a fantastically old-school Danish inn where the Béarnaise sauce is thick and the herring served with a side of lard. Slip into dining rooms adorned with old flasks, pot plants and Poul Henningsen lamps and tuck into faithful, delicious classics like fried eel with boiled potato in white wine sauce, hash with fried egg, and golden schnitzels.

From Stege, catch bus 684, which stops right in front of the inn.

Bogø

The island of Bogø, west of Møn, is somewhere you pass through on the way to somewhere else. It's connected to Møn by a causeway, and to Zealand and Falster via the impressive Farø bridges.

Bicycles are not allowed on the Farø bridges, so cyclists need to take the summer-only **car ferry** (☑ 30 53 24 28; www.idas-venner.dk; one way adult/child Dkr25/15, car/bicycle Dkr65/20; ⊙ May–mid-Sep) that shuttles between southern Bogø and Stubbekøbing in Falster. Ferries run from Bogø hourly between 9.15am and 6.15pm, and from Stubbekøbing between 9am and 6pm. From early to mid-May, ferries from Bogø run from 10.15am to 2.15pm, and from Stubbekøbing between 10am and 1.30pm.

FALSTER

POP 43,400

The southeastern coast of Falster is a summer haven where white-sand beaches act as a magnet for German and Danish holidaymakers. Marielyst in particular is a popular family seaside destination, with the emphasis on gentle activity holidays. A short drive away, Nykøbing's Middelaldercentret is another winner with the kids, where they can spend a pleasant half-day watching giant catapults being fired, cheering on jousting knights and exploring the medieval town.

You might fancy a car or bike ride through Falster's rather repetitive agricultural interior to the tip of the island, where Denmark's most southerly point is acknowledged by Sydstenen (the South Stone), a big rock with a bench in front of it.

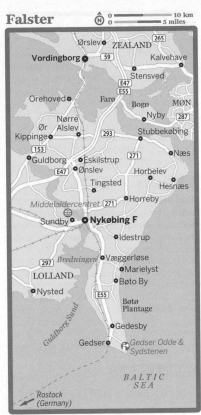

Falster

❶ Getting There & Away

Nykøbing F is 128km southwest of Copenhagen. The north–south E55 highway goes directly through Nykøbing F, while Rte 9 connects Nykøbing F with Lolland via the Frederik IX bridge.

Trains leave Copenhagen hourly for Nykøbing F (Dkr171, two hours).

There are ferries from Gedser (26km south of Nykøbing F) to Rostock in Germany. Bus 740 runs to Gedser (Dkr36, 40 minutes), with one to two services per hour Monday to Saturday, and one service every two hours on Sunday.

❶ Getting Around

From Nykøbing F train station it's a 25-minute bus ride to Marielyst (Dkr24) on bus 741. The service runs hourly on weekdays and every two hours on weekends. Bus 742 also runs between Nykøbing F and Marielyst.

Bicycles can be hired from the Marielyst tourist information office for Dkr60 per day.

Nykøbing F

POP 16,450

Falster's only large town is Nykøbing F, which sprawls over the Frederick IX bridge and onto the island of Lolland. The best thing about it is its Medieval Centre, complete with jousting knights, which makes a very entertaining family day out. Otherwise, Nykøbing F is a modern town with few tourist attractions.

The 'F', incidentally, stands for Falster and is used to differentiate the town from Denmark's two other Nykøbings.

◉ Sights

Middelaldercentret   THEME PARK

(Medieval Centre; www.middelaldercentret.dk; Ved Hamborgskoven 2, Sundby L; adult/child/family Dkr125/65/300; ⊙10am-5pm Jul–mid-Aug, to 4pm May, Jun & mid-Aug–Sep, closed Mon May & Sep; ⊕) Time-travel to the days of damsels and knights at this recreated early-15th-century medieval village – great fun, especially if you have kids. The site includes four brutal-looking siege engines (fired off at noon), a merchant's house with its own harbour and boats, a marketplace surrounded by craft workshops, and a playground complete with medieval-inspired play equipment. Try to visit during the knights' tournaments, which occur at 1.45pm daily from late June to mid-August (1.30pm Tuesday, Wednesday, Thursday, Saturday and Sunday outside those months).

The Medieval Centre is on the outskirts of Nykøbing F, across the bridge on Lolland. Bus 702 runs from Nykøbing F train station roughly half-hourly on weekdays and hourly on weekends.

Museet Falsters Minder   MUSEUM

(Langgade 2; admission Dkr50; ⊙10am-5pm Mon-Fri, to 4pm Sat mid-Jun–Aug, 10am-4pm Tue-Sat rest of yr) This is a nicely presented local-history museum, occupying one of Nykøbing F's oldest houses. It includes costumes, toys, glass, ceramics and reconstructed 19th- and early 20th-century rooms and shops – look for the elegant, Pompeiian-themed goldsmith shop. Most labelling is in Danish.

⌁ Sleeping

The tourist office keeps a list of rooms available in private homes; prices start at Dkr300 per person, with a Dkr25 booking fee.

WORTH A TRIP

OREBY KRO & MØLLE

Down a bucolic country road, 4km northwest of the town of Sakskøbing, lie two of Lolland's best-kept secrets. The first is **Oreby Kro** (☑54 17 44 66; Orebygaard 2, Sakskøbing; lunch Dkr89-180, dinner mains Dkr180; ⊙noon-4pm & 5.30-10pm Tue-Sat, noon-4pm Sun Jun-Sep, shorter hrs rest of yr). Set in a thick-walled, fjord-flanking inn dating from 1847, its snug, elegant dining rooms, adorned with oil paintings, antique furniture, and the odd mounted deer, set a suitable scene for soulful, produce-driven Danish fare like butter-fried plaice with onions, capers, grilled lemon and Danish potatoes, or *koldskål* (cold buttermilk soup) with *kammerjunker* biscuit and strawberries.

Beside Oreby Kro lies **Oreby Mølle** (☑54 70 70 88; www.orebymolle.dk; Orebygaard 4, Sakskøbing; s/d with bathroom incl breakfast Dkr995/1195, s without bathroom incl breakfast from Dkr595; P🞲), an aristocratic manor house set on handsome grounds with views of the fjord. Restored under the guidance of Hans Michael Jebsens, a Danish businessman famed for reviving historic properties, it is now one of the Denmark's most romantic hotels, its elegant, time-warped rooms lavished with valuable art, antiques and textiles. Communal spaces include a beautiful old library, its soaring shelves lined with old books which can be browsed on velvet sofas. Four rooms have their own bathroom, some have their own toilet, and all others have a shared bathroom. The most beautiful rooms are those in the main building, also home to the sublimely spacious Bridal Suite (Dkr1995), which comes with its own fireplace and private dining room.

Sakskøbing lies 17km west of Nykøbing F and 9km east of Maribo. The town is connected to Oreby Kro and Oreby Mølle via Orebyvej, which runs off the main street of Brogade. Although local trains to Sakskøbing run half-hourly to hourly from both Nykøbing F (Dkr36, 16 minutes) and Maribo (Dkr24, 7 minutes), Oreby Kro and Oreby Mølle are an inconvenient 4.7km walk from Sakskøbing station, making the use of public transport less than ideal.

Falster City Camping
CAMPGROUND €

(☑ 54 85 45 45; www.fc-camp.dk; Østre Allé 112; campsites per adult/child Dkr80/40, small/large huts Dkr160/230; ☺ Easter-Sep; 🛜) A very non-urban city camping ground, this two-star place is down a quiet tree-lined lane, near the hostel and Nykøbing's excellent swimming pool. There are small red huts for rent, a playground with bouncy pillows, and free wi-fi. Bike hire costs Dkr50 per day.

Danhostel Nykøbing Falster
HOSTEL €

(☑ 54 85 66 99; www.danhostel.dk/nykoebing-falster; Østre Allé 110; dm/s/d Dkr300/350/450; P 🛜) Probably one of the few hostels in the world where you can hear the rusty belch of tigers, this modern 94-bed place is near the zoo, 1km east of the centre. An overhanging roof makes rooms quite dark, but all have toilets, and facilities include a washing machine and TV lounge. Take bus 741 (Dkr24) from Nykøbing F train station.

Hotel Falster
HOTEL €€

(☑ 54 85 93 93; www.hotel-falster.dk; Skovalléen 2; s/d incl breakfast Dkr765/955; P @) This is a family-run place with friendly management and 69 comfortable, albeit dated rooms. Although its location just off a busy main road is not appealing, it's relatively central. In mid-2014 the hotel's restaurant and lobby were undergoing reconstruction after a fire in the restaurant kitchen.

✖ Eating

Café Vandtårnet
CAFE €

(Hollandsgård 20; sandwiches Dkr45; ☺ 10am-4pm Mon-Fri) Channelling Copenhagen with its boldly coloured furniture, low-slung table lamps, and contemporary art, this cool, laid-back hang-out sits at the bottom of the town's old water tower. Tuck into fresh sandwiches, muffins, biscuits and tarts, and wash it all down with the town's best coffee. Customers get a 50% discount to the art gallery (vandtaarnet.multicentersyd. dk; adult/child Dkr20/10; ☺ 10am-4pm Mon-Fri) upstairs.

★ La Comida
DANISH €€

(☑ 54 85 09 10; www.lacomida.dk; Slotsgade 22; mains Dkr210; ☺ 5-9pm Tue-Sat) Set in a white-washed, 19th-century wine cellar and run by a young, talented team, La Comida is by far one of the top dining options in the south islands. The short, seasonal evening menu is determined by the morning's market produce, put to outstanding use in sophisticated

yet simple dishes like 15-hour slow-cooked veal served with green tomatoes cooked in apple vinegar, cardamon and vanilla.

The wine list offers some inspired, lesser-known selections; trust the waitstaff's recommendations.

❶ Information

Torvet, the town centre, is a 10-minute walk west of the train station.

Tourist Office (☑ 51 21 25 08; www.visitlol-land-falster.com; Langgade 2; ☺ 10am-5pm Mon-Fri, to 2pm Sat; 🛜) Located in the Museet Falsters Minder, the tourist office provides information and free wi-fi.

Marielyst

POP 705

With its glorious stretch of beach, Marielyst is one of Denmark's prime vacation areas. Thankfully, the beach is long enough to absorb the crowds, and you should be able to find a relatively private patch of your own. For the most convenient parking, follow the main street until it dead-ends.

The town itself is one long strip of bucket-and-spade shops, bars, pizza places and ice-cream kiosks running perpendicularly down towards the beach. In high season there are loads of different activities to try around Marielyst, from windsurfing classes to paintball. The tourist office has information on all activities.

⚊ Sleeping

The tourist office has a list of available rooms in private homes, updated daily. Expect to pay around Dkr800 for a double room.

Marielyst Feriepark & Camping
CAMPGROUND €

(☑ 70 20 79 99; www.marielyst-camping.dk; Marielyst Strandvej 36; campsites per adult/child Dkr75/35; ☺ Apr-Sep; @) This centrally located camping ground is off the main road. Hedges break up the pitches, but also make it feel slightly cramped.

Hotel Nørrevang
HOTEL €€€

(☑ 54 13 62 62; www.norrevang.dk; Marielyst Strandvej 32; d from Dkr995, cottages from Dkr1450; P 🛜 ☺) Marielyst's most upmarket hotel offers classic rooms under a low-slung thatched roof. Standard rooms have a toilet, phone, satellite TV and free wireless internet. There are 54 cottages with kitchens that can accommodate four to six people, as well as an indoor pool with spa and water slide. The 'upmarket' restaurant is best avoided.

✗ Eating

Many of Marielyst's eating places are closed for lunch and on Mondays out of the high season. On the corner of Bøtøvej and Marielyst Strandvej you'll find several ice-cream and hot-dog kiosks.

Larsen's Plads INTERNATIONAL **€€**
(☑ 54 13 21 70; Marielyst Strandvej 53; pizzas Dkr52-85, mains Dkr149-169, dinner buffet Dkr159; ⊘ 10am-9pm daily) 'My wife left me for my best friend. God, I miss him.' If you find that funny, there are plenty more jokes plastering the walls of idiosyncratic Larsen's Plads. It offers hearty beef, chicken and fish dishes, several vegetarian offerings, a big brunch (Dkr99) and takeaway pizzas. For fresh bread and pastries, head to **Larsen's Bageri** (pastries Dkr12; ⊘ 6am-5pm) across the street.

ⓘ Information

Tourist Office (☑ 54 13 62 98; www.visitmarielyst.com; Marielyst Strandpark 3; ⊘ 10am-4pm Mon-Fri, to 5pm Sat, to 2pm Sun late Jun–mid-Aug, shorter hrs rest of yr; 🛜) By the bowling alley on the outskirts of town. Offers extensive information, as well as free internet and wi-fi.

LOLLAND

POP 65,580

Lolland's flat farmland is enlivened by a smattering of family-friendly attractions – parents with their own transport should take the kids to see monkeys and tigers at Knuthenborg Safari Park, and to the vast, slide-filled waterpark of Lalandia. The most appealing of Lolland's towns is Maribo, nestled on the shores of a bird-filled lake.

ⓘ Getting There & Around

The main east–west railway line runs between Nykøbing F (on Falster) and Nakskov (Dkr84, 45 minutes), with half-hourly to hourly trains during the week (hourly on weekends).

The other railway line runs between Nykøbing F and the Rødby ferry (Dkr48, 25 minutes). Trains leave Rødbyhavn several times a day in conjunction with the ferry service to Puttgarden, Germany; most of the trains continue on from Nykøbing F to Copenhagen.

LangelandsFærgen (☑ 70 23 15 15; www.faergen.dk; adult/child/car with up to nine passengers one-way Dkr80/40/260) runs a car ferry between Tårs (in the far west of Lolland) and Spodsbjerg (in Langeland) once an hour. Travel time is 45 minutes. See the website for up-to-date sailing times.

There's a direct ferry service to Puttgarden (Germany) from Rødbyhavn, a small harbourside

Lolland

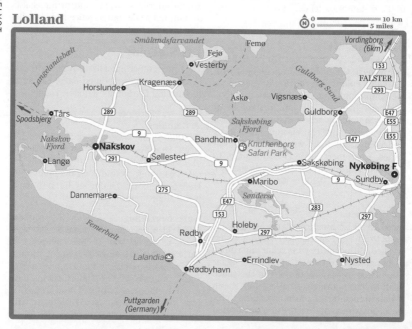

FUGLSANG KUNSTMUSEUM

Fuglsang Kunstmuseum (www.fuglsangkunstmuseum.dk; Nystedvej 71; adult/child Dkr70/free; ⊗10am-5pm Jun-Aug, shorter hrs rest of yr) Lolland's cultural cred received a much-needed boost with the opening of Fuglsang Kunstmuseum, considered one of Denmark's most comprehensive regional art museums. White, abstract and dramatically framed by Lolland's trademark green fields, its permanent collection spans Danish painting, illustration and sculpture from 1780 to today.

You'll find landscape paintings from prolific 19th-century artists like Jens Juel and PC Skovgaard, including the latter's iconic *View from the Cliffs of Møn* (1852). The museum has a particularly impressive collection of early-20th-century works, among them Jais Nielsen's striking Futurist painting *Afgang!* (1918).

Permanent collection aside, Fuglsang Kunstmuseum hosts around three temporary exhibitions annually, and houses a cafe and small, savvy gift shop.

You'll find the museum 4.5km south of the town of Sakskøbing, itself 9km east of Maribo.

town in the south. It provides the link in the inter-Europe E47 highway between Germany and Denmark.

Maribo

POP 5925

Maribo is easily the most agreeable of Lolland's towns, with a picture-perfect setting on the shores of a large inland lake, **Søndersø**. Its historic cathedral, thick beech woods, waterside walking paths and a few small museums are the main attractions – it's really a place for slow strolling, breathing deeply and letting all that tension slide away.

◉ Sights & Activities

Maribo Domkirke   CATHEDRAL
(⊗9am-3pm Mon, 8am-6pm Tue-Sat, 8am-4pm Sun Apr-Oct, shorter hrs rest of yr) Founded in the 15th century, Maribo's cathedral was once part of a larger monastic complex. Countess Leonora Christine, daughter of Christian IV, joined the convent in 1685 after she was released from a 22-year imprisonment in Copenhagen Castle. She lived the rest of her life here, editing the prison journals that record her tribulations – rat infestations, a flea-infested cell, a randy jailer and the vindictiveness of the queen, Sophia Amelia. Leonora Christine's crypt is in the cathedral, marked by a plainly lettered tombstone.

Frilandsmuseet Maribo   MUSEUM
(www.aabne-samlinger.dk; Meinckesvej 5; adult/child incl admission to Stiftsmuseum Maribo Dkr60/free; ⊗10am-4pm Tue-Sun May-Sep) Alfresco Frilandsmuseet Maribo is made up of buildings plucked from elsewhere in Denmark, from a farm, fire station and windmill, to a dairy, schoolhouse and smithy. Old-fashioned games are scattered about the gardens – who could resist a round of Poke Out Palle's Eye? The museum is 1km from Torvet, close to the camping ground.

Stiftsmuseum Maribo   MUSEUM
(www.aabne-samlinger.dk; Banegårdspladsen 5; adult/child incl admission to Frilandsmuseet Maribo Dkr60/free; ⊗11am-4pm Thu-Sat) ✎ Beside Maribo's train station, this little museum contains Stone Age arrowheads, Viking combs, Iron Age glass-bead necklaces, and clothes, toys and furniture. Several rooms explore the experience of 18th-century Polish immigrants, who settled in the area to work in the cane fields and sugar refineries. Most of the information is in Danish and German.

Anemonen   BOAT TOUR
(☑54 78 04 96; uk.naturparkmaribo.dk; adult/child return ticket to Borgø Dkr75/30) The good ship *Anemonen* sails on Maribo's island-dotted lake in summer. Some of the trips stop at Borgø, which hides the ruins of an 11th-century fortress destroyed by a medieval peasants' uprising. Trips run from the jetty outside the cathedral from May to September, at least once weekly (increasing to four times weekly in July and August). See the website for the latest sailing schedule.

✪ Festivals & Events

Maribo Jazz Festival   MUSIC
(www.maribojazz.dk in Danish) The four-day Maribo Jazz Festival adds to the town's laid-back ambience on the third weekend in July.

🛏 Sleeping

The well-organised tourist office can book single/double rooms in private homes for around Dkr300/500, plus a Dkr25 booking fee.

Maribo Sø Camping   CAMPGROUND €
(☑54 78 00 71; www.maribo-camping.dk; Bang-shavevej 25; campsites per adult/child Dkr78/42; ☺Apr–mid-Oct; 🛜) Maribo's appealing three-star camping ground has a prime position on Søndersø, with arresting views of the cathedral across the water. It's very well equipped, with a shop, kitchen, coin laundry and TV lounge, and it's accessible to people in wheelchairs. The camping ground is 500m southwest of town.

Danhostel Maribo   HOSTEL €
(☑54 78 33 14; www.maribo-vandrerhjem.dk; Søndre Blvd 82B; dm/s/d Dkr180/350/400; ☺Feb–mid-Dec; 🅿) About 2km southeast of Torvet, this modern hostel near Søndersø has 96 beds. There's a lakeside trail to town, and you can hire bicycles (Dkr85 per day) to get you about.

Ebsens Hotel   HOTEL €€
(☑54 78 10 44; www.ebsens-hotel.dk; Vestergade 32; s/d incl breakfast from Dkr595/695; 🅿@🛜) Rooms at Ebsens are small and straightforward, but it's a friendly family-run place and relatively good value, especially the four cheaper rooms without toilets. The hotel also has a cosy, wood-panelled lunch and dinner **restaurant** (mains Dkr149-Dkr268) serving mostly Danish fare.

🍴 Eating

Restaurant Svanen   INTERNATIONAL €€
(2-/3- course dinner Dkr345/395; ☺6-9pm) White-linen tables and a lakeside location befit Maribo's top restaurant, located inside Hotel Maribo Søpark. Savour the likes of lime-marinated salmon or saltimbocca-style hake with ham and Brie in a white-wine sauce.

Panya Thai   THAI €€
(Vesterbrogade 55; mains Dkr94-115; ☺4-9.30pm) While it mightn't deliver the zing of true Thai food, tasty Panya makes for a refreshing change from the stock-standard burgers and Danish standbys. Best of all, vegetarians are well catered for.

ℹ Information

Tourist Office (☑54 78 04 96; www.visitlolland-falster.com; Rådhuset, Torvet; ☺10am-4.30pm Mon-Fri, to 2pm Sat mid-Jun–Aug, shorter hrs rest of yr) Located on the main town square.

Around Lolland

Knuthenborg Safari Park

Drive-through **Knuthenborg Safari Park** (www.knuthenborg.dk; Knuthenborg Allé, Bandholm; adult/child Dkr199/109; ☺10am-6pm Jul-early Aug, shorter hrs rest of yr), 7km north of Maribo via Rte 289, is northern Europe's biggest safari park and one of Denmark's top attractions. Its collection of over 1200 wild animals includes free-roaming zebras, antelopes, giraffes, rhinoceroses, wallabies and other exotic creatures. The park occupies what was once Denmark's largest private estate and has an arboretum, aviary, a tiger forest (complete with free-roaming tigers) and a big adventure playground for your own little monkeys. The savannah is off limits to anyone not inside a vehicle. Just as well!

Lalandia

As this **amusement park** (www.lalandia.dk; Lalandia Centret 1, Rødby; adult/child Dkr200/150; ☺waterpark 1-7pm late May-late Aug, shorter hrs rest of yr) has Denmark's largest swimming area, Lalandia really undersells itself using the term waterpark. Sure it has indoor pools, outdoor pools, water slides, Jacuzzis and a wave machine, but there are also all kinds of other satellite attractions: mini golf, bowling, a fitness centre, pitch and field sports, an indoor ski slope, restaurants, supermarket, indoor playground Monky Tonky Land, and children's shows and discos. Most people come on an accommodation package, with a minimum two-night stay (from around Dkr2050 in high season). 'Residents' get in free to the waterpark and indoor playground, and enjoy priority hours. Lalandia is 5km northwest of the small port of Rødbyhavn, in the south of the island.

Bornholm

Includes ➡

Rønne 143
Åkirkeby 145
Dueodde 146
Snogebæk 147
Nexø 147
Svaneke 148
Gudhjem & Melsted . . 150
Sandvig & Allinge 153
Hammershus Slot . . . 154
Hammeren 155
Christiansø 155

Best Places to Eat

➡ Kadeau (p146)

➡ Lassens (p153)

➡ Nordbornholms Røgeri (p153)

➡ Hallegård (p147)

➡ Café Sommer (p154)

Best Places to Stay

➡ Stammershalle Badehotel (p152)

➡ Byskrivergaarden (p153)

➡ Jantzens Hotel (p150)

➡ Christiansø Gæstgiveriet (p156)

➡ Hotel Romantik (p153)

Why Go?

The sunniest part of Denmark, Bornholm lies way out in the Baltic Sea, 200km east of Copenhagen. But it's not just (relatively) sunny skies that draw the hordes each year. Mother Nature was in a particularly good mood when creating this Baltic beauty, bestowing on it arresting chalk cliffs, soothing forests, bleach-white beaches and a pure, ethereal light that painters do their best to capture.

Humankind added the beguiling details, from medieval fortress ruins and thatched fishing villages, to the iconic *rundkirker* (round churches) and contemporary Bornholms Kunstmuseum. The island's ceramic and glassware artisans are famed throughout Denmark, as are its historic smokehouses and ever-expanding league of food artisans. It's no wonder that seven out of 10 visitors to Bornholm return.

From October to April, many places close, so always do your homework (www.bornholm.info).

When to Go

Bornholm blooms from June to mid-September, with attractions, tourist offices, transport and cultural events operating at full steam. Long days and warmer weather are ideal for hiking, cycling and getting wet on Bornholm's beautiful beaches. On the food front, June plays host to Denmark's most famous one-day cook-off, Sol over Gudhjem. Outside of these warmer months, the island slows down, with many attractions, restaurants and accommodation options reducing their hours or closing down for the season. Needless to say, prebook accommodation in the summer, especially in the most crowded month, July.

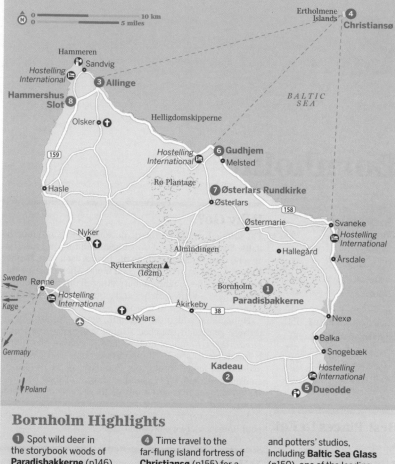

Bornholm Highlights

1 Spot wild deer in the storybook woods of **Paradisbakkerne** (p146)

2 Feast on extraordinary New Nordic cuisine at culinary hotspot **Kadeau** (p146)

3 Tuck into traditionally smoked fish in a Bornholm *røgeri*, or smokehouse, like the one in **Allinge** (p153)

4 Time travel to the far-flung island fortress of **Christiansø** (p155) for a taste of cosy village life

5 Wiggle the finest white sand between your toes on the sweeping beach at **Dueodde** (p146)

6 Shop for one-off creations at the island's plethora of glass-blowers'

and potters' studios, including **Baltic Sea Glass** (p150), one of the leading glass-blowing ateliers

7 Hit the bike pedal from Gudhjem to the striking, whitewashed **Østerlars Rundkirke** (p152)

8 Snoop around the commanding clifftop ruins of **Hammershus Slot** (p154)

ⓘ Getting There & Away

Bornholm can be reached by air, boat or a combination that couples the boat with a bus or train via Sweden.

AIR

Danish Airport Transport (DAT; ☏ 76 92 30 40; www.dat.dk) operates several flights a day between Copenhagen and Rønne. Book ahead for cheaper flights.

BOAT

BornholmerFærgens (☏ 70 23 15 15; www.faergen.dk; adult/child 12-15/under 11 Dkr290/145/free, car incl 5 passengers Dkr1625) operates an overnight ferry service from Køge, 39km south of Copenhagen, to Bornholm. The ferry departs daily at 12.30am and arrives at 6am. The upside is that you travel while you sleep (a berth costs an extra Dkr278). The downside is the trip out to Køge, about 30 minutes by train south of Copenhagen, adds additional time and cost.

BUS & BOAT

Graahundbus (www.graahundbus.dk) runs buses several times daily between Copenhagen's Central Station and Ystad in Sweden (bus route 866), where it connects with a catamaran (adult/child Dkr290/150). The bus takes around one hour and 10 minutes to Ystad, followed by the standard 1¼-hour catamaran service to Rønne on Bornholm.

TRAIN & BOAT

DSB (www.dsb.dk) offers a combined train/catamaran service (adult/child Dkr328/149) to Rønne. You catch a train from Copenhagen's Central Station to Ystad in Sweden, then connect with the catamaran to Rønne. It's also possible to drive to Ystad and cross with a car from there. The total trip should take no more than 3½ hours.

❶ Getting Around

TO/FROM THE AIRPORT

The island's airport, Bornholms Lufthavn, is 5km southeast of Rønne, on the road to Dueodde. Buses 6 and 7 connects the airport to Rønne.

BICYCLE

Bornholm is ideal for cycling, with over 230km of bike trails crisscrossing the island. Some of the trails go over former train routes, some slice through forests, and others run alongside main roads. You can start right in Rønne, where bike routes fan out to Allinge, Gudhjem, Nexø, Dueodde and the Almindingen forest.

If you don't feel like pedalling the entire way, you can take your bike on public buses for an additional Dkr24.

The tourist office in Rønne sells the 82-page English-language *Bicycle Routes on Bornholm* (Dkr129), which maps out routes and describes sights along the way. It also provides a free, simple map of cycling routes on the island.

You'll find bike rental outlets in most major towns. **Bornholms Cykeludlejning** (bike rental per 1/2/7 days Dkr70/140/390; ⏰9.30am-5.30pm Mon-Fri, 9am-noon & 2-5.30pm Sat) is the handiest one, close to the Rønne ferry terminal and next door to the island's main tourist office.

BUS

Bornholms Amts Trafikselskab (BAT; www.bat.dk; pass per day adult/child Dkr150/75, per week Dkr500/250) operates bus services on the island. Fares are based on a zone system, with

the maximum fare being for five zones. Tickets cost Dkr13 per zone, and are valid for unlimited trips within one zone for 30 minutes. Another 15 minutes validity is added for each added zone. The multiride 'RaBATkort' ticket is good for 10 rides and can be used by more than one person. Day/week passes cost Dkr150/500. Children travel for half-price. Buses operate all year, but schedules are less frequent from October to April. All ticket types can be purchased on board.

Buses 7 and 8 circumnavigate the island, stopping at all major towns and settlements. Other buses make direct runs from Rønne to Nexø, Svaneke, Gudhjem and Sandvig.

CAR & MOTORCYCLE

Europcar (📞56 95 43 00; www.europcar.com; Nordre Kystvej 1, Rønne) is at the Q8 petrol station and rents cars from around Dkr600 per day, as well as scooters. It has another branch at the airport.

Rønne

POP 13,570

Rønne is Bornholm's largest settlement and the main harbour for ferries from Ystad in Sweden and Køge in Denmark. The town has been the island's commercial centre since the Middle Ages, and while the place has expanded and taken on a more suburban look over the years, a handful of well-preserved quarters still provide pleasant strolling. Especially appealing is the old neighbourhood west of Store Torv with its handsome period buildings and cobblestone streets, among them Laksegade and Storegade.

◎ Sights

Bornholms Museum MUSEUM
(www.bornholmsmuseum.dk; Sankt Mortensgade 29; adult/child incl entry to Hjorths Fabrik Dkr70/free; ⏰10am-5pm Jul–mid-Aug, closed Sun mid-May–Jun & mid-Aug–mid-Oct, shorter hrs rest of yr) Prehistoric finds including weapons, tools and jewellery are on show at Bornholm's main museum, which has a surprisingly large and varied collection of local history exhibits, including some interesting Viking finds. A good maritime section is decked out like the interior of a ship and there's a hotchpotch of nature displays, antique toys, Roman coins, pottery and paintings.

Hjorths Fabrik MUSEUM
(www.bornholmsmuseum.dk/hjorths; Krystalgade 5; adult/child incl entry to Bornholms Museum Dkr70/free; ⏰museum 10am-5pm Jul–mid-Aug, closed Sun mid-May–Jun & mid-Aug–mid-Oct,

Rønne

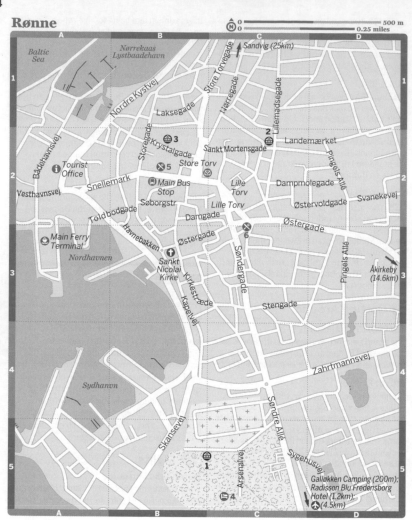

Rønne

⊙ Sights
1 Bornholms Forsvarsmuseum C5
2 Bornholms Museum C2
3 Hjorths Fabrik.....................................B2

🛏 Sleeping
4 Danhostel Rønne C5

✕ Eating
5 Jensen's Bageri..................................B2
6 Oste-Hjørnet.......................................C3

shorter hrs rest of yr, studio 10am-4pm mid-May–mid-Oct) This ceramics museum features a working studio, and watching the master artisans turn clay into beautifully moulded works of art is the real highlight. You'll find some fetching, locally made wares for sale in the shop in front (which is free to enter).

★ **Nylars Rundkirke**   CHURCH
(Kirkevej 10K, Nylars; ⊙ 7am-6pm Apr-Sep, 8am-3.30pm Oct-Mar) Built in 1150, Nylars Rundkirke is the most well-preserved and easily accessible round church in the Rønne area. Its central pillar is adorned with wonderful

13th-century frescoes, the oldest in Bornholm. The works depict scenes from the Creation myth, including Adam and Eve's expulsion from the Garden of Eden. The cylindrical nave has three storeys, the top one a watchman's gallery that served as a defence lookout in medieval times.

Inside the church, the front door is flanked by two of Bornholm's 40 rune stones; carved memorial stones that date back to the Viking era. Nylars Rundkirke is about 8km from Rønne, on the road to Åkirkeby, and a 15- to 20-minute trip from Rønne on bus 5 or 6; alight at Nylars bus stop and turn north on Kirkevej for the 350m walk to the church. The cycle path between Rønne and Åkirkeby also passes the church.

Bornholms Forsvarsmuseum   MUSEUM
(Defence Museum; www.bornholmsforsvarsmuseum. dk; Arsenalvej 8; adult/child Dkr55/35; ⊙10am-4pm Tue-Sat mid-May–early Oct) A 17th-century citadel called Kastellet houses the Forsvarsmuseum, south of the town centre. The museum has extensive displays of guns, blades, bombs and military uniforms, but the historical context they are given is usually scant. Some brief explanatory notes in English are available from the ticket desk. There are especially large displays on the Nazi occupation of the island and on the bombing of Rønne and Nexø by the Soviets at the end of WWII.

🛏 Sleeping

The tourist office can book rooms (singles/doubles Dkr225/400) in private homes in Rønne; there's no booking fee.

Galløkken Camping   CAMPGROUND €
(☑56 95 23 20; www.gallokken.dk; Strandvejen 4; campsites per adult/child Dkr72/37; ⊙May-Aug) Just over 1km south of the town centre, this well-equipped, family-orientated camping ground also has basic but attractive four-bed wooden cabins (from Dkr550 per day) and bikes for rent (per day Dkr70).

Danhostel Rønne   HOSTEL €
(☑56 95 13 40; www.danhostel-roenne.dk; Arsenalvej 12; dm/s/d/tr Dkr200/350/450/530; ⊙Apr-late Oct; [P][🖥]) The immaculately kept 140-bed hostel near Galløkken Camping is a secluded, whitewashed building with a neatly tended garden. Expect small, tidy, if somewhat soulless dorms.

Radisson Blu Fredensborg Hotel   HOTEL €€
(☑56 90 44 44; www.bornholmhotels.dk; Strandvejen 116; r incl breakfast from Dkr1125; [P][@][🖥])

🖉 Perched on a pleasant knoll overlooking wave-pounded rocks at the southern end of Rønne, the Fredensborg has 72 comfortable rooms with classic 20th-century Scandi style (admittedly, some rooms are due for a revamp) – all with sea views, some with rather pokey '70s-style toilets and a few with access for people in wheelchairs. There's also a sauna, tennis court, and restaurant.

🍴 Eating

There's a reasonable variety of restaurants and cafes in and around the main square of Store Torv, though no standout venues.

Oste-Hjørnet   DELI €
(Ostergade 40B; cheese boards from Dkr70; ⊙9am-5.30pm Mon-Thu, to 6pm Fri, to 1pm Sat) This gut-rumbling little deli stocks both local and foreign slabs of gourmet cheeses, as well as locally made charcuterie, stuffed savoury pancakes, and fresh bread – the perfect ingredients for a picnic.

Jensen's Bageri   BAKERY €
(Snellemark 41; focaccias Dkr16, pastries Dkr10; ⊙6am-5.30pm Mon-Fri, to 3pm Sat & Sun) Nibble on freshly baked focaccias, sausage rolls and Danish pastries at this petite bakery, located between the tourist office and the main town square, Store Torv.

ℹ Information
Bornholms Centralsygehus (☑56 95 11 65; Sygehusvej 9) The island's hospital is at the southern end of town.
Library (Pingels Allé; ⊙9.30am-6pm Mon-Fri, to 2pm Sat) Free internet access.
Post Office (Store Torv 11; ⊙10am-4.30pm Mon-Fri, 9.30am-noon Sat) Inside the Eurospar supermarket.
Tourist Office (Bornholms Velkomstcenter; ☑56 95 95 00; www.bornholm.info; Nordre Kystvej 3; ⊙9am-6.30pm late Jun-early Aug, shorter hrs rest of yr) A few minutes' walk from the harbour, this large, friendly office has masses of information on all of Bornholm and Christiansø.

Åkirkeby
POP 2050

The inland town of Åkirkeby is a mix of old half-timbered houses and newer homes with less pull factor.

The tourist office, car park and a couple of simple eateries are at the eastern side of the church on Jernbanegade. The town square is 150m east of the tourist office.

◎ Sights

★ NaturBornholm MUSEUM
(www.naturbornholm.dk; Grønningen 30; adult/
child Dkr100/60; ◎10am-5pm Apr-Oct) Natur-
Bornholm offers a terrific geological and
biological narrative of the island spanning
back to its fledgling days as a cooling slab
of magma. The museum is packed with
interesting facts and lively interactive displays, making it especially popular with
families. Aptly, the centre is perched atop
the ancient fault line where Bornholm's
sandstone south is fused with its gneiss
and granite north. The building itself was
designed by Henning Larsen, whose claims
to fame also include the Copenhagen Opera
House.

Aa Kirke CHURCH
(Nybyvej 2; ◎8am-5pm) The town takes its
name from its main sight, the 12th-century
Romanesque stone church Aa Kirke. Occupying a knoll overlooking the surrounding
farmland, this is Bornholm's largest church.
Slip inside for a number of historic treasures, including a 13th-century baptismal
font of carved sandstone depicting scenes of
Christ and featuring runic script. The ornate
pulpit and altar date from about 1600.

✕ Eating

★ Kadeau MODERN SCANDINAVIAN €€€
(☑56 97 82 50; www.kadeau.dk; Baunevej 18; lunch
dishes Dkr125-150, 4-/6-/8-course dinner from
Dkr600/750/950; ◎noon-4pm & 5.30pm-mid-
night Jul–mid-Aug, shorter hrs rest of yr) Book
ahead to experience one of Denmark's most
exciting and innovative destination restaurants. The menu is a confident, creative
celebration of Nordic produce and foraged
ingredients, including wild herbs from the
adjacent beach and woods. Lunch options
are limited but inspired, though the true
tour de force is dinner, where dishes such as
sugar-cured scallops in chamomile-infused
milk, served with pickled celeriac, will have
you swooning.

Take note that although Kadeau's address
is in Åkirkeby, the restaurant is actually 8km
southeast of the town, right on the beach.

Interior Woodlands

A fifth of Bornholm is wooded, making it the
most forested county in Denmark. Beech,
fir, spruce, hemlock and oak are dominant.
There are three main areas, each laid out

with walking trails (you can pick up free
maps at tourist offices). A single bicycle trail
connects them all.

Almindingen, the largest forest (2412
hectares), is in the centre of the island
and can be reached by heading north from
Åkirkeby. It's the site of Bornholm's highest
point, the 162m hill **Rytterknægten**, which
has a lookout tower called Kongemindet
from where you can view the surrounding
countryside.

Paradisbakkerne (Paradise Hills) contains wild deer and a trail that passes an
ancient monolithic gravestone. It's 2km
northwest of Nexø. **Rø Plantage**, about
5km southwest of Gudhjem, has a terrain of
heather-covered hills and woodlands.

Dueodde

Dueodde, the southernmost point of Bornholm, is a vast stretch of breathtaking beach
backed by deep green pine trees and expansive dunes. Its soft sand is so fine-grained
that it was once used in hourglasses and ink
blotters.

There's no real village at Dueodde – the
bus stops at the end of the road where
there's a hotel, a casual steakhouse restaurant, a couple of food kiosks and a boardwalk across the marsh to the beach. The
only 'sight' is a **lighthouse** on the western
side of the dunes; you can climb the 197
steps for a view of endless sand and sea.

The **beach** at Dueodde is a fantastic place
for children: the water is generally calm and
is shallow for about 100m out, after which
it becomes deep enough for adults to swim.
During July and August it can be a crowded
trek for a couple of hundred metres along
boardwalks to reach the beach. Once there,
simply head left or right to discover your
own wide-open spaces.

⌂ Sleeping

**Dueodde Vandrerhjem & Camping
Ground** HOSTEL, CAMPGROUND €
(☑56 48 81 19; www.dueodde.dk; Skorkkegårdsve-
jen 17; s/d/tr/q Dkr225/375/450/530, campsites
per adult/child Dkr72/37, tent Dkr30-40; ◎May-
Sep; 🅿🛜🏊) This upbeat beachside hostel
and camping ground combo is a 10-minute
walk east of the bus stop. The place also offers pleasant, pine-clad cabins/apartments
for rent at Dkr4500 per week for two persons. Perks include an indoor swimming
pool.

HALLEGÅRD

It might be right off the tourist radar, but artisanal charcuterie **Hallegård** (☑56 47 02 47; www.hallegaard.dk; Aspevej 3, Østermarie; tapas plate Dkr150; ☺10am-6pm late Jun–mid-Sep, shorter hrs rest of yr) is a darling of Danish locavores. Indeed, many of Copenhagen's top chefs procure their meats from this bucolic farmhouse, hidden away down a country lane 8km southwest of Svaneke. It's run by the affable Jørgen Toft Christensen, his wife Lis Frederiksen, and their family. Together they have built quite a reputation for both carnivorous concoctions, both traditional and modern. Among the classics is the 'Rita' sausage, made with pork, beef, cherry wine and dried onions. According to Jørgen's son-in-law, Christian, this is Hallegård's 'political sausage', named after a former minister of agriculture's wife, who offered the recipe and who still drops in for the odd 'quality control'.

In all, Hallegård produces around 30 types of charcuterie, some of which are smoked in traditional brick ovens. In the case of its cold smoked ham (a Bornholm 'prosciutto' of sorts), the smoking takes four to six months, with the hams stored in former WWII bunkers located nearby.

Peckish? The farmhouse deli/cafe offers a 'tapas' plate with a selection of its products, tailored to your taste buds. Pair it with a glass of the organic house wine (Dkr40) and you have one of Bornholm's best feeds.

To get here from Svaneke, head southwest along Korshøje, turning right into Ibskervej at the 'T' intersection, then left into Lyrsbyvej (look out for the 'Hallegård' sign) and left again at Aspevej. Keep in mind that opening times in the low season can vary so it's a good idea to call ahead.

Dueodde Badehotel APARTMENTS €€
(☑56 95 85 66; www.dueodde-badehotel.dk; Sirenevej 2; d per 3 nights incl breakfast Dkr2184-3744, self-catering apt per 3 days Dkr1444-3805; P❄) These smart, modern, Ikea-style apartments 150m from the beach have terraces or balconies overlooking the pleasant garden. Sleeping between two and five people, they're an especially good bet for families. The complex also offers double rooms, and those with terraces or balconies also feature a sofa and kitchenette. On-site perks include a coin laundry, tennis court and sauna.

Snogebæk

POP 706

A quaint seaside village with a pretty sweeping beach, Snogebæk makes a satisfying little detour if you are travelling by car or bike between Nexø and Dueodde. Right in town, **Kjærstrup Chocolate By Hand** (www.kjaerstrup.dk in Danish; Hovedgade 9; ☺11am-9pm daily) keeps sweet tooths purring (and dentists wealthy) with its heavenly cocoa concoctions. Taste-test the sublimely flavoured ganaches and the Danish speciality *flødebolle* (the Danish version of chocolate snowballs with whipped sugary egg whites inside a crisp chocolate dome).

Down by the water, at the southern end of Havnevej and further along Hovedgade, you'll find a small cluster of shops selling clothes and quality, reasonably priced hand-blown glass. You'll also find a good **smokehouse** (Hovedgade 6; lunch/dinner buffet Dkr120/180; ☺noon-10pm Jul, to 9pm Jun & Aug, shorter hrs rest of yr) where you can get smoked fish, deli items and cold beer. Just to the right of it is another Bornholm foodie pit stop, **Boisen Is** (www.boisen-is.dk; Hovedgade 4; 2 scoops Dkr28; ☺10am-sunset late Jun-Aug, shorter hrs rest of yr), justifiably famous for its organic, seasonally inspired ice cream.

The end of the road is a good site for spotting migratory ducks and other water birds. If you're feeling exploratory (or in need of burning some calories), follow the coastal footpath leading north along the beach.

Nexø

POP 3685

Nexø (Neksø) is Bornholm's second-largest town and like Rønne it makes up for its comparative lack of aesthetic charm with a bustling nature. It has a large modern harbour where fishing vessels unload their catch. The town and harbour were reconstructed after being destroyed by Soviet bombing in WWII. Despite taking a back seat to more touristy towns such as Gudhjem and Svaneke, Nexø has its fair share of picturesque buildings.

◎ Sights & Activities

Nexø Museum   MUSEUM
(Havnen 2; adult/child Dkr30/10; ⊘10am-4pm Mon-Fri, to 1pm Sat Jul & Aug, shorter hrs rest of yr) In a handsome 1796 sandstone building opposite the waterfront, the modest yet endearing Nexø Museum features intriguing exhibits on Nexø's history, including photos of Nexø before the bombs of WWII and wartime artefacts such as Nazi and Russian military helmets. Other curiosities include cannons, vintage toiletries and an old-school 150kg diving suit.

Martin Andersen Nexø's House   MUSEUM
(cnr Andersen Nexøvej & Ferskeøstræde; adult/child Dkr30/10; ⊘10am-4pm Mon-Fri mid-May–mid-Oct, also 10am-2pm Sat Jul & Aug) Snoop around the childhood home of the author of *Pelle the Conqueror* (the book that inspired the 1988 Oscar-winning film). The house is in the southern part of town and displays photos of the author, along with some of his letters and other memorabilia.

Balka   BEACH
Although Nexø's central waterfront is industrial, 2km south of town you'll find a popular seaside area called Balka with a gently curving, white-sand beach.

⌖ Sleeping

Because the beaches on the outskirts are much more appealing, few people stay in Nexø proper.

Hotel Balka Søbad   HOTEL €€
(✆56 49 22 25; www.hotel-balkasoebad.dk; Vester Strandvej 25; s incl breakfast Dkr850, d incl breakfast Dkr1050-1300; ⊘May-Sep; P@🛜🛋) Boasting its own bathing beach, this hotel has 106 commodious rooms in two-storey buildings. Rooms might recall the late '70s, but they're pleasant and clean, and have at least two twin beds, a sofa bed, balcony and kitchenette; some even have a second bedroom. Facilities include a tennis court, swimming pool, bar and restaurant.

Hotel Balka Strand   HOTEL €€
(✆56 49 49 49; www.hotelbalkastrand.dk; Boulevarden 9; s/d incl breakfast Dkr875/1075; P🛜🛋)

Only 200m from Balka's sandy beach, this smart, friendly hotel has double rooms and cheery apartments, all with modern decor. On-site pluses include a pool, massage treatments, bar and restaurant.

✗ Eating

You'll find a handful of eateries on and around Torvet (the main square), as well as by the harbour, though none are particularly noteworthy.

Kvickly   SUPERMARKET €
(Købmagergade 12; ⊘8am-8pm) If you want to pack a lunch for the beach, this supermarket has a bakery and deli section. You'll find it near the bus stop in the town centre.

❶ Information

Tourist Office (✆56 49 70 79; www.bornholm. info; Sdr Hammer 2G; ⊘10am-5pm Mon-Fri, to 2pm Sat & Sun Jul & Aug, closed Sun May, Jun, Sep & Oct, shorter hrs rest of yr) Opposite the main bus station, this helpful office has information on Nexø, Snogebæk, Svaneke and Dueodde.

Svaneke

POP 1060

Svaneke is a super-cute harbour town of red-tiled 19th-century buildings that has won international recognition for maintaining its historic character. Popular with yachters and landlubbing holidaymakers, its pretty harbourfront is lined with mustard-yellow half-timbered former merchants' houses, some of which have been turned into hotels and restaurants. Svaneke is also home to the island's most famous smokehouse and a notable microbrewery, both of which are highly recommended.

◎ Sights & Activities

Glastorvet   CRAFT STUDIOS
If you're interested in crafts, there are a number of pottery and handicraft shops dotted around town, and at Glastorvet in the town centre there's a workshop where you can watch glass being melted into orange glowing lumps and then blown into clear, elegant glassware.

Svaneke Kirke   CHURCH
(Kirkepladsen 2; ⊘8am-3pm Mon-Fri) You'll find some interesting period buildings near

Svaneke Kirke, a few minutes' walk south of Svaneke Torv, the town square. The watermelon-hued church, home to a rune stone, dates from 1350, although it was largely rebuilt during the 1880s.

Windmills
HISTORIC BUILDINGS

The easternmost town in Denmark, Svaneke is quite breezy and has a number of windmills. To the northwest of town you'll find an old **post mill** (a type of mill that turns in its entirety to face the wind) and a **Dutch mill**, as well as an unusual three-sided **water tower** designed by architect Jørn Utzon (of Sydney's Opera House fame). On the main road 3km south of Svaneke in the hamlet of Årsdale, there's a working windmill where grains are ground and sold.

🛏 Sleeping

Hullehavn Camping
CAMPGROUND €

(🗹 56 49 63 63; www.hullehavn.dk; Sydskovvej 9; campsite per adult/child Dkr72/36; ☺ Apr-late Sep) Has the more natural setting of Svaneke's two camping grounds, including its own sandy beach. Three-star rating and just 400m south of Danhostel Svaneke.

Danhostel Svaneke
HOSTEL €

(🗹 56 49 62 42; www.danhostel-svaneke.dk; Reberbanevej 9; dm/s/d Dkr160/450/510; ☺ Apr-late Oct; 🅿🛜) A basic but modern low-roofed hostel, 1km south of the centre of Svaneke. Facilities include a communal kitchen and laundry facilities.

Hotel Siemsens Gaard
HOTEL €€

(🗹 56 49 61 49; www.siemsens.dk; Havnebryggen 9; s incl breakfast Dkr850, d incl breakfast from Dkr1275; ☺ closed Jan & Feb; 🅿📶🛜) Although the straightforward rooms at this harbourside hotel are a little dowdy, they are comfortable and equipped with fridge and toilets (some doubles even have kitchenettes). Request a room in the old wing, a beautiful half-timbered building that dates from the mid-17th century. Service is friendly and guests can rent bikes for Dkr75 per day.

🍴 Eating & Drinking

Just off Torv you'll find a **Dagli'Brugsen** (Nansensgade 11; ☺ 8am-8pm) supermarket.

★ Rogeriet i Svaneke
SEAFOOD €

(Fiskergade 12; counter items Dkr35-115; ☺ 9am-8.30pm Jul & Aug, shorter hrs rest of yr) You'll find a fine selection of excellent, smoked fare at the long counter here, including wonderful smørrebrød (open sandwiches), great trout, salmon, herring, shrimp, fried fish cakes and tasty *frikadeller* (Danish meatballs). Chow inside with a view of the massive, blackened doors of the smoking ovens or at the outdoor picnic tables overlooking the old cannons.

You'll find the smokehouse by the water at the end of Fiskergade, just north of the town centre.

Svaneke Chokoladeri
CHOCOLATE €

(www.svanekechokoladeri.dk; Torv 5; chocolate truffles Dkr11; ☺ 10am-5pm Mon-Fri, 10am-3pm Sat, 11am-3pm Sun; 🎫) Located at the entrance to Bryghuset is one of Bornholm's top chocolatiers. Freshly made on the premises, the seductive concoctions include a white chocolate, coconut and lime truffle, as well as a very Bornholm *stout øl* (stout beer) truffle. We dare you to resist!

Bryghuset
MICROBREWERY

(Torv 5; lunch Dkr69-129, dinner mains Dkr149-298; ☺ 10am-midnight, kitchen closes 9.30pm) This is one of the most popular dining and drinking options on the island, known throughout Denmark for its excellent beers brewed on the premises. If you haven't already eaten, it also serves decent, hearty pub grub. Danish lunch classics include smørrebrød (open sandwiches) and *fiske-frikadeller* (fish cakes) with rye bread remouldade. Dinner mains are mostly juicy, fleshy affairs.

Hotel Siemsens Gaard
DANISH €€

(www.siemsens.dk; Havnebryggen 9; lunch Dkr68-196, dinner mains Dkr218-272; ☺ 11.30am-9pm) With patio dining overlooking the harbour, this hotel's restaurant makes an ideal lunch choice on a sunny day. There is a focus on local produce, and it does good light lunches such as daintily presented smørrebrød (open sandwiches), smoked and marinated salmon, and other more substantial fresh fish and meat dishes.

ℹ Information

Post Office (Nansensgade 11; ☺ 8am-6pm) At the Dagli'Brugsen supermarket.

Tourist Office (🗹 56 49 70 79; Peter F Heerings Gade 7; ☺ 10am-4pm Mon-Fri mid-Jun–mid-Sep) Svaneke's tourist office is located by the harbour.

Gudhjem & Melsted

POP 710

Gudhjem is the best-looking of Bornholm's harbour towns. Its rambling high street is crowned by a squat windmill standing over half-timbered houses and sloping streets that roll down to the picture-perfect harbour. The town is a good base for exploring the rest of Bornholm, with cycling and walking trails, convenient bus connections, plenty of places to eat and stay, and a boat service to Christiansø. Interestingly, the harbour was one of the settings for the Oscar-winning film *Pelle the Conqueror,* based on the novel by Bornholm writer Martin Andersen Nexø, whose childhood home (p148) is in nearby Nexø.

◉ Sights & Activities

Gudhjem's shoreline is rocky, though sunbathers will find a small sandy **beach** at Melsted, 1km southeast. A 4km **bike path** leads south from Gudhjem to the thick-walled stoutly buttressed Østerlars Rundkirke, the most impressive of the island's round churches.

★ Oluf Høst Museet   MUSEUM

(www.ohmus.dk; Løkkegade 35; adult/child Dkr75/35; ◷11am-5pm mid-Jun–Aug, shorter hrs rest of yr; ▣) This wonderful museum contains the workshops and paintings of Oluf Høst (1884–1966), one of Bornholm's best-known artists. The museum occupies the home where Oluf lived from 1929 until his death. The beautiful back garden is home to a little hut with paper, paints and pencils for kids with a creative itch.

Baltic Sea Glass   GLASSWORKS, GALLERY

(www.balticseaglass.com; Melstedvej 47; ◷10am-5pm Fri-Wed, to 7pm Thu) Wherever you travel on Bornholm you will come across small independent ceramicists' and glass-blowers' studios. A couple of kilometres south of Gudhjem is one of the best: Baltic Sea Glass. It's a large, modern workshop and showroom with regularly changing exhibitions, as well as a permanent display showcasing the work of Maibritt Jönsson and Pete Hunner.

Gudhjem Glasrøgeri   GLASSWORKS

(☑56 48 54 68; Ejnar Mikkelsensvej 13A; ◷10am-8pm Mon-Fri, to 5pm Sat & Sun Easter-Nov, shorter hrs rest of yr) Watch top-quality Bornholm glass being hand-blown at Gudhjem Glasrøgeri at the dockside.

Walks   WALKING

A short five-minute climb up the heather-covered hill, **Bokul** provides a fine view of the town's red-tiled rooftops and out to sea.

From the hill at the southeastern end of Gudhjem harbour you'll be rewarded with a **harbour view**. You can continue along this path that runs above the shoreline 1.5km southeast to Melsted, where there's a little **sandy beach**. It's a delightful nature trail, with swallows, nightingales and wildflowers.

🛏 Sleeping

Danhostel Gudhjem   HOSTEL €

(☑56 48 50 35; www.danhostel-gudhjem.dk; Løkkegade 7; dm/s/d Dkr220/385/490; 🛜) Right by the harbour, this hostel has cosy, bright six-bed dorms. The reception is at a small grocery shop on Løkkegade, about 75m northwest of the hostel. Bikes can be hired for Dkr90 per day.

Sannes Familie Camping   CAMPGROUND €

(☑56 48 52 11; www.familiecamping.dk; Melstedvej 39; campsite per adult/child Dkr90/60, 4-person cabin per week Dkr3050-7850; ◷Apr–mid-Sep; 🅿🛜) This lovely four-star site right beside the beach also boasts a sauna for when the weather doesn't deliver. Camping aside, the site offers comfortable cabins accommodating three to 10 people; the new, four-person 'luxury huts' come with Siemens kitchen appliances. The place also offers bikes (Dkr65/250 per day/week) and wi-fi (Dkr20 per day).

Gudhjem Camping   CAMPGROUND €

(☑56 48 50 71; www.slettenscamping.dk; Melsted Langgade 36A; campsite per adult/child Dkr72/37; ◷mid-May–mid-Sep; 🅿) This is the nearest camping ground to town, a 15-minute walk south of Gudhjem harbour. Furnished four-person tents – complete with beds, kitchen and electricity – are available for Dkr2075 to Dkr3550 per week. Another option is the on-site furnished caravans, costing from Dkr3095 to Dkr4765 per week.

Jantzens Hotel   HOTEL €€

(☑56 48 50 17; www.jantzenshotel.dk; Brøddegade 33; s Dkr850, d Dkr1200-1300; 🛜) One of the island's true charmers, Jantzens offers smallish but supremely cosy, stylish rooms in a handsome period building. Some rooms have sea views and the breakfast is one of Bornholm's best.

Therns Hotel   HOTEL €€

(☑56 48 50 99; www.therns-hotel.dk; Brøddegade 31; s Dkr650, d Dkr750-1050; 🛜) This reasonably

Gudhjem & Melsted

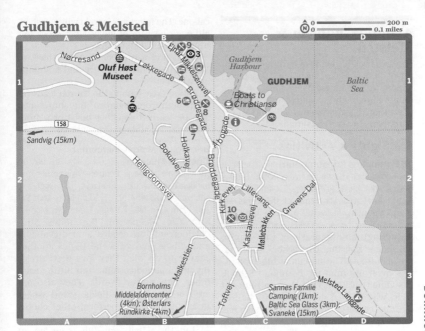

priced, two-star hotel has 30 pleasant rooms in a very central location. The hotel also rents out bikes (Dkr90 per day).

✕ Eating

You'll find a **Spar** (Kirkevej; ☺8am-10pm) supermarket just off Brøddegade.

Gudhjem Rogeri SEAFOOD €
(Gudhjem Harbour; lunch/dinner buffet Dkr120/180; ☺10am-9pm Jul-Aug, shorter hrs rest of yr) Gudhjem's popular smokehouse serves deli-style fish and salads, including the classic Sol over Gudhjem (Sun over Gudhjem; smoked herring with a raw egg yolk). There's both indoor and outdoor seating, some of it very challenging to get to (the upper floor is reached by a rope ladder!). There's live folk, country or rock music most nights in the summer.

Café Klint INTERNATIONAL €€
(☏56 48 54 59; Ejnar Mikkelsensvej 20; light meals Dkr45-129, dinner Dkr139-189; ☺10am-9pm mid-Jun–mid-Aug, shorter hrs rest of yr; ☏) On a sunny day the patio here is the spot to kick back with a beer and a harbour view. Tasty edibles include salads, sandwiches, tapas and gutsy steaks. It's a popular summertime hang-out, with live music Monday to Saturday night from mid-June to mid-August.

Gudhjem & Melsted

◉ **Top Sights**
  1 Oluf Høst Museet B1

◎ **Sights**
  2 Bokul B1
  3 Gudhjem Glasrøgeri B1

🛏 **Sleeping**
  4 Danhostel Gudhjem B1
  5 Gudhjem Camping D3
  6 Jantzens Hotel B1
  7 Therns Hotel B1

✕ **Eating**
  8 Café Klint B1
  9 Gudhjem Rogeri B1
  10 Spar C2

ℹ Information

There are toilets and showers at the harbour and a car park just northwest of it.

Post Office (☺8am-6pm) Inside the Spar supermarket.

Tourist Office (☏56 48 64 48; www.allinge. dk; Ejnar Mikkelsensvej 17; ☺10.30am-4pm Jul & Aug, shorter hrs rest of yr) Small tourist office right by the harbour, with information on Gudhjem and the rest of Bornholm.

Around Gudhjem & Melsted

The area around Gudhjem harbours a number of cultural riches, including the island's impressive art museum, its most striking round church, and an intriguing medieval re-creation. It's also where you'll find one of Bornholm's top two restaurants.

⊙ Sights & Activities

★**Bornholms Kunstmuseum** MUSEUM
(www.bornholms-kunstmuseum.dk; Otto Bruuns Plads 1; adult/child Dkr70/free; ⊙10am-5pm Jun-Aug, closed Mon Apr, May, Sep & Oct, shorter hrs rest of yr) Occupying a svelte, modern building and overlooking sea, fields and (weather permitting) the distant isle of Christiansø, Bornholms Kunstmuseum echoes Copenhagen's Louisiana. The museum exhibits paintings by artists from the Bornholm School, including Olaf Rude, Oluf Høst and Edvard Weie, who painted during the first half of the 20th century. The art museum also has works by other Danish artists, most notably paintings of Bornholm by Skagen artist Michael Ancher.

There's a cafe on-site. Buses stop in front of the museum (bus 2 from Rønne; bus 4 or 8 between Gudhjem and Sandvig).

Østerlars Rundkirke CHURCH
(Vietsvej 25; admission Dkr10; ⊙9am-5pm Mon-Sat) The largest and most impressive of Bornholm's round churches dates back to at least from 1150, and its seven weighty buttresses and upper-level shooting gallery give away its former role as a fortress. The roof was originally constructed with a flat top to serve as a battle platform, but the excessive weight this exerted on the church walls saw it eventually replaced with its present conical one. The interior is largely whitewashed, although a swath of medieval frescoes has been uncovered and restored.

You'll find a rune stone dating back to 1070 at the church entrance and a sundial above it.

A 4km cycle path to the church leads inland south from Gudhjem; the church can also be reached on either bus 1 or 9 from Gudhjem. From Rønne, catch bus 4.

Bornholms Middelaldercenter Open-Air Museum MUSEUM
(Bornholm's Medieval Centre; www.bornholms-middelaldercenter.dk; Stangevej 1, Gudhjem; adult/child Dkr145/110; ⊙10am-5pm Mon-Sat Jul, 10am-4pm Mon-Fri Aug, 11am-3pm Mon-Fri Sep) The 10.5-hectare Bornholms Middelaldercenter re-creates a medieval fort and village, and gives the Danes another chance to do what they love best: dressing up in period costume and hitting each other with rubber swords. They also operate a smithy, tend fields, grind wheat in a water mill and perform other chores of yore throughout the summer months. In July the activity schedule is beefed up to include falconry presentations, archery demonstrations and hands-on craft activities for children.

The medieval centre is 500m north of Østerlars Rundkirke and can be reached by either bus 1 or 9 from Gudhjem, or bus 4 from Rønne.

🛏 Sleeping & Eating

★**Stammershalle Badehotel** BOUTIQUE HOTEL **€€**
(📞56 48 42 10; www.stammershalle-badehotel.dk; Sdr Strandvej 128, Rø; s/d incl breakfast from Dkr700/900; 🅿🛜) Bornholm's most fabulous slumber spot occupies an imposing, early

---

READY, STEADY, COOK

Whet your appetite at **Sol over Gudhjem** (www.solovergudhjemkonkurrence.dk), Gudhjem's famous harbourside cook-off. Taking place on a Saturday afternoon in late June, it sees four of Denmark's hottest chefs battle it out as they use Bornholm produce to create a tantalising two-course menu.

Competitive chefs aside, the event also features an appetising food market, with over 40 stalls showcasing the best of Danish produce and specialities, from herring to honey and cheeses. Various competitions means you might just walk away with new kitchen equipment, art or (better still) a free meal at one of Copenhagen's 'It' nosh spots. Best of all, the event is free! The official cook-off usually starts at 1pm, so it's a good idea to head in at around noon to get a good seat. After all, you'll want to taste-test the entries, right?

Check the website for festival dates and details.

ROUND CHURCHES

As the windmills are to Mykonos or the stone heads are to Easter Island, so are the four 12th-century round churches to Bornholm. The *rundkirker* (round churches) are the symbols of the island, immediately familiar to every Dane. Each was built with 2m-thick whitewashed walls and a black conical roof at a time when pirating Wends from eastern Germany were ravaging coastal areas throughout the Baltic Sea. They were designed not only as places of worship but also as refuges against enemy attacks – their upper storeys doubled as shooting galleries. They were also used as storehouses to protect valuable possessions and trading goods from being carried off by the pirates.

Each church was built about 2km inland, and all four are sited high enough on knolls to offer a lookout to the sea. These striking and utterly unique churches have a stern, ponderous appearance, more typical of a fortress than of a place of worship. All four churches are still used for Sunday services. You'll find them at Østerlars, Olsker, Nyker and Nylars.

20th-century bathing hotel overlooking a rocky part of the coast a few kilometres north of Gudhjem. It's a calming blend of whitewashed timber and understated Cape Cod–esque chic, not to mention the home of one of Denmark's up-and-coming New Nordic restaurants, Lassens. Book well ahead, especially in the summer high season.

★ **Lassens**　　　　MODERN SCANDINAVIAN €€€
(☑56 48 42 10; www.stammershalle-badehotel.dk; Sdr Strandvej 128, Rø; small/large tasting menu Dkr450/550; ☺6-11pm Jul & Aug, closed Mon May, Jun & Sep, shorter hrs rest of yr) There are two restaurants foodies cannot afford to miss on Bornholm: Kadeau and Lassens, located at Stammershalle Badehotel. The latter is home to award-winning chef Daniel Kruse, whose pure, showstopping compositions might include smoked scallops with Icelandic *skyr* (strained yoghurt), dehydrated olives, truffle mayonnaise, parsley sauce and malt chips. Service is knowledgeable and personable, and the sea-and-sunset panorama is as inspired as the kitchen's creations. Bookings are essential.

Sandvig & Allinge

POP 1635

Sandvig is a quiet little seaside hamlet with storybook older homes, many fringed by rose bushes and tidy flower gardens. It's fronted by a gorgeous sandy bay and borders a network of interesting walking trails.

Allinge, the larger and more developed half of the Allinge-Sandvig municipality, is 2km southeast of Sandvig. Although not as quaint as Sandvig, Allinge has the lion's share of commercial facilities, including banks, grocery shops and the area's tourist office.

Seven kilometres southeast of Sandvig, in the small village of **Olsker**, is the most slender of the island's four round churches. If you take the inland bus to Rønne, you can stop off en route to visit the church or catch a passing glimpse of it as you ride by.

🛏 Sleeping & Eating

Byskrivergarden　　　　GUESTHOUSE €€
(☑56 48 08 86; www.byskrivergaarden.dk; Løsebækegade 3, Allinge; s/d incl breakfast Dkr750/1000; ☺mid-May–mid-Sep; P🐾) This enchanting, white-walled, black-beamed converted farmhouse right on the water is our choice of places to stay in Allinge. The rooms (try to get the sea-facing not the road-facing ones) are simply yet smartly decorated in a contemporary style. There's a pleasant garden, a large, cheerful breakfast room and kelp-filled rock pools nearby if you fancy taking a dip.

Hotel Romantik　　　　HOTEL €€
(☑20 23 15 24; www.hotelromantik.dk; Stranvejen 68, Sandvig; s/d from Dkr650/800, 2- to 4-person apt per week from Dkr3402; P@🐾) The coast-hugging Romantik offers smart, comfortable hotel rooms, some with sea views. Even better are the 40 stylish apartments, complete with modern kitchenettes. The hotel also offers simple, satisfactory budget rooms (singles/doubles from Dkr600/700) in a nondescript annexe across the street.

Nordbornholms Røgeri　　　　SEAFOOD €
(Kæmpestranden 2, Allinge; buffet Dkr180; ☺11am-9pm daily; 🐾) Several of Bornholm's top chefs

praise this smokehouse as the island's best. Not only does it serve a drool-inducing buffet of locally smoked fish, salads and soup, but its waterside setting makes it the perfect spot to savour Bornholm's Baltic flavours. Kids aged between five and 11 can tackle the buffet at half price.

Café Sommer INTERNATIONAL €€
(Havnegade 19, Allinge; lunch Dkr95-150, dinner 2/3 courses Dkr245/295; ⊙10am-9.30pm Jul, 11.30am-9.30am Jun & Aug) Sporting a popular, harbour-facing terrace and slinky, urbane interiors, Café Sommer is a sound spot for tasty lunchtime salads and burgers, not to mention delicious smørrebrød (three for Dkr135 including fried local salted herring with beets, onions and mustard). Dinner options are warming and meaty; think crumbed cod fillet baked with herbs and served with seasonal vegetables and a dill and lemon cream.

❶ Information

Allinge has the lion's share of commercial facilities, including banks, grocery shops and the tourist office.

Tourist Office (📝56 48 64 48; www.allinge. dk; Kirkegade 4, Allinge; ⊙9am-4pm Mon-Fri, 11am-3pm Sat Jul & Aug, shorter hrs rest of yr) The area's tourist office.

Hammershus Slot

The 13th-century ruins of Hammershus Slot, dramatically perched on top of a sea cliff, are the largest in Scandinavia. Construction probably began around 1250 under the archbishop of Lund, who wanted a fortress to protect his diocese against the Crown, engaged at the time in a power struggle with the Church. In the centuries that followed, the castle was enlarged, with the upper levels of the square tower added on during the mid-16th century.

Eventually, improvements in naval artillery left the fortress walls vulnerable to attack and in 1645 the castle temporarily fell to Swedish troops after a brief bombardment. Hammershus served as both military garrison and prison – King Christian IV's daughter, Leonora Christine, was imprisoned here on treason charges from 1660 to 1661.

In 1743 the Danish military abandoned Hammershus and many of the stones were carried away to be used as building materials elsewhere. Still, there's much to see and you shouldn't miss a stroll through these extensive fortress ruins. The grounds are always open and admission is free.

LOCAL KNOWLEDGE

DANIEL KRUSE – CHEF & BORNHOLM NATIVE

My favourite part of Bornholm...
...is the north coast. It's particularly diverse with its cliffs, beaches and forests. I'm a very visual person and my dishes are usually inspired by images. Once I have the forms and shapes in my head, I find the ingredients that not only fit the image, but that work wonderfully together. I use a lot of herbs from the island's forests and coast. My favourite is called *skovsyre* (forest acid). It's zesty, versatile and has a refreshing kick.

Food lovers on Bornholm shouldn't miss...
...eating at New Nordic restaurant Kadeau (p75), or at one of Bornholm's famous *røgeri* (smokehouses). My favourite is Nordbornholms Røgeri (p153) in Allinge. The guys there are genuinely passionate about the smoking process and the quality is wonderful. Stop for a local beer at Bryghuset (p149) in Svaneke, and taste some amazing hams and sausages at Hallegård (p147), a fantastic rural butcher near Østermarie. Then there's my restaurant, Lassens.

Beyond Bornholm, book a table at...
...Noma (p75) in Copenhagen. Not only is the food incredible, but the staff are intuitive and approachable. Another favourite of mine is Søllerød Kro, just north of Copenhagen. It's not so much New Nordic as French-Danish fusion. Just like at Noma, you know you're going to be taken good care of as soon as you walk through the door. They do lunch but go in the evening to get the full experience.
As told to Cristian Bonetto

ℹ Getting There & Away

There's an hourly bus (2 or 8) from Sandvig to Hammershus Slot, but the most enjoyable way to get here is via footpaths through the hills of Hammeren – a wonderful hour's hike. The well-trodden trail begins by the Sandvig Familie camping ground and the route is signposted.

If you're coming from Rønne, bus 2 makes the trip to Hammershus Slot about once an hour. Bus 7 makes the trip every two hours.

Hammeren

Hammeren, the hammerhead-shaped crag of granite at the northern tip of Bornholm, is crisscrossed by **walking trails** leading through hillsides thick with purple heather. Some of the trails are inland, while others run along the coast. The whole area is a delight for people who enjoy nature walks.

For something a little more challenging, follow the trails between Sandvig and Hammershus Slot. The shortest route travels along the inland side of Hammeren and passes **Hammer Sø**, Bornholm's largest lake, and **Opaløsen**, a deep pond in an old rock quarry. A longer, more windswept route goes along the rocky outer rim of Hammeren, passes a **lighthouse** at Bornholm's northernmost point and continues south along the coast to **Hammer Havn**.

From Hammershus Slot there are walking trails heading south through another heather-clad landscape in a nature area called **Slotslyngen**, and east through public woodlands to **Moseløkken granite quarry**. Moseløkken is also the site of a small **museum** (www.moseloekken.dk; Moseløkkevej 4; adult/child Dkr70/60; ⏱9am-4pm Mon-Fri Apr–mid-Sep) which showcases the work of local stonemasons, sculptures by sculptors Anker Hansen and Ole Christensen, and occasional demonstrations of traditional rock-cutting techniques.

For a detailed map of the trails and terrain, pick up the free *Hammeren og Hammershus, Slotslyng* forestry brochure at any one of the island's tourist offices.

Christiansø

POP 90

If you think Bornholm is as remote as Denmark gets, you'd be wrong. Even further east, way out in the merciless Baltic, is tiny Christiansø, an intensely atmospheric 17th-century island fortress about 500m long and an hour's sail northeast of Bornholm. There is

THERE BE TROLLS

As you travel around Bornholm you will almost certainly spot drawings and figures of the island's mascot: a disreputable-looking horned troll called Krølle Bølle who originated in stories told by local writer Ludvig Mahler to his son in the early 1940s. Usually depicted with a ready-smoked herring dangling from his fishing rod (a neat trick that, even for a troll), Krølle Bølle is said to live with his parents, Bobbasina and Bobbaraekus, beneath Langebjerg Hill, close to Hammershus Slot, appearing on the stroke of midnight when an owl hoots three times.

something of the Faroe Islands about Christiansø's landscape, with its rugged, moss-covered rocks, historic stone buildings and even hardier people. There is a real sense, too, that you are travelling back in time when you visit here, particularly if you stay overnight at the charming atmospheric Christiansø Gæstgiveriet and get to experience the island once most of the day-trippers have gone.

A seasonal fishing hamlet since the Middle Ages, Christiansø fell briefly into Swedish hands in 1658, after which Christian V turned it into an invincible naval fortress. Bastions and barracks were built; a church, school and prison followed.

Christiansø became the Danish Navy's forward position in the Baltic, serving to monitor Swedish trade routes and in less congenial days as a base for attacks on Sweden. By the 1850s, though, the island was no longer needed as a forward base against Sweden, and the navy withdrew. Those who wanted to stay on as fishermen were allowed to live as free tenants in the old cottages. Their offspring, and a few latter-day fisherfolk and artists, currently make up Christiansø's circa 100 residents. The entire island is an unspoiled reserve – there are no cats or dogs, no cars and no modern buildings – allowing the rich birdlife, including puffins, to prosper.

If the hectic pace of life on Christiansø is getting to you, try escaping to a smaller island, **Frederiksø**, by the footbridge.

Græsholm, the island to the northwest of Christiansø, is a wildlife refuge and an important breeding ground for guillemots, razorbills and other sea birds. It has to be one of the most remote places in Denmark and the locals protect its environment fiercely.

Together these three are known as the Ertholmene Islands, and they serve as spring breeding grounds for up to 2000 eider ducks. The ducks nest near coastal paths and all visitors should take care not to scare mothers away from their nests because predator gulls will quickly swoop and attack the unattended eggs. Conservation laws forbid the removal of any plants from this unique ecosystem. Interestingly, the islands have been also attracting a colony of seals since 2011.

◉ Sights & Activities

A leisurely walk of around an hour is all that's needed to explore both Christiansø and Frederiksø, making this a satisfying day trip.

Towers

The main sights are the two stone circular defence towers.

Lille Tårn   LANDMARK, MUSEUM
(Little Tower; museum adult/child Dkr20/5; ⊗ museum 11.30am-4pm Jul-Aug, 11.30am-4pm Mon-Fri, 11.30am-2pm Sat & Sun May-Jun & Sep) Lille Tårn on Frederiksø dates from 1685 and is now the local history museum. The ground floor features fishing supplies, hand tools and ironworks; upstairs there are cannons, vintage furniture pieces, models and a display of local flora and fauna.

Store Tårn   LANDMARK
(Great Tower; ⊗ noon-4pm Jun-Aug) **FREE** Built in 1684, Christiansø's Store Tårn is an impressive structure measuring a full 25m in diameter, and the tower's 100-year-old **lighthouse** offers a sweeping 360-degree view of the island. On our last visit, the tower was set for major restoration work, due for completion in 2017.

Walking

The main activity on Christiansø is the walk along the fortified stone walls and cannon-lined batteries that mark the island's perimeter. There are skerries (rocky islets) with nesting sea birds and a secluded **swimming cove** on Christiansø's eastern side.

🛏 Sleeping & Eating

There's a small food store and snack shop beside Christiansø Gæstgiveriet.

Christiansø Teltplads   CAMPGROUND €
(☎ 24 42 12 22; campsites Dkr75-100; ⊗ May-Aug) Camping is allowed in summer in a small field called the Duchess Battery at the northern end of Christiansø, but limited space means it can be difficult to book a site. The camping ground has a recently renovated kitchen for guests.

Christiansø Gæstgiveriet   GUESTHOUSE €€
(☎ 56 46 20 15; www.christiansoekro.dk; s/d without bathroom Dkr1050/1150; ⊗ closed late Dec-Jan) Built in 1703 as the naval commander's residence, this is the island's only inn, with six simple rooms and a traditional Danish **restaurant** open for lunch and dinner daily. Most of the rooms come with harbour views.

❶ Getting There & Away

Christiansøfarten (☎ 56 48 51 76; www. bornholmexpress.dk; return ticket adult/child Dkr250/125) operates passenger ferries to Christiansø from Gudhjem year-round. From July to late August, ferries depart Gudhjem daily at 10am, 12.30pm and 3pm. Return ferries depart Christiansø at 2pm, 4.15pm and 7.30pm. Sailing time is around an hour. Services are reduced outside the high season – check the ferry website for times.

Dogs or other pets are forbidden on Christiansø island.

Funen

Includes ➡

Odense	159
Ladby	169
Egeskov Slot	170
Faaborg	170
Svendborg	173
Langeland	177
Northern Langeland	178
Southern Langeland	179
Ærø	180
Ærøskøbing	181

Best Places to Eat

➡ Fiske Restaurant Rudolf Mathis (p169)

➡ Skovsgaard MadMarked (p180)

➡ Falsled Kro (p172)

➡ Café Aroma (p183)

➡ Restaurant no.61 (p164)

Best Places to Stay

➡ Pension Vestergade 44 (p182)

➡ Falsled Kro (p172)

➡ Vesteraas Bed & Nature (p182)

➡ På Torvet (p182)

➡ Odense City B&B (p163)

Why Go?

Funen (Fyn in Danish) is Denmark's proverbial middle child. Lacking Zealand's capital-city pull or Jutland's geographic dominance, it's often overlooked by visitors, who perhaps make a whistle-stop visit to Hans Christian's Andersen's birthplace and museum in the island's capital, Odense.

Sure, the master of fairy tales is a worthy favourite son, and Odense is a lively cultural and commercial centre. But there is much more to Funen: thatched farmhouses, picture-book coastal towns and grand Renaissance castles dot the island's patchwork of fields and woods.

Rolling southern pastures and orchards grow some of the country's best produce (Funen is called 'Denmark's garden'), while handsome harbour towns give access to a yacht-filled archipelago and idyllic seafaring islands like Ærø. It's not hard to understand why many describe this region as a microcosm of the very best of Denmark.

When to Go

As elsewhere in Denmark, Funen really comes alive in the summer months. Yachties descend on Funen's southern harbours from July onward, giving these towns an especially festive air. Odense's excellent museums and quality dining have year-round appeal; festivals peak in August, but the lead-up to Christmas is also sparkly and sweet. Egeskov Slot is open mid-April to mid-October, plus two weekends in November for its fairy tale–worthy Christmas market.

Foodies will eat well year-round (think fresh asparagus, new potatoes, orchards in bloom and plump berries from spring through summer). The local bounty from nearby farms and woods is at its best in early autumn.

Funen Highlights

1 Explore **Egeskov Slot** (p170), a moat-encircled castle with a garden full of mazes, museums and marvels

2 Immerse yourself in the fairy-tale world of Hans Christian Andersen in **Odense** (p159)

3 Visit Denmark's only Viking Age ship grave,

Vikingemuseet Ladby (p169), the last resting place of a 10th-century chieftain

4 Sail away to one of the country's friendliest islands, **Ærø** (p180), with undulating country lanes perfect for cycling

5 Marvel at Cold War manoeuvring as you visit

bunkers and battleships at **Langelandsfort** (p179)

6 See wooden ships on the **Svendborg** (p173) waterfront before cruising the South Funen Archipelago

7 Stop at roadside produce stalls while touring southern Funen before refreshments at **Falsled Kro** (p172)

ODENSE

POP 172,500

Funen's millennium-old capital is a cheerful, compact city ideal for feet or bicycles, with enough diversions to keep you hooked for a couple of days.

The city makes much ado about being the birthplace of Hans Christian Andersen. There's a profusion of Andersen-related attractions, including museums, children's centres and sculptures of his most famous stories – even the lights at pedestrian crossings feature Andersen in silhouette. Yet there's much more to the place than hatted storytellers, including art hub Brandts, Denmark's best zoo, and a buzzing cafe scene.

The city is the transport hub for the rest of the island, making it the best base if you're exploring without your own wheels.

History

Odense translates as 'Odin's shrine', for the god of war, poetry and wisdom. Despite having no harbour, Odense was Denmark's largest provincial town by the middle of the 18th century. In 1800 it was finally linked to the sea by a large canal. The city went from strength to strength, becoming an important textile centre.

◎ Sights & Activities

The tourist office has good brochures: pick up *In HC Andersen's footsteps* for coverage of attractions, parks and events related to Odense's favourite son. Ask about the City Pass (Dkr169), valid for 24 hours and giving free admission to most sights (50% off zoo entry).

Note that most museums are closed Mondays from September to May.

★**HC Andersens Hus**   MUSEUM
(www.museum.odense.dk; Bangs Boder 29; adult/child Dkr95/free; ◎10am-5pm Jul & Aug, 10am-4pm Tue-Sun Sep-Jun) Lying amid the miniaturised streets of the old poor quarter (now often referred to as the HCA Quarter), this museum delivers a thorough, lively telling of Andersen's extraordinary life and times. His achievements are put into an interesting historical context and leavened by some engaging audiovisual material and quirky exhibits (such as the display on his height – HCA was 25cm taller than the national average at the time).

The attraction incorporates Andersen's rather sparse birthplace. There's also a re-

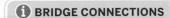

ⓘ BRIDGE CONNECTIONS

Funen is connected to Zealand by the Storebælts Bro (Great Belt Bridge), and to Jutland by the Lillebælts Bro (Little Belt Bridge).

If you're driving, there is a toll (Dkr235 for a regular car) to cross the impressive 18km-long Storebælts Bro. See www.storebaelt.dk for more.

construction of his Copenhagen study, displays of his pen-and-ink sketches and paper cuttings, and a voluminous selection of his books, which have been translated into some 140 languages (more than any other author).

The ticket gets you same-day entry to HC Andersens Barndomshjem.

Børnekulturhuset Fyrtøjet   CULTURAL CENTRE
(www.museum.odense.dk; Hans Jensens Stræde 21; admission Dkr80-95; ◎10am-4pm Fri-Sun Feb–mid-Dec, daily during school holidays; ⊞) Next to HC Andersens Hus is the charming Fyrtøjet (The Tinderbox culture house for children), where kids are encouraged to explore the world of Hans Christian Andersen through storytelling and music (the storytelling is in Danish, but the activities are suitable for all languages). Kids can dress up, have their face painted, act out stories and draw fairytale pictures in the art studio.

HC Andersens Barndomshjem   MUSEUM
(www.museum.odense.dk; Munkemøllestræde 3-5; adult/child Dkr30/free; ◎10am-5pm Jul & Aug, to 3pm or 4pm Tue-Sun Sep-Jun) The small childhood home of Hans Christian Andersen paints a picture of the writer's poverty-stricken childhood. He lived here from 1807 to 1819, aged two to 14.

Odense Zoo   ZOO
(www.odensezoo.dk; Sønder Blvd 306; adult/child Dkr175/95; ◎from 10am daily; ⊞) Denmark's showpiece zoo borders both banks of the river, 2km south of the city centre. It's an active supporter of conservation and education programs, and its residents include tigers, lions, giraffes, zebras and chimpanzees, plus an 'oceanium' with penguins and manatees.

The highlight is the zoo's Kiwara area, an open space that aims to mimic the African savannah. You can feed giraffes (Dkr70) or take in the views from the upper deck of the excellent visitor centre.

Child-friendly drawcards include a playground and lots of animal-related games.

FUNEN ODENSE

Odense

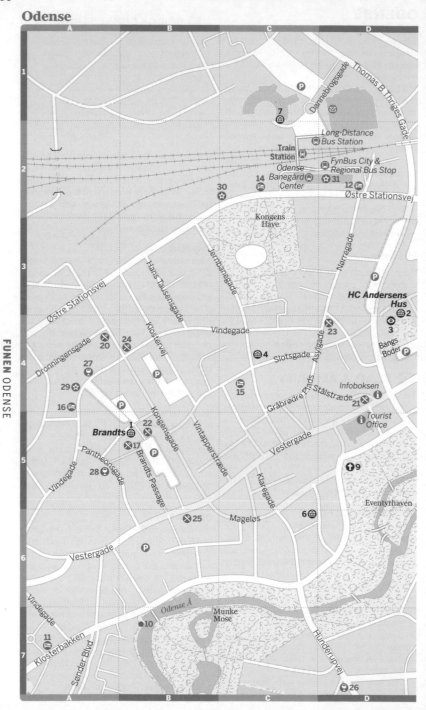

Check the website's calendar for details of feeding times and daily events. Closing time varies – generally from 4pm (winter) to 7pm (summer).

Odense Aafart boats stop at the zoo during high season. A number of buses run here frequently (40, 42, 51, 52, 151, 152; Dkr23), or you can walk or cycle the 2km-long wooded riverside path that begins at Munke Mose.

★Brandts   MUSEUM

(www.brandts.dk; Brandts Torv; combined ticket adult/child Dkr90/free; ⊙10am-5pm Tue, Wed & Fri-Sun, noon-9pm Thu) The former textile mill on Brandts Passage has been beautifully converted into a sprawling art centre, with thought-provoking, well-curated changing displays (including a riveting exhibition on tattooing when we last stopped by). Note: there's free entry after 5pm Thursday.

Brandts Samling (the permanent collection) traces 250 years of Danish art, from classic to modern, and includes an impressive assemblage of international photography.

Art highlights include portraits by Christoffer Wilhelm Eckersberg (the 'father of Danish painting'), plus HA Brendekilde's powerful *Udslidt* ('Worn Out'; 1889), depicting a collapsed farm worker, and PS Krøyer's radiant *Italienske markarbejdere* ('Italian Field Laborers'; 1880). Funen artists also feature – Johannes Larsen's *Svanerne letter, Fiil Sø* is a stunning depiction of swans taking flight.

On the third floor, **Danmarks Mediemuseum** traces the history of the Danish media (primarily in Danish, but with a tablet provided for coverage in other languages).

The area around Brandts is worth a wander for great street art and murals.

Brandts 13   MUSEUM

(www.brandts.dk; Jernbanegade 13; adult/child Dkr13/free; ⊙10am-5pm Wed & Fri-Sun, noon-9pm Thu) In a stately building from 1884, this offshoot branch of Brandts presents changing contemporary art exhibitions: the likes of multimedia, video etc are nicely juxtaposed against the neoclassical architecture.

Møntergården   MUSEUM

(www.museum.odense.dk; Mønterstræde; adult/child Dkr50/free; ⊙10am-5pm Jun-Aug, 10am-4pm Tue-Sun Sep-May) This revamped city showcase is a model of good museum design (something the Danes excel at). In 'Funen – Centre of the Universe', you walk through a chronological display of world events and see how Funen experienced them – including

FUNEN ODENSE

Odense

◎ **Top Sights**
1 Brandts	B5
2 HC Andersens Hus	D3

◎ **Sights**
3 Børnekulturhuset Fyrtøjet	D4
4 Brandts 13	C4
5 Carl Nielsen Museet	E3
6 HC Andersens Barndomshjem	C6
7 Jernbanemuseet	C1
8 Møntergården	E4
9 Sankt Knuds Kirke	D5

🏃 **Activities, Courses & Tours**
10 Odense Aafart	B7

🛏 **Sleeping**
11 Ansgarhus Motel	A7
12 CabInn Odense Hotel	D2
13 City Hotel	E3
14 Danhostel Odense City	C2
15 First Hotel Grand	C4
16 Odense City B&B	A4

🍴 **Eating**
17 Cafe Biografen	B5
18 Den Gamle Kro	E4
19 Fresh-Produce Market	E3
20 Goma	A4
21 Lagkagehuset	D4
22 LE:K	B5
23 Odense Chokoladehus	D4
24 Restaurant no.61	B4
25 Simoncini	B6

🍷 **Drinking & Nightlife**
26 Carlsens Kvarter	D7
27 Den Smagløse Café	A4
28 Nelle's Coffee & Wine	A5

🎭 **Entertainment**
Cafe Biografen	(see 17)
29 Dexter	A4
30 Musikhuset Posten	C2
31 Nordisk Film Biografer Odense	D2
Odense Koncerthus	(see 5)
32 Odeon (under construction)	E3

the effects of the Industrial Revolution on villages, and how locals experienced WWII occupation and the Cold War. Plus there are Viking-era finds, and information on how Funen came to be known as 'Denmark's garden' (hint: apples play a key role).

Separate buildings include exhibits on Odense in the Middle Ages and Renaissance period, the inside of a restored 1646 townhouse; and a 17th-century almshouse.

Sankt Knuds Kirke CHURCH
(www.odense-domkirke.dk; Klosterbakken; ⊙10am-5pm Apr-Oct, to 4pm Nov-Mar) Odense's imposing 14th-century Gothic cathedral reflects the city's medieval wealth and stature. Its most intriguing attraction lies in the chilly crypt, down an inconspicuous staircase to the right of the altar. Here you'll find a glass case containing the 900-year-old skeleton of Denmark's patron saint, King Canute (Knud) II, alongside the bones of his younger brother Benedikt.

Both were killed by Jutland peasants during a revolt against taxes; legend holds that Knud was murdered whilst kneeling in prayer. Although Knud was less than saintly, the pope canonised him in 1101 in a move to secure the Catholic Church in Denmark.

Carl Nielsen Museet MUSEUM
(www.museum.odense.dk; Claus Bergs Gade 11; ⊙11am-3pm Wed-Sun May-Aug & 3-7pm Thu-Fri, 11am-3pm Sat & Sun Sep-Apr) FREE In Odense's concert hall, displays detail the career of the city's native son Carl Nielsen (1865–1931), Denmark's best-known composer, and a skilled conductor and violinist. His music includes six symphonies, several operas and numerous hymns and popular songs.

Jernbanemuseet MUSEUM
(www.jernbanemuseet.dk; Dannebrogsgade 24; adult/child Dkr90/45; ⊙10am-4pm) Clamber aboard a diverting collection of 19th-century locomotives at the Danish Railway Museum, just behind the train station. The museum has two dozen engines and wagons, including double-decker carriages and the Royal Saloon Car belonging to Christian IX, fully kitted out with everything a king might need.

Den Fynske Landsby MUSEUM
(www.museum.odense.dk; Sejerskovvej 20; adult/ child Dkr85/free; ⊙10am-6pm daily Jul-Aug, 10am-5pm Tue-Sun Apr-Jun & Sep-Oct) Wind back the clock at this delightful open-air museum, which has relocated period houses from around Funen and created a small country village, complete with barnyard animals, a duck pond, apple trees and flower gardens. Costumed 'peasants' tend to the geese, while children in knickerbockers play with hoops.

The museum is in a green zone 4km south of the city centre; buses 110 and 111 (Dkr23) run nearby. The best way to get here is by boat – from May to August, Odense Aafart boats sail hourly from Munke Mose past

FUNEN ODENSE

the zoo to the end station at Fruens Bøge, from where it's a 15-minute woodland walk to reach the museum.

Odense Aafart
BOAT TOUR

(☑ 66 10 70 80; www.aafart.dk; adult/child return Dkr80/60) The riverside Munke Mose park is an attractive place for a picnic, stroll or boat trip. From May to August Odense Aafart runs 30-minute river rides to the wooded Fruens Bøge area, where there's a 'nature playground' full of giant wooden toadstools and centipedes. From here, it's a 15-minute walk to Den Fynske Landsby. The boat stops at Odense Zoo en route.

Trips leave Munke Mose on the hour from 10am to 5pm (6pm in July and early August).

On Saturday in high summer, the experience is enriched by live jazz on board (bookings advised; tickets Dkr120). The 2pm boat journey on weekdays in July is a family-focused one with fairy-tale performances. See the website for more details.

Independent or energetic types can paddle their own craft in Munke Mose, with rowing boats and pedalos for hire (per hour Dkr100) from the boat kiosk from May to August.

🎪 Festivals & Events

Odense Blomsterfestival
FLOWERS

(www.blomsterfestival.dk) For five days in mid-August, Odense is a riot of colour and perfume during the Flower Festival.

HC Andersen Festivals
CULTURAL

(http://hcafestivals.com/) Are you at all surprised that the city celebrates its famous native son? This week-long program in mid-August features plenty of HCA performances and lectures, plus concerts, comedy and loads of family-friendly events.

Odense International Film Festival
CINEMA

(OFF; www.filmfestival.dk) Popular festival in late August celebrating short films.

🛏 Sleeping

Odense offers good-value and well-located budget and midrange accommodation but is less well served at the higher end. The large hotel chains in town generally don't inspire, and in many cases are not very central.

It's a good idea to ask about parking when you book; oftentimes this is not available onsite, or carries an additional fee.

The tourist office has details of rooms in private homes for around Dkr350/500 for singles/doubles.

★ Odense City B&B
B&B €

(www.odensecitybb.dk; Vindegade 73B; s/d from Dkr200/300; ☎) We're almost reluctant to share the secret of this ace B&B. In a prime central location (Brandts and eating options are just outside the door), a well-travelled couple have established this guesthouse above their home, with five fresh rooms sharing two toilets and a small kitchenette. The prices are wonderful value; breakfast costs Dkr50.

Danhostel Odense City
HOSTEL €

(☑ 63 11 04 25; www.odensedanhostel.dk; Østre Stationsvej 31; dm/d from Dkr250/470; @☎) Perfectly placed for travellers, with the train and bus stations as neighbours and Kongens Have (a large park) directly opposite. All rooms at this large, modern hostel have toilets, and there's a guest kitchen, laundry and a basement TV room.

FUNEN ODENSE

ⓘ BIG CITY CHANGES

Odense is in the process of reinventing itself, with some grand projects underway: redeveloping the harbour and university, plus the construction of a new hospital, and a new concert hall, too.

In mid-2014, part of the four-lane Thomas B Thriges Gade (a main arterial road through the city centre) was closed to traffic permanently to enable the city's historic heart to reconnect – over the coming years, the road will be closed as far south as the river. In its place, transformative new green spaces, buildings, bike lanes and underground car parks are planned, and eventually a 14km light-rail to connect north and south.

It's a model for town planners everywhere: how to give a city back its heart, and give over central areas to pedestrians and cyclists. It's not been without its critics, but political consensus has helped.

In short, expect change in the city centre (and construction, too). If you're driving, get your hands on an up-to-date map (or better yet, park on the centre's fringe and walk in). Check the projects online at www.odense.dk/storby and www.fragadetilby.com, and look out for the big red **Infoboksen** (Fisketorvet) in town, where lots of info is disseminated.

CabInn Odense Hotel
HOTEL €

(☑63 14 57 00; www.cabinn.com; Østre Stations-vej 7; s/d from Dkr495/625; @⊚) Facing off with the nearby Danhostel, fighting for the budget-conscious, train-travelling custom, is this member of the popular budget-bed chain. Sure, the beds are narrow and the no-frills rooms lack charm, but at these prices it's decent value.

DCU-Odense City Camp
CAMPGROUND €

(☑66 11 47 02; www.camping-odense.dk; Odensevej 102; campsites per adult/child/tent Dkr80/50/48, cabins from Dkr560; @⊚≋) A neat camping ground in a wooded area (close to walking and cycling paths), with TV lounge, outdoor swimming pool, and kids' amusements. There are also simple cabins for rent. It's about 4km south of the city centre, not far from Den Fyn-ske Landsby museum. Take bus 21, 22 or 23.

City Hotel
HOTEL €€

(☑66 12 12 58; www.city-hotel-odense.dk; Hans Mules Gade 5; s/d incl breakfast from Dkr735/1035; P@⊚) Handy for the gems of the HCA Quarter (museums, concert hall, farmers market), this hotel has friendly service and free parking, plus unremarkable but comfort-able rooms. Its best features: the rooftop ter-race, bike hire, and discounts at Den Gamle Kro (under the same ownership). Discounted weekend and summer rates are good value.

Ansgarhus Motel
HOTEL €€

(☑66 12 88 00; www.ansgarhus.dk; Kirkegårds Allé 17; s/d incl breakfast Dkr575/745; P⊚) A solid choice, this is a small, family-run place in a quiet residential area near the river and parkland, with cosy rooms and an inviting, plant-filled courtyard. Most rooms have pri-vate toilets, but there are four cheaper sin-gles that don't (Dkr450).

First Hotel Grand
HOTEL €€

(☑66 11 71 71; www.firsthotels.dk; Jernbanegade 18; r from Dkr750; P⊚) Odense's grand dame dates from 1897 and her exterior is still a head-turner; she's had a skilful makeover in recent times, bringing the interior up-to-date, with lots of warm chocolate tones in the crisp, business-style room decor. The lo-cation is good and the breakfast excellent; the lovely lounge and brasserie areas are the best features. Online deals are good.

🍴 Eating

The pedestrianised main street Vestergade houses several good restaurants and cafes, and there's a cluster of buzzing bars/bistros around Kongensgade and in Brandts Pas-sage. Many stay open until at least midnight (often 2am or 3am on the weekend), but for drinking only. Kitchens stop taking food or-ders at 9pm or 10pm.

Odense Chokoladehus
CHOCOLATE €

(www.odensechokoladehus.dk; Nørregade 32; sweet treats around Dkr20; ⊙10am-5pm Tue-Fri, 10am-1.30pm Sat) Happiness, it turns out, is one of the rainbow-hued macarons sold from this tiny den of sweetness. Or maybe happiness is the lemon and white-chocolate tart. Or the brownies. Or possibly the home-made ice cream...

Bazar Fyn
INTERNATIONAL €

(www.bazarfyn.dk; Thriges Plads 3; ⊙10am-9pm Tue-Sun) More than just a great place to buy groceries, Bazar Fyn offers an insight into the multicultural side of Odense. The roofed market is about five minutes' walk from the train station. There's fresh fruit and veg and deli items (stores close 6pm), plus a food court where you can eat cheaply: Lebanese shwarma, Greek souvlaki, Indian curries, Vi-etnamese pho.

Lagkagehuset
BAKERY €

(Vestergade 1; sandwiches & salads around Dkr60; ⊙6.30am-7pm Mon-Fri, to 6pm Sat & Sun) Who doesn't love a good bakery-cafe? Here you'll score decent coffee, delectable buttery pas-tries, and good lunchtime salads and sand-wiches.

Cafe Biografen
CAFE €

(www.cafebio.dk; Brandts Passage 43; meals Dkr64-145; ⊙11am-11pm) The diverse clientele makes for great people-watching at this large, cheerful place beside Brandts (there's an amphitheatre outside that gets put to good use with summer concerts). The well-priced menu sings classic hits (burgers, salads, pas-ta, sandwiches). Weekend brunches (Dkr109) attract a crowd, as does the bargain buffet dinner (Dkr139) from 5pm Wednesday to Friday.

⭐ Restaurant no.61
EUROPEAN €€

(☑61 69 10 35; www.no61.dk; Kongensgade 61; 2/3 courses Dkr255/295; ⊙from 5pm Tue-Sat) Winning plaudits for its embrace of classic European cooking, this cosy, farmhouse-chic bistro has a menu that changes monthly and is short, simple and seasonal. Each course presents two options: dishes plucked straight from the Funen fields might include white asparagus with truffle-infused hollandaise

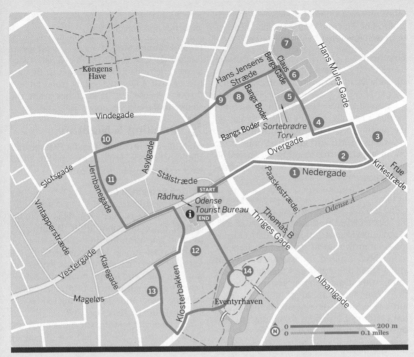

City Walk
Storybook Odense

START RÅDHUS
END RÅDHUS
LENGTH 1.5KM
DURATION 2-3 HOURS

From the rådhus (town hall) head east on Vestergade, cross over Thomas B Thriges Gade, then turn onto **1 Nedergade**, a cobblestoned street lined with crooked half-timbered houses and antique stores, including **2 Kramboden**.

At the end of Nedergade, a left turn brings you to **3 Vor Frue Kirke**, traditionally the oldest church in Odense (records are hazy). Most of the interior dates to the 13th century.

From the church turn back onto Overgade; you'll soon reach **4 Møntergården** (p161), a museum that's well worth a browse. Turn right into Claus Bergs Gade, which spills out onto **5 Sortebrødre Torv** – this square is the setting for Odense's farmers market.

Opposite the square is the Radisson hotel. Check out the **6 sculptured benches** out the front, celebrating HC Andersen.

Immediately north of the hotel is the **7 Odense Koncerthus** (p167), with a museum

dedicated to celebrated composer Carl Nielsen. The concert hall, Odeon, is under construction nearby (due for completion in 2016).

From the concert hall, turn onto Ramsherred to reach **8 HC Andersens Hus** (p159), Hans Christian Andersen's birthplace, and the children's centre **9 Fyrtøjet** (p159). The museum is in a neighbourhood of coloured houses – Bangs Boder is storybook pretty.

Follow Gravene west to Slotsgade; contemporary-art exhibitions are held in **10 Brandts 13** (p161), on the corner of Jernbanegade. Turn left and follow Jernbanegade to Vestergade, passing the site of **11 Gråbrødre Kloster**, a medieval monastery turned home for the elderly.

Reaching Vestergade, dogleg south to e **12 Sankt Knuds Kirke** (p162), Odense's cathedral. From here, take Munkemøllestræde, where you'll find **13 HC Andersens Barndomshjem** (p159), the writer's childhood home.

Loop back on Klosterbakken and take the path into **14 Eventyrhaven** ('Fairy-tale Garden'), a riverside park with a statue of HCA. Walk north through the park to return to the rådhus.

sauce, or a confection of strawberry, rhubarb, white chocolate and crème anglais. Reservations recommended.

Simoncini
ITALIAN €€

(☑66 17 92 95; www.simoncini.dk; Vestergade 70; pasta Dkr110-140, mains Dkr195-250; ⏱from 5.30pm Mon-Sat) Seasonal, local produce with an authentic Italian spin is on offer in this rustically elegant dining space off the main drag. Guinea-fowl-filled ravioli, asparagus risotto and grilled octopus bring on an appetite; the monthly set menu offers excellent value (two/three/four courses Dkr199/249/299).

LEI:K
INTERNATIONAL €€

(☑66 11 66 12; www.leik.dk; Brandts Passage 33-35; lunch Dkr99-119, dinner mains Dkr185-395; ⏱noon-11pm Mon-Wed, to 1am Thu-Sat) Odense looks all grown up at this scene-y hotspot, with a NYC-inspired, industrial-chic interior and a menu of burgers and fine cuts of beef (pimp your steak with fois gras or langoustine). Long hours are kept: lunch is served until 4pm, and a late-night kitchen opens until midnight Thursday to Sunday (to feed the cocktail-supping crowd).

Den Gamle Kro
DANISH, FRENCH €€

(☑66 12 14 33; www.dengamlekro.eu; Overgade 23; smørrebrød Dkr71-135, dinner mains Dkr218-348; ⏱11am-10pm Mon-Sat, to 9pm Sun) The romantic Gamle Kro spreads through several half-timbered 17th-century houses, with a glass-roofed courtyard and medieval cellar. Lunch options include classic smørrebrød, while dinner is a decadent French affair: terrine of fois gras, duck breast with truffle sauce, plaice *meunière*, tournedos rossini. Seasonal set menus represent the best value (two/three courses Dkr298/385).

Goma
JAPANESE €€€

(☑66 14 45 00; www.goma.nu; Kongensgade 66 3; set menus Dkr300-500; ⏱5.30pm-late Tue-Sat) Goma is straight from an interiors magazine, all blond wood, cool lighting and interesting chairs. At ground level there's a bar serving snacks and cocktails (house speciality: gin); downstairs is a restaurant putting an inventive, California-style spin on Japanese cuisine. The 16-piece sushi plate is a thing of beauty; alternatively, the kitchen has set menus from Dkr300 to Dkr500 per person.

Self-Catering

The train station contains a small grocery store that opens until 10pm, and a reason-able bakery. Bazar Fyn (p164) is great for groceries and cheap grub.

Fresh-Produce Market
FOOD MARKET

(Sortebrødre Torv; ⏱8am-1pm Wed & Sat) Twice a week, there's a farmers market in the picturesque HCA Quarter, selling fruit and veg, flowers, cheese etc. It stretches from the square to the concert house.

🍷 Drinking & Nightlife

Nightlife is centred on Brandts Passage and Vintapperstræde, pedestrian corridors lined with restaurants, bars and cafes.

★Den Smagløse Café
BAR

(http://densmagloesecafe.dk; Vindegade 57; ⏱noon-midnight or later; 🛜) This friendly, offbeat place describes itself as 'bringing to mind your grandmother's living room or your German uncle Udo's campervan'. It's *hyggelig* (cosy) in a slightly mad, wonderful way: old sofas and lamps, books and bric-a-brac. It serves all manner of drinks (coffee, cocktails, beer) and you can bring food if you like (there are pizzerias nearby).

Our favourite feature: the 'pølsemuseum' (or *wurstwelt,* if you prefer) – a display of sausages in jars. Yes.

Nelle's Coffee & Wine
BAR

(www.nelles.dk; Pantheonsgade; ⏱9am-10pm Mon-Thu, to midnight Fri & Sat, 9am-5.30pm Sun; 🛜) Get your morning caffeine fix here (Nelle's brews the city's best coffee), then return at wine-time, to select from some 20 wines-by-the-glass (from Dkr45). Nelle's doesn't serve meals but you won't go hungry: there are morning pastries, afternoon cakes and wine-time nuts or cheese boards.

Carlsens Kvarter
PUB

(www.carlsens.dk; Hunderupvej 19; ⏱noon-1am Mon-Sat, 1-7pm Sun; 🛜) If soulful sipping appeals more than party crowds, this cosy neighbourhood pub has you covered. Friendly staff recommendations help ease you into the huge selection of microbrewed beer and whiskies – 138 on the beer menu alone, including Trappist ales and plenty of local stuff. If bad weather strikes, this could well be a place to hole up.

☆ Entertainment

Nordisk Film Biografer Odense
CINEMA

(www.nfbio.dk; Østre Stationsvej 27) Mainstream and arthouse flicks, on the 2nd floor of the train station.

Cafe Biografen CINEMA
(www.cafebio.dk; Brandts Passage 39) Behind Brandts, this cinema shows first-run movies and art-house flicks.

Dexter LIVE MUSIC
(www.dexter.dk; Vindegade 65) An intimate live-music venue, where the music is primarily (but not exclusively) jazz, blues, folk and world, from Danish and international artists. There are jam sessions every Monday (free entry). Check the concert calendar online.

Musikhuset Posten LIVE MUSIC
(www.postenlive.dk; Østre Stationsvej 35) In an old postal warehouse close to the station, Posten presents live music (rock, pop, hip-hop etc) from established and upcoming artists. There's often something interesting going on in one of its two halls – check listings online.

Odense Koncerthus CONCERT VENUE
(www.odensesymfoni.dk; Claus Bergs Gade 9) Home of the Odense Symphony Orchestra. The classical music program commonly includes works by native son Carl Nielsen. Ticket prices vary according to the concert (generally starting around Dkr140). Check the program online, and note the new concert hall/theatre, **Odeon**, being built in the vicinity.

ⓘ Information

The train station is in a large modern complex, the Odense Banegård Center (OBC), containing cafes, shops, the public library and travel facilities (eg lockers). The tourist office is a short walk south from here.

INTERNET ACCESS
Galaxy Net Café (Østre Stationsvej; 1hr Dkr17; ☉9-12.30am) On the 2nd floor of the train station.
Odense Centralbibliotek (www.odensebib.dk; Østre Stationsvej; ☉10am-7pm Mon-Thu, to 4pm Fri, to 2pm Sat, also to 2pm Sun Oct-Mar) Library inside the train station, with free internet use and foreign-language newspapers.

MONEY
Plenty of banks along the main shopping street, Vestergade, have ATMs.
Forex (Østre Stationsvej; ☉9.30am-5.30pm Mon-Fri, 10am-3pm Sat) Foreign exchange inside the Banegård Center.

POST
Main Post Office (Dannebrogsgade 2; ☉10am-6pm Mon-Fri, to 1pm Sat) North of the train station.

TOURIST INFORMATION
Tourist Office (☑ 63 75 75 20; www.visi-todense.com; Vestergade 2; ☉9.30am-6pm Mon-Fri, 10am-3pm Sat, 11am-2pm Sun Jul & Aug, 10am-4.30pm Mon-Fri, to 1pm Sat Sep-Jun) Helpful, well-stocked office, in the town hall about 700m from the train station.

ⓘ Getting There & Away

Odense is 44km northwest of Svendborg and 50km east of the bridge to Jutland.

BUS
Long-distance buses (*rutebiler*) to destinations beyond Funen leave from Dannebrogsgade, at the rear of the train station. **FynBus** (☑ 63 11 22 00; www.fynbus.dk) runs bus services in Funen, within Odense and to/from all major towns on the island – these buses generally arrive and depart from stops directly behind the Odense Banegård Center. Information is online (mostly in Danish), or via the bus station info desk, staffed from 9.30am to 5pm Monday, to 4pm Tuesday to Friday.

Key destinations, with frequent services (at least hourly) include Faaborg (Dkr71, one hour) and Kerteminde (Dkr41, 40 minutes). To reach Svendborg, take the train.

CAR & MOTORCYCLE
The cross-country E20 motorway from Copenhagen to Esbjerg (west-coast Jutland) runs south of Odense, with plenty of exits indicated.

TRAIN
There's a **ticket office** (☉7am-6pm Mon-Fri, 9am-4pm Sat, 10am-6pm Sun) on the 2nd floor of the train-station complex, and plenty of automatic machines.

Odense is accessible by the main railway line between Copenhagen (Dkr276, 1½ hours, at least hourly), Aarhus (Dkr240, 1¾ hours, at least hourly) and Esbjerg (Dkr218, 1½ hours, hourly).

Trains between Odense and Copenhagen stop at Nyborg (Dkr53, 15 minutes). The only other train route in Funen is the half-hourly run between Odense and Svendborg (Dkr78, 40 minutes).

ⓘ Getting Around

BICYCLE
Odense is a delight to explore by bike, especially along the many riverside bike paths. The tourist office has free cycling maps.

The city council runs an extensive bike-share scheme – if you don't have a Danish mobile phone, you need to register online with your credit card details, then use your mobile phone to access bikes. Full instructions are on

FUNEN ODENSE

www.cibi.dk – scroll down to find 'Bycykel turist' under Odense.

It's a longwinded process if all you want is a bike for a couple of hours – a simpler alternative is to rent bikes at **Odense Cykeludlejning** (☑ 29 29 25 89; www.odensecykler.dk; Nedergade 36; ☺ 9am-1pm Mon-Fri May-Aug) for Dkr100 per day. Outside of opening hours, you can book via the website, or rent bikes through City Hotel (p164).

BOAT

There are boats (p163) from Munke Mose park in Odense to the zoo or Den Fynske Landsby.

BUS

The main transit point for city buses is behind the Odense Banegård Center (OBC). Buy your ticket from the driver (Dkr23) – exact change is recommended. Alternatively, a one-day Odense-billet costs Dkr40; there is also the option of a one-day ticket covering all of Funen (including Langeland services) for Dkr170.

The very handy, free CityBus (route 10) does a regular loop of Odense from 11am to 5pm weekdays, until 4pm Saturday. It runs every eight to 10 minutes – use it as a free sightseeing tour!

CAR & MOTORCYCLE

Outside rush hour, driving in Odense is not difficult, but many central sights are on pedestrian streets. It's best to park your car and explore on foot.

In and around the city centre, there's time-restricted metered parking along the streets, usually charged from 9am to 6pm Monday to Friday and 9am to 2pm Saturday. There are large undercover car parks around Brandts (access from Vindegade) and by the train station. Parking costs around Dkr12 per hour.

TAXI

Taxis are available at the train station, or by phoning **Odense Taxa** (☑ 66 15 44 15).

AROUND FUNEN

Woodlands and agricultural fields claim most of Funen, with surprises hiding in the rural landscape – a Viking ship slumbering in an isolated mound, the fairy-tale castle Egeskov, an enigmatic 2000-year-old passage grave.

Funen's sleepy towns curl themselves around fortified mansions and medieval houses. Offshore, scattered islets are home to small communities – sometimes of people, sometimes just birds, rabbits and deer. Things liven up in Svendborg, the largest settlement outside Odense, whose bars and cafes are popular with visiting yachties.

Kerteminde

POP 5860

Small, sleepy Kerteminde has much to offer beyond its pleasant cobbled heart of timbered houses. The impressive aquarium, sandy beaches and yacht-filled harbour make for pleasant diversions, and there's a radiant collection of work by 'peasant painter' Johannes Larsen.

Kerteminde is also a base for visiting the superb Viking ship at Ladby, or for getting away from it all on Romsø.

◎ Sights & Activities

★ **Johannes Larsen Museet**　　ART MUSEUM
(www.johanneslarsenmuseet.dk; Møllebakken 14; adult/child Dkr80/free; ☺ 10am-5pm Jun-Aug, closed Mon Sep-May) The vivid naturalistic paintings of wildlife and provincial Danish scenes that flowed from the brush of Johannes Larsen are on show in his former home north of town. Larsen (1867–1961) painted near obsessively from his studio here, while his wife, Alhed, also an artist, captured the lush blooms of her greenhouse.

This is a quality attraction for a town of this size. Beside the house there's an impressive purpose-built exhibition hall showcasing more of their work, alongside paintings by 50 other artists from the Fyn school. The tiny cafe (in an old washhouse) at the end of the flower- and duck-filled garden serves light lunches and homebaked cakes.

Fjord & Bælt　　AQUARIUM
(www.fjord-baelt.dk; Margrethes Plads 1; adult/child Dkr140/60; ☺ Feb-Nov; ⊞) This family-friendly harbourside marine centre houses aquariums, a 40m-long underwater tunnel, touch pools for kids, and seals and porpoises. It's best to go at feeding times (usually around 11am and 1pm). Note: confirm opening days online, as the aquarium is closed Mondays outside of Danish school holidays.

Romsø　　ISLAND
The idyllic wooded island of Romsø, whose only residents are deer, rabbits and birds, is a 30-minute boat ride from Kerteminde. You can walk a coastal trail around the 1-sq-km island or just soak up the solitude. Bring a picnic lunch – there are no facilities.

The **Romsø-Båden** (☑ 23 43 63 04; www.romsoe.dk; adult/child return Dkr240/120) boat service takes passengers to the island on Wednesday and Saturday from April to

August, departing Kerteminde at 9am and Romsø at 2pm. Reservations required.

🛏 Sleeping

★ Købmandsgård B&B   GUESTHOUSE €
(☑ 65 32 46 51; www.bnb-kerteminde.dk; Andresens Købmandsgård 4; s/d without bathroom Dkr500/600; 🛜) Købmandsgård is a photogenic 16th-century merchant's house set around a cobbled courtyard in the middle of town. Part of it houses an excellent-value guesthouse, with four double rooms that share a kitchen-living space and two toilets. It's fresh and inviting, with friendly owners. Breakfast is Dkr75.

Danhostel Kerteminde   HOSTEL €
(☑ 65 32 39 29; www.dkhostel.dk; Skovvej 46; dm/d Dkr275/595; 🛜) More like a rural retreat and sweetly nestled by a wooded area, this well-run hostel is a five-minute walk from a sandy beach and 15 minutes' walk south of town. The 30 rooms all have toilets. Breakfast is Dkr70. Dorm beds are available in high season.

Tornøes Hotel   HOTEL €€
(☑ 65 32 16 05; www.tornoeshotel.dk; Strandgade 2; s/d incl breakfast Dkr775/975; 🛜) In a prominent redbrick building at the entrance to the town, this bright, cheerful place has well-equipped, if anonymously decorated, rooms, plus a restaurant with a prime outlook over the water – try the beer, made by the hotel owners at their microbrewery, Kerteminde Bryghus.

🍴 Eating

Thorsteds   SEAFOOD €€
(☑ 21 36 13 33; www.thorsteds.com; Hindsholmvej 5; lunch/dinner buffet Dkr149/219; ⊘ 10am-10pm daily Jun-Jul, closed Tue in Aug, shorter hours Sep; 🚸) Sit waterside, or as close to the buffet as you can – this is a three-ship spread that covers loads of piscatorial pleasures, including lobster soup, shrimp, mussels and smoked fish (salmon, herring, mackerel). There's plenty o'potatoes (veggies are a little sparse), but it's all delicious. Non-fishy folks can choose meat options from the short à la carte menu.

Check the website for closing days outside of the summer high season. Weekend brunch buffets are also bumper (Dkr139).

★ Fiske Restaurant Rudolf Mathis   SEAFOOD €€€
(☑ 65 32 32 33; www.rudolf-mathis.dk; Dosseringen 13; mains Dkr345, 3-course lunch/dinner

Dkr395/575; ⊘ noon-2pm & 6-9.30pm Tue-Sat Mar-Dec) One of Funen's best restaurants occupies a striking waterside building south of Kerteminde harbour. This is classic seafood served in innovative ways that recognise delicate flavours and pair perfectly with locally grown produce (springtime asparagus or summer berries, for example). Staples are home-smoked salmon, fresh fish cooked over an open wood fire, and a starter of scallops, langoustine and citron-mayo.

ℹ Information

Kerteminde Tourist Office (☑ 65 32 11 21; www.visitkerteminde.dk; Hans Schacksvej 5; ⊘ 10am-6pm Mon-Fri, 10am-3pm Sat & Sun Jun-Aug, 11am-5pm Mon-Fri, 10am-noon Sat Sep-May) Shares a building with the post office. Rents bikes (Dkr100 per day).

ℹ Getting There & Away

Kerteminde is on Rte 165, 22km northwest of Nyborg and 19km northeast of Odense.

Buses 151 and 885 connect Kerteminde with Odense (Dkr41, 40 minutes).

Ladby

Denmark's only Viking Age ship grave, known as **Ladbyskibet** (the Ladby Ship, named for the tiny village where it was found), is a captivating site. Around the year 925, a Viking chieftain was laid to rest in a splendid 21.5m warship, surrounded by weapons, jewellery, clothing and other fine possessions. Archaeologists have ascertained that not long after his burial the grave was plundered and the chieftain's body was removed. But what was left behind is amazing: all the wooden planks from the ship decayed long ago, leaving the perfect imprint of hull moulded into the earth, along with 2000 rivets, an anchor, iron curls from the ship's dragon-headed prow, and the grinning skulls of sacrificed dogs and horses.

The site of the find – under a turfed-over mound – gives an eerie sense of time and place, compounded by a dimly-lit airtight chamber that holds the compelling relic. The site's adjacent museum, **Vikingemuseet Ladby** (www.vikingemuseetladby.dk; Vikingevej 123; adult/child Dkr60/free; ⊘ 10am-5pm Jun-Aug, 10am-4pm Tue-Sun Sep-May), does a great job recounting what is known of the story. It displays finds from the grave and a reconstructed mock-up of the boat before it was interred, complete with slaughtered cattle, giving a vivid sense of the scale and trouble taken over the burial of the chieftain.

In a neighbouring field, a group of boat-building enthusiasts is building a replica of *Ladbyskibet,* using techniques from the Viking era.

ℹ Getting There & Away

By car or bike, follow Rte 315 out of Kerteminde, then the signs to Ladby. In Ladby village, 4km southwest, turn north onto Vikingevej, a one-lane road through fields that ends after 1.2km at the museum car park. The ship mound is a few minutes' walk along a field path.

Local bus 482 (Dkr23) makes the six-minute trip from Kerteminde to Ladby (you'll have to walk the Vikingevej section) but it operates only on school days, so hiring a bike is a better summertime option.

Egeskov Slot

Whatever you do, don't miss a day exploring Egeskov Slot, squarely aimed at families but with plenty of thrills for all ages.

◉ Sights

★**Egeskov Slot**   CASTLE
(www.egeskov.dk; Egeskov Gade 18, Kværndrup; adult/child castle & grounds Dkr210/130, grounds only Dkr180/110; ⊙10am-7pm Jul–mid-Aug, to 5pm mid-Apr–Jun & mid-Aug–mid-Oct) Egeskov Castle, complete with moat and drawbridge, is a magnificent example of the lavish constructions that sprang up during Denmark's 'Golden Age'. It was built in 1554 on a foundation of thousands of upright oak trunks.

There are enough sights and activities in the grounds to keep anyone happily occupied for a day. Inside the castle itself, 12 rooms plus the attic are open to visitors. These are full of antique furnishings, grand period paintings and an abundance of macabre hunting trophies.

In the attic is a beautiful collection of old toys, and a model train set from the early 20th century. The castle's pride and joy is **Titania's Palace**. This jaw-dropping doll's house was commissioned by English officer Sir Nevile Wilkinson, who filled it with miniature works of art over a 15-year period. This is Downton Abbey, rendered in miniature (and far grander). You could study its marvels – including handcarved mahogany furniture, tiny tapestries, glass mosaic windows, a miniature chess set, an illus-trated Bible no bigger than a thumbnail – for hours.

➡ **The Grounds**
Designed in the 18th century, the castle's expansive 15-hectare park contains century-old privet hedges, a herd of deer, space-age sculptures and manicured English-style gardens. Visitor attractions include a handful of first-class museums displaying outstanding collections of vintage cars and aircraft, antique motorcycles and bikes, emergency vehicles and horse-drawn vehicles, plus a wartime grocery shop.

There's also the cheesy **Dracula's Crypt**; a fabulous children's playground and a trio of mazes; and a treetop walk with shaky bridges and push-button birdsong.

The castle grounds usually stay open an hour longer than the castle. Check the website for 'Open By Night' events (usually Wednesdays in peak summer), when the grounds stay open until 11pm, with a program of evening concerts and fireworks. There's also pre-Christmas activity.

🛏 Sleeping & Eating

Just outside the gates there's a free **camping ground** for tents only. Buy shower tokens from the ticket office.

In the grounds are a couple of **kiosks** selling hot dogs and ice cream. More-substantial Italian-leaning fare is on offer at **Cafe Jomfru Rigborg** (meals Dkr49-165, picnic hamper adult/child Dkr95/145). The cafe will also arrange picnic hampers, but these must be ordered with 48 hours' notice.

ℹ Getting There & Away

Egeskov Slot is 2km west of Kværndrup on Rte 8, and is well signposted.

If you're in Nyborg or Faaborg, bus 920 (roughly hourly) runs 500m from the castle – ask the driver where to alight. Otherwise, take a train to Kværndrup station and catch the 920 bus, walk, or take a taxi.

Faaborg

POP 7200

In its 17th-century heyday, Faaborg claimed one of the country's largest commercial fishing fleets. It might be a lot sleepier these days, but vestiges of those golden years live on in cobblestone streets like Holkegade, Adelgade and Tårngade. Add to this a couple of good museums and a reinvigorated waterfront, and you have a winning pitstop.

Faaborg

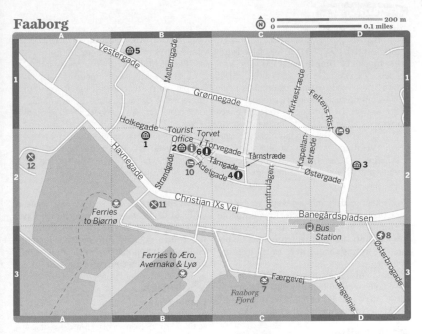

⊙ Sights

Faaborg Museum
MUSEUM

(www.faaborgmuseum.dk; Grønnegade 75; adult/child Dkr60/free; ⊙10am-4pm daily Jun-Aug, closed Mon Sep-May) You'll find a notable collection of Funen art, including works by Johannes Larsen, Peter Hansen, Jens Birkholm and Anna Syberg, and a flower-filled garden and cafe inside this handsome, imposing building. Kai Nielsen's original granite sculpture of the *Ymerbrønd* is also here.

Faaborg Arrest
MUSEUM

(www.ohavesmuseet.dk; Torvet 19; adult/child Dkr50/free; ⊙10am-5pm daily Jul-Aug, 11am-3pm Tue-Sun Feb-Jun & Sep-Oct) This museum occupies the former prison cells (in service until 1989) in the town hall, where displays cover the justice system and prison life.

Den Gamle Gaard
HISTORIC BUILDING

(www.ohavemuseet.dk; Holkegade 1; ⊙11am-3pm Mon-Wed Aug–mid-Sep) **FREE** Den Gamle Gaard is a beautiful timber-framed house that dates back to about 1720. Inside are 22 rooms, arranged to show how a wealthy merchant lived in the early 19th century – full of antique furniture, porcelain, toys, and maritime objects. When we visited it was open only limited hours – check the website.

Faaborg

⊙ Sights
1 Den Gamle Gaard	B2
2 Faaborg Arrest	B2
3 Faaborg Museum	D2
4 Klokketårnet	C2
5 Vesterport	B1
6 Ymerbrønd	B2

⊕ Activities, Courses & Tours
7 Sea-Bathing Pavilion	C3
8 Syd Fyenske Veteranjernbane	D3

⊟ Sleeping
9 Danhostel Faaborg	D2
10 Hotel Faaborg	B2

⊗ Eating
11 Det Hvide Pakhus	B2
12 Faaborg Røgeri	A2

Torvet & Around
SQUARE

The star of Faaborg's main square, is sculptor Kai Nielsen's striking bronze fountain **Ymerbrønd**, which caused a minor uproar on its unveiling. It depicts a Norse creation myth: the naked frost giant Ymir (from whose body the sky and earth were made) suckling at the udder of a cow.

Nearby, the recently refurbished **Klokketårnet** (Bell Tower; Tårnstræde; adult/child

WORTH A TRIP

FALSLED KRO

Falsled Kro (☑ 62 68 11 11; www.falsledkro.dk; Assensvej 513, Falsled; r from Dkr2800; lunch mains Dkr175-245, dinner four-/six-course menu Dkr825/1025) Ten kilometres west of Faaborg is Falsled Kro, in 2014 awarded Denmark's most 'travel-worthy' gourmet destination by the *White Guide* restaurant almanac. It's a picture-perfect historic inn dating from 1744, sitting cosily under a thatched roof, with impeccable decor, position, accommodation and food (oh the food – the four- or six-course menu utilises prime locally harvested ingredients, and French techniques with Nordic twists).

A night or two here, in this coastal countryside idyll, would be entirely memorable – but if your budget doesn't stretch that far, stop by for lunch or coffee in the cobbled, flower-bedecked courtyard, then amble down to the small marina behind the kro. And then you'll probably appreciate the 'fairy-tale' label that's often applied to rural Funen.

Dkr20/free; ⊙ daily mid-Jun–Aug) was once part of a medieval church. It's climbable in summer. From late June to mid-August, you can join the nightwatchman as he begins his rounds from here every evening at 9pm.

The medieval town gateway **Vesterport** (West Gate) was built in the 15th century to allow entry into Faaborg and is one of only two such gates remaining in Denmark.

🏃 Activities

Don't miss the new improved waterfront area, with a timber **sea-bathing pavilion**.

The countryside north of Faaborg, Svanninge Bakker, has been dubbed – a little optimistically – the 'Funen Alps'. It's made up of rolling hills and woodland crossed with **cycling and walking trails**.

Syd Fyenske Veteranjernbane   TRAIN RIDE
(☑ 62 61 17 09; www.veteranbanen-faaborg.dk; adult/child return Dkr80/40) This antique train makes summer runs from the old Faaborg train station (departs from near the Lidl supermarket, on Østebrogade) northeast to Korinth. It departs at 1pm and 3.30pm Sunday from late June to August, and also on Tuesdays and Thursdays in July. The return trip lasts 90 minutes.

🛌 Sleeping

Danhostel Faaborg   HOSTEL €
(☑ 62 61 12 03; www.danhostelfaaborg.dk; Grønnegade 71-72; dm/d Dkr175/375; ⊙ Apr-Sep; 🛜) This is a simple, oh-so-cosy hostel, based in two historic buildings – an old cinema and a half-timbered poorhouse, both full of sunshine and creaking woodwork. There are few frills (toilets are shared). Dorm beds are available in high summer.

Hotel Faaborg   HOTEL €€
(☑ 62 61 02 45; www.magasingaarden.dk; Torvet; s/d incl breakfast Dkr750/950; 🛜) Plumb in the centre square, this pretty-as-a-picture boutique-style hotel has fresh rooms and a lovely downstairs courtyard and cafe.

🍴 Eating

Faaborg Røgeri   SEAFOOD €
(www.faaborgroegericafe.com; Vestkaj 3; fish dishes Dkr32-76; ⊙ 10am-9pm daily mid-Jun–mid-Aug, reduced hrs rest of yr) Nothing says 'Danish holiday' better than eating *fiskefrikadeller* (fishballs) and remoulade from a paper plate in the salty-smelling harbourside sunshine.

Det Hvide Pakhus   DANISH €€
(☑ 62 61 09 00; www.dethvidepakhus.dk; Christian IXs Vej 2; lunch Dkr88-135, dinner mains Dkr155-265; ⊙ 11.30am-10pm daily mid-Jun–Aug, reduced hrs rest of yr) Set in a light, airy harbourside warehouse, Det Hvide Pakhus is as much a hit with locals as it is with out-of-towners. Lunch is a lesson in old-school Danish cuisine (heavy on the fish, direct from local fishermen), while dinner gets a bit fancier and skews towards fine cuts of beef. Kitchen closes 8pm.

ℹ️ Information

Tourist Office (☑ 63 75 94 44; www.visit-faaborgmidtfyn.com; Torvet 19; ⊙ 9am-5pm Mon-Fri, 9am-2pm Sat Jun-Aug, 10am-4pm Mon-Fri Sep-May) With bike hire, cycling and hiking maps, fishing licences etc. Can book accommodation and ferry tickets for a small fee.

ℹ️ Getting There & Away

Faaborg is a scenic 28km drive west of Svendborg (Rte 44) and 42km south of Odense on Rte 43.

BOAT

Aerøfærgerne (☑ 62 52 40 00; www.aeroe-ferry.dk) runs daily ferries to Søby at the northwestern end of the island of Ærø (one hour). There are one to three services a day – check schedules online. One-way adult/child tickets are Dkr130/82; transporting a car/bicycle one way costs Dkr280/27; drivers are advised to book ahead.

BUS

Faaborg's bus station is on Banegårdspladsen, at the defunct train station on the southern side of town.

From Odense, buses 111 and 141 (Dkr71) run regularly (bus 141 is the most direct, and takes an hour). From Svendborg, take frequent bus 931 (Dkr51, 55 minutes).

Svendborg

POP 26,700

Darling of the Danish yachting fraternity, who pack the town's cafe-dotted streets each summer, Svendborg is a major sailing centre. There are more Danish boats registered here than anywhere else outside Copenhagen, and the town is the main gateway to Funen's beautiful southern archipelago.

Although it's predominantly a modern industrial settlement, Svendborg possesses wooded cycling areas, popular beaches, a great natural-history museum and a first-rate hostel – not to mention a harbour packed with old wooden boats from across the Baltic.

◉ Sights & Activities

Maritimt Center Danmark HISTORIC BUILDING
(☑ 63 75 94 92; www.maritimt-center.dk; Havnepladsen 2; cruises adult/child Dkr270/170) At the Ærø ferry dock is the Maritime Centre, with its HQ inside a candy-striped timber warehouse (Pakhuset) from the late 19th century. The centre arranges cruises on historic sailing ships in high summer (late June to mid-August), with the possibility of sailing from various ports in the area (Svendborg, Faaborg, Marstal and Ærøskøbing on Ærø, Rudkøbing on Langeland). The website outlines the schedule.

Pakhusbutikken, the centre store, sells a range of souvenirs, including local produce from the area (try the delectable Skarø ice cream).

★ Sejlskibsbroen WATERFRONT
Don't miss Sejlskibsbroen, a jetty lined with splendidly preserved wooden sailing ships, and with an adjoining marina catering for the great number of yachts that sail local waters.

Naturama MUSEUM
(www.naturama.dk; Dronningemaen 30; adult/child Dkr140/free; ☉ Feb-Nov; ♿) Make a date with nature at Svendborg's impressive natural-history museum. Its three levels focus on water, land and air: whale skeletons dominate the basement, Scandinavian mammals congregate on the middle floor, and birds soar above it all. There's state-of-the-art sound and lighting, plus regular film shows and a good hands-on section for kids.

Note: confirm opening days online, as the museum is closed Mondays outside Danish school holidays.

Anne Hvides Gård HISTORIC BUILDING
(Fruestræde 3) 🆓 The oldest house in Svendborg, dating from 1560, is a bumblebee-coloured structure that leans tipsily to one side, highlighting its antiquity when all around is quite modern. The interior is only open by appointment; enquire with **Svendborg Museum** (☑ 62 21 02 61; info@svendborgmuseum.dk).

Forsorgsmuseet MUSEUM
(www.forsorgsmuseet.dk; Grubbemøllevej 13; adult/child Dkr50/free; ☉ 10am-4pm Tue-Sun May-Dec, shorter hrs Jan-Apr) A thought-provoking place, the Welfare Museum is housed in Svendborg's old poorhouse, which was home to paupers during its century of operation (from 1872). There were two ways to be admitted to this institution – the 'worthy' poor (disabled or old, for example), or the 'unworthy poor' (capable of work but unemployed, alcoholics, vagrants, 'women of easy virtue').

It's hard to reconcile such an equitable society (today's Denmark) with such harsh judgments, and this museum does a good job in explaining the times. There's also a section on life in children's homes and orphanages.

M/S Helge BOAT TRIPS
(www.mshelge.dk) From mid-May to mid-September, the vintage vessel *Helge* sails three or four times daily on a schedule that makes five stops in the area, at Svendborg Sund camping ground on the northern tip of Tåsinge, then at Christiansminde, a popular beach area east of Svendborg, before continuing to Troense and Valdemars Slot on Tåsinge. It turns around at Valdemars Slot to retrace its steps back to Svendborg harbour.

The boat leaves Svendborg harbour at 10am, 12.30pm and 2.30pm from mid-May to mid-September (with an additional sailing at 4.30pm in July); the total sailing time to the final stop is 55 minutes. Use it as a long sightseeing tour (Dkr60 one way), or a short-hop transport option (riding two stops for Dkr30).

FUNEN SVENDBORG

Svendborg

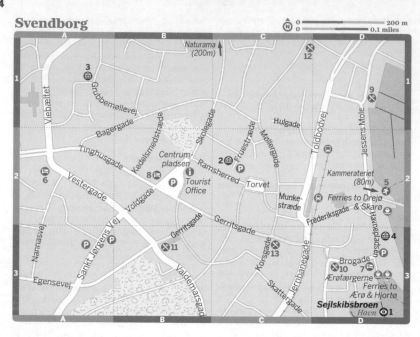

Svendborg

◉ Top Sights
1 Sejlskibsbroen......................................D3

◉ Sights
2 Anne Hvides Gård.................................C2
3 Forsorgsmuseet.....................................A1
4 Maritimt Center Danmark..................D3

◉ Activities, Courses & Tours
5 M/S Helge..D2

◉ Sleeping
6 Danhostel Svendborg.........................A2
7 Hotel Ærø..D3
8 Hotel Svendborg..................................B2

◉ Eating
9 Bendixens Fiskehandel....................... D1
10 Jettes Diner...D3
11 Kvickly...B3
12 Pizzeria La Pupa.................................C1
13 Vintapperiet...C3

🛏 Sleeping

Svendborg and its surrounds have good, inexpensive B&Bs, many of which are listed in the *Funen and the Islands* B&B brochure (found in tourist offices across Funen and online at www.bed-breakfast-fyn.dk).

The nearest camping ground is on Tåsinge (p177), on the southern side of Svendborg Sound.

★**Danhostel Svendborg**   HOSTEL €€
(☑62 21 66 99; www.danhostel-svendborg.dk; Vestergade 45; dm/d incl breakfast & linen Dkr275/750; P@🛜) This is a slick, professional hostel – more like a hotel really, and prices reflect this. Simple, spotless rooms, each with toilet and TV, are based in a renovated 19th-century iron foundry in the city centre. It's a popular conference centre in winter, and has oodles of facilities: laundry, kitchen, garden, breakfast buffet (Dkr75) and plentiful lounge nooks.

A double room without breakfast and linen costs Dkr600. Parking is off Nannavej.

Hotel Ærø   HOTEL €€
(☑62 21 07 60; www.hotel-aeroe.dk; Brogade 1; s/d incl breakfast Dkr850/1025; 🛜) This handsome mustard-and-white hotel occupies an unbeatable harbourside position (right by where the Ærø ferry docks), and has bags of atmosphere. The annexe of large, modern rooms is light and airy. The 'British-colonial' style – big comfy wooden beds, mock mahogany desks and wood floors – is restrained and relaxed. Harbour views cost Dkr100 extra.

Hotel Svendborg HOTEL €€
(📋 62 21 17 00; www.hotel-svendborg.dk; Centrumpladsen 1; s/d from Dkr995/1225; @ 🛜) Best Western offers smart, minimalist Scandi style n the centre of town. It's well-equipped, and predominantly a business hotel during the week, so summertime and weekend rates are more accommodating (single/double Dkr875/975).

🍴 Eating & Drinking

Bendixens Fiskehandel SEAFOOD €
(www.bendixens-fiskehandel.dk/; Jessens Mole 2; meals Dkr40-95; ⊙grill 11am-8pm or 9pm Mon-Sat) What could be better than fish and chips for Dkr70, and a boat-filled harbour as your view? This fish shop has an attached bargain-priced grill where you can buy fresh fish dishes to down at alfresco picnic tables.

Jettes Diner BURGERS €
(www.jettesdiner.dk; Kullinggade 1; burgers Dkr66-85; ⊙11.30am-9pm Sun & Mon, to 9.30pm Tue-Sat) It's all about bumper burgers at Jettes, a popular and inexpensive spot favoured by everyone, from workers nipping in for a beer to yachties from the nearby harbour. There's a good selection, too – from standard beef to chicken, pulled pork, and even some vegetarian options (and gluten-free buns).

Kvickly SUPERMARKET €
(Gerritsgade 33; ⊙9am-8pm Mon-Fri, 8am-6pm Sat & Sun) For self-catering; home to a decent bakery (opens 7am).

★Vintapperiet FRENCH €€
(📋 62 22 34 48; Brogade 37; lunch Dkr70-125, 2/3/4 courses Dkr200/250/300; ⊙11am-5.30pm Mon, 11am-10pm Tue-Sat Jun-Aug, shorter hrs rest of yr) There's a clever blend of rustic-France-meets-Denmark at this little bistro, tucked into a half-timbered house. Cheese or charcuterie for lunch, a small menu of selections for dinner (coq au vin, braised lamb nicoise), and always lots of wine options by the glass – perhaps even some live music to accompany it.

Pizzeria La Pupa ITALIAN €€
(www.lapupa.dk; Møllergade 78; pizzas Dkr80-130, mains Dkr200-250; ⊙5.30-10pm) Run by a real-deal Italian family, this rustic pizzeria-trattoria is a short walk back from the harbour and is a local favourite for its warm-hearted hosts as much as for its excellent pasta and pizza.

Kammerateriet BAR
(www.kammerateriet.com; Svendborg Havn; ⊙2-11pm Mon-Thu, 2pm-2am Fri, 11-2am Sat, noon-11pm Sun Jun-Aug, shorter hrs rest of yr) Walk across the bridge from the ferry area to find the town's hottest new bar and live-music venue, opened for summer 2014 in an old shipyard building. The local guys behind Kammerateriet have put together a place full of good vibes, booze, tapas and live music – and a cool artifical strand completes the chilled holiday scene.

ℹ Information

Tourist Office (📋 63 75 94 80; www.visitsvendborg.dk; Centrumpladsen 4; ⊙10am-4pm or 5pm Mon-Fri, to 1pm Sat) Has lots of information on south Funen; can book accommodation, ferry tickets etc.

ℹ Getting There & Away

Svendborg is the transit point between Odense and the South Funen Archipelago. It's 44km southeast of Odense on Rte 9.

BOAT

Ærøfærgerne (📋 62 52 40 00; www.aeroe-ferry.com) runs up to 12 ferries a day between Svendborg and Ærøskøbing (on Ærø); the crossing takes 75 minutes, and a one-way ticket costs Dkr130/82 for an adult/child. Transporting a car/bike one way costs Dkr280/27. Drivers should book their car passage in advance, especially in peak summer.

The M/S *Helge* (p173) sails between Svendborg and Tåsinge.

BUS & TRAIN

The bus and train stations are north of the Ærø ferry terminal, on Toldboldvej.

There are frequent bus services between Svendborg and Faaborg (bus 931, Dkr51, 55 minutes). Trains leave Odense for Svendborg twice an hour (Dkr78, 40 minutes).

ℹ Getting Around

Svendborg Cykeludlejning (📋 30 17 69 27; www.svendborgcykeludlejning.dk; Jernbanegade 10; ⊙9am-1pm Jun-Aug, shorter hrs rest of yr) Has bikes for rent (per day Dkr90) – check the website for opening hours.

The Svendborg tourist office has maps and brochures that outline scenic bike paths around the area.

Tåsinge

POP 6200

The island of Tåsinge is connected to Svendborg and Langeland by road bridges. Its main sights are in the northeast: the pretty sea-captain's village of Troense and palatial

THE SOUTH FUNEN ARCHIPELAGO

The South Funen Archipelago (in Danish, Det Sydfynske Øhav) is the name given to the 55 islands and uninhabited islets south of Faaborg and Svendborg. These are some of Denmark's true gems, and with some time and a sense of exploration, you could visit a few to pick a favourite.

Islands

Other than the larger islands of Tåsinge and Langeland (connected to Funen by road) and Ærø (everyone's favourite nautical-but-nice isle, accessible by ferry only), there are a handful of smaller islands that can easily be reached by scheduled summertime boat services from Faaborg and Svendborg.

These are wee gems designed for cycling, sailing, strolling, swimming and relaxation – most have summertime bike rental. Daytrips are a delight, but overnighting opportunities (including camping grounds and small marinas) also exist on many islands (check beforehand!).

➡ **From Faaborg** The Visit Faaborg site (www.visitfaaborg.dk) has information on the islands **Lyø**, **Avernakø** and **Bjørnø**.

➡ **From Svendborg** The Visit Svendborg site (www.visitsvendborg.dk) has information on **Drejø**, **Skarø** and **Hjortø**.

Tourist offices in the area provide information, maps and ferry schedules – other useful planning resources are Visit Fyn (www.visitfyn.com), and the excellent Archipelago Map (available online at www.archipelagomap.dk).

Activities

The Archipelago Map outlines the great activities in the area, including sea kayaking, windsurfing, angling, sailing and – of course – cycling, as well as companies that can help you access the outdoors.

One of the headline acts in this area is the 220km **Øhavssti** (Archipelago Trail), a long-distance walking trail that snakes its way from west to east along the southern edges of Funen and across to northern Langeland; the final section spans the length of Ærø. The trail takes in some of the most beautiful countryside in the region. It can be tackled in sections or attempted from start to finish.

Tourist offices in the region carry the seven-pamphlet series of free map guides (which each cover 25km to 35km of the trail's length; in Danish, German or English) or you can buy a detailed guidebook. There is information and PDF downloads online at www.detsydfynskeoehav.dk, although some of the English information is not as up-to-date as the Danish material.

17th-century Valdemars Slot. The rest of the island is a mixture of woods, hedges and open fields, cut through by Rte 9.

◉ Sights

Troense
VILLAGE

Troense is a well-to-do seaside village with a small yachting harbour and quaint thatched houses: two particularly pretty streets are Grønnegade and Badstuen.

Valdemars Slot
CASTLE

(www.valdemarsslot.dk; Slotsalléen 100, Troense; adult/child Dkr85/45; ⊙10am-5pm daily Jun-Aug, closed Mon May & Sep) One of Christian IV's lavish palaces, Valdemars Slot was built for his son in 1644. Valdemar never actually lived here – he died on a Polish battlefield at age 34 – and the castle itself was badly damaged in the Danish-Swedish wars. It was gifted to the naval hero Niels Juel, who transformed it into the baroque mansion you see today.

The palatial interior is crammed with antique furniture and eccentricities – lavish Venetian glass, 17th-century Gobelin tapestries, a toilet hidden in a window frame, a secret ammo store, Niels Juels' sea chest pasted with engravings, and autographed photos of visiting celebs. In the attic is the grisly **Jagt- & Trofæmuseet**, featuring ethnographical objects and animal trophies collected by hunter Børge Hinsch and others.

Another museum can be found in the pond-filled courtyard: **Danmarks Museum for Lystsejlads** (Yachting Museum; www.lystsejlads.dk; adult/child incl castle Dkr99/55; ⊙ 10am-5pm Jun-Aug) contains a collection of sleek, varnish sailboats.

There's no admission charge to the grounds of the castle or the sandy beach, just outside the southern gate. There is mini golf here, plus a casual cafe, and in the castle's vaulted cellars, a smart lunchtime **restaurant** (lunch Dkr95-185; ⊙ 11.30am-4pm Tue-Sun Apr-Nov).

You can get to Valdemars Slot by bus (route 250 stops 1km short), but a better way is via M/S *Helge* (p173), a boat that ferries passengers from Svendborg.

Bregninge   VILLAGE
The small village of Bregninge, on Rte 9, is home to one of Denmark's most-visited churches, the medieval **Bregninge Kirke**. Its attraction lies in the panoramic views from the **tower**.

Tåsinge Museum (www.taasinge-museum.dk; Kirkebakken 1; adult/child Dkr40/free; ⊙ 10am-4pm Tue-Sun Jun-Aug), across the road from the church, is a local-history museum telling the story of Lieutenant Sixten Sparre and artist Elvira Madigan, Denmark's real-life Romeo and Juliet. Facing separation, the tragic lovers committed suicide in 1889. They are buried together on Tåsinge in the churchyard at Landet, 3km south of Bregninge, where brides still throw bouquets on their grave.

🛏 Sleeping & Eating

Svendborg Sund Camping   CAMPGROUND €
(☑ 21 72 09 13; www.svendborgsund-camping.dk; Vindebyørevej 52; adult/child Dkr80/50 per campsite Dkr35; ⊙ Apr-Sep; 🛜) This well-kept seaside facility is the closest camping ground to Svendborg (there are also cottages for hire – weekly only in peak summer). It's at the northern tip of Tåsinge, about 2km northeast of the Svendborg bridge, and it's super scenic and family-friendly. The ferry M/S *Helge* docks out front; you can hire bicycles, kayaks and motorboats.

Hotel Troense   HOTEL €€
(☑ 62 22 54 12; www.hoteltroense.dk; Strandgade 5; s/d incl breakfast from Dkr875/1075; 🛜) Perched above the harbour, Hotel Troense has rooms divided between the main building (with sea views) and modern blocks at the back (with private seating areas in the garden). Rooms are quite plain but the setting is lovely. The dated decor of the restaurant could almost be retro – the food is also classic Danish fare. The restaurant is open noon to 9pm April to October, for dinner Monday to Saturday the rest of the year.

🚍 Getting There & Away

Route 9 connects Tåsinge with Svendborg on Funen, and Rudkøbing on Langeland. There are cycle paths running the entire way.

Buses run from Svendborg to Tåsinge (route 250), but the bus stops 1km short of the castle – and the vintage ferry M/S *Helge* (p173) is much more fun.

LANGELAND

Langeland is a long, narrow stretch of beach-fringed green, connected by bridge to Tåsinge. It's a grain-producing island: small farming villages and windmills dot the countryside, and everything moves at an unhurried pace.

Langeland

Langeland's major town, Rudkøbing, is unremarkable; the real attractions lie north at the Tickon sculpture park and south at the former military stronghold of Langelandsfort. This is good country for meandering exploration, bird-watching, and paddling in clear waters on the island's beaches.

❶ Getting There & Away

Route 9 connects Langeland to Tåsinge, via the Langeland bridge.

Bus 930 makes the 20km run from Svendborg to Rudkøbing (Dkr41, 30 minutes) at least hourly. See www.fynbus.dk for schedules.

A ferry operates from Spodsbjerg to Tårs on Lolland. The ferry service from Rudkøbing to Marstal on Ærø has ceased – to reach Ærø you need to return to Svendborg and take the ferry from there.

❶ Getting Around

Route 305 runs from Lohals to Bagenkop, nearly the full length of the island.

BICYCLE

There are sealed cycle paths running from the Rudkøbing area north to Lohals, east to Spodsbjerg and south to Bagenkop. The tourist office in Rudkøbing sells a bicycle map of Langeland (Dkr30) outlining six routes, and you can hire bikes from **Lapletten** (⌨ 62 51 10 98; www.lapletten.dk; Engdraget 1), also in Rudkøbing, and from camping grounds on the island.

BUS

From Rudkøbing, local bus 913 travels north to Lohals and 912 travels south to Bagenkop; these services connect all of Langeland's major villages and run about every two hours.

Rudkøbing

POP 4500

Rudkøbing's tumbledown streets are pleasant enough for a brief meander, but there's no need to spend much time here (unless you're travelling by bus, or stocking up on info or supplies).

Between Torvet and the harbour are a series of narrow cobbled streets lined with tiny tilting houses. Combining three of the most interesting, Ramsherred, Smedegade and Vinkældergade, makes a fine stroll.

🛏 Sleeping & Eating

Hotel Rudkøbing

Skudehavn HOTEL, APARTMENTS €€
(⌨ 62 51 46 00; www.rudkobingskudehavn.dk; Havnegade 21; s/d incl breakfast Dkr575/795; ℗)

Down by the modern marina, this bright holiday centre includes small, stylish hotel rooms, but the nicest options are the two-bedroom apartments (sleeping six, and all with toilet, kitchen, TV and private balcony or terrace). A two-night stay in these costs from Dkr1500, with significant discounts for extra nights (and low-season stays). There's also a restaurant and bar.

Slagterpigerne DELI €
(www.slagterpigerne.dk; Torvet 6; smørrebrød Dkr22-45; ☉ 9am-5pm Mon-Thu, to 6pm Fri, to 1pm Sat) Put a picnic together with some takeaway smørrebrød (open sandwiches) and deli items from this butcher's shop on the main square.

Super Brugsen SUPERMARKET €
(Ahlefeldtsgade 5; ☉ 8am-7pm) Large supermarket with a cheapo cafe, and good bakery section that opens at 6.30am.

❶ Information

Tourist Office (⌨ 62 51 35 05; www.langeland. dk; Torvet 5; ☉ 9.30am-4.30pm Mon-Fri year-round, also 9.30am-2.30pm Sat Jul & Aug) Comprehensive info on the island. Helpful staff can book ferry tickets or accommodation for Dkr25.

Northern Langeland

The main sight in northern Langeland is Tranekær. Lohals, at the island's northern tip, has facilities and beaches nearby, but it's not as charming as Tranekær and the southern beaches are better.

◉ Sights

Tranekær Slot CASTLE
(www.tranekaergods.dk) The little village of Tranekær stretches between its church and the salmon-coloured Tranekær Slot, which has been in the hands of one family since 1659 (there's been a fortification here since the 13th century). The castle's interior is only open to the public on tours conducted over two weeks in July (see the website) – but the grounds are open daily and known as Tickon.

Tickon GARDEN
(Tranekær International Centre for Art & Nature; adult/child Dkr25/free; ☉ sunrise-sunset) The wooded grounds of Tranekær Slot are home to the magical Tickon, a collection of outdoor art installations. You can wander around the lake and arboretum, inhabited

by a herd of red deer. There are surprises round every corner: a unicorn's horn sprouts in a glade, a river of tree trunks floods down a hillside. There are 19 sculptures to enjoy, and the fun is finding them in the landscape.

🛏 Sleeping & Eating

There are some lovely B&Bs around Tranekær – see 'Private Accommodation' on www.langeland.dk, or contact Rudkøbing's tourist office.

Æblegaarden　　　　　　　　B&B €€
(✆59 64 02 44; www.aeblegaarden.dk; Fæbækvej 25; per person incl breakfast Dkr385; 🛜) On a beautiful, bountiful rural property (the name means 'The Apple Farm') about 8km north of Tranekær Slot, friendly hosts offer two stylish, light-filled rooms for rent (shared kitchenette and toilet). Breakfast is a highlight, utilising farm-fresh produce; dinners are also possible (advance notice usually required).

Tranekær Gæstgivergaard　GUESTHOUSE €€
(✆62 59 12 04; www.tranekaerkro.dk; Slotsgade 74; s/d Dkr750/950; 🅿) This village inn 200m south of the castle dates from 1802 and retains its period ambience. Most rooms have peaceful garden views (they're in a more-modern annex out the back). The highly rated restaurant (mains Dkr250 to Dkr390) is strong on local game, such as venison and pheasant.

Southern Langeland

Southern Langeland's pastoral landscape contains some gentle diversions. The island's favourite Blue Flag beach is at the thatched seaside hamlet of **Ristinge**. Other pitstops include a manor house and a Cold War-era relic.

At the tip of Langeland, you might spy **wild horses** (follow signs for 'Vilde Heste'): two herds of Exmoor ponies have been introduced to keep the coastal meadows cropped. The area here and around Bagenkop also contain excellent bird-watching sites connected by footpaths, and there's a coastal nature reserve, **Tryggelev Nor**, midway between Bagenkop and Ristinge.

Humble, Bagenkop and Lindelse are all reasonable sized villages – they each have a nondescript *kro* (inn) providing accommodation and food, plus small supermarkets. Humble is closer to Ristinge beach but

Bagenkop has more charm, plus an idyllic small harbour for wandering.

◉ Sights

Skovsgaard　　　　　　　　　MUSEUM
(www.danmarksnaturfond.dk; Kågårdsvej 12; adult/child Dkr60/free; ⏱10am-5pm Mon-Fri, 11am-5pm Sun mid-May–Sep) If you've been touring Denmark's decadent palaces, it's refreshing to visit Skovsgaard. The kitchen cellars, servants' dining room and housekeeper's room of the old manor house have been furnished with dummies and props, giving an interesting glimpse of how the 'downstairs' staff lived.

The stables hold a collection of horse-drawn vehicles and tractors. There's also an organic food cafe.

Skovsgaard estate is off Rte 305 (the main road) around 3km southeast of Lindelse.

Langelandsfort　　　　　　HISTORIC SITE
(www.langelandsfort.dk; Vognsbjergvej 4B, Bagenkop; adult/child Dkr95/free; ⏱10am-5pm May-Sep, to 3pm Apr & Oct) There are few better Danish examples of Cold War paranoia than unique Langelandsfort, built in 1952–53 to defend the western Baltic against the Russians. You can descend into various bunkers and command centres, board a claustrophobic U-boat, explore a minesweeper and peer inside two fighter planes. The solid grey masses of concrete, rusting barbed wire and camouflage-green emplacements and anti-aircraft guns are in startling contrast to the picnic-perfect countryside in which they are set.

The site is big (to see everything involves a walk of about 2km) and you'll need a couple of hours to look around. A new exhibition covers espionage during the era. The fort is just north of Bagenkop.

🛏 Sleeping & Eating

Ristinge SommerCamp　CAMPGROUND €
(✆62 57 13 29; www.ristinge.dk; Ristingevej 104, Ristinge; per adult/child/campsite Dkr74/49/65; ⏱May-Sep; 🌐🛜🏊) The long sandy beach at Ristinge is often cited as one of Denmark's best. Within walking distance is this super camping ground, with swimming pool, playground, mini golf, tennis court, bike hire and loads more. There are also caravans and huts for hire (from Dkr400 per night).

Bagenkop Kro　　　　　　　　　INN €€
(✆62 56 13 04; www.bagenkopkro.dk; Østergade 15, Bagenkop; s/d Dkr500/800; 🛜) Smart but

very petite rooms are on offer here, at this handsome grey *kro* on the main drag. Good, traditional meals are available at lunch and dinner, and there's a well-frequented buffet on Friday, Saturday and Sunday nights, with plenty of local fish and seafood for Dkr199.

★ **Skovsgaard MadMarked**   CAFE, DELI €
(www.danmarksnaturfond.dk; Kågårdsvej 12; lunch plate Dkr75; ⊘10am-5pm mid-May–Sep, until 9pm Thu) 'MadMarked' sounds worrying but in fact means 'food market', and this bright, pretty cafe-deli at the entrance to the Skovsgaard estate is brimming with fresh, organic local produce (some of it grown on the estate). You can lunch on a plate of various meats and salads; we'll understand if you go straight for coffee and dessert (eg rhubarb crumble).

Stock up on gourmet picnic supplies, or drop by on Thursday nights for a simple, low-cost buffet dinner (from 5.30pm; Dkr98).

ÆRØ

Just 30km long and 9km wide, Ærø (pronounced 'with difficulty' – or *air-rue*) is the frontrunner for the title of loveliest Danish island.

The island is rich in maritime history, and home to some good beaches and photogenic bathing huts. Add the picturebook town of Ærøskøbing and the country roads that roll through gentle countryside peppered with thatched-roofed, half-timbered houses and old windmills, and you'll really capture the feeling of stepping back in time.

It helps that Ærø is populated by some of the friendliest people in Denmark: in a gesture of kindness, the local bus is free. Still, the three main towns (Ærøskøbing, Marstal and Søby) are within perfect cycling distance of each other, and cycling is a great way to get around – not least as this is in keeping with the spirit of an island that is run almost entirely on sustainable energy sources such and wind and solar power.

In summer the place comes alive. There is a lively **jazz festival** (www.aeroejazzfestival.dk) in late July/early August, and it's a favourite yachtie destination. It's also developing a reputation as the wedding capital of Denmark: Vegas it ain't (it's a whole lot more sedate), but more than 2000 couples from all over the world got married on the island in 2013. (Curious? See www.getmarriedindenmark.com.)

ⓘ Getting There & Away

Ærøfærgerne (☑ 62 52 40 00; www.aeroeferry.dk) runs year-round car ferries:

Ærø

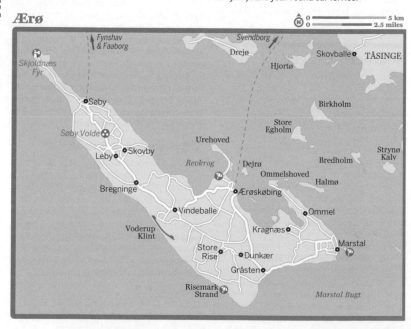

→ **Svendborg-Ærøskøbing** The main service, running up to 12 times daily. Journey time: 75 minutes.

→ **Faaborg-Søby** Runs two to three times a day. Journey time: one hour.

→ **Fynshav-Søby** From Fynshav on the island of Als (southern Jutland). Runs two to three times a day. Journey time: 70 minutes.

Prices are the same on all three routes:

Adult one-way/return Dkr130/199

Child one-way/return Dkr82/115

Car one-way/return Dkr280/437

Bicycle one-way/return Dkr27/41

If you have a car it's a good idea to reserve, particularly on weekends and in summer (you can do this online).

The ferry link between Marstal and Rudkøbing (on Langeland) no longer operates.

ℹ Getting Around

BICYCLE

Cycling is the perfect way to enjoy Ærø, with three well-signposted cycle routes creating a 60km circuit:

→ **Route 90:** Ærøskøbing to Søby (17.5km)

→ **Route 91:** Søby to Marstal (31.5km)

→ **Route 92:** Marstal to Ærøskøbing (10.5km)

Ærø's tourist offices sell an inexpensive English-language cycling map of the island (Dkr20), listing sights along the way.

Bike Erria (☑ 32 14 60 74; www.bike-erria. dk) is a useful company that promotes bicycle tourism on the island and can help you plan a cycle-tour itinerary (one day or longer) – delivering bikes to you, delivering your bags to your accommodation etc.

Note that you can take bikes on the bus after 9am.

You can rent bikes for around Dkr60 to Dkr75 per day across Ærø – try the following places:

→ **Pilebækkens Cykler** (☑ 62 52 11 10; Pilebækken 11, Ærøskøbing)

→ **Nørremarks Cykeludlejning** (☑ 62 53 14 77; Møllevejen 77, Marstal)

→ **Søby Cykelforretning** (☑ 40 33 91 14; Havnevejen 2, Søby)

BUS

Bus 790 runs the length of the island, from Søby harbour to Marstal harbour and vice versa, via Ærøskøbing (a full journey takes just under an hour). The bus is free, and operates hourly from 5am to 9pm weekdays (slightly less frequently and shorter hours on weekends). Pick up the schedule at tourist offices.

Ærøskøbing

POP 930

A prosperous 17th-century merchants' town, Ærøskøbing has bucketloads of character. Cobblestone streets meander between crooked houses, cheerfully painted and gently skewed, with hand-blown glass windows, doorways bursting with bright hollyhocks, and half-hidden courtyards offering glimpses into snug, private worlds.

The town has outstanding accommodation and makes the best base for a stay on Ærø.

◎ Sights & Activities

The three local museums are outlined at www.arremus.dk; a combined ticket for all three is Dkr85.

Wandering the timeless streets of Ærøskøbing is like winding the clock back a century or two. The oldest house, at Søndergade 36, dates to 1645. Other fine streets for strolling are Vestergade and Smedegade; there's a particularly charming house known as Dukkehuset ('The Doll's House') at Smedegade 37.

Hammerichs Hus   MUSEUM
(www.arremus.dk; Gyden 22; adult/child Dkr30/ free; ⊙noon-3pm Thu Jul & Aug, by appointment rest of year) Our favourite of Ærøskøbing's museums, half-timbered Hammerichs Hus is the most gnarled, creaky hobbit-hole of a home imaginable (mind your head). Its snug interior is full of antiques collected by sculptor Gunnar Hammerich: most impressive are the walls, lined with around 3000 beautiful 17th- and 18th-century Dutch tiles.

It's not open long hours, but staff at the nearby Ærø Museum will open it for you during their opening hours.

Ærø Museum   MUSEUM
(www.arremus.dk; Brogade 3-5; adult/child Dkr30/ free; ⊙11am-4pm Mon-Fri, 11am-3pm Sat & Sun Jul-Aug, by appointment rest of yr) This sweet assemblage includes maritime paraphernalia, plus traditional clothing, furniture and household utensils.

Flaske Peters Samling   MUSEUM
(www.arremus.dk; Smedegade 22; adult/child Dkr40/free; ⊙10am-4pm Jul-Aug, 11am-3pm Mon-Sat mid-Apr–Jun & Sep–mid-Oct, by appointment rest of yr) The former poorhouse displays the amazing life's work of Peter Jacobsen ('Bottle Peter'), who crafted 1700 ships-in-a-bottle.

FUNEN ÆRØSKØBING

Vesterstrand BEACH

(Vestre Strandvej) Walk or cycle to the beach, a few minutes north from town (take Strandvejen or Sygehusvejen), for a swim, or sunset-watching amid the brightly painted bathing huts.

🛏 Sleeping

The *Ærø Guide,* available in tourist offices, lists B&Bs around the island, as does www. aeroe.dk. There are also plenty of holiday cottages for rent.

Andelen Guesthouse GUESTHOUSE €

(☑61 26 75 11; www.andelenguesthouse.com; Søndergade 28A; s/d/tr without bathroom Dkr600/700/900) After big renovations, a young, well-travelled Danish-English family have opened this great option: wooden floors, timber beams, stylish modern (shared) toilets, pretty courtyard. It's in a building with lots of history and character – it houses Bio Andelen, the sweet local 50-seat cinema (complimentary tickets for guests) that's been the venue for many jazzfest gigs. Breakfast is Dkr75.

Ærøskøbing Camping CAMPGROUND €

(☑62 52 18 54; www.aeroecamp.dk; Sygehusvej 40; campsites per site adult/child Dkr78/48) Near Vesterstrand beach (about 1km north of the town centre), this green camping ground has hedges for shelter, plus neat facilities, playground

BED & NATURE

Vesteraas Bed & Nature (☑61 28 62 52; www.vesteraas.dk; Voderup 41; cottage Dkr750-1250; ☺May-Sep) A young family runs this sustainable farm (raising grass-fed cattle) in a lush, view-blessed area where cows and chickens roam. Two atmospheric, family-friendly self-contained cottages are available here, sleeping up to six. One is in the stylishly converted old stables, and one is in a magnificent 'greenhouse', of sorts (part of which spies on the cowshed interior).

These are unique, creative and restful options where the appeal of rural escape becomes crystal clear – in peak of summer, the rental period is generally one week. Vesteraas is in Voderup, signposted off the main road from the hamlet Vindeballe – it's about 8km southwest of Ærøskøbing.

and bike rental. The small, cute, no-frills huts are great if you'd like a roof over your head. Marstal and Søby also have camping grounds.

★ Pension Vestergade 44 GUESTHOUSE €€

(☑62 52 22 98; www.vestergade44.com; Vestergade 44; s/d without bathroom incl breakfast Dkr990/1090; ☏) The large timbered house was built in 1784 by a sea captain for his daughter. It's now owned and run as a guesthouse by lovely Susanna (originally from England), and she gets it right, down to the finest detail: the six rooms are decorated with period charm, the large garden is delightful, and the breakfast comprises freshly laid eggs and homemade jam.

In a nutshell, it's close to perfect; booking ahead is advised.

På Torvet APARTMENTS, CAFE €€

(☑62 52 40 50; www.paatorvet.dk; Torvet 7; d studio Dkr750-950; ☏) Friendly new owners have renovated a grand old building on the idyllic village square, and turned it into a light-filled cafe-bar. They also rent accommodation in an annex at the back: eight studio apartments, all with small kitchen and sitting area, and stylish furnishings. Families should ask about the excellent, two-bedroom apartments (sleeping four) above the cafe. Highly recommended.

🍴 Eating

Ærøskøbing Røgeri SEAFOOD €

(Havnen 15; meals Dkr36-82; ☺10am-9pm Jul–mid-Aug, 11am-7pm mid-Apr–Jun & mid-Aug–mid-Oct) Get an authentically salty-dog feel at this traditional fish smokehouse, adjacent to the harbour. It serves bargain-priced smoked-fish plates (the halibut with potato salad is delicious) or fish-stuffed sandwiches. Wash it down with a plastic cup full of locally brewed beer.

Ærøskøbing Bageri BAKERY €

(Vestergade 62; ☺7am-5pm Mon-Fri, to 2pm Sat & Sun) A cut above even Denmark's high bakery standards for bread, sandwiches and assorted deli products, behind a fab retro facade.

Den Gamle Købmandsgaard DELI €

(www.dengamlekoebmandsgaard.com; Torvet 5; ☺10am-4.30pm Mon-Fri, to 2pm Sat) The Old Merchant's Court is a hub for local produce – an indoor farmers market selling fine local produce (bread, beer, salami, ice cream, honey, chocolate). Stop in for coffee, cake and a tastebud-tempting browse.

Netto SUPERMARKET €

(Vestre Allé 4; ⊘8am-10pm) For self-caterers; by the harbour.

Café Aroma INTERNATIONAL €€

(☑62 52 40 02; www.cafe-aroma.dk; Havnepladsen; mains Dkr72-225; ⊘11am-10pm Jul & Aug, to 8pm Apr-Jun & Sep-Oct) This cafe's interior is the essence of *hyggelig* (cosy): film posters, old cinema seats, a battered sofa, even a barber's chair – but on warm summer evenings, the outdoor terrace is in hot demand. There's a good all-day menu where local produce shines – try fish (of course) or the gourmet hotdog, then follow with delicious homemade ice cream.

Above the cafe, **Hotel Aroma** offers outstanding rooms and apartments (double from Dkr695), stylish and colourful with plenty of character.

ℹ️ Information

Ærøskøbing Tourist Office (☑62 52 13 00; www.visitaeroe.dk; Havnen 4; ⊘9am-4pm Mon-Fri) Near the ferry terminal. This is the main info centre for the island, with smaller summertime branches in Marstal and Søby.

Marstal

POP 2400

Marstal, at the eastern end of Æro, is larger and more modern than Ærøskøbing, but it's one of the island's big draws thanks to its living maritime history. In its 19th-century heyday, more than 300 merchant ships pulled into port annually and eight shipyards were operating. It's still a seafaring town with a busy shipyard, marina and excellent nautical museum.

Appropriately enough, acclaimed author Carsten Jensen partly set his bestselling maritime epic *We, the Drowned* here. You can buy the novel at the museum and in the tourist offices. It's a great way to steep yourself in Marstal's seafaring history.

⊙ Sights & Activities

Marstal Søfartsmuseum MUSEUM

(www.marmus.dk; Prinsensgade 1; adult/child Dkr60/free; ⊘9am-5pm Jun-Aug, 10am-4pm Apr, May, Sep & Oct, 11am-3pm Mon-Sat Nov-Apr) If you don't know a barquentine from a brig, the absorbing nautical collection here will make everything (almost) clear. It's stuffed full of ships' models, sea chests and sailors' souvenirs from around the world, plus tales of life for the families left behind by the seafarers.

WORTH A TRIP

ISLAND BREWS

Rise Bryggeri (☑62 52 11 32; www.risebryggeri.dk; Vandværksvej 5; ⊘shop 11am-3pm Jul-Sep, cafe 11am-9pm Jul-Aug, 11am-3pm Sep) Well worth a cycling excursion is the island's wee microbrewery, pumping out delicious brews including stout, pilsner, India pale ale and dark ale. Its bock-style walnut beer comes highly recommended. You can sample Rise beer throughout the island, or you can drop in to visit its shop and dine rustically in its idyllic garden.

Find it signposted just off the main road in the hamlet of Store Rise, about 7km south of Ærøskøbing.

There's even some climbable rigging in the courtyard. Take a walk to the nearby waterfront to see the newly restored, century-old schooner *Bonavista*, built in Marstal in 1914.

Havkayak Center Marstal KAYAKING

(☑50 21 94 60; www.havkajakcenter-marstal.dk; Marstal Marina; ⊘Apr–mid-Aug) Kayaking is a great way to explore the usually calm waters around the island; this centre offers lessons, weekly guided trips (a two-hour paddle at 4pm Wednesday in peak summer), or just kayak hire for experienced paddlers. It's mostly local enthusiasts – call or email to find out what's possible. The centre is down at the marina – look for the beach volley signs.

Eriks Hale BEACH

South of town, on a strip of sand that juts into the sea, is this popular beach. It's a must-visit for its bathing huts, particularly Denmark's most photogenic: painted red with green shutters, sitting pretty under a thatched roof.

🛏 Sleeping

Danhostel Marstal HOSTEL €

(☑62 53 39 50; www.marstalvandrerhjem.dk; Færgestræde 29; dm Dkr220, d without/with bathroom Dkr400/550; ⊘May–mid-Sep; 🛜) Nicely positioned halfway between the harbour and the beach, this is a well-run, high-quality hostel with a pretty cobbled courtyard and stylish dining area with wood fire. A handful of rooms have toilets; some also have sea views. Dorms are available in high season. A fine choice.

Ærø Hotel
HOTEL €€

(☑62 53 24 06; www.aeroehotel.dk; Egehovedvej 4; s/d incl breakfast Dkr750/850; 🎧🏊) When all the boutique options are full, the island's largest hotel (100 rooms) comes into its own. It lies a little way out of Marstal and has been newly taken over by a local family. They're friendly, service-oriented folks with plans to modernise what are good, light-filled rooms. There's an on-site restaurant and funky indoor pool.

🍴 Eating

As with the rest of the island, restaurant opening hours outside the peak summer period are somewhat erratic, but there are a handful of year-round options. Your accommodation will be able to point you in the right direction, or the tourist office.

From May to September, look out for the Thai food van that operates down at the marina.

Ø-Smageriet
CAFE €

(Kirkestræde 6; meals Dkr65-135; ⊙9am-10pm daily Jul-Aug, 10am-7pm Mon-Thu, to 5pm Fri & Sat Sep-Jun) Part of a pastel-coloured collective at the end of Kirkestræde. Stop here for quality homemade gelato, smørrebrød and deli treats for picnickers. One gelato flavour uses the candy made in the cute yellow building opposite, called Ø-Bolcher. Pop in to see the sweets being made.

Super Brugsen
SUPERMARKET €

(cnr Kirkestræde & Skovgyden; ⊙8am-7pm Mon-Fri, 8am-6pm Sat & Sun) At the northern end of the pedestrian shopping street, Kirkestræde, where most services are also located (post, bank etc).

Kongensgade 34
INTERNATIONAL €€

(www.kongensgade34.dk; Kongensgade 34; meals Dkr85-169; ⊙10am-midnight Sun-Thu, to 2am Fri & Sat Jul-Aug, shorter hrs rest of yr; 🎧) A relaxed, all-day bar-bistro that moves from lunch into dinner then late-night drinks. There's a menu of Danish and global classic hits: sit in the sun and enjoy a burger, steamed mussels or a pile of *pilselv rejer* (unpeeled prawns) with citron-mayo.

Restaurant Edith
MODERN DANISH €€€

(☑62 25 25 69; www.restaurantedith.dk; Kirkestræde 8; 3-/5-/7-course menu Dkr445/599/699; ⊙6-11pm) Pretty, mint-green Edith is a smart showcase for regional produce (locally caught fish, island-reared meat, plenty of herbs, vegetables and summer berries), put to good use in innovative creations. Outside the summer season it's only open for dinner Friday and Saturday, and only if booked ahead.

ℹ Information

Marstal Tourist Office (Skolegade 26; ⊙10am-6pm Mon-Fri, to 4pm Sat, 5pm Sun Jun-Aug, shorter hrs rest of yr) Inside the library on Skolegade, a small street running between the harbour and the pedestrian street (Kirkestræde).

Søby
POP 540

The shipyard, fishing fleet and marina dominate the small village of Søby, but it lacks the tourist charm of either Ærøskøbing or Marstal. There are some excellent B&Bs in the countryside between here and Ærøskøbing.

Skjoldnæs Fyr
LIGHTHOUSE

(adult/child Dkr20/10) An excellent destination for a drive or cycle, Skjoldnæs Fyr is a 19th-century, granite-block lighthouse 5km northwest of Søby, next to the small clubhouse for the scenic golf course. You can climb the narrow stairway (it's rarely locked during the day) for exhilarating views of wind-tossed swallows and the sea. A few minutes' walk beyond the lighthouse is a pebble beach and bird breeding area.

Søbygaard
MANOR

(www.arremus.dk; Søbygaardsvej; adult/child Dkr50/free; ⊙10am-4pm daily mid-Apr–mid-Oct, to 5pm Jul & Aug, by appointment rest of yr) The earthen ramparts of Søby Volde, once part of a 12th-century fortress, hunch to one side of the main road, 3km south of Søby. Across the lane is 16th-century Søbygaard, a compact manor house with a dry moat, reputedly haunted by a white lady. It stages art exhibitions, and musical events in summer.

Southern Jutland

Includes ➡

Kolding 186
Esbjerg 188
Fanø 191
Ribe. 193
Wadden Sea
National Park 198
Rømø 198
Tønder 200
Møgeltønder 202
Sønderborg 203

Best Places to Eat

➡ Sønderho Kro (p192)

➡ Otto & Ani's Fisk (p200)

➡ Sælhunden (p197)

➡ Hjerting Badehotel (p189)

➡ Kolvig (p197)

Best Places to Stay

➡ Hotel Koldingfjord (p187)

➡ Sønderho Kro (p192)

➡ Schackenborg Slotskro (p202)

➡ Weis Stue (p196)

➡ Danhostel Ribe (p196)

➡ Den Gamle Arrest (p196)

Why Go?

Southern Jutland gets its inspiration from a few sources – from the North Sea, naturally, but also a little from the south. This is the only part of Denmark connected to mainland Europe (by a 68km-long border), and in some places you can feel the historic ties with Germany.

This is a region of salty offshore islands, understated royal palaces and character-filled historic towns, with unexpectedly modern treats in the form of edgy art and architecture, and offbeat design museums. The jewel in the crown is Ribe, the country's oldest town, and historic Denmark at its most photogenic. The islands of Als, Fanø and Rømø have clear-cut appeal for beach-going holidaymakers, and birdwatchers also love this region. The tidal rhythms of the Wadden Sea bring an abundance of feathered friends (and their fanciers). An eclectic mix of royal-watchers, castle-collectors and design-enthusiasts will also be ticking must-sees off their list.

When to Go

If it's sunshine and beaches you're after, June to August is the obvious time to join the crowds on islands such as Rømø, Fanø and Als. The region's biggest festival (Tønder Festival) farewells summer in style in late August.

Ribe charms at any time of year – December is delightful, with a Christmas market and festivities that make the atmosphere extra-*hyggelig* (cosy). The attractions of larger towns (Kolding, Esbjerg, Sønderborg, Tønder) are also year-round. Note that in spring (March to April) and autumn (mid-September to October) there's some unique bird-watching by the Wadden Sea.

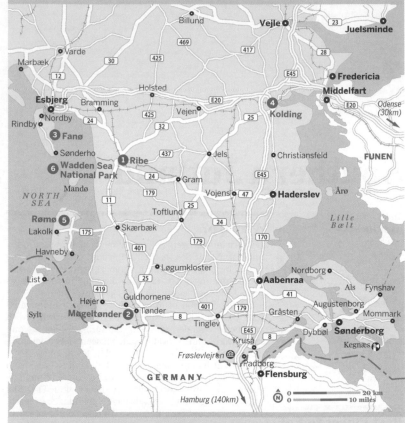

Southern Jutland Highlights

1 Join the night-watchman on an evening walk through historic **Ribe** (p194)

2 Dial the cuteness factor up to 11 in fairytale **Møgeltønder** (p202)

3 Head from modern, Esbjerg to salty-dog **Fanø** (p191) in only 12 minutes

4 Envy **Kolding** (p186) its appealing mix of the old and the new

5 Check out the wind-driven blokarts and kitebuggies at Sønderstrand on **Rømø** (p198)

6 See birds 'dance' during the 'Sort Sol' in the **Wadden Sea National Park** (p198)

Kolding

POP 58,000

Kolding is an eminently likeable mid-sized town with a crowd-pleasing mix of old and new, encapsulated in one of its major drawcards, the hilltop castle Koldinghus. After a stroll through the town's old quarters, head to Trapholt to admire the modern furniture design for which Denmark is renowned.

⊙ Sights

Koldinghus CASTLE, MUSEUM

(www.koldinghus.dk; Markdanersgade; adult/child Dkr80/free; ⊙10am-5pm) Koldinghus is the town's extravagant showpiece, with the requisite turbulent history. A fortress occupied the land in 1268, while parts of the castle you see today can be traced to the mid-15th century. After a huge fire in 1808, the prevailing school of thought was that the castle would be left in ruins (at the time, the Danish state was at war and bankrupt). Now, however, the reborn castle shines, and the interplay between old and new architectural styles is a highlight.

There are good displays, including collections of art and silverware, and changing contemporary exhibits – grab a floor plan to help find your way around. It's a climb to the top of the tower but you'll be rewarded with a panoramic view of the town.

★ **Trapholt**   MUSEUM
(www.trapholt.dk; Æblehaven 23; adult/child Dkr80/ free; ⊙10am-5pm Tue-Sun, to 8pm Wed) The Trapholt museum of modern art, applied art and furniture design is housed in an architectural wonder in Kolding's residential northeastern outskirts. There are a couple of classics from the Skagen artists, vibrant modern pieces and a sculpture garden. Downstairs, the furniture collection has examples of covetable Danish chairs, with many fine examples by the likes of iconic designers Hans Wegner, Verner Panton and Arne Jacobsen.

One of Trapholt's more intriguing exhibits is Jacobsen's prototype summerhouse, **Kubeflex** (the only one of its kind). It was designed by Jacobsen in 1969-70 and involves cubic modules designed to be added to as the need arose. The house is open at 1pm and 3pm daily (also at 11am weekends).

All in all, Trapholt is one of the most impressive museums in Jutland – and the view-enriched cafe and giftshop are also topnotch. Take bus 4 to get here.

Historic Buildings   HISTORIC BUILDINGS
The red-and-green half-timbered house close to the tourist office on Akseltorv is **Borchs Gård**, a decorative Renaissance building dating from 1595. Kolding's oldest house is nearby and immensely photogenic, at **number 18** on the shopping strip of Helligkorsgade. It's a wonky, orange-coloured, half-timbered affair built in 1589.

🛏 Sleeping

Danhostel Kolding   HOSTEL €
(☑75 50 91 40; www.danhostelkolding.dk; Ørnsborgvej 10; dm Dkr215, d without/with bathroom Dkr475/575; ⊙mid-Jan–Nov; @🛜) This top option is above a park about 1.5km north of the city centre (a 15-minute walk). There are pleasant rooms in the older-style main building, and a newer annexe with private bathrooms and modern kitchen-dining area. It's deservedly popular with families and backpackers; bus 3 stops nearby.

★ **Hotel Koldingfjord**   HOTEL €€
(☑75 51 00 00; www.koldingfjord.dk; Fjordvej 154; r from Dkr1125; @🛜🏊) Play lord of the manor at this grand, castle-like estate (a former sanatorium) 7km east of the city, amid the forest on Kolding Fjord (2km past Trapholt museum; take bus 4). It's a gorgeously restful spot, with first-class facilities (indoor pool, free bikes, cafe, terrace and restaurant) and the rooms are an ode to Scandi minimalism and design.

Kolding Hotel Apartments   APARTMENTS €€
(☑75 54 18 00; www.koldinghotelapartments.dk; Kedelsmedgangen 2; d/f apt from Dkr895/1295; 🛜) This central lakeside complex does family holidays in style. On offer are stylishly furnished apartments of various sizes (sleeping up to six) in funky three-storey buildings – triangular, circular, octagonal and star-shaped (great when admired from the Koldinghus tower). Parking, linen and breakfast cost extra.

🍴 Eating & Drinking

Den Blå Café   INTERNATIONAL €€
(www.denblaacafe.dk; Slotsgade 4; mains Dkr78-188; ⊙10am-10pm Mon-Wed, to 11pm Thu, to 2am Fri & Sat, to 4pm Sun) This casual all-day spot offers a large alfresco area and a menu of easy-pleasing favourites (burgers, salads, nachos). If the weather doesn't favour the great outdoors, get cosy in the cute French-bistro interior. Visit for its daily brunch buffet (Dkr98), or late-night drinks.

Nicolai Biograf & Café   ITALIAN €€
(www.nicolaibio.dk; Skolegade 2, entry on Blæsbjerggade; mains Dkr75-198; ⊙lunch & dinner) Inside a renovated old school, the Nicolai cultural centre houses an art-house cinema alongside a cool cafe serving gourmet pizza and pasta. The weekend brunch buffet (Dkr148) is a hit with in-the-know locals, as is the good-value Sunday-night pasta buffet (Dkr98).

You'll Never Walk Alone Pub   PUB
(www.denengelskepub.dk; AL Passagen 2; ⊙2-8pm Sun & Mon, noon-midnight Tue-Thu, 11am-late Fri & Sat) Known in town simply as 'the English pub', this traditional boozer lies in a passage between Jernbanegade and Klostergade. Outdoor seating, meals, live music and big-screen football matches give it an appeal beyond the 300-plus beers on the menu (including Danish microbrews). AL Passagen is home to other good eating and drinking options, too.

Kolding

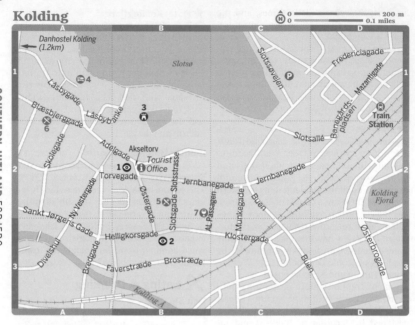

Kolding

⊙ Sights
1 Borchs Gård B2
2 Helligkorsgade 18 .... B3
3 Koldinghus B1

🛏 Sleeping
4 Kolding Hotel Apartments A1

✖ Eating
5 Den Blå Café B2
6 Nicolai Biograf & Café A1

⊖ Drinking & Nightlife
7 You'll Never Walk Alone Pub B2

ℹ Information

Tourist Office (☑76 33 21 00; www.visitkold
ing.dk; Akseltorv 8; ⊙10am-5pm Mon-Fri, to
2pm Sat) Knowledgeable staff; good info on
nearby activities.

ℹ Getting There & Away

Kolding is 72km east of Esbjerg and 82km north
of the German border. The E20 (which continues
east to Funen) and the E45 connect Kolding with
other major towns in Jutland. If you're travelling
by road north to south, Rte 170 is a pleasant
alternative to the E45.

There are regular train services to most places
in Jutland. There's a useful line west to Esbjerg
(Dkr99, 50 minutes) or east to Odense (Dkr121,
40 minutes) and on to Copenhagen; travel east
may involve a change of train in Fredericia.

ℹ Getting Around

Buses leave from next to the train station. If you're
driving, a ring road encircles the heart of town,
with Ndr Ringvej and Slotssøvejen marking the
northern and northeastern boundaries. There's
parking off Slotssøvejen, opposite the library.

Esbjerg

POP 71,600

Esbjerg (pronounced *es*-be-air) has a touch
of the 'wild frontier' about it – a new city (by
Danish standards) that's grown big and af-
fluent from oil, fishing and trading. Its business focus lies to the west, to the oilfields of
the North Sea, but its ferry link with the UK
ceased in 2014.

Esbjerg fails to pull heartstrings on first im-
pressions – its silos and smokestacks hardly
compete with the storybook streets of nearby
Ribe. However, Esbjerg redeems itself with
some quirky attractions and easy access to
the beautiful, time-warped iand of Fanø, just
a 12-minute ferry ride away.

◉ Sights & Activities

Musikhuset Esbjerg ARCHITECTURE
(www.mhe.dk; Havnegade 18) Famed Danish architect Jørn Utzon (he of the Sydney Opera House) designed Esbjerg's Music House together with his son, Jan. The performing arts centre opened in 1997 and is the city's main venue for cultural events including concerts, opera and ballet.

Esbjerg Kunstmuseum MUSEUM
(www.eskum.dk; Havnegade 20; adult/child Dkr60/free; ⊙10am-4pm) The Utzon-designed Musikhuset is home to the modern-art collection of Esbjerg Kunstmuseum. In an admirable display of openness (and a nod to restricted space), the Åbne Magasiner (Open Stores) downstairs allows you to look up undisplayed works from the collection. Another benefit: from the museum it's easy to admire the angles and details of the Utzons' architectural prowess.

Esbjerg Vandtårn TOWER
(Havnegade 22; adult/child Dkr20/free; ⊙10am-4pm daily Jun–mid-Sep, 10am-4pm Sat & Sun Apr–May & mid-Sep–Oct) Esbjerg self-consciously attempted to manufacture a medieval appearance in 1897 when the town architect built the water tower now conveniently (for tourists) located next door to Musikhuset Esbjerg. Climb up the tower to get your bearings and check out the sweeping port.

Fiskeri- og Søfartsmuseet AQUARIUM
(www.fimus.dk; Tarphagevej 2; adult Dkr100-130, child free; ⊙from 10m daily; 🅿) For an up-close look at North Sea marine life, head 4km northwest of the city centre to the saltwater aquarium at the Fisheries & Maritime Museum (take bus 3 or 6). Here you can see assorted local fish species getting along swimmingly, plus seals being fed at 11am and 2.30pm daily.

Mennesket ved Havet MONUMENT
(Hjertingvej) On the waterfront opposite Fiskeri- og Søfartsmuseet is Esbjerg's most interesting landmark, *Mennesket ved Havet* ('Man Meets the Sea'): four stark-white, 9m-high, stylised human figures, sitting rigid and staring out to sea. They were created by Danish sculptor Svend Wiig Hansen to commemorate the city's centennial in 1995 and they make a striking backdrop to holiday snaps.

Seal Safari BOAT TRIPS
(www.faergen.com/sealsafari; adult/child Dkr130/70; ⊙Esbjerg departures 10.45am & 1.45pm Mon-Thu, 10.45am Fri Jul-Aug; 🅿) In July and August you can enjoy a 2½-hour sightseeing cruise around the harbour and into Ho Bugt (Ho Bay), with a chance of seeing seals in their natural habitat. Tours operate once or twice a day, Monday to Friday, and depart from the ferry harbour in Esbjerg (by the Fanø ferry).

There is also the option to join the tour from Fanø (boats depart Nordby 20 minutes before the Esbjerg departure times listed here).

🛏 Sleeping

CabInn Esbjerg BUDGET HOTEL €
(☎75 18 16 00; www.cabinn.com; Skolegade 14; s/d from Dkr545/675; @🛜) Esbjerg's best value is found in this classy century-old building that's been thoroughly renovated and sits in a prime inner-city location. It's a hit with international and local visitors, who enjoy its good rates and light-filled rooms, all with bathroom, kettle and TV. Free parking, a decent breakfast buffet (Dkr70) and free wi-fi add up to a good deal.

Danhostel Esbjerg HOSTEL €
(☎75 12 42 58; www.esbjerg-danhostel.dk; Gammel Vardevej 80; dm Dkr230, d without/with bathroom Dkr560/720; @🛜) An excellent choice if you don't mind being out of the city centre. It's in a spiffy location, neighbouring a sports stadium, swimming pool, park and cinema. The old building is lovely and the communal facilities top-notch; rooms in the new wing all have private bathrooms. It's 3km northwest of the city centre on bus 4.

Hotel Britannia HOTEL €€€
(☎75 13 01 11; www.britannia.dk; Torvegade 24; s/d Dkr1460/1660; @🛜) The town's largest and most business-oriented hotel has professional service, smart rooms and well-regarded eateries in a central location, but its rack rates are clearly pitched at expense-account business travellers. Weekend and summer rates (late June to August) are better value at Dkr860/960 per single/double.

🍴 Eating & Drinking

★ Hjerting Badehotel INTERNATIONAL €€
(☎75 11 70 00; www.hjertingbadehotel.dk; Strandpromenaden 1; 3/5 courses Dkr429/569, cafe mains Dkr119-249; 🛜) If Esbjerg's industry has you yearning for a little trademark Danish *hygge* (cosiness), make your way 10km north of town to this delightful 'bathing hotel' on the beach. There's a gourmet restaurant here, the well-regarded **Strandpavillonen**

Esbjerg

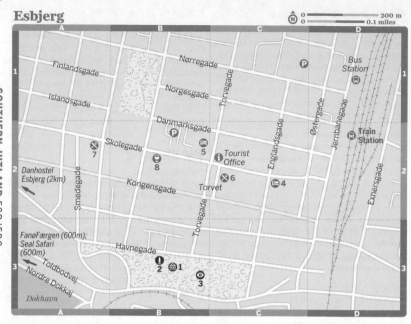

Esbjerg

⊙ Sights
1 Esbjerg Kunstmuseum	B3
2 Esbjerg Vandtårn	B3
3 Musikhuset Esbjerg	B3

🛏 Sleeping
4 CablInn Esbjerg	C2
5 Hotel Britannia	B2

✖ Eating
6 Dronning Louise	C2
7 Sand's Restaurant	A2

🍷 Drinking & Nightlife
8 Paddy Go Easy	B2

(open Monday to Saturday evening; bookings advised), plus the **Ship Inn**, an inviting cafe-bar open from 11am to midnight daily.

The hotel is also a great option for accommodation, with fresh, elegant hotel rooms (single/double Dkr1195/1395) and stylish beachhouses sleeping four. There's a wellness centre too, plus kayaks and bikes for hire.

Sand's Restaurant   DANISH €€
(www.sands.dk; Skolegade 60; lunch Dkr42-139, dinner mains Dkr109-249; ⊙11.30am-9.30pm Mon-Sat) The menu at this classy 100-year-old restaurant is an ode to old-school Danish favourites: lunchtime smørrebrød and herring platters, evening fish (try the *bakskuld*, a local fish not unlike a flounder) and plenty of classic *bøf* (beef).

Dronning Louise   INTERNATIONAL €€
(www.dr-louise.dk; Torvet 19; lunch Dkr90-145, dinner mains Dkr190-300; ⊙10am-1am Mon-Wed, to 3am Thu, 4am Fri, 5am Sat, midnight Sun; 🖥) Jack-of-all-trades, the Queen Louise commands a great central position on Torvet: she's a restaurant, pub and even a nightclub (Friday and Saturday), with occasional live music, too. You can dine from the broad, classic-hits menu on the square, inside or in the rear courtyard. Kitchen closes 10.30pm Monday to Saturday, 9.30pm Sunday.

Paddy Go Easy   PUB
(Skolegade 42) Skolegade is where to head to when you're thirsty; it's virtually wall-to-wall bars. We like Paddy Go Easy for the real Irish accents behind (and often in front of) the bar, Kilkenny and Guinness on tap, and decent *craic* all round.

ⓘ Information

Torvet, the city square, can be found where Skolegade and Torvegade intersect. The train and bus stations are about 300m east of Torvet; the Fanø ferry terminal is 1km southwest.

Tourist Office (☑ 75 12 55 99; www.visit esbjerg.dk; Skolegade 33; ⊙ 10am-4pm Mon-Fri) On the corner of Torvet. Offers self-service screens, plus racks of brochures and maps.

❶ Getting There & Away

AIR

Esbjerg airport (www.esbjerg-lufthavn.dk) is 10km east of the city centre, with daily connections to two other North Sea oil bases, Stavanger (Norway) and Aberdeen (Scotland).

BOAT

In September 2014, the passenger ferry between Esbjerg and Harwich (UK) ceased operating.

There are frequent **boats** to nearby Fanø. For more information see p192.

BUS

The **bus station** (local and long distance) is on Jernbanegade, by the train station.

Thinggaard Express (www.expressbus.dk) operates bus 980 from Esbjerg to Frederikshavn once daily (Dkr340, 5¼ hours), calling at Viborg and Aalborg en route.

Bus 915X is a handy service, connecting Esbjerg with Ribe (Dkr60, 30 minutes) before travelling on to the southeast Jutland town of Sønderborg (Dkr180, 2½ hours), via Gråsten.

CAR

Esbjerg is 77km north of Tønder, 31km northwest of Ribe, 59km southwest of Billund and 92km west of the Funen–Jutland bridge.

If you're driving into Esbjerg, the E20 (the main expressway from the east) leads directly into the heart of the city and down to the ferry harbour.

TRAIN

There are regular services running south to Ribe (Dkr60, 35 minutes) and Tønder (Dkr110, 1½ hours); and east to Kolding (Dkr99, 45 minutes) and Aarhus (Dkr265, two hours).

❶ Getting Around

Most city buses can be boarded at the train station; it's Dkr20 for a local ticket (available from the driver). Bus 5 runs to the harbour every 20 minutes.

Fanø

POP 3200

The intimate island of Fanø holds more charm than the larger, more-popular island of Rømø, further south. It may have something to do with the means of arrival (is it just us, or is a boat more romantic than a 10km-long causeway?). And this island backs it up with two traditional seafaring settlements full of idyllic thatch-roofed houses, blooming gardens and cobblestone streets lined with boutiques and cafes.

Beach-goers are blessed with wide, welcoming strips of sand on the exposed west coast, and a lively summer-season atmosphere. All this, and it's just 12 minutes from Esbjerg – too easy.

◉ Sights

The main villages of Nordby and Sønderho lie at each end of the 16km-long island; ferries from Esbjerg arrive at **Nordby**. **Sønderho** in particular is one of Denmark's most charming villages. It dates from the 16th century and has more than a hint of Middle Earth to its jumble of thatched houses.

The tourist office can provide brochures and maps outlining on-foot exploration of Nordby and Sønderho. The villages are home to a few low-key **museums** detailing Fanø's rich maritime history. Fanø's golden age peaked in the late 19th century, when it boasted the largest fleet outside Copenhagen; over a period of 150 years it was the site for the construction of more than 1000 vessels.

With time and interest, check out Nordby's maritime or history museum. Sønderho has an art museum and an original 19th-century sea-captain's house known as Hannes Hus.

🏃 Activities

If you're here on a day trip, it can be enjoyable to wander around Nordby to soak up the charm, then jump on the bus to Sønderho, or hire a bike, visit the beach, take a boat trip or see where the mood takes you – maybe to the local links **golf course** (www.fanoe-golf-links.dk), the oldest golf course in Denmark. Other options include horse riding and sea kayaking – ask at the tourist office.

Fanø is also a mecca for kite-flyers from around the world. The island hosts a photogenic kite festival in mid-June, when thousands of kites are flown from various beaches (see www.kitefliersmeetingfanoe.de).

Beaches   BEACHES

Families and water-sports fans (and amber-hunters, too) come to Fanø above all else for the great beaches – the best swimming is found between **Rindby Strand** and **Fanø Bad** (Denmark's first international seaside resort). Further north is the vast sand spit, Søren Jessens Sand. South of Rindby, the beach is full of activity: windsurfing, kitesurfing and blokarts.

Fanø Klitplantage NATURE RESERVE

Wildlife-watchers and nature-lovers will feel at home in the centre of the island, where 1162 hectares make up this nature reserve. Hit the walking tracks and you'll find birds, deer and rabbits in abundance. Stop by the popular picnic site and forest playground near Pælebjerg.

🛏 Sleeping

There are seven campgrounds on Fanø, virtually all within a short walk of the coast. All are family-focused and most have cabins for rent. For more information, see www.visit fanoe.dk.

For information on booking summer holiday flats and houses (which typically sleep four to six people and are rented by the week), contact the tourist office. There are booking agents (eg www.danibo.dk), but their websites are generally only in Danish and German.

★Møllesti B&B GUESTHOUSE €

(☑75 16 29 49; www.mollesti.dk; Møllesti 3, Nordby; s/d Dkr300/450-500; ☺Jun-Aug; ☎) This well-priced B&B is hidden away in the atmospheric lanes of Nordby. It's home to four simple, stylish bedrooms sharing two bathrooms and a kitchenette/lounge, in a restored sea-captain's house from 1892. It can open for guests on weekends outside of summer, but you'll need to arrange this in advance. Breakfast costs an additional Dkr50; there's a two-night minimum stay.

Fanø Krogaard INN €€

(☑76 66 01 66; www.fanoekrogaard.dk; Langelinie 11, Nordby; d from Dkr895; ☎) In operation since 1664, this charming inn on the Nordby waterfront has cosy antique-filled rooms (plus more modern ones in a newer annex) and an intimate atmosphere, plus a large, sunny terrace and an appealing menu of local specialities (lunch Dkr79 to Dkr139, dinner mains Dkr129 to Dkr239).

★Sønderho Kro INN €€€

(☑75 16 40 09; www.sonderhokro.dk; Kropladsen 11, Sønderho; s/d inc breakfast from Dkr1195/1495; ℗) The loveliest place to stay on the island (and renowned around the country) is this thatched-roof slice of *hyggelig* heaven. It dates from 1722, and its 14 individually decorated rooms feature local antiques. The inn

has an acclaimed gourmet restaurant (lunch Dkr129 to Dkr179, dinner three/five courses Dk495/695), which showcases local and seasonal specialities in a steeped-in-time dining room.

🍴 Eating

As well as the inns serving food, take a stroll along Nordby's Hovedgaden and Sønderho's Sønderland and you'll be tripping over inviting little eateries and sunny courtyard gardens.

There are supermarkets and bakeries in the main villages on the island. Heather honey is a local speciality, as is lamb, and it's worth seeking out beer brewed at the local microbrewery, Fanø Bryghus.

Slagter Christiansen DELI

(www.fanoeslagteren.dk; Hovedgaden 17; ☺8am-5.30pm Mon-Thu, to 6pm Fri, to 1pm Sat) The Nordby butcher, Slagter Christiansen, is known throughout Denmark for his *Fanø skinke* (Fanø ham), a ham in the style of Italian parma. The store is a delicatessen full of local gourmet produce.

ⓘ Information

Nordby's main street, Hovedgaden, is a block west of the ferry terminal; along here you'll find banks, stores and eateries.

Tourist Office (☑70 26 42 00; www.visitfanoe. dk; Skolevej 5, Nordby; ☺9am-5pm Mon-Fri, 10am-4pm Sat & Sun Jul-Aug, 10am-5pm Mon-Fri Sep-May) In Nordby, about 700m from the ferry harbour (via Hovedgaden).

ⓘ Getting There & Around

It's expensive to take a car across to Fanø. If you're doing a day trip or overnight stay from Esbjerg, you're better off leaving your car on the mainland and hiring a bike or taking the bus once you reach the island.

FanøFærgen (☑70 23 15 15; www.fanoefaergen.dk) shuttles a car ferry between Esbjerg and Nordby one to three times hourly from 5am to 2am. Sailing time is 12 minutes. A return ticket for a foot passenger/bike is Dkr45/40. It costs Dkr300/415 in low/high season to transport a car (return trip, including passengers).

There's a local bus service (route 431) from the ferry dock that runs about once an hour, connecting Nordby with Fanø Bad (Dkr20), Rindby Strand (Dkr20) and Sønderho (Dkr30).

Bicycles can be hired from a number of places, including **Fri BikeShop** (☑75 16 24 60; Mellemgaden 12, Nordby). Taxis can be reached on ☑75 16 62 00.

Ribe

POP 8200

The crooked cobblestone streets of Ribe (pronounced *ree*-buh) date from the late 9th century, making it Denmark's oldest town. It's easily one of the country's loveliest spots in which to stop and soak up some history. It's a delightfully compact chocolate-box confection of crooked half-timbered 16th-century houses, a sweetly meandering river and lush water meadows, all overseen by the nation's oldest cathedral. Such is the sense of living history that the entire 'old town' has been designated a preservation zone, with more than 100 buildings registered by the National Trust. Don't miss it.

History

Founded around AD 700, Ribe evolved into a key post of the hailed Viking era. It began when the Apostle of the North, Ansgar, was given a parcel of land by the Danish king around 860 with permission to erect a church. It's not known when the church was built, but the earliest record of the existence of a bishop in Ribe is 948 – and bishops have cathedrals. During the Viking era, Ribe, linked to the sea by its river, flourished as a centre of trade between the Frankish empire and the Scandinavian states to the north.

In the 12th century the Valdemar dynasty fortified the town, building a castle and establishing Ribe as one of the king's Jutland residences.

The end of the medieval period saw Ribe enter its most torrid time. Two factors combined to send the town into 250 years of decline. A fire ripped through in 1580, and the relocation of the royal family to Copenhagen saw royal money leave the town. In turn the population diminished, and the bustling trade port turned into a struggling town with little regional importance or influence.

This economic downturn was something of a blessing – there was no finance available for building bigger and better houses, so the old town remained virtually untouched. In 1899 a tourist and conservation organisation (showing remarkable foresight) was established, and in 1963 the town council issued a preservation order covering the core of the old town. Their good sense has been well rewarded, with tourists flocking to soak up Ribe's old-world charm.

◉ Sights

Ribe Domkirke CHURCH
(www.ribe-domkirke.dk; Torvet; tower adult/child Dkr20/10; ⊙10am-5pm Mon-Sat, noon-5pm Sun May-Sep, shorter hours Oct-Apr) Dominating Ribe's skyline is the impressive Ribe Cathedral, which dates back to at least 948 (the earliest record of a bishop residing in Ribe) – making it the oldest in Denmark. The cathedral was largely rebuilt in 1150 when Ribe was at the heart of royal and government money, which in turn paved the way for some fine architectural structures.

The new cathedral was constructed primarily from tufa, a soft porous rock quarried near Cologne and shipped north along the Rhine. It took a century for the work to reach completion. Later additions included several Gothic features, but the core of the cathedral is decidedly Romanesque, a fine example of medieval Rhineland influences in architecture.

The interior decor is a hotchpotch of later influences. There's an organ with a facade designed by renowned 17th-century sculptor Jens Olufsen, a baptismal font from 1375, and an ornate pulpit created in 1597 (a mark on the pillar behind the pulpit shows where the flood of 1634 reached). You can find remains of paintings from the 16th century on the last two pillars on the northern side of the cathedral, while in the apse are modern-day frescoes, stained-glass windows and seven mosaics created in the 1980s by artist Carl-Henning Pedersen. The funky mosaics enliven the church and add a fascinating contrast to the more sombre features.

For a view over the countryside, climb the 248 steps (52m) up the cathedral **tower** which dates from 1333. A survey of the surrounding marshland makes it easy to understand why the tower once doubled as a lookout station for floods. New **museum exhibits** in the tower cover the cathedral's long history.

A new architecturally designed exhibition space, **Kannikegården**, is planned for near the cathedral. This museum will explain the significance of excavations recently performed in the area, which found evidence of Christianity arriving in Ribe a century earlier than historians had believed.

For added atmosphere, look out for summer classical-music concerts held in the cathedral.

Ribe

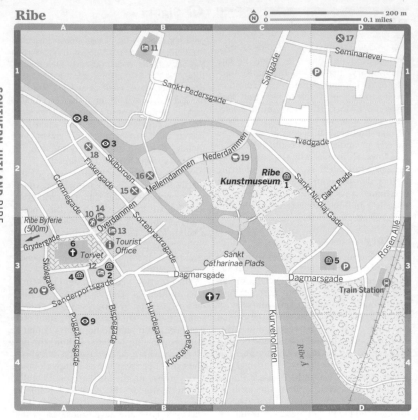

Historic Ribe
HISTORIC NEIGHBOURHOOD
For a leisurely stroll that takes in some of Ribe's handsome half-timbered homes and idyllic cobbled lanes, head along any of the streets radiating out from Torvet (note that the night-watchman walks cover much of this ground).

To help you appreciate the surrounds, drop by the tourist office and pick up a copy of the free *Town Walk in Old Ribe* brochure; it's available in Danish, English, German, Dutch, Italian and French.

On Puggårdsgade is a privately owned 16th-century manor house, the charmingly skew-whiff **Taarnborg**, where no corner is 90 degrees. Next door at No 5 is a half-timbered house from 1550. From Grønnegade, narrow alleys lead down and across pretty Fiskergade to Skibbroen and the picturesque old harbour.

Riverfront Area
HISTORIC NEIGHBOURHOOD
Along the riverfront is **Stormflodssøjlen** (Skibbroen), a wooden flood column com-

memorating the numerous floods that have swept over Ribe. The ring at the top indicates the water's depth during the record flood of 1634 (6m above normal!), which claimed hundreds of lives. Although these days a system of dikes affords low-lying Ribe somewhat more protection, residents are still subject to periodic flood evacuations.

Not far from here is **Johanne Dan**, an old sailing ship designed with a flat bottom that allowed it to navigate through the shallow waters of the Ribe Å; an onboard visit is usually only possible in conjunction with a guided tour (enquire at the tourist office).

Sankt Catharinæ Kirke
CHURCH
(www.ribe-kloster.dk; Sankt Catharinæ Plads; ⊙10am-5pm May-Sep, 10am-4pm Tue-Sun Oct-Apr) Founded by Spanish Blackfriars in 1228, St Catharine's Church was originally built on reclaimed marshland, but it eventually collapsed. The present structure dates from the 15th century. Of the 13 churches built during

Ribe

⊙ Top Sights
1 Ribe Kunstmuseum.............................C2

⊙ Sights
2 Den Gamle Rådhus..............................A3
3 Johanne Dan.......................................A2
4 Kannikegården....................................A3
5 Museet Ribes Vikinger.......................D3
6 Ribe Domkirke....................................A3
7 Sankt Catharinæ Kirke.......................B3
8 Stormflodssøjlen................................A1
9 Taarnborg...A4

⊙ Activities, Courses & Tours
10 Night-Watchman Tour........................A3

⊖ Sleeping
11 Danhostel Ribe...................................B1
12 Den Gamle Arrest...............................A3
13 Hotel Dagmar......................................A3
14 Weis Stue..A2

⊗ Eating
15 Isvaflen...B2
16 Kolvig..B2
17 Kvickly...D1
18 Sælhunden..A2
   Vægterkælderen......................... (see 13)
   Weis Stue.................................... (see 14)

⊙ Drinking & Nightlife
19 Postgaarden..C2
20 Ribe Bryghus.......................................A3

the pre-Reformation period in Ribe, Sankt Catharinæ Kirke and Ribe Domkirke are the only survivors.

In 1536 the Reformation forced the friars to abandon Sankt Catharinæ Kirke and, in the years that followed, the compound served as an asylum for the mentally ill and a wartime field hospital, to name a couple of its incarnations. These days the abbey provides housing for the elderly.

In the 1920s Sankt Catharinæ Kirke was restored at tremendous cost (due to its still-faulty foundations) and was reconsecrated in 1934. The interior boasts a delicately carved pulpit dating to 1591 and an ornate altarpiece created in 1650.

For a Dkr5 fee you can enter the tranquil cloister garden and enjoy a few minutes of contemplative silence.

Den Gamle Rådhus HISTORIC BUILDING
(www.detgamleraadhusiribe.dk; Von Støckens Plads; adult/child Dkr15/free; ⊙1-3pm daily Jun-Aug) This is the oldest town hall (1496) in Denmark and was used as a courthouse until

2006 – these days it's a popular spot for civil weddings. As well as ceremonial artefacts, there's an exhibit on local law and order (including a collection of medieval weapons and the executioner's axe).

★Ribe Kunstmuseum MUSEUM
(www.ribekunstmuseum.dk; Sankt Nicolaj Gade 10; adult/child Dkr70/free; ⊙10am-5pm Thu-Tue, to 8pm Wed Jul & Aug, 11am-4pm Tue-Sun Sep-Jun) An undeniable benefit of being the oldest town in the land is the opportunity to amass an impressive art collection. Ribe's beautifully restored art museum has been able to acquire some of Denmark's best works, including those by 19th-century 'Golden Age' painters.

The gallery's riverside garden presents a glorious backdrop to collection pieces by big-name Danish artists. It's worth exploring the delightfully verdant area behind the art gallery (open to all), where paths pass over the river and lead either to Sankt Catharinæ Kirke or Nederdammen.

Museet Ribes Vikinger MUSEUM
(www.ribesvikinger.dk; Odins Plads 1; adult/child Dkr70/free; ⊙10am-6pm Thu-Tue, to 9pm Wed Jul & Aug, 10am-4pm rest of yr, closed Mon Nov-Mar; ⊞) To better come to grips with Ribe's Viking and medieval history, visit the informative displays of the Museum of Ribe's Vikings. Two rooms provide snapshots of the town in 800 and during medieval times in 1500. These portrayals are complemented by rare archaeological finds and good explanations, which add real substance to the tales.

Ribe VikingeCenter MUSEUM
(www.ribevikingecenter.dk; Lustrupvej 4; adult/child Dkr100/50; ⊙11am-5pm late Jun-late Aug, 10am-3.30pm Mon-Fri early May-late Jun & late Aug–mid-Oct; ⊞) Embrace your inner Viking (ignore any pillaging tendencies, ok?) at this hands-on, open-air museum. It attempts to re-create a slice of life in Viking-era Ribe using various reconstructions, including a 34m longhouse. The staff, dressed in period clothing, bake bread over open fires, demonstrate archery and Viking-era crafts such as pottery and leatherwork, and offer falconry shows and 'warrior training' (for kids, using a sword and shield). You'll undoubtedly learn more about Viking life than you could from a textbook.

The centre is 3km south of town; bus 417 runs out here.

SOUTHERN JUTLAND RIBE

DON'T MISS

NIGHT-WATCHMAN TOURS

One of the best free activities in Denmark is Ribe's 45-minute **night-watchman tour** (⊙ 8pm May–mid-Sep, also 10pm Jun-Aug;) FREE, which departs from out the front of Weis Stue, on Torvet, once or twice a night in the warmer months. Nowadays, it's a stroll through the town's historic streets, designed to entertain and educate visitors to Ribe, but the night-watchman's walk was originally born of necessity.

As early as the 14th century these watchmen made their nightly rounds in Ribe, ensuring the streets were safe for locals to walk. They were also charged with being on the lookout for fires or floods threatening the town. The job was abolished in Ribe in 1902, but reinstated in 1935 as a tourist attraction. Interesting factual titbits, singing and colourful stories of memorable Ribe citizens (in Danish and English) are just part of the act. Throw in narrow streets, pretty-as-a-picture houses and a late sundown, and it's a great way to end a history-soaked day.

𝒞 Tours

Town Walks   WALKING TOUR
(adult/child Dkr75/free; ⊙11.30am Mon-Fri Jul-Aug) The tourist office stages guided 90-minute town walks in high season. At the time of research these were being conducted in Danish and German only.

Ghost Walks   WALKING TOUR
(www.ribesvikinger.dk; adult/child Dkr50/free; ⊙ 9pm Wed Jul-Aug) The weekly summertime ghost walks operated by (and departing from) Museet Ribes Vikinger show the town in a whole new light – listen out for tales of Maren Spliid, who was burned at the stake in 1641, the last victim of Denmark's witch-hunt persecutions.

🛏 Sleeping

The tourist office's brochure lists some 35 private homes in and around Ribe that rent great-value rooms and apartments – doubles cost Dkr350 to Dkr600, excluding breakfast. You can see pictures of the accommodation online at www.visitribe.dk.

There are also rooms for rent above the Sælhunden and Postgaarden eateries.

Danhostel Ribe   HOSTEL €
(⊉75 42 06 20; www.danhostel-ribe.dk; Sankt Pedersgade 16; dm Dkr220, s/d from Dkr435/470; P@🛜) 🚲 An ideal location, knowledgeable staff, sparkling rooms (all with bathroom) and impressive facilities make this a top option suited to both backpackers and families. It rents bikes and is a stone's throw from Ribe's historic centre; equally impressive is its commitment to the environment, from the Good Origin coffee in its vending machines to its promotion of sustainable travel in the Wadden Sea region.

Weis Stue   GUESTHOUSE €
(⊉75 42 07 00; www.weisstue.dk; Torvet; s/d Dkr395/495) An ancient wooden-beamed house from 1600, Weis Stue has eight small, crooked rooms (with shared bathrooms) above its restaurant. They have lashings of character: creaking boards, sloping walls and low overhead beams.

Ribe Camping   CAMPGROUND €
(⊉75 41 07 77; www.ribecamping.dk; Farupvej 2; per adult/child/site Dkr80/50/70; @🛜⛱) Just 2km north of the train station lies this busy, well-equipped campground bursting with good cheer and excellent amenities; a summertime outdoor heated swimming pool, rental bikes and playground are at your disposal. There are also some pretty swanky cabins for hire (with Jacuzzis!), from Dkr600.

★**Den Gamle Arrest**   GUESTHOUSE €€
(⊉75 42 37 00; www.dengamlearrest.dk; Torvet 11; d incl breakfast Dkr740-1090) You need to be creative when turning jail cells into guestrooms, and Annitha, the lovely owner of this place, can take a bow. This superbly positioned building served as a jail until 1989; now it holds cells converted into bright, simple rooms that maximise space (a mezzanine level holds table and chairs above a petite roll-away bed).

Most former cells have a washbasin but share bathroom facilities; there are also wardens' rooms with full bathroom. Pics are on the website.

Ribe Byferie   APARTMENTS €€
(⊉79 88 79 88; www.ribe-byferie.dk; Damvej 34; apt for 4 people Dkr895-1395; P@🛜) This is a well-run 'village' of modern apartments in a quiet part of town, a short walk southwest of Torvet. Roomy self-catering apartments

sleep from two to seven; families are catered to with a wellness centre, games room, bike and canoe hire, kids' club, playground and lovely barbecue area. Prices fluctuate with season; linen and breakfast cost extra.

Hotel Dagmar   HOTEL €€€
(✍75 42 00 33; www.hoteldagmar.dk; Torvet; s/d incl breakfast from Dkr1095/1295; @ 📶) Classy, central Hotel Dagmar is Denmark's oldest hotel (founded in 1581) and exudes all the charm you'd expect. There's a golden hue to the hallways and rooms, with old-world decor alongside tiling, artworks and antiques. See the website for packages involving meals and accommodation.

✖ Eating & Drinking

Isvaflen   ICE CREAM €
(Overdammen 11; 2/3 scoops Dkr23/29; 🖈) Pizza places and ice-cream sellers aren't hard to find along the main drag. On a warm day, Isvafeln is swamped with holidaymakers devouring the great ice-cream flavours.

Kvickly   SUPERMARKET €
(Seminarievej; ⊘8am-8pm Mon-Fri, to 6pm Sat & Sun) Well placed for self-caterers staying at the hostel; the post office is inside.

Sælhunden   DANISH €€
(www.saelhunden.dk; Skibbroen 13; lunch Dkr99-159, dinner mains Dkr135-220; ⊘11am-10pm) This handsome old black-and-white restaurant is by the riverfront, with outdoor seating by the *Johanne Dan* boat. *Sælhund* means seal, so it's no surprise this place dedicates itself to serving quality seafood in traditional Danish guises. Try the delicious house specialty, *stjerneskud* (one fried and one steamed fillet of fish both served on bread with prawns, caviar and dressing).

Weis Stue   TRADITIONAL DANISH €€
(www.weisstue.dk; Torvet 2; lunch Dkr84-118, dinner mains Dkr154-208; ⊘11.30am-10pm) Don't come here looking for modern, could-be-anywhere cuisine. As befits the setting (one of Denmark's oldest inns, wonky and charming), the menu is a traditionalist's dream. The large meat-and-potatoes portions are full of northern European flavour (pepper pork medallions, Wiener schnitzel), best washed down with locally brewed beer. There's bags of atmosphere, but little joy for vegetarians.

Vægterkælderen   EUROPEAN €€
(Torvet; mains Dkr100-225; ⊘noon-10pm) In summer you won't catch anyone down in the 'night-watchman's cellar' at Hotel Dagmar – they're all dining alfresco on the main square. The cellar's timber-heavy decor seems made for cold weather – soft leather banquettes and booths. The 'keep it simple' menu does exactly that (mains of burger or Caesar salad, for example), with two/three courses costing Dkr150/200.

Kolvig   MODERN DANISH €€€
(www.kolvig.dk; Mellemdammen 13; lunch Dkr77-163, dinner mains Dkr163-245; ⊘11am-midnight Mon-Sat) Kolvig's alfresco terrace overlooks the river, offering prime Ribe-watching. The menu is the most ambitious in town, showcasing local produce; most interesting is the delicious tapas plate of Wadden Sea flavours, including shrimp, salmon and cold-smoked lamb. Desserts, too, are local and creative: try the 'bread pie' (made with rye bread) served with vanilla mousse and blackberries.

Postgaarden   CAFE €
(www.postgaarden-ribe.dk; Nederdammen 36; meals Dkr69-119; ⊘10am-5.30pm Mon-Fri, to 4pm Sat) Postgaarden has a range of Danish and international microbrews for sale in its delicatessen, and a changing selection of boutique (and sometimes obscure) brews on tap to accompany its cafe-style menu, best enjoyed in the photogenic 1668 courtyard.

Ribe Bryghus   BREWERY
(www.ribebryghus.dk; Skolegade 4B; ⊘10am-2pm Sat) Look out for this label's locally brewed beers at restaurants and bars around town, or pop into the brewery (by the courtyard) during its limited opening hours. Note it's also 'open' whenever the brewers are inside working their hoppy magic.

❶ Information

Tourist Office (✍75 42 15 00; www.visitribe. dk; ⊘9am-6pm Mon-Fri, 10am-5pm Sat Jul-Aug, reduced hrs rest of yr) Has an abundance of information on the town and surrounding areas, plus internet access. Ask here about the RibePas (adult/child Dkr20/10, or free from a handful of accommodation providers) that grants the holder up to 20% discount at many local attractions. It may be superseded by a new type of pass by the time you visit.

❶ Getting There & Away

Ribe is 31km south of Esbjerg via Rte 24, and 47km north of Tønder via Rte 11.

Trains from Ribe run hourly on weekdays and less frequently at weekends north to Esbjerg (Dkr60, 35 minutes), and south to Skærbæk for Rømø (Dkr30, 20 minutes) and Tønder (Dkr78, 65 minutes).

❶ Getting Around

Ribe is a tightly clustered town, so it's easy to explore. Everything, including the hostel and the train station, is within a 10-minute walk of Torvet, the central square that's dominated by the huge cathedral.

Central parking is free but generally has a two-hour daytime limit; there is four-hour parking by the hostel, and just north of the hostel on Saltgade is 48-hour parking. North of the train station (on Rosen Alle) is another area of 48-hour parking.

Bicycles can be hired from Danhostel Ribe and cost Dkr80/140 for one/two days.

Wadden Sea National Park

One of the new national parks created in Denmark in the last few years is **Nationalpark Vadehavet** (Wadden Sea National Park; www.danmarksnationalparker.dk). Stretching along Jutland's west coast from Ho Bugt (west of Esbjerg) to the German border, and incorporating the holiday islands of Rømø and Fanø, its marshlands provide food and rest for millions of migratory birds. In 2014, the park was admitted to the Unesco World Heritage list.

The Wadden Sea extends 450km, from west Jutland south and west to the Dutch island of Texel. Large parts of the Dutch and German Wadden Sea have been national parks for years; with the Danish area now also protected, this is one of the largest national parks in Europe.

It is one of the most important areas for fish, birds and seals. Ten to 12 million waterbirds pass through the area on their way to/from their breeding grounds in northern Scandinavia, Siberia or Greenland. The birds forage in the sea's tidal flats, which are exposed twice every 24 hours.

🏃 Activities

Ask at tourist offices on the west coast for ways to access the offerings of the park.

A few operators and activity centres run tours to explore different facets of the park – for example seal-spotting, bird-watching, oyster-collecting, and tidal walks exploring the sandflats.

One of the most popular options is to experience the '**Sort Sol**' (Black Sun) in spring (approximate dates March to April) and autumn (mid-September to late October). This describes the phenomena of large numbers of migrating starlings (up to a million) gathering in the marshes outside Ribe and Tønder. 'Sort Sol' takes place in the hours just after sunset, when the birds gather in large flocks and form huge formations in the sky before they decide on a location to roost for the night. The movements of the formations have been likened to a dance and the birds are so numerous they seem to obliterate the sunset.

VadehavsCentret   ACTIVITY CENTRE
(☑ 75 44 61 61; www.vadehavscentret.dk; Okholmvej 5, Vester Vedsted; adult/child Dkr70/35; ⏱ 10am-4pm or 5pm mid-Feb–Oct; ♿) This is the best source on information about the park. About 10km southwest of Ribe, VadehavsCentret is an information and activity centre, reached by bus 411 from Ribe. There are **exhibitions** on the tides, flora and fauna of the national park, plus an excellent calendar of **tours** (five-hour oyster safari for Dkr260; Sort Sol viewing Dkr65).

From here, there are tractor-buses running 6km across the tidal flats at low tide to the small outlying island of **Mandø** (return Dkr60; timetables at www.mandoebussen.dk). It's possible to hire bikes to explore the island, and to stay at a local campground, B&B or *kro* (inn; see www.mandoetourist.dk).

Naturcenter Tønnisgaard   ACTIVITY CENTRE
(☑ 74 75 52 57; www.tonnisgaard.dk; Havnebyvej 30, Rømø; adult/child Dkr22/11; ⏱ 10am-4pm Mon-Fri mid-Mar–Oct, 10am-3pm Mon-Wed Nov–mid-Mar; ♿) Based on Rømø, this information and activity centre for the national park has exhibitions, plus family-friendly tour offerings depending on the season (eg bird-watching, shrimp-, oyster- or mushroom-collecting).

Rømø

POP 650

Summer sees the large island of fill with tourists (predominantly from Germany). This is hardly surprising given the entire west coast is one long, sandy beach that's prime happy-holiday turf, perfect for sun-bathing and sunset-watching or something more active. Rømø is connected to the mainland by a 10km causeway (with cycle lane). During the colder months it's a windswept sleeper with get-away-from-it-all charm that couldn't be further removed from its busy summer incarnation.

◉ Sights

Kommandørgården HISTORIC BUILDING

(www.natmus.dk; Juvrevej 60, Toftum; ⊙10am-5pm Tue-Sun May-Sep, to 3pm Oct) **FREE** The handsome thatched Kommandørgården, 1.5km north of the causeway, is the preserved home of one of Rømø's 18th-century whaling captains. It stands as testimony to the prosperity that such men brought to the island through their whaling expeditions. It has Dutch tiles lining many walls and woodwork painted in rococo style (there is minimal labelling in English, however). In the barn is the skeleton of a 13m-long sperm whale that was stranded on Rømø in 1996.

Rømø Kirke CHURCH

(Havnebyvej, Kirkeby) The 18th-century Rømø Church is on the main road in Kirkeby. It's noted for its unique Greenlandic gravestones (lining the northern wall of the churchyard), erected by sea captains and decorated with images of their boats and families.

🏃 Activities

Windsports

The long west-coast beach is divided into activity areas, with **windsurfing** a popular pursuit near Lakolk. Most enthusiasts arrive with their own equipment, but if you come without, enquire at the tourist office about rental possibilities.

At the southwest corner of the island is **Sønderstrand**, a remarkable sight – full of cars, colour and land-based activities making great use of the air that blows in fresh from the North Sea. There's a small area for parking your car where the sealed road reaches the sand, or you can continue driving on the beach itself (north as far as Lakolk).

As the sealed road reaches Sønderstrand, to your left is an area dedicated to *strandsejlads,* aka land-yachts or blokarts (a three-wheeled go-kart that utilises a sail to capture the wind). To the right, it's all about *kitebuggy kørsel* – buggies with attached parachutelike kites. Great speeds are reached, and it's quite a spectacle. If you want a crack at either, there are companies that can help with lessons and/or gear rental (usually open from about late April to early October, if weather and conditions are agreeable).

Windriders ADVENTURE SPORTS

(☑22 34 13 85; www.windriders.dk; Havnebyvej 60, Kongsmark) Offers introductory lessons to blokarts (Dkr225 per hour), or simple rental (Dkr150 for 30 minutes).

KiteSyd ADVENTURE SPORTS

(☑20 88 83 85; www.kitesyd.dk) About the kites: kitesurfing, kitebuggies and kite landboarding (riding an oversized skateboard using a kite and the power of the wind).

Horse Riding

The beaches are perfect for a horse ride into the sunset.

Kommandørgårdens Islændercenter HORSE RIDING

(☑74 75 51 22; http://islander.kommandoer gaarden.dk; Havnebyvej 201; 🖈) Affiliated with Hotel Kommandørgården, this centre has a stable full of Icelandic horses and a range of rides to appeal to kids, beginners and more-experienced horse-folk, through forest and along the beach. A three-hour sunset tour costs Dkr350; a full-day tour to the north of Rømø costs Dkr895.

Other Activities

Rømø's interior has walking trails through heather moors and wooded areas, offering quiet hiking spots.

Enjoy Resorts Rømø (☑74 75 56 55; www. enjoyresorts.dk; Vestergade 31, Havneby), en route to Sønderstrand, is home to a relaxation-inducing wellness spa (Dkr250 for nonguests); indoor swimming pool and fitness centre (adult/child Dkr75/35); bowling alley (one hour Dkr120); and a challenging links golf course (18 holes Dkr300).

🛏 Sleeping

The vast majority of accommodation is found in some 1600 summerhouses and apartments scattered around the island, which are usually rented by the week in the high season (outside this period there's often a three-night minimum). Prices vary, depending on the season and the degree of luxury. The tourist office can provide a catalogue and also handle bookings.

Danhostel Rømø HOSTEL €

(☑74 75 51 88; www.danhostel.dk/romo; Lyngvejen 7, Østerby; dm Dkr250, d without/with bathroom Dkr420/520; ⊙Apr–mid-Oct) A picturesque red, thatched-roof complex (another old sea-captain's house) that's well hidden off the main road and set among pines, but walking distance to a supermarket and bakery. The rooms (a few with bathroom) are basic but spick-and-span, and the outdoor areas beckon for a complete holiday wind-down.

Lakolk Strand Camping   CAMPGROUND €
(☑74 75 52 28; www.lakolkcamping.dk; Lakolk; campsite per adult/child Dkr90/56; ☺mid-Apr–Oct; @☎) In high summer, the beachside campground and shopping centre at Lakolk is holiday heaven or hell, depending on your outlook. It's bursting at the seams with families praying for good weather; the huge campground is wall-to-wall with campervans and all the requisite facilities, including rental of on-site caravans and cabins.

Hotel Kommandørgården   HOTEL, CAMPGROUND €€
(☑74 75 51 22; www.kommandoergaarden.dk; Havnebyvej, Østerby; per adult/child/site Dkr82/48/75, hotel s/d from Dkr875/925; @☎☒) This astonishingly big complex has everything from camping and cabins to hotel rooms and apartments, and a restaurant and bar. Plus there are activities laid on thick, including a wellness centre, bike hire, kayaking, horse riding, kids' play centre, and indoor and outdoor swimming pools.

Enjoy Resorts Rømø   RESORT €€€
(☑74 75 56 55; www.enjoyresorts.dk; Vestergade 31, Havneby; houses Dkr1760-2098; ☎☒) A luxury-leaning, activity-rich playground for families enjoying the golf course, wellness centre, restaurant and large complex of two-bedroom, fully equipped houses (sleeping up to eight). There's a a two-night minimum, plus plenty of weekly deals and golf/wellness packages.

✖ Eating

Havneby is the island's culinary hotspot, with a large supermarket and good array of mostly family-oriented eateries. At Lakolk there's a small supermarket and some casual refuelling spots including a bistro, summer nightclub, pizzeria, ice creamery and cafes.

On menus, keep an eye out for Rømø produce, particularly *marsklam* (marsh-grazing lamb) and *rejer* (shrimps).

Otto & Ani's Fisk   SEAFOOD €
(Havnespladsen, Havneby; meals Dkr65-195; ☺11am-8pm) This no-frills cafeteria is right on the harbourside at Havneby, so the fish are as fresh as they come. Pull up a pew outside and feast on fish and chips (Dkr65) or a breadroll filled with Rømø shrimp (Dkr75).

You can also buy fresh uncooked fish and seafood, and smoked fishy delicacies.

Holms Røgeri & Restaurant   SEAFOOD €€
(www.holmsrogeri.dk; Nordre Havnevej 1, Havneby; lunch Dkr59-148, dinner mains Dkr123-208; ☺11.30am-9pm) It's hard to go past the lunchtime *stjerneskud* at this fish specialist, or a plate full of local shrimp. At dinnertime the menu broadens to offer hefty steak options too. Book your seat for the popular piscatorial pile-up at Friday and Sunday night fish buffets (Dkr228).

❶ Information

Tourist Office (☑74 75 51 30; www.romo.dk; Nr Frankel 1, Havneby; ☺9am-5pm Mon-Sat, to 3pm Sun Jul-Aug, 9am-4.30pm Mon-Sat, to noon Sun Sep-Jun) In central Havneby; can arrange cottage rental.

❶ Getting There & Away

Rømø is on Rte 175, 14km west of Skærbæk. Bus 285 runs from Skærbæk to Havneby (Dkr30, 40 minutes) a handful of times daily. Hourly trains link Skærbæk with Ribe, Tønder and Esbjerg.

The **Sylt Ferry** (☑73 75 53 03; www.sylt-ferry. com) operates between Havneby and the nearby German island of Sylt several times a day (one-way car ticket including passengers Dkr354, adult return Dkr77); journey time is 40 minutes.

❶ Getting Around

Roads allow cars to access the beaches at Lakolk and Sønderstrand, and you can drive up and down the west coast along the sand.

The Havneby–Skærbæk bus (route 285) isn't particularly useful for local travel; your best option is to rent a bike from **Rømø Cykler** (☑22 34 13 85; www.romocykler.dk; Havnebyvej 60, Kongsmark; per day/week from Dkr60/300; ☺10am-5pm Apr-Oct, to 6pm Jul & Aug), as Rømø is as flat as a pancake and perfect for cycling.

Tønder

POP 7700

Tønder is an inviting place that's had a rocky journey through serious flooding to German annexation; strong German links remain (not surprising, given Tønder's proximity to the border, just 4km south).

During the 16th century a series of dikes were erected to prevent the imminent threat of flooding. In doing so the town isolated itself from its sea-port connection and turned elsewhere for economic prosperity. Lace-making was introduced – an economic windfall that employed up to 12,000 workers during its peak in the 18th century.

◎ Sights

Tønder Museum — MUSEUM
(www.museum-sonderjylland.dk; Kongevej 51; adult/child Dkr50/free; ☺10am-5pm Jun-Aug, closed Mon Sep-May) Three-in-one Tønder Museum houses **Kulturhistorie Tønder**, a collection of delicate Tønder lace and decoratively painted furniture. In the adjacent wing is **Kunstmuseet i Tønder**, home to changing art exhibitions. Our favourite feature is the 1902 **Vandtårnet** (water tower), with panoramic views. Take the lift up and walk down – on each of the tower's eight floors are the fabulous chair designs of locally born Hans Wegner, one of the most innovative and prolific of all Danish furniture designers.

You will have seen Wegner's designs on your travels through Denmark – check out the Ox Chair on the 5th floor, the quirky Valet Chair on the 4th floor, and the Peacock and Wishbone chairs on the 2nd floor.

Historic Buildings — HISTORIC BUILDINGS
For a glimpse of the past, head south from Torvet along Søndergade and turn right into **Uldgade**. The cobbled street has Tønder's best collection of unique gabled houses. On the main pedestrian street, **Drøhses Hus** (Storegade 14; adult/child Dkr30/free; ☺10am-5pm Mon-Fri, 10am-2pm Sat Apr-Dec) dates from 1672; it's been meticulously restored and is open to the public, exhibiting lace and arts and crafts. **Det Gamle Apotek** (The Old Pharmacy; Østergade 1), beside Torvet, has an elaborate 1671 baroque doorway flanked by two lions that stand guard over the extensive giftshop collection inside.

Kristkirken — CHURCH
(Kirkepladsen; ☺10am-4pm Mon-Sat) The grand Kristkirken on the northeastern side of Torvet dates back to 1592. Its opulent interior came courtesy of the town's rich cattle and lace merchants, who donated generously between the late 17th and 18th centuries.

✿ Festivals & Events

Tønder Festival — MUSIC
(www.tf.dk) Growing in reputation and scale each year, the four-day Tønder Festival takes place in the last week of August and draws some 20,000 attendees from all corners of the globe. It's regarded as one of the best folk music festivals in Europe, with top-quality international folk and roots music.

⊨ Sleeping

B&Bs in the area can be found online at www.toenderbb.dk. For something special, head to the old *kro* in Møgeltønder.

Danhostel Tønder — HOSTEL €
(☑74 92 80 01; www.danhostel-tonder.dk; Sønderport 4; dm Dkr220, s & d with bathroom Dkr495; @🛜) Cut from the same cloth as other southern Jutland Danhostels, this is a plain, low-slung brick building with plentiful rooms (all with bathroom), friendly staff, appealing communal areas and fresh, clean facilities. It's a few minutes' walk southeast of the town centre. The campground is next door.

Hostrups Hotel — HOTEL €
(☑74 72 21 29; www.hostrupshotel.dk; Søndergade 30; s/d from Dkr380/490; 🛜) The low prices, then the worn carpet in the halls, may set off alarm bells, but there's no need – rooms here are pretty good for the price. This pretty green-coloured hotel is opposite a small lake – try for a room that overlooks it.

✗ Eating & Drinking

Café Engel — CAFE €
(www.cafe-engel.dk; Frigrunden 3; sandwiches Dkr39-89; ☺11am-5pm Tue-Sat) At the end of Uldgade, this cafe has a simple, streamlined interior, pretty outdoor seating, good coffee and a small but tempting menu (cutely hand-drawn) of sandwiches (try one with salmon and homemade tzatziki).

Kloster Caféen — CAFE €
(www.klostercafeen-toender.dk; Torvet 11; ☺10am-5pm Mon-Fri, 11am-5pm Sat, 11am-4pm Sun) Options around Torvet include Kloster Caféen, in Tønder's oldest house (from 1520 and boasting beautiful old tiles). The square is also home to a photogenic market selling fruit, vegetables and cheese on Tuesday and Friday mornings.

Victoria — INTERNATIONAL €€
(www.victoriatoender.dk; Storgade 9; mains Dkr65-199; ☺11am-10pm Mon-Thu, to 4am Fri, 2am Sat, noon-10pm Sun) At the turn of the 19th century, Tønder had a world-beating one bar for every 49 inhabitants. Only the Victoria kicks on now as a jack-of-all-trades pub/cafe/restaurant. It's a winner, with an all-ages crowd, old-world timber-rich decor and a good range of international and local beers. The menu is long, varied (burgers, burritos, pasta, sandwiches) and well priced.

WORTH A TRIP

GRÅSTEN PALACE

For three weeks each summer the sleepy town of Gråsten (population 4200) is abuzz as Queen Margrethe and Prince Henrik (and usually the extended family) head for some R&R at their summer residence. When they're not visiting, the lovely **palace gardens** (🕐 from 7.30am year-round) are open to the public (seasonal closing times vary, from 4.30pm in winter to 8pm in summer).

Gråsten Palace (www.slke.dk; Slotsgade) is on the banks of the lake, Slotssø. It was originally built in the middle of the 16th century but destroyed by fire in 1603. It was rebuilt, only to be ravaged by fire again in 1757; in 1842 the main building you see today was constructed, and in 1935 the rights to the castle were handed to the royal family.

The only part of the palace open to the public is the richly adorned **chapel** (🕐 11am-2pm Wed, 10am-noon Sat, 2-4pm Sun Apr-Oct). Built between 1699 and 1702, it's the only section of the old castle to survive the fire of 1757.

Trains between Kolding and Sønderborg stop at Gråsten (from Sønderborg Dkr40, 12 minutes). Buses 100, 223 and 915X cover the 16km between Gråsten and Sønderborg (Dkr40).

ℹ Information

Tourist Office (☎ 74 72 12 20; www.visittonder. dk; Storegade 2-4; 🕐 10am-5pm Mon-Fri, 10am-2pm Sat) Helpful office with information on the town and Møgeltønder.

ℹ Getting There & Around

Tønder is on Rte 11, 4km north of the border with Germany and 77km south of Esbjerg.

The train station is on the western side of town, about 1km from Torvet via Vestergade. Trains run regularly to/from Ribe (Dkr78, 65 minutes) and Esbjerg (Dkr111, 1½ hours).

Bus 266 runs regularly to Møgeltønder (Dkr20, 15 minutes).

Møgeltønder

This little village is impossibly cute – if you could, you'd wrap it up and take it home for your grandmother. A royal castle, one of the most beautiful main streets in Denmark, and a church rich in frescoes are some of the gems to be found here.

⊙ Sights

Schackenborg   CASTLE
(Schackenborgvej) On the eastern edge of the village is Schackenborg, a small castle from the late 17th century that for the past 20 years has been home to Queen Margrethe's youngest son, Prince Joachim, and his family. In 2014, however, Joachim and his wife, Princess Marie, announced plans to move to Copenhagen with their two small children, so the castle will be handed over to the newly formed Schackenborg Foundation.

You'll need to make enquiries locally (start with Tønder's tourist office) to find out whether the castle and/or its grounds are open to the public. In previous summers there have been popular guided tours of the castle gardens once or twice a week.

★ Møgeltønder Kirke   CHURCH
(www.moegeltoender-kirke.dk; Slotsgade 1; 🕐 8am-4pm May-Sep, 9am-4pm Oct-Apr) At the western end of Slotsgade is Møgeltønder Kirke, its lavish interior a feast for the senses. The Romanesque nave dates back to 1180 and the baptismal font is from 1200. The church has had many additions, however, as the Gothic choir vaults were built during the 13th century, the tower dates from about 1500 and the chapel on the northern side was added in 1763. The interior is rich in frescoes, gallery paintings and ceiling drawings.

You'll also find the oldest functioning church organ in Denmark, dating from 1679. The detailed gilt altar dates from the 16th century. Note the 'countess' bower', a balcony with private seating for the Schack family, who owned the church from 1661 until 1970.

🛏 Sleeping & Eating

Schackenborg Slotskro   HOTEL €€
(☎ 74 73 83 83; www.slotskro.dk; Slotsgade 42; s/d Dkr1099/1359; 🛜) With the palace as its neighbour and Prince Joachim as a part-owner, this classy inn can claim tip-top royal connections. It has 25 rooms, at the inn and in three nearby houses; rooms are elegant and well equipped. It also has a fine reputation for traditional Danish cooking and makes a lovely spot for a lunch (Dkr119 to Dkr189) of

salmon or herring, or the full-blown evening treatment (three/six course degustation menu Dkr414/669).

Mormors Lille Café
CAFE €

(Slotsgade 9; cakes Dkr30-45; ⊙ 11am-6pm Jun-Aug) 'Grandma's little cafe' is perfectly in keeping with the village's character, cute as a button under its low, thatched roof, surrounded by outdoor tables and flowerbeds. Old-school *lagkage* (layer cake) or *æblekage* (apple cake) are the order of the day.

❶ Getting There & Away

Møgeltønder is 5km west of Tønder via Rte 419. Bus 266 connects Tønder with Møgeltønder (Dkr20, 15 minutes).

Sønderborg

POP 27,400

Sønderborg, nestled on both sides of the Als Sund (Als Sound), nurtures a modern ambience despite its medieval origins. In the mid-12th century Valdemar I (the Great) erected a castle fortress along the waterfront and the town has since spread out from there.

To some degree the town has shaped Denmark, acting as the battleground for two wars against Germany in the middle of the 19th century. In 1864, during the battle of Dybbøl, Danish forces gathered here while a bombardment of 80,000 German shells paved the way for the German occupation of Jutland for some 60 years. After WWI the region once again became Danish soil.

Postwar reconstruction of the city has led to its modern feel and a bombardment of another kind – the annual descent of German and Danish holidaymakers. There's not as much English spoken in these parts; understandably, German is the second language for many.

⊙ Sights

Sønderborg Slot
CASTLE, MUSEUM

(ww.museum-sonderjylland.dk; Sønderbro 1; adult/child Dkr60/free; ⊙ 10am-4pm or 5pm Apr-Oct, 1-4pm Tue-Sun Nov-Mar) Sønderborg Castle dates from the mid-12th century, when a stronghold was built on the site; later bastions were added for further fortification. It's rich in lore, and nowadays it houses a **museum** of regional history with exhibits on the wars of 1848 and 1864, as well as paintings from the Danish 'Golden Age' and insight into the political history of the region.

Between 1532 and 1549 the castle was used to hold the deposed king, Christian II. In the late 16th century the fortified castle was turned into a royal residence (the 1568 chapel rates as one of Europe's oldest preserved royal chapels). It took on its baroque appearance during further restorations in 1718. During the German occupation it was used as a German barracks.

Historiecenter Dybbøl Banke
MUSEUM

(www.museum-sonderjylland.dk; Dybbøl Banke 16; adult/child Dkr110/60; ⊙ 10am-5pm Apr-Oct) On 18 April 1864 the German army steamrolled the Danes and took control of southern Jutland until the end of WWI. On the western

---

WORTH A TRIP

FRØSLEVLEJREN

The town of Padborg (population 4500), right by the German border, is the site of Frøslevlejren (Frøslev Camp), an internment camp opened near the end of WWII following negotiations with Germany to keep Danish POWs in Denmark (despite this agreement, 1600 Danish patriots were deported to concentration camps in Germany). During its nine months in operation, Frøslev held 12,000 prisoners.

Frøslevlejrens Museum (www.froeslevlejrensmuseum.dk; Lejrvej 83; ⊙ 9am-5pm mid-Jun–mid-Aug, shorter hrs rest of yr, closed Dec-Jan) **FREE** tells fascinating stories of the Danish Resistance movement and daily prison life at Frøslev. If you've visited other German-run wartime camps, you're in for a surprise here. A shining light among the German POW camps, Frøslev had ample food, no torture and no executions (prisoners were even allowed one visitor per month). The only real horror was the threat of deportation across the border. Interestingly, when the war ended, the camp's name was changed and the new inmates were suspected Nazi collaborators.

Frøslevlejren is on the northwestern outskirts of Padborg, 1km west of the E45 (take exit 76). Bus 110 connects Sønderborg with Padborg, but there are no buses to the museum – you'll need to walk or take a taxi the 4km from Padborg.

edge of town, this history centre gives an informative glimpse into the bloody war of 1864, with demonstrations and storytelling. Although it offers typically high-quality displays of a very important time, if you're not Danish, German or have no interest in military history, it can probably be skipped. Bus 1 runs out here from town.

Dybbøl Mølle   LANDMARK
(Dybbøl Banke 7; adult/child Dkr45/30; ☺ daily mid-Apr–mid-Oct) The Dybbøl windmill has been bombed twice and now stands as a beloved national symbol. Exhibits cover the mill's history and explain the symbolism of the site.

🛏 Sleeping

Danhostel Sønderborg City   HOSTEL €
(☑ 74 42 31 12; www.sonderborgdanhostel.dk; Kærvej 70; dm 175kr, s/d Dkr435/570; @ 🛜) A 15-minute walk north of the town centre, this modern hostel is built around garden areas, complete with barbecues. All rooms have bathrooms. It's a classy place for a budget bed – note that dorm beds are only available from June to August. Town bus 6 stops nearby.

Sønderborg Camping   CAMPGROUND €
(☑ 74 42 41 89; www.sonderborgcamping.dk; Ringgade 7; per adult/child/site Dkr75/30/30; ☺ Apr-Sep) Set in an idyllic position next to the yacht marina, and a lovely 10-minute walk into town along the waterfront. It's a family-friendly, amenity-rich place where sites are in demand come summer – book ahead. Cabins and caravans can be hired.

Hotel Sønderborg Garni   HOTEL €€
(☑ 74 42 34 33; www.hotelsoenderborg.dk; Kongevej 96; s/d from Dkr650/875; 🛜) Friendly service and a prime location in an upmarket residential neighbourhood sweeten the gloomy appearance of this small hotel (complete with turret). The 1904 building has 18 rooms, all different (the cheapest singles are tiny) and with a homely, relaxed feel.

✖ Eating & Drinking

You'll find a good selection of eateries down by the harbour (on Havnegade) and on Rådhustorvet. Stairs link the two areas.

Café Ib Rehne Cairo   INTERNATIONAL €€
(www.ibrehnecairo.dk; Rådhustorvet 4; meals Dkr72-145; ☺ 10am-11pm Mon-Wed, to midnight Thu, to 2am Fri & Sat, to 9pm Sun) Named after the sign-off of a veteran Danish correspondent, this all-day cafe-bar sports fresh decor and a classic-hits menu (bagels, burgers, salads). The

alfresco tables on the square get a workout from brunch-time, but there's also a loungey area inside, perfect for evening cocktails.

OX-EN Steakhouse   STEAK €€€
(www.ox-en.dk; Brogade 2; mains Dkr159-349; ☺ 5.30-11pm Mon-Sat) Prime Australian steaks have found themselves halfway across the globe to be salivated over (and paired with New World wines) at this chic, busy harbour restaurant. If you don't get your kicks from lavastone-grilled meat, there are a few non-steak concessions on the menu.

❶ Information

Sønderborg spreads along both sides of the Als Sund, joined by two bridges. The town centre and Sønderborg Slot are to the east, on the island of Als. The Dybbøl area and the train station are on the western side (part of mainland Jutland).

Services can be found on the pedestrian street Perlegade, immediately north of Rådhustorvet.

Tourist Office (☑ 74 42 35 55; www.visitson derborg.com; Rådhustorvet 7; ☺ 10am-5pm Mon-Fri, 10am-1pm Sat) On the main square. Lots of info on walking and cycling in the region.

❶ Getting There & Around

Sønderborg is 30km northeast of the German border crossing at Kruså, via Rte 8. It's connected by trains to Kolding (Dkr160, 1½ hours) and the rest of Jutland.

The train station is on the western side of town, by the modern Alsion building. Town bus 1 connects the train station with the east-side bus station (on Jernbanegade, a block east of Perlegade).

Als

The island of Als, separated from Jutland by the thin Als Sund, is relatively untouched by large-scale tourism and provides visitors with a snapshot of a laid-back Danish country lifestyle. It's a good region for lazy drives or cycling (bus schedules can be erratic). Down south is where the best beaches lie (nice and sheltered – locals recommend Kegnæs); up the east coast you'll encounter engaging little villages. And campgrounds are everywhere, heaving in summer with Danes and Germans.

Information and maps for the area can be obtained from the Sønderborg tourist office. For island-hoppers there are ferries connecting Fynshav on Als' east coast to Søby on the island of Ærø (see www.aeroe-ferry.com), or to Bøjden on Funen (www.faergen.dk).

Central Jutland

Includes ➡

Aarhus	208
Djursland	221
Ebeltoft	221
The Lake District	224
Silkeborg	224
The Interior	230
Jelling	230
Billund & Legoland	231
Central West Coast	238
Hvide Sande	238

Best Places to Eat

➡ Kähler Villa Dining (p216)

➡ Restaurant Gastronomisk Institut (p228)

➡ St Pauls Apothek (p216)

➡ Molskroen (p222)

➡ Hotel Julsø (p229)

➡ Henne Kirkeby Kro (p238)

Best Places to Stay

➡ Niels Bugges Hotel (p237)

➡ Hotel Guldsmeden (p215)

➡ Hotel Legoland (p233)

➡ Legoland Holiday Village (p232)

➡ Villa Zeltner (p227)

Why Go?

Easily the largest and most varied of all Danish regions, central Jutland encompasses dramatically different features, from the calm beaches of the sheltered east coast to the wild and woolly west coast, battered by North Sea winds. Lying in between, offering visual stimulation among the flatness, are the rolling hills and forests of the Lake District.

The real beauty of this region is that you can skip between themes depending on your mood. Fancy world-class art and top-notch restaurants? Aarhus, Jutland's main city and Denmark's second-largest metropolis, can provide. How about Viking history? Set sail for Hobro. Religious history? Off to Jelling. Want to explore the great outdoors? Head for Rold Skov or Silkeborg. Care to tackle nature's forces? Let loose on the waters of Hvide Sande. And OK, you've suppressed that inner child long enough – make a beeline for plastic-fantastic Legoland, and beware the accompanying pangs of childhood nostalgia.

When to Go

Warm weather is the key to enjoying much of this region (the beaches, theme parks, music festivals, activities), but Aarhus holds year-round appeal. Its museums, cafes and boutiques entertain in all weather, but the city's bars are in fact quieter in summer, when Aarhus University has its break.

If you're visiting in the shoulder season (May, June, September), it's worth checking when the various safari and amusement parks are open. Legoland, central Jutland's star attraction, is open daily May to August and most days in April, September and October (it's closed November to March).

Winter sees the big-ticket family attractions close, but cultural life steps up, with plenty of live theatre and music. December is rich with Christmas markets and good cheer.

New Carlisle Public Library
New Carlisle, IN 46552
574-654-3046

Central Jutland Highlights

1 View Aarhus rooftops through rose-coloured glass atop **ARoS Aarhus Kunstmuseum** (p218)

2 Explore the sights of **Aarhus** (p208), then eat superbly and drink plentifully while sampling the nightlife

3 Revel in the great outdoors on a canoe trip in the **Lake District** (p225)

4 Marvel at microcosmic Miniland at **Legoland** (p231) before jumping on a few rides

5 Enjoy the wind in your hair – and sails – while learning to windsurf at **Hvide Sande** (p238)

6 Feel the weight of history at **Jelling** (p230), the spiritual home of the Danish royal family

7 Hop between beaches, theme parks and animal parks in the prime family-holiday territory of **Djursland** (p221)

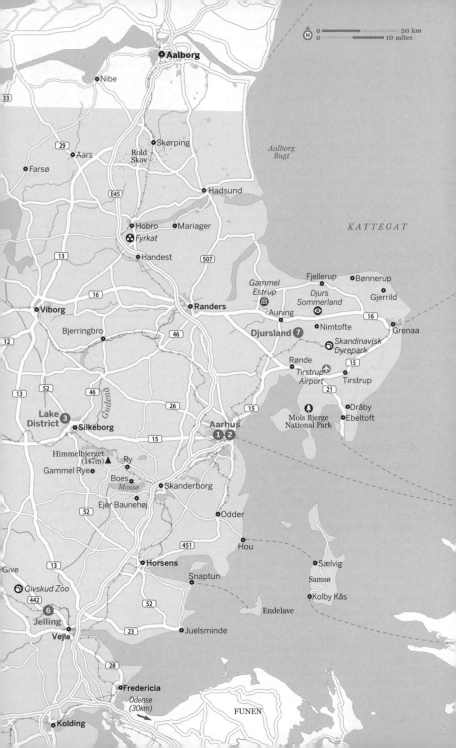

AARHUS

POP 310,000

Sure, Aarhus (*oar*-hus) may be Denmark's second-largest city, but it feels more like a relaxed and friendly big town, a little bashful in the shadow of its glamorous big sister, Copenhagen.

The museums and restaurants are first-rate, while the sizable student population (around 40,000) enlivens Aarhus' parks and cobblestone streets (and fill its bars). There's a growing number of excellent festivals, and savvy travellers are coming to appreciate the city's charms. Expect its stature to grow in the lead-up to 2017, when it is one of the European Capitals of Culture (more information at www.aarhus2017.dk).

History

Due to its central seaside location, Aarhus has always been a busy trading town. Its name comes from Aros, meaning 'place at the river's mouth'. Excavations from the mid-1960s suggest the city was founded around 900 AD.

Medieval times were Aarhus' most turbulent, as the town was wedged in the middle of feuding neighbouring states. Prosperity was kept in check over the following centuries by raids from rival Vikings and attacks by fearsome Wend pirates. Stability then prevailed until the 1500s, and it was during this time that Aarhus flourished as a centre of trade, art and religion.

◎ Sights

★ ARoS Aarhus Kunstmuseum   ART MUSEUM
(www.aros.dk; Aros Allé 2; adult/child Dkr110/free; ⊙10am-5pm Tue-Sun, to 10pm Wed; ⊕) Inside the cubist, red-brick walls of Aarhus' showpiece art museum are nine floors of sweeping curves, soaring spaces and white walls, showcasing a wonderful selection of Golden Age works, Danish modernism, and an abundance of arresting and vivid contemporary art. The museum's cherry-on-top is the spectacular **Your Rainbow Panorama**, a 360-degree rooftop walkway offering technicolour views of the city through its glass panes in all shades of the rainbow.

Intriguingly, ARoS' main theme is Dante's *The Divine Comedy;* the entrance is on level 4, and from there you either descend into Hell or climb towards Heaven. Hell is **De 9 Rum** (The 9 Spaces), on the bottom floor, painted black and home to moody installation pieces; Heaven is the rooftop rainbow halo, the brainchild of Olafur Eliasson, a

CENTRAL JUTLAND AARHUS

AARHUS VS ÅRHUS

In 2011, the city of Århus reverted to the old spelling of its name: Aarhus. The letter å was officially introduced to the Danish alphabet in 1948 and represents the sound 'aa', pronounced as the 'a' in the English 'walk'. You may still encounter Århus on a number of signs, maps etc.

Danish-Icelandic artist famed for big, conceptual pieces.

Another iconic piece is Ron Mueck's **Boy** on level 1, an astoundingly lifelike, oversized (5m-high) sculpture of a crouching boy.

The museum stages varied special exhibitions – check what's on when you're in town. ARoS also houses a great giftshop and light-filled cafe on level 4 (free entry), and a restaurant on level 8.

Den Gamle By   MUSEUM
(The Old Town; www.dengamleby.dk; Viborgvej 2; adult/child Dkr135/free; ⊙10am-5pm; ⊕) The Danes' seemingly limitless enthusiasm for dressing up and re-creating history reaches its zenith at Den Gamle By. It's a picturesque open-air museum of 75 half-timbered houses brought here from all corners of Denmark and reconstructed as a provincial market town from the era of Hans Christian Andersen. Re-created neighbourhoods from 1927 and 1974 are the latest additions.

You can take a **horse-drawn wagon ride** (adult/child Dkr40/30) around the site, and then visit each building, store and workshop to see craftspeople practising their trade. Small museums cater to different interests – the **Danish Poster Museum** has some fabulous retro pieces, the **Toy Museum** showcases antique playthings, and the **Gallery of Decorative Arts** displays silverware, porcelain and clocks. Don't miss the apartment block from 1974 for a peek into past lives, or the TV and hi-fi store stocking authentic 1970s gear.

The website details kid-friendly activities for visitors – these peak in July and August, and in the lead up to Christmas.

Den Gamle By is 1.5km west of the city centre (a 20-minute walk from the train station); buses 3A, 19 and 44 stop nearby. There's a detailed schedule of opening hours and admission prices (set according to the museum's activities) outlined on the website. Outside of opening hours you can stroll the cobbled streets for free.

Botanisk Have   GARDENS

(Vesterbrogade) `FREE` Behind Den Gamle By is the Botanical Garden, with its funky walk-through greenhouses (one housing a cafe) and re-created Jutland environments. Reach it through an exit from Den Gamle By or directly from Vesterbrogade.

★**Moesgård Museum**   MUSEUM

(www.moesmus.dk; Moesgård Allé; adult/child Dkr110/free; ⊘10am-5pm Tue-Sun, to 9pm Wed, open Mon Jul-Sep) Don't miss the reinvented Moesgård Museum, 10km south of the city. It reopened in October 2014 in a spectacularly designed, award-winning modern space, next door to the manor house that once accommodated its excellent prehistory exhibits. The museum's star attraction is the 2000-year-old **Grauballe Man**, whose astonishingly well-preserved body was found in 1952 in the village of Grauballe, 35km west of Aarhus.

The superb display on the Grauballe Man is part history lesson, part *CSI: Crime Scene Investigation* episode. Was he a sacrifice to Iron Age fertility gods, an executed prisoner, or simply a victim of murder? Either way, the broken leg and the gaping neck wound suggest his death, sometime around 290 BC (give or take 50 years), was a violent one. His body and skin, tanned and preserved by the unique chemical and biological qualities of the peat bog in which he was found, are remarkably intact, right down to his hair and fingernails.

Aside from the Grauballe Man, the museum brings various eras (from the Stone Age to the Viking era) to life with well-designed archaeological and ethnographic displays. Bus 18 runs here frequently; with your own wheels, it's a lovely drive – take Strandvejen south, then Oddervej, and follow the signs.

Moesgård   OUTDOORS

The Moesgård area, 10km south of the city centre, is a must for the Moesgård Museum, but the area's natural attractions warrant investigation, too. An enjoyable **walking trail**, dubbed the 'Prehistoric Trackway' (Oldtidsstien) leads from behind the museum across fields of wildflowers, past grazing sheep and through beech woods down to **Moesgård Strand**, one of Aarhus' best sandy beaches.

Pick up a brochure and trail map at the museum. You can walk one way and catch a bus from the beach back to the city, or follow the trail both ways as a 4km round-trip.

Frequent bus 18 from Aarhus terminates at the museum. Bus 31 runs in summer and terminates at Moesgård Strand.

Aarhus Domkirke   CHURCH

(www.aarhus-domkirke.dk; Bispetorv; ⊘9.30am-4pm Mon-Sat May-Sep, 10am-3pm Mon-Sat Oct-Apr) With a lofty nave spanning nearly 100m in length, Aarhus Domkirke is Denmark's longest church. The original Romanesque chapel at the eastern end dates from the 12th century, while most of the rest of the church is 15th-century Gothic.

Like other Danish churches, the cathedral was once richly decorated with frescoes that served to convey biblical parables to unschooled peasants. After the Reformation in 1536, church authorities, who felt the frescoes smacked too much of Roman Catholicism, had them all whitewashed, but many have now been uncovered and restored. They range from fairy-tale paintings of St George slaying a dragon to scenes of hellfire.

A highlight of the cathedral is the ornate, five-panel gilt altarpiece made in Lübeck by the renowned woodcarver Bernt Notke in the 15th century.

CENTRAL JUTLAND AARHUS

AARHUS IN...

Two Days

Start by mixing the old with the new at Aarhus' two big-ticket attractions – **ARoS** for cutting-edge art and architecture, **Den Gamle By** for a taste of yesteryear. Finish with alfresco dinner along Åboulevarden. Next day, visit the remarkable **Moesgård Museum**, then return to town to visit the **cathedral** and poke around the Latin Quarter, where you'll have no trouble finding a cool spot to refuel or hear live music.

Four Days

Follow the two-day itinerary, and on the third day grab a free city bike and venture further afield, south to **Marselisborg**, or north to **Risskov**. Take your swimsuit if it's warm enough. Later, check out the boutiques and restaurants of the **Frederiksbjerg** neighbourhood. On day four, consider taking a train or bus to check out the waterways of **Silkeborg** or the beaches or funparks of **Djursland**.

Aarhus

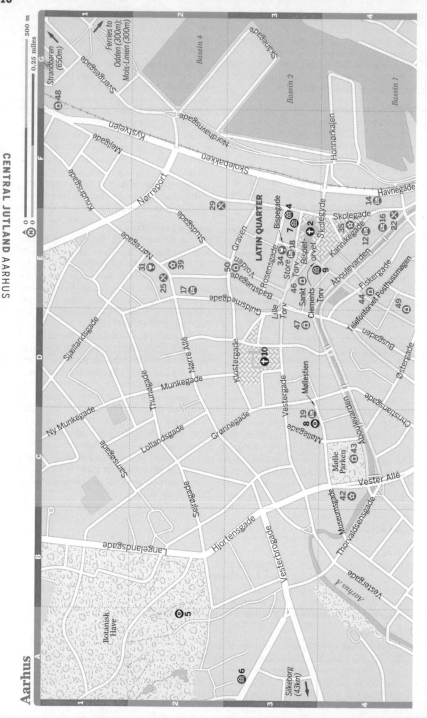

CENTRAL JUTLAND AARHUS

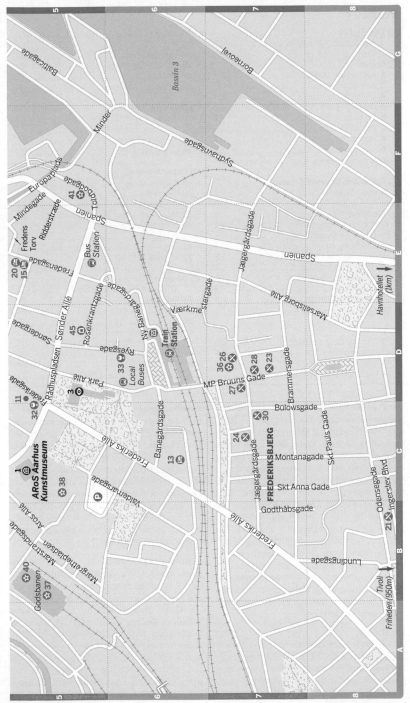

Aarhus

◉ **Top Sights**
1 ARoS Aarhus Kunstmuseum C5

◉ **Sights**
2 Aarhus Domkirke E3
3 Aarhus Rådhus D5
4 Besættelsesmuseet E3
5 Botanisk Have A2
6 Den Gamle By A3
7 Kvindemuseet E3
8 Møllestien C3
9 Vikingemuseet E3
10 Vor Frue Kirke D3

◉ **Activities, Courses & Tours**
11 Cycling Aarhus D5

◉ **Sleeping**
12 CabInn Aarhus Hotel E4
13 City Hotel Oasia C6
14 City Sleep-In F4
15 Hotel Aarhus City Apartments E5
16 Hotel Ferdinand E4
17 Hotel Guldsmeden E2
18 Hotel Royal E3
19 Møllestien Cottages C3
20 Villa Provence E5

◉ **Eating**
21 Fresh-Produce Market B8
22 Globen Flakket E4
23 Kähler Spisesalon D7
24 Klassisk 65 Bistro & Vinbar C7

25 Klassisk Fisk E2
26 Kvickly D7
27 Lagkagehuset D7
28 Nordisk Spisehus D7
29 Oli Nico F2
30 St Pauls Apothek C7

◉ **Drinking & Nightlife**
31 Løve's Bog- & VinCafé E2
32 Sherlock Holmes Pub C5
33 Sigfred's Kaffebar D6
34 Under Masken E3

◉ **Entertainment**
35 Aarhus Teater E4
36 Cinemaxx D7
37 Godsbanen B5
38 Musikhuset Aarhus C5
39 Øst for Paradis E2
40 Radar B5
41 Train F5
42 VoxHall & Atlas C4

◉ **Shopping**
ARoS Aarhus Kunstmuseum ....(see 1)
43 Flagstang Markeder C4
44 Georg Jensen E4
45 HAY D5
46 Kristian F Møller E3
47 Magasin du Nord D3
48 Paustian G1
49 Salling E4
50 Summerbird Chocolaterie E3

Vor Frue Kirke   CHURCH
(www.aarhusvorfrue.dk; Frue Kirkeplads; ⊙10am-4pm Mon-Fri, to 2pm Sat May-Sep; shorter hrs Oct-Apr) Set back from Vestergade, the Church of Our Lady is like a Russian *matryoshka* (nesting doll), opening to reveal multiple layers. It was here that the original Aarhus cathedral was erected shortly after 1060. That cathedral stood until about 1240, when it was replaced by the current red-brick church, whose main treasure lies in it basement: the vaulted **crypt** of the original cathedral (enter via the stairs beneath the chancel), uncovered by chance in 1955 during a restoration. Vor Frue Kirke has yet another **chapel**, this one exhibiting early 16th-century frescoes. It can be entered through the garden courtyard – take the left door.

Møllestien   STREET
While you're exploring the old part of town, be sure to wander idyllic Møllestien, easily Aarhus' prettiest street – all cobblestones, pastel-coloured cottages and climbing roses.

Kvindemuseet   MUSEUM
(www.kvindemuseet.dk; Domkirkeplads 5; adult/child Dkr45/free; ⊙10am-5pm Tue-Sat, to 8pm Wed; ⊞) Denmark is today a model for equality, but this hasn't always been the case. In a fresh, engaging exhibition inside the old town hall, the Women's Museum charts women's lives in Denmark and their hard-won achievements. It's inspiring stuff, but it's not just one for the ladies – families will love the hands-on kids' exhibits in the 'History of Childhood' section. There's also a pretty cafe here.

Besættelsesmuseet   MUSEUM
(www.besaettelsesmuseet.dk; Mathilde Fibigers Have 2; adult/child Dkr30/free; ⊙11am-4pm Tue-Sun Jun-Aug, 11am-4pm Tue, Sat & Sun Sep-May) For those interested in the German Occupation of Denmark during WWII, the small Occupation Museum is inside the building that the Germans once used to interrogate and house prisoners (entrance is just behind Kvindemuseet). It has well-presented displays of military equipment, Nazi and Danish propaganda, and insights into everyday

life during the war. Labels are in Danish – ask for the explanatory guide in English.

Vikingemuseet MUSEUM
(www.moesmus.dk; Sankt Clements Torv 6; ☉10.15am-5pm Mon-Fri) **FREE** There's more than the expected vaults in the basement of Nordea bank, a stone's throw from the cathedral. In the mid-1960s this site was excavated and artefacts from the Viking era were unearthed. Concise exhibits include a skeleton, a reconstructed pithouse, 1000-year-old carpentry tools and pottery.

Aarhus Rådhus ARCHITECTURE
(Rådhuspladsen) Aarhus' controversial town hall was designed by renowned architect Arne Jacobsen, a pioneer of Danish modernism, and completed in 1942. It's clad in Norwegian marble and has a distinctive grey appearance. Jacobsen also designed many of the interiors (along with Verner Panton) – for design buffs, it's worth a look inside.

Marselisborg OUTDOORS
A green belt begins 2km south of the centre and runs nearly 10km south, hugging the coast – it's a great place for hiking and cycling. The northern end is known as Marselisborg, the midsection Moesgård and the southern end Fløjstrup – names taken from the former estates of which they were once part.

Landmark features at the northern end are the Marselisborg Palace, Tivoli Friheden amusement park, Jysk Væddeløbsbane (horse-trotting track) and Atletion (sports complex).

Marselisborg Palace & Park PALACE
(Kongevejen 100; ☉park 8am-9pm Apr-Sep, 9am-4pm Oct-Mar) Marselisborg Palace is a summer home of the royal family, and when they're not in residence the public can explore the English-style grounds and rose garden (free admission). When the blue-bloods are here, watch the changing of the guard at noon from a vantage point on the road. The palace is reached on bus 19.

Tivoli Friheden AMUSEMENT PARK
(www.friheden.dk; Skovbrynet; adult/child Dkr110/90; ☉mid-Apr–Sep; ⊞) Neither as big nor as fabulous as Copenhagen's major drawcard, Aarhus' Tivoli is still a fun, wholesome family attraction, full of childhood favourites (dodgem cars and a Ferris wheel) as well as newer, faster rides. You can buy a multi-ride pass (adult/child Dkr220/200, including admission) and go hard, or pay for each ride individually. The park is at the northern edge of Marselisborg woods, reached on bus 16.

Check the website for the park's changing opening hours (as late as 11pm in peak summer). Friday nights from May to August see popular outdoor concerts from big-name Danish performers as part of the Fed Fredag ('Fat Friday') program.

🏃 Activities
The easiest, most enjoyable way to experience the great outdoors surrounding Aarhus is on foot or by bike, and the best hiking and cycling is along the green belt south of the city.

If the weather's good, popular family-friendly beaches lie on the town's outskirts and feature clean, calm (but often cool) waters. The best-loved spots to the north are the traditional seabaths known as **Den Permanente**, in Risskov not far from the hostel. **Bellevue**, further north of Den Permanente (about 4km north of the city centre), is also popular; buses 17 and 20 will get you there.

Otherwise head south to **Moesgård Strand** about 7km from the centre on bus 31. Den Permanente tends to draw a younger crowd; families head to Moesgård.

AARHUS FOR KIDS

Aarhus – and indeed all of Jutland – is an incredibly family-friendly place to travel. Entry to most museums is free for kids, and you won't have to minimise your time in culture-vulture places – almost every attraction has factored kids into its audience, with displays and activities designed especially to keep them entertained. And then there are places designed *solely* with families in mind – Tivoli Friheden (p213) in Aarhus, for example, but also parks in Djursland (p222), Randers (p234) and, of course, Legoland (p231).

Other factors point to a relatively stress-free experience: many hotels have family rooms (Danhostel Aarhus (p214), CabInn Aarhus (p215) and Aarhus City Apartments (p215) are good options); many restaurants have a *børnemenu* (children's menu); the outdoors is gentle and the beaches calm; and you can hire kids' bikes or seats from Bikes 4 Rent (p220). Go forth and multiply!

 CITY DISCOUNTS

If you're planning to tick off city sights, the **AarhusCard** is a worthwhile investment. The bus station and most accommodation providers sell the pass (adult/child 24-hour pass Dkr129/69, 48-hour pass Dkr179/79), which allows unlimited transport on local buses as well as free or discounted admission to most sights.

In a city full of students, an ISIC or ID card from your home university is an asset. If you have one, flaunt it. From pubs to restaurants to museums, students are given favourable prices.

Tours

It's worth checking with VisitAarhus to see if summertime walking tours are scheduled.

Cycling Aarhus   CYCLING TOURS
(27 29 06 90; www.cycling-aarhus.dk; Frederiksgade 78) This company offers comprehensive cycling tours from April to October. The Grand Tour takes in Aarhus' highlights over 12km and three hours, departing at 10am and 2pm daily from the company's central base (where bike rental is also available). Shorter (90-minute) tours also run occasionally, including one that takes in the rapidly changing harbourfront.

Festivals & Events

Spot Festival   MUSIC
(www.spotfestival.dk) This annual event, held in May, showcases up-and-coming Danish and Nordic musical talent, in and around Musikhuset.

Sculpture by the Sea   CULTURAL
(www.sculpturebythesea.dk) This month-long festival is held biennially (June in odd-numbered years) and transforms the city's southern beachfront into an outdoor gallery, with dozens of sculptures from Danish and foreign artists displayed beside (and in) the water.

NorthSide Festival   MUSIC
(www.northside.dk) A three-day music festival in mid-June that's building a big reputation – line-ups rival the legendary Roskilde Festival.

Aarhus Jazz Festival   MUSIC
(www.jazzfest.dk) This week-long jazz celebration in mid-July sees big-name local and international acts doing their thing in various theatres, cafes and squares.

Viking Moot   CULTURAL
(www.moesmus.dk) A Viking-style market is held at Moesgård Strand over a weekend in late July. There are crafts, food and equestrian events, plus Vikings of all nationalities competing to out-fight one another.

Aarhus Festival   ARTS
(www.aarhusfestuge.dk) The city dons its shiniest party gear at the end of August, when this festival transforms the town for 10 days, celebrating music, food, short film, theatre, visual arts and outdoor events for all ages (many of which are free).

Sleeping

A number of smart new chain hotels have set up in Aarhus, catering to the business and conference crowd and offering good weekend rates. If you're after something special, book early at one of the boutique hotels.

The 'Where to Sleep' section of the VisitAarhus website (www.visitaarhus.com) lists rooms in private homes, as well as private apartments for rent. Many of these are central and well priced. AirBnB (www.airbnb.com) also has an excellent selection of rooms and apartments.

Note that where parking is indicated in reviews below, it is rarely free.

City Sleep-In   HOTEL €
(86 19 20 55; www.citysleep-in.dk; Havnegade 20; dm Dkr180, d without/with bathroom Dkr450/500; @) The most central hostel option has small, basic rooms – you'll be more drawn to the communal areas, such as the pretty courtyard or 1st-floor TV room. There are helpful staff, a global feel and decent amenities (lockers, kitchen, pool table, laundry).

The doubles are pricey for what you get – if you need to rent bed linen (Dkr50) and a towel (Dkr20), it might pay to look at the cheaper hotels. Breakfast is Dkr70.

Danhostel Aarhus   HOSTEL €
(86 21 21 20; www.aarhus-danhostel.dk; Marienlundsvej 10; dm Dkr250, d without/with bathroom Dkr550/720; ☉ mid-Jan–mid-Dec; P@) The main building here is as pretty as a picture: it's a large octagonal room that was once a dancehall. Accommodation is bright and basic; some rooms have private bathrooms (linen costs extra). Breakfast costs Dkr64. The hostel is 3km north of the city centre, in pretty woods close to the beach; take bus 17, 18 or 20.

Havnhotellet
HOTEL €

(www.bbhotels.dk; Marselisborg Havnevej 20; s/d/tr incl breakfast Dkr600/600/825; Ⓟ 🛜) These fresh, good-value rooms at the marina are straight off the Ikea production line. All booking is done online (hence no phone number), and check-in is via a computer. The hotel is 1.5km south of the centre (off Strandvejen; catch bus 19) and walking distance to Marselisborg; at your doorstep is a handful of restaurants (and free parking).

Tip: choose a room on the 1st floor (1.sal), as ground-floor rooms lack privacy. The price drops for second and subsequent nights.

CabInn Aarhus Hotel
BUDGET HOTEL €

(Ⓙ 86 75 70 00; www.cabinn.com; Kannikegade 14; s/d/tr from Dkr495/625/805; Ⓟ @ 🛜) 'Best location, best price' is the CabInn chain's motto, and given that this branch doubled in size in 2014, it's clearly doing something right. The functional rooms are based on ships' cabins (hence the name) – the cheapest is *tiny*, but all come with bathroom, kettle and TV. The location is indeed top-notch. Breakfast costs Dkr70.

DCU-Camping Blommehaven
CAMPGROUND €

(Ⓙ 86 27 02 07; www.blommehaven.dk; Ørneredevej 35; adult/child/site Dkr80/50/48-70; ☉ late Mar–late Oct; 🛜) This big beachside campground 6km south of the city centre lies in the scenic Marselisborg woods en route to Moesgård. It's got loads of family-oriented facilities, plus simple four-berth huts (Dkr635). If you're driving, follow Strandvejen south; otherwise, take bus 18 or (in summer) 31.

★ Hotel Guldsmeden
BOUTIQUE HOTEL €€

(Ⓙ 86 13 45 50; www.hotelguldsmeden.com; Guldsmedgade 40; d without/with bathroom from Dkr995/1395; 🛜) A top pick for its excellent location, warm staff, French Colonial–style rooms with Persian rugs, pretty garden oasis and relaxed, stylish ambience. Bumper breakfasts (mainly organic) are included, as is Guldsmeden's own organic toiletries range. *Guldsmed* means both goldsmith and dragonfly in Danish – look for sweet use of the dragonfly motif in the decor.

★ Villa Provence
BOUTIQUE HOTEL €€

(Ⓙ 86 18 24 00; www.villaprovence.dk; Fredens Torv 12; s/d/ste incl breakfast from Dkr1095/1295/2300; Ⓟ 🛜) Elegant rooms (individually decorated in Provençal country style) for a mature, well-heeled crowd. The suites are large and lovely; standard rooms are smaller but with the same attention to detail – all have flat-screen TVs, French linen and original French movie posters. Besides the gourmet breakfast, our favourite feature is the courtyard, with flowering potplants and fairy-lit trees.

Møllestien Cottages
COTTAGES €€

(Ⓙ 86 13 06 32; www.house-in-aarhus.com; Møllestien 49 & 51; d Dkr800-900) On Aarhus' prettiest street, a ceramicist rents out two neighbouring cottages – small, homely places each with courtyard, kitchen, lounge and bathroom (the cheaper of the two is more rustic); be warned that the staircases to the upstairs bedrooms are steep. One-night stays cost an extra Dkr300. Book early.

City Hotel Oasia
HOTEL €€

(Ⓙ 87 32 37 15; www.hoteloasia.com; Kriegersvej 27; d weekdays/weekend incl breakfast Dkr1295/975kr; Ⓟ @ 🛜) Clearly a subscriber to the minimalist school of design, Oasia offers bright modern rooms full of clean lines and the best of Scandinavian fittings (Hästens beds, Bang & Olufsen TVs, designer chairs). It's well placed for the train station.

Hotel Ferdinand
BOUTIQUE HOTEL €€

(Ⓙ 87 32 14 44; www.hotelferdinand.dk; Åboulevarden 28; s/d studio from Dkr950/1150, ste from Dkr1100/1300; 🛜) Ferdinand is in the centre of the Åboulevarden action, with a swank French brasserie downstairs. There are eight suites where the restaurant (large and luxurious); in the neighbouring building are five studio apartments, with kitchen, washing machine and balconies.

Hotel Aarhus
City Apartments
APARTMENTS €€

(Ⓙ 86 27 51 30; www.hotelaca.dk; Fredensgade 18; d from Dkr799, studio from Dkr989, apt from Dkr1189; Ⓟ 🛜) Good for families and long-stayers, this three-storey apartment block is home to modern rooms, studios and apartments. All have kitchens (kitchenettes in the rooms) and cable TV. There's no reception, so you need to book ahead and arrange to be met.

Hotel Royal
HOTEL €€€

(Ⓙ 86 12 00 11; www.hotelroyal.dk; Store Torv 4; s/d incl breakfast from Dkr1295/1495; Ⓟ 🛜) If you've come to expect restrained Scandi style in your top-end Danish hotels, prepare to be surprised. From the over-the-top entrance portico to the chandelier-lit reception area and incredible murals, the Royal seems a little, well, gaudy in parts. But fun, too – we love the fish-tank reception desk and the rich colour schemes. The rooms are appropriately lavish.

✖ Eating

Away from the same-same feeling you may get along Åboulevarden, fertile hunting grounds come dinnertime include the Latin Quarter (good for bistro-style cafes); Mejlgade (home to some excellent budget options); and the cool Frederiksbjerg neighbourhood, south of the train station (centred on MP Bruuns Gade and Jægergårdsgade).

★ **Oli Nico** INTERNATIONAL €
(www.olinico.dk; Mejlgade 35; dishes Dkr55-125; ⊗11.30am-2pm & 5.30-9pm Mon-Fri, noon-2pm & 5.30-9pm Sat, 5.30-9pm Sun) You may need to fight for one of the sought-after tables at Oli Nico, a small deli-restaurant with a menu of classic dishes at astoundingly good prices (*moules frites* for Dkr60, rib-eye steak for Dkr125 – both with homemade chips!). The daily-changing three-course dinner menu (for a bargain Dkr130) may be Aarhus' best-kept food secret. No reservations; takeaway available.

Lagkagehuset BAKERY €
(MP Bruunsgade 34; sandwiches & salads around Dkr60; ⊗6.30am-7pm Mon-Fri, to 6pm Sat & Sun) There's a whole lot of baked-good deliciousness going on here – take a number and wait for your chance to order from the display of breads, cakes and pastries. Lunchtime sandwiches and salads are decent value, and the coffee is good.

Kähler Spisesalon MODERN SCANDINAVIAN €€
(www.spisesalon.dk; MP Bruuns Gade 33; open sandwich Dkr75, 3-/4-course menu Dkr279/325; ⊗9am-10pm Mon-Sat, 10am-10pm Sun) This elegant 'salon' is filled with plants, lamps, mirrors and covetable ceramics (made by Kähler, a 175-year-old ceramic company with its flagship store down the road, at No 41). It's a great choice at any time of day, for its weekday breakfast buffet (Dkr80), excellent coffee, artful reinterpretation of the classic smørrebrød, or long-simmered *boeuf bourguignon*.

**Klassisk 65
Bistro & Vinbar** FRENCH, DANISH €€
(⊡86 13 12 21; www.klassiskbistro.dk; Jægergårdsgade 65; mains Dkr165-205; ⊗lunch & dinner daily, plus brunch Sun) Heavy on rustic, shabby-chic charm, this tightly packed place is all about carefully mismatched furniture and crockery, and shelves laden with wine. The locals flock for the much-prized *hyggelig* (cosy) atmosphere and value for money. The kitchen puts a Danish spin on French country cook-

ing, and the three-course menu of the day is perfect at Dkr295.

Globen Flakket CAFE, RESTAURANT €€
(www.globen-flakket.dk; Åboulevarden 18; dinner mains Dkr129-189; ⊗8.30am-midnight Mon-Thu, to 2am Fri & Sat, 9am-11pm Sun; ▣) Pitching to a broad demographic, this upbeat riverside venue is a decent option at any hour. As well as a classic-hits menu of burgers, pasta etc, plenty of good-value buffet options draw in the punters (including the weekday breakfast buffet for Dkr39, weekend brunch for Dkr119, and afternoon cake buffet for Dkr39).

★ **St Pauls Apothek** MODERN SCANDINAVIAN €€
(⊡86 12 08 33; www.stpaulsapothek.dk; Jægergårdsgade 76; 2/3-course menu Dkr245/295; ⊗5.30pm-midnight Tue-Thu, to 2am Fri & Sat) What was once a pharmacy is now one of Aarhus' hottest, best-value dining destinations: a Brooklyn-esque combo of hipster mixologists, vintage architectural detailing, and slinky mood lighting. The menu is small on choice but big on Nordic produce and confident food pairings – and for Dkr595, you can enjoy three courses matched with inspired, delicious cocktails. Book ahead.

The Apothek is also in hot demand as a luxe drinking den – visit in the wee hours to sample a few of the killer cocktails.

★ **Kähler Villa Dining** MODERN DANISH €€€
(⊡86 17 70 88; www.villadining.dk; Grenåvej 127; 4-course dinner incl wine Dkr599; ⊗6.30-9.30pm Mon-Sat) Aarhus' culinary A-lister lies about 5km north of the centre, in a gracious old villa where gustatory magic happens, at a delightfully accessible price. It's a clever concept: for a flat rate of Dkr599, and at a set starting time, diners enjoy a set menu of appetiser, starter, main, dessert and coffee, plus as much wine as they fancy.

Take Skovvejen north past Risskov (the pretty forest where the Danhostel is), and the road becomes Grenåvej. Plenty of local buses serve this route, including 17, 18 and 100.

Nordisk Spisehus MODERN DANISH €€€
(⊡86 17 70 99; www.nordiskspisehus.dk; MP Bruuns Gade 31; 3-/5-course lunch Dkr199/299, 3-/5-/8-course dinner Dkr399/599/799; ⊗noon-10pm Mon-Sat) Another clever concept restaurant, where the menu is usually geographically themed ('Rome', for example, or 'New York Meets Paris') and dishes are loaned from (consenting) Michelin-starred restaurants around the globe, then given a Nordic twist. Menus change every two

months – it's no doubt a huge challenge, but the kitchen handles it with aplomb. Lunch is excellent value.

Klassisk Fisk
SEAFOOD €€€

(☑ 28 71 99 95; www.klassiskfisk.dk; Nørregade 38; lunch Dkr65-160, dinner mains Dkr215-245; ☺ noon-4pm & 5.30-10pm Mon-Sat) Elegant decor, a relaxed feel and a menu of fresh fishy treats – it's as simple, and as delicious, as that. The crew behind French bistro Klassisk 65 turn their attention to seafood here: oysters naturel, lobster, tuna carpaccio, softshell crab and bouillabaisse vie for menu attention, or opt for the three-course menu of the day for Dkr295.

Self-Catering
Supermarkets generally open from 8am, closing between 8pm and 10pm. Bakeries inside supermarkets open from 7am.

Kvickly
SUPERMARKET

(MP Bruuns Gade 25; ☺ 8am-8pm Mon-Fri, to 6pm Sat & Sun) Bruun's Galleri shopping centre is connected to the train station; there's a large supermarket on the lower level.

Fresh-Produce Market
FOOD MARKET

(Ingerslevs Boulevard; ☺ 8am-2pm Wed & Sat) In the cool Frederiksbjerg neighbourhood, this twice-weekly farmers market sells fruit and veg, flowers, fish, cheese etc.

🍸 Drinking & Nightlife

Aarhus' large student contingent guarantees the bars fill up from Thursday onwards. There are a few streets lined with wall-to-wall drinking dens: the north side of Åboulevarden is full of chic restaurant-bars and a fashionable crowd, while the south side has big drinking dens open late on Friday and Saturday nights and drawing lots of students. Nearby Skolegade has a handful of intimate boozers and dive bars; Frederiksgade gives you more boisterous English/Irish pubs than you can poke a pint at, all attempting to woo students with discounted beer (Dkr30 for a pint of Carlsberg) and schedules of live music, jam sessions, televised sports, quiz competitions and karaoke.

★ Strandbaren
BAR

(facebook.com/strandbarenaarhus; Havnebassin 7, pier 4; ☺ May-Sep) Plonk shipping containers and sand on a harbourfront spot and voila: beach bar. This chilled hang-out at Aarhus Ø (just beyond the ferry port) offers food, drink, flirting and weather-dependent activities and events. Check hours and location on the Facebook page (harbour redevelopment may require an annual location change; opening hours are 'when the sun is shining').

Bus 33 runs out this way. While you're here, check out the new architectural developments of Aarhus Ø, including the head-turning 'Iceberg'.

★ Løve's Bog- & VinCafé
BAR

(www.loeves.dk; Nørregade 32; ☺ 9am-midnight Mon-Fri, from 10am Sat, 10am-5pm Sun) This snug 'book and wine cafe' is full of book-lined shelves and old furniture, and reading and laptopping regulars. Occasional poetry readings and jazz bands add to the cultured air, while the short, simple tapas menu nicely fills in any writer's-block moments.

Sigfred's Kaffebar
COFFEE BAR

(www.sigfreds.dk; Ryesgade 28; ☺ 8am-6pm Mon-Thu, to 7pm Fri, 10am-5pm Sat) Sigfred's repeatedly wins awards for the best coffee in town, brewed by expert baristas and sipped by ever-faithful regulars. Its original outlet caffeinates the pedestrianised shopping street; a second branch is in the Latin Quarter, at Guldsmedgade 20.

Under Masken
BAR

(Bispegade 3; ☺ noon-2am Mon-Sat, 2-10pm Sun) Artist-run Under Masken keeps things kooky with its jumble of gilded mirrors, African tribal masks, sailor pictures and glowing fishtanks. Slide in a for a loud, smoky and fun night on the tiles. Note: no food served.

Sherlock Holmes Pub
PUB

(www.sherlock-holmes.dk; Frederiksgade 76; ☺ noon-late) This is a real English-style pub, dim and cosy and with a calendar full of live music, karaoke, jam sessions and televised football. You can pop next door to the **Golden Lion** for a dose of English pub grub, while close by are popular Irish pubs: **Tir na Nog**, at Frederiksgade 40, and **Waxies** at No 16.

☆ Entertainment
Live Music
Aarhus is considered Denmark's music capital, so aside from the diverse offerings of Musikhuset Aarhus and the live-music events of club venues such as Train, it's not hard to track down music being played in more intimate venues. Look for summertime outdoor concerts too, in venues such as Tivoli Friheden amusement park; festivals also are a boon to live-music lovers.

Websites for the venues may be in Danish, but the events calendars should be easy enough to follow.

Musikhuset Aarhus
LIVE MUSIC

(www.musikhusetaarhus.dk; Thomas Jensens Allé 2) Aarhus' concert hall is a large, glass-fronted venue that hosts a range of musical events, from Rod Stewart to *Rigoletto,* performances from Den Kongelige Ballet (the Royal Danish Ballet) or the Aarhus Symphony Orchestra.

Train
LIVE MUSIC, CLUB

(www.train.dk; Toldbodgade 6; ☺ club from midnight Fri & Sat) Aarhus' premier club, Train is first and foremost a concert venue, with shows a couple of nights a week and some big international acts on the program. Train opens as a late-night club as well, on Friday and Saturday nights, with room for up to 1700 party-people and top-notch DJ talent. The complex also incorporates Kupé, a funky lounge club.

Radar
LIVE MUSIC

(www.radarlive.dk; Godsbanen, Skovgaardsgade 3) Radar offers a glimpse into Aarhus' indie scene with a wide range of music (including rock, techno, punk and folk) from its home inside the very cool Godsbanen freight yard, a new cultural hub for the city. **Godsbanen** (www.godsbanen.dk; Skovgaardsgade 3) is home to stages, workshops and a quality cafe, and hosts exhibitions and events – it's worth a look.

VoxHall & Atlas
LIVE MUSIC

(www.fondenvoxhall.dk; Vester Allé 15) VoxHall is a well-established live-music locale (capacity 700) hosting an eclectic range of acts. Attached is the more-intimate Atlas (capacity 300), specialising in jazz and world-music performers.

Theatre

Aarhus Teater
THEATRE

(www.aarhusteater.dk; Bispetorv) This is a suitably theatrical building dating from 1900, embellished with gargoyles and other extravagant decor. Performances are largely in Danish, but musical and dance productions are also staged.

Cinema

Cinema tickets cost from Dkr70 to Dkr95 – it's cheaper to see a daytime session.

★ Øst for Paradis
CINEMA

(www.paradisbio.dk; Paradisgade 7-9) Art-house cinema in the northern reaches of the Latin Quarter. It shows films in original language, with Danish subtitles.

Cinemaxx
CINEMA

(www.cinemaxx.dk/aarhus; MP Bruuns Gade 25) Inside Bruun's Galleri shopping centre (connected to the train station); screens blockbusters alongside smaller local films.

🔒 Shopping

The shopping is excellent, but you may be surprised by the limited opening hours. Some smaller stores don't trade on weekends (except for a few hours on Saturday morning).

Søndergade, the 850m-long busy pedestrian street (known as Ryesgade at its starting point opposite the train station), is lined with mainstream shopping and chain stores.

The Latin Quarter is a cobblestone, largely pedestrianised area offering original finds in cool fashion and design boutiques. Check out Badstuegade and Volden, and west along Vestergade.

Frederiksbjerg has more eclectic clothing and design stores, including some retro stores and artisan studios. Stroll Bruuns Gade, Sankt Pauls Kirkeplads and Jægergårdsgade.

Central department stores open longer hours and offer everything from cosmetics to fashion to homewares, including big-name Danish brands (Lego toys, Royal Copenhagen porcelain, Holmegaard glass etc). Be sure to ask about VAT refunds. Stores include **Magasin du Nord** (wwww.magasin.dk; Immervad 2-8; ☺ 8am-8pm) and **Salling** (www.salling.dk; Søndergade 27; ☺ 9am-8pm Mon-Fri, to 6pm Sat & Sun).

ARoS Aarhus Kunstmuseum
BOOKS, GIFTS

(Aros Allé 2; ☺ 10am-5pm Tue-Sun, to 10pm Wed) The art museum's giftshop has an extensive range of art books, homewares, accessories and nifty knick-knacks.

Georg Jensen
DESIGN

(www.georgjensen.com; Søndergade 1; ☺ 10am-5.30pm Mon-Thu, to 6pm Fri, to 3pm Sat) Exquisite silverware and jewellery from the Danish master; next door is Georg Jensen Damask, selling classic linen pieces.

HAY
DESIGN

(www.hay.dk; Rosenkrantzgade 24; ☺ 10am-6pm Mon-Fri, 10am-4pm Sat) Well-chosen examples of the latest Danish furniture as well as fabulous designer homewares, textiles and rugs.

Kristian F Møller BOOKS
(Store Torv 5; ⏲10am-6pm Mon-Thu, to 7pm Fri, to 4pm Sat) Well-priced English-language books and a range of travel guides.

Paustian DESIGN
(www.paustian.dk; Skovvejen 2; ⏲10am-6pm Mon-Fri, to 3pm Sat & Sun) A shrine to the best of Danish (and international) design. Prepare to desire everything that couldn't possibly fit in your suitcase...

Summerbird Chocolaterie CHOCOLATE
(Volden 31; ⏲10am-5.30pm Mon-Thu, to 6pm Fri, to 3pm Sat) Exquisite choc-shop in the Latin Quarter. The pretty packaging makes these a classy souvenir for someone back home.

Flagstang Markeder FLEA MARKET
(www.flagstang-markeder.dk; Mølleparken; ⏲10am-4pm Sun monthly) Scour Aarhus' monthly flea market for anything from Cheap Monday jeans to Royal Copenhagen porcelain and plastic-fantastic '70s Danish kitchenware (plus a good deal of junk). Check the website calendar for dates. In winter, the market moves inside, to the foyer of Musikhuset.

ℹ Information

The AarhusCard offers discounts to sights and entertainment venues, and free transport.

EMERGENCY

Police/Ambulance (☎112)

Police Station (☎87 31 14 48; Ridderstræde 1)

INTERNET ACCESS

Gate 58 (Vestergade 58B, 1st fl; per hr Dkr18-28; ⏲10am-midnight Mon-Fri, noon-midnight Sat & Sun) Much more a gamers' den than an internet cafe.

Hovedbiblioteket (www.aakb.dk; Europaplads; ⏲10am-6pm Mon-Fri, 10am-2pm Sat) Get online for free at the main public library, which in early 2015 moved into its new home – an impressive new harbourfront building known as Dokk1. Read about the plans for Dokk1 at www.urbanmediaspace.dk.

LEFT LUGGAGE

Coin-operated lockers are available at the train and bus stations; a small/large locker costs Dkr20/40 for a 24-hour period.

MEDICAL SERVICES

Aarhus Universitetshospital (☎78 45 00 00; Nørrebrogade 44) Hospital with a 24-hour emergency ward; call before arriving.

Emergency Doctor Service (☎70 11 31 31; ⏲4pm-8am Mon-Fri, all day Sat & Sun) After-hours medical assistance.

Løve Apotek (Store Torv 5; ⏲24hr) Convenient pharmacy.

MONEY

There are banks and ATMs all over town, with a good concentration near the train station, along the pedestrianised shopping strip (Ryesgade/Søndergade) and around the cathedral.

Forex (Banegårdspladsen 20; ⏲9am-6pm Mon-Fri, 10am-3pm Sat) Foreign exchange close to the train station.

POST

Post Office (Banegårdspladsen; ⏲10am-6pm Mon-Fri, 10am-1pm Sat) Next to the train station.

TOURIST INFORMATION

VisitAarhus (☎87 31 50 10; www.visitaarhus.com) no longer has a central tourist office, but aims to reach travellers via its website, phone line, mobile info booths (in peak periods), and touch-screen computers at many of the town's attractions, transport hubs and accommodation providers.

If you have questions and want face-to-face help, staff at the bus station can usually help. Otherwise, do some advance prep: visit the website, download the app, check social media pages for up-to-date info (see 'This is why I love Aarhus' on Facebook; follow @VisitAarhus on Twitter).

ℹ Getting There & Away

AIR

Aarhus Airport (AAR; www.aar.dk), also known as Tirstrup airport, is 45km northeast of the city.

Scandinavian Airlines (SAS) has daily flights to/from Copenhagen; Sun-Air (affiliated with British Airways) operates direct connections to Stockholm, Gothenburg and Oslo. Ryanair has daily connections to/from London (Stansted).

BOAT

Mols-Linien (☎70 10 14 18; www.mols-linien.dk) Operates high-speed ferries between Aarhus and Odden in north Zealand (one-way adult/child/car Dkr349/175/699, 70 minutes, minimum five sailings daily). Rates for car passage include passengers.

BUS

All regional and long-distance buses stop at Aarhus **bus station** (Rutebilstation; Fredensgade 45), 300m northeast of the train station. From Aarhus you can reach most Jutland towns of note on the X-bus network – information is online at www.midttrafik.dk, or via the bus station info desk, staffed from 7am to 10pm.

Abildskou (☎70 21 08 88; www.abildskou.dk) Express bus line 888 runs up to 10 times daily between Aarhus and Copenhagen's Valby station (Dkr310, three to 3½ hours), with connections to Copenhagen airport. Good fare discounts are available – see the website.

CAR & MOTORCYCLE

The main highways to Aarhus are the E45 from the north and south, and Rte 15 from the west. The E45 doesn't make it into the city itself – take exits 46 to 50.

TRAIN

Inside the train station (hovedbanegård) you'll find the **ticket office** (⊙7.10am-6pm Mon-Fri, 10.15am-5pm Sat & Sun) with its orderly ticket-queuing system: red for domestic journeys, green for international. For domestic journeys, skip the queues by using one of the ticket machines (instructions available in English; credit cards accepted). Friday trains are busy, and it's best to reserve a seat (Dkr30) for long journeys.

Trains to Copenhagen (one way Dkr382, three to 3½ hours), via Odense (Dkr240, 1¾ hours), leave Aarhus roughly half-hourly.

Other frequent services are Aalborg (Dkr194, 1½ hours), Frederikshavn (Dkr252, 2¾ hours; may involve a change of train in Aalborg), Grenaa (Dkr100, 1¼ hours) and Silkeborg (Dkr85, 50 minutes).

⊙ Getting Around

A new light-rail line (known as the Aarhus Letbane) is expected to open in 2016. Phase 1 includes the construction of a 12km tramway from Aarhus train station via the harbour to Nørreport, where it will divide into two tracks to the north. The rail link to Grenaa in Djursland will carry trams. The opening of the letbane will impact upon bus services – the Midttrafik website (www.midttrafik.dk) will keep you informed; its phone line and the service counter at the bus station are your best bets for info.

ON YOUR BIKE

OK, so you've found yourself a bycykel and are looking to explore. Good two-wheeled trips:

➡ South to Marselisborg, taking in the palace and park. Stop off to refuel at the marina en route.

➡ North to check out the green campus of Aarhus University.

➡ Further north to Risskov, to explore the pretty woodlands and beach.

➡ Aarhus Ø and the northern harbour-side developments, full of impressive architectural designs (the 'Iceberg' complex is a head-turner).

TO/FROM THE AIRPORT
Aarhus

A bus service (route 925X) connects Aarhus with the airport at Tirstrup (Dkr100, 50 minutes). Buses depart outside the train station (close to the post office) and the changeable schedule is geared to meet all incoming and outgoing flights – phone ☑ 70 21 02 30 for up-to-date information or see www.midttrafik.dk. A taxi between the airport and the city centre will set you back a hefty Dkr650.

Billund

Aarhus is connected by bus with the large airport at Billund, about 100km southwest and a two-hour bus ride away (Dkr160). Buses 912X and 913X depart from the Aarhus bus station.

It's quicker to take a frequent train to Vejle, where there are plenty of buses to the airport.

BICYCLE

Free **Aarhusbycykel** (www.aarhusbycykel.dk) city bikes are available from locations around the city from April to October (download a map from the website, or ask at your accommodation). There are a few bikes close to the Subway store opposite the train station, and some outside the town hall. You need to put a Dkr20 coin into the slot to obtain the bike (refunded when you return it).

If you're visiting from November to March, or you want a better-quality bike for a lengthy period, **Bikes 4 Rent** (☑ 20 26 10 20; www.bikes4rent.dk; per day/week Dkr95/250) can help. Staff deliver bikes to a central city location (the Radisson hotel by Musikhuset).

BUS

Aarhus has an extensive, efficient local bus network. Most in-town (yellow) buses stop close to the train station on Park Allé. Buy your ticket from the on-board machine (Dkr20, allowing up to two hours' travel). Information on tickets, routes and schedules is available from the bus station on Fredensgade, via the website www.midttrafik.dk (good info in English) or by dialling ☑ 70 21 02 30.

CAR & MOTORCYCLE

A car is convenient for getting to sights such as Moesgård on the city outskirts, although the city centre is best explored on foot.

Parking

There's paid undercover parking in municipal car parks, including one near Musikhuset Aarhus and at Bruun's Galleri shopping centre. Such car parks generally charge by the hour. There are also numerous billetautomat (parking meters) along city streets. You'll usually need to pay for street parking from 9am to 7pm Monday to Friday and 9am to 4pm Saturday (outside those hours parking is generally free). Parking costs Dkr12/17 for the first/second hour, and Dkr22 per hour after that. Press a button on the *billetautomat* for English instructions.

Rental

All the major players (Europcar, Budget, Hertz, Sixt and Avis) have car-rental desks at Aarhus airport. In town, **Europcar** (⌨ 89 33 11 11; www.europcar.com; Sønder Allé 35) has a central office across from the bus station.

TAXI

Taxis are available at the train station and at a rank by the cathedral; you can also flag one on the street or order one by phone (89 48 48 48). All taxis have a meter – expect to pay up to Dkr100 for destinations within the inner city.

DJURSLAND

Djursland, the large peninsula north-east of Aarhus (Jutland's 'nose'), is prime summer-holiday territory for hordes of beach-going Danish, Swedish and German families. The area's standout towns are Ebeltoft and Grenaa. Sprawling Grenaa (connected by ferry to Varberg in Sweden) is the larger of the two and the surrounding beaches are better, but Ebeltoft has more charm.

There are some top-notch sandy beaches all over the peninsula (particularly in the north, at Fjellerup, Bønnerup and Gjerrild, and just south of Grenaa), while family-focused, land-based activities range from historic manor houses to animal parks, shark pools and a hugely popular funpark.

Djursland's public-transport connections with Aarhus are excellent. If you have your own wheels, Rte 15 heads out of Aarhus towards Ebeltoft (via Rte 21) and on to Grenaa – but with a little time up your sleeve we recommend taking the rural back roads.

Ebeltoft

POP 7500

Ebeltoft has all the ingredients you need for a summer getaway. Cobblestone streets lined with half-timbered houses, white-sand beaches and a classic warship attract large numbers of ice-cream-eating holidaymakers.

The tourist office, *Fregatten Jylland* (below) and the harbour are along Strandvejen. From the harbour walk a block east on Jernbanegade to reach Adelgade, the main shopping street. Torvet, the town square, is at the southern end of Adelgade.

⊙ Sights & Activities

Fregatten Jylland MUSEUM, SHIP
(www.fregatten-jylland.dk; SA Jensens Vej 4; adult/child Dkr125/80; ⊙ from 10am; ⌨) *Fregatten Jylland* has quite a presence. From bow to stern the frigate is 71m, making it the world's longest wooden ship. It played an instrumental role in Denmark's navy in the 19th century; today it's been restored for visitors – step inside and experience the life of a crew member. Closing time varies, from 3pm in winter to 6pm in peak summer.

Glasmuseet Ebeltoft MUSEUM
(www.glasmuseet.dk; Strandvejen 8; adult/child Dkr85/free; ⊙ 10am-5pm or 6pm daily Apr-Oct, 10am-4pm Wed-Sun Nov-Mar) Contemporary glass art is beautifully showcased at the sleek Glasmuseet, with stunning permanent pieces plus changing exhibitions gracing its light-filled interior. You can also watch glass-blowers working their magic on-site.

Adelgade STREET
Cobbled Adelgade is one of the loveliest main streets in Jutland, lined with pastel-coloured cafes and stores, and pretty courtyards. At its southern end is the diminutive old town hall, built in 1789. It has a half-timbered, chocolate-box appearance (it's a popular spot for weddings) and is now home to local history exhibits (free admission).

Beaches BEACHES
Ebeltoft sits on a calm, protected bay, fringed with white-sand beaches; you'll find a nice stretch right along Ndr Strandvej, the coastal road that leads north from the town centre.

Ree Park Safari SAFARI PARK
(www.reepark.dk; Stubbe Søvej 15; adult/child Dkr160/90kr; ⊙ 10am-4pm or 6pm mid-Apr–mid-Oct; ⌨) Ree Park houses an impressive collection of animals from all corners of the globe, with Africa taking more than the lion's share (pun intended). Visitors can pay extra to ride a camel (Dkr30) or take a Land Rover tour through the 'African savannah' (Dkr45); there are plenty of animal feedings throughout the day. The park is 10km northeast of Ebeltoft (no bus service).

🛏 Sleeping & Eating

Good dining options can be found on Adelgade and at the marina, but it's well worth a trip 6km northwest to the village of Femmøller, a fab fine-dining destination.

★ **Danhostel Ebeltoft**   HOSTEL €
(☑ 86 34 20 53; www.ebeltoft-danhostel.dk; Egedalsvej 5; s/d/tr/q Dkr480/520/570/620; @ 🛜) A map is almost compulsory to find this hostel, perched above the town (3km by road, or about a 25-minute walk). But it's worth the trip, with hotel-standard accommodation (all rooms with bathroom and TV) and some cool design features. Breakfast is Dkr65.

Hotel Ebeltoft Strand   HOTEL €€
(☑ 86 34 33 00; www.ebeltoftstrand.dk; Ndr Strandvej 3; d from Dkr1195; 🛜) In a plum position on the beachfront and close to the tourist office, this sprawling hotel offers good facilities and a range of price options, including standard and deluxe seaview rooms, plus 16 family-sized apartments.

Glascaféen   CAFE €
(www.glasmuseet.dk; Strandvejen 8; mains Dkr48-146; ⊙ daily Apr-Oct, Wed-Sun rest of yr, closed Jan) Behind Glasmuseet Ebeltoft, this small, sleek cafe has a glorious deck overlooking the water. There's a short, flavourful menu

---

MOLS BJERGE NATIONAL PARK

• •

One of the five new national parks created in Denmark in the last few years, **Mols Bjerge National Park** (http://eng.nationalparkmolsbjerge.dk) covers 180 sq km of Djursland forests, moors and open grasslands as well as lakes, coastal areas and the sea. It encompasses the town of Ebeltoft and nearby villages, and is named after the best-known natural feature of the region, Mols Bjerge (Mols Hills – rising to all of 137m).

The Ebeltoft tourist office can give you the necessary literature if you're interested in exploring the park. A dedicated information centre is likely to be built in the not-too-distant future, and will probably be in the vicinity of Kalø (south of Rønde), where you can explore typical park highlights such as forest, an 18th-century manor and ruins of a 14th-century castle.

---

of sandwiches, tapas and *fiskefrikadeller* (fishballs), plus locally brewed beer and soft drinks. The weekend brunch is a beauty, plus it's open until 10pm from July to mid-August (otherwise, closing time is around 4pm).

Molskroen Brasserie   FRENCH, DANISH €€
(www.molskroen.dk; Hovedgaden 31A, Femmøller Strand; mains Dkr195-295; ⊙ 11.30am-9pm Wed-Sun) Molskroen's owners have rejuvenated Femmøller's beach hotel, **Strandhotellet**, with fresh, blue-hued rooms (doubles from Dkr1180) and outstanding dining choices. The **Brasserie** here has perfect pedigree, with Michelin-starred chef Michel Michaud calling the shots. The Franco-Danish menu proffers perfect Gallic classics (duck confit, steak tartare) and lunchtime smørrebrød, or you can opt for a set, three-course feast (Dkr435).

A second restaurant inside Strandhotellet is the high-quality steakhouse **A Hereford Beefstouw**.

★ **Molskroen**   FRENCH €€€
(☑ 86 36 22 00; www.molskroen.dk; Hovedgaden 16, Femmøller; mains Dkr325-445; ⊙ 6-9pm Mon-Sat) For something special, make your way to this acclaimed *kro* (inn), renowned throughout the country and a popular gourmet destination. The restaurant is now under the helm of the same Michelin-starred chef as the Brasserie (above): Michel Michaud. Sample his sublime creations as part of a four-course menu for Dkr595, or go all out with the signature six-course menu including wine for Dkr1795. There are equally impressive suites here, with beautiful, design-heavy doubles starting from Dkr1580.

🛈 Information

Tourist Office (☑ 86 34 14 00; www.visitdjursland.com; SA Jensens Vej 3; ⊙ 9am-4.30pm Mon-Fri, 10am-1pm Sat) Off Strandvejen, next to *Fregatten Jylland*.

🛈 Getting There & Around

Ebeltoft is on Rte 21, 52km east of Aarhus and 33km southwest of Grenaa.

BOAT

Mols-Linien (☑ 70 10 14 18; www.mols-linien.dk) Operates a daily high-speed car ferry between Ebeltoft and Odden in north Zealand (one-way adult/child/car Dkr349/175/699, 70 minutes). Rates for car passage include passengers.

BUS

➜ Bus 123 runs between Aarhus (Nørreport) and Ebeltoft (Dkr85, 1¼ hours).

➜ Bus 212 links Randers and Ebeltoft (Dkr105, 1½ hours).

➜ Bus 351 links Ebeltoft and Grenaa (Dkr57, one hour).

Grenaa

POP 14,600

A purpose-built harbour complete with (captive) sharks, a historic old town and 7km of fine, sandy beaches are the defining attractions of Grenaa. The old town, radiating out from Torvet, is the economic and shopping hub of the district. It's about 3km west of the harbour, where the waterfront is peopled by shark-fanciers and Sweden-bound ferry-goers.

◎ Sights & Activities

Beaches   BEACHES

Grenaa's 7km of Blue Flag–winning beach runs south of town and is where it's at on hot days; this area is known for its child-friendly shallow waters. To get here, follow the coast south from the harbour. The northern end of the beach is a hive of activity, but as you go south it becomes a little more private.

Kattegatcentret   OCEANARIUM

(www.kattegatcentret.dk; Færgevej 4; adult/child Dkr160/90; ⊙10am-4pm or 5pm; ⬥) If you fancy being just inches from a shark and in total control, you'll love the glass tunnel at Kattegatcentret, where the focus is on surrounding sealife. At 1pm you can watch the shark-feeding session – a good way to see just why sharks are at the top of the food chain. There is also a seal pool (and feeding sessions), and a kid-friendly touchpool. Check the website for winter closing dates.

⛺ Sleeping & Eating

The Djursland tourist brochure (published annually) lists private rooms and beachside holiday cottages (usually rented by the week). The region is blanketed with camping grounds.

Grenaa Strand Camping   CAMPGROUND €

(☑86 32 17 18; www.grenaastrandcamping.dk; Fuglsangvej 28; site/adult/child Dkr100/82/60; ⊙Apr–mid-Sep; ⬡⬢⬣⬤) A super option if your visit to Grenaa is all about the beach, this site is in pole beachside position a few kilometres south of town. A pirate theme

(aarghh!), high-season activities for kids, plus minigolf and a swimming pool will keep families happy. Cabins and on-site caravans are well priced; there's also a minimarket and summertime cafe.

Hotel Grenaa Havlund   HOTEL €€

(☑86 32 26 77; www.hotelgrenaahavlund.dk; Kystvej 1; s/d Dkr695/895; 🛜) This sunny little beachfront hotel offers comfy, no-frills rooms about 1km south of the Grenaa harbour area.

Restaurant Skakkes Holm   SEAFOOD €€

(☑86 30 09 89; www.skakkesholm.dk; Lystbådehavnen; dinner buffet incl drinks adult/child Dkr229/72; ⊙lunch Tue-Fri, dinner daily; ⬥) Over a footbridge by Kattegatcentret is the marina, a pleasant little place to explore. Of an evening you'll find hungry folks loading their plates from the impressive buffet at Restaurant Skakkes Holm. Given the surroundings, it's only fitting that the emphasis here is on fish.

❶ Information

Tourist Office (☑87 58 12 00; www.visitdjursland.com; Torvet 6; ⊙10am-4pm Mon-Fri, 10am-1pm Sat) Close to the cathedral, in the main square.

❶ Getting There & Around

Grenaa is 65km northeast of Aarhus on Rte 15 and 58km east of Randers along Rte 16.

BOAT

Stena Line (www.stenaline.com) connects Grenaa with Varberg in Sweden. For more info see p300.

BUS

Buses 120 and 122 run from Aarhus (Nørreport) to Grenaa. Train services also link the two towns (Dkr89, 1¼ to 1½ hours); the train is sightly faster than the bus, but the prices are the same. In Grenaa, buses and trains leave from the station at Stationsplads, a short walk from Torvet; local buses 1 and 2 cover the ground between the centre and the harbour.

Around Djursland

From a base in Djurland's nicest coastal towns (Ebeltoft and Grenaa) you're within easy daytripping distance of yet more family attractions – including one of Denmark's biggest summertime magnets, Djurs Sommerland.

◉ Sights

Gammel Estrup   MUSEUM
(www.gammelestrup.dk; Randersvej 2, Auning; manor & museums adult/child Dkr95/free; ⊙10am-5pm daily mid-Apr–mid-Oct, 10am-3pm or 4pm Tue-Sun rest of yr, closed Jan) On the outskirts of Auning, 33km west of Grenaa, lies this grand manor house, home to two museums, splendid gardens and an aura of Danish gentility.

The moat-encircled manor that is home to **Herregårdsmuseet** (the Manor Museum) has been preserved and presented in much the same way as it was in the 17th century, with antique furniture, elaborate tapestries, historic portraits and glorious views.

Unless you're a farmer, the **Dansk Landbrugsmuseum** (Danish Agricultural Museum; www.gl-estrup.dk) may hold less appeal, but its high-quality exhibits tell the story of Danish farming, food and food culture.

To get here, take bus 212 or 214 from Randers. If you're driving, take Rte 16 between Grenaa and Randers.

Djurs Sommerland   AMUSEMENT PARK
(www.djurssommerland.dk; Randersvej 17, Nimtofte; admission Dkr235-255; ⊙from 10am daily mid-Jun–mid-Aug, also open select days in May, Sep & Oct; ♿) One of Djursland's biggest drawcards is this much-hyped amusement park with arguably the best outdoor rides in Jutland (more than 60, including Denmark's longest roller coaster), plus a waterpark, with pools and waterslides for all ages.

Everyone over the age of three pays the entrance fee; once this is paid, you're free to play to your heart's content. Closing hours vary (from 5pm to 9pm); check the website to confirm opening days and hours.

The park lies 20km west of Grenaa in Nimtofte. Plenty of bus options will get you there – from Aarhus, bus 400 runs directly to the park during the summer peak.

Skandinavisk Dyrepark   ZOO
(www.skandinaviskdyrepark.dk; Nødagervej 67B, Nødagervej; adult/child Dkr175/95; ⊙from 10am mid-Apr–mid-Oct; ♿) Nordic species are top of the food chain here, where the biggest attraction is the impressive polar-bear facility. Other star performers: brown bears, moose, musk ox and wolves. Fallow deer, reindeer and goats can be fed by hand. To reach the park, follow the signs from Kolind or from Rte 15, 2km north of Tirstrup. Bus 120 runs between Aarhus and Grenaa and stops near the park.

THE LAKE DISTRICT

One of Jutland's most prized areas is the Lake District (Søhøjlandet), gently dazzling with hills, forests and lakes not found elsewhere in Denmark. This region is home to Denmark's longest river (the Gudenå, 160km long), Jutland's biggest lake (Mossø) and Denmark's highest point, Møllchøj (a smidge under 171m, bless its cotton socks). It's unlikely to induce nosebleeds, but its a delightful area for rambling and enjoying the superbly pretty scenery.

Silkeborg

POP 43,200

In a flat country, the modern town of Silkeborg is something of a black sheep, surrounded as it is by hills, sitting on an expansive lake and spaciously laid out. Modern-art lovers and history boffins will find cause to stop here, but nature lovers have the most to celebrate. It's Silkeborg's surrounding landscapes that draw tourists – not thrill-seekers but rather families and outdoorsy folk drawn to the lush forests and waterways that are perfect for cycling, rambling and, especially, canoeing.

◉ Sights

Museum Silkeborg   MUSEUM
(www.museumsilkeborg.dk; Hovedgårdsvej 7; adult/child Dkr50/free; ⊙10am-5pm daily May–mid-Oct, noon-4pm Sat & Sun Nov-Apr) Here you can check out the amazingly well-preserved body of the 2350-year-old **Tollund Man**, the central (albeit leathery) star in an otherwise smart but predictable collection. The well-preserved face of the Tollund Man is hypnotic in its detail, right down to the stubble on his chin. Like the Grauballe Man at Aarhus' Moesgård Museum, the life (and death) of the Tollund Man remains a mystery.

His intact remains were found in the outskirts of Silkeborg in 1950, and have been radiocarbon dated to around 350 BC. The autopsy suggests he had been hanged, yet he was placed as though lying asleep with only a leather hat over his face and a thin leather noose around his neck. Was he an executed prisoner, or a sacrifice to the gods? That's the big unanswered question, but the accompanying displays aren't as engrossing as those at Moesgård.

Museum Jorn   ART MUSEUM
(www.museumjorn.dk; Gudenåvej 7-9; adult/child Dkr80/free; ⊙11am-5pm Tue-Fri, 10am-5pm Sat &

Sun) This wonderful art space contains some striking works. It displays many of the works of native son Asger Jorn and other modern artists, including Max Ernst, Le Corbusier and Danish artists from the influential Co-BrA group. It's 1km south of the town centre.

KunstCentret Silkeborg Bad ART MUSEUM
(www.silkeborgbad.dk; Gjessøvej 40; adult/child Dkr60/free; ⊙10am-5pm Tue-Sun May-Sep, noon-4pm Mon-Fri, 11am-5pm Sat & Sun Oct-Apr) This former spa dates from 1883 and is now a beautiful, modern art space, with permanent works and changing exhibitions of art, sculpture, ceramics, glassware, design and architecture, surrounded by parkland (always open) featuring contemporary sculpture. It's about 2km southwest of town; catch local bus 10.

Aqua AQUARIUM
(www.visitaqua.dk; Vejlsøvej 55; adult/child Dkr140/75; ⊙10am-6pm Jul-Aug, shorter hrs rest of yr; ♿) Aqua, 2km south of the town centre, is an entertaining aquarium and exhibition centre built into several outdoor lakes. It explores the ecosystems of the area, with lots of touch-tanks and fishy creatures, cute otters and birds among the imaginative displays.

★**Indelukket** PARK
(Åhave Allé; ♿) Don't miss a stroll through this picturesque riverside park – follow Åhavevej south to reach it. There's a kiosk here, as well as minigolf, a marina and an open-air stage. If you're on foot, it's the desired route to get to Museum Jorn, the campground and points further south.

🏃 **Activities**

The tourist office has oodles of information on the following activities and more (including options such as golf, horse riding and fishing). A good purchase is the *Silkeborg Aktivitetskort* (Activities Map; Dkr50).

Boat Trips

Hjejlen Boat Company BOAT TRIPS
(☑86 82 07 66; www.hjejlen.com; one-way/return Dkr90/140; ⊙May-Sep) The *Hjejlen*, the world's oldest operating paddle steamer, has been plying the waters of the Lake District since it was first launched in 1861. These days the boat shuttles tourists from Silkeborg to the foot of Himmelbjerget during the summer season (10am and 2pm daily, July to mid-August). The operators also have other boats plying the route during this period, and from May to September.

The route takes in a wealth of river and lake scenery and is one of the most popular outings in the Lake District. Boats also stop at Indelukket park and Aqua aquarium.

Canoeing & Kayaking

In the warmer months (May to September), self-guided canoe tours are popular. These take you through some magnificent countryside, and options range from a couple of hours to a couple of days.

You can plan your own tour and consult the various canoe hirers for the finer details – they are a wealth of information and will rent canoes by the hour (Dkr100) or day (Dkr400) and help with transport of gear to the chosen departure point, if necessary. If you don't have your own camping gear, you should also enquire about tent rental (usually possible if arranged a few days in advance).You can expect an average, leisurely day of canoeing to cover about 15km to 20km.

If all you have is a day, recommended options are the 24km round-trip across the lakes east to Himmelbjerget (a harder, more exposed route), or a gentler option travelling with the currents north from Silkeborg to Kongensbro (and taking the bus back to town). Make enquiries with **Silkeborg Kanocenter** (☑86 80 30 03; www.silkeborgkanocenter.dk; Østergade 36; ⊙9am-8pm Jun-Aug, to 5pm Apr, May, Sep; ♿). You can also hire motorboats here (per hour/day Dkr200/900) if the exertion of canoeing doesn't appeal.

Silkeborg Kanocenter has a range of tour options, too (adaptable from two to five days): a **Family Tour** takes you along a route staying in camping grounds where your tent is pre-erected for you. A **Pioneer Tour** is a more challenging option, sleeping at primitive tent sites along the way. If you're a softie who prefers a real bed, a **Luxury Tour** has accommodation and meals arranged at atmospheric old lakeside inns.

Silkeborg Kanocenter also has one-person kayaks for hire (Dkr275 per day), while Silkeborg Kayak og Cykel Udlejning (p226), at the northern end of Indelukket park, has family kayaks available for multiday rental, plus motor dinghies, mountain bikes and lots of good ideas for combining cycling and kayaking in a day tour.

Hiking & Cycling

The tourist office has plenty of brochures on hiking and cycling routes – a worthwhile purchase is either *12 Beautiful Bicycle*

Silkeborg

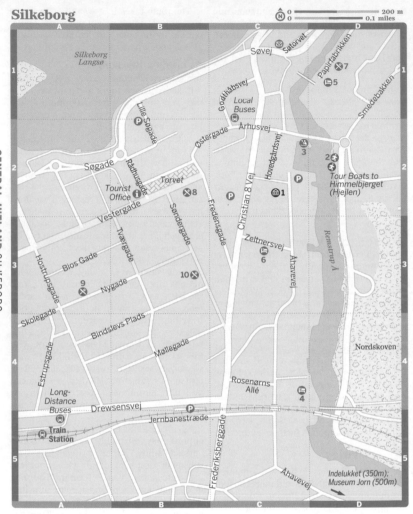

Tours or *12 Lovely Walks in the Lakelands* (Dkr40 each). **Silkeborg Kayak og Cykel Udlejning** (www.skcu.dk; Åhave Allé 7; kayak/ mountain bike per day Dkr350/175; ☺9am-8pm Jun-Aug, to 5pm May, by arrangement Sep, Oct, Apr;) has mountain bikes for hire; for a taster, they suggest taking a bike on the boat to Himmelbjerget and cycling back (15km).

The beech forest of **Nordskoven** is criss-crossed with hiking and bike trails. To reach Nordskoven head south down Åhavevej from the tourist office, then go left over the old railway bridge near the hostel.

The track of the old railway from Silke-borg to Horsens is now an excellent walking and cycling trail of about 50km or so.

The **Hærvej** (www.haervej.com), the Old Military Road, passes through the region (west of Silkeborg). This is a 250km historic route from the German border north to Viborg along the backbone of Denmark; it's been converted into a cycling, hiking and horse-riding trail.

Swimming

For idyllic swimming, head to the lakeshore of **Almindsø**. Head south of town on Fred-eriksberggade and take a left at the roundabout in the direction of Horsens. The swimming area is signposted on your right after 1km; there are bathing jetties, change rooms and a kiosk here.

🎭 Festivals & Events

Riverboat Jazz Festival   MUSIC
(www.riverboat.dk) Scandis love jazz, and Silkeborg has embraced it with the five-day Riverboat Jazz Festival, held in late June. It's not quite New Orleans, but you can buy a ticket and take a cruise down the river, or stroll the streets and take advantage of the free performances.

🛏 Sleeping

Budget and midrange choices in town are limited, making B&B accommodation an especially good (and good-value) option. The website www.silkeborg.com lists all the choices, and the tourist office can help. There are oodles of camping grounds in the region.

★ Villa Zeltner   B&B €
(☑ 29 82 58 58; www.villa-zeltner.dk; Zeltnersvej 4; s/d/apt from Dkr350/500/600; 🛜) Super-central and with loads of style, this great-value B&B houses a handful of rooms with shared bathroom and kitchen access, plus a couple of small apartments with private kitchen and bathroom.There's garden access and a grill, too, plus a few bikes for guest use. Breakfast can be arranged at additional cost.

★ Danhostel Silkeborg   HOSTEL €
(☑ 86 82 36 42; www.danhostel-silkeborg.dk; Åhavevej 55; dm Dkr275, d without/with bathroom Dkr520/720; ☼Mar-Nov; @🛜) The gorgeous riverbank location, good facilities and lack of budget alternatives in town make this hostel popular, so book ahead. Once here, enjoy the outdoor tables and homely communal areas alongside cyclists, families, school groups and Euro-backpackers. Dorm beds are available July to mid-September; breakfast costs Dkr75.

Gudenåens Camping   CAMPGROUND €
(☑ 86 82 22 01; www.gudenaaenscamping.dk; Vejlsøvej 7; per adult/child/site Dkr85/52/70; @🛜🏊) Follow the signs for Aqua to find this tree-filled riverside park, about 2km south of the town centre (just south of Indelukket). Cabins and caravans are available for hire (only by the week in July & August), and there's a lovely natural pool for swimming. Local bus 4 runs down this way.

Silkeborg

◎ Sights	
1 Museum Silkeborg	C2

✦ Activities, Courses & Tours	
2 Hjejlen Boat Company	D2
3 Silkeborg Kanocenter	C2

🛏 Sleeping	
4 Danhostel Silkeborg	C4
5 Radisson BLU Hotel	D1
6 Villa Zeltner	C3

✖ Eating	
7 Café Evald	D1
8 Føtex Supermarket	B2
9 Okkels Is	A3
10 Restaurant Gastronomisk Institut	B3

Radisson BLU Hotel   HOTEL €€
(☑ 88 82 22 22; www.radissonblu.com/hotel-silkeborg; Papirfabrikken 12; d incl breakfast Dkr1125-1575; @🛜) This polished performer lives in the redeveloped paper factory that was once the backbone of the local economy. It's right on the river, among a clutch of restaurants, and the designer rooms are petite but comfy and well equipped. Weekend rates are cheaper than midweek.

✖ Eating

There are two areas to investigate when scouting for eating (and drinking) options: the reinvigorated Papirfabrikken (the old paper factory) and the fast food and international cuisines found on Nygade. End-of-week nightlife clusters around the corner of Nygade and Hostrupsgade.

Okkels Is   ICE CREAM €
(Nygade 26E; 2/3 scoops Dkr28/34; ☼11.30am-10pm Mon-Sat, 12.30-10pm Sun May-Jul, shorter hrs rest of yr; 🚸) Excellent homemade Italian-style ice cream.

Café Evald   INTERNATIONAL €€
(www.evald.nu; Papirfabrikken 10B; lunch Dkr100-150, dinner mains Dkr150-290; ☼11am-midnight or 1am Mon-Sat, 9.30am-9.30pm Sun) Among the family restaurants, cinema and cafe-bars of Papirfabrikken is bustling Evald, wooing patrons with a crowd-pleasing menu. Sit at a riverside table, order a beer from the local Grauballe Bryghus (brewery) and try the 'tapas' plate – a sampler plate comprising five small tastes of seasonal favourites.

HERNING & THE HEART OF ART

If you're a fan of modern art, chances are you've heard of Italian conceptual artist Piero Manzoni (1933–63). What you may not know is that the biggest public collection of his work is not in Milan, but on the eastern fringe of Herning (population 48,000), a regional centre 40km west of Silkeborg. You'll find Manzoni's work, and that of visionaries such as Mario Merz and Man Ray, at **HEART** (www.heartmus.dk; Birk Centerpark 8, Herning; adult/child Dkr75/free; ⊙10am-5pm Tue-Sun), Herning's striking contemporary-art museum. Designed by US architect Steven Holl, its crumpled exterior walls and sleeve-inspired roof honour the collection's founder, Danish shirt manufacturer and passionate art collector Aage Damgaard (1917–91). In the summers of 1960 and 1961, Damgaard invited Manzoni to indulge his creative spirit in Herning. The result: Herning's Manzoni legacy.

Across the street, the **Carl-Henning Pedersen and Else Alfelt Museum** (www. chpeamuseum.dk; Birk Centerpark 1; adult/child Dkr40/free; ⊙10am-4pm Tue-Sun) showcases the riotously colourful paintings, watercolours, mosaics, ceramics and sculptures of artists Carl-Henning Pedersen (1913–2007) and Else Alfelt (1910–74); there's a large sculpture park beyond the museum. Next door to HEART stands Danish architect Jørn Utzon's 1970-designed **Prototype House** (closed to the public), while further south you'll witness artist Ingvar Cronhammar's ominous **Elia**. Attracting lightning, shooting random flames of gas, and looking straight off a *Dr Who* set, it's northern Europe's largest sculpture.

HEART and its neighbours aside, another reason to head to Herning is for an event at **Boxen** (www.mch.dk; Kaj Zartows Vej 7, Herning), a slick indoor sporting arena and concert venue hosting big-name international touring acts (Lady Gaga, for example).

You might consider Herning as a day trip from Silkeborg, easily reached by train (Dkr65, 40 minutes). For the museums, alight at Birk Centerpark station (not Herning station), from where the sights are a short walk. Boxen arena is south of the city, off Hwy 15 (take the train to Herning Messecenter).

★ **Restaurant Gastronomisk Institut** EUROPEAN €€€

(☑86 82 40 97; www.gastronomiske.dk; Søndergade 20; lunch Dkr117-199, dinner mains Dkr199-299; ⊙11.30am-3pm & 5.30-9.30pm Tue-Sat) The ambitious name creates high expectations, and this elegant central restaurant delivers, with changing menus highlighting seasonal produce (and good-value set menus, including four evening courses for Dkr399). Leisurely lunchers might like crayfish soup; dinner ranges from suckling calf to fresh fish. Dinner bookings recommended.

Self-Catering

Føtex Supermarket SUPERMARKET €
(Torvet; ⊙8am-9pm) Central supermarket with on-site bakery and cafe.

ℹ️ Information

Banks and other services are found along the main shopping strip, Vestergade.

Tourist Office (www.silkeborg.com; Torvet 2A; ⊙10am-5pm Mon-Fri, 10am-2pm Sat Jul-Aug, shorter hrs Sep-Jun) Well-stocked office on the main square.

ℹ️ Getting There & Around

Silkeborg is 44km west of Aarhus on Rte 15. Half-hourly trains connect Silkeborg with Aarhus (Dkr85, 50 minutes) via Ry (Dkr39, 15 minutes).

Ry

POP 5700

Mellow, more-rural Ry lies in the heart of the Lake District. It has a pretty duck-filled marina, where you'll find tourist boats to Himmelbjerget and nearby canoe hire. It's surrounded by lovely landscapes and quaint villages perfect for exploring.

🏃 Activities

Ask at Ry's tourist office for leaflets detailing walking, cycling and boating options.

Hjejlen Boat Company BOAT TRIPS
(☑86 82 07 66; www.hjejlen.com; one-way/return Dkr70/100) Schedules three or four boats daily from Ry to Himmelbjerget, operating most days June to August (and weekends in May and September). Boats leave Ry at 10.15am, 12.15pm and 2.15pm (plus 4.15pm

in July), and sail from Himmelbjerget one hour later. It's good to book a day in advance.

Ry Kanofart CANOEING
(☑ 86 89 11 67; www.kanoferie.dk; Kyhnsvej 20; ☺ 9am-6pm daily Jun-Aug, 9am-6pm Sat & Sun May & Sep) Ry Kanofart has canoes for hire, costing Dkr100/400 per hour/day. As with the operators in Silkeborg, staff here can help you plan multiday river trips on the Gudenå and lakes.

Hiking & Cycling

One of the best trails from Ry is the two-hour, 7km walk west to Himmelbjerget. The starting point for the hike is Munkedalsvej, which branches off Rodelundvej just south of the Ry bridge. The signposted path leads to the Himmelbjerget boat dock before climbing the hill to the tower. A nice option is to hike out and catch a boat back to Ry or on to Silkeborg.

Cycling allows you to explore the low-key charms of the area. **Ry Cykler** (☑ 86 89 14 91; Parallelvej 9B; regular/mountain-bike rental per day Dkr75/200; ☺ 8.30am-5.30pm Mon-Fri, 9.30am-noon Sat) is 1.5km east of the train station, towards Skanderborg.

🛏 Sleeping & Eating

Camping grounds are plentiful in the area. There are a few takeaway options and Italian restaurants on Skanderborgvej, or pack a picnic lunch for your hike or ride.

Hotel Blicher HOTEL €€
(☑ 86 89 19 11; www.hotelblicher.dk; Kyhnsvej 2; d standard/superior Dkr990/1250; P @ 🛜) There are two room categories at Ry's only hotel – the superior rooms are newly renovated and a fresher option than the older, unrenovated wing. It's a large, pleasant place, popular for conferences and weddings, and staff can help arrange canoeing and cycling.

Le Gâteau BAKERY €
(Klostervej 12; sandwiches Dkr45; ☺ 7am-5.30pm Mon-Fri, to 2pm Sat, to noon Sun) Flaky pastries, good coffee and handy sandwiches await at this smart little bakery, opposite the Ry train station and tourist office.

La Saison DANISH €
(Kyhnsvej 2; lunch smørrebrød 1/3 pieces Dkr49/125, dinner mains Dkr175; ☺ 11am-9pm) Easily Ry's fanciest dining option, this shiny outfit is attached to Hotel Blicher and has a

lunchtime menu of smørrebrød classics, and a short but high-quality dinner menu.

Kvickly SUPERMARKET €
(Siimtoften 2; ☺ 8am-8pm Mon Fri, 8am-6pm Sat, 10am-6pm Sun) Good for picnic supplies; just back from the marina.

❶ Information

Tourist Office (☑ 86 69 66 00; www.visit skanderborg.com; Klostervej 3; ☺ 10am-4pm Mon-Fri, 10am-noon Sat May-Aug, 10am-2pm Mon-Fri Sep-Apr) Helpful office at the train station.

❶ Getting There & Around

Ry is on Rte 445, 22km southeast of Silkeborg and 35km west of Aarhus. Half-hourly trains connect Ry with Silkeborg (Dkr39, 15 minutes) and Aarhus (Dkr66, 30 minutes).

Himmelbjerget

There's something quite endearing about a country that names one of its highest points Himmelbjerget (meaning 'sky mountain'), especially when that peak only hits 147m. It's a mere hillock to non-Danes, but it does afford charming vistas of the surrounding forests and lakes and is a popular tourist spot, complete with ice-cream kiosks and souvenir stalls ringing the car park.

It costs Dkr10 to park your vehicle. Once you've completed the brief pilgrimage from the car park to the mountaintop, you could climb the 25m tower (another Dkr10), but the view from outside the tower is just as panoramic.

There are a number of memorials in the vicinity, plus marked hiking trails. One trail leads 1km from the mountaintop down to the lakeshore where boats from Ry and Silkeborg dock.

At the boat dock you'll find **Hotel Julsø** (☑ 86 89 80 40; www.hotel-julso.dk; Julsøvej 14; lunch Dkr98-145, 3-course dinner Dkr385; ☺ 11.30am-10pm Mon & Wed-Sat, 11.30am-5pm Tue & Sun, shorter hrs Apr, May, Sep, Oct), a photogenic timber *kro* with a watery panorama and a gourmet menu that highlights the talents of the Italian-born chef. The *kro* can also be reached by road off Rte 445. Events are held here during the summer peak; it's worth calling ahead to reserve a table – and to ensure it's open.

ⓘ Getting There & Away

Himmelbjerget is a 10-minute drive west of Ry on Rte 445. It can also be reached by a pleasant 7km hike from Ry, or by a scenic boat ride from either Ry or Silkeborg.

THE INTERIOR

The landscape of Jutland's interior ranges from hilly woodland up the middle to rolling fields in the east. Industry is prominent throughout, and there are plenty of medium-sized towns that are pleasant enough places to while away a day, but are not particularly worth going out of your way for (no offence to the towns themselves, mind, but we're talking about the likes of Fredericia, Vejle, Horsens, Skive and Holstebro).

Our advice is pretty straightforward – with limited holiday time, head to the towns with the most visitor appeal, be it in the form of Viking relics, historic churches or theme parks.

Jelling

POP 3400

A sleepy town with a big history, Jelling is revered as the birthplace of Christianity in Denmark, the monarchy and all that is truly Danish. The town served as the royal seat of King Gorm during the Vikings' most dominant era; Gorm the Old was the first in a millennium-long chain of Danish monarchs that continues unbroken to this day. The site of Gorm's ancient castle remains a mystery, but other vestiges of his reign can still be found at Jelling Kirke.

The town is a kind of spiritual touchstone for the Danes, Virtually all of them will visit at some point, to pay homage at the church, inspect the two rune stones and climb the burial mounds. The area became a Unesco World Heritage Site in 1994.

◉ Sights

Jelling Kirke   CHURCH
(www.jellingkirke.dk; Vejlevej; ⊙ 8am-8pm May-Aug, to 6pm Sep-Oct & Mar-Apr, to 5pm Nov-Feb) Inside this small whitewashed church, erected around 1100, are some vividly restored 12th-century **frescoes**; the main attractions, however, are the two well-preserved **rune stones** just outside the church door.

The smaller stone was erected in the early 10th century by King Gorm the Old in honour of his wife. The larger one, raised by Gorm's son, Harald Bluetooth, is adorned with the oldest representation of Christ found in Scandinavia and is commonly dubbed 'Denmark's baptismal certificate'.

The stone reads: 'King Harald ordered this monument to be made in memory of Gorm his father and Thyra his mother, the Harald who won for himself all Denmark and Norway and made the Danes Christians.' A replica of the stone (in full colour, as the original would once have appeared) is at Kongernes Jelling, opposite the church.

Harald Bluetooth did, in fact, succeed in routing the Swedes from Denmark and began the peaceful conversion of the Danish people from the pagan religion celebrated by his father to Christianity.

Two large **burial mounds** flank Jelling Kirke. The barrow to the north was long believed to contain the bones of Gorm and his queen, Thyra, but when it was excavated in 1820 no human remains were found. The southern mound was excavated in 1861 but, again, no mortal remains unearthed.

In the 1970s archaeologists dug beneath Jelling Kirke itself and hit pay dirt. They found the remains of three earlier wooden churches; the oldest is thought to have been erected by Harald Bluetooth. A burial chamber was also unearthed and human bones and gold jewellery were discovered. Archaeologists now believe that the remains are those of Gorm, who had originally been buried in the northern mound but was later reinterred by his son. Presumably Harald Bluetooth, out of respect, moved his parents' remains from pagan soil to a place of honour within the church. The bones of Queen Thyra have yet to be found.

Archaeological investigations in the area are ongoing. Read about them online (http://jelling.natmus.dk), or learn more at Kongernes Jelling.

Kongernes Jelling   MUSEUM
(http://natmus.dk/en/royal-jelling; Gormsgade 23) **FREE** In summer 2015, a newly expanded visitors centre will open opposite the church. Expect high-quality interactive exhibitions: before its expansion, Kongernes Jelling provided enthralling insight into the town's monuments and their importance to Danish royal history. The museum is part of the National Museum organisation; check the website for opening hours.

✖ Eating

Sleeping options are best in nearby Givskud or Billund (about 20km west). There's a supermarket and a bakery for picnic supplies.

Byens Café   CAFE €€
(www.byenshus.com; Møllegade 10; lunch Dkr50-95, dinner mains Dkr80-219; ⊙ noon-9pm Tue-Sat, 11am-5pm Sun) Byens Hus (The Town's House) is home to the local library, cinema, gallery and a spacious cafe serving quality all-day dishes. Inside you'll see the big copper vats of the local microbrewery, Jelling Bryggeri, and you can also sample the wares.

Jelling Kro   TRADITIONAL DANISH €€
(www.jellingkro.dk; Gormsgade 16; lunch Dkr75-125, dinner mains Dkr98-210; ⊙ 11am-9.30pm daily Jun-Aug, shorter hrs rest of yr) In a 1780 bright-yellow building bristling with character, this country inn serves up traditional, meat-heavy Danish fare.

ℹ Information

Jelling Kirke is in the centre of town, a three-minute walk due north from the train station along Stationsvej. Tourist information will likely be offered at Kongernes Jelling when it reopens. There is online information at www.visitvejle.com.

ℹ Getting There & Away

Jelling is 10km northwest of Vejle on Rte 442. From Vejle, trains run at least hourly on weekdays, less frequently at weekends (Dkr30, 15 minutes). Bus 211 covers the same ground for the same price.

Givskud

It's a decent leap from Christianity to lions (or is it?), but if you're in need of a fun family distraction, **Givskud Zoo** (www.givskudzoo.dk; Løveparkvej 3, Givskud; adult/child Dkr190/100; ⊙ from 10am daily mid-Apr–mid-Oct; ⚑), 8km northwest of Jelling, can provide. It's an entertaining safari park with plenty of African animals, and you can explore certain areas from the comfort of your own car or in the park-run safari buses (Dkr30). Walking trails take you past elephant and gorilla enclosures; for littlies there's a petting zoo. Closing times vary (from 4pm to 8pm). Bus 211 runs regularly to the zoo from Vejle, via Jelling.

Close to the zoo's entrance is the **Danhostel Givskud Zoo** (☎ 75 73 05 00; www.givskud-zoo.dk; Løveparkvej 2B; dm/s/d Dkr200/580/680; ⊛), which makes a useful budget option for the region (it's only 23km from here to Legoland). All rooms have bathrooms, and the decor is littered with cheerful hints of wild animals. Breakfast costs Dkr70.

Billund & Legoland

POP 6200

The attractions of the 'company town' of Billund (built around a little Danish product you might know: Lego) are so geared to families you might feel a little, well, underdressed if you visit without your own set of excited offspring; but don't let that stop you from embracing your inner child and allocating Legoland some generous time in your itinerary.

◉ Sights & Activities

★**Legoland**   AMUSEMENT PARK
(www.legoland.dk;   Nordmarksvej;   adult/child Dkr309/289; ⊙ 10am-8pm or 9pm Jul–mid-Aug, shorter hrs Apr-Jun & Sep-Oct, closed Nov-Mar; ⚑) Mind-blowing Lego models, fun rides and the happy-family magic associated with great theme parks have transformed Legoland into Denmark's most visited tourist attraction outside of Copenhagen. It's a great day outing (you'll need a day to do it justice), and it sits smack-bang in the middle of Jutland, 1km north of Billund.

The heart of Legoland is **Miniland** – 20 million plastic Lego blocks snapped together to create miniature cities and replicate global icons (and recreate scenes from *Star Wars* movies).

You can't help but marvel at the brilliant Lilliputian models of the Kennedy Space Centre, Amsterdam, Bergen or a Scottish castle, and you'll no doubt vow to head home and drag your Lego out of storage to see what masterpiece you can create (surely it's not that hard?). In Miniland you can also do some advance sightseeing of Danish landmarks including Copenhagen's Nyhavn, Ribe, Skagen or various royal palaces. Or take a trip in miniboats past landmarks such as the Statue of Liberty, the Acropolis and an Egyptian temple. The reconstructions are on a scale of 1:20 to 1:40 and the attention to detail is incredible. The park's largest piece, a model of Indian chief Sitting Bull, was built with 1.4 million Lego bricks. (The smallest piece? A Miniland dove, built of four small white bricks.)

ℹ LEGOLAND PRACTICALITIES

Legoland is no doubt the reason you're in Billund. To maximise your time, consider buying your tickets online to avoid the queues (you can also buy tickets at most accommodation providers in the area). Note that adult tickets are for those aged 13 and over; infants under two years are free. Seniors over 65 pay the child's price. To enable a cheaper second day at the park, visit a ticket booth with your ticket and pay an additional Dkr99. Car parks in the area charge Dkr50.

Inside Legoland you'll find a bank, ATMs, lockers, a baby room, pushchair rental and almost anything else you might need. Do we need to mention there's a huge, busy Lego shop?

Closing times vary – from 6pm to 9pm. Also worth knowing (and not well publicised) is that the park opens its gates a half-hour before the rides close, and no ticket is necessary to enter at this time. Rides normally close one or two hours before the park itself (check the website), so with a bit of luck you could end up with 2½ hours to browse and check out Miniland for free.

Pick up a map to assist with further exploration. The park is divided into themed areas, including **Legoredo Town**, a Wild West area that's home to a cool new haunted house; **Knights' Kingdom**, where a medieval castle awaits; **Pirate Land**, which hosts ships, sword-play and a swimming area; **Adventure Land**, a strange hybrid of Indiana Jones meets Egypt; **Polar Land**, with a big new roller coaster and a penguin habitat; and **Duplo Land**, with plenty of safe, simple rides and activities for littlies.

For some downtime stop by **Atlantis**, an aquarium built around Lego models of divers and submersibles. For the chilled park-goer there are placid rides, from merry-go-rounds to a tranquil train ride; adrenalin-junkies should seek out the roller coasters. Once the entrance fee is paid, all rides are free – the only exception is the SEAT Driving School (Dkr70), for kids aged seven to 13.

Lego House   CULTURAL CENTRE

Expected to open in 2016 in the heart of Billund town, Lego House is an 'experience centre' with a bold and *fun* design that resembles a stack of gigantic Lego bricks. It will incorporate exhibition areas, rooftop gardens, a cafe, a Lego store and a covered public square, and is expected to attract 250,000 visitors annually.

Lalandia   ENTERTAINMENT COMPLEX

(www.lalandia.dk; Ellehammers Allé; Aquadome adult/child Dkr220/170, Monky Tonky Dkr50; 🚼) Adding to the extreme family-friendly focus of Billund is Lalandia, a showy entertainment complex that's like Vegas for kids (there's also a Lalandia in southern Lolland).

This huge roofed complex (where the sky is always blue and temperature warm) is free to enter – once inside, you pay for activities such as the Aquadome waterpark, Monky Tonky playland, minigolf, tenpin bowling and a smorgasbord of sports activities. There are free kids concerts, too, and a handful of restaurants and shops.

There's also an associated estate of holiday houses for rent ('residents' access the Aquadome and Monky Tonky for free) – see the website for more information.

🛌 Sleeping

Billund hotels are pricey, but they're all busy catering to a market focused firmly on family fun (colourful decor, playrooms, peak-summer activities etc). A good nearby budget option is Danhostel Givskud Zoo (p231). Advance bookings are recommended.

★ Legoland Holiday
Village   CAMPGROUND, HOSTEL €€

(📞 75 33 27 77; www.legoland-village.dk; Ellehammers Allé; campsite Dkr258, d room/cabin Dkr1750/1175; @ 🛜) Taking everything up a notch with marvellous Lego detail, this outstanding 'village' encompasses the **Pirate's Inn Hotel** and a huge campground. In the hotel, pirate-themed rooms sleep up to five and include bathroom, wi-fi, TV and linen, plus kitchen access. Self-contained cabins are available (choose standard or with a 'Wild West' theme) plus Indian-style tepee tents.

The campground is enormous, and well-equipped. Families will love the minigolf, playground and petting zoo. There's also a restaurant on-site (breakfast buffet adult/child Dkr80/40; hostel rates include breakfast).

Zleep Hotel   HOTEL €€

(☑ 24 61 06 35; www.zleephotels.com; Billund Airport; d Dkr599-1299; @ 🖝) If you can do without the frills, bright Zleep (part of a chain) is beside the airport terminal and offers simple, comfy rooms sleeping up to four, all with bathroom and TV. Advance online bookings bring the best rates; breakfast costs Dkr75. There's also bike rental available (handy for covering the 2km to Legoland).

Hotel Propellen   HOTEL €€

(☑ 75 33 81 33; www.propellen.dk; Nordmarksvej 3; s/d/f Dkr1348/1498/1948; @ 🖝 🛋) Compared to other places in town, Propellen has a grown-up feel, but still caters to families with its indoor pool, playroom and playground. Adults will enjoy the sauna, Jacuzzis, fitness centre and restaurant.

★ Hotel Legoland   HOTEL €€€

(☑ 75 33 12 44; www.hotellegoland.dk; Aastvej 10; d standard/themed room from Dkr1655/2955; @ 🖝) Lego is *everywhere* here, alongside spectacular kid-friendly detail – but there's also plenty of appeal for grown-ups in this 223-room hotel. Standard rooms are unremarkable, though high quality. Where this place shines is in the family rooms, and the utterly fabulous themed rooms (choose from knight, princess, pirate and kingdom themes) – but these come at a premium.

Packages usually include parking, buffet breakfast and two days' park admission.

✖ Eating

There are offerings within Legoland and inside Lalandia, and restaurants attached to the hotels, or you can head into the town-ship of Billund itself, which has a big supermarket, good bakery-cafe, pizzerias and a few other options (priced more for locals than for tourists).

Within Legoland there are picnic spots, plus restaurants and outlets selling the usual takeaway fare. The names of these simple eateries – Burger House, The Hotdog Company – should cause no confusion over what they serve. Options for sit-down fare include the Family Buffet (adult/child Dkr199/119) or Italian Pizza & Pasta (mains Dkr89 to Dkr179), both near the park entrance. From the park you can also access the Legoland Hotel Restaurant.

Legoland Hotel Restaurant   BUFFET €€€

(☑ 75 33 12 44; Aastvej 10; dinner mains Dkr220-295; ☺ lunch & dinner; ♨) A large, light-filled place with a comprehensive kids' menu. The buffet lunch (adult/child Dkr198/78) and dinner (Dkr285/135) represent decent value, and kids (adults, too) will love the potatoes shaped like Lego bricks. An à la carte menu is also offered. Reservations recommended.

Pirate's Inn   BUFFET €€

(Ellehammers Allé 2; buffet adult/child Dkr198/99; ☺ dinner; ♨) At the Holiday Village is this more-economical option, serving an Italian buffet every evening. It also offers takeaway options.

❶ Information

Legoland Holidays (☑ 96 23 47 92; www.legolandholidays.dk) Official agency that can organise accommodation packages.

PLASTIC FANTASTIC

A carpenter by trade, Ole Kirk Christiansen turned his tools to making wooden toys in Billund when business was slow during a Depression-era slump in 1932. Christiansen came up with the business name Lego, a contraction of *leg godt,* meaning 'play well' in Danish (in a beautiful piece of symmetry, *lego* can mean 'I put together' in Latin). What followed was a heart-warming story showing that 'from little things big things grow'. By the late 1940s Lego became the first Danish company to acquire a plastics-injection moulding machine for toy production and began making interlocking plastic blocks called 'binding bricks' – the forerunner of today's Lego blocks.

In 1960 the wooden-toy warehouse went up in flames, and Lego decided to focus production on its plastic toys instead. Lego blocks soon became the most popular children's toy in Europe – in 2000 *Fortune* magazine named the Lego brick 'toy of the century'.

The statistic are incredible: enough Lego has been produced to supply 52 bricks to every person on the planet. And seven Lego boxes are sold every second.

The company (but not the theme park) is still owned by Ole Kirk's descendants; primary concept and development work takes place at the Billund headquarters.

Tourist Office (⏾79 72 72 99; www.visit
billund.dk; Hans Jensensvej 6; ⊘9am-3pm
Mon-Fri year-round, until 5.30pm in Jul plus
10am-2pm Sat) In Billund township, 1km southwest of Legoland.

❶ Getting There & Away

AIR

Billund airport (www.billundairport.dk) sits almost right outside Legoland's gate, serving not
only Legoland but most of Jutland. Because of
its central location, it has grown into Denmark's
second-busiest airport.

There's a comprehensive schedule of direct
flights from Billund to various Scandinavian and
European cities, provided by SAS and British
Airways. **Ryanair** (www.ryanair.com) connects
Billund with London (Stansted), Milan, Rome,
Barcelona and more.

BUS

There's no train service to Billund (a new rail
connection is planned, but this won't be completed until 2020).

If you're travelling by train, the most common
route is to disembark at Vejle and catch a bus
from there. Bus 43 runs between Vejle and Billund airport (Dkr60, 30 minutes); bus 143 runs
a slower route from Vejle and stops at Legoland
(Dkr60, 40 minutes), Billund town centre and
the airport.

Buses run up to 10 times daily between Aarhus
and Billund airport (Dkr160kr, one hour). Other
buses run to the airport from major Jutland
towns including Esbjerg, Ribe and Kolding.

To plan your travel, use www.rejseplanen.dk.

CAR

Billund is on Rte 28, 59km northeast of Esbjerg
and 28km west of Vejle.

International car-rental agencies have offices
at the airport.

❶ Getting Around

Billund Bike (⏾72 18 55 70; www.billundbike.dk;
Butikstorvet 6; ⊘10am-6pm Mon-Fri, 10am-noon
Sat & Sun) offers bike rental for Dkr80 per day.

Most local buses stop at Billund town centre,
Legoland and the airport. A free summertime
shuttle bus (late June to mid-August) connects
the accommodation and attractions of Billund
with the town centre and airport.

Randers

POP 61,200

Randers' appeal lies predominantly in its
most flaunted attraction – a triple-domed
zoo that mesmerises families and wild-
life-enthusiasts alike. Industrial pursuits
are still the heartbeat of the city but there's
also history and culture if you know where
to look.

⊙ Sights & Activities

Randers Regnskov   ZOO
(www.regnskoven.dk; Tørvebryggen 11; adult/child
Dkr170/100; ⊘10am-4pm or later; ⏺) Randers' most-visited attraction is this dome-
enclosed tropical zoo (*'regnskov'* translates
to rainforest), where the temperature is always a humid 20°C to 30°C (remember to
dress accordingly). Trails within the sultry
domes pass through impressive enclosures
housing crocodiles, monkeys, pythons,
iguanas, orchids, hibiscus and other rainforest flora and fauna. The South American
dome is a standout (the others represent
Africa and Asia), as waterfalls and an abundance of wildlife engulf you. Closing times
vary, from 4pm to 6pm, check the website
for more information.

**Graceland
Randers**   MUSEUM, ENTERTAINMENT COMPLEX
(www.elvispresley.dk; Graceland Randers Vej 3;
museum adult/child Dkr99/69; ⊘10am-9pm)
Two kilometres southeast of Randers'
town centre is the **Elvis Presley Museum**, housed in a replica Graceland mansion (double the size of the original) that
opened in 2011. True, you don't expect to
find a shrine to the King in regional Denmark, but one mad-keen local fan has
proved his dedication in building this
showcase for his personal collection of
memorabilia. Inside the kitschy complex
there's also a well-stocked Elvis shop,
American diner and mini movie theatre.
Thankyouverymuch.

**Historic
Buildings**   HISTORIC NEIGHBOURHOOD
The most interesting part of Randers is
its central area, a hotchpotch of architecture with some antique gems alongside
more-modern eyesores. Hunt down the
pearls, and the stories behind them, with
the *Star Route* brochure, free from the
tourist office. It outlines a self-guided tour
around town, highlighting the likes of the
late-15th-century **Paaskesønnernes Gård**
(Rådhustorvet 7); **Helligåndshuset** (Eric Men-
veds Plads), once part of a medieval monastery; and the imposing red medieval **Sankt
Mortens Kirke** (Kirketorvet).

🛏 Sleeping

There's not a great deal of accommodation in town; many families visit Randers Regnskov from nearby holiday hotspots such as Djursland.

Stephansen Hotel & Restaurant BOUTIQUE HOTEL €€
(☑86 44 27 77; www.stephansenshotel.dk; Møllestræde 4; s/d incl breakfast Dkr750/1095) Just 200m north of the tourist office is this petite, family-owned gem of a hotel, with seven fresh, pristine-white rooms. A sweet courtyard garden and small restaurant are attached.

Hotel Randers HOTEL €€
(☑86 42 34 22; www.hotel-randers.dk; Torvegade 11; d/ste Dkr1145/1495; 🛜) This is an old-world, art deco treasure. It was built in 1856, refurbished in the 1920s and has retained its unique style. The decor is rich and individualised – if you can afford to upgrade to an 'antique room' you can live the high life for a night. Online deals available.

🍴 Eating

At mealtimes, good hunting grounds are around Rådhustorvet and along Storegade.

Café Borgen CAFE €
(Houmeden 10; light meals Dkr39-67; ⊘10am-10pm Mon-Thu, to 2am Fri & Sat, 11.30am-6pm Sun) Borgen offers a little slice of Euro-life, with Parisian-style outdoor seating and a low-lit interior. Home to rich coffee and lazy lunches, it morphs into an inviting spot for evening drinks.

Café Mathisen INTERNATIONAL €€
(www.cafemathisen.dk; Torvegade 11; lunch Dkr89-139, dinner mains Dkr139-269; ⊘11am-11pm Mon-Sat) Part of the delightful Hotel Randers, the Mathisen has elegant black-and-white decor that brings to mind the art deco era. Its lunch offerings are light and simple (club sandwich, Caesar salad), and it's not too fancy to put a burger next to stuffed poussin on the evening menu.

❶ Information

The train station is west of the city centre. It's a 12-minute walk from there via Vestergade to Rådhustorvet, the central square.

Tourist Office (☑86 42 44 77; www.visitranders.com; Rådhustorvet 4; ⊘10am-5pm Mon-Fri, 10am-1pm Sat Apr-Oct, 10am-5pm Mon-Fri

Nov-Mar) Plenty of local information; offers bike hire.

❶ Getting There & Around

Randers is 76km south of Aalborg and 36km north of Aarhus on the E45, and 41km east of Viborg on Rte 16. All trains between Aarhus (Dkr58, 30 minutes) and Aalborg (Dkr111, 50 minutes) stop here, at the station on Jernbanegade, west of the city centre.

Rebild Bakker & Rold Skov

The heart-warming story of Rebild Bakker (the Rebild Hills) dates back to 1912, when a group of Danish-Americans presented 200 hectares of (previously privately owned) forest to the Danish government on the proviso that it would remain in a natural state, be open to all visitors and be accessible to Danish-Americans for celebration of US holidays.

This act of goodwill inspired the Danish forest service to acquire adjacent woodland and collectively the 80-sq-km area is now known as **Rold Skov** (Rold Forest; Denmark's largest). The area has good walks and mountain-biking trails that take you through rolling heather-covered hills, while its woods contain European aspen, beech and oak trees.

Rebild Bakker is a sleepy, albeit scenic, place (more a day-trip destination), but it's now positioning itself as an outdoor-activity centre for cross-country runners and mountain-bikers. The tourist office has info on all activities in the area, including canoeing, fishing, horse riding and golf.

Restaurants and a couple of small museums are close to the striking new building known as RebildPorten, housing the tourist office and some nicely done local exhibits. RebildPorten is beside the car park at the national park's entrance.

🏃 Activities

Walking

There are numerous walking trails criss-crossing the park. One 4km route begins in a sheep meadow west of the car park. It goes past **Tophuset**, a small century-old thatched house (now a cafe) that was built by the first caretakers; the neighbouring **Blokhusmuseet**, modelled on the log cabin that US president Abraham Lincoln grew up in; a large glacial boulder called **Cimbrerstenen**, sculpted in the form of a Cimbrian

WORTH A TRIP

HOBRO & FYRKAT

The pleasant but unremarkable town of Hobro (populaton 11,700) lies at the mouth of the Mariager Fjord, well connected by train and road to the larger towns of Randers (27km southeast) and Aalborg (49km north).

Hobro's biggest asset lies in a rural setting 3km southwest of the town centre and stems from the Viking era: **Fyrkat** (www.nordmus.dk; Fyrkatvej; adult/child entry to Vikingecenter Fyrkat Dkr60/free; ☺10am-5pm Jun-Aug, to 4pm May, to 3pm Sep), a 10th-century ring fortress. Although it's smaller than the better-known Trelleborg in Zealand, Fyrkat so closely resembles Trelleborg that both fortresses are presumed to have been built by the Viking king Harald Bluetooth around 980. Fyrkat was excavated by archaeologists in the 1950s, but its function remains a mystery – it may have been a regional power centre or barracks.

Today, as you walk out onto the grass-covered 3m-high circular ramparts, you can absorb the fort's impressive symmetrical design and note the four cuts in its earthen walls, formerly imposing gates that faced the four points of the compass.

Although no structures remain within the ramparts, just outside is a replica Viking longhouse built utilising a stave-style construction technique. At the entrance to Fyrkat there are some period farm buildings, including a 200-year-old working water mill.

Complementing the fortress is **Vikingecenter Fyrkat** (www.nordmus.dk; Fyrkatvej; adult/child incl entry to Fyrkat Dkr60/free; ☺10am-5pm Jun-Aug, to 4pm May, to 3pm Sep; 👪), a Viking-style farmstead 1km north. Archaeologists believe such farms existed around the fortress walls, supplying encamped Vikings with fresh produce. This complex took more than a decade to erect, using only materials and tools authentic to the period; the 33m longhouse is particularly impressive. Costumed interpreters provide demonstrations of silverwork, archery, breadmaking, music and other Viking crafts.

Travellers with kids in tow will love the fabulous **mythical playground** next door to the complex.

To find out more about ring fortresses, see the Trelleborg section (p122).

bull's head by Anders Bundgaard; a hollow where 4th of July celebrations are held; and **Sønderland**, the park's highest hill (102m). It's a particularly lovely stroll in summer and autumn, when the heather adds a purple tinge to the hillsides.

Mountain Biking

The park is a magnet for mountain-bikers, and there are loads of bike trails. The popular 25km 'Blue Route' journeys past lakes and through forested hills.

Skørping Cykler   BIKE HIRE
(✆98 39 13 05; www.skørpingcykler.dk; Møldrupvej 10) Bike hire and route info is available from this operator in Skørping; city/mountain bikes cost Dkr125/250 per day.

✯ Festivals & Events

Rebild Festival   CULTURAL
(www.rebildfesten.dk) The Rebild Festival is an annual 4th of July celebration (held since 1912) that is the biggest outside the USA and features musicians and high-profile guest-speakers (Danish and American). The

festival's popularity has waned over the decades; attendances have dropped from highs of 10,000 to around 4000. International guests tend to stay in Aalborg.

🛏 Sleeping & Eating

Danhostel Rebild   HOSTEL €
(✆98 39 13 40; www.danhostelrebild.dk; Rebildvej 23; dm/s/d Dkr250/395/450; @ 🀢) Sitting pretty under its thatched roof, this hostel is of a typically good standard. Rooms are in an annexe behind the old main building and all have their own bathroom.

Comwell Sport Rebild Bakker   HOTEL
(✆98 39 12 22; www.comwellsport.dk; Rebildvej 36; d Dkr900; 🀢🏊) Marketing itself as a 'sports hotel', this sprawling complex promotes active holidays and backs it up with an indoor pool, sauna, gym, healthy options in its restaurant, free mountain bikes for guest use, and daily training sessions (yoga, boxing, water aerobics, running, cycling). Rooms are modern and comfy. Best rates are found online.

ℹ Information

Tourist Office (☏ 99 88 90 00; www.visit rebild.dk; Rebildvej 25a; ⊙10am-5pm Tue-Sun) Helpful staff, based inside the information centre known as RebildPorten. Has maps and brochures of the area, plus exhibits on the nature and folklore of the forest.

ℹ Getting There & Away

Rte 180 runs through the Rold Skov forest, connecting Rebild Bakker with Hobro, 23km to the south.

Trains running between Aalborg (Dkr50, 25 minutes) and Aarhus (Dkr160, 70 minutes) stop in Skørping, from where it's 3km west to Rebild Bakker. Bus 104 runs a handful of times between Skørping and Rebild Bakker (Dkr20) on weekdays only.

By train from Skørping, you can also reach nearby towns such as Hobro and Randers.

Viborg

POP 38,600

Rich in religious history and bordering two idyllic lakes, Viborg is a sweetly romantic getaway. During its holiest period (just prior to the Reformation), 25 churches lined the streets. Nowadays, only two can be found in the town centre.

◉ Sights & Activities

Viborg Domkirke   CHURCH
(www.viborgdomkirke.dk; Sankt Mogens Gade 4; admission Dkr10; ⊙11am-5pm Mon-Sat, noon-5pm Sun May-Aug, until 3pm Sep-Apr) The striking, twin-towered cathedral is equally impressive inside and out, with **frescoes,** painted over five years (1908–13) by artist Joakim Skovgaard, evocatively portraying the story of the Protestant bible. In 1876 the cathedral was almost entirely rebuilt, becoming the largest granite church in Scandinavia (an enduring claim to fame). The crypt is all that survives from its birth date of 1100.

Skovgaard Museet   MUSEUM
(www.skovgaardmuseet.dk; Domkirkestræde 2-4; adult/child Dkr50/free; ⊙10am-5pm Tue-Sun Jun-Aug, 11am-4pm Tue-Sun Sep-May) Just outside the cathedral, this museum highlights further work of cathedral-artist Joakim Skovgaard, among other works by his contemporaries, plus changing exhibitions.

Historic Quarter   HISTORIC NEIGHBOURHOOD
The old part of town lies just to the north and west of the cathedral; the tourist-office

brochure outlines a map and important monuments and buildings. **Sankt Mogens Gade** has a charming pocket of homes from the mid-16th century, including Den Hauchske Gård at No 7, Villadsens Gård at No 9A, and Den Gamle Præstegård at No 11. B&Bs can also be found here.

Viborg Museum   MUSEUM
(www.viborgmuseum.dk; Hjultorvet 4; adult/child Dkr40/free; ⊙11am-5pm Tue-Sun Jul–mid-Aug, shorter hrs rest of yr) This local history museum tells the story of Viborg's rich religious past.

Margrethe I   BOAT TRIPS
(adult/child Dkr50/30; ⊙2pm mid-May–Aug) Jump onboard the *Margrethe I* for a one-hour cruise of the town lakes. There are additional cruises from mid-June (at 3.15pm); the boat departs from outside Golf Salonen on Randersvej. The surrounding park is lovely; from mid-May to September you can rent canoes and rowboats from the park kiosk for lake exploration.

🛏 Sleeping & Eating

Danhostel Viborg   HOSTEL €
(☏86 67 17 81; www.danhostelviborg.dk; Vinkelvej 36; dm/s/d Dkr210/415/515; ⊙mid-Jan–Nov; @🛜) This well-run place feels like a country escape, 3km from town in green surrounds and backed by botanic gardens down to the lakeshore. Rooms are top-notch, too (most with bathrooms). Note that the town's camping ground is next door. No bus services.

Oasen   GUESTHOUSE €€
(☏86 62 14 25; www.oasenviborg.dk; Nørregade 13; s/d Dkr400/550, with bathroom Dkr450/650; 🛜) Oasen is an inviting complex of central rooms and apartments, nicely bridging the gap between hostels and business hotels. Some rooms have shared bathroom, but all have cable TV and free wi-fi, plus kitchen access. Breakfast (Dkr75) is taken in a sweet little 'cafe' in the garden.

★ Niels Bugges Hotel   BOUTIQUE HOTEL €€
(☏86 63 80 11; www.nielsbuggeskro.dk; Egeskovvej 26, Hald Ege; d Dkr1250-1450, without bathroom Dkr790; 🛜) This old inn, set amid forest on the outskirts of town, is a destination hotel where design and gastronomy are taken seriously and the result is something special. Rooms epitomise farmhouse chic, all florals, patchworks and antiques. Add a library, romantic grounds and wonderful New Nordic–inspired restaurant, **Skov** (meaning 'forest'), and you too will be dreading checkout.

WORTH A TRIP

HENNE KIRKEBY KRO

Tucked away in a scenic, off-the-radar part of west Jutland, about halfway between Esbjerg (40km south) and Hvide Sande (36km north) is Henne Kirkeby. This tiny hamlet is home to the idyllic **Henne Kirkeby Kro** (🖂 75 25 54 00; hennekirkebykro.dk; Strandvejen 234, Henne; dinner Dkr975), the kind of historic inn that Copenhagen gourmands will happily travels hours to reach. In the kitchen at the *kro* is Paul Cunningham, a British-born chef who has worked in many of Denmark's best kitchens, and whose previous restaurant, Copenhagen's The Paul, was awarded a Michelin star. Deluxe, design-driven accommodation here befits the status of destination inn (rooms from Dkr1475); the menu is a thing of beauty, drawing on the enormous kitchen garden and excellent local produce.

Skov has a great seafood buffet on Friday nights, year-round, (Dkr348; reservations required). The hotel's owners also have the nearby **Niels Bugges Kro** in lakeside Dollerup. The *kro* houses a more traditional **restaurant** (open noon-9pm daily) and offers row-boat rental, plus there's an annexe in the countryside with yet more idyllic accommodation.

To reach the hotel from Viborg, take Rte 13 south then follow signs for 'Hald Ege'. Bus 53 runs out this way.

Café Morville   INTERNATIONAL €€
(www.cafemorville.dk; Hjultorvet; lunch Dkr69-124, dinner dishes Dkr69-179; ⊙10am-10pm Mon & Tue, to 11pm Wed & Thu, to 1am Fri & Sat, 11am-5pm Sun; 🛜) One of those chic all-day cafes that seem compulsory in Danish towns. You can park yourself on the leather banquettes for a mid-morning coffee or late-night drink and everything in between.

❶ Information

Banks and other services can be found on Sankt Mathias Gade.

Tourist Office (🖂 87 87 88 88; www.visit viborg.dk; Skottenborg 12-14; ⊙10am-5pm Mon-Fri, to 2pm Sat Jun-Aug, 10am-4pm Mon-Fri Sep-May) Clued up on the area, with good brochures and maps, plus bike hire (Dkr100 per day). This office is a little out of the centre;

there's a smaller second branch inside the Viborg Museum on central Hjultorvet.

❶ Getting There & Away

Viborg is 66km northwest of Aarhus on Rte 26 and 44km west of Randers on Rte 16. Regular trains run to/from Aarhus (Dkr138, 70 minutes). The train station is 1km southwest of the cathedral.

CENTRAL WEST COAST

The sweeping, windswept coastline of the central west is dotted with small settlements full of campgrounds and holiday houses, catering primarily to German and Danish summer tourists. The fjordside town of **Ringkøbing** (population 9700) is a pleasant, if unremarkable, place acting as a service centre for the beachside communities – it's connected to the Danish train network and regular buses link it with towns down the coast.

Ringkøbing's marina is a good spot for wandering: old fishermen's huts contrast with modern development and there's a handful of restaurants. There's an excellent hostel and a central old hotel in town, but the holiday activity is happening elsewhere.

The coast's most flaunted area is Holmsland Klit, the thin neck of sand and dunes stretching nearly 35km from north to south and separating the North Sea from Ringkøbing Fjord.

Hvide Sande

POP 3050

Hvide Sande (meaning 'white sands') owes its existence to the wind. Wind caused the sand migration that forced the construction of a lock here in 1931 to assure a North Sea passage for the port of Ringkøbing. And wind continues to be the big drawcard for the large number of tourists who come here to windsurf.

Aside from the wind, it's all about the fish. Hvide Sande has a busy deep-sea fishing harbour, with trawlers, fish-processing factories and an early-morning fish auction. There's also a small fishing museum/aquarium adjacent to the tourist office. Ask at the tourist office about fishing trips with local anglers, and the fish auctions (held weekly in summer for tourists).

🏃 Activities

Westwind
WINDSURFING, KITESURFING

(☑97 31 25 99; www.westwind.dk; ☺May-Oct) A consistent, howling westerly coupled with both an invitingly safe lake in Ringkøbing Fjord and the wild North Sea around Hvide Sande make this area ideal for windsurfers of all skill levels.

Westwind has two bases on the outskirts of town (one north, the other just south). It offers instruction (in English, German or Danish) in surfing, windsurfing, kitesurfing and stand-up paddle (SUP) surfing, plus gear rental.

A three-hour introductory windsurfing lesson costs Dkr400; a nine-hour course (in three three-hour blocks) costs Dkr995 – and they guarantee you can windsurf after those nine hours.

Kabel Park
WATERSKIING, WAKEBOARDING

(☑30 29 56 56; www.kabelpark.dk; ☺mid-Apr–Oct) Next to the northern branch of Westwind (in what's labelled the 'Aqua Sports Zone') is this entertaining waterpark, where waterskiers and wakeboarders are pulled by cable rope-tow along an 800m-long course, complete with jump-ramps for the experienced. There's a two-hour intro class for novices (Dkr375), otherwise one/two hours on the course costs Dkr150/200; BYO skis/wakeboard and wetsuit, or hire here.

It's also pretty cool to watch the waterpark antics – there's a cafe here for that purpose.

Vinterlejegaard Ridecenter
HORSE RIDING

(☑75 28 22 77; www.vinterlejegaard.dk; Vesterledvej 9) Hvide Sande is perfect for viewing a coastal sunset on horseback. Contact this riding centre for details; it's about 8km south of Hvide Sande and offers one-hour beach rides for Dkr200.

🛏 Sleeping

The tourist office rents out sexy state-of-the-art houseboats, as well as summer cottages and rooms in private homes (houseboats and cottages are generally rented by the week in summer).

Danhostel Hvide Sande
HOSTEL €

(☑97 31 21 05; www.danhostel-hvidesande.dk; Numitvej 5; dm Dkr189, d without/with bathroom Dkr385/455; @🛜) Tucked away from the crowds in a side street on the northern side of the channel, this homely, well-equipped hostel offers no-frills rooms (many with bathroom) and access to the nearby sports centre with which it is affiliated.

Hvide Sande Camping
CAMPGROUND €

(☑97 31 12 18; www.hvidesandecamping.dk; Karen Brandsvej 70; per adult/child/site Dkr78/40/40; ☺Apr-Oct) If you're here for the windsurfing, this is the campground for you. It's on the southern side of town, across the road from the Westwind operation, and offers good facilities including cabins and bike hire (bikes for nonguests, too; Dkr65 per day).

Hvide Sande Hotel
HOTEL €€

(☑97 31 10 33; www.hssh.dk; Bredgade 5; s/d/f Dkr745/945/1145; @🛜) The only hotel in town has fresh, simple rooms (all with bathroom and TV) in an old seamen's home down at the bustling harbour. Online bookings obtain decent discounts (as low as single/double Dkr545/645).

🍴 Eating

At the harbour there's a supermarket and no shortage of cafes, ice-creameries and bakeries competing for holidaymakers' appetites.

Edgar Madsen Fiskebutik
SEAFOOD €

(www.edgarmadsen.dk; Metheasvej 10; ☺9am-5.30pm Mon-Fri, 9am-3pm Sat & Sun) A proud and long-standing purveyor of all things fishy. Build your own picnic – breadrolls filled with shrimp, salmon or *fiskefrikadeller* sell for a bargain Dkr30.

Restaurant Under Broen
SEAFOOD €€

(www.underbroen.dk; 1 fl, Toldbodgade 20; lunch Dkr85-198kr, dinner mains Dkr128-198kr; ☺11.30am-9pm) Given the prime harbourside location of this elegant dining room, and the fishing boats moored just metres away, it doesn't take a brainiac to know the menu will feature superfresh fish options. The downstairs Cafe Marina has simpler fare at cheaper prices.

ℹ Information

Tourist Office (☑70 22 70 01; www.hvide sande.dk; Nørregade 2; ☺9am-4pm Mon-Fri, 11am-2pm Sat) On the northern side of the channel.

ℹ Getting There & Away

Hvide Sande is on Rte 181. Bus 580 runs between Hvide Sande and Ringkøbing station (Dkr39, 30 minutes) roughly hourly on weekdays, less frequently at weekends.

Northern Jutland

Includes ➡

Aalborg	241
Frederikshavn	248
Sæby	249
Skagen	251
Råbjerg Mile	255
Hirtshals	255
Hjørring	257
Løkken	257
Hanstholm	259
Klitmøller	260

Best Places to Eat

➡ Mortens Kro (p246)

➡ Skagens Museum Cafe (p254)

➡ Det Gamle Røgeri (p259)

➡ Abbey Road (p245)

➡ Ruths Gourmet (p254)

Best Places to Stay

➡ Villa Vendel (p258)

➡ Villa Rosa (p245)

➡ Aahøj (p250)

➡ Badepension Marienlund (p253)

➡ Ruths Hotel (p254)

Why Go?

Northern Jutland, split from the rest of Jutland by the Lim-fjord, wows visitors with its magnificent light and beautiful barren landscapes of shifting sands. The region is promoted as 'Lysets Land', or the Land of Light, and if you witness the soft blue nuances by the water as day turns into night, you'll understand why (and begin to comprehend the region's appeal to artists).

But it's not just painters who flock here. Windsurfers and beach-goers make a beeline for the north the minute the weather turns kind. Families head off to the zoos, aquariums and funparks, and seafood-lovers rejoice in the fresh-off-the-boat catch.

The area's most coveted tourist destination is Skagen, at Denmark's northern tip. It's both a civilised haven of chichi restaurants and art museums, and a wild place where nature calls the shots – which sums up the entire region, really.

When to Go

Summer is prime time to visit the north. The beaches, theme parks, festivals and activities are in full swing in July and August, when accommodation prices hit their peak. The shoulder season (May, June, September) usually offers decent weather and smaller crowds.

Aalborg has year-round attractions and events, including its popular Carnival celebrations in May, and plenty of performances in its arresting new concert hall. There's also some appeal to the notion of rugging up and braving the cooler weather someplace such as Skagen, where you can admire the turbulent tides and shifting sands without the summer crowds and high-season prices. Winter is better for the Danish art of *hygge* (cosiness), after all.

Aalborg

POP 130.900

Things are on the way up for Aalborg, Denmark's fourth-largest city. It sits at the narrowest point of the Limfjord (the long body of water that slices Jutland in two), and recent developments have seen the waterfront become the focal point of the town. A concerted effort is being made to rejuvenate the central industrial areas and turn neglected spaces into something far more appealing.

Traditionally Aalborg has flown under the traveller's radar, but that could easily change. There are enough low-key diversions here to occupy a few days for most visitors, from architecture fans to families, and party animals to history boffins.

◎ Sights & Activities

★**Utzon Center**   ARCHITECTURE, MUSEUM
(www.utzoncenter.dk; Slotspladsen 4; adult/child Dkr60/free; ⊘10am-5pm Tue-Sun, open Mon in Jul) An impressive 700-sq-metre design and architecture space, the Utzon Center, with its distinctive silver roofscape, sits pretty on the waterfront. It bills itself as 'a dynamic and experimental centre of culture and knowledge' and is the last building designed by celebrated Danish architect, Jørn Utzon (1918–2008). Utzon famously designed the Sydney Opera House; he grew up in Aalborg and died shortly after this eponymous centre was finished.

The centre hosts a changing program of exhibitions on architecture, design and art; there's also a high-quality restaurant.

★**Waterfront**   LANDMARK
The Aalborg waterfront promenade, extending east from Limfjordsbroen, is a good example of urban regeneration, taking what was a scruffy dockside area and opening it up to locals. Here you'll find restaurants, a park, playground, basketball courts and moored boats (including an old ice-breaker, now a restaurant-bar). One of the best features is the **Aalborg Havnebad** (Jomfru Ane Parken 6; ⊘daily mid-Jun–Aug) **FREE**, a summertime outdoor pool that lets you take a dip in the Limfjord.

East of the Utzon Center there's more new development, including university buildings and smart, low-cost housing for the city's growing student population. The latest addition is the shiny new **Musikkens Hus** (www.musikkenshus.dk; Musikkens Plads 1), a first-class, futuristic-looking concert hall that opened in 2014.

An anachronism among all this new development, the mid-16th-century, half-timbered **Aalborghus Slot** (Slotspladsen; ⊘dungeon 8am-3pm Mon-Fri May-Oct) **FREE** is more an administrative office than a castle, but there's a small dungeon you can visit.

Nordkraft   CULTURAL CENTRE
(www.nordkraft.dk; Kjellerups Torv; ⊘7am-11pm) Once a power station, this cultural centre is home to a theatre, concert venue, art-house cinema, gallery, fitness centre, plus a couple of eateries. The small tourist office is also here, so it's worth popping in to see what's happening locally.

Budolfi Domkirke   CHURCH
(www.aalborgdomkirke.dk; Algade 40; ⊘9am-4pm Mon-Fri, to 2pm Sat Jun-Aug, 9am-3pm Mon-Fri, 9am-noon Sat Sep-May) This 12th-century cathedral marks the centre of the old town and its elegant carillon can be heard every hour, on the hour. Its whitewashed interior creates an almost Mediterranean ambience.

As you enter the cathedral from Algade, look up at the foyer ceiling to see colourful frescoes from around 1500. The interior boasts some beautifully carved items, including a gilded baroque altar and a richly detailed pulpit.

Aalborg Historiske Museum   MUSEUM
(www.nordmus.dk; Algade 48; adult/child Dkr30/ free; ⊘10am-5pm Tue-Sun Apr-Dec, to 4pm Jan-Mar) Just west of Budolfi Domkirke is the town's history museum, with artefacts from prehistory to the present, and furnishings and interiors that hint at the wealth Aalborg's merchants enjoyed during the Renaissance.

Gråbrødrekloster Museet   MUSEUM
(www.nordmus.dk; Algade 19; ⊘10am-5pm Tue-Sun Apr-Oct, to 4pm Nov-Mar) This underground museum allows you to step off one of Aalborg's busiest shopping streets to explore the life of a Franciscan friary in medieval times. Entry is via an **elevator** outside Salling department store on Algade; the museum is free to enter, but you pay to ride the elevator (Dkr40 per group).

Helligåndsklostret   MONASTERY
(CW Obels Plads; adult/child Dkr50/free; ⊘tours 2pm Tue & Thu Jul-Aug) An alley off Algade leads to the rambling Monastery of the Holy Ghost, which dates from 1431 and is home to

Northern Jutland Highlights

1 Stand at the meeting place of two seas at Denmark's northernmost point, **Grenen** (p251)

2 Find inspiration in the treasured artworks of **Skagens Museum** (p251)

3 Discover the new, improved appeal of waterfront **Aalborg** (p241)

4 Let the wind take you places at **Klitmøller** (p260)

5 Take in the sunset and a memorable meal at **Gammel Skagen** (p252)

6 Loll about on lovely **Løkken beach** (p258) or **Tornby Strand** (p256)

7 Play amid Mother Nature's sandcastles at **Rubjerg Knude** (p258); and **Råbjerg Mile** (p255)

some fascinating frescoes. The interior can only be visited on a guided tour.

Historic Buildings HISTORIC BUILDINGS

Aalborg has lost chunks of its historical quaintness to industrial and commercial development, but the centre contains enough ancient half-timbered buildings to give you an idea of the kind of affluence its Renaissance merchants enjoyed.

East of Budolfi Domkirke are three noteworthy buildings: the baroque-style **old town hall** (c 1762), at the corner of Østerågade and Gammel Torv; the five-storey **Jens Bangs Stenhus** (c 1624) at Østerågade 9; and **Jørgen Olufsens House** (c 1616) at Østerågade 25. The latter two are lovely Renaissance buildings – Jens Bang's house was built by a well-heeled merchant and now functions as a pharmacy; Jørgen Olufsen's house was built by a wealthy mayor and now operates as a cosy Irish pub.

In addition, the neighbourhood around **Vor Frue Kirke** (Peder Barkes Gade) is worth seeing, particularly the cobbled L-shaped street of Hjelmerstald. Halfway down the street is **Langes Gård** (Hjelmerstald 15), a courtyard full of sculptures and ceramics.

Ask at the tourist office for the English-language *Good Old Aalborg* booklet, which maps out two walking tours and provides details of buildings and sights along the way.

Lindholm Høje VIKING SITE

(Vendilavej; ☉dawn-dusk) **FREE** The Limfjord was a kind of Viking motorway providing easy, speedy access to the Atlantic for longboat raiding parties. It's not surprising, then, that the most important piece of Aalborg's historical heritage is a predominantly Viking one.

The atmospheric Lindholm Høje is a Viking burial ground, where nearly 700 graves from the Iron Age and Viking Age are strewn around a hilltop pasture ringed by a wall of beech trees.

Many of the Viking graves are marked by stones placed in the oval outline of a Viking ship, with two larger end stones as stem and stern. At the end of the Viking era the whole area was buried under drifting sand and thus preserved until modern times.

Lindholm Høje Museet (www.nordmus. dk; Vendilavej 11; adult/child Dkr60/free; ☉10am-5pm daily Apr-Oct, 10am-4pm Tue-Sun Nov-Mar) adjoins the site and explains its history, and has displays on finds made during its exca-

vation. Murals behind the exhibits speculate on how the people of Lindholm lived.

Lindholm Høje is 15 minutes north of central Aalborg via bus 2. With your own wheels, head north from the centre over Limfjordsbroen to Nørresundby, and follow the signs.

Kunsten MUSEUM

(www.kunsten.dk; Kong Christians Allé 50) Housed in a modular, marble building designed by the great Finnish architect Alvar Aalto, Kunsten is Aalborg's museum of modern and contemporary art. The building's light-filled interior complements a fine collection of predominantly Danish works.

Kunsten will reopen after major renovations in October 2015 (before then, you can see some of its collection inside the train station). Check the website for opening hours and prices.

To get to Kunsten, take the tunnel beneath the train station, which emerges into Kildeparken, a green space with statues and water fountains. Go directly through the park, cross Vesterbro and continue through a wooded area to the museum, a 10-minute walk in all. Alternatively, take bus 15.

Aalborg Zoo ZOO

(www.aalborgzoo.dk; Mølleparkvej 63; adult/child Dkr170/100; ☉10am-7pm Jun-Aug, shorter hrs rest of yr; ⓐ) Teeming with feathered, furry and four-legged friends, it's no surprise this zoo is one of Denmark's most popular. Some 1200 animals call it home, including tigers, zebras, elephants, giraffes, chimpanzees, penguins and polar bears. It's southwest of the city and can be reached by bus 11; closing times vary, check the website.

🎭 Festivals & Events

Aalborg Karneval CULTURAL

(www.aalborgkarneval.dk) Each year in late May, Aalborg kicks up its heels hosting this week-long festival (the biggest Carnival celebrations in northern Europe), when up to 100,000 participants and spectators shake their maracas and paint the town red.

🛏 Sleeping

If only the sleeping options matched the quality of the eating choices! With few exceptions, Aalborg's hotel scene is lacklustre.

The tourist office has details of budget-priced rooms in private homes.

Aalborg

200 m
0.1 miles

Vestre Havnepromenade

Tourist Office

28

11

19

17

Limfjord

16

Utzon Center
1

15

Friis Shopping Centre

Nørregade

Danmarksgade

Slotspladsen

3

Kochs Kiosk

Gabels Torv

Fjordgade

Slotsgade

Bredegade

Vor Frue Stræde

Det Danske Udvandrerarkiv

13

Niels Ebbesens Gade

Peder Barkes Gade

10

14

Vestre Havnepromenade

City Bus Stop

Nytorv

Østeråagade

9

Algade

5

Møllegade

6

Mølleå

23

Maren Turis Gade

Ved Stranden

8

12

Mølleplads

21

Rantzausgade

Mølleå Arkaden

Brandtrupsgade

Adelgade

24

26

25

20

7

CW Obels Plads

Jomfru Ane Gade

Vesterå

Bispensgade

Gravensgade

4

Algade

2

Vingårdsgade

Sankelmarksgade

Boulevarden

Toldbodgade

Kattesundet

Jernbanegade

Danmarksgade

Korsgade

Holbergsgade

Dalgasgade

Vesterbro

Stengade

27

18

Grønnegangen

Prinsensgade

(300m);
(500m)

Kunsten (800m);
Aalborg Zoo
(1.6km)

Aalborg

◉ Top Sights
1 Utzon Center E2

◉ Sights
2 Aalborg Historiske Museum................B3
3 Aalborghus Slot D2
4 Budolfi Domkirke C3
5 Elevator to Gråbrødrekloster
    Museet..C3
6 Gråbrødrekloster Museet C3
7 Helligåndsklostret B2
8 Jens Bangs Stenhus............................C3
9 Jørgen Olufsens House........................C2
10 Langes Gård D4
11 Nordkraft F4
12 Old Town Hall C3
13 Vor Frue Kirke D4

⊕ Activities, Courses & Tours
14 Aalborg Havnebad D1

⊜ Sleeping
15 CabInn Aalborg E3
16 First Hotel Aalborg..............................E3
17 Hotel Aalborg......................................G4
18 Villa Rosa...A4

⊗ Eating
19 Abbey Road F4
20 Café KlosterTorvet C2
21 Caféministeriet C4
22 Føtex..D3
23 Mortens Kro...C4
24 Penny Lane C3
25 Pingvin Tapas & Vincafé B2

◉ Drinking & Nightlife
Irish House.....................................(see 9)
26 Søgaards Bryghus C2
27 The Wharf B1

⊕ Entertainment
28 Musikkens Hus F3

but it's hardly central. The surrounds are green and the accommodation is basic (all rooms have bathrooms); dorm beds are available in summer. There's an adjoining campground with budget cabins. It's in the marina area about 3km west of the town centre; take bus 13 (which stops short of the hostel).

Villa Rosa
GUESTHOUSE €€
(✆98 12 13 38; www.villarosa.dk; Grønnegangen 4; r & apt Dkr500-800; P☏) Book early to snare one of only six theatrically decorated rooms over three floors (no lift) at this late-19th-century villa. The three small self-contained apartments are the stand-out bargain here – the English Room is especially lovely. Three rooms share a large bathroom and guest kitchen. It's the most interesting option in town, so the reasonable rates and central location are added bonuses.

First Hotel Aalborg
HOTEL €€
(✆98 10 14 00; www.firsthotels.com; Rendsburggade 5; d incl breakfast from Dkr740; P@☏) Some of the newly renovated rooms at this smart fjordside hotel near the Utzon Center have water views, and the (limited) free parking is a bonus, as is the central location, and on-site gym and bar. Best rates are found online.

Hotel Aalborg
HOTEL €€
(Sømandshjemmet; ✆98 12 19 00; www.hotel-aalborg.com; Østerbro 27; s/d from Dkr715/760; P☏) This old seamen's hotel was once oddly placed, but encroaching harbourside redevelopment now sees it in the heart of the action, with Nordkraft and Musikkens Hus as neighbours. Comfortable, no-frills rooms are on offer, but there are exciting plans for a big extension and dramatic makeover (including the addition of high-end rooms). Free parking and friendly staff, too.

✕ Eating

★ Abbey Road
CAFE €
(http://abbeyroadcafe.dk; Kjellerupsgade 1A; meals Dkr89-135; ☺8am-10pm Mon-Sat) Opposite Nordkraft is this near-perfect all-day cafe: quality coffee and tea, mismashed furniture, and *hygge* by the bucketload. A new little sister to the long-established Penny Lane, Abbey Road dispenses salads, sandwiches and tapas plates, plus some seriously tasty baked goods (including healthy seeded breads – but hello pear-and-chocolate tart).

CabInn Aalborg
HOTEL €
(✆96 20 30 00; www.cabinn.com; Fjordgade 20; s/d/tr from Dkr495/625/835; @☏) The cheap, reliable CabInn chain added Aalborg to its portfolio with this large, central hotel across the road from the Utzon Center and neighbouring the Friis shopping centre. All 239 rooms have TV and bathrooms, but there's little room for cat-swinging in the cheaper rooms. Breakfast costs Dkr70.

Danhostel Aalborg
HOSTEL €
(✆98 11 60 44; www.bbbb.dk; Skydebanevej 50; dm/d Dkr345/590; P@☏) The hostel is handy for boating activities on the fjord (you can hire kayaks here in summer)

> ### ⓘ AALBORG CARD
>
> If you're in town for a couple of days, the Aalborg Card may be worth considering – it gives free entry to many of the sights, plus free parking (at Kennedy Arkaden, southeast of the train station) and free use of public transport. A 48-hour pass costs Dkr225. It's particularly worthwhile if you plan to visit expensive sights such as the zoo; buy it from the tourist office.

Penny Lane   CAFE, DELI €
(http://pennylanecafe.dk; Boulevarden 1; meals Dkr89-135; ☺8am-6pm Mon-Thu, to 7pm Fri, to 4pm Sat) This ace cafe-delicatessen has an in-house bakery, so its freshly baked bread, local cheeses and cured meats are extremely picnic-worthy. There's an in-house cafe offering a cracker brunch platter (Dkr105) or lunchtime sandwiches, salads and tarts. Leave room for something sweet.

Café KlosterTorvet   CAFE €
(www.klostertorvet.dk; CW Obels Plads 14; meals Dkr39-108; ☺10am-11pm Mon-Wed, to 1am Thu, to 3am Fri & Sat, to 10pm Sun) On a square full of great choices, KlosterTorvet is a laid-back cafe-bar with a studenty feel, thanks largely to its budget-friendly meals (baguettes, salads, pasta etc; kitchen closes 9pm), strong coffee, well-priced beer, and backgammon-playing clientele.

Pingvin Tapas & Vincafé   INTERNATIONAL €€
(☎98 11 11 66; www.cafepingvin.dk; Adelgade 12; dinner 4/6/8 tapas Dkr198/238/268; ☺noon-11pm Mon-Sat) This chic restaurant-bar offers a selection of up to 30 'tapas' (not so much shared dishes, but more of an individual tasting-plate approach). Enjoy small portions of lobster soup, grilled prawns with Vietnamese mango salad, or smoked duck breast. There's an excellent global wine list, plus lunchtime offers.

Caféministeriet   CAFE €€
(www.cafeministeriet.dk; Mølleplads; dinner mains Dkr95-175; ☺10am-midnight Mon-Thu, to 2am Fri & Sat, to 10pm Sun) A fashionable crowd enjoys classic cafe fare here, preferably on the summer terrace in the centre of the traffic-free square. The menu courses from fruity breakfasts to burgers by way of smørrebrød and tapas selections (the kitchen closes at 9pm); drop by for late-night alfresco drinks.

★**Mortens Kro**   MODERN DANISH €€€
(☎98 12 48 60; www.mortenskro.dk; Møllea 4-6; 4-course menu Dkr598; ☺5.30-10pm Mon-Sat) Hands down both the best and priciest in town, sleek Mortens Kro is owned by celebrity chef Morten Nielsen. It's a stylish, well-hidden place where top-quality local, seasonal produce is showcased: home-smoked trout and salmon, Norwegian lobster soup, cherry meringue with raspberry sorbet. Book ahead and dress to impress. Mølleå Arkaden is accessed from Peder Barkes Gade 40A or Mølleplads.

Morten Nielsen is also the chef behind the excellent restaurant at the Utzon Center – a great place to go for top-shelf smørrebrød or weekend brunch.

Self-Catering

Føtex   SUPERMARKET
(Slotsgade 8; ☺8am-9pm) Central supermarket. Bakery opens from 7am.

🍺 Drinking & Nightlife

If it's a flirt, a drink or loud beats you're after, trawl Jomfru Ane Gade, Aalborg's take-no-prisoners party street, jammed solid with bars. The venues themselves are pretty homogenous, so it's best to explore until you hear your kind of music or spy your type of crowd. Things are pretty tame early in the week, but get rowdy later from Thursday night onward.

You won't have trouble finding somewhere to wet your whistle along Jomfru Ane Gade, so we've listed a few places away from the main strip that you might not track down on your own (also check out the venues listed under Eating).

Irish House   PUB
(www.theirishhouse.dk; Østerågade 25; ☺1pm-1am Mon-Wed, noon-4am Fri & Sat, 2pm-midnight Sun) It's almost too beautiful a setting in which to get sloshed. Inside a 17th-century building loaded with timber carvings and stained glass, this cheerful pub offers live music Thursday to Saturday, cheap pub grub and a big range of beers.

Søgaards Bryghus   MICROBREWERY
(www.soegaardsbryghus.dk; CW Obels Plads 4; ☺11am-11pm Mon-Thu, until late Fri & Sat, 11.30am-10pm Sun) Every Danish town worth its salt has a microbrewery, and Aalborg's is a cracker. With loads of outdoor seating and a long menu of beer accompaniments, you could

easily lose an afternoon sampling Søgaard's impressive array of brews.

The Wharf   PUB
(Borgergade 16; ⊘2pm-midnight Mon-Wed, to 1am Thu, noon-2am Fri & Sat, 3-8pm Sun) Beer-lovers' heaven, this surprising slice of the UK in deepest Jutland is dedicated to cask ale and serves up to 42 different British, Belgian, Danish, Irish and German beers the length of its capacious bar. Pub food is served weekdays until 7.30pm.

ⓘ Information

Aalborg spreads along both sides of the Limfjord, with its two sections linked by bridge and tunnel. The business, shopping and dining hub and most traveller amenities are on the southern side.

MONEY
ATMs can be found all over the city, with a concentration around Nytorv.
Forex (Ved Stranden 22; ⊘9am-5.30pm Mon-Fri, 10am-2pm Sat) Foreign exchange.

POST
Post Office (Slotsgade 14; ⊘9.30am-6pm Mon-Fri, to 1pm Sat) Inside Føtex supermarket.

TOURIST INFORMATION
Det Danske Udvandrerarkiv (The Danish Emigration Archives; ☑99 31 42 20; www.udvandrerarkivet.dk; Arkivstræde 1; ⊘10am-4pm Mon-Wed, to 5pm Thu, to 3pm Fri) Behind Vor Frue Kirke; keeps records of Danish emigration history and (for a fee) helps foreigners of Danish descent trace their roots.
Tourist Office (☑99 31 75 00; www.visitaalborg.com; Nordkraft, Kjellerups Torv 5; ⊘10am-5.30pm Mon-Fri, to 2pm Sat) A small but well-stocked office inside Nordkraft. In summer, information is also dispensed from the delightful 1896 Kochs Kiosk (Gabels Torv).

ⓘ Getting There & Away

AIR
Aalborg airport (www.aal.dk) is 6.5km northwest of the city centre. There are plentiful direct connections with Copenhagen, and direct flights to/from Oslo and Amsterdam. **Norwegian** (www.norwegian.com) has daily connections with London (Gatwick).

BUS
Long-distance buses stop at the **bus station** (Fredensgade) south of JF Kennedys Plads (behind the Kennedy Arkaden shopping centre), not far from the train station.

From Aalborg you can reach most Jutland towns of note on the X-bus network – info is online at the site of the regional transport company, **Nordjyllands Trafikselskab** (NT; www.nordjyllandstrafikselskab.dk) or via the helpful **bus station information desk** (☑98 11 11 11; ⊘7am-5pm Mon-Fri, 9.30am-4pm Sat, 10.30am-5.30pm Sun) and its customer-service phone line.

In summer, the good-value NT Travel Pass covers 24/72 hours of transport in northern Jutland (train and bus) for Dkr150/250. Two children under 12 years can accompany a paying adult for free. Buy the pass online (www.nordjyllandstrafikselskab.dk) and it's delivered to your phone.

Abildskou (☑70 21 08 88; www.abildskou.dk) Express bus line 888 operates once or twice daily from Aalborg to Copenhagen's Valby station (Dkr360, 5½ hours). Good fare discounts are available – see the website.

Thinggaard Express (☑98 11 66 00; www.expressbus.dk) Bus 980 from Esbjerg to Frederikshavn once or twice daily, calling at Viborg and Aalborg en route.

CAR & MOTORCYCLE
Aalborg is 117km north of Aarhus and 65km southwest of Frederikshavn. The E45 bypasses the city centre, tunnelling under the Limfjord, while Rte 180 (which links up with the E45 both north and south of the city) leads into the centre.

To get to Lindholm Høje, or points north of the centre, take Rte 180 (Vesterbro), which crosses Limfjordsbroen.

TRAIN
Trains run about hourly north to Frederikshavn (Dkr100, 70 minutes), where there are onward connections to Skagen (from Aalborg Dkr120, two hours), and south to Aarhus (Dkr194, 1½ hours) or to Copenhagen (Dkr431, 4½ to five hours).

ⓘ Getting Around

TO/FROM THE AIRPORT
Town buses 2A, 2B, 70 and 71 run frequently between the city centre and the airport (Dkr20).

BICYCLE
Free **city bikes** (www.aalborgbycyklen.dk) are available from various spots around town from May to October (look for 'Bycyklen' signs). You put a Dkr20 coin into the slot to obtain the bike, which is refunded when you return it.

Bikes can be hired from **Munk's Eftf** (☑98 12 19 46; www.munk-aalborg.dk; Løkkegade 25; per day/week Dkr80/400). Note, however, that the store is closed for most of July.

BUS

For about eight weeks in peak summer (late June to late August) there is a **free City Circle bus** running half-hourly from 10am to 6pm (until 2pm Saturday and Sunday). The circuit takes in major sights such as the zoo, Kunsten and the waterfront.

Almost all city buses leave from south of JF Kennedys Plads and pass the city-centre stops on Østerågade and Nytorv, near Burger King. The standard local bus fare is Dkr20; buy tickets from the driver.

Information on tickets, routes and schedules is available at the helpful bus station information desk (p247).

CAR

Car-rental companies Hertz, Avis and Europcar have booths at the airport or in town.

Apart from a few one-way streets, Aalborg is easy to travel around by car. There's free (but time-restricted) parking along many side streets, and metered parking in the city centre. There are also several large commercial car parks, including at Ved Stranden 11 (opposite the Radisson hotel), at Kennedy Arkaden (enter from Østre Allé), and under the Friis shopping centre (enter from Nyhavnsgade). These aren't cheap (up to Dkr18 per hour, maximum Dkr160 for a 24-hour period).

TAXI

You can order a **taxi** (☑ 98 10 10 10), or just pick one from the rank at the train station.

Frederikshavn

POP 23,300

A transport hub rather than a compelling destination, Frederikshavn shuffles more than three million people through its port each year, making it Jutland's busiest international ferry terminal. The majority of visitors are Scandinavians raiding Denmark's supplies of relatively cheap booze and meat.

The town itself lacks the historical glamour of its coastal neighbours but can successfully entertain you for a few hours with its feature attraction, Bangsbo – still, Skagen or even Sæby make for more appealing overnight options.

◉ Sights

Bangsbo　　　　　　　　　　MUSEUM
(www.kystmuseet.dk; Dronning Margrethesvej 6; adult/child Dkr50/free; ⊙10am-4pm Mon-Fri, 11am-4pm Sat & Sun Jun-Aug, Mon-Fri only Sep-May) It's well worth exploring the Bangsbo area, 3km south from the town centre. The main draw-card is **Bangsbo Museum**, an old country estate with an interesting mix of exhibits. The manor house displays antique furnishings and collectibles, while the old farm buildings house ship figureheads, military paraphernalia and exhibits on the Danish Resistance during WWII.

The most intriguing exhibit is the Ellingå ship, the reconstructed remains of a 12th-century Viking-style merchant ship that was dug up from a nearby streambed.

Bus 3 from central Frederikshavn stops near the entrance to the estate, from where it's an enjoyable 500m walk through the woods to the museum. The adjoining **Bangsbo Botaniske Have** (Botanic Gardens) has a deer park and is a picturesque place to stroll or picnic.

Bangsbo Fort, about 800m over the wooded ridge from the gardens, is an atmospheric WWII bunker complex housing some big guns and commanding wonderful views across to Frederikshavn and out to sea.

🛏 Sleeping

⭐ **Danhostel**
Frederikshavn City　　　　　　HOSTEL €
(☑ 98 42 14 75; http://danhostelfrederikshavn. dk; Læsøgade 18; dm/s/d Dkr220/530/590; 🅿 @ 🛜) Frederikshavn's hostel is perfectly positioned behind the tourist office, with a supermarket and cafe-bar as neighbours. It's busy with ferry passengers enjoying the fresh new facilities (all rooms have bathrooms). Communal areas are top-notch, as is the courtyard garden with barbecue. Breakfast costs Dkr60.

Best Western
Hotel Herman Bang　　　　　　HOTEL €€
(☑ 98 42 21 66; www.hermanbang.dk; Tordenskjoldsgade 3; standard s/d from Dkr795/995; 🛜) The standard rooms here are bright and comfortable, and the most expensive ('business') rooms are quite luxurious. The cheapest (called 'budget' rooms) are poor value – you're better off at the hotel's newly decorated budget annex, **Herman Bang Bed & Breakfast** (www. hbbb.dk; Skolegade 2; d with/without bathroom Dkr650/500). The hotel has an upmarket spa and American-style diner.

🍴 Eating

Karma Sushi　　　　　　JAPANESE €€
(www.karmasushi.dk; Lodsgade 10; 8-piece sushi Dkr98-135; ⊙5-10pm Tue-Thu, to 11pm Fri & Sat)

When hunger strikes, head for the eastern end of Lodsgade, which has oodles of eating options. The standout is good-looking Karma, an oasis of calm and elegance among the strange hybrid Mexican-Italian buffets – but its beautifully presented sushi morsels don't come cheap.

Møllehuset   DANISH €€
(www.mollehuset.dk; Skovalléen 45; lunch Dkr110-205, dinner mains Dkr205-235; ☉11am-6pm Sun & Mon, to 10pm Tue-Sat) This handsome old mill house from the mid-18th-century is in a leafy setting in the Bangsbo area (though its modern extension does lack a little soul). The menu has plenty of appeal in the form of tapas tasters, cheese platters and fresh fish. Bus 3 from central Frederikshavn stops here.

ℹ Information

An overhead walkway leads from the ferry terminals to the tourist office, which sits at the edge of the central commercial district. The train station and the adjacent bus terminal are a 10-minute walk north of the ferry terminal. Danmarksgade is the pedestrian shopping strip, with banks and other services.

Tourist Office (☎98 42 32 66; www.visit frederikshavn.dk; Skandiatorv 1; ☉9am-4pm Mon-Fri, 10am-1pm Sat) Over the walkway from the ferry terminal, it offers the low-down on the town and surrounds.

ℹ Getting There & Around

BICYCLE
The tourist office arranges bike rental (Dkr80 per day).

BOAT
Stena Line (☎96 20 02 00; www.stenaline. com) connects Frederikshavn with Gothenburg (Sweden) and Oslo (Norway). See p299 for more information on international ferries.

BUS
Bus routes in northern Jutland extend as far afield as Hirtshals, Hjørring and Løkken. **Thinggaard Express** (☎98 11 66 00; www.express bus.dk) operates bus 980 from Frederikshavn to Esbjerg once or twice daily, calling at Viborg and Aalborg en route.

CAR
Frederikshavn is 65km northeast of Aalborg on the E45 and 41km south of Skagen on Rte 40.

TRAIN
Frederikshavn is the northern terminus of Danske Statsbaner (DSB) train lines (the na-tional rail network); however, a private train line operates hourly trains north to Skagen (Dkr60, 35 minutes). DSB trains depart about hourly south to Aalborg (Dkr100, 1¼ hour) and Aarhus (Dkr252, 2¾ hours).

Sæby
POP 8800

While Skagen is the inspiration behind world-renowned Scandinavian artists, Sæby could well be called the spiritual home (or at least the holiday house) of Danish literature. The pretty town was the inspiration behind Herman Bang's *Sommerglæder* (Summer Pleasure) and Henrik Ibsen's renowned work *Fruen fra havet* (The Lady from the Sea). In summer, Sæby's harbour and old town are packed with ice-cream-toting holidaymakers. It's a sleeper compared with Skagen further up the road, but it has plenty of charm.

◎ Sights & Activities

Algade   STREET
Soak up Sæby's living history with a walk along the town's oldest street. Algade links the small museum with the church and is lined with gardens, half-timbered houses and a handful of artists' studios and craft shops.

Sæby Museum   MUSEUM
(www.kystmuseet.dk; Algade 1; adult/child Dkr50/free; ☉10am-4pm Mon-Fri, 11am-4pm Sat & Sun Jun-Aug, shorter hrs rest of yr) This small, sweet museum occupies a 17th-century timber-frame house. Expect to see an amber collection, a 1920s classroom and a classically furnished Victorian sitting room.

Sæby Klosterkirke   CHURCH
(Strandgade 5; ☉8am-6pm Mon-Sat, 8am-4pm Sun Apr-Oct, 8am-4pm Mon-Sat, 9am-noon Sun Nov-Mar) Sæby Klosterkirke is all that remains of a four-winged Carmelite monastery dating from 1470. Its visually imposing exterior is coupled with an interior that boasts beautiful frescoes from the Middle Ages and a 16th-century pulpit and canopy.

From the church you can readily access the harbour (take the path marked 'Kirkestien').

Harbour   HARBOUR
The photogenic, yacht-filled harbour is home to plenty of fish-peddling restaurants and ice-cream kiosks. For those disappointed with the physical size of the Little Mermaid in Copenhagen, Sæby's symbol of protection, **the Lady from the Sea statue,**

LOVELY LÆSØ

The appeal of the island of Læsø (population 1840) lies in its ability to stay firmly entrenched in the past. It may be just 28km off the coast of Frederikshavn, but it seems 100 years in arrears. It's home to small farms, sandy beaches, heathlands, dunes, much-loved traditions and charming small communities.

Island tradition continues in the making of Læsø salt. At one time an island export, the salt is now sold in small souvenir bags and is respected for its medicinal qualities as well as its gourmet potential. On the island you can visit the **saltworks**, and take a salt bath at **Læsø Kur** (☑ 98 49 13 22; www.saltkur.dk; Vesterø Havnegade 28), a wellness centre inside a former church.

The island has a few small towns (Vesterø Havn, Byrum and Østerby Havn), a couple of medieval churches, and a smattering of museums (including a seaweed-roofed farm museum). South of the main island is **Rønnerne**, an area of tidal wetlands with extensive seaside meadows and heathland, impressive birdlife and unique flora and fauna.

Day Trips to Læsø

A good way to experience Læsø is by day trip from Frederikshavn, departing on the 7.50am ferry and landing at Vesterø Havn. There are four options, all outlined on the ferry company's website (www.laesoe-line.dk). These include a bus tour of major sights, a self-guided cycling tour, a tractor-pulled cart ride into Rønnerne with a nature guide, or a seal-watching boat ride. The day trips cost between Dkr255 and Dkr400, including return ferry passage (if you're staying on the island you can also join the tours and pay a lower rate).

Staying on Læsø

The **tourist office** (☑ 98 49 92 42; www.visitlaesoe.dk; Vesterø Havnegade 17; ⊗ 9am-3pm Mon-Fri, to 2pm Sat & Sun mid-Jun–Aug, shorter hrs rest of yr) is 300m east of the ferry terminal and can help organise holiday cottages around the island; book in advance for July and August.

There are plenty of small hotels and a Danhostel. We're fond of the idyllic beachside **Strandgaarden Badehotel** (☑ 98 49 90 35; www.badehotel.eu; Strandvejen 8; d without/with bathroom from Dkr800/1150, incl breakfast), pretty as a picture under its thatched roof, and with beds for most budgets plus bike hire and an excellent restaurant.

Transport

Færgeselskabet Læsø (☑ 98 49 90 22; www.laesoe-line.dk; return adult/child Jul & Aug Dkr230/115, Sep-Jun Dkr180/80) sails three to seven times daily year-round between Læsø and Frederikshavn (1½ hours).

A free public bus runs between the villages of Vesterø Havn, Byrum and Østerby Havn; it operates in connection with ferry departure and arrival times.

Bicycles can be rented from **Jarvis Cykler** (☑ 98 49 94 44; www.jarvis-laesoe.dk; Vesterø Havnegade 29; per day Dkr80), close to the ferry terminal. The tourist office has cycling maps outlining various routes.

---

has presence *and* stature. It's based on Henrik Ibsen's play of the same name, which he wrote after a summer spent in and around Sæby.

🛏 Sleeping

★ **Aahøj** GUESTHOUSE €€
(☑ 98 46 11 27; www.aahoj.dk; Hans Aabelsvej 1; s/d incl breakfast from Dk575/650; 🛜) The top pick in town, for its intimate atmosphere (nine homely rooms in an elegant 1896 villa) and central location. The sunroom is the perfect place for breakfast, while the idyllic riverside garden beckons for a lazy afternoon with a book.

Sæby Fritidscenter-Danhostel HOSTEL €
(☑ 98 46 36 50; www.saebyfritidscenter.dk; Sæbygaardvej 32; dm from Dkr155, d without/with bathroom from Dkr350/570; @🛜) This hostel is 1.5km west of the town centre, at a large sports centre and with plenty of open space. Facilities are of the usual high standard, and there's a choice of rooms – the cheapest have

shared bathrooms, while the A++ rooms (Dkr660) have bathroom, balcony, TV and fridge. There are also simple cottages (sleeping five).

✖ Eating

Jensens Fiskerestaurant   SEAFOOD €€
(☑ 98 46 11 56; www.jensensfisk.dk; Havnen 7; buffet lunch/dinner Dkr139/199; ⊙ 11.30am-11.30pm) In the harbour area, restaurants woo you with tables loaded with fresh fish bounty. Upstairs at Jensens is a smart, light-filled restaurant offering buffet or à la carte choices (buffets are the best value-for-money); downstairs is a more casual cafe/takeaway serving fish and chips to a beer-drinking, sun-seeking crowd. Restaurant reservations advised.

Frøken Madsen's Spisehus   DANISH €€
(☑ 98 40 80 36; http://frk-madsen.dk; Pindborggade 1; mains Dkr189-299; ⊙ 5pm-9pm Wed-Sat, plus noon-2pm Sat & Sun) Frøken Madsen serves up Danish favourites in a cosy old building a block from the main street. On a warm evening, a table on the flower-filled garden terrace above the small river is in demand. Kind to the purse-strings is the weekend lunch buffet (Dkr129) or the Friday-night dinner buffet (Dkr199); book ahead for both.

ⓘ Information

The main shopping area is around Vestergade. **Tourist Office** (☑ 98 46 12 44; www.visitsaeby. dk; Algade 14; ⊙ 9.30am-4pm Mon-Fri, 10am-1pm Sat) Sharing space with some galleries on the town's oldest street.

ⓘ Getting There & Away

Sæby is 12km south of Frederikshavn on Rte 180. There is no train line but the frequent buses 73 and 973X between Aalborg and Frederikshavn stop at Sæby (Dkr30 from Frederikshavn).

The Sæby bus station is 300m southwest of the town centre (take Stationsvej off Grønnegade).

Skagen

POP 8200

With its rich art heritage, fresh seafood, photogenic neighbourhoods and classic characters, Skagen (pronounced Skain) is an utterly delicious slice of Denmark.

In the mid-19th century artists flocked here, charmed by the radiant light's impact on the ruggedly beautiful landscape.

Now tourists come in droves, drawn by an intoxicating combination of busy working harbour, long sandy beaches and buzzing holiday atmosphere. The town gets packed in summer but maintains its charm, especially in the intimate, older neighbourhoods, filled with distinctive yellow houses framed by white-picket fences and red-tiled roofs.

Catering to the tourist influx are numerous museums, art galleries, bike-rental outlets, ice-creameries and harbourside restaurants. Come and see why half the Danish population lights up whenever the town's name is mentioned.

⊙ Sights & Activities

★**Skagens Museum**   MUSEUM
(www.skagensmuseum.dk; Brøndumsvej 4; adult/child Dkr90/free; ⊙ 10am-5pm daily May-Aug, Tue-Sun Sep-Apr) This wonderful gallery (undergoing major renovation and expansion from late 2014 into 2015) showcases the outstanding art that was produced in Skagen between 1870 and 1930.

Artists discovered Skagen's gorgeous light and its wind-blasted heath-and-dune landscape in the mid-19th century, and fixed eagerly on the romantic imagery of the area's fishing life that had earned the people of Skagen a hard living for centuries.

Painters such as PS Krøyer and Anna and Michael Ancher followed the contemporary fashion of painting *en plein air* (out of doors). Their work established a vivid figurative style of painting that became known internationally as the 'Skagen School'.

PS Krøyer's work is quite incredible, particularly his efforts to 'paint the light'. He was particularly transfixed by the 'blue hour', the transition between day and night, when the sky and the sea seem to merge into each other in the same shade of blue.

Overall, the paintings here evoke a sense of place and demonstrate a real community of artists in Skagen who worked and played together. The gallery also houses the former dining room of the Brøndums Hotel, one-time hang-out of many of the Skagen artists. The portrait-filled room was moved in its entirety in 1946 from the hotel across the road.

Grenen   OUTDOORS
Appropriately enough for such a neat and ordered country, Denmark doesn't end untidily at its most northerly point, but on a neat finger of sand just a few metres wide. You can actually paddle at its tip, where the

Skagen

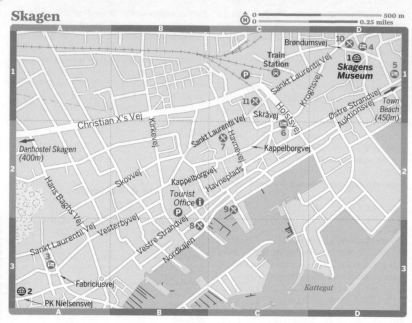

waters of the Kattegat and Skagerrak clash, and you can put one foot in each sea – but not too far. Bathing here is forbidden because of the ferocious tidal currents.

The tip is the culmination of a long, curving sweep of sand at Grenen, about 3km northeast of Skagen along Rte 40. Where the road ends there's a car park (Dkr13 per hour), excellent restaurant and small art gallery. From the car park the 30-minute walk up the long, sweeping stretch of sand passes the grave of writer Holger Drachmann (1846–1908).

The tractor-pulled bus, the **Sandormen** (adult/child return Dkr25/15; ☺ Apr-Oct), can take you out to the point; it leaves from the car park at Grenen from 10am daily and runs regularly all day, according to demand.

Gammel Skagen   VILLAGE, BEACH
There's a touch of Cape Cod in refined Gammel Skagen ('Old Skagen', also known as Højen), renowned for its gorgeous sunsets, upmarket hotels and well-heeled summer residents.

It was a fishing hamlet before sandstorms ravaged this windswept area and forced many of its inhabitants to move to Skagen on the more protected east coast. It's a pleasant bike ride 4km west of Skagen: head towards Frederikshavn and turn right at Højensvej, which takes you to the waterfront.

Skagen By- og Egnsmuseum   MUSEUM
(www.kystmuseet.dk; PK Nielsensvej 8; adult/child Dkr50/free; ☺ 10am-4pm Mon-Fri, 11am-4pm Sat & Sun Jun-Aug, closed weekends rest of yr) Evocatively presented, this open-air museum, 200m southwest of the harbour, depicts Skagen's maritime history and gives an insight into the traditional fishing community that so transfixed the Skagen artists (but without the romanticism!).

Den Tilsandede Kirke   RUIN
The 'sand-covered church', built during the late 14th century, was once the region's biggest church. It fell victim to a sand drift that began in the 17th century and became progressively worse – so much so that churchgoers eventually had to dig their way in. In 1795 the relentless sand drift broke the will of the congregation and the church was closed. The main part of the church was torn down in 1810 but the whitewashed **tower** (adult/child Dkr20/3; ☺ 11am-5pm daily Jun-Aug, weekends only Apr, May & Sep) still stands.

The photogenic tower and the surrounding area comprise part of **Skagen Klitplantage**, a nature reserve. It's about 5km south of Skagen and well signposted from Rte 40. The nicest way to get here is by bike; take Gammel Landevej from Skagen.

Skagen

◎ Top Sights
1 Skagens Museum D1

◎ Sights
2 Skagen By- og Egnsmuseum A3

🛏 Sleeping
3 Badepension Marienlund A3
4 Brøndums Hotel................................. D1
5 Finns B&B D1
6 Hotel Plesner C2

🍴 Eating
Brøndums Hotel.......................... (see 4)
7 Jakobs Café & Bar C2
8 Pakhuset B3
9 Skagen Fiskerestaurant......................C2
Skagens Museum Cafe ....(see 1)
10 Slagter Munch.................................... D1
11 SuperBrugsen C1

Skagen Odde Naturcenter   NATURE CENTRE
(www.skagen-natur.dk; Bøjlevejen 66; adult/child Dkr65/30; ⏰10am-4pm Mon-Fri, 11am-4pm Sat & Sun May–mid-Oct) In a beautiful Utzon-designed building on the northern outskirts of town, this centre gives an insight into the natural elements that surround Skagen and make it unique. It's pricy, but worth a visit if you're into architecture. There are also changing art exhibitions, and family activities.

Town Beach   BEACH
The closest beach to town is accessed from Østre Strandvej; east-coast beaches are sheltered and good for families, while the west coast is wilder.

✯✯ Festivals

Skagen Festival   MUSIC
(www.skagenfestival.dk) Since 1971 the Skagen Festival has seen the town packed with performers, buskers and appreciative visitors, and acts encompassing rock to folk music. It's held on the first weekend of July; book accommodation well in advance.

🛏 Sleeping

You'll need to book ahead in summer, when hotel accommodation can be scarce (and at its highest rate; outside July to August most prices drop).

Danhostel Skagen   HOSTEL €
(☑98 44 22 00; www.danhostelskagen.dk; Rolighedsvej 2; dm/s/d Dkr180/525/625; ⏰Mar-Nov; Ⓟ🛜) Always a hive of activity, this hostel is modern, functional and spick-and-span. It's decent value, particularly for families or groups. Low-season prices drop sharply. It's 1km towards Frederikshavn from the Skagen train station (if you're coming by train, get off at Frederikshavnsvej).

Grenen Strand Camping   CAMPGROUND €
(☑98 44 25 46; www.campone.dk/grenen; Fyrvej 16; campsite from Dkr50, plus per adult Dkr90; ⏰Apr–mid-Sep; @🛜) This busy, well-organised place is in a fine seaside location on the outskirts of town towards Grenen. There's plenty of tree cover and good facilities, including wee four-bed cabins.

★ Badepension Marienlund   GUESTHOUSE €€
(☑28 12 13 20; www.marienlund.dk; Fabriciusvej 8; s/d incl breakfast Dkr650/1100; ⏰Apr-Oct; Ⓟ🛜) A cosy atmosphere, idyllic garden and pretty lounge and breakfast areas make Marienlund a top option. There are only 14 rooms, all light, white and simply furnished (all with bathrooms). You'll find the hotel in a peaceful residential neighbourhood west of the centre; bike hire available.

Finns B&B   GUESTHOUSE €€
(☑98 45 01 55; www.finns.dk; Østre Strandvej 63; s/d incl breakfast from Dkr525/750; ⏰May–mid-Sep; 🛜) Take a 1923-vintage 'log cabin' built for a Norwegian count, fill it with art, antiques and memorabilia, and you have this fabulously quirky slumber spot. Gay-friendly, TV-free and adults-only (no kids under 15), Finns is a stone's throw from the beach and has six individually decorated rooms (a few with shared bathroom).

Brøndums Hotel   HOTEL €€
(☑98 44 15 55; www.broendums-hotel.dk; Anchersvej 3; s/d with shared bathroom incl breakfast Dkr935/1485; 🛜) This charming hotel is steeped in history – it had close associations with the Skagen artists in its heyday. There have been recent renovations to bring the decor up to date, but prices are high given bathrooms are shared. There's a cheaper nearby annex, **Admiralgaarden**, with more rooms (some with bathrooms). The hotel's breakfast buffet is something special. Open year-round.

Hotel Plesner   BOUTIQUE HOTEL €€
(☑98 44 68 44; www.hotelplesner.dk; Holstvej 8; s/d incl breakfast Dkr1395/1495; 🛜) Candy-striped designer touches run throughout this boutique hotel, home to 16 fresh, petite guestrooms.

NORTHERN JUTLAND SKAGEN

Highlights include an alluring garden lounge (where afternoon tea is served).

★ Ruths Hotel · HOTEL €€€

(☑ 98 44 11 24; www.ruths-hotel.dk; Hans Ruths Vej 1; r incl breakfast from Dkr1750) One of Denmark's grand bathing hotels – beautifully positioned in chichi Gammel Skagen, with acclaimed restaurants, a wellness centre and stylish modern-meets-traditional decor. Rooms and apartments are spread over a campus of buildings.

✗ Eating & Drinking

Perhaps a dozen seafood shacks line the harbour, selling fresh seafood. Prawns/shrimp *(rejer)* are the favourite order, costing around Dkr100 for a generous helping.

Havnevej, the road connecting the harbour and the town centre, has a cluster of eateries and bars. At Havneplads things get a little seedier (well, as seedy as Denmark gets), with some late-opening summertime nightclubs.

It's a good idea to make dinner reservations in summer, when the town is heaving.

★ Skagens Museum Cafe · CAFE €

(www.skagensmuseum.dk; Brøndumsvej 4; lunch Dkr85-100; ⊙10am-5pm) For lunch or a cuppa in a magical setting, head to the Garden House cafe at Skagens Museum, serving lunchtime dishes plus a super spread of homebaked cakes and tarts. Note: you don't need to pay the museum's admission if you're just visiting the cafe.

Pakhuset · SEAFOOD €€

(☑ 98 44 20 00; www.pakhuset-skagen.dk; Rødspættevej 6; lunch Dkr85-230, mains Dkr170-240; ⊙11am-late) Seafood is the star at Pakhuset, from simple fishcakes with remoulade to swoon-inducing flambéed Norwegian lobster tails. It has long hours and superb ambience both outdoors (slap bang on the harbour) and indoors (think wooden beams and cheerful ship mastheads). Fine-dine in the restaurant upstairs (from 6pm), or keep it cheaper in the downstairs cafe. Keep an eye out for live music, too.

Skagen Fiskerestaurant · SEAFOOD €€

(☑ 98 44 35 44; skagenfiskerestaurant.dk/; Fiskehuskaj 13; lunch Dkr80-225, dinner Dkr120-259; ⊙10am-late Apr–mid-Oct, shorter hrs rest of yr) This dockside place has the same approach as nearby Pakhuset – casual cafe fare at lunch and dinner (*fiskefrikadeller*, or fresh-off-the-boat prawns you peel yourself), an

in-demand outdoor terrace, and a smarter upstairs area for fancy-pants evening dining. Downstairs is rustic and fun – you know a place doesn't take itself too seriously when the floor is covered in sand.

Ruths Brasserie · FRENCH €€

(www.ruths-hotel.dk; Gammel Skagen; meals Dkr95-325; ⊙11.30am-9pm) If your holiday dollar doesn't quite stretch to Ruths Gourmet, the Brasserie is a *très bon* backup option. Here, you can enjoy the marvellous terrace and an all-day menu of classic French dishes. The Brasserie's bakery starts wooing customers with pastries from 7.30am.

Jakobs Café & Bar · INTERNATIONAL €€

(www.jakobscafe.dk; Havnevej 4; lunch Dkr75-155, dinner mains Dkr190-280; ⊙9am-1am Sun-Thu, to 3am Fri & Sat; ☎) The terrace of this relaxed cafe-bar is primed for people-watching, and the comprehensive menu has favourites such as burgers, Caesar salad, *moules frites* and steaks (the kitchen closes at 10pm). On summer nights the place is generally heaving with young Danes enjoying warm-up drinks; there's live music on weekends.

Ruths Gourmet · MODERN DANISH €€€

(☑ 98 44 11 24; www.ruths-hotel.dk; Gammel Skagen; 3/5/9 courses Dkr595/865/1395; ⊙6pm-late Tue-Sat Jul & Aug, Thu-Sat Apr-Jun & Sep, Fri & Sat Oct-Mar) New Nordic cuisine is in the spotlight at this intimate restaurant at Ruths Hotel, under the leadership of acclaimed chef Thorsten Schmidt. The menu has a regional focus, utilising fine local produce to stunningly innovative and creative effect (choose menus from three to nine courses). You'll need to book ahead to score one of only 22 seats.

Brøndums Hotel · FRENCH, DANISH €€€

(☑ 98 44 15 55; www.broendums-hotel.dk; Anchersvej 3; lunch Dkr155-225, dinner mains Dkr210-385; ⊙11.30am-9pm) French cuisine is the main influence on otherwise classic Danish dishes here. Meals are served in the old-world ambience of the dining room – it has a special-occasion feel, but you can just as easily pop in for classic lunchtime smørrebrød or afternoon coffee and cake. There's also a picture-perfect garden for alfresco dining.

Self-catering

SuperBrugsen · SUPERMARKET €

(Sankt Laurentii Vej 28; ⊙8am-10pm) In-house bakery opens from 7.30am. The post office is inside.

Slagter Munch BUTCHER, DELI €
(www.munch-skagen.dk; Sankt Laurentii Vej 1;
⊕ 9am-5.30pm Mon-Fri, 8am-1pm Sat) The
queues out the door attest to this butcher's reputation for award-winning *skinke*
(ham) and sausages. There's also a selection
of picnic-worthy salads and deli produce
for sale.

❶ Information

Sankt Laurentii Vej, the main street, runs almost the entire length of this long, thin town
and is never more than five minutes' walk from
the waterfront. The train station is on Sankt
Laurentii Vej, 100m north of the pedestrianised
town centre.

Tourist Office (☑ 98 44 13 77; www.skagen-
tourist.dk; Vestre Strandvej 10; ⊕ 9am-4pm
Mon-Sat, 10am-2pm Sun late Jun–mid-Aug,
shorter hrs rest of yr) In front of the harbour,
with loads of info on regional sights, attractions
and activities.

❶ Getting There & Away

BUS
The summertime bus 99 connects Skagen with
other northern towns and attractions.

CAR
Skagen is 41km north of Frederikshavn on Rte
40, and 49km northeast of Hirtshals via Rtes
597 and 40.

TRAIN
Trains run hourly to Frederikshavn (Dkr60, 35
minutes), where you can change for destinations
further south.

❶ Getting Around

BICYCLE
The best way to get around is by bike, and loads
of places offer rental. **Skagen Cykeludlejning**
(www.skagencykeludlejning.dk; Banegårdspladsen, Sankt Laurentii Vej 22; bike hire per day/
week Dkr90/375) is adjacent to the train station
and has a range of bikes. It has a second outlet
close to the harbour, in the bike shop at Fisker-
gangen 10.

CAR
Parking is at a premium in summer – there's
paid parking (Dkr13 per hour, from 9am to 6pm)
beside and in front of the tourist office, and
beside the train station.

TAXI
Taxis (☑ 98 43 34 34) are available at the
station.

Råbjerg Mile

Denmark's largest expanse of drifting sand
dunes, **Råbjerg Mile** is an amazing natural
phenomenon. These undulating, 40m-high
hills are fun to explore and almost big
enough to lose yourself in. The dunes were
formed on the west coast during the great
sand drift of the 16th century and have
purposefully been left in a migratory state
(moving towards the forest at a rate of 15m
per year). The dunes leave a low, moist layer of sand behind, stretching westwards to
Skagerrak.

Råbjerg Mile is 16km southwest of Skagen, signposted off Rte 40 on the road to
Kandestederne. It's about 4km from Hulsig
station, on the Frederikshavn–Skagen train
line.

Hirtshals

POP 6000
Beloved by discount-hungry Norwegians
and largely inhabited by hardened Hirtshals
seamen, this modern town makes a reasonable base for sightseeing, but its appearance
won't take your breath away. It has ferry
connections to points further north (way
north, such as Iceland, the Faroe Islands and
Norway); beaches and an impressive show
of sea life may add to the appeal.

◉ Sights & Activities

Nordsøen Oceanarium AQUARIUM
(www.nordsoenoceanarium.dk; Willemoesvej 2;
adult/child Dkr170/90; ⊕ 9am-6pm daily Jul-Aug,
10am-4pm or 5pm rest of yr, closed Dec–early Jan;
▣) If you've always wondered what lurks
beneath, head to the impressive North Sea
Oceanarium, home to one of the largest
aquariums in northern Europe. Here, 4.5
million litres of seawater is home to thousands of elegantly balletic mackerel and herring in a huge, four-storey tank. Check the
website for feeding times: in summer, these
are 11am and 3pm in the oceanarium (done
by a diver with a video camera), and noon
and 4pm at the outdoor seal pool.

Touchpools and an excellent playground
make this a perfect family excursion.

By car the E39 passes close to the aquarium (signposted); if you're coming by train
from Hjørring, get off at Lilleheden station,
from where it's a five-minute walk.

Tornby Strand   BEACH

If all you're after is a long stretch of white sand, Tornby Strand delivers it in spades (and buckets), 5km south of Hirtshals. As the sand is compact enough to drive on, many park next to the breakers. Hiking is possible among the high mounded dunes and into the coastal woodlands that back the southern side of the beach.

Tornby Strand can be reached from Hirtshals via Rte 55 and Tornby Strandvej. The village here has a summer campground and a handful of sleeping and eating options.

🛏 Sleeping & Eating

Danhostel Hirtshals   HOSTEL €

(☑98 94 12 48; www.danhostelhirtshals.dk; Kystvejen 53; dm Dkr160, d without/with bathroom Dkr520/575; @🕾) This is a good budget option, 1km southwest of the train station, with helpful staff and the usual high-standard Danhostel facilities. Its best feature is its location, across the road from a beach. Dorm beds are available July to September.

Hotel Hirtshals   HOTEL €€

(☑98 94 20 77; www.hotelhirtshals.dk; Havnegade 2; s/d/f from Dkr695/795/1295; 🕾) On the main square above the fishing harbour, Hotel Hirtshals has bright, comfortable rooms with steepled ceilings – try for one with a sea view (at the time of research a new wing was under construction). It's well-positioned for enjoying the town's restaurants and is heavily peopled by ferry-going Norwegians.

Hirtshals Fiskehus   SEAFOOD €€

(http://hirtshalsfiskehus.dk; Sydvestkajen 7; meals Dkr59-129; ⊘11am-9pm Jun-Aug, to 8pm May & Sep) There's a popular *kro* (inn) on the main square, Grønne Plads, but we recommend you take the steps down to the fishing harbour come mealtime. Here, a fishmonger-cafe enjoys a prime quayside position and offers a menu of good-value fish dishes (*fiskefrikadeller*, fish burger, etc) to eat in or takeaway.

ℹ Information

The main pedestrian street is Nørregade, southwest of the train station and the ferry terminals. The seaward end of Nørregade opens out into Den Grønne Plads (Green Square), with stairs leading down to the fishing harbour. There are banks and services along Nørregade.

The **tourist office** (☑98 94 22 20; www.visit hirtshals.dk; Dalsagervej 1; ⊘9am-6pm Mon-Sat Jul, 9am-4pm Mon-Sat Aug, 9am-4pm Mon-Fri, to 1pm Sat Sep-Jun) is part of a 'Velkomstcenter' (Welcome Centre) 2.5km southeast of the train station off the E39 (to Aalborg), catering to motorists fresh off the Norwegian ferries. A small, more-central **museum** (www.vhm.dk; Sophus Thomsens Gade 6; 10am-4pm Mon-Fri, to 2pm Sat Jul, 10am-4pm Mon-Fri Aug, shorter hrs rest of yr), off Nørregade, also has maps and brochures, and a complex schedule of opening hours.

ℹ Getting There & Around

BOAT

The following international ferries use Hirtshals as their main port.

Color Line (www.colorline.com) Service to/from the Norwegian ports of Kristiansand and Larvik.

Fjordline (www.fjordline.com) Fast catamaran to Kristiansand from mid-May to August, plus year-round ferry to Stavanger and Bergen, and to Langesund (all in Norway).

Smyril Line (www.smyril-line.com) Weekly departures to the Faroe Islands and Iceland.

BUS

Summer bus 99 stops at Nordsøen Oceanarium, Tornby Strand and Hirtshals station.

CAR

Hirtshals is 49km southwest of Skagen via Rtes 597 and 40, and 41km northwest of Frederikshavn via the E39 and Rte 35.

ℹ SUMMER BUSES

The Danish train system doesn't extend to northwest Jutland. If you're holidaying in the area in summer and don't have your own transport, you may come to rely on 'Toppen af Denmark' (Top of Denmark) – the number 99 bus that runs a few times daily from the top tip of Jutland (Grenen) along the northwest coast, taking in Skagen, Gammel Skagen, Hirtshals, Tornby Strand, Hjørring, Lønstrup, Løkken, Fårup Sommerland (where it connects with bus 200 to Aalborg) and Blokhus. Naturally, it also does the route in reverse.

The service runs only for about six weeks (the height of the summer season) from late June/early July to mid-August. Pick up a timetable or call ☑98 11 11 11; the website for **Nordjyllands Trafikselskab** (www.nordjyllandstrafikselskab.dk) is in Danish, but timetables should be easy enough to access (just look for 'Sommerbus').

TRAIN

Hirtshals' train station is on Havnegade, west of the ferry terminals. A private railway connects Hirtshals with Hjørring at least hourly (Dkr30, 20 minutes). At Hjørring you can connect with DSB trains to Aalborg, Frederikshavn or destinations further south.

Hjørring

POP 25,100

That the inland town of Hjørring has few hotels speaks volumes – the holiday action is going on elsewhere, at the surrounding seaside towns. Still, if you don't have your own wheels, Hjørring may be an OK base, given its good transport connections. And it's a handsome service town, far more atmospheric than Hirtshals, with medieval churches, street sculptures, and good eating and shopping opportunities.

If you're using Hjørring as a base, the attractive midrange **Hotel Phønix** (🖉98 92 54 55; www.phoenix-hjoerring.dk; Jernbanegade 6; s/d incl breakfast Dkr895/995; @🛜) is a better choice than the out-of-town hostel, thanks to its position close to the train and bus stations.

ℹ️ Information

Springvandspladsen (Hjørring's main square) is a five-minute walk north of the train station along Jernbanegade; stroll 200m further north on Strømgade to reach Sankt Olai Plads, which is bordered by three medieval churches.

Tourist Office (🖉72 33 48 78; www.visithjoer ring.dk; Østergade 30; ⊘10am-6pm Mon-Fri, to 3pm Sat) At the library, inside the Metropol shopping centre.

ℹ️ Getting There & Away

BUS

Hjørring is well served by regional buses operated by **Nordjyllands Trafikselskab** (NT, North Jutland Transport Association; www.nordjylland-strafikselskab.dk), with services to many parts of northern Jutland. The bus station is across the road from the train station, accessed from Asylgade.

CAR

Hjørring is 35km west of Frederikshavn on Rte 35, and 17km south of Hirtshals on Rte 55 or the E39.

TRAIN

Hjørring is on the Aarhus–Frederikshavn DSB train line and is also the terminus of a short private train line to Hirtshals. Destinations by train (services run at least hourly) include:

JUTLAND'S BEST BEACHES

The water's never going to be as warm as the Med, but Denmark has long coastal stretches of white sand. Following are some of our fave Jutland beach-going spots:

➡ southern Als

➡ western Fanø

➡ Grenaa

➡ Løkken

➡ Moesgård Strand (Aarhus)

➡ western Rømø

➡ Skagen

➡ Tornby Strand (Hirtshals)

Aalborg (Dkr80, 45 minutes)
Aarhus (Dkr230, 2¼ hours)
Frederikshavn (Dkr50, 30 minutes)
Hirtshals (Dkr30, 20 minutes)
Skagen (Dkr60, 1½ hours) Change trains at Frederikshavn.

Løkken

POP 1600

A generation of Danish holidaymakers may raise an eyebrow when they read this, but Løkken is now an appealing holiday spot for all ages. It was once the renowned summer habitat of teenage party-animals, but has matured considerably since those heady days and now draws a tamer crowd.

The former fishing town's biggest drawcard is its wide, sandy beach, and the requisite shops, ice-creameries and cafes welcome the summer bombardment. Colder months see the town go into hibernation.

◎ Sights & Activities

Fårup Sommerland   AMUSEMENT PARK
(www.faarupsommerland.dk; Pirupvejen, Blokhus; admission Dkr240-265; ⊘from 10am daily mid-Jun–mid-Aug, also open select days in May, Sep & Oct) One of the most-visited Danish attractions, this wholesome (and pricey) amusement park caters to holidaying families in search of distractions – of which there are plenty, from roller coasters to kiddie-safe rides and a huge waterpark with wave pool and waterslides. Everyone over the age of three pays the same entrance fee. Consider visiting just in the afternoon, when the entry price drops

WORTH A TRIP

RUBJERG KNUDE

About 13km north of Løkken (en route to the town of Lønstrup) is Rubjerg Knude, an area of sand dunes that show just how Mother Nature calls the shots on this wind-whipped coast. **Rubjerg Knude Fyr** (the lighthouse) stood 200m inland when it opened in 1900, some 60m above sea level. Over time the sea moved closer, and by the late 1960s the lighthouse had to be closed because frequent heavy sand drifts were making its light near-impossible to see from the sea. In 1980 it opened as a museum with exhibitions about the migrating sands, but had to close in 2002 as the sand drift was burying the museum buildings. Today it attracts tourists as a photogenic landmark and curiosity, partly submerged in sand. It is expected that the lighthouse will fall into the sea in the coming decade or so, due to coastal erosion. There's good information online at www. rubjergknude.dk.

To reach Rubjerg Knude, take Rte 55 northeast from Løkken and turn left after about 6km, onto Lønstrupvej (signposted). It's quite a walk from the car park to the lighthouse (a good half-hour). Summer bus 99 passes through the area.

to Dkr175 to Dkr200 (depending on the time of year).

Closing hours vary (from 5pm to 8.30pm); check the website to confirm opening days and hours.

The park is on the outskirts of Blokhus, about 15km south of Løkken. Such is its popularity, frequent summer buses run here from Aalborg (bus 200), Frederikshavn (bus 77) and Skagen (bus 99, via Hirtshals, Hjørring and Løkken).

Løkken Beach   BEACH
Go looking for your own (free) beachside fun at Løkken's lovely long strand, lined with neat rows of white wooden beach huts and a few stout little fishing vessels (interestingly, these 480-plus beach huts are stored inland during winter). Check out the kitesurfers taking advantage of west-coast winds (BYO gear).

🛏 Sleeping & Eating

The tourist office has loads of holiday houses on its books, usually rented out weekly in high season. Hotels and apartments are also generally geared to long-stayers rather than overnighters passing through; the tourist office has details of private rooms for rent.

★ **Villa Vendel**   GUESTHOUSE €€
(☑ 98 99 14 56; www.villavendel.dk; Harald Fischers Vej 12; r & apt Dkr500-850; 🛜) East of Torvet is this delightful option, a member of the Small Elegant Hotels group (an apt description), with four rooms (all with bathrooms) and two apartments. There's a classy old-world feel with wooden floors and neutral decor,

plus a guest kitchen, a courtyard for alfresco breakfast (Dkr65) and a large garden.

A friendly owner, plenty of local info, good-value prices and year-round opening make for an impressive package.

Bolcheriet   SWEETS €
(www.bolcheriet.dk; Torvet 1; ⊙ 10am-5pm daily Jul-Aug, shorter hrs rest of yr) On the main square, be sure to pop into Bolcheriet, a colourful, sweet-smelling Willy Wonka world where you can see candy being made (and of course purchase the stuff).

Restaurant Løkken Badehotel   DANISH €€
(www.restaurantlb.dk; Torvet 8; lunch Dkr69-149, dinner mains Dkr139-259; ⊙ from 11.30am daily) You'll have no problem finding a place to eat on Torvet, brimming with alfresco tables. This sunshine-yellow hotel sits in pole position, with a huge terrace and a menu that wins locals' hearts with well-prepared, old-school Danish favourites, from lunchtime *smørrebrød* to *stegt rødspætte* (pan-fried plaice). The hotel itself is home to family-sized holiday apartments.

ℹ Information

Tourist Office (☑ 98 99 10 09; www.loekken. dk; Jyllandsgade 15; ⊙ 10am-4pm Mon-Fri, 9am-4pm Sat Jul-Aug, 10am-3pm Mon-Fri, 9am-noon Sat Sep-Jun) Helpful office beside the SuperBrugsen supermarket on the way into town. Has a wealth of knowledge on activities in the area and can book hotels and summer-houses.

ℹ Getting There & Away

Løkken is on Rte 55, 18km southwest of Hjørring. Bus 71 runs frequently between Løkken and

Hjørring (Dkr40, 30 minutes), and Løkken and Aalborg (Dkr60, 70 minutes).

Løkken is also on the summertime bus 99 route.

Hanstholm

POP 2160

Despite its interesting wartime museum and status as the northern boundary of one of Denmark's new national parks, modern Hanstholm is a charmless place – thanks largely to the fact that a small, lacklustre shopping centre serves as the town's heart.

There's still plenty of fish-factory action down at the harbour, and some excellent places to eat there, but overnighting is better down the west coast at Klitmøller or Nørre Vorupør.

◉ Sights

Viewpoint   VIEWPOINT

Hanstholm's impressive commercial harbour was completed in 1967; since then the town has developed into one of Denmark's largest fishing ports and prominent industrial centres. There's a good viewpoint over the harbour at the end of Helshagevej (follow the signs for 'Havneudsigt').

MuseumsCenter Hanstholm   MUSEUM

(www.museumscenterhanstholm.dk; Molevej 29; adult/child Dkr75/25; ⊙10am-5pm Jun-Aug, to 4pm Feb-May & Sep-Oct) Hanstholm was a key player in the German occupation of Denmark and this impressive museum is based around a German bunker. Hitler used this as part of his 'Atlantic Wall' system, a series of fortifications that spread from Kirkenes in Norway to the Pyrenees. Along with the bunker you can visit the Documentation Centre, which outlines this period in more detail and provides an insight into the way of life for locals under Hitler's rule.

🛏 Sleeping & Eating

Hotel Hanstholm   HOTEL €€

(☑ 97 96 10 44; www.hotelhanstholm.dk; Christian Hansens Vej 2; s/d Dkr795/995; @ 🛜 🏊) Rooms are of a good standard and facilities are laid on thick, including indoor pool, sauna and on-site restaurant (dinner mains Dkr179 to Dkr288).

★ Det Gamle Røgeri   SEAFOOD €

(http://roegeriet.dk/hanstholm/; Kuttergade 7; meals Dkr65-135; ⊙10am-6pm Sun-Thu, to 7pm Fri & Sat) If you're anywhere near Hanstholm,

head to the harbour then follow the signs to this unprepossessing cafeteria. On the menu are some spectacular fishy treats – the *stjerneskud* is the house speciality: two fried and one steamed piece of fish, plus smoked salmon, shrimp and asparagus on bread. It's so good we had to visit again the next day for seconds.

❶ Information

Tourist Office (☑ 97 92 19 00; www.visitthy. dk; Tårnvej 21; ⊙10am-4pm Mon-Fri, 11am-2pm Sat mid-Jun–Jul, 11am-4pm Mon-Fri, 11am-2pm Sat & Sun Aug–mid-Sep) The summertime tourist office is at the local lighthouse dating from 1843 (which you can climb, for Dkr10). It's often run by volunteers, so hours may be slightly erratic.

❶ Getting There & Away

By road, Hanstholm is at the terminus of Rtes 181, 26 and 29. Thisted, 21km to the south via Rte 26, has the nearest train station. Buses 90 and 322 regularly connect Thisted and Hanstholm (Dkr30, 45 minutes); bus 322 runs via Klitmøller.

THY NATIONAL PARK

One of Denmark's handful of newly protected spaces, **Thy National Park** (www.nationalparkthy.dk) stretches 55km south along the North Sea coast from Hanstholm to Agger Tange, covering an area of 244 sq km of coastline, dunes, lakes, pine forest and moors. There are plenty of windswept, wide-open spaces to access: marked hiking, cycling and horse-riding trails, bird-watching opportunities, plus a good dose of history in fishing hamlets and WWII-era German bunkers.

Local tourist offices can help with information on activities within the park, or check out www.visitthy.dk. A small park information centre (open 1pm to 5pm April to November) lives at **Stenbjerg Landingsplads**, an atmospheric cluster of fishermen's huts off Rte 181 halfway between Agger and Klitmøller.

Also worth a stop is the small beach resort of **Nørre Vorupør**, where fishing vessels are winched up onto the sand. In mid-2014 Denmark's first *havbad* (sea baths) opened here, with a concrete pool built in the North Sea shallows to enable safe swimming.

Klitmøller

POP 820

Klitmøller's windy ways and curving waves have transformed the small fishing village into one of Europe's premier surfing destinations, known colloquially as 'Cold Hawaii'. It's a small holiday settlement of summerhouses, where wetsuit-clad surfers roam the streets and outdoorsy folk get around on bikes, seemingly oblivious to the cracking wind.

Klitmøller hosts a PWA (Professional Windsurfing Association) world cup event each September.

Activities

Don't despair if you're not world-championship windsurfing material. In addition to the challenging waves of the North Sea, the calmer waters of the lake Vandet Sø or the Limfjord are close by, so there are conditions suitable for all levels.

Westwind Klitmøller
WINDSURFING, KITESURFING

(✐97 97 56 56; http://klitmoller.westwind.dk; Ørhagevej 150) Long-established Westwind has enthusiastic surfers keen to show you the ropes of windsurfing, kitesurfing, surfing and stand-up paddle boarding (SUP), in English, German or Danish. A three-hour introductory windsurfing course costs Dkr375; a 4½-hour introduction to kitesurfing is Dkr899. For those who know what they're doing, gear rental is available from Westwind's well-stocked surf shop.

Cold Hawaii Surf Camp
SURFING

(✐29 10 88 73; www.coldhawaiisurfcamp.com; Ørhagevej 151) There's an excellent backstory to how this young Israeli-Tahitian couple with fine surfing pedigrees ended up in Klitmøller. They run a cool cafe and surf shop, along with learn-to-surf lessons (90 minutes, Dkr290) and multiday surf camps (accommodation included; five days from Dkr2500). There's also gear rental.

☞ Sleeping & Eating

Gaarden Klitmøller
GUESTHOUSE €

(✐97 97 56 80; http://gaardenklitmoller.dk; Kalles Mark 2; r without bathroom Dkr400-550; ☺Apr-Oct;

☎) Part of this old building has been newly converted into a colourful guesthouse, with three bedrooms sharing a bathroom, living space and kitchenette. It's lovely and homely; linen is additional (Dkr35), as is breakfast (Dkr50).

Nystrup Camping
CAMPGROUND €

(✐97 97 52 49; www.nystrupcamping.dk; Trøjborgvej 22; per adult/site Dkr84/30-80; ☺Mar-Oct; ⊛☎) Populated by windblown types and littered with surfing kit, this popular ground has plenty of trees for shelter and decent facilities including cabins, bike hire and a playground.

N151
CAFE €

(Ørehagevej 151; meals Dkr35-99; ☺8am-5pm) In a bright, inviting space, Vahine from Cold Hawaii Surf Camp has set up a fun cafe, with good coffee, homebaked cakes and authentic French pastries. Plus, topping the list of things you *don't* expect to find in northwest Jutland: *poisson crú*, a Tahitian dish of raw fish marinated in lime and coconut milk served with warm rice.

Klitmøller Røgeri
SEAFOOD €

(http://klitmoeller-roegeri.dk; Ørhagevej 152; meals Dkr29-119; ☺11.30am-9pm Jul–mid-Aug, shorter hrs May, Jun & Sep) Offers a sensational selection of fresh and smoked seafood, not far from the beach – grab some fish and chips or a prawn-stuffed baguette and watch the water acrobatics in full swing.

Fiskerestaurant Niels Juel
SEAFOOD €€

(http://nielsjuel.com; Ørhagevej 150; fish buffet Dkr149; ☺from 5.30pm Tue-Sun May-Sep) The large terrace of this elevated restaurant – whitewashed under a thatched roof – is the best spot to watch the surfing action. The good-value fish buffet heaves with herrings, prawns and salmon. Downstairs from the restaurant is a casual all-day cafe-bar with draught beer and fast food.

❶ Getting There & Away

Klitmøller is 11km southwest of Hanstholm on Rte 181, and 18km northwest of Thisted on Rte 557. Bus 322 runs frequently between the three towns; Thisted has a rail connection for journeys south.

Understand Denmark

DENMARK TODAY 262
Racial tensions, contentious politics and ambitious environmental goals: contemporary Denmark is a complex creature.

HISTORY 264
Relics from Denmark's past abound: bog bodies, Viking forts, ancient churches and magnificent castles. Piece together the history jigsaw here.

THE DANISH LIFESTYLE. 273
From neighbourly trust and *hygge* (cosiness), to winter blues and gender equality: exactly what shapes and challenges the world's happiest populace?

DANISH DESIGN. 276
Groundbreaking modern architecture, statement furniture and homewares – get acquainted with Denmark's coveted lines and curves.

FOOD & DRINK 279
'New Nordic' ingenuity, old-school pork and spuds, and sweet, sticky cinnamon snails: take your taste buds on a tour around the Danish table.

LITERATURE, FILM & TV 285
Fairy tales, existentialist enlightenment, brooding Nordic noir and envelope-pushing films: Denmark's creative output is a spellbinding mix.

Denmark Today

The Danes are, overwhelmingly, a happy bunch. If you believe those contentment surveys and liveability lists, Denmark is one of the happiest nations on earth, with some of the best quality of life. It's not hard to see why: despite the bumps of the global financial crisis, it has among the highest per-capita GDP in the European Union and unemployment is relatively low. Education is free, and Danish social-welfare programs are the envy of many.

Best in Print

The Complete Fairy Tales (Hans Christian Andersen; 1874) The most famous Danish book in the world.

Either/Or (Søren Kierkegaard; 1843) The first great work of the father of existentialism.

Miss Smilla's Feeling for Snow (Peter Høeg; 1992) A worldwide hit set largely in Copenhagen.

We, the Drowned (Carsten Jensen; 2006) An epic tale of sailors from seafaring Marstal on Ærø.

The Almost Nearly Perfect People (Michael Booth; 2014) Explores the stories behind the 'Nordic miracle'.

Best on Film

Babette's Feast (1987) Set in a rugged west-coast village in 1871.

Pelle the Conqueror (1987) Award-winning depiction of the hard life of an immigrant in 19th-century Denmark.

Festen (The Celebration; 1998) First of the Dogme95 movies, from celebrated writer-director Thomas Vinterberg.

Italian for Beginners (2000) Diverse but damaged Danes learning the language of love.

In a Better World (2010) Playground bullying, conflicting moral choices – engineered to question the cosy stereotype of Denmark.

Happiness & Harmony?

There is more to the Danes' story of contentment. Stroll around Copenhagen or almost any Danish town and you'll experience some of the most harmonious civic spaces anywhere. Look a bit closer, however, and – as in a Hans Christian Andersen fable – you'll find a darker side, too. As with other European nations, there's been a gradual shift to the political right in this famously liberal nation. Concern has grown over immigration – particularly from Muslim countries – and an erosion of traditional values.

For all the talk of assimilation and the comprehensive state effort to achieve it, racial, cultural and religious fault lines and prejudices remain. This challenge to tolerance has unnerved many Danes, while many of them avoid confronting their underlying resentment towards non-European newcomers. In mid-2014, the issue was highlighted when the anti-immigration Danish People's Party won the European Parliament election with four seats and nearly 27% of the vote.

Internal 'class divisions' (of a sort) have also appeared – fanned by the media, it is alleged – between urban and rural Denmark. There is much marginalising talk about the so-called '*udkantsdanmark*', the sparsely populated, 'peripheral' areas of the country. These outlying regions are often portrayed in the media as home to the poor (and poorly educated, and/or unemployed), while the wealthy are concentrated in the larger cities. Urbanisation is not a new phenomenon, but Copenhagen's population is increasing by about 10,000 people annually. This is placing pressure on the city's infrastructure, while also posing questions about the future prospects of *udkantsdanmark*.

Politics & Economics

After a decade of conservative rule and with a sluggish economy due to the global financial crisis, Denmark's political pendulum again moved left in its most recent parliamentary elections, held in 2011. After a close election (fought largely over which side was better equipped to steer the Danish economy out of its malaise), a new, centre-left coalition took government.

Since the 2011 election, the new government coalition has been led by Social Democrat Helle Thorning-Schmidt, the country's first female prime minister (and FYI: the prescient Danish political drama *Borgen* premiered in 2010). During the first year in office her government rolled back anti-immigration legislation enacted by the previous government, and passed a tax-reform with support from the liberal-conservative opposition.

Taxation and immigration have remained controversial issues among the parties of Thorning-Schmidt's ruling coalition. It has not been all smooth sailing: her government was weakened in early 2014 when the small Socialist People's Party left the coalition amid disagreements over plans to sell off a stake in the state utilities giant Dong Energy to investment bank Goldman Sachs, among others.

The next elections must take place no later than mid-September 2015. Opinion polling at the time of our research (a long way out from elections) showed voters favouring the conservative parties.

Sustainability

As well as their admirable attitudes to civic duties (voter turnout at the last parliamentary election was around 87%; there is relatively low tax evasion), Danes go about their business with a green conscience.

While some Western governments continue to debate the veracity of climate-change science, Denmark gets on with (sustainable) business. Wind power generates around 30% of Denmark's energy supply, and the country is a market leader in wind-power technology, exporting many wind turbines.

The long-term goal for Danish energy policy is clear: the entire energy supply – electricity, heating, industry and transport – is to be covered by renewable energy by 2050. The city of Copenhagen has pledged to go carbon-neutral by 2025.

The cycling culture is another example of Denmark's green outlook. Copenhagen has around 430km of continuous, safe cycle paths, and 52% of all Copenhageners cycle to their place of work or education every day. The network of paths continues to expand and improve – beautifully illustrated by the innovative Cykelslangen elevated bike track over the harbour, which opened in mid-2014.

POPULATION: **5.57 MILLION**

AREA: **43,094 SQ KM**

COASTLINE: **7314KM**

UNEMPLOYMENT: **6%**

GDP PER CAPITA: **US$37,800**

if Denmark were 100 people

80 would be Lutheran
15 would be no denomination

4 would be Muslim
1 would be other

population distribution
(%)

87 Urban
13 Rural

population per sq km

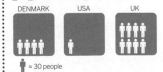

DENMARK   USA   UK

≈ 30 people

History

Denmark's size is deceptive. It might be Europe's 30th largest country, but this corner of Scandinavia has played a significant role in shaping the region. By the late 4th century, the Jutes had invaded and settled in England, followed centuries later by the Vikings, whose own presence spanned from Newfoundland to Baghdad. By the beginning of the 19th century, Denmark's colonial power reached four continents. Yet even with the dramatic shrinking of Danish territory, the Danes have continued to inspire, influence and shape the global sphere, from science, philosophy and medicine, to social justice.

Of Stone, Bronze & Iron

So fearsome were the Vikings that the English introduced a special prayer into church services: 'From the fury of the Northmen, good Lord, deliver us'.

Humans first trod the Danish earth and dug the region's flint tens of thousands of years ago as retreating glaciers let lichen and mosses grow, attracting herds of reindeer. Permanent settlements sprang up in about 12,000 BC.

Stone Age culture relied primarily on hunting, but as the climate gradually warmed these hunters resettled near the sea, subsisting on fish, sea birds and seals. Small-scale agriculture followed and villages developed around the fields.

Around 1800 BC the first artisans began fashioning weapons, tools, jewellery and finely crafted works of art in the new metal, bronze, traded from as far away as Crete and Mycenae.

Locally available iron led to superior ploughs, permitting larger-scale agricultural communities. Present-day Denmark's linguistic and cultural roots date to the late Iron Age arrival of the Danes, a tribe thought to have migrated south from Sweden in about AD 500.

At the dawn of the 9th century, the territory of present-day Denmark was on the perimeter of Europe, but Charlemagne (r 768–814) extended the power of the Franks northward to present-day northern Germany. Hoping to ward off a Frankish invasion, Godfred, king of Jutland, reinforced an impressive earthen rampart called the Danevirke. However, the raiding Franks breached the rampart, bringing Christianity to Denmark at sword point.

TIMELINE	c 12,000 BC	c 4000 BC	c 1800 BC
	The first permanent settlements are established on Jutland and the nearby Baltic islands.	People begin to grow more food crops. The advent of agriculture sees woods cleared by slash-and-burn and grain is sown in the resulting ash.	Bronze is introduced to Denmark, giving rise to skilled artisans who fashion weapons, tools, jewellery and works of art. Trade routes to the south bring the supply of bronze.

The Vikings

To the modern imagination, the word 'Viking' commonly conjures images of bearded thugs in horned helmets, jumping from longships and pillaging their way through early Christendom. While some of these Northmen (as they were known in Britain) were partial to a spot of looting and slaughter – not to mention slave trading – the real history of these Scandinavian seafarers is far more complex.

The Viking era spanned several centuries and took on different characteristics throughout the time. Although unrecorded raids had probably been occurring for decades, the start of the Viking Age is generally dated from AD 793, when Nordic Vikings ransacked Lindisfarne Monastery, off the coast of Northumbria in northeastern England. Survivors described the Vikings' sleek square-rigged vessels as 'dragons flying in the air' and the raiders as 'terrifying heathens'.

Early Viking raiders often targeted churches and monasteries for their wealth of gold and jewels. Books and other precious but perishable cultural artefacts were just some of the raids' collateral damage. Roughing up monks – who wrote the history of the age – hardly endeared the Vikings to posterity.

The Vikings were initially adventurous opportunists who took advantage of the region's turmoil and unstable political status quo but in time their campaigns evolved from piratical forays into organised expeditions that established far-flung colonies overseas.

They were successful traders, extraordinary mariners and insatiable explorers whose exploits took them to Byzantium, Russia and North Africa, and even as far as the Caspian Sea and Baghdad. They also established settlements in Iceland, Greenland and Newfoundland.

The Vikings settled in several places too, including Northern France and the British Isles, proving to be able farmers. They were also shrewd political players, establishing their own kingdoms and intermarrying with local nobles or squeezing protection money from local kings. Even the historically pivotal 1066 Battle of Hastings can be thought of not as a battle between England and France, but essentially a fight between two leaders descended from this Nordic stock (William and Harald).

Settlement and assimilation was one reason for a decline in raiding and fighting. The Jelling Stone of Harald I (Bluetooth) that still stands in the churchyard in Jelling is the document of an even more important factor: the embrace in the 10th century of Christianity in Scandinavia and thus closer cultural ties and a degree (very relatively speaking) of 'civilisation'.

Human trafficking was not uncommon among the Vikings, who captured and enslaved women and young men while pillaging Anglo-Saxon, Celtic and Slavic settlements. These captives were subsequently sold in giant slave markets in Europe and the Middle East.

HISTORY THE VIKINGS

c AD 500	793	950–985	985–1014
Arrival of the Danes in the late Iron Age. This tribe, thought to have migrated south from Sweden, forms present-day Denmark's linguistic and cultural roots.	The first documented raid at Lindisfarne Monastery on north-eastern England by Danish Vikings.	King Harald I (Bluetooth), son of Gorm the Old, unifies Denmark. He spearheads the conversion of Danes to Christianity from his court at Jelling.	During the reigns of Harald Bluetooth's son Sweyn Forkbeard and grandsons Harald II and Canute the Great, England is conquered and a short-lived Anglo-Danish kingdom formed.

A (Quasi) Unified Denmark

By the early 9th century Jutland (and parts of southern Norway) were more or less united under a single king. In the late 9th century unification of the territories that make up modern-day Denmark inched forwards when warriors, led by the Norwegian chieftain Hardegon, conquered the Jutland peninsula; Hardegon then began to extend his power base across the rest of Denmark's territory.

The current Danish monarchy traces its roots back to Gorm the Old, Hardegon's son, who reigned in the early 10th century from Jelling in central Jutland. His son, Harald Bluetooth, who ruled for 35 years, concluded the conquest of Denmark and also completed Denmark's adoption of Christianity, partly to appease his powerful Frankish neighbours to the south who, a century earlier, had sent the missionary Ansgar to build churches in the Danish towns of Ribe and Hedeby.

Harald Bluetooth's son Sweyn (Svend) Forkbeard (r 987–1014) and grandsons Harald II (r 1014–18) and Canute the Great (r 1019–35) conquered England, establishing a short-lived Anglo-Danish kingdom over much of the British Isles. Canute the Great was the first true Danish king to sit on the throne of England, reigning in much the same manner as an English king except that he employed Scandinavian soldiers to maintain his command.

When Canute's son Hardecanute died, the balance of power shifted to the English heirs of Alfred the Great, although many of the Danes who had settled in England elected to stay on.

Unsuccessful attempts by the Danes to reclaim England followed, and the defeat of the Norwegian Vikings by Harold II of England at the Battle of Stamford Bridge in 1066 heralded the end of the Viking era.

The Bloody Middle Ages

Internal strife, plots, counter plots and assassinations involving rival nobles, wealthy landowners and corrupt church leaders blighted the early medieval era.

King Valdemar I eventually united a war-weary country and enacted Denmark's first written laws, known as the Jyske Lov (Jutland Code) in Vordingborg, southern Zealand. His successors enacted other laws that were quite progressive for their time: no imprisonment without just cause, an annual assembly of the *hof* (national council), and the first supreme court.

Margrethe, who had assumed de facto control of the Crown after her young son Oluf died in 1387, became the official head of state and Denmark's first ruling queen. The next year Swedish nobles sought Margrethe's assistance in a rebellion against their unpopular German-born

---

Key Viking Sights

Lindholm Høje (p243)

Viking Ship Museum (p109)

Ladbyskibet (p169)

Nationalmuseet (p45)

Trelleborg (p122)

Stone Age villagers buried their dead in dolmen, a type of grave monument comprising upright stones and topped by a large capstone; features still common to Denmark's meadows.

1066	1137–1157	1219	1363
The defeat of Norwegian Vikings by Harold II of England at the Battle of Stamford Bridge heralds the end of the Viking era.	Civil strife, assassinations, plots and general skulduggery continues until Valdemar, son of Knud Lavard, takes the throne in 1157, introducing progressive policies in the Jyske Lov (Jutland Code).	The Dannebrog (Danish flag; today the oldest national flag in the world) is raised for the first time, its creation supposedly divinely provided and firing the Danes to victory in Estonia under Valdemar II.	Norway's King Haakon marries Margrethe, daughter of the Danish King Valdemar IV, who is to become an influential and powerful queen.

DENMARK'S BOG BODIES

The people of Iron Age Denmark left little evidence and precious little by way of written records of themselves. Thankfully, some extraordinary discoveries in the last couple of centuries offer tantalising insights into this culture.

Drainage and peat cutting in Denmark's bogs has yielded hundreds of often amazingly well-preserved bodies of men, women and children, mostly from the Iron Age (the early centuries BC and AD).

Many of the bodies are also compelling historical who- and why-dunnits. Burial was unusual (cremation was common at the time) and some appear to have been ritually killed, perhaps due to the supernatural power the Iron Age people are thought to have attributed to the bogs.

If it was ritual killing, were these people victims or willing participants? Windeby I, for example, discovered in 1950 in Germany and aged about 16, was found underneath rocks and branches, presumably used to push down the body and suggesting some kind of ritual. Others may have simply been waylaid, murdered and dumped.

The Grauballe Man certainly died a nasty death that suggests a brutal execution. It's a history and forensics conundrum, brilliantly illustrated at his current resting place, the Moesgård Museum (p209) in Aarhus. In Copenhagen's Nationalmuseet (p45), the Woman from Huldremose met a seemingly horrific end, a vicious cut almost severing her right upper arm. Twenty-two centuries after her death, she remains wrapped in her skirt, scarf and snug-looking capes.

The most famous body of all is that of the Tollund Man. On show at the Museum Silkeborg (p224), his head is extraordinarily preserved, right down to the stubble on his chin. He died, aged in his 30s, naked but for the beautifully plaited leather noose used to strangle him and the leather cap he has worn for 2000 years. It frames an utterly serene face. Was he a holy sacrifice or a punished prisoner? The mystery remains unsolved.

king. The Swedes hailed Margrethe as their regent, and in turn she sent Danish troops to Sweden, securing victory over the king's forces.

A decade later Margrethe established a formal alliance between Denmark, Norway and Sweden known as the Kalmar Union, to counter the powerful German-based Hanseatic League that had come to dominate regional trade.

In 1410 King Erik of Pomerania, Margrethe's grandson, staged an unsuccessful attack on the Hanseatic League, which sapped the Kalmar Union's vitality. This, together with Erik's penchant for appointing Danes to public office in Sweden and Norway, soured relations with aristocrats in those countries. The Swedish council withdrew from the union, whereupon the Danish nobility deposed Erik in 1439.

Learn everything you ever wanted to know about a millennium of Danish royals at www.danmark skonger.dk.

1375–87	1396–1439	1534	1588–1648
Five-year-old Oluf becomes king of Denmark following the death of Valdemar IV, and five years later also becomes king of Norway. His mother assumes de facto control on his death.	Reign of King Erik of Pomerania, Margrethe's grandson. He stages an unsuccessful attack on the Hanseatic League, which exhausts the resources of the Kalmar Union. The Danish nobility depose Erik in 1439.	Following King Frederick I's death, Hanseatic mercenaries from Lübeck (now in Germany) invade southern Jutland and Zealand. Danish peasants and members of the middle class welcome the invaders.	The early prosperous and peaceful years of Christian IV's long reign end in 1625 when Christian attempts to neutralise Swedish expansion by beginning the Thirty Years' War. Denmark suffers crippling losses.

Erik's successor, King Christopher III, made amends by pledging to keep the administrations of the three countries separate. However, the union continued to be a rocky one, and in 1523 the Swedes elected their own king, Gustav Vasa. The Kalmar Union was permanently dissolved, but Norway would remain under Danish rule for another three centuries.

The Lutheran Reformation & Civil War

The monarchy and Catholic Church played out a pivotal power struggle during the Danish Reformation. Caught in the middle of this religious and political foment was King Frederik I, who over the course of 10 years went from promising to fight heresy against Catholicism to inviting Lutheran preachers to Denmark. When Frederik died, the lack of a clear successor left the country in civil war.

The following year (1534) Hanseatic mercenaries from Lübeck (now in Germany) invaded southern Jutland and Zealand. By and large the Lübeckers were welcomed as liberators by peasants and members of the middle class, who were in revolt against the nobility.

Alarmed by the revolt, a coalition of aristocrats and Catholic bishops crowned the Lutheran Christian III as king. Still, the rebellion raged on. In Jutland, manor houses were set ablaze and the peasants made advances against the armies of the aristocracy.

Christian's general, Rantzau, took control, cutting Lübeck off from the sea and marching northward through Jutland, brutally smashing peasant bands. Rantzau's troops besieged Copenhagen, where merchants supported the uprising and welcomed the prospect of becoming a Hanseatic stronghold. Cut off from the outside world, Copenhagen's citizens suffered starvation and epidemics before surrendering after a year in 1536.

Christian III quickly consolidated his power, offering leniency to the merchants and Copenhagen burghers who had revolted in exchange for their allegiance. Catholic bishops, on the other hand, were arrested, and monasteries, churches and other ecclesiastical estates became the property of the Crown.

Thus the Danish Lutheran Church became the only state-sanctioned denomination and was placed under the direct control of the king. Buoyed by a treasury enriched by confiscated Church properties, the monarchy emerged from the civil war stronger than ever.

War & Absolute Monarchy

A period of peace marked the early reign of Christian IV who then spoiled it by embarking on what would become the ruinous Thirty Years' War. The aim of the war was to neutralise Swedish expansion; its outcome for Denmark was morale- and coffer-sapping losses.

> The Danish Monarchy can be traced back to Viking king Gorm the Old, who ruled from c 936 to his death in c 958. The monarchy is the oldest in Europe.

> The Order of the Elephant was instituted by King Christian I in the 1470s to celebrate the battle elephants of the Christian crusades.

1658	1660–65	1675–1720	1784
Denmark signs the Treaty of Roskilde, the most lamented humiliation in its history, losing a third of its territory, including the island of Bornholm and all territories on the Swedish mainland.	King Frederik III establishes absolute monarchy. He introduces an absolutist constitution called the Kongeloven (Royal Act), which becomes the law of the land for most of the following two centuries.	The monarchy rebuilds the military and fights three more wars with Sweden (1675–79, 1699–1700 and 1709–20), without regaining its lost territories. A period of relative peace follows.	The young Crown Prince Frederik VI assumes control, brings progressive landowners into government and introduces a sweeping series of reforms improving rights for the masses.

Seeing a chance for revenge against Sweden, following its troubled occupation of Poland, Christian IV's successor, Frederik III, once again declared war in 1657. For the Danes, ill-prepared for battle, it was a tremendous miscalculation.

Sweden's King Gustav led his troops back from Poland through Germany and into Jutland, plundering his way north. During 1657–58 – the most severe winter in Danish history – King Gustav marched his soldiers across the frozen seas of the Lille Bælt between Fredericia and the island of Funen. King Gustav's uncanny success unnerved the Danes and he proceeded without serious resistance across the Store Bælt to Lolland and then on to Falster.

The Swedish king had barely made it across the frozen waters of the Storstrømmen to Zealand when the thawing ice broke away behind him, precariously separating him and his advance detachment from the rest of his forces. However, the Danes failed to recognise their sudden advantage; instead of capturing the Swedish king, they sued for peace and agreed to yet another disastrous treaty.

In 1658 Denmark signed the humiliating Treaty of Roskilde, ceding a third of its territory, including the island of Bornholm and all territories on the Swedish mainland. Only Bornholm, which eventually staged a bloody revolt against the Swedes, would again fly the Danish flag.

Absolute monarchy returned in 1660, when King Frederik III cunningly convened a gathering of nobles, placed them under siege, and forced them to nullify their powers of council. Frederik declared his right of absolute rule, declaring the king the highest head on earth, above all human laws and inferior to God alone.

In the following decades the now all-powerful monarchy rebuilt the military and continued to pick fruitless fights with Sweden. Peace of a sort eventually descended and for much of the 18th century the Danes and Swedes managed to coexist without serious hostilities.

> A polar bear was included in the Danish coat of arms in the 1660s to symbolise the country's claim of sovereignty over Greenland.

Revolution

By the turn of the 19th century, Denmark's trading prowess was worrying Britain, by now the world's pre-eminent sea power. When Denmark signed a pact of armed neutrality with Sweden, Prussia and Russia, Britain's navy attacked Copenhagen in 1801, heavily damaging the Danish fleet and forcing Denmark to withdraw from the pact.

Denmark managed to avoid further conflicts and actually profited from the war trade until 1807, when a new treaty between France and Russia once again drew the Danes closer to the conflict.

Wary of Napoleon's growing influence in the Baltic, Britain feared that Denmark might support France. Despite Denmark's neutrality, the British fleet unleashed a devastating surprise bombardment on Copenhagen,

> When Napoleon fell in 1814, the Swedes, then allied with Britain, successfully demanded that Denmark, an ally of France, cede Norway to them.

1790s	1800–01	1846	1849
Feudal obligations of the peasantry are abolished. Large tracts of land are broken up and redistributed to the landless. Education is made compulsory for all children under the age of 14.	Denmark signs a pact of armed neutrality with Sweden, Prussia and Russia. In response, Britain's navy attacks Copenhagen, battering the Danish fleet and forcing Denmark to leave the pact.	Political ferment sweeps Europe; two growing Danish factions (farmers and liberals) join forces to form a liberal party.	The Danish constitution is enacted and absolute monarchy is abolished.

setting much of the city ablaze, destroying its naval yards and confiscating the entire Danish fleet.

Although the unprovoked attack was unpopular enough back home to have been roundly criticised by the British parliament, Britain nonetheless kept the Danish fleet. The British then offered the Danes an alliance – they unsurprisingly refused the offer and instead joined the continental alliance against Britain, who retaliated by blockading both Danish and Norwegian waters, causing poverty in Denmark and famine in Norway.

Despite the disastrous early years of the 19th century, by the 1830s Denmark was flourishing again, economically and culturally. Philosopher Søren Kierkegaard, theologian Nikolaj Frederik Severin Grundtvig and writer Hans Christian Andersen emerged as prominent figures. Sculptor Bertel Thorvaldsen bestowed his grand neoclassical statues on Copenhagen, and Christoffer Wilhelm Eckersberg introduced the Danish school of art.

> In 2000 Denmark resoundingly rejected the adoption of the euro by a referendum. In the same year, the Øresundsbron (Øresund Bridge) was opened, connecting Denmark and Sweden by road and rail.

Democracy

When revolution swept Europe in the spring of 1848, Denmark's new political parties, which had arisen from the debating chambers of the new provincial assemblies, waxed with the waning power of the monarchy. The new Danish king, Frederik VII, under pressure from the new liberal party, abolished the absolute monarchy and drew up a democratic constitution, establishing a parliament with two chambers, Folketing and Landsting, whose members were elected by popular vote.

Although the king retained a limited voice, parliament took control of legislative powers. The constitution also established an independent judiciary and guaranteed the rights of free speech, religion and assembly. Denmark had changed overnight from a virtual dictatorship to one of the most democratic countries in Europe.

When Denmark's new constitution threatened to incorporate the border duchy of Schleswig as an integral part of Denmark, the German

DENMARK'S FINEST HOUR

Soon after taking full control of the country in October 1943, Denmark's Nazi occupiers planned, as they did in the other parts of Europe they occupied, to round up Jewish Danes and deport them to their deaths in the concentration camps. The Danish resistance had other ideas and in an extraordinarily well co-ordinated operation smuggled some 7200 Jews – about 90% of those left in Denmark – into neutral Sweden. In recognition of its actions in saving its Jewish population, Denmark is remembered as one of the Righteous Among the Nations at the Yad Vashem Holocaust Memorial in Jerusalem.

1901	1943	1953	1973
The Venstrereformparti (Left Reform Party) sweeps to power and embarks on an ambitious social reform program, including amending the constitution to give women the right to vote.	In a hastily planned operation, the Danish resistance successfully smuggles some 7200 Jews into Sweden after hearing of Nazi plans to round them up and transport them to its European concentration camps.	The Danish constitution is amended to allow a female monarch, paving the way for Margrethe II to become queen, Denmark's first female monarch since the 14th century.	Denmark joins the European Community (now the European Union).

population in the duchy allied with neighbouring Holstein, sparking years of unrest. In 1864 the Prussian prime minister, Otto von Bismarck, declared war on a militarily weak Denmark and captured Schleswig. Further eroding Denmark's sovereignty, it raised doubts about Denmark's survival as a nation.

In the wake of that defeat, a conservative government took and retained power until the end of the century. The conservatives oversaw a number of economic advances: extending the railway throughout the country and rapid industrialisation that established large-scale shipbuilding, brewing and sugar-refining industries.

The 20th Century

Denmark declared neutrality at the outbreak of WWII, but Germany, threatened by the growing Allied presence in Norway, coveted coastal bases in northern Jutland and in April 1940 seized key Danish strategic defences and occupied the country.

Managing to retain a degree of autonomy, the Danes trod a thin line, running domestic affairs under close Nazi supervision until August 1943 when the Germans took outright control. A Danish resistance movement quickly mushroomed.

Although the island of Bornholm was heavily bombarded by Soviet forces, the rest of Denmark emerged from WWII relatively unscathed. With the country officially free from German control on 5 May 1945, Danes took to the streets, burning the black shades used to cover their windows during bombing raids.

The Social Democrats led a comprehensive social-welfare state in postwar Denmark and cradle-to-grave medical care, education and public assistance was established. As the economy grew and the labour market increased, women entered the workforce in unprecedented numbers and household incomes reached new heights.

In the 1960s a rebellion by young people, disillusioned with growing materialism, the nuclear arms race and an authoritarian educational system, took hold in the larger cities. The movement came to a head in Copenhagen in 1971, when protesters tore down the fence of an abandoned military base at the east side of Christianshavn and turned the site into the still-thriving commune of Christiania.

Denmark's external relationships were not without their troubles either. It joined the European Community, the predecessor of the European Union (EU), in 1973, but has been rather more hesitant about the subsequent expansion of the EU's powers. Denmark rejected the 1992 Maastricht Treaty (which set the terms for much greater economic and political cooperation) as well as the adoption of the euro.

The word 'Denmark' (*Danmark* in Danish) dates back to the Viking Age and its first recorded use is on the famous Jelling Stones from c 900. The larger stone is affectionately known as the nation's baptismal certificate.

1989	2000	2000	2004
Denmark passes a bill legalising registered partnerships, becoming the world's first country to legally recognise same-sex unions.	Reaching the limits of their tolerance for the extent of the European project, Denmark votes against adopting the new European currency, the euro.	The Øresundsbron and adjoining Drogden tunnel are officially opened, providing a direct road and rail link between Denmark and Sweden. The project becomes the longest combined road and rail bridge in Europe.	Crown Prince Frederik weds Australian-born Mary Elizabeth Donaldson in a fairy-tale ceremony watched by millions of people around the world.

Meanwhile, Denmark maintained its leadership stance for socially liberal policies, including same-sex unions (instituted in 1989) and aggressive implementation of alternative energy sources.

In the late 1990s and early 2000s, the government was a coalition of the centre-right Venstre party and the Conservative People's Party, sometimes also calling on the support of the generally nationalist right-wing Danish People's Party (DPP). This new power structure led Denmark to impose some of the toughest immigration laws in Europe in 2002, including restrictions on marriage between Danes and foreigners.

Modern Times

The first decade of the 21st century proved somewhat turbulent by Danish standards. Concerns over immigration – particularly from Muslim countries – saw a resurgence of the political right and increased support for the traditionalist DPP. In practical terms, the DPP's participation contributed to Denmark's joining the USA, UK and other allies in the 2003 Iraq War and Denmark's commitment to maintain its role in Afghanistan.

A History of Denmark by Palle Lauring is a well-written excursion through the lives and times of the Danish people.

In 2006 Denmark found itself in the unfamiliar role of villain in the eyes of many Muslims following the publication of cartoons depicting the prophet Mohammed – a deep taboo for many Muslims but an issue of freedom of speech for liberal news editors – in the *Jyllands-Posten* newspaper. The depiction sparked violent demonstrations across the world, the beamed images of protestors burning Danish flags shocking a nation not accustomed to such intense, widespread vitriol.

By 2010 the political pendulum began swinging to the left again as discontent over the country's stuttering economic performance grew. In September 2011, parliamentary elections saw a new, centre-left coalition take over after a closely fought election. At the helm was Denmark's first female prime minister, Helle Thorning-Schmidt.

Despite her officially left-wing leanings, Thorning-Schmidt has followed a largely centralist agenda, resulting in a number of controversial policy implementations. Her tax reform included an increase in the top tax threshold, effectively lowering tax rates for the country's high-income earners. By 2016 the corporate tax rate was expected to drop to 22%, down from 24.5% in 2014. Other reforms have included cuts to early-retirement and unemployment benefits, all of which – according to the government – are designed to increase labour output and avoid a projected shortage within the next decades.

2005–06	2011	2011	2014
Denmark becomes a villain to many Muslims, and the focus of violent demonstrations following the publication of cartoons depicting the prophet Mohammed in *Jyllands-Posten*.	Helle Thorning-Schmidt, leader of the Social Democrats, defeats incumbent prime minister Lars Løkke Rasmussen in the Danish general election, becoming Denmark's first female prime minister.	Plans are approved for the Femern Bælt-forbindelsen (Fehmarn Belt Fixed Link), an underwater road and rail tunnel linking the Danish island of Lolland to the German island of Fehmarn.	The Socialist People's Party quits the ruling coalition over plans to sell part of the state-controlled company Dong Energy to investment bank Goldman Sachs and others.

The Danish Lifestyle

You'd be forgiven for thinking the Danes are pretty much perfect. Not only are they impossibly good-looking, they're famously civic minded, egalitarian, and masters of mood lighting. What makes these Nordic role models tick? And just how perfect are their enlightened Scandinavian lives?

The Happiness Index

As if those perfect cheekbones weren't enough, Denmark wowed once more in 2013 when a report published by the Earth Institute at Columbia University proclaimed it to be the world's happiest nation. Taking into account six factors – including real GDP per capita, healthy life expectancy, social support, freedom from corruption, and generosity – the country scored a total of 7.693 on a scale from 0 to 10. Fellow Nordic nations Norway and Sweden also made it into the Top 5, a long way off from the US at 17 and Britain at 22.

So, what's the secret? According to *Det er et lykkeligt land* (It Is a Happy Country), a study released in 2013 by Denmark's Institut for Lykkeforskning (Institute for Happiness Research), the nation's high happiness rating is driven by its robustly democratic civil society. Most Danes feel genuinely empowered to make changes and improvements, both in their own lives and in the communities in which they live. The result is a general sense of collective satisfaction.

Research also points to the Danes' high level of trust. Globally, only one in four people feel that they can trust others. In Denmark, the figure is three in four. This remarkable abundance of trust in one's fellow citizens goes a long way in explaining the common Danish sight of infants left snoozing in their prams while mum or dad pop inside to buy groceries or sip a coffee. Less time worrying about the negative leaves more time to focus on the positive.

Putting the Well in Welfare

When it comes to explaining their enviable lifestyle, most Danes will point proudly to their nation's famous welfare system. Despite recent controversial reforms, it's a system that remains one of the world's most generous. Danes enjoy equal access to medical services, with free GP visits and numerous state subsidised goods and services, including prescription medicines, dental care and physiotherapy. Childcare for children aged 0 to six is heavily subsidised and the public school system offers free education to children from the age of six to 16. It's a deal too good to refuse for most, with almost 90% of all Danish children attending state-financed public schools.

Even in adulthood, minds are kept active with state-supported access to Denmark's iconic *højskole* (folk high school), arts-focused schools offering courses in everything from philosophy, debating, and creative writing, to dance, applied arts, cooking, and even gardening. One in 10

Denmark's love of civic mindedness is mirrored in the Danish board game Konsensus. In it, players are required to put themselves in the mindset of other participants in order to work out what they are thinking and give the same answer to win points.

HYGGE

Befriend a Dane or two and chances are you'll be invited to partake in a little *hygge*. Usually it translates as 'cosy', which goes a long way to explain the not uncommon scenario of even the gruffest, toughest of Danish men inviting his buddies over for beers and cosiness. In reality, *hygge* (pronounced hoo-guh) means much more than that. Indeed, there really is no equivalent in English. *Hygge* refers to a sense of friendly, warm companionship of a kind fostered when Danes gather together in groups of two or more, although you can actually *hygge* yourself if there is no one else around. The participants don't even have to be friends (indeed, you might only have just met), but if the conversation flows – avoiding potentially divisive topics like politics and the best way to pickle a herring – the bonhomie blossoms and toasts are raised before an open fire (or, at the very least, some candles), you are probably coming close. Many cafes, bars and restaurants do their utmost to foster a *hyggelig* atmosphere, with open fires, tealights lit no matter what time of day or year and, of course, a nonstop supply of alcohol. Interestingly, the word's origin is not Danish but Norwegian. Originally meaning something along the lines of 'well-being', it first appeared in Danish writing around the end of the 18th century.

Danish adults make use of these institutions, either to explore an interest or to simply meet new people.

The origins of the *højskole* stretch back to the mid-19th century and the revered Danish theologian and political figure Nikolaj Frederik Severin Grundtvig (1783–1872). Arguing that a newly democratic Denmark would only succeed if all its citizens were able to partake in the country's political life, Grundtvig went about establishing liberal arts colleges for the rural poor. These schools would eventually develop into the folk high schools dotted across the country today.

Grundtvig's ideas would play a formidable role in developing modern Denmark's value of egalitarianism and civic responsibility. While class divisions do exist in Denmark, the gap between rich and poor is much narrower than it is in many other developed countries. Income disparity is also relatively narrow, discouraging the snooty judgment of less-profitable jobs.

Yet, as happy and holistic as Denmark is, it is not flawless. According to a Gallup poll released in late 2014, only 43% of those under 45 feel like they are part of the community as a whole, while a mere 24% of those in the same age bracket felt that they were thriving socially. What this means for Denmark's long-term happiness remains to be seen.

According to the 2013 Corruption Perceptions Index released by Transparency International (www.transparency.org), Denmark and New Zealand are the least corrupt countries in the world.

Seasonal Moods

A friendly shoulder to lean on can come in quite handy as autumn's leaves flutter to the ground and another long, gloomy Danish winter looms. It's a feeling succinctly and wittily captured in *Året har 16 måneder* (The Year Has 16 Months), a poem by the great living Danish poet Henrik Nordbrandt: 'The year has 16 months: November, December, January, February, March, April, May, June, July, August, September, October, November, November, November, November'.

It's in November that Mother Nature usually unfurls her thick, winter fog over the country, extinguishing all hope of just one more mild autumnal day. As the celebrated writer and television chef Adam Price puts it: 'It's in November, when the light leaves us, that the blue notes really hit. It becomes a state of mind. There's a longing, a sense of nostalgia, perhaps a little sadness. As Danes, we live it. It's part of us'.

For around 12% of the population, that little sadness is in fact Seasonal Affective Disorder (SAD), a seasonally triggered depression most prolific in the autumn and winter months. Whether affected or not, many Danes combat the winter blues with escapes to warmer climes, from nearby Malaga to the far-flung beaches of Thailand. At home, however, it's *hygge* (cosiness) to the rescue as flickering candles, soft lighting, and toasty catch-ups with friends turn the darkness into a celebration of all things snug. It's a Danish tradition that reaches fever pitch at Christmas, when Christmas markets, twinkling lights and hot, flowing *gløgg* (mulled wine) turns cities and towns into winter wonderlands.

Not surprisingly, Denmark's short, sweet summers are embraced with fervent gusto, the long nights of winter replaced by deliciously long, invigorating days. Parks become veritable seas of bronzing flesh, outdoor festivals are in full swing, and those with a *sommerhus* (summer house) or *grill* (barbeque) dust them down for another much-awaited season.

Equality

In 2013 Denmark ranked number eight internationally in the gender gap index, a report on gender equality released by the World Economic Forum. Of the numerous factors taken into account, the country ranked first for educational attainment, 11th for political empowerment, and 25th for economic participation and opportunity.

While it scored lowest of the Nordic countries, Denmark remains one of the world's most gender-equal societies. Women students outnumber men at tertiary level, while figures released by the OECD (Organisation for Economic Co-operation and Development) in 2013 showed that the average Danish man spends three hours and 37 minutes a day cooking, cleaning or caring for loved ones. In total, Danish men undertake 47% of domestic chores, giving Denmark the narrowest gap in the division of housework between the sexes. Policies including mandatory paternal leave and post-maternity re-entry programmes have also helped shape a society in which women can more easily balance a career and family.

Despite these admirable statistics, sexism has not been fully relegated to the history books. One high-profile Dane all too aware of this is prime minister Helle Thorning-Schmidt, whose well-documented love of designer labels has earned her the nickname 'Gucci Helle' in the media and by some of her political opponents. While Thorning-Schmidt's detractors argue that her passion for expensive fashion undermines the core principles of her party – the Social Democrats – others point to the fact that her male counterparts never face the same scrutiny when it comes to their appearance.

Such seeming double standards are not restricted to the wardrobe either. Speaking to Adam Price (creator of the TV political drama *Borgen*) in 2009, Thorning-Schmidt referred to a media interview with then-prime minister Lars Løkke Rasmussen. In it, the leader stated that it was satisfactory to see his family only once or twice a week as they understood the challenges of his job. Musing on the comment, Thorning-Schmidt remarked that a female politician could never make the same statement for fear of being judged as a bad wife and mother willing to sacrifice everything. Even in progressive Denmark, deep-rooted prejudices can be hard to erase.

Anne and Peter are the most common first names in Denmark today, and Jensen the most common surname. The current average age of Danish women is 41.8 years and 40 years for men. Life expectancy is 81.9 years for women and 78 years for men.

THE DANISH LIFESTYLE EQUALITY

Danish Design

Is there a more design-conscious nation than Denmark, or a more design-obsessed capital than Copenhagen? Sure, the Italians like a nice sofa and the French have their frocks, but in Denmark the passion for excellent design runs deeper than that.

The Danish Architecture Centre (www.dac.dk) is a brilliant source of information about new architecture, innovation and urban development in the capital. Its website offers download-able podwalks for archi-buffs, as well as information about its architecture walking tours in Copenhagen.

One of the country's most inspirational qualities is its love and mastery of the applied arts. Along with its Scandinavian neighbours, Denmark has had a massive influence on the way the world builds its public and private spaces, and on the way it designs interiors, furniture and home-wares.

While modern Danish design bloomed in the 1950s, its roots are firm-ly planted in the 1920s and the work of pioneering Danish Modernist Kaare Klint (1888–1954). The architect spent much of his career studying the human form and modified a number of chair designs for added func-tionality. Klint's obsession with functionality, accessibility and attention to detail would ultimately drive and define Denmark's mid-20th-century design scene and its broader design legacy.

Architecture

Denmark's architectural portfolio is rich and eclectic, graced with the millennia-old military precision of Trelleborg, the medieval curves of Bornholm's round churches, the Renaissance whimsy of Copenhagen's Kronborg Slot, and the rococo elegance of the city's Marble Bridge.

On the world stage, Danish architecture has shone especially bright since the mid-20th century, its enlightened, innovative approach to de-sign pushing boundaries and enjoying accolades across the globe.

Among its deities is Arne Jacobsen (1902–71). An innovator in inter-national modernism, the pipe-smoking architect pioneered Danish in-terpretations of the Bauhaus style. Among his celebrated works are the Radisson Blu Royal Hotel in Copenhagen, the functionalist town hall he designed for Aarhus (with interiors by Hans Wegner), and his Kubeflex prototype summerhouse at Kolding's Trapholt museum, all of which en-capsulate Jacobsen's masterful sense of proportion.

Equally famous is Jørn Utzon (1918–2008), whose work reflects the organic trend within modernism. Creator of the World Heritage–listed Sydney Opera House, constructed in the 1960s, Utzon famously incor-porated elements as wide-reaching as Mayan, Japanese and Islamic influences into traditional Danish design. In Jutland you can admire Utzon's work in Esbjerg and Skagen, but the best place to visit is the Utzon Center in Aalborg. This impressive design and architecture space was the last building designed by the celebrated architect before his death in 2008.

Utzon is not the only Dane to design an architectural icon for a foreign city, with Viborg-born architect Johan Otto von Spreckelsen (1929–87) responsible for Paris' cube-like, monument-cum-skyscraper La Grande Arche. Completed in 1989, the building's ability to balance the dramatic and the unorthodox with a sense of purity and harmony underscores the work of many contemporary Danish creations. Among these is Henning Larsen's award-winning The Wave, a striking yet soothing housing development in Vejle, Jutland, sculpted like giant white waves.

An even more recent example is Denmark's National Maritime Museum in Helsingør, a concrete and glass complex ingeniously built in and around a former dry dock. The museum is the work of prolific firm BIG (Bjarke Ingels Group), whose groundbreaking creations also include the Copenhagen apartment complex VM Bjerget (Mountain Dwellings), a stepped, pyramidal structure whose clever configuration gives each apartment a sense of spaciousness and privacy more akin to detached suburban abodes.

Furniture & Interiors

As wonderful as Danish design-focused stores, museums, hotels and restaurants are, the very best place to see Danish design is in its natural environment: a Danish home. To the Danes, good design is not just for museums and institutions; they live with it and use it every day.

Visit a Danish home and you'll invariably find a Bang & Olufsen stereo and/or TV in the living room, Poul Henningsen lamps hanging from the ceiling, Arne Jacobsen or Hans Wegner chairs in the dining room, and the table set with Royal Copenhagen dinner sets, Georg Jensen cutlery and Bodum glassware.

Modern Danish furniture focuses on a practical style and the principle that its design should be tailored to the comfort of the user. This smooth, unadorned aesthetic traces its roots to architect Kaare Klint, founder of the furniture design department at the Royal Academy of Fine Arts in Copenhagen.

INDEX: Design to Improve Life is a Danish-based nonprofit organisation that works to promote design and design processes that have the capacity to improve the lives of people worldwide. Read more about its inspiring work at designtoimprovelife.dk.

DANISH DESIGN FURNITURE & INTERIORS

CAPITAL DRAMA

Functional, humanistic, organic and sympathetic are all adjectives that might be used to describe the defining features of classic postwar Danish architecture, best embodied in the work of architects such as Jørn Utzon and Arne Jacobsen. Their usually restrained take on modernism has been superseded since the 1990s, often by a much bolder, brasher, even aggressive type of building.

Here are a handful of Copenhagen's most iconic modern buildings.

Radisson Blu Royal Hotel (Arne Jacobsen) Not content with merely creating a building, Jacobsen designed every item in the hotel, down to the door handles, cutlery, and the famous Egg and Swan chairs. Room 606 remains entirely as it was on opening day in 1960.

The Black Diamond (Schmidt, Hammer & Lassen) Completed in 1999, Copenhagen's monolithic library extension offers a sharp contrast to the original red-brick building. While the latter sits firmly and somberly, the black granite extension floats on a ribbon of raised glass, leaning towards the harbour as if wanting to detach and jump in.

Operaen (Henning Larsen) It seems to be the rule that any large commissioned public building must be marked by the word 'controversial' and the opera house (completed in 2005) is no exception. While its squat exterior has drawn comparisons to a toaster, the maple-wood and Sicilian marble interior is a triumph.

Royal Danish Playhouse (Lundgaard & Tranberg) Completed in 2008 and facing Operaen, the award-winning Skuespilhuset is dark, subdued and elegant. Its glass-house design includes a projected upper floor of coloured glass, a playful contrast to the building's muted-grey, English clay bricks.

Den Blå Planet (3XN) Denmark's new National Aquarium has made quite a splash with its spiral, whirlpool-inspired design. Hitting the scene in 2013, its gleaming silver facade is clad in shingles; diamond-shaped aluminium plates designed to adapt to the building's organic form.

FOUR LEGS GOOD: CLASSIC DANISH CHAIRS

Labouring with an almost fetishistic obsession, the great Danish designers such as Arne Jacobsen could spend long, angst-ridden months, even years, perfecting a single chair. Still, the results made the world sit up straight; in the 1950s *Time* magazine even devoted a cover to the phenomenon. There are dozens to choose from, but some of the classics follow.

The Round Chair (Hans Wegner) In 1950 US *Interiors* magazine put the chair on its cover, calling it 'the world's most beautiful chair'. It became known simply as 'the Chair', and began making high-profile appearances such as the televised 1960 presidential debates between Nixon and Kennedy.

The Ant Chair (Jacobsen) Perhaps the most (in)famous chair in the world, thanks to the 1960s Lewis Morley photograph of call girl Christine Keeler (from the British Profumo Affair) sitting on one.

The Egg Chair (Jacobsen) This represents the essence of jetsetting 1950s modernity. Jacobsen designed the Egg Chair for the Radisson Blu Royal Hotel.

The Panton Chair (Verner Panton) After helping with Jacobsen's Ant Chair, Panton went on to do great things in plastic, the most iconic being his Panton Chair.

Nxt Chair (Peter Karpf) Beech plywood moulded into angular planes is the defining characteristic of this striking design, which took 30 years to reach production. It helped spawn the Voxia line, which is still going strong.

With two stores in Copenhagen and one in Aarhus, design firm Hay (hay.dk) is a well-known showcase for contemporary Danish designers, among them Thomas Bentzen, Hee Welling, and Lee Storm.

In 1949 one of Klint's contemporaries, Hans Wegner (1914–2007), created the Round Chair. Its fluid, curving lines made it an instant classic and a model for many furniture designers to follow, as well as helping establish the first successful overseas export market for Danish furniture. A wonderful array of Wegner-designed chairs is displayed in the Tønder Museum in the designer's home town.

A decade after Wegner's Round Chair, Arne Jacobsen created the Ant, a form of chair designed to be mass-produced, which became the model for the stacking chairs now found in schools and cafeterias worldwide. Jacobsen also designed the Egg and the Swan; both are rounded, uncomplicated upholstered chairs with revolving seats perched on pedestal stands.

Danish design prevails in stylish lamps as well. The country's best-known lamp designer was Poul Henningsen (1894–1967), who emphasised the need for lighting to be soft, for the shade to cast a pleasant shadow and for the light bulb to be blocked from direct view. His PH5 lamp created in 1958 remains one of the most popular hanging lamps sold in Denmark today.

The clean lines of industrial design are also evident in the avant-garde sound systems and televisions produced by Bang & Olufsen; and in Danish silver and cutlery design generally. The father of modern Danish silverwork was the sculptor and silversmith Georg Jensen (1866–1935), who artistically incorporated curvilinear designs; his namesake company is still a leader in the field.

Despite the large shadow cast by the modernists, a new generation of Danish designers are making their mark. While some remain influenced by the heroes of the 1950s, others are challenging their hegemony, with fresh designs that are often bold and irreverent. Among the latter is prolific designer Thomas Bentzen (b 1969), whose whimsical furniture and lighting hum with an almost animated personality.

Food & Drink

In little over a decade, Denmark has gone from dining dowager to culinary darling. New Nordic cuisine continues to wow food critics and foodies alike, while Danish classics are enjoying resurgent popularity and modern interpretations. Copenhagen is home to the world's number-one restaurant (Noma; p75), taking top spot in the S Pellegrino World's 50 Best Restaurants rankings in 2010, 2011, 2012 and 2014) and no less than 15 Michelin-starred restaurants; a record-breaking number for the city. Word is spreading: Denmark has produce to be proud of, and chefs with the training and skills to make the most of it. Old recipes are being rediscovered and interest in traditional food culture continues to soar. The result is an ever-evolving culinary landscape, ripe for exploration.

New Nordic Innovation

Despite some claims of overexposure, Denmark's New Nordic cuisine continues to thrill food critics, editors, bloggers and general gluttons across the globe.

The cuisine itself stems from 2004, when Nordic chefs attending a food symposium in Copenhagen created a 10-point manifesto defining the cuisine's aims. According to the manifesto, New Nordic cuisine is defined by seasonality, sustainability, local ingredients and produce, and the use of Nordic cooking methods to create a cuisine that originally and distinctly reflects Scandinavian culture, geography and history.

The movement has thrown the spotlight on Denmark's fantastic raw ingredients, from excellent pork products, beef, game and seafood, to root vegetables, wild berries and herbs. It also serves as a showcase for rarer ingredients from the wider Nordic region, among them Greenlandic musk ox, horse mussels from the Faroe Islands, obscure berries from Finland, and truffles from the Swedish island of Gotland.

The world's most famous New Nordic restaurant remains Noma, where owner-chef René Redzepi eschews all nonindigenous produce in his creations, including olive oil and tomatoes. He plays with modest, often-overlooked ingredients and consults food historians, digging up long-lost traditions. Famously, he also forages in the wilderness for herbs and plants. The ingredients are then skilfully prepared using traditional techniques (curing, smoking, pickling and preserving) alongside contemporary experiments that have included, among other things, ants.

Despite Redzepi's strict faithfulness to Nordic produce, a newer wave of chefs – many of whom are Noma alumni – seem to be taking a less dogmatic approach, their own seasonal, Nordic menus splashed with the odd foreign ingredient. Among these is chef Matt Orlando, of the Copenhagen restaurant Amass, a place where burnt kale and beach plants might be punctuated by foie gras or Indian gherkins. While some may argue that this compromises the very concept of New Nordic cuisine, others see it as the next step in the evolution of contemporary Danish cooking.

The Scandinavian Kitchen, by Danish chef and media personality Camilla Plum, outlines over 100 essential Scandi ingredients and 200 recipes. Plum is a household name in Denmark; she runs an organic farm north of Copenhagen that's open to visitors on Saturdays and Sundays. See www.fuglebjerg gaard.dk.

Danish Staples & Specialities

Reindeer moss and hay-smoked quail eggs may be the norm on New Nordic menus, but traditional Danish tables serve up a much heartier cast of classics. Grab a fork and knife and plunge into the following Danish faithfuls.

Turf

Traditional Danish grub has a soft spot for the carnivorous. Pork (*flæsk* or *svinekød*) is ubiquitous, served as *flæskesteg* (roast pork), *mørbradbøf* (pork tenderloin) and comfort-food favourite *frikadeller* – fried minced-pork meatballs commonly served with boiled potatoes and red cabbage. Watch nostalgia wash over Danish eyes at the mere mention of crispy *flæskesvær* (pork crackling), eaten as a salty snack and now back in vogue on some of Copenhagen's trendiest bar menus. Equally wicked is *æbleflæsk*, a heady concoction of fried bacon, onions and apples served on *rugbrød* (rye bread) best paired with dark beer and snaps.

Beef (*bøf or okse*) is also popular, ranging from cheaper comfort-food dishes using mince to expensive cuts of steak, often served with Béarnaise sauce. *Hakkebøf* is a dish of minced-beef burger, usually covered with fried onions and served with boiled potatoes, brown sauce and beets. Also finding its way back onto menus is *pariserbøf*, a rare beef patty topped with capers, raw egg yolk, beets, onions and horseradish.

Surf

Expansive coastlines mean no shortage of excellent surf options. Herring (*sild*) is a staple. Often served marinated in numerous ways, including in sherry, mustard, orange or curry, it's also commonly served smoked, fried or charred. Cured or smoked salmon (*laks*) is also prolific, a favourite dish being *gravad laks;* cured or salted salmon marinated in dill and served with a sweet mustard sauce.

Then there's *stegt rødspætte,* fried breaded plaice, often served with parsley potatoes; *kogt torsk,* poached cod married with mustard sauce and boiled potatoes; and the ubiquitous *fiskefrikadeller,* pan-fried fish patties served with thick remoulade or tartar sauce and fresh lemon wedges. Equally iconic is the majestic *stjerneskud.* Literally 'Shooting Star', it's a belt-busting combination of both steamed and fried fish fillets, topped with smoked salmon, shrimp and caviar, and served on buttered bread.

The Danes are great fish smokers, and the wonderfully woody flavour of smoked seafood is one of Scandinavia's most distinctive culinary

Apart from Copenhagen, another first-rate destination for foodies is Bornholm – home to excellent smokehouses, nationally renowned charcuterie Hallegård (p147), modern Danish restaurant marvels Kadeau (p146) and Lassens (p153), and scores of local specialities, from caramel to microbrewed beer.

ESSENTIAL DANISH FLAVOURS

New Nordic flavours Sample Nordic produce cooked with groundbreaking creativity at hotspot restaurants like Copenhagen's Noma, Kadeau or Geranium.

Smørrebrød Rye or white bread topped with anything from beef tartar to egg and shrimp, the open sandwich is Denmark's most famous culinary export.

Sild Smoked, cured, pickled or fried, herring is a local staple, best washed down with generous serves of akvavit (an alcoholic spirit commonly made with potatoes and spiced with caraway).

Kanelsnegl A calorific delight, the 'cinnamon snail' is a sweet, buttery pastry, sometimes laced with chocolate.

Koldskål A cold, sweet buttermilk soup made with vanilla and traditionally served with crunchy biscuits such as *kammerjunkere*.

Beer Carlsberg may dominate, but Denmark's expanding battalion of microbreweries include Mikkeller, Amager Bryghus and Bryghuset Møn.

highs. You'll find smokehouses (*røgeri*) all around Denmark's coast, preserving herring, eel, shrimp and other fresh seafood. The most renowned are on Bornholm.

Across on the northern tip of Jutland, salubrious Skagen is a top spot to feast on fresh shrimp *(rejer)* and lobster *(hummer)*.

Smørrebrød

Although the earliest recorded mention of smørrebrod is in the 13th-century Hakonar Saga, the elaborate Danish open sandwich known today stems back to the late 19th century. As the number of posh-nosh restaurants grew in Copenhagen, the city's modest beer and wine cellars began sprucing up their bread and butter standard with fancy new toppings, in turn creating Denmark's most celebrated culinary export.

The basic smørrebrød is a slice of rye bread topped with any number of ingredients, from roast beef or pork, to juicy shrimps, pickled herring, liver pâté, or fried fish fillet. The garnishes are equally variable, with the sculptured final product often looking too good to eat. In the laws of Danish smørrebrød, smoked salmon is served on white bread, and herring on rye bread. Whatever the combination, the iconic dish is best paired with akvavit (alcoholic spirit) and an invigorating beer.

Smørrebrød is a lunchtime staple in countless restaurants and cafes, the most famous of which is Copenhagen's Schønnemann (p74), a celebrated 19th-century veteran whose offerings span the classical to modern, with twists like cold-smoked venison leg paired with porcini remoulade and beetroot chips.

Generally speaking, smørrebrød is cheapest in bakeries or specialised smørrebrød takeaway shops found near train stations and office buildings. Try to pronounce smørrebrød as 'smuhr-bruth', but don't feel bad if your pronunciation doesn't match a native Dane's (it never will).

The Sweet Stuff

Denmark is Valhalla for lovers of all things flaky, sticky and sweet, and its bakeries are a constant source of temptation.

Ironically, what is commonly known as a 'Danish pastry' abroad is known to the Danes as a *wienerbrød* ('Viennese bread'), and nearly every second street corner has a *bageri* (bakery) with different varieties. As legend has it, the naming of the pastry can be traced to a Danish baker who moved to Austria in the 18th century, where he perfected the treats of flaky, butter-laden pastry. True to their collective sweet tooth, Danes eat them for breakfast.

Not that Denmark's pastry selection ends there. Other famous treats include *kanelsnegle,* a luscious cinnamon scroll sometimes laced with thick, gooey chocolate, and the equally popular *tebirkes,* a flaky, croissant-like pastry filled with a marzipan spread and sprinkled with poppy seeds.

Where to Eat & Drink

From René Redzepi and Rasmus Kofoed, to Nicolai Nørregaard and Claus Henriksen, a wave of contemporary Danish chefs continue to transform seasonal ingredients into evocative, idiosyncratic dishes that capture the flavours, textures, colours and moods of the region.

While much of the ingenuity remains centred in Copenhagen, a number of destination restaurants dot the country, from urban nosheries like St Pauls Apothek in Aarhus, to eat-and-slumber castles and manor-houses, among them Dragsholm Slot in Zealand and Falsled Kro in Funen.

That said, you *can* eat badly in Denmark, particularly in the provinces, where dry schnitzels, rubbery pizzas and inauthentic pasta remain the chief outsourced foodstuff for the masses. To help avoid such disappointment,

FOOD & DRINK WHERE TO EAT & DRINK

As you drive around rural areas in the summer months, keep an eye out for roadside stalls selling fresh farm produce (usually with an honesty-box system in place). *Jordbær* are strawberries, *kirsebær* are cherries, *ærter* are peas, and *kartofler* are potatoes.

SIP, SUP & SLUMBER: DENMARK'S TOP GOURMET RETREATS

The only thing better than a long, indulgent dinner is a long, indulgent dinner with a beautiful room or suite waiting just steps away from your table. The following castles and inns combine atmospheric slumber and inspired, seasonal menus for a getaway worth any detour.

Dragsholm Slot (p113) Take an ancient castle, add ex-Noma chef Claus Henriksen, and you have this celebrated culinary retreat on the edge of fertile Lammefjorden (Denmark's 'vegetable garden') in northwest Zealand. Fine dine on the likes of watercress and crayfish with radish and smoked lard, or opt for pared-back, rustic grub in the less-expensive Eatery.

Falsled Kro (p172) A former smugglers' inn in southern Funen, Falsled Kro sees top-tier local produce shine brightly in strictly seasonal dishes like lightly smoked and salted cod with caviar, horseradish and apple.

Henne Kirkeby Kro (p238) Snuggle up at this hip, revamped inn in western Jutland's heathlands. At your table are the clean, contemporary New Nordic flavours of expat Brit, Michelin-starred chef Paul Cunningham.

Molskroen (p222) Close to Aarhus in seaside Djursland, renovated Molskroen serves up Gallic-inspired, Scandi-refined brilliance like foie gras terrine with roasted brioche bread and pear chutney, or lobster fricassee with celery purée.

Ruths Gourmet (p254) Skagen's light-washed maritime beauty meets New Nordic ingenuity at Ruths. Heading the kitchen is revered chef Thorsten Schmidt, who lets the ebb and flow of regional produce dictate his light, exquisitely composed creations.

here are a few tips: in coastal areas, look for a traditional *røgeri* (smokehouse), where you can get great, inexpensive seafood. In many villages, you can often find classic Danish home cooking in a traditional *kro* (inn). Also, hit a *bageri* (bakery) – the Danes are master bakers, especially when it comes to *rugbrød* (rye bread).

Wherever you dine, be aware that kitchens close relatively early in Denmark compared with other European countries, so aim to eat before 10pm (9pm in smaller towns). For many restaurants and cafes, the closure of the kitchen signals a move into 'bar mode', with drinks available until late (along with live music or a DJ in some venues).

Cheap Eats

Dining out can be expensive in Denmark, with coveted, high-end nosh spots often more costly than comparable restaurants in Paris and London. In Copenhagen, a number of top-end restaurants (or their alumni chefs) have launched relatively cheaper, more casual spin-offs serving innovative, New Nordic food. Among the best are Pony (p76) and Rebel (p74). Keep in mind that alcohol is also spectacularly costly in fashionable places, and can easily double the price of your meal.

Aside from smokehouses, bakeries and cafes, there are other options for a cheaper feed. Thai and Chinese restaurants are common, though rarely authentic. Pizza is another option, though very few serve the woodfired perfection you may be hoping for, while simple Lebanese and Turkish eateries selling inexpensive *shawarma* (a filling pitta-bread sandwich of shaved meat) are another option. Equally common (if not particularly healthy) are the *pølsevogn;* wheeled carts peddling a variety of hot dogs.

Brunch

Danes rarely eat breakfast out. They do, however, embrace brunch with gusto. Many cafes and restaurants put on lavish buffets on weekends, running from about 10am to 2pm and generally priced between Dkr110 and Dkr175.

Claus Meyer is a superstar on the Danish food front. Founder of the New Nordic food movement, he is also a TV chef, food educator, co-founder of Noma restaurant, cookbook author, and general gastro-entrepreneur. His website (www.clausmeyer.dk) outlines the fascinating manifesto for New Nordic cuisine.

On weekdays, numerous eateries offer a 'brunch plate' (*brunch tall-erken*) on their menu. Served from 10am through to lunch, these often consist of samplings of brunch classics, from muesli and yoghurt, to cold cuts, bread, cheese and something sweet (pastry or pancakes), all served on the one plate.

Vegetarians & Vegans

Despite the countrywide adoration of all things pork, vegetarians should be able to get by comfortably throughout Denmark (although in smaller towns the options will be limited). Danish cafes commonly serve a variety of salads, and vegetarians can usually find something suitable at the smørrebrød counter. Most restaurants will have at least one herbivorous dish on the menu, or can whip something up if requested.

Drinks

The Danes are enthusiastic drinkers, with beer *(øl)*, wine *(vin)* and spirits served in most restaurants and cafes. Alcohol is available at grocery shops during normal shopping hours, with prices quite reasonable compared with those in other Scandinavian countries.

Beer

The Danes are prodigious producers and consumers of beer. The oldest trace of beer in Denmark dates back to 2800 BC, with Copenhagen's first brewing guild established in 1525. Copenhagen-based Carlsberg Breweries markets the Carlsberg and Tuborg labels, and is one of the world's largest brewery groups. It's also the largest exporter of beer in Europe.

While the best-selling beers in Denmark are pilsners, a lager with an alcohol content of 4.6%, there are scores of other beers to choose from. These range from light beers with an alcohol content of 1.7% to hearty stouts that kick in at 8%. Essential beer terms you should know include:

øl – beer
pilsner – lager
lyst øl – light beer
lagerøl – dark lager
fadøl – draught
porter – stout

In the last decade, locals have developed a growing taste for microbrews and craft beers, and there are now more than 120 small breweries around the country. Indeed, any Danish town worth its salt will have its

FOOD & DRINK DRINKS

Denmark is home to two high-calibre food festivals: Copenhagen Cooking (p65), held annually in February and August, and Denmark's biggest chef competition, Sol over Gudhjem (p152), held on the island of Bornholm in June.

YULETIDE FEASTING

Not only does the traditional Danish Christmas (*jul*) ooze *hygge* (cosiness), it explodes with festive grub.

The biggest festivities are on Christmas Eve, when gift giving and songs sung around the Christmas tree are fuelled with copious amounts of akvavit (alcoholic spirit) and specially brewed Yuletide beers. The culinary centrepiece is roast pork, duck or goose, served with red cabbage and boiled potatoes cooked in butter and sugar. After the meal it's time for warming *risengrød* (rice pudding), inside of which lies a single whole almond. The person who finds the almond in his or her bowl gets a prize, such as a sweet made of marzipan. Come 25 December, the leftovers from Christmas Eve make for an excellent *koldt bord* (cold table) lunch.

Of course, the Yuletide treats begin well before Christmas Eve and Day, with common Advent bites including *brunekager* and *pebernødder* (spice cookies), golden *klejner* (deep-fried knotted dough), and *æbleskiver* – small, spherical pancakes traditionally served with *gløgg* (mulled wine).

DINNER WITH DANES

Three agencies offer visitors the chance to spend an evening in the home of locals, sampling traditional Danish food and learning about Denmark straight from the horse's mouth. The hosts are mainly in Copenhagen, and the agencies usually attempt to match you with people of similar ages and interests. The price is around Dkr420 to Dkr520 for two courses, wine and coffee. If you're interested, fill in an online request, preferably a month in advance.

The agencies are as follows:

Dine with the Danes (www.facebook.com/DineWithTheDanes)
Meet the Danes (meetthedanes.dk)
Meet Gay Copenhagen (www.meetgaycopenhagen.dk)

own *bryghus* (brewery), and these are often innovators producing a wide variety of styles.

A growing number of bars, pubs and restaurants proudly list their boutique bottled offerings and changing draught beers, with obscure local drops getting a run next to the better-known brands. Various bars cater to the more discerning beer-drinker, among them Mikkeler in Copenhagen. Then of course there's the country's largest beer festival, Ølfestival (beerfestival.dk), held in May in Copenhagen, with over 700 suds on offer.

Wine

A few important customs: make eye contact with everyone during a toast. And before you leave the table, *always* thank your host or hostess for any food or drink, even if it's just a cup of coffee.

Despite its northerly latitude, Denmark is home to a small but thriving wine-making industry. It has its own industry association, Danske Vingårde (Danish Vineyards), and over 50 wine-growers, including Zealand's Kelleris Vingaard (www.kellerisvingaard.dk), Dyrehøj Vingård (www.dyrehoj-vingaard.dk) and Dansk VinCenter (www.vincenter.dk).

Curiously, it's not global warming driving the industry's growth, but the development of grape varieties that bud and mature early, making them ideal for the region's short growing season. Among these is the commonly used hybrid grape Rondo and the Regent, the latter producing richly coloured wines that are vigorous and intense. That said, it's Denmark's white and sparkling wines that show the most promise, with common white grape varieties including the Riesling-like Johanitter.

Even more notable, however, are the apple-based wines made by Jutland's innovative Cold Hand Winery (www.coldhandwinery.dk). Among these is the award-winning Malus X – Feminan, a beautifully balanced dessert wine with crisp minerality and toffee-like overtones.

Currently, the vast majority of Denmark's homegrown drops are sold on the local market, with several showcased at Modern Danish restaurants like Copenhagen's Kanalen (p75), as well as at Copenhagen's gourmet food market Torvehallerne KBH (p79).

Akvavit

The most popular spirit in Denmark is the Aalborg-produced akvavit. There are several dozen types, the most common of which is made from potatoes and spiced with caraway seeds. In Denmark akvavit is not sipped but is swallowed straight down as a shot, usually followed by a chaser of beer.

Literature, Film & TV

Like so many Danish forays onto the world stage, Denmark's contribution to Western culture has been in inverse proportion to the country's size.

On Page
The Golden Age

Dubbed the 'Golden Age', the first half of the 19th century saw Denmark flourish both culturally and economically. Among the writers of the period were two icons of the Danish literary legacy: Hans Christian Andersen (1805–75), whose fairy tales have been translated into more languages than any other book except the Bible; and noted philosopher and theologian Søren Kierkegaard (1813–55), considered the father of existentialism.

Once Upon a Time...

As well as single-handedly revolutionising children's literature, Hans Christian Andersen wrote novels, plays and several fascinating travel books. Stories such as *The Little Mermaid*, *The Emperor's New Clothes* and *The Ugly Duckling* have been translated into over 170 languages and are embedded in the global literary consciousness like few others.

Andersen infused his animals, plants and inanimate objects with a magical humanity. His antagonists are not witches or trolls, but human foibles such as indifference and vanity, and it's often his child characters who see the world most clearly. The result is a gentleness that crosses borders and generations. His work is said to have influenced Charles Dickens, Oscar Wilde and innumerable modern-day authors.

Andersen was born in Odense, the son of a cobbler and a washerwoman. In his autobiographies he mythologised his childhood as poor but idyllic. His father died when Andersen was 11, and Andersen left for Copenhagen soon after, an uneducated 14-year-old on a classic fairy-tale mission: to make his fortune in the big city. He tried and failed at various occupations until he eventually found success with his writing, initially with his poems and plays, and then his first volume of short stories.

A neurotic, sexually ambivalent, highly strung hypochondriac, Andersen lived a troubled life. It may go some way to explaining why he was such a restless nomad to the last. Andersen's collected works (156 in all) include poems, novels, travel books, dramatic pieces and three autobiographies. Succumbing to liver cancer, his final resting place is Copenhagen's Assistens Kirkegård.

Realism & Modern Times
Acclaimed Prose

Around 1870 a trend towards realism emerged in Danish literature, dubbed the 'modern breakthrough'. Focused on contemporary issues, the movement's leading figure was Georg Brandes (1842–1927), a writer and social critic who called passionately for a style of literature designed to spark debate and challenge societal norms. Among those who achieved

How to tackle Kierkegaard's works? Consider starting with *Kierkegaard* by Michael Watts, which gives a short biography of the philosopher's life and family, plus tips and ideas on how to read and analyse his complex work.

this was Jens Peter Jacobsen (1847–85), his novel *Marie Grubbe* being the first in Denmark to deal with women's sexuality.

Another realist was Henrik Pontoppidan (1857–1943), who won a Nobel Prize for Literature (shared with compatriot Karl Gjellerup) in 1917 for 'his authentic descriptions of present-day life in Denmark'. The prize would be given to Johannes Vilhelm Jensen in 1944, his historical novel *The Fall of the King* acclaimed as the best Danish novel of the 20th century in 1999.

The most famous Danish writer of the 20th century is Karen Blixen (1885–1962). Starting her career with *Seven Gothic Tales*, published under the pen name Isak Dinesen, she is best known for *Out of Africa*, the memoirs of her farm life in Kenya. Penned in 1937, it was made into an Oscar-winning movie in 1985. Her Danish estate in Rungsted is now a museum dedicated to her life and work.

One of Denmark's leading contemporary novelists is Peter Høeg, whose works focus on nonconformist characters on the margins of society. In 1992 he published the global hit *Miss Smilla's Feeling for Snow* (published as *Smilla's Sense of Snow* in the USA and made into a movie in 1997), a suspense mystery about a Danish-Greenlandic woman living in Copenhagen.

The Nordic Whodunnits

Although the hugely popular genre of Scandinavian crime fiction seems dominated by Swedes (most notably Henning Mankell and Stieg Larsson) and the odd Norwegian (Jo Nesbø), noteworthy Danish authors are contributing to the genre.

Among them is Jussi Adler-Olsen, winner of the 2011 Glass Key award, a prestigious literary prize dedicated to Nordic crime fiction. The first of his series dealing with the intriguing cold case squad Department Q was published in English in 2011 – in the UK with the title *Mercy,* and in the US as *The Keeper of Lost Causes*. His latest installment in the series – titled *Guilt* in the UK and *The Purity of Vengeance* in the US – revolves around protagonist Nete Hermansen, who plots revenge against her abusers on Sprogø, a Danish island infamous for its since-defunct reformatory for young women deemed 'dangerous' or 'immoral'.

Another notable contemporary crime writer is Copenhagen-based journalist Erik Valeur, whose debut novel *The Seventh Child* won the 2012 Glass Key prize. Intricately crafted, its plot revolves around the mysterious death of woman, an orphanage, and seven unidentified orphans suspected to be the abandoned children of Denmark's elite.

Hans Christian Andersen Sites

Den Gamle Gaard (p171), Faaborg

Fyrtøjet (p159), Odense

HC Andersens Barndomshjem (p159), Odense

HC Andersens Hus (p159), Odense

Assistens Kirkegård (p60), Copenhagen

On Screen

New Nordic Noir

Over the past 15 years, Denmark has cemented its reputation for superlative TV crime drama, characterised by gripping plot twists and a dark, moody atmosphere.

Planting the seed of success was the four-season drama *Unit One.* Based around an elite mobile police task force, the show won an Emmy Award for best non-American television drama series in 2002. On its tail was *The Eagle*, its 24 episodes revolving around a small Danish investigation unit solving everything from terrorist threats to international fraud. The show would also go on to receive an Emmy in 2005.

Come 2007 audiences were introduced to *The Killing* and its protagonist Sarah Lund, a Copenhagen police detective known for her astute crime solving abilities and love of Faroese knitwear. During its three seasons, the series became an international cult hit, screening in almost 20 countries, winning a BAFTA Award, and spawning an American remake.

Police tape gave way to spin doctors with the acclaimed political drama *Borgen*. Launched in 2010, the three-season hit stars much-loved Danish actor Sidse Babett Knudsen as Birgitte Nyborg, an idealistic politician suddenly thrown into the oft-challenging position of the country's *statsminister* (prime minister). Praised for its strong female characters, the show's string of awards include a Prix Italia (2010) and a BAFTA (2012).

Debuting in 2011, Danish-Swedish crime thriller *The Bridge* hooked viewers from its very first scene, in which a pair of severed corpses are discovered on the Øresund Bridge, at the very border between Sweden and Denmark. Screened in over 170 countries to date, the series would also spawn American and British-French versions.

Academy Success

Although Danish cinema stretches back to the end of the 19th-century, it wasn't until the 1980s that Danish directors attracted a broader international audience, with a swag of trophies to prove it.

Director Gabriel Axel's *Babette's Feast* (1987) won the Academy Award for Best Foreign Film in 1998. An exploration of the impact a French housekeeper has on two pious sisters, the film is an adaptation of a story by Karen Blixen, whose novel *Out of Africa* had been turned into an Oscar-winning Hollywood movie just three years earlier.

Remarkably, just a year later, a Danish film again won Best Foreign Film at the Academy Awards (as well as the Cannes Film Festival's Palme d'Or): *Pelle the Conqueror* was directed by Bille August and adapted from Martin Andersen Nexø's book about the harsh life of an immigrant in 19th-century Denmark.

The award fell into Danish hands once again in 2011 with *In a Better World*. Directed by Susanne Bier, the contemplative drama begins with playground bullying and takes in infidelity, bereavement, evil warlords and revenge – a plot engineered by Bier to question the cosy stereotype of her homeland.

Among the trio of films competing to be Denmark's Best Foreign Film contender at the 2015 Academy Awards was director Niels Arden Oplev's offbeat 1970s period flick *Speed Walking* (2014), featuring *Borgen* actors Sidse Babett Knudsen and Pilou Asbæk.

Acclaimed for its rich visual textures and innovative use of close-ups, *La Passion de Jeanne d'Arc* (1928) by director Carl Theodor Dreyer (1889–1968) was named the most influential film of all time in a list of the 'Essential 100' published by the Toronto International Film Festival in 2010.

LITERATURE, FILM & TV ON SCREEN

ADAM PRICE – CREATOR OF TV SERIES BORGEN

How close is Borgen to real-life Danish politics?

The tone of the series and the dilemmas are quite true to Danish politics. We spoke to several spin-doctors, politicians, and political journalists when researching, and we'd pitch every finished storyline to the political editor of the DR (Danish Broadcasting Corporation) news department, who was our barometer of realism. We'd call him the show's 'evil uncle'.

Why do you think the series resonates internationally?

People can see themselves in the characters' lives. Protagonist Birgitte Nyborg's main challenge is balancing her private and professional life. This is a common dilemma for modern people. Her pain is real. She is not the typical, cynical stereotype of a politician.

What's the secret to the success of Danish TV drama?

The DR has been behind most of Denmark's international successes. It's hard to get the green light from them, but once they agree to a show, they give full power to the producer and head writer. You'll never have a senior executive come and personally want to influence your writing. This saves the work from being distorted by too many compromises.

Directors of Note

Denmark has produced some high-profile directors, many of whom have crossed over from local Danish-language films to Hollywood productions.

Bille August Known for his literary adaptations: *Pelle the Conqueror* (1987); *The House of the Spirits* (1993), based on the novel by Chilean writer Isabel Allende; *Smilla's Sense of Snow* (1997), from the bestseller by Peter Høeg; *Les Misérables* (1998), adapted from Victor Hugo's classic tale; and *Night Train to Lisbon* (2013), based on Pascal Mercier's philosophical novel.

Susanne Bier One of Denmark's leading directors, she has made a name for herself internationally with respected local films *Brothers* (remade into an American production with the same name), *After the Wedding* (2006), *In a Better World* (2010) and *A Second Chance* (2014).

Lone Scherfig Scherfig's romantic comedy *Italian for Beginners* (2000) dealt with diverse but damaged Danes learning the language of love, and became an international hit. She also directed the dark comedy *Wilbur Wants to Kill Himself* (2002), a Danish-Scottish co-production, as well as the UK films *An Education* (2009) and *The Riot Club* (2014).

Thomas Vinterberg Co-founder of the Dogme95 movement, Vinterberg conceived, wrote and directed the first of the Dogme movies, *Festen* (The Celebration; 1998), to wide acclaim. Although subsequent films flopped, *The Hunt* (2012) won the 2013 Nordic Council Film Prize, as was also nominated for Best Foreign Language Film at the 2014 Academy Awards.

Nicolas Winding Refn Famous for directing the gritty and violent *Pusher* trilogy, which explores the criminal underworld of Copenhagen. His film, the US 'art-house noir' *Drive*, won him the Best Director award at the 2011 Cannes Film Festival.

And then there's Lars von Trier...

Top Danish Films

Pelle the Conqueror (1987)

Babette's Feast (1987)

Breaking the Waves (1996)

In a Better World (2010)

The Hunt (2012)

Speed Walking (2014)

Lars von Trier & Dogme95

Whether he's depicting explicit sexual encounters in *Nymphomaniac* (2013), the apocalypse in *Melancholia* (2011), or framing female genital mutilation in the polarising *Antichrist* (2009), there is little doubt that the leading Danish director and screenwriter of the 21st century remains Lars von Trier, who continues to live up to his label as the film world's *enfant terrible*.

Von Trier's better-known films include the melodrama *Breaking the Waves* (1996), which featured Emily Watson and took the Cannes Film Festival's Grand Prix; *Dancer in the Dark* (2000), a musical starring Icelandic pop singer Björk and Catherine Deneuve, which won Cannes' Palme d'Or in 2000; and the frequently difficult and experimental *Dogville* (2003), starring Nicole Kidman.

Von Trier is a cofounder of Dogme95, sometimes dubbed the 'vow of chastity'. This artistic manifesto pledged a minimalist approach to filmmaking using only hand-held cameras, shooting on location with natural light and rejecting the use of special effects and pre-recorded music. It attracted both ardent fans and widespread dismissal, but its impact and influence on modern cinema cannot be underestimated.

Survival Guide

DIRECTORY A–Z ... 290

Accommodation........ 290

Customs
Regulations............ 292

Electricity 292

Embassies &
Consulates 293

Food 293

Gay & Lesbian
Travellers 293

Health................. 293

Insurance.............. 293

Internet Access........ 294

Legal Matters 294

Money................. 294

Opening Hours 295

Public Holidays........ 295

Telephone 295

Time 296

Tourist Information 296

Travellers with
Disabilities............ 296

Visas................. 296

TRANSPORT 297

GETTING THERE &
AWAY 297

Entering the Country.... 297

Air 297

Land 298

Sea 299

GETTING AROUND...... 300

Air 300

Bicycle 300

Boat 300

Bus 301

Car & Motorcycle....... 301

Local Transport........ 302

Train 303

LANGUAGE 304

GLOSSARY............. 309

Directory A–Z

Accommodation

High standards of comfort and convenience are the norm in Denmark whether you're camping, hostelling or staying in a guesthouse or hotel, although nothing is particularly cheap.

➡ Campgrounds, hostels and B&B accommodation generally offer an excellent standard of accommodation and are good ways to secure comfort on a budget.

➡ Self-catering apartments, cottages and summerhouses make appealing and cost-effective alternatives for families and groups planning to stay in one place for a while.

➡ Airbnb (www.airbnb. com) is a great resource for private rooms, apartments, cottages and houses all over the country.

➡ Staff at local tourist offices can provide lists of local accommodation and may be able to arrange bookings. Fees may apply.

➡ During July and August it's advisable to book ahead. Even campgrounds can fill up.

➡ Many hotels, hostels and restaurants are also members of the Green Key eco accreditation scheme (www.green-key.org), in which they aim to cut their use of energy, chemicals and use of nonrenewable resources.

➡ We list prices for the summer high season (generally June to August). From September to May, many guesthouses and hotels offer substantial discounts on these rates – websites list up-to-date rates.

➡ There is no hard-and-fast rule about the inclusion of breakfast in prices – many hotels include it in their price, but for others it is optional. It is never included in the price of hostels and budget hotels, and ironically it is usually *not* included in B&B rates.

Bed & Breakfast & Private Rooms

➡ There's a growing number of B&Bs – some are traditional homestay arrangements, where you stay in the hosts' house, but many more are private rooms in small guesthouses, where you may share a toilet and kitchen with other guests, or have a studio-style apartment to yourself.

➡ A great example of this is in Ribe, where 35 private homes rent out rooms and apartments (some of them in beautifully restored old houses).

➡ The number and quality of these places is on the increase. They're often cheaper than a private room at a hostel or budget hotel, at around Dkr350/600 for a single/double. The rate generally includes linen but excludes breakfast, which can often be purchased (around Dkr60 to Dkr70).

➡ Staff at tourist offices maintain lists of B&B options in their area – check the local tourism websites for links.

➡ Many B&Bs that operate more like small guesthouses are bookable on sites like booking.com.

➡ Best online resource: www. bedandbreakfastguide.dk.

Camping

➡ Denmark is very well set up for campers, with nearly 600 camping grounds. Some are open only in the summer months, while others operate from spring to autumn. About

---

SLEEPING PRICE RANGES

The following price ranges refer to a double room in high season. Unless otherwise noted, rooms have private toilets.

€ less than Dkr700

€€ Dkr700–1500

€€€ more than Dkr1500

200 stay open year-round (and have low-season rates).

➡ You need a camping card (Dkr110) for stays at all camping grounds. You can buy a card at the first camping ground you arrive at, at local tourist offices, or from the Danish Camping Board (see www. danishcampsites.dk). The cost for an annual pass for couples is Dkr110; it covers all accompanied children aged under 18.

➡ The per-night charge to pitch a tent or park a caravan typically costs around Dkr75 for an adult, and about half that for each child. In summer some places also tack on a site charge of Dkr50 per tent/caravan; some also have a small eco tax.

➡ Many camping grounds rent cabins (a few offer on-site caravans) sleeping four to six people. Cabins range from simple huts with bunk beds to full cottages with kitchen and toilet. You generally BYO linen or pay to hire it. In the summer high season (mid-June to mid-August), many cabins can only be hired by the week (around Dkr3500, but it very much depends on the cabin's size and facilities).

➡ Backpackers and cyclists, note: even if a camping ground is signposted as fully booked, there may be sites for light-travelling campers.

➡ Throughout Denmark camping is restricted to established camping grounds or private land with the owner's permission. You risk a fine camping in a car or caravan at the beach or in a car park.

➡ If you're touring around, look for camping grounds offering 'QuickStop', a cheaper rate whereby you arrive after 8pm and leave again by 10am.

➡ Check www.smaapladser. dk for a list of 35 camping grounds that are smaller and more intimate, with a

maximum of 145 camping sites.

➡ Best online resources: www.danishcampsites.dk and www.dk-camp.dk

Farmstays

➡ A great way to get a feel for rural Denmark is on a farmstay, which can simply mean bed and breakfast accommodation or actually helping out with farm activities.

➡ The website of **Landsforeningen for Landboturisme** (www. visitfarmen.dk) links to 90 farms throughout Denmark that offer accommodation (from farmhouse rooms to family-sized self-contained flats and small rural houses – click on the map of the region you wish to visit, then see the selection. You book directly with the farm owner.

➡ Although it's best to plan in advance, if you're cycling or driving around Denmark you may well come across farmhouses displaying *værelse* (room) signs.

Hostels

➡ Some 88 hostels make up the **Danhostel association** (☑ 33 31 36 12; www.danhostel.dk), which is affiliated with Hostelling International (HI). Some are dedicated hostels in holiday areas, others are attached to sports centres (and hence may be busy with travelling sports teams etc).

➡ If you hold a valid national or international hostel card, you receive a 10% discount on rates (these can be purchased from hostels and cost Dkr70 for Danish residents, Dkr160 for

BOOK YOUR STAY ONLINE

For more accommodation reviews by Lonely Planet authors, check out http://lonelyplanet.com/hotels/. You'll find independent reviews, as well as recommendations on the best places to stay. Best of all, you can book online.

foreigners). We list prices for non-cardholders.

➡ Danish hostels appeal to all ages and are oriented as much towards families and groups as to budget travellers. Hiring a private room is the norm. All hostels offer dorm beds in shared rooms from July to mid-September; outside these months, availability of dorm beds varies from hostel to hostel.

➡ Typical costs are Dkr200 to Dkr275 for a dorm bed. For private rooms, expect to pay Dkr400 to Dkr600 per single, Dkr450 to Dkr720 per double, and up to Dkr100 for each additional person in larger rooms. All hostels offer family rooms; many rooms come with toilets.

➡ Duvets and pillows are provided, but you'll have to bring or hire your own sheets (typically between Dkr50 and Dkr70 per stay).

➡ All hostels provide an all-you-can-eat breakfast costing around Dkr70, and some also provide dinner. Most hostels have guest kitchens with pots and pans.

➡ Advance reservations are advised, particularly in summer. In a few places, reception closes as early as 6pm. In most hostels the reception office is closed, and the phone not answered, between noon and 4pm.

➡ Between May and September, hostels can get crowded with children on school excursions, or sports groups travelling for tournaments.

➡ Many Danish hostels close for at least part of the low season.

Hotels

➡ A few brands tend to dominate in the hotel business. For budget hotels, look for CabInn (www.cabinn.dk) across the country, and Wake Up (www.wakeupcopenhagen.com) in Copenhagen. Business-standard hotel chains include Scandic (www.scandichotels.com), Radisson (www.radisson.com), Comwell (www.comwell.dk) and First Hotels (www.firsthotels.com).

➡ There's a good range of boutique hotels in larger cities and popular upmarket destinations (Bornholm, for example, and Skagen), but true luxury or design hotels are not especially common outside the capital. If you're looking for something more memorable than a chain hotel room, consider staying in a castle, historic manor house or farm. Look out for *badehotel*, too (old seaside 'bathing inn') – many of these are now restored. Great resources for something a little special: www.historichotels.dk and www.smalldanishhotels.com.

➡ Be careful: the inclusion of *kro* in a name usually implies a country inn, but it is also (less commonly) the Danish version of a motel, found along major motorways near the outskirts of town.

➡ Some hotels have set rates published on their websites; others have rates that fluctuate according to season and demand. Most hotel websites offer good deals, as do booking engines such as booking.com (most Danish sleeping options are on booking.com).

➡ Many business hotels offer cheaper rates on Friday and Saturday nights year-round, and during the summer high season (from about mid-summer in late June until the start of the school year in early/mid-August).

➡ There is no hard-and-fast rule about the inclusion of breakfast in accommodation prices. It is never included in the price of budget hotels (but can be purchased for around Dkr70). Hotel breakfasts are usually decent all-you-can-eat buffets.

Manor Houses

➡ Denmark is simply stuffed with castles and manor houses, some of them offering atmospheric accommodation set in beautiful grounds. The website of the **Danske Slotte & Herregaarde association** (www.slotte-herregaarde.dk) has links to 14 atmospheric manor houses and small castles around Denmark that offer accommodation.

Rental Accommodation

➡ Many seaside resort areas are filled with cottage and apartment accommodation. These are generally rented out by the week and require reservations. Rates vary greatly, depending on the type of accommodation and the season, but generally they're cheaper than hotels.

➡ **DanCenter** (☏70 13 00 00; www.dancenter.com) handles holiday-cottage bookings nationwide. Many tourist offices can also help make reservations. Alternatively, try **Novasol** (☏70 42 44 24; www.novasol.dk), which organises self-catering options in cottages and summer houses.

➡ Hundreds of places (summer cottages, inner-city apartments, family-friendly houses) can be rented direct from the owner via **Airbnb** (www.airbnb.com).

Customs Regulations

➡ Coming from outside the EU, you can bring into Denmark 200 cigarettes, and 1L of spirits or 4L of wine or 16L of beer.

➡ Coming from an EU country, you are allowed to bring in 800 cigarettes, and 10L of spirits or 90L of wine or 110L of beer.

Electricity

Denmark uses the two-pin continental plug like most other European countries – it has two round pins and operates on 230V (volts) and 50Hz (cycles) AC.

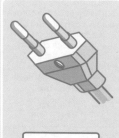

230V/50Hz

230V/50Hz

Embassies & Consulates

Australian Embassy (☑70 26 36 76; www.denmark. embassy.gov.au; Dampfærgevej 26, Copenhagen)

Canadian Embassy (☑33 48 32 00; www.denmark.gc.ca; Kristen Bernikows Gade 1, Copenhagen)

French Embassy (☑33 67 10 00; www.ambafrance-dk. org; Kongens Nytorv 4, Copenhagen)

German Embassy (☑35 45 99 00; www.kopenhagen. diplo.de; Stockholmsgade 57, Copenhagen)

Irish Embassy (☑35 47 32 00; www.embassyofireland.dk; Østbanegade 21, Copenhagen)

Netherlands Embassy (☑33 70 72 00; www.nlembassy.dk; Toldbodgade 33, Copenhagen)

New Zealand Consulate (☑33 37 77 00; www.nzconsulate.dk; Store Strandstræde 21, Copenhagen)

UK Embassy (☑35 44 52 00; http://ukindenmark.fco.gov. uk; Kastelsvej 36-40, Copenhagen)

US Embassy (☑33 41 71 00; http://denmark.usembassy. gov/; Dag Hammarskjölds Allé 24, Copenhagen)

Food

Denmark, and Copenhagen in particular, has become Scandinavia's culinary powerhouse, boasting plenty of Michelin stars in the capital and many more excellent new places throughout the coun-

try. For more information see p279.

Gay & Lesbian Travellers

➡ Given Denmark's high degree of tolerance for alternative lifestyles of all sorts, it's hardly surprising that Denmark is a popular destination for gay and lesbian travellers.

➡ Copenhagen in particular has an active, open gay community with a healthy number of venues, but you'll find gay and lesbian venues in other cities as well.

➡ For general info, contact **Landsforeningen for Bøsser, Lesbiske, Biseksuelle og Transpersoner** (www.lgbt. dk), the Danish national association for the GLBT community.

➡ A useful website for travellers with visitor information and listings in English is www.copenhagen-gay-life.dk. Also see www.out-and-about.dk.

➡ The main gay and lesbian festival of the year is **Copenhagen Pride** (www.copenhagenpride.dk), a five-day queer fest that takes place in August. There's also the gay and lesbian film festival **Mix Copenhagen** (mixcopenhagen.dk), held each October.

Health

Denmark is a relatively healthy place and travellers shouldn't need to take any unusual health precautions.

EMERGENCIES

For police, fire and ambulance services in Denmark, dial ☑112.

Availability & Cost of Health Care

➡ You can get medical treatment anywhere in the country by contacting a doctor, during consultation hours.

➡ If you're in urgent need of medical care outside office hours, you can contact an emergency doctor (Lægevagten). Visit the website www.laegevagten.dk/kontakt-laegevagten, and click where you are on the map to find the telephone number of the emergency doctor in your area.

➡ For minor ailments, pharmacists can give advice and sell over-the-counter medication. They can also advise when more specialised help is required and point you in the right direction. Look for the sign *apotek* (pharmacy).

INSURANCE

➡ If you're an EU citizen, the European Health Insurance Card covers you for most medical care but not for nonemergencies or for emergency repatriation to home. Apply online via your government's health department website.

➡ Citizens from other countries should find out if there is a reciprocal arrangement for free medical access in Denmark. Make sure your health insurance covers you for the worst possible scenario, such as an accident requiring an emergency flight home.

Insurance

➡ Although Denmark is a safe place to travel, theft does occasionally happen, and illness and accidents

---

EATING PRICE RANGES

The following price ranges refer to a standard main course.

€ less than Dkr125

€€ Dkr125–250

€€€ more than Dkr250

are always a possibility. A travel insurance policy to cover theft, loss and medical problems is strongly recommended.

Internet Access

⇒ With the proliferation of wi-fi, and most locals and travellers carrying iPads and/or smartphones, the internet cafe is a dying breed in Denmark. There may be a couple catering to gamers and to laptop-less travellers in the major cities, but public libraries are your best bet in midsized and small towns for free use of computers with internet access.

⇒ Libraries also have free wi-fi (you will need a code), as do many cafes, bars, and even trains and buses. Wi-fi is common in hotels and hostels (indicated in listings using the 🛜 icon) and is usually free.

Some hostels and hotels will offer a computer for guests to use, free or for a small charge (indicated in our reviews with the @ symbol).

Legal Matters

⇒ Authorities are strict about drink driving, and even a couple of drinks can put you over the legal limit of 0.05% blood-alcohol level. Drivers detected under the influence of alcohol are liable to receive stiff penalties and a possible prison sentence.

⇒ Always treat drugs with a great deal of caution. In Denmark all forms of cannabis are officially illegal.

Money

⇒ Although Denmark is an EU member nation, Denmark's citizens rejected adopting the euro in a referendum in 2000.

⇒ Denmark's currency, the krone, is most often written with the symbol DKK in international money markets, Dkr in northern Europe and Dkr within Denmark.

⇒ One krone is divided into 100 øre. There are 50 øre, Dkr1, Dkr2, Dkr5, Dkr10 and Dkr20 coins. Notes come in denominations of 50, 100, 200, 500 and 1000 kroner.

ATMs

⇒ Most banks in Denmark have 24-hour automated teller machines (ATMs) that give cash advances on Visa and MasterCard credit cards as well as Cirrus and Plus bank cards.

⇒ Typically, you'll get a good rate when withdrawing money directly from a Danish ATM, but keep in mind that your home bank may charge you a fee for international transactions or for using another bank's ATM – check before you leave.

⇒ A few banks, especially in Copenhagen, have 24-hour cash machines that change major foreign currencies into Danish kroner.

Credit Cards

⇒ Credit cards such as Visa and MasterCard are widely accepted in Denmark (American Express and Diners Club less so).

⇒ In many places (hotels, petrol stations, restaurants, stores) a surcharge may be imposed on foreign cards (up to 3.75%). If there is a surcharge, it must be advertised (eg on the menu, at reception).

⇒ If a card is lost or stolen, you should inform the issuing company as soon as possible.

AmEx (☏80 01 00 21)
Diners Club (☏36 73 73 73)
MasterCard (☏80 01 60 98)
Visa (☏80 01 85 88)

PRACTICALITIES

⇒ **Discount cards** Seniors and students qualify for discounts on some transport fares and museum entry fees, but you'll need to show proof of student status or age.

⇒ **Newspapers and magazines** *Jyllands-Posten*, *Politiken* and *Berlingske Tidende* are the leading Danish-language newspapers. Danish news in English is available in the *Copenhagen Post* (www.cphpost.dk), published weekly.

⇒ **Numbering** A comma indicates a decimal point; points indicate thousands. So 12,345.67 in English would be written 12.345,67 in Danish.

⇒ **Smoking** Danes are surprisingly heavy smokers, but smoking in restaurants, bars and clubs is banned. Some hospitality venues have separate smoking rooms. As of mid-2014, smoking is banned on train platforms. Hotels determine their own smoking rules but most are non-smoking.

⇒ **TV** Danish TV broadcasts local and international programs, with English-language programs usually presented in English with Danish subtitles. International cable channels such as CNN and BBC World are available in many hotels.

⇒ **Weights and measures** Denmark uses the metric system. Fruit is often sold by the piece (*stykke* or 'stk').

Tipping

➡ Hotel and restaurant bills and taxi fares include service charges in the quoted prices.

➡ Further tipping is unnecessary, although rounding up the bill is not uncommon when service has been especially good.

Opening Hours

➡ Opening hours vary throughout the year. We've provided high-season opening hours; in tourist areas and establishments, hours will generally decrease in the shoulder and low seasons.

➡ Family-friendly attractions (museums, zoos, fun parks) in holiday hotspots will generally open from June to August (possibly May to September), and for the spring and autumn school holidays.

➡ Standard opening hours are as follows:

Banks 10am-4pm Monday to Friday

Bars 4pm-midnight, to 2am or later Friday & Saturday (clubs on weekends may open until 5am)

Cafes 8am-5pm or midnight

Restaurants noon-10pm (maybe earlier on weekends for brunch)

Shops 10am-6pm Monday-Friday (possibly until 7pm on Friday), to 4pm Saturday. Some larger stores may open Sunday.

Supermarkets 8am-8pm or 9pm (many with bakeries opening around 7am)

Public Holidays

Many Danes take their main work holiday during the first three weeks of July, but there are numerous other holidays as well.

Banks and most businesses close on public holidays and transport schedules are commonly reduced.

New Year's Day (Nytårsdag) 1 January

Maundy Thursday (Skærtorsdag) Thursday before Easter

Good Friday (Langfredag) Friday before Easter

Easter Day (Påskedag) Sunday in March or April

Easter Monday (2. Påskedag) Day after Easter

Great Prayer Day (Stor Bededag) Fourth Friday after Easter

Ascension Day (Kristi Himmelfartsdag) Sixth Thursday after Easter

Whitsunday (Pinsedag) Seventh Sunday after Easter

Whitmonday (2. Pinsedag) Seventh Monday after Easter

Constitution Day (Grundlovsdag) 5 June

Christmas Eve (Juleaften) 24 December (from noon)

Christmas Day (Juledag) 25 December

Boxing Day (2. Juledag) 26 December

New Year's Eve (Nytårsaften) 31 December (from noon)

School Holidays

In addition to the public holidays noted above, schools generally close as follows:

Winter holidays A week in February (week 7 or 8)

Spring holidays A week around Easter time

Summer holidays From the last Saturday in June to around 10 August

Autumn holidays A week in mid-October (week 42)

Christmas and New Year Two weeks

VAT REFUNDS

The value-added tax (VAT; called MOMS in Danish) on all goods and services in Denmark is 25%. Citizens from countries outside the EU can claim a VAT refund on goods as they leave the EU (as long as they spend a minimum of Dkr300 per shop, and the shop participates in one of the refund schemes). Get the shop to fill in a refund form, then present it, together with your passport, receipts and purchases, at the airport upon departure.

Telephone

➡ Public phones are elusive in Denmark. There may be a payphone outside the local train or bus station, and some bigger attractions, but few others. You pay by the minute. Phones accept coins, credit cards or prepaid phonecards (available from kiosks and post offices).

Mobile Phones

➡ The cheapest and most practical way to make calls at local rates is to purchase a Danish SIM card and pop it into your own mobile phone (tip: bring an old phone from home for that purpose). Before leaving home, make sure that your phone isn't blocked from doing this by your home network.

➡ If you're coming from outside Europe, also check that your phone will work in Europe's GSM 900/1800 network (US phones work on a different frequency).

➡ You can buy a prepaid SIM card at supermarkets, post offices, kiosks and petrol stations throughout the country. Top-up credit is available from the same outlets.

➡ Danish mobile service providers (starter SIM-card packages cost from Dkr29) include the following:

TDC (tdc.dk)

Telenor (www.telenor.dk)

Telia (telia.dk)

Phone Codes

➧ All telephone numbers in Denmark have eight digits; there are no area codes. This means that all eight digits must be dialled, even when making calls in the same city.

➧ For local directory assistance dial ☑118. For overseas enquiries, including for rates and reverse charge (collect) calls, dial ☑113.

➧ The country code for Denmark is ☑45. To call Denmark from another country, dial the international access code for the country you're in followed by ☑45 and the local eight-digit number.

➧ The international access code in Denmark is ☑00. To make direct international calls from Denmark, dial ☑00 followed by the country code for the country you're calling, the area code, then the local number.

Time

➧ Time in Denmark is one hour ahead of GMT/UTC, the same as in neighbouring European countries.

➧ Clocks are moved forward one hour for daylight-saving time from the last Sunday in March to the last Sunday in October.

➧ Denmark uses the 24-hour clock system and all timetables and business hours are posted accordingly.

➧ *Klokken,* which means o'clock, is abbreviated as kl (kl 19.30 is 7.30pm).

➧ The Danes number their weeks, and refer to them as such – eg schools break for winter holidays in week 7;

some businesses are closed for summer holidays in weeks 29 and 30. It might be hard to wrap your head around – www.ugenr.dk can help.

Tourist Information

➧ Denmark is extremely well served by helpful, well-informed tourist offices and multilingual staff. See the local listings for details.

➧ Each town and region publishes a glossy annual brochure that covers most of the things travellers need to know, and has a website full of sights, accommodation options and practical info.

➧ Important websites for visitors to Denmark include www.denmark.dk and www.visitdenmark.com.

➧ Regional tourist offices include the following:

Bornholm (www.bornholm. info)

Copenhagen (www.visit copenhagen.com)

East Jutland (www.visit aarhus.com)

Funen (www.visitfyn.com)

Northern Jutland (www. visitnordjylland.com)

Southern Jutland (www. sydvestjylland.com)

West Jutland (www.visitden mark.com/west-jutland)

Zealand, Møn, Falster & Lolland (www.visiteastden mark.com)

Travellers with Disabilities

➧ Denmark is improving access to buildings,

transport and even forestry areas and beaches all the time, although accessibility is still not ubiquitous.

➧ The official www. visitdenmark.com website has a useful series of links for travellers with disabilities, and explains how to access detailed information – click on the 'Special Travel' section under 'Practical Information'.

➧ A useful resource is **God Adgang** (www.godadgang.dk), which lists service providers who have had their facilities registered and labelled for accessibility.

Visas

➧ No entry visa is needed by citizens of EU and Nordic countries.

➧ Citizens of the USA, Canada, Australia and New Zealand need a valid passport to enter Denmark, but they don't need a visa for tourist stays of less than 90 days.

➧ Citizens of many African, South American, Asian and former Soviet bloc countries do require a visa. The Danish Immigration Service publishes a list of countries whose citizens require a visa at its website at www. nyidanmark.dk.

➧ If you're in the country and have questions on visa extensions or visas in general, contact the Danish Immigration Service, **Udlændingestyrelsen** (www.nyidanmark.dk).

Transport

Getting to Denmark is simple. The capital, Copenhagen, has worldwide air links, and some carriers fly into regional airports around the small nation. Train, road and bridge links exist to Germany and Sweden, and there are ferry connections to/from several countries.

Once you get to Denmark, transport stays hassle-free. Most journeys by train, car or bus are so short you can reach regional destinations before your next meal.

Flights, tours and rail tickets can be booked online at www.lonelyplanet.com/bookings.

GETTING THERE & AWAY

Entering the Country

➡ Denmark is part of the Schengen agreement, which eliminated border passport control between Schengen countries in Europe. This means you no longer need to stop or show your passport when travelling between Denmark and Germany or Denmark and Sweden. You must still have your passport with you, however, when travelling in Schengen countries, as a form of identification.

➡ There is passport control when entering Denmark from a country outside the Schengen area and some nationalities need a visa to enter Denmark.

➡ If you're arriving by ferry, particularly from a neighbouring country, passports are not usually checked.

Passport

➡ For entry into the Schengen area, you must have a passport valid for three months beyond your proposed departure date.

Air

Airports

The majority of overseas flights into Denmark land at **Copenhagen International Airport** (www.cph.dk) in Kastrup, about 9km southeast of central Copenhagen.

A number of international flights, mostly those coming from other Nordic countries or the UK, land at smaller regional airports, in Aarhus, Aalborg, Billund, Esbjerg and Sønderborg.

Airlines

Dozens of international airlines fly to/from Danish airports; the airport websites have up-to-date information on all the relevant carriers.

Airlines that use Denmark as their primary base:

Scandinavian Airlines (SAS; www.flysas.com) The flag carrier of Denmark (and Norway and Sweden).

CLIMATE CHANGE & TRAVEL

Every form of transport that relies on carbon-based fuel generates CO_2, the main cause of human-induced climate change. Modern travel is dependent on aeroplanes, which might use less fuel per kilometre per person than most cars but travel much greater distances. The altitude at which aircraft emit gases (including CO_2) and particles also contributes to their climate change impact. Many websites offer 'carbon calculators' that allow people to estimate the carbon emissions generated by their journey and, for those who wish to do so, to offset the impact of the greenhouse gases emitted with contributions to portfolios of climate-friendly initiatives throughout the world. Lonely Planet offsets the carbon footprint of all staff and author travel.

RIDESHARING

To find passengers to share fuel costs, try www.carpooling.co.uk, which has an international search option.

Land

Technically, Denmark's only land crossing is with Germany, although the bridge over the Øresund from Sweden functions in the same way.

Bicycle

You can carry your bicycle into Denmark aboard a boat, plane or train.

Ferries Boats into Denmark are all well equipped for passengers with bicycles, usually for a nominal fee.

Flights Bicycles can travel by air, but airline baggage regulations seem to be in constant flux and their approach can be inconsistent. If you intend to travel with your bike, check with the airline well in advance, preferably before you pay for your ticket.

Trains You will generally need to buy a ticket to transport your bike on a train to Denmark, and in peak times reserve a place for it.

Bus

➡ Copenhagen is well connected to the rest of Europe by daily (or near daily) buses. Major Jutland cities also have links – from Norway south via Hirtshals ferry port to Aalborg and Aarhus.

➡ The most extensive European bus network is maintained by **Eurolines** (☎33 88 70 00; www.eurolines. dk), a consortium of 30 bus operators. Eurolines Scandinavia offers connections to more than 500 major European cities in 26 countries. Destinations, timetables and prices are all online; advance reservations are advised.

➡ Not under the Eurolines umbrella, **Abildskou** (☎70 21 08 88; www.abildskou.dk) links Aarhus and Berlin (one way Dkr495, nine hours, daily) with stops in Kolding and Vejle (Denmark) and Flensburg and Neumünster (Germany) en route. There is an option to connect to services to Hamburg.

Car & Motorcycle

➡ Requirements for bringing your own vehicle into Denmark are: a valid driver's licence, certificate of registration and nationality plate, and proof of third-party insurance.

➡ Insurance requirements are outlined on the website of the **Danish Motor Insurers' Bureau** (DFIM; www.dfim.dk).

GERMANY

➡ The E45 motorway is the main road link with Germany, although there are several smaller crossings. The E45 runs from the German border north through Jutland to Frederikshavn.

➡ With a bridge linking the Jutland peninsula to the island of Funen, and a toll bridge from Funen to Zealand, it's possible to drive all the way from mainland Europe to Copenhagen (and on to Sweden).

➡ There are also car ferries to Danish islands from Germany (see p300).

NORWAY

➡ Unless you fancy a road trip through southern Sweden to cross the Øresund Bridge, car ferries are still the most efficient way to arrive from Norway (see p300).

SWEDEN

➡ The remarkable 16km Øresundsbron (Øresund Bridge) joins Copenhagen with Malmö in Sweden, via the E20 motorway. It's actually a combination of a tunnel beneath the sea, an artificial island (Peberholm), and a suspension bridge catering for cars and trains.

➡ The Øresund Bridge's toll station is situated on the Swedish side. The toll for a regular car/motorcycle is Dkr335/175; campervans or cars towing a caravan pay Dkr670. You can pay by cash (at the yellow manned stations, using Danish or Swedish currency, or the euro), credit/pay cards (automatic stations) or via a 'BroPas' transponder affixed to your windscreen (for regular commuters). Read more at www.oresundsbron. com.

➡ You can also take a car ferry (see p300).

UK

➡ You could take the Channel Tunnel to the continent then make your way northeast through France, Belgium and Germany to Denmark.

➡ The car ferry from Harwich to Esbjerg ceased operating in September 2014.

Train

➡ The Danish state railway, **Danske Statsbaner** (DSB; ☎70 13 14 15; www.dsb.dk) can provide schedule and fare information.

BRIDGING THE GAP

With the bridge-tunnel connection between Denmark and Sweden such a success, there are plans for a similar link between the German island of Fehmarn and the Danish island of Lolland. Planning is underway for a tunnel to close the 19km Fehmarn Belt, considerably shortening travel time between Hamburg and Copenhagen. Read about the project at www.femern.com.

RAIL PASSES

It may be hard to get your money's worth on a rail pass if you're travelling most of the time in tiny Denmark, although a pass may make sense if you're visiting other countries as well.

There's a dizzying variety of passes, depending on where you reside and where you're going to travel. In addition to the websites listed below, details about rail passes can be found at www.railpass.com. And remember, if you buy a rail pass, read the small print.

Note: prices depend on age and class of travel. There are cheaper rates for children (aged four to 11), youths (12 to 25 years) and seniors (over 60).

Supplements (eg for high-speed services, night trains, seat reservations) are not covered by passes.

Eurail Passes

Eurail passes (www.eurail.com) are for residents of non-European countries, and can only be bought outside Europe. They are available from larger travel agencies and online. There are a variety of passes available, including the following:

➡ **Global Pass** Covers 23 European countries (not including the UK), and can be purchased for a range of durations, including 10 or 15 days within a two-month period, 15 or 21 consecutive days, or for one, two or three months. Prices vary; unlimited travel for one month costs adult/youth €595/913 (Note: this pass is much better value for under-26s. If you're older than 26, you have to buy a 1st-class pass.)

➡ **One Country Pass** Covers only one country (ie Denmark) and is valid for three or seven days during a one-month period. Price for an adult travelling in 2nd class for three/seven days €111/152.

Other Eurail passes to consider include the **Select Pass** (covers three to five bordering countries), **Two-country regional pass** (covering Denmark and Sweden, or Denmark and Germany) and the **Scandinavia Rail Pass** (valid for Norway, Sweden, Finland and Denmark).

InterRail Passes

InterRail passes (www.interrail.eu) are available only to European residents and can be purchased from most major train stations, student travel outlets and online.

➡ **InterRail Global Pass** Covers 30 countries and comes in five versions, from five days of travel in 10 days, to a full month's unlimited travel. Price for an adult travelling in 2nd class for one month is €56.

➡ **InterRail One Country Pass** Covers one country (ie Denmark) and is valid for three, four, six or eight days during a one-month period. The price for an adult travelling in 2nd class for eight days is €255.

➡ A great reference for Europe-wide rail travel is the website **The Man In Seat 61** (www.seat61.com).

➡ Eurail and InterRail tickets are valid on the DSB.

Sea

Ferry connections are possible between Denmark and Norway, Sweden, Germany, Poland (via Sweden), Iceland and the Faroe Islands. The ferry link with the UK ceased in 2014.

Fares on these routes vary wildly, by season and by day of the week. The highest prices tend to occur on summer weekends and the lowest on winter weekdays. Discounts are often available, including for return tickets, car and passengers, holders of rail passes or student cards, and seniors. Child fares are usually half the adult fares.

If travelling in peak times, in particular if you are transporting a car, you should always make reservations well in advance – this is doubly true in summer and on weekends. Taking a bicycle incurs a small fee.

Faroe Islands & Iceland

Smyril Line (www.smyrilline.com) Sails from the northern Jutland port of Hirtshals to Tórshavn, the capital of the Faroe Islands (once weekly year-round, twice weekly in summer high season; 36 hours), and from Hirtshals to Seyðisfjörður (Iceland) via Tórshavn (once weekly April to October; 47 hours).

Germany

BornholmerFærgen (www.bornholmerfaergen.dk) Sails from Rønne (on Bornholm) to Sassnitz (four to 11 times a week April to October; 3½ hours).

Scandlines (www.scandlines.com) Sails from Rødbyhavn (on Lolland) to Puttgarden (every half hour; 45 minutes) and from Gedser (on Falster) to Rostock (up to 11 daily; two hours).

SyltExpress (www.syltfaehre.de) Sails from Havneby (on west-coast Rømø) to the German island of Sylt (up to nine daily; 40 minutes).

Norway

Color Line (www.colorline.com) Sails from Hirtshals to Kristiansand (once or twice daily; 3¼ hours) and Larvik (once or twice daily; 3¾ hours).

DFDS Seaways (www.dfdsseaways.com) Copenhagen to Oslo (once daily; 17 hours).

Fjordline (www.fjordline.com) Offers a fast catamaran service from Hirtshals to Kristiansand (two or three services daily mid-May to August; 2¼ hours). Also sails from Hirtshals to Bergen via Stavanger (once daily; Stavanger 10½ hours, Bergen 16½ hours), and Langesund (once daily; 4½ hours).

Stena Line (www.stenaline.com) Frederikshavn to Oslo (daily; nine hours).

Poland

Polferries (www.polferries.com) Connects Świnoujście with Ystad in southern Sweden (once or twice daily; seven to eight hours). From Ystad there is a free connecting shuttle-bus service to Copenhagen via the Øresund Bridge for foot passengers; those in cars receive a pass for passage across the bridge. From Ystad there are frequent ferries to Bornholm.

Sweden

BornholmerFærgen (www.bornholmerfaergen.dk) Rønne (Bornholm) to Ystad (up to nine times daily; 80 minutes).

Scandlines (www.scandlines.com) Helsingør to Helsingborg (up to four sailings an hour; 20 minutes).

Stena Line (www.stenaline.com) Sails from Frederikshavn to Gothenburg (up to six times a day; 3½ hours) and from Grenaa to Varberg (once or twice daily; four to five hours).

GETTING AROUND

Air

Denmark's small size and efficient train network mean that domestic air traffic is limited, usually to business travellers and people connecting from international flights through Copenhagen.

Still, domestic carriers offer frequent services between Copenhagen and a few of the more distant corners of the country.

Scandinavian Airlines (SAS; www.flysas.com) Connects Copenhagen with Aarhus, Aalborg and Billund.

Bicycle

➜ Cyclists in Denmark are very well catered for, and there are excellent cycling routes throughout the country. For more information see p30.

➜ It's easy to travel with a bike anywhere in Denmark, even when you're not riding it, as bicycles can be taken on ferries and trains for a modest fee.

➜ Be aware on intercity trains that reservations should be made at least three hours prior to departure because bikes generally travel in a separate section of the train.

Hire

➜ Rest assured, you'll be able to hire a bike in almost every Danish town and village. Some tourist offices, hostels and camping grounds rent them out, and some bike shops provide a hire service. A few upmarket hotels have free bikes for guest use, while the largest cities (Copenhagen, Aarhus, Odense, Aalborg) have a free *bycykler* (town bike) scheme.

➜ Bike-rental prices average around Dkr100/400 per day/week for something basic. Note that helmets are generally not included with hired bicycles (they are not compulsory in Denmark).

Boat

Boats link virtually all of Denmark's populated islands; see listings for details. These range from large high-speed car ferries sailing several times daily, year-round, between Aarhus and Odden in north Zealand, to small summertime boats ferrying daytrippers to minor

---

THE ESSENTIAL TRANSPORT WEBSITE

For getting around in Denmark, the essential website is www.rejseplanen.dk. This excellent resource allows you to enter your start and end point, date and preferred time of travel, and will then give you the best travel option, which may involve walking or taking a bus or train. Bus routes are linked, travel times are given, and fares listed. You can also compare travel times and costs (and even carbon emissions) for public transport versus driving your own vehicle. You can't travel without it! Download the app for easy mobile access.

ROAD DISTANCES (KM)

	Aalborg	Copenhagen	Esbjerg	Frederikshavn	Grenaa	Helsingør	Kalundborg	Kolding	Næstved	Nyborg	Odense	Ringkøbing	Rødby	Skagen	Thisted	Tønder	Viborg	Århus (Aarhus)
Aalborg	---																	
Copenhagen	402	---																
Esbjerg	216	298	---															
Frederikshavn	65	465	278	---														
Grenaa	136	367	216	193	---													
Helsingør	443	47	339	506	408	---												
Kalundborg	345	103	241	408	310	139	---											
Kolding	199	230	72	261	164	271	173	---										
Næstved	342	85	238	405	307	125	71	152	---									
Nyborg	274	228	170	337	239	169	71	102	68	---								
Odense	243	165	139	306	208	206	108	71	105	37	---							
Ringkøbing	174	336	81	236	188	377	279	115	276	208	177	---						
Rødby	410	181	306	473	375	221	176	238	105	136	173	344	---					
Skagen	105	505	319	41	233	546	448	302	445	377	346	277	513	---				
Thisted	90	399	185	138	186	440	342	196	339	271	240	123	407	172	---			
Tønder	284	315	77	347	249	356	258	86	255	187	156	148	323	387	252	---		
Viborg	80	323	136	142	100	354	266	119	263	195	164	94	331	183	87	205	---	
Århus (Aarhus)	112	304	153	171	63	345	ferry	101	244	176	145	127	312	212	153	186	66	---

islands in the South Funen Archipelago.

A number of islands can only be reached by ferry; expect there to be a year-round service. Popular routes include Køge–Bornholm, Svendborg–Ærø, Frederikshavn–Læsø, and Esbjerg–Fanø, but this list is far from exhaustive. It's a good idea to book car passage in advance, at any time of year (but especially summer).

Bus

➡ Long-distance buses run a distant second to trains. Still, some cross-country bus routes work out to about 25% cheaper than trains.

➡ Daily express buses include connections between Copenhagen and Aarhus (Dkr310, three to 3½ hours) and Copenhagen and Aalborg (Dkr360, five to 5½

hours), stopping at a number of Jutland towns en route. These generally use the ferry service from Odden to Jutland, but some services run via Odense.

➡ Full timetables, cities served, and fares (including discounts) are online at www. abildskou.dk.

Car & Motorcycle

➡ Denmark is an excellent destination for a driving holiday. Roads are high quality and usually well signposted. Except during rush hour, traffic is quite light, even in major cities.

➡ One thing to be aware of is the large number of cyclists – they often have the right of way. It is particularly important that you check cycle lanes before turning right.

➡ Access to and from Danish motorways is straightforward: roads leading out of town centres are named after the main city that they lead to (eg the road heading out of Odense to Faaborg is called Faaborgvej).

➡ Petrol stations, with toilets, baby-changing facilities and minimarkets, are at 50km intervals on motorways.

➡ Denmark's extensive ferry network carries vehicles at reasonable rates. Fares for cars average three times the passenger rate. It's wise to make ferry reservations in advance, even if it's only a couple of hours ahead of time. On weekends and holidays, ferries on prime crossings can be completely booked.

Driving Licence

Short-term visitors may hire a car with only their home

country's driving licence (so long as the licence is written in Roman script; if not, an international driving licence is necessary).

Fuel

➡ Unleaded petrol and diesel fuel are available. Although prices fluctuate somewhat, per-litre prices at the time of research were around Dkr12.

➡ In towns, petrol stations may be open until 10pm or midnight, but there are some 24-hour services. Some have unstaffed 24-hour automatic pumps operated with credit cards.

Hire

➡ Rental cars are relatively expensive in Denmark, but a little research can mean big savings. Walk-in rates start at about Dkr600 per day for a small car, although naturally the per-day rates drop the longer you rent.

➡ You may get the best deal on a car rental by booking with an international rental agency before you arrive. Be sure to ask about promotional rates, pre-pay schemes etc. Ensure you get a deal covering unlimited kilometres.

➡ Avis, Budget, Europcar and Hertz are among the largest operators in Denmark, with offices in major cities, airports and other ports of entry. There are very few local budget operators. If you'll be using a rental car for a while, you might consider hiring your car in cheaper Germany and either returning it there afterwards, or negotiating a slightly more expensive one-way deal.

➡ Rental companies' weekend rates, when available, offer real savings. For about Dkr1000, you can hire a small car from Friday to Monday, including VAT and insurance. These deals may have restrictions on the amount of kilometres included (often around 300km) – request a plan

that includes unlimited kilometres if you'll need it.

Road Rules

➡ Drive on the right-hand side of the road.

➡ Cars and motorcycles must have dipped headlights on at all times.

➡ Drivers are required to carry a warning triangle in case of breakdown.

➡ Seat belt use is mandatory. Children under 135cm must be secured with approved child restraint appropriate to the child's age, size and weight.

➡ Motorcycle riders (but not cyclists) must wear helmets.

➡ Speed limits: 50km/h in towns and built-up areas, 80km/h on major roads, up to 130km/h on motorways. Maximum speed for vehicles with trailers: 80km/h. Speeding fines can be severe.

➡ Using a hand-held mobile phone while driving is illegal; hands-free use is permitted.

➡ It's illegal to drive with a blood-alcohol concentration of 0.05% or more.

➡ Use of a parking disc (P-skive) is required where time-limited parking is allowed – this is a device that looks like a clock, which you place on the dashboard of your car to indicate the time you arrived at a car-parking space. Discs are often available from petrol stations and tourist offices.

➡ Motorways have emergency telephones at 2km intervals, indicated by arrows on marker posts. From other telephones, dial ☑112 for emergencies.

Tolls

There are two toll routes in Denmark:

➡ The 18km motorway bridge across the Storebælt (Great Belt) linking Funen and Zealand (www.storebaelt.dk). Casual one-way passage for a

regular car/motorcycle is Dkr235/125.

➡ The 16km motorway bridge/tunnel across the Øresund between Denmark and Sweden (www.oresundsbron.com). Casual one-way passage for a regular car/motorcycle is Dkr335/175.

➡ Note that you can't travel on either of these toll routes on foot or by bicycle – you'll need to travel by bus or train if you don't have your own car.

Local Transport

Local transport in Denmark is of a high standard. There are excellent train, metro and bus options within Copenhagen; outside the capital, larger towns have local bus networks, and most small towns have bus connections to their regional hub.

Rejsekort

➡ The multiple-use paper local transport ticket known as the klippekort has been gradually phased out, with a move to an electronic ticketing system for travelling by bus, train and metro. You load up your card with money, then 'check in' at card-reading devices as you enter and exit transport, and reload your card as your funds run low. Denmark's card is known as the Rejsekort – see www. rejsekort.dk for information.

➡ Rejsekorts are designed for local users, so non-residents may find them a hassle to obtain and use. The good news is that there are still 'cash tickets' (kontantbilleter) available for all journeys (no Rejsekort

---

TIP!

Nearly all Danish train stations have left-luggage lockers (from Dkr20 for 24 hours).

required), and there are still options to buy a one-day or three-day travel pass covering Copenhagen city transport, for example. For short-stay visitors, these are generally a simpler option. We quote cash ticket prices.

➡ If you are visiting Denmark for a lengthy period, you can buy a Rejsekort Anonymous. The card costs Dkr80, but you must then add Dkr170 to the card to cover the cost of travel (which you then top-up as needed). You can buy a Rejsekort Anonymous at vending machines placed at every metro station, at Copenhagen airport and at Copenhagen Central Station.

Bus

Nearly every town in Denmark supports a network of local buses, which circulate around the town centre and also connect it with outlying areas. In smaller towns, the local bus terminal is often adjacent to the train station and/or long-distance bus terminal. Cash fares are around Dkr20 to Dkr25 per local ride, but daily travel passes may be useful.

Taxi

➡ Taxis are generally readily available for hire in city centres, near major shopping centres and at train stations. If you see a taxi with a lit *fri* sign (or a green light), you can wave it down, or you can phone for a taxi instead – hotels and tourist offices have numbers for local companies.

➡ Tipping is included in the fare.

➡ You can pay by cash or credit card.

Train

➡ Denmark has a very reliable train system with reasonable fares and frequent services. The network extends to most corners of the country, with the exception of the southern islands and a pocket of northwestern Jutland. In these areas, a good network of local buses connects towns.

➡ Most long-distance trains on major routes operate at least hourly throughout the day. **Danske Statsbaner** (DSB; ☑70 13 14 15; www.dsb. dk) runs virtually all trains in Denmark. Types of DSB trains include the following:

InterCity (IC) Modern comforts.

InterCityLyn (ICL) On certain well-travelled routes. Same facilities as InterCity, but with fewer stops.

Regionaltog Regional trains; reservations generally not accepted.

S-tog The combined urban and suburban rail network of Greater Copenhagen.

Fares & Discounts

Standard train fares work out to be a fraction over Dkr1 per kilometre, with the highest fare possible between any two points in Denmark topping out at around Dkr500 (Copenhagen to Skagen, a road distance of 525km).

➡ The reservation fee for a seat *(pladsbillet)* is Dkr30.

➡ Note that the 'Stillezone' on trains is a quiet zone.

➡ Bikes can be taken on many trains, but you need to buy a ticket *(cykelbillet)* for them on regional and intercity trains (price varies with distance travelled, but is generally quite cheap).

It's free to take a bike on the S-tog.

➡ A **DSB 1** (1st-class ticket) generally costs about 50% more than the standard fare. DSB 1 tickets give an automatic seat guarantee on IC or ICL services. Discounts include the following:

Children (under 12) Travel free if they are with an adult travelling on a standard ticket (each adult can take two children free).

Children (under 15) Pay half the adult fare.

Group *'Minigruppe'* offers a 20% discount for groups of three to seven people travelling on the same ticket (minimum two adults); there are also *'gruppebillet'* rebates for eight or more adults travelling together (contact DSB to access these).

Orange *Orange-billetter* discounted tickets (as low as Dkr149 for lengthy IC and ICL journeys – Copenhagen to Aarhus, for example) – although the number of tickets available at that price is limited. To find the cheapest fares, buy your ticket well in advance (up to two months before your travel date), travel outside peak hours, and travel Monday to Thursday or on a Saturday.

Seniors (65 and over) A 25% discount on Friday and Sunday and a 50% discount on other days.

Youth (aged 16 to 25) Can buy a DSB WildCard (youth card) valid for one year for Dkr185; it allows a 25% discount on Friday and Sunday and a 50% discount on other days.

Train Passes

Some rail passes should be bought before you arrive in the country. For more information on rail passes see p299).

Language

As a member of the Scandinavian or North Germanic language family, Danish is closely related to Swedish and Norwegian. With about 5.5 million speakers, it's the official language of Denmark and has co-official status – alongside Greenlandic and Faroese respectively – in Greenland and the Faroese Islands. Until 1944 it was also the official language of Iceland and today is taught in schools there as the first foreign language. Danish is also a minority language in the area of Schleswig-Holstein in northern Germany, where it has some 30,000 speakers.

Most of the sounds in Danish have equivalents in English, and by reading our coloured pronunciation guides as if they were English, you're sure to be understood. There are short and long versions of each vowel, and additional 'combined vowels' or diphthongs. Consonants can be 'swallowed' and even omitted completely, creating (together with vowels) a glottal stop or stød *steudh* which sounds rather like the Cockney pronunciation of the 'tt' in 'bottle'. Note that ai is pronounced as in 'aisle', aw as in 'saw', eu as the 'u' in 'nurse', ew as the 'ee' in 'see' with rounded lips, ow as in 'how', dh as the 'th' in 'that', and r is trilled. The stressed syllables are in italics in our pronunciation guides. Polite and informal forms are indicated with 'pol' and 'inf' respectively.

BASICS

Hello.	*Goddag.*	go·*da*
Goodbye.	*Farvel.*	faar·*vel*
Yes./No.	*Ja./Nej.*	ya/nai
Please.	*Vær så venlig.*	ver saw *ven*·lee
Thank you.	*Tak.*	taak
You're welcome.	*Selv tak.*	sel taak
Excuse me.	*Undskyld mig.*	awn·skewl mai
Sorry.	*Undskyld.*	awn·skewl

How are you?
Hvordan går det?   vor·*dan* gawr dey

Good, thanks.
Godt, tak.   got taak

What's your name?
Hvad hedder   va *hey*·dha
De/du? (pol/inf)   dee/doo

My name is ...
Mit navn er ...   mit nown ir ...

Do you speak English?
Taler De/du   ta·la dee/doo
engelsk? (pol/inf)   *eng*·elsk

I don't understand.
Jeg forstår ikke.   yai for·*stawr* i·ke

ACCOMMODATION

Where's a ...?	*Hvor er der ...?*	vor ir deyr ...
campsite	*en camping-plads*	in *kaam*·ping·plas
guesthouse	*et gæstehus*	it *ges*·te·hoos
hotel	*et hotel*	it hoh·*tel*
youth hostel	*et ungdoms-herberg*	it *awng*·doms·heyr·beyrg
Do you have a ... room?	*Har I et ... værelse?*	haar ee it ... *verl*·se
single	*enkelt*	*eng*·kelt
double	*dobbelt*	*do*·belt
How much is it per ...?	*Hvor meget koster det per ...?*	vor *maa*·yet *kos*·ta dey peyr ...
night	*nat*	nat
person	*person*	per·*sohn*

WANT MORE?

For in-depth language information and handy phrases, check out Lonely Planet's *Western Europe Phrasebook*. You'll find it at shop.lonelyplanet.com.

DIRECTIONS

Where's the ...?
Hvor er ...?   vor ir ...

What's the address?
Hvad er adressen?   va ir a·*draa*·sen

Can you show me (on the map)?
Kan De/du vise mig   kan dee/doo *vee*·se mai
det (på kortet)? (pol/inf) dey (paw *kor*·tet)

How far (away) is it?
Hvor langt (væk) er det? vor laangt (vek) ir dey

How do I get there?
Hvordan kommer   vor·*dan* ko·ma
jeg derhen?   yai deyr·*hen*

Turn ...	*Drej ...*	drai ...
at the corner	*ved hjørnet*	vi *yeur*·nedh
at the traffic lights	*ved trafik-lyset*	vi traa·*feek*·lew·set
left	*til venstre*	til *vens*·tre
right	*til højre*	til *hoy*·re

It's ...	*Det er ...*	dey ir ...
behind ...	*bag ...*	ba ...
far (away)	*langt (væk)*	laangt (vek)
in front of ...	*foran ...*	*fo*·ran ...
left	*til venstre*	til *vens*·tre
near (to ...)	*nær (ved ...)*	ner (vi ...)
next to ...	*ved siden af ...*	vi *see*·dhen a ...
on the corner	*på hjørnet*	paw *yeur*·net
opposite ...	*på modsate side af ...*	paw *mohdh*·sa·te *see*·dhe a ...
right	*til højre*	til *hoy*·re
straight ahead	*lige ud*	*li*·e oodh

EATING & DRINKING

What would you recommend?
Hvad kan De/du   va kan dee/doo
anbefale? (pol/inf) an·*bey*·fa·le

What's the local speciality?
Hvad er den lokale   va ir den loh·*ka*·le
specialitet?   spey·sha·lee·*teyt*

Do you have vegetarian food?
Har I vegetarmad? haar ee vey·ge·*taar*·madh

Cheers!
Skål!   skawl

I'd like (the) ..., please.	*Jeg vil gerne have ..., tak.*	yai vil *gir*·ne ha ... taak
bill	*regningen*	*rai*·ning·en
drink list	*vinkortet*	*veen*·kor·tet

SIGNS

Indgang	Entrance
Udgang	Exit
Åben	Open
Lukket	Closed
Forbudt	Prohibited
Toilet	Toilets
Herrer	Men
Damer	Women

menu	*menuen*	me·*new*·en
that dish	*den ret*	den ret

Could you prepare a meal without ...?	*Kan I lave et måltid uden ...?*	kan ee *la*·ve it *mawl*·teedh oo·dhen ...
butter	*smør*	smeur
eggs	*æg*	eg
meat stock	*kød-boullion*	*keudh*·boo·lee·yong

Key Words

bar	*bar*	baar
bottle	*flaske*	*flas*·ke
breakfast	*morgenmad*	*morn*·madh
cafe	*café*	ka·*fey*
children's menu	*børne-menu*	*beur*·ne·mey·new
cold	*kold*	kol
cup	*kop*	kop
daily special	*dagens ret*	*da*·ens rat
dinner	*middag*	*mi*·da
drink	*drink*	drink
food	*mad*	madh
fork	*gaffel*	*gaa*·fel
glass	*glas*	glas
hot	*varm*	vaarm
knife	*kniv*	kneev
lunch	*frokost*	*froh*·kost
market	*marked*	*maar*·kedh
menu	*menu/spisekort*	me·*new*/*spee*·se·kort
plate	*tallerken*	ta·*ler*·ken
restaurant	*restaurant*	res·toh·*rang*
snack	*mellem-måltid*	me·lem·*mawl*·teedh
spoon	*ske*	skey
teaspoon	*teske*	*tey*·skey

with	med	me
without	uden	oo·dhen

Meat & Fish

beef	oksekød	ok·se·keudh
chicken	hønsekød	heun·se·keudh
cod	torsk	torsk
eel	ål	orl
fish	fisk	fisk
herring	sild	seel
lamb	lammekød	la·me·keudh
lobster	hummer	haw·ma
meat	kød	keudh
mutton	fårekød	faw·re·keudh
pork	svinekød	svee·ne·keudh
salmon	laks	laks
seafood	skaldyr	skal·dewr
steak	engelsk bøf	eng·elsk beuf
trout	forel/ørred	foh·rel/eur·redh
tuna	tunfisk	toon·fisk
veal	kalvekød	kal·ve·keudh

Fruit & Vegetables

apple	æble	eb·le
apricot	abrikos	a·bree·kohs
banana	banan	ba·nan
beans	bønner	beu·na
cabbage	kål	kawl
carrots	gulerødder	goo·le·reu·dha
cauliflower	blomkål	blom·kawl
cherry	kirsebær	keer·se·ber
corn	majs	mais
cucumber	agurk	a·goork
fruit	frugt	frawgt
leek	porre	po·re
lemon	citron	see·trohn
mushroom	champignon	sham·peen·yong

nuts	nødder	neu·dha
onion	løg	loy
orange	appelsin	a·pel·seen
peach	fersken	fers·ken
peanut	jordnød	jor·neudh
pear	pære	pe·re
peas	ærter	er·ta
pineapple	ananas	a·na·nas
plum	blomme	blo·me
potato	kartoffel	ka·to·fel
spinach	spinat	spee·nat
strawberry	jordbær	jor·ber
vegetable	grønsag	greun·saa
watermelon	vandmelon	van·mey·lon

Other

bread	brød	breudh
butter	smør	smeur
cake	kage	ka·e
cheese	ost	awst
cream	fløde	fleu·dhe
egg	æg	eg
garlic	hvidløg	veedh·loy
honey	honning	ho·ning
ice	is	ees
jam	syltetøj	sewl·te·toy
noodles	nudler	noodh·la
pepper	peber	pey·wa
rice	ris	rees
salad	salat	sa·lat
soup	suppe	saw·pe
sugar	sukker	saw·ka

Drinks

beer	øl	eul
buttermilk	kærnemælk	ker·ne·melk
coffee	kaffe	ka·fe
(orange) juice	(appelsin-) juice	(aa·pel·seen·) joos
lemonade	citronvand	see·trohn·van
milk	mælk	melk
mineral water	mineralvand/ danskvand	mee·ne·ral·van/ dansk·van
red wine	rødvin	reudh·veen
soft drink	sodavand	soh·da·van
sparkling wine	mousserende vin	moo·sey·ra·ne veen
tea	te	tey

QUESTION WORDS

How?	Hvordan?	vor·dan
What?	Hvad?	va
When?	Hvornår?	vor·nawr
Where?	Hvor?	vor
Who?	Hvem?	vem
Why?	Hvorfor?	vor·for

| water | *vand* | van |
| white wine | *hvidvin* | *veedh*·veen |

EMERGENCIES

| Help! | *Hjælp!* | yelp |
| Go away! | *Gå væk!* | gaw vek |

Call ...!	*Ring efter ...!*	ring *ef*·ta ...
a doctor	*en læge*	in *le*·ye
the police	*politiet*	poh·lee·*tee*·et

It's an emergency!
Det er et nødstilfælde! dey ir it *neudhs*·til·fe·le

I'm lost.
Jeg er faret vild. yai ir *faa*·ret veel

I'm sick.
Jeg er syg. yai ir sew

It hurts here.
Det gør ondt her. dey geur awnt heyr

I'm allergic to (antibiotics).
Jeg er allergisk over yai ir a·*ler*·geesk o·va
for (antibiotika). for (an·tee·bee·*oh*·tee·ka)

Where's the toilet?
Hvor er toilettet? vor ir toy·*le*·tet

SHOPPING & SERVICES

Where's the ...?	*Hvor er ...?*	vor ir ...
ATM	*der en hæve-automat*	deyr in *he*·ve·ow·toh·mat
bank	*der en bank*	deyr in baank
local internet cafe	*den lokale internet café*	den loh·*ka*·le *in*·ta·net ka·*fey*
nearest public phone	*den nærmeste telefonboks*	den *ner*·mes·te te·le·*fohn*·boks
post office	*der et postkontor*	deyr it *post*·kon·tohr
public toilet	*der et offentligt toilet*	deyr it o·*fent*·leet toy·*let*
tourist office	*turist-kontoret*	too·*reest*·kon·toh·ret

I'm looking for ...
Jeg leder efter ... yai *li*·dha *ef*·ta ...

Can I have a look?
Må jeg se? maw yai sey

Do you have any others?
Har I andre? haar ee *aan*·dre

How much is it?
Hvor meget koster det? vor *maa*·yet *kos*·ta dey

That's too expensive.
Det er for dyrt. dey ir for dewrt

NUMBERS

1	*en*	in
2	*to*	toh
3	*tre*	trey
4	*fire*	feer
5	*fem*	fem
6	*seks*	seks
7	*syv*	sew
8	*otte*	*aw*·te
9	*ni*	nee
10	*ti*	tee
20	*tyve*	*tew*·ve
30	*tredive*	*traadh*·ve
40	*fyrre*	*fewr*·re
50	*halvtreds*	hal·*tres*
60	*tres*	tres
70	*halvfjerds*	hal·*fyers*
80	*firs*	feers
90	*halvfems*	hal·*fems*
100	*hundrede*	*hoon*·re·dhe
1000	*tusind*	*too*·sen

What's your lowest price?
Hvad er jeres laveste va ir ye·res *la*·ve·ste
pris? prees

There's a mistake in the bill. (restaurant/shop)
Der er en fejl i deyr ir in fail ee
regningen/ *rai*·ning·en/
kvitteringen. kvee·*tey*·ring·en

TIME & DATES

What time is it?
Hvad er klokken? va ir *klo*·ken

It's (two) o'clock.
Klokken er (to). *klo*·ken ir (toh)

Half past (one).
Halv (to). (lit: half two) hal (toh)

At what time ...?
Hvad tid ...? va teedh ...

At ...
Klokken ... *klo*·ken ...

am (morning)	*om morgenen*	om *mor*·nen
pm (afternoon)	*om eftermiddagen*	om ef·*taa*·mi·da·en
pm (evening)	*om aftenen*	om *aaft*·nen
yesterday	*i går*	ee gawr
today	*i dag*	ee da
tomorrow	*i morgen*	ee morn

ROAD SIGNS

Ensrettet	One Way
Indkørsel Forbudt	No Entry
Motorvej	Freeway
Omkørsel	Detour
Parkering Forbudt	No Parking
Selvbetjening	Self Service
Vejarbejde	Roadworks
Vigepligt	Give Way

Monday	*mandag*	man·da
Tuesday	*tirsdag*	teers·da
Wednesday	*onsdag*	awns·da
Thursday	*torsdag*	tors·da
Friday	*fredag*	fre·da
Saturday	*lørdag*	leur·da
Sunday	*søndag*	seun·da

January	*januar*	ya·noo·ar
February	*februar*	feb·roo·ar
March	*marts*	maarts
April	*april*	a·preel
May	*maj*	mai
June	*juni*	yoo·nee
July	*juli*	yoo·lee
August	*august*	ow·gawst
September	*september*	sip·tem·ba
October	*oktober*	ohk·toh·ba
November	*november*	noh·vem·ba
December	*december*	dey·sem·ba

TRANSPORT

Public Transport

Is this the ... to (Aarhus)?	*Er dette ... til (Århus)?*	ir dey·te ... til (awr·hoos)
boat	*båden*	baw·dhen
bus	*bussen*	boo·sen
plane	*flyet*	flew·et
train	*toget*	taw·et

What time's the ... bus?	*Hvad tid er den ... bus?*	va teedh ir den ... boos
first	*første*	feurs·te
last	*sidste*	sees·te
next	*næste*	nes·te

One ... ticket (to Odense), please.	*En ... billet (til Odense), tak.*	in ... bee·let (til oh·dhen·se) taak
one-way	*enkelt*	eng·kelt
return	*retur*	rey·toor

At what time does (the train) arrive/leave?
Hvornår ankommer/ afgår (toget)? — vor·nawr an·ko·ma/ ow·gawr (taw·et)

Does it stop at (Østerport)?
Stopper den/det på (Østerport)? — sto·pa den/dey paw (eus·ta·port)

What's the next station/stop?
Hvad er næste station/ stoppested? — va ir nes·te sta·shohn/ sto·pe·stedh

Please tell me when we get to (Roskilde).
Sig venligst til når vi kommer til (Roskilde). — see ven·leest til nawr vee ko·ma til (ros·kee·le)

Please take me to (this address).
Vær venlig at køre mig til (denne adresse). — ver ven·lee at keu·re mai til (de·ne a·draa·se)

Please stop here.
Venligst stop her. — ven·leest stop heyr

Driving & Cycling

I'd like to hire a ...	*Jeg vil gerne leje en ...*	yai vil gir·ne lai·ye in ...
bicycle	*cykel*	sew·kel
car	*bil*	beel
motorbike	*motorcykel*	moh·tor· sew·kel

air	*luft*	lawft
oil	*olie*	ohl·ye
park (car)	*parkere*	paar·key·ra
petrol	*benzin*	ben·seen
service station	*benzinstation*	ben·seen· sta·shohn
tyres	*dæk*	dek

Is this the road to (Kronborg Slot)?
Fører denne vej til (Kronborg Slot)? — feu·ra de·ne vai til (krohn·borg slot)

Can I get there by bicycle?
Kan jeg cykle derhen? — kan yai sewk·le deyr·hen

I need a mechanic.
Jeg har brug for en mekaniker. — yai haar broo for in mi·ka·ni·ka

I've run out of petrol.
Jeg er løbet tør for benzin. — yai ir leu·bet teur for ben·seen

I have a flat tyre.
Jeg er punkteret. — yai ir pawng·tey·ret

GLOSSARY

Note that the Danish letters æ, ø and å fall at the end of the alphabet.

akvavit – schnapps
allé – avenue
amt – county
apotek – pharmacy, chemist

bad – bath, bathroom
bageri – bakery
bakke – hill
banegård – train station
bibliotek – library
billet – ticket (P-billet means parking ticket required)
billetautomat – automated parking-ticket dispenser

bro – bridge
bryggeri – brewery
bugt – bay
by – town
børnemenu – children's menu

campingplads – camping ground
cykel – bicycle

dag – day
dagens ret – dish of the day
dansk – Danish
domkirke – cathedral
DSB – Danske Statsbaner (Danish State Railway), Denmark's national railway
dyrepark – animal park, zoo

Fyn – Funen
fyr – lighthouse
færge – ferry
færegehavn – ferry harbour

gade – street
gård – courtyard, farm

hav – sea, ocean
have – garden

havn – harbour
hus – house
hygge – to make cosy (verb), cosiness (noun)
hyggelig – cosy (adjective)
hytte – hut, cabin

IC – intercity train
IR – inter-regional train

jernbane – railway
Jylland – Jutland

kart – map
keramik – ceramic, pottery
kirke – church
kirkegård – churchyard, cemetery
klint – cliff
klit – dune, sand hill
kloster – monastery
kort – card
kro – inn
kunst – art
køreplan – timetable

lufthavn – airport
lystbådehavn – marina

mad – food
magasin – department store
morgenmad – breakfast
museet – museum
møntvask – coin laundry

nat – night
nord – north
ny – new

og – and

plads – place, square
plantage – plantation, tree farm, woods
pris – price

retter – dishes, courses

rundkirke – fortified round church, found on Bornholm
rutebilstation – bus station (for long-distance buses)
røgeri – fish smokehouse
rådhus – town hall, city hall

samling – collection, usually of art
Sjælland – Zealand
skov – forest, woods
slagter – butcher
slot – castle
smørrebrød – open sandwich
sti – path, walkway
strand – beach, shoreline
sund – sound
svømmehal – swimming pool
syd – south
sø – lake

teater – theatre
tog – train
torv, torvet – square, marketplace
turistkontor – tourist office
tårn – tower

udsigt – view, viewpoint
uge – week

vandrerhjem – youth and family hostel
vej – street, road
vest – west
værelse – room (to rent)

wienerbrød – Danish pastry, literally 'Vienna bread'

ø – island, usually attached as a suffix to the proper name
øl – beer
øst – east

å – river
år – year

Behind the Scenes

SEND US YOUR FEEDBACK

We love to hear from travellers – your comments keep us on our toes and help make our books better. Our well-travelled team reads every word on what you loved or loathed about this book. Although we cannot reply individually to postal submissions, we always guarantee that your feedback goes straight to the appropriate authors, in time for the next edition. Each person who sends us information is thanked in the next edition – the most useful submissions are rewarded with a selection of digital PDF chapters.

Visit **lonelyplanet.com/contact** to submit your updates and suggestions or to ask for help. Our award-winning website also features inspirational travel stories, news and discussions.

Note: We may edit, reproduce and incorporate your comments in Lonely Planet products such as guidebooks, websites and digital products, so let us know if you don't want your comments reproduced or your name acknowledged. For a copy of our privacy policy visit lonelyplanet.com/privacy.

OUR READERS

Many thanks to the travellers who used the last edition and wrote to us with helpful hints, useful advice and interesting anecdotes:

Gillians Jeens, Henrik Hytteballe, Jackie Mc-Cormack, Julie Woods, Krill Koroteev, Matthias Vogel, Rosette Claes

AUTHOR THANKS

Carolyn Bain

At Lonely Planet, my thanks to DE Gemma Graham for encouraging and accommodating further Nordic wanderings. Big bouquets to my genius co-author, Cristian Bonetto, for being equally passionate about Denmark and generous with your knowledge. Heartfelt gratitude goes to my Danish family, the Østergaards – your warm welcome and generosity in Skagen, Sunds and Svendborg mean the world to me. To the good folks of Ærø, thanks for a most *hyggelig* island stay. To all the Danes who rented me apartments, answered my questions, indulged my Eurovision fixation and generally made this trip such a joy: *tusind tak*.

Cristian Bonetto

Tusind tak to Martin Kalhoj, Christian Struckmann Irgens, Mette Cecilie Perle Smedegaard, Grete Seidler, Mia Hjorth Lunde, Jens Lunde, Henrik Lorentsen, Gitte Kærsgaard, Henrik Sieverts Ørvad, Brian Jakobsen and René Ørum for their insights and generosity. Last but not least, a big thank you to my ever-diligent co-writer and friend, Carolyn Bain.

ACKNOWLEDGMENTS

Climate map data adapted from Peel MC, Finlayson BL & McMahon TA (2007) 'Updated World Map of the Köppen-Geiger Climate Classification', *Hydrology and Earth System Sciences*, 11, 163344

Cover photograph: Beach house in Ærø; Andrew Rich, Getty Images.

'The year has 16 months' © Henrik Nordbrandt 1986. Used by permission of the publisher.

THIS BOOK

This 7th edition of Lonely Planet's *Denmark* was researched and written by Carolyn Bain and Cristian Bonetto. The 6th edition was researched and written by Carolyn Bain, Cristian Bonetto and Andrew Stone. This guidebook was produced by the following:

Destination Editor
Gemma Graham

Coordinating Editor
Samantha Forge

Product Editor
Stephanie Ong

Senior Cartographer
Valentina Kremenchutskaya

Book Designer Wendy Wright

Assisting Editors
Jodie Martire, Jenna Myers

Cartographer
James Leversha

Cover Researcher
Naomi Parker

Thanks to Claire Naylor, Samantha Tyson, Ryan Evans, Larissa Frost, Jouve India, Martine Power, Wayne Murphy

Index

The Danish language places the letters æ, ø and å at the end of the alphabet.

A

Aalborg 241-8, **244**
  accommodation 243, 245
  activities 241, 243
  drinking 246-7
  festivals & events 243
  food 245-6
  information 247
  sights 241, 243
  travel to/from 247
  travel within 247-8
Aalborg Karneval 21, 243, **22**
Aarhus 15, 18, 208-21, **210-11, 15**
  accommodation 214-15
  activities 213
  children, travel with 213
  drinking 217
  entertainment 217-18
  festivals & events 214
  food 216-17
  history 208
  information 219
  itineraries 209
  shopping 218-19
  sights 208-9, 212-13
  tours 214
  travel to/from 219-20
  travel within 220-1
Aarhus Domkirke 209
Aarhus Festival 23, 214
accommodation 290-2, see also individual locations
activities 19-20, 21-4, 30-4, see also individual activities
air travel 297, 300

Map Pages **000**
Photo Pages **000**

akvavit 284
Allinge 153-4
Als 204
Amalienborg Slot 56
amusement & theme parks 36
  Bakken 92
  Djurs Sommerland 224
  Fårup Sommerland 257-8
  Lalandia (Billund) 232
  Lalandia (Lolland) 140
  Legoland 12, 18, 231-4, **12**
  Middelaldercentret 136
  Tivoli Friheden 213
  Tivoli Gardens 24, 45, 66
Andersen, Hans Christian 59, 285
  festivals 24, 163
  museums 159
  sites 286
aquariums
  Aqua 225
  Den Blå Planet 18, 63
  Fiskeri- og Søfartsmuseet 189
  Fjord & Bælt 168
  Kattegatcentret 223
  Nordsøen Oceanarium 255
architecture 20, 276-8, see also individual architects
area codes 17, 296
Arken Museum of Modern Art 92
ARoS Aarhus Kunstmuseum 208
art museums
  Arken Museum of Modern Art 92
  ARoS Aarhus Kunstmuseum 208
  Bornholms Kunstmuseum 152
  Brandts 161
  Carl-Henning Pedersen & Else Alfelt Museum 228
  Davids Samling 59-60

Esbjerg Kunstmuseum 189
Faaborg Museum 171
Fuglsang Kunstmuseum 139
Glasmuseet Ebeltoft 221
HEART 228
Hirschsprung 60
Johannes Larsen Museet 168
KunstCentret Silkeborg Bad 225
Kunsten 243
Louisiana 91
Museum Jorn 224-5
Nikolaj Kunsthal 50
Ny Carlsberg Glyptotek 48-9
Ordrupgaard 92
Ribe Kunstmuseum 195
Skagens Museum 251
Statens Museum for Kunst 58-9
Thorvaldsens Museum 50
V1 Gallery 61
Assistens Kirkegård 60
ATMs 294

B

Bakken 92
Bangsbo 248
beaches
  Copenhagen 61
  Dueodde 146, **14**
  Ebeltoft 221
  Fanø 191-2
  Funen 182
  Gammel Skagen 14, 252
  Gilleleje 106
  Grenaa 223
  Hornbæk 105
  Hvide Sande 14, 238
  Klintholm Havn 134
  Klitmøller 14, 260
  Køge 115
  Løkken 258

Marstal 183
  northern Jutland 257
  Tisvildeleje 107
  Tornby Strand 256
  Ulvshale Strand 131
beer 21, 280, 283-4, see also breweries
bicycle travel, see cycling
Billund 231-4
bird-watching
  Christiansø 155-6
  Fanø 192
  Funen 179
  Møn 131
  Wadden Sea National Park 198
Black Diamond 54, 277, **20**
Blixen, Karen 96, 97, 287
blokarts 192, 199
boat travel 299-301, see also kayaking & canoeing, sailing
boat trips
  Copenhagen 62, 63
  Esbjerg 189
  Maribo 139
  Odense 163
  Ry 228-9
  Silkeborg 225
  Svendborg 173
  Viborg 237
bog bodies
  Grauballe Man 13, 209, 267
  Tollund Man 13,224, 267, **13**
Bogø 135
books 262, 272, 279, see also literature
border crossings 297
Bornholm 10, 39, 141-56, **142, 10**
  accommodation 141
  climate 141
  food 141
  highlights 142
  travel seasons 141

travel to/from 142-3
travel within 143
Bornholms Kunstmuseum 152
Boxen 228
Brahe, Tycho 49, 61
Brandts 161
Bregninge 177
breweries 61, 183, 283-4
budgeting 17
burial mounds & passage graves
    Grønsalen 134
    Jelling Kirke 230
    Klekkende Høj 134
    Kong Asgers Høj 134
    Lindholm Høje 243
    Møn 134
bus travel 298, 301
bushwalking, *see* hiking
business hours 295
Bycyklen 90

C
camping 290-1
canoeing, *see*
    kayaking & canoeing
car travel 298, 301-2
Carlsberg Visitors Centre 61
castles & palaces, *see also* fortresses
    Amalienborg Slot 56
    Dragsholm Slot 113
    Egeskov Slot 170
    Fredensborg Slot 103
    Frederiksborg Slot 101-2
    Gråsten Palace 202
    Koldinghus 186-7
    Kronborg Slot 12, 97, **12**
    Marselisborg Palace & Park 213
    Rosenborg Slot 59
    Schackenborg 202
    Søbygaard 184
    Sønderborg Slot 203
    Tranekær Slot 178
    Valdemars Slot 176-7
    Vallø Slot 119
cathedrals, *see* churches & cathedrals
cell phones 16, 295
central Jutland 40, 205-39, **206-7**
    accommodation 205
    climate 205
    food 205
    highlights 206
    travel seasons 205

Charlottenlund 92
children, travel with 19, 35-7, 67, 213, *see also* amusement & theme parks, aquariums, zoos & safari parks
Christiansø 155-6
churches & cathedrals, *see also* monasteries
    Aarhus Domkirke 209
    Bregninge Kirke 177
    Budolfi Domkirke 241
    Elmelunde Kirke 132
    Fanefjord Kirke 134
    Holmens Kirke 55
    Jelling Kirke 230
    Keldby Kirke 131-2
    Kristkirken 201
    Maribo Domkirke 139
    Marmorkirken 56-7
    Møgeltønder Kirke 202
    Nylars Rundkirke 144-5
    Ribe Domkirke 193
    Roskilde Domkirke 109-11
    Rømø Kirke 199
    Sankt Bendts Kirke 117
    Sankt Catharinæ Kirke 194-5
    Sankt Knuds Kirke 162
    Sankt Mariæ Kirke & Karmeliterklostret 99
    Sankt Nicolai Kirke 114-15
    Sankt Olai Domkirke 99
    Sorø Kirke 120-1
    Stege Kirke 129
    Sæby Klosterkirke 249
    Viborg Domkirke 237
    Vor Frelsers Kirke 58
    Vor Frue Kirke 49-50, 212
    Østerlars Rundkirke 152
climate 16, 21-4, 34, 42, *see also individual regions*
climate change 297
consulates 293
Copenhagen 9, 38, 42-91, **44, 46-7, 52-3, 8**
    accommodation 42, 66-70
    activities 61-3
    children, travel with 67
    Christiania 57-8
    drinking 42, 78, 80-2
    entertainment 82-5
    festivals & events 65-6
    food 42, 70-8, 79
    free activities 56

highlights 44
history 43, 45
information 88-9
itineraries 43
shopping 85-8
sights 45, 48-51, 54-61
tours 63, 65
travel seasons 42
travel to/from 89
travel within 89-91
walking tour 64, **64**
Copenhagen Blues Festival 24, 65-6
Copenhagen Fashion Week 21
Copenhagen Jazz Festival 11, 23, 65, 84
Copenhagen Pride 23, 65
costs 17, *see also* money
CPH:PIX 21, 65
credit cards 294
culture 262, 273, 275
currency 16
customs regulations 292
cycling 10, 30-1
    Aarhus 214, 220
    Bornholm 31
    Copenhagen 57, 62-3, 65, 66, 90
    Dyrehaven 92
    Funen 172
    mountain biking 236
    routes 31, 32
    rules 66
    Ry 229
    Silkeborg 225-6
    travel to/from Denmark 298
    travel within Denmark 300
Cykelslangen 57

D
Danmarks Borgcenter 18, 124-5
Davids Samling 59-60
De Kongelige Repræsentationslokaler 50-1
Den Blå Planet 18, 63
Den Gamle By 208
Den Gamle Rådhus 195
design 14, 20, 276-8
Designmuseum Danmark 56
Det Kongelige Bibliotek 54
disabilities, travellers with 296
discount cards 294

Aalborg 246
Aarhus 214
    Copenhagen 89
Djursland 221-4
Dragsholm Slot 113
drinks 283-4, *see also* beer, breweries
driving 298, 301-2
Dueodde 146-7, **14**
Dybbøl Mølle 204

E
Ebeltoft 221-3
economy 263
Egeskov Slot 170
electricity 292
Elmelunde 132
Elmelunde Kirke 132
Elmelundemesteren 132
embassies 293
emergencies 17, 307
environmental issues
    climate change 297
    sustainability 263
    Thomas B Thriges Gade 163
Ertholmene Islands 155-6
Esbjerg 188-91, **190**
Esrum Kloster 102
Esrum Sø 104
events 21-4, *see also* festivals
    Art Copenhagen 24, 65
    Christmas Fairs 24
    Copenhagen Fashion Week 21
    Kulturhavn 65
    Kulturnatten 24, 66
    Sculpture by the Sea 22, 214
exchange rates 17

F
Faaborg 170-3, **171**
Falster 39, 126, 135-8, **127, 135**
    accommodation 126
    climate 126
    food 126
    highlights 127
    travel seasons 126
    travel to/from 135
    travel within 135
Fanø 191-2
farmstays 291
ferries 299-301
festivals 21-4, *see also* events

festivals *continued*
Aalborg Karneval 21, 243, **22**
Aarhus Festival 23, 214
Aarhus Jazz Festival 214
beer 21
Copenhagen Blues Festival 24, 65-6
Copenhagen Jazz Festival 11, 23, 65, 84
Copenhagen Pride 23, 65
CPH:PIX 21, 65
film 21, 65, 66, 163
food 23, 24, 283
Hamlet Summer Plays 12, 23, 99
HC Andersen 24, 163
Maribo Jazz Festival 139
Midsummer Eve 22, 65
NorthSide Festival 23, 214
Rebild Festival 23, 236
Riverboat Jazz Festival 22, 227
rock & pop music 11, 23, 112, 201, 214, 253
Roskilde Festival 23, 112, **11**
Skagen Festival 23, 253
Skt Hans Aften 22, 65
Smukfest 23
Sol over Gudhjem 23, 152
Sort Sol 21, 198
Sorø Jazz 121
Strøm 24, 65
Tønder Festival 23, 201
Viking Moot 23, 214
Vinter Jazz 21, 65
Ærø Jazz Festival 180
Ølfestival 21
films 262, 286-8
festivals 21, 65, 66, 163
food 19, 279-83, 293, *see also individual locations*
festivals 23, 24, 283
highlights 19, 282
language 305-7
New Nordic cuisine 9, 18, 279, **9**
Noma 9, 75, 279
fortresses, *see also* castles & palaces
Fyrkat 236
Hammershus Slot 154-5

Kastellet 57
Trelleborg 122-3
Fredensborg 103-4
Frederiksborg Slot 101-2
Frederikshavn 248-9
Frøslevlejren 203
Frøslevlejrens Museum 203
Fuglsang Kunstmuseum 139
Funen 39, 157-84, **158**
accommodation 157
climate 157
food 157
highlights 158
travel seasons 157

G
galleries, *see* art museums
Gammel Estrup 224
gardens, *see* parks & gardens
gay travellers 23, 65, 293
Geocenter Møns Klint 133
Gilleleje 106-7
Givskud 231
golf 191
Gorm the Old 230, 268
Graceland Randers 234
Grauballe Man 13, 209, 267
Grenaa 223
Grenen 251-2, **13**
Gråbrødrekloster Museet 241
Gråsten 202
Gråsten Palace 202
Gudhjem 150-1, **151**

H
Hallegård 147
Hamlet 12, 23, 99
Hammeren 155
Hammershus Slot 154-5
Hanstholm 259
HC Andersens Hus 159
health 293
HEART 228
Helsingør 97-101, **98**
Henne Kirkeby 238
Herning 228
hiking 30, 34
Aarhus 213
Archipelago Trail 34, 176
Bornholm 146, 150, 155
central Jutland 229, 235-6
Copenhagen 92
Funen 172
Silkeborg 225-6

Rømø 199
Zealand 105, 106, 107, 118, 125
Øhavssti 34, 176
Hillerød 101-3
Himmelbjerget 229-30
Hirtshals 255-7
history 264-72
20th century 271-2
21st century 272
books 272
Bronze Age 264
civil war 268
conflict with Britain 269-70
democracy 270-1
Iron Age 264
Lutheran Reformation 268
Middle Ages 266-8
monarchy 267, 268-9
Stone Age 264
Thirty Years' War 268
Treaty of Roskilde 269
Vikings 193, 265
war with Sweden 268-9
WWII 270, 271-2
Hjørring 257
Hobro 236
holidays 295
Holmens Kirke 55
Hornbæk 104-6
horse riding 199, 239
Humlebæk 91
Hvide Sande 14, 238-9
hygge 274
Høeg, Peter 262, 286, 288

I
Imax Tycho Brahe Planetarium 61
immigration 296, 297
insurance 293-4
internet access 294
internet resources 17
cycling 31
transport 300
Ishøj 92
islands 19, 176, *see also individual islands*
itineraries 25-9, **25**, **26**, **28**, **29**

J
Jacobsen, Arne 213, 276, 277
Jacobsen, Carl 59

jazz music
Aarhus Jazz Festival 214
Copenhagen Jazz Festival 11, 23, 65, 84
Maribo Jazz Festival 139
Riverboat Jazz Festival 22, 227
Sorø Jazz 121
Vinterjazz 21
Ærø Jazz Festival 180
Jelling 230-1
Jelling Kirke 230
Jelling Stones 230, 271
Jutland, *see* central Jutland, northern Jutland, southern Jutland

K
Kadeau (Copenhagen) 18, 75
Karen Blixen Museet 96-7
Kattegatcentret 223
kayaking & canoeing 33-4
central Jutland 225, 229
Copenhagen 63
Funen 183
Keldby 131-2
Keldby Kirke 131-2
Kerteminde 168-9
Kierkegaard, Søren 60, 106, 270, 285
kitesurfing
central Jutland 239
northern Jutland 260
southern Jutland 192, 199
Klampenborg 92
Klintholm Havn 134
Klitmøller 14, 260
Knuthenborg Safari Park 140
Kolding 186-8, **188**
Koldinghus 186-7
Kommandørgården 199
Kongernes Jelling 230
Korsør 124
Kronborg Slot 12, 97, **12**
Krølle Bølle 155
Kulturnatten 24, 66
Kunsten 243
Kvindemuseet 212
Køge 114-19, **115**

L
Ladby 169-70
Ladbyskibet 14, 169-70
Lake District 224-30

Langeland 177-80, **177**
language 16
  accommodation 304-5
  emergencies 307
  food 305-7
  transport 308
Larsen, Henning 277
legal matters 294
Legoland 12, 18, 231-4, **12**
Lejre 113-14
lesbian travellers 23, 65, 293
literature 97, 285-6, *see also* books
Little Mermaid 59
Lolland 39, 138-40, **127, 138**
  accommodation 126
  climate 126
  food 126
  highlights 127
  travel seasons 126
  travel to/from 138-9
  travel within 138-9
Louisiana 91
Lyngby 92
Læsø 250
Løkken 257-9

M
magazines 294
Marchal 18, 68
Maribo 139-40
Marielyst 137-8
Marstal 183-4
measures 294
medical services 293
Melsted 150-1, **151**
Mennesket ved Havet 189
Midsummer Eve 22, 65
mobile phones 16, 295
Moesgård 209
Moesgård Museum 209, 267
Mols Bjerge National Park 222
monarchy 267, 268-9
monasteries, *see also* churches & cathedrals
  Esrum Kloster 102
  Helligåndsklostret 241
money 16, 17, 294-5
motorcycle travel 298, 301-2
mountain biking 236, *see also* cycling
M/S Museet for Søfart 18, 99

museums, *see also* art museums, open-air museums, war museums
Aalborg Historiske Museum 241
Bangsbo Museum 248
Bornholms Museum 143
Danmarks Borgcenter 18, 124-5
Danmarks Rockmuseum 18, 111
Den Gamle By 208
Designmuseum Danmark 56
Elvis Presley Museum 234
Empiregården 129-30
Forsorgsmuseet 173
Fregatten Jylland 221
Frilandsmuseet Maribo 139
Gammel Estrup 224
Geocenter Møns Klint 133
Gråbrødrekloster Museet 241
Hammerichs Hus 181
HC Andersens Barndomshjem 159
HC Andersens Hus 159
Helsingør Bymuseum 99-100
Karen Blixen Museet 96-7
Koldinghus 186-7
Kongernes Jelling 230
Kongernes Lapidarium 51, 54
Kvindemuseet 212
Køge Museum 114
Maritimt Center Danmark 173
Marstal Søfartsmuseum 183
Moesgård Museum 209, 267
M/S Museet for Søfart 18, 99
Museet Ribes Vikinger 195
Museum Silkeborg 224, 267
Møntergården 161-2
Nationalmuseet 45, 267
NaturBornholm 146
Oluf Høst Museet 150
Rock & Roll Museum 18, 111
Ribe VikingeCenter 195
Rudolph Tegners Museum & Statuepark 106
Skovgaard Museet 237

Skovsgaard 179
Sorø Kunstmuseum 121
Stevns Museum 118
Sæby Museum 249
Teatermuseet 51
Thorsvang 129
Trapholt 187
Tønder Museum 201
Utzon Center 241
Viking Ship Museum 109, **15**
Vikingemuseet (Aarhus) 213
Vikingemuseet Ladby 169-70
music, *see also* jazz music, rock & pop music
Copenhagen Blues Festival 24, 65-6
Sorø International Music Festival 121
Strøm 24, 65
Tønder Festival 23, 201
Musikhuset Esbjerg 189
Musikkens Hus 241
Møgeltønder 202-3
Møgeltønder Kirke 202
Møn 39, 128-35, **127, 128**
  accommodation 126
  climate 126
  highlights 127
  travel seasons 126
  travel to/from 128
Møns Klint 132-3

N
national parks
  Mols Bjerge National Park 222
  Rebild Bakker 235-7
  Thy National Park 259
  Wadden Sea National Park 18, 198, 222
Nationalmuseet 45, 267
Naturama 173
NaturBornholm 146
New Nordic cuisine 9, 18, 279, **9**
newspapers 294
Nexø 147-8
Nielsen, Carl 162
Nordby 191
Nordkraft 241
Nordsøen Oceanarium 255
northern Jutland 40, 240-60, **242**
  accommodation 240
  climate 240
  food 240

highlights 242
travel seasons 240
travel within 256
Nykøbing F 136-7
Nylars Rundkirke 144-5
Nyord 131
Nørre Vorupør 18, 259

O
Odense 18, 159-68, **160-1**
  accommodation 163-4
  drinking 166
  entertainment 166-7
  festivals & events 163
  food 164, 166
  history 159
  information 167
  sights 159, 161-3
  travel to/from 167
  travel within 167-8
  walking tour 165, **165**
Oluf Høst Museet 150
open-air museums
  Bornholms Middelaldercenter Open-Air Museum 152
  Den Fynske Landsby 162-3
  Frilandsmuseet 92
  Ribe VikingeCenter 195
  Sagnlandet Lejre 113-14
  Skagen By- og Egnsmuseum 252
  Vikingecenter Fyrkat 236
opening hours 295
opera 83
Operaen 83
Ordrupgaard 92
Oreby Kro 136

P
Padborg 203
palaces, *see* castles & palaces
parks & gardens
  Bangsbo Botaniske Have 248
  Botanisk Have (Aarhus) 209
  Botanisk Have (Copenhagen) 60
  Fredensborg Slotshave 103-4
  Indelukket 225
  Kongens Have 59
  Liselund 133
  Marselisborg Palace & Park 213
  Tickon 178-9

passage graves, see burial mounds & passage graves
passports 296, 297
planning, see also individual regions
budgeting 17
calender of events 21-4
children, travel with 19, 35-7, 67, 213
Denmark basics 16-17
Denmark's regions 38-40
internet resources 17
itineraries 25-9, **25**, **26**, **28**, **29**
outdoor activities 30
repeat visitors 18
travel seasons 16, 21-4, 34, 42
politics 263
pop music, see rock & pop music
population 263
Presley, Elvis 234
public holidays 295

R
Randers 234-5
Rebild Bakker 235-7
Rebild Festival 23, 236
religion 263
Ribe 13, 193-8, **194**, **13**
Ribe Domkirke 193
Ribe Kunstmuseum 195
Ribe VikingeCenter 195
Ringkøbing 238
Riverboat Jazz Festival 22, 227
rock & pop music 11
Danmarks Rockmuseum 18, 111
NorthSide Festival 23, 214
Rock & Roll Museum 18, 111
Roskilde Festival 23, 112, 11
Skagen Festival 23, 253
Tønder Festival 23, 201
Rock & Roll Museum 18
Rold Skov 235-7
Romsø 168-9
Rosenborg Slot 59
Roskilde 108-13, **110**

Map Pages **000**
Photo Pages **000**

Roskilde Domkirke 109-11
Roskilde Festival 23, 112, **11**
round churches 153
Rubjerg Knude 258
Rudkøbing 178
Ruinerne under Christiansborg 51
Rundetårn 49
rundkirker 153
Rungsted 96
Ry 228-9
Rømø 198-200
Rønne 143-5, **144**
Råbjerg Mile 255
Rådhus 49

S
safari parks, see zoos & safari parks
sailing 33
Sandvig 153-4
Sankt Bendts Kirke 117
Sankt Catharinæ Kirke 194-5
Sankt Knuds Kirke 162
Sankt Nicolai Kirke 114-15
Sankt Olai Domkirke 99
Schønnemann 74
Sculpture by the Sea 22, 214
Sejlskibsbroen 173
shopping, see individual locations
Silkeborg 224-8, **226**
Skagen 13, 251-5, **252**
Skagen Festival 23, 253
Skagens Museum 251
Skjoldnæs Fyr 184
Skovsgaard 179
Skt Hans Aften 22, 65
smoking 294
Smukfest 23
smørrebrod 74, 281
Snogebæk 147
social system 273-5
Sol over Gudhjem 23, 152
Sorø 119-22, **120**
Sorø Kirke 120-1
South Funen Archipelago 176
southern Jutland 40, 185-204, **186**
accommodation 185
climate 185
food 185
highlights 186
travel seasons 185
Statens Museum for Kunst 58-9

Stege 129-31, **130**
Stenbjerg Landingsplads 259
Stevns Klint 118
Storebælts-forbindelsen 124
Strøm 24, 65
surfing 260
sustainability 263
Svaneke 148-9
Svendborg 173-5, **174**
swimming 31-2, see also beaches
central Jutland 226-7
Copenhagen 61-2
northern Jutland 241
Sæby 249-51
Søby 184
Søllerød Kro 71
Sønderho 191

T
telephone services 16, 295-6
theme parks, see amusement & theme parks
Thomas B Thriges Gade 163
Thorvaldsens Museum 50
Thy National Park 259
time 296
tipping 295
Tisvildeleje 107-8
Tivoli Friheden 213
Tivoli Gardens 24, 45, 66
Tollund Man 13, 224, 267, **13**
Torvehallerne KBH 79
tourist information 296
tours, see also individual locations
southern Jutland 196
Wadden Sea National Park 198
train travel 298-9, 303
Traphott 187
travel seasons 16, 21-4, 34, 42
travel to/from Denmark 297-300
travel within Denmark 300-3
trekking, see hiking
Trelleborg 122-4
Trier, Lars von 288
Troense 176
trolls 155
TV 294
Tønder 200-2

Tønder Festival 23, 201
Tåsinge 175-7

U
Ulvshale 131
Utzon Center 241
Utzon, Jørn 149, 189, 228, 241, 276, 277

V
vacations 295
Valdemars Slot 176-7
Vallø 119
vegetarian & vegan travellers 283
Viborg 237-8
Viborg Domkirke 237
Viking Ship Museum 109, **15**
Vikingecenter Fyrkat 236
Vikings 266
Fyrkat 236
highlights 19
history 193, 265
Jelling burial mounds 230
Jelling rune stones 230, 271
Ladbyskibet 14, 169-70
Lindholm Høje 243
Museet Ribes Vikinger 195
Ribe VikingeCenter 195
Trelleborg 122-4
Viking Moot 23, 214
Viking Ship Museum 109, **15**
Vikingecenter Fyrkat 236
Vikingemuseet 213
Vikingemuseet Ladby 169-70
visas 16, 296
von Trier, Lars 288
Vordingborg 124-5

W
Wadden Sea National Park 18, 198, 222
walking, see hiking
war museums
Besættelsesmuseet 212-13
Bornholms Forsvarsmuseum 145
Frøslevlejrens Museum 203
Historiecenter Dybbøl Banke 203
Langelandsfort 179

MuseumsCenter Hanstholm 259
watersports 30, 239
weather 16, 21-4, 34, 42, see also individual regions
websites, see internet resources
Wegner, Hans 201
weights 294
windsurfing
  central Jutland 239
  northern Jutland 260
  southern Jutland 192, 199
wine 284

WWII 270, 271-2, see also war museums

Y
Your Rainbow Panorama 15, 208

Z
Zealand 38, 93-125, **94**
  accommodation 93
  climate 93
  food 93
  highlights 94
  travel seasons 93

travel to/from 96
travel within 96
zoos & safari parks 36-7
  Aalborg Zoo 243
  Copenhagen Zoo 18, 61
  Givskud Zoo 231
  Knuthenborg Safari Park 140
  Odense Zoo 159, 161
  Randers Regnskov 234
  Ree Park Safari 221
  Skandinavisk Dyrepark 224

Æ
Ærø 10, 180-4, **180**, **11**
Ærøskøbing 181-3

Ø
Ølfestival 21
Øresundsbron 270
Østerlars Rundkirke 152

Å
Åkirkeby 145-6
Århus, see Aarhus

Map Legend

Sights
- Beach
- Bird Sanctuary
- Buddhist
- Castle/Palace
- Christian
- Confucian
- Hindu
- Islamic
- Jain
- Jewish
- Monument
- Museum/Gallery/Historic Building
- Ruin
- Shinto
- Sikh
- Taoist
- Winery/Vineyard
- Zoo/Wildlife Sanctuary
- Other Sight

Activities, Courses & Tours
- Bodysurfing
- Diving
- Canoeing/Kayaking
- Course/Tour
- Sento Hot Baths/Onsen
- Skiing
- Snorkelling
- Surfing
- Swimming/Pool
- Walking
- Windsurfing
- Other Activity

Sleeping
- Sleeping
- Camping

Eating
- Eating

Drinking & Nightlife
- Drinking & Nightlife
- Cafe

Entertainment
- Entertainment

Shopping
- Shopping

Information
- Bank
- Embassy/Consulate
- Hospital/Medical
- Internet
- Police
- Post Office
- Telephone
- Toilet
- Tourist Information
- Other Information

Geographic
- Beach
- Hut/Shelter
- Lighthouse
- Lookout
- Mountain/Volcano
- Oasis
- Park
- Pass
- Picnic Area
- Waterfall

Population
- Capital (National)
- Capital (State/Province)
- City/Large Town
- Town/Village

Transport
- Airport
- Border crossing
- Bus
- Cable car/Funicular
- Cycling
- Ferry
- Metro station
- Monorail
- Parking
- Petrol station
- S-Bahn/S-train/Subway station
- Taxi
- T-bane/Tunnelbana station
- Train station/Railway
- Tram
- Tube station
- U-Bahn/Underground station
- Other Transport

Note: Not all symbols displayed above appear on the maps in this book

Routes
- Tollway
- Freeway
- Primary
- Secondary
- Tertiary
- Lane
- Unsealed road
- Road under construction
- Plaza/Mall
- Steps
- Tunnel
- Pedestrian overpass
- Walking Tour
- Walking Tour detour
- Path/Walking Trail

Boundaries
- International
- State/Province
- Disputed
- Regional/Suburb
- Marine Park
- Cliff
- Wall

Hydrography
- River, Creek
- Intermittent River
- Canal
- Water
- Dry/Salt/Intermittent Lake
- Reef

Areas
- Airport/Runway
- Beach/Desert
- Cemetery (Christian)
- Cemetery (Other)
- Glacier
- Mudflat
- Park/Forest
- Sight (Building)
- Sportsground
- Swamp/Mangrove

OUR STORY

A beat-up old car, a few dollars in the pocket and a sense of adventure. In 1972 that's all Tony and Maureen Wheeler needed for the trip of a lifetime – across Europe and Asia overland to Australia. It took several months, and at the end – broke but inspired – they sat at their kitchen table writing and stapling together their first travel guide, *Across Asia on the Cheap*. Within a week they'd sold 1500 copies. Lonely Planet was born.

Today, Lonely Planet has offices in Franklin, London, Melbourne, Oakland, Beijing and Delhi, with more than 600 staff and writers. We share Tony's belief that 'a great guidebook should do three things: inform, educate and amuse'.

OUR WRITERS

Carolyn Bain
Coordinating Author, Funen, Southern Jutland, Central Jutland, Northern Jutland

As a teenager, Melbourne-born Carolyn spent a year living smack in the heart of Jutland, and today speaks (often mangled) Danish with a *jysk* (Jutlandish) accent, according to those who know such things. Since her year amongst the Danes, Carolyn has frequently returned to dose up on history, hospitality and *hygge*, and she drops in while updating guidebooks to various parts of northern Europe (including Iceland, Sweden and Estonia – see more at carolynbain.com.au). She also covered Jutland for the previous two editions of this book. As with every Denmark visit, on this trip she was in heaven revisiting favourite haunts such as Skagen and Ribe, discovering new favourites like Ærø, coveting designer chairs, rummaging in flea markets and lingering over brunch plates. Carolyn also wrote the Planning and Survival sections of this book.

Read more about Carolyn Bain at:
lonelyplanet.com/members/carolynbain

Cristian Bonetto
Copenhagen, Zealand, Møn, Falster & Lolland, Bornholm

Cristian has been writing passionately about Danish lamps, bikes and bites for almost a decade. Indeed, the Australian-born scribe has contributed to almost 20 Lonely Planet titles, including Scandinavia, Italy, New York City and Singapore. Beyond Lonely Planet, his musings have featured everywhere from Britain's Telegraph and BBC Travel, to Dubai Eye 103.8's *The Travel Show*. Cristian also wrote the History, Danish Lifestyle, Danish Design, Food & Drink, and Literature, Film & TV chapters. Follow him on Twitter @CristianBonetto

Published by Lonely Planet Publications Pty Ltd
ABN 36 005 607 983
7th edition – May 2015
ISBN 978 1 74220 621 9
© Lonely Planet 2015   Photographs © as indicated 2015
10 9 8 7 6 5 4 3 2 1
Printed in China

Although the authors and Lonely Planet have taken all reasonable care in preparing this book, we make no warranty about the accuracy or completeness of its content and, to the maximum extent permitted, disclaim all liability arising from its use.

All rights reserved. No part of this publication may be copied, stored in a retrieval system, or transmitted in any form by any means, electronic, mechanical, recording or otherwise, except brief extracts for the purpose of review, and no part of this publication may be sold or hired, without the written permission of the publisher. Lonely Planet and the Lonely Planet logo are trademarks of Lonely Planet and are registered in the US Patent and Trademark Office and in other countries. Lonely Planet does not allow its name or logo to be appropriated by commercial establishments, such as retailers, restaurants or hotels. Please let us know of any misuses: lonelyplanet.com/ip.